Oracle® XSQL
Combining SQL, Oracle Text, XSLT, and Java to Publish Dynamic Web Content

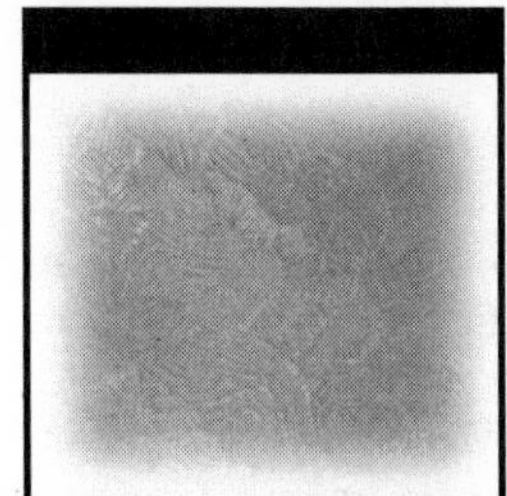

Oracle® XSQL
Combining SQL, Oracle Text, XSLT, and Java to Publish Dynamic Web Content

Michael D. Thomas

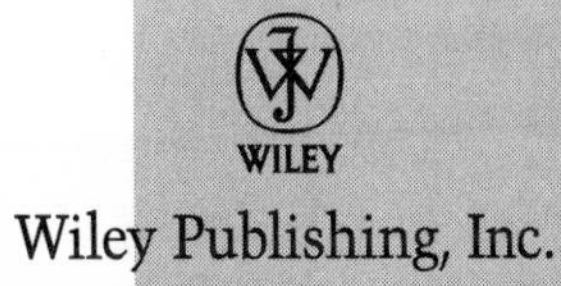

Wiley Publishing, Inc.

Publisher: Robert Ipsen
Editor: Theresa Hudson
Developmental Editor: Kathryn A. Malm
Managing Editor: Micheline Frederick
Text Design & Composition: Wiley Composition Services

This book is printed on acid-free paper. ♾

Published by Wiley Publishing, Inc., Indianapolis, Indiana

Published simultaneously in Canada

For general information on our other products and services please contact our Customer Care Department within the United States at (800) 762-2974, outside the United States at (317) 572-3993 or fax (317) 572-4002.

Wiley also publishes its books in a variety of electronic formats. Some content that appears in print may not be available in electronic books.

ISBN 0-471-27120-9

Printed in the United States of America

10 9 8 7 6 5 4 3 2 1

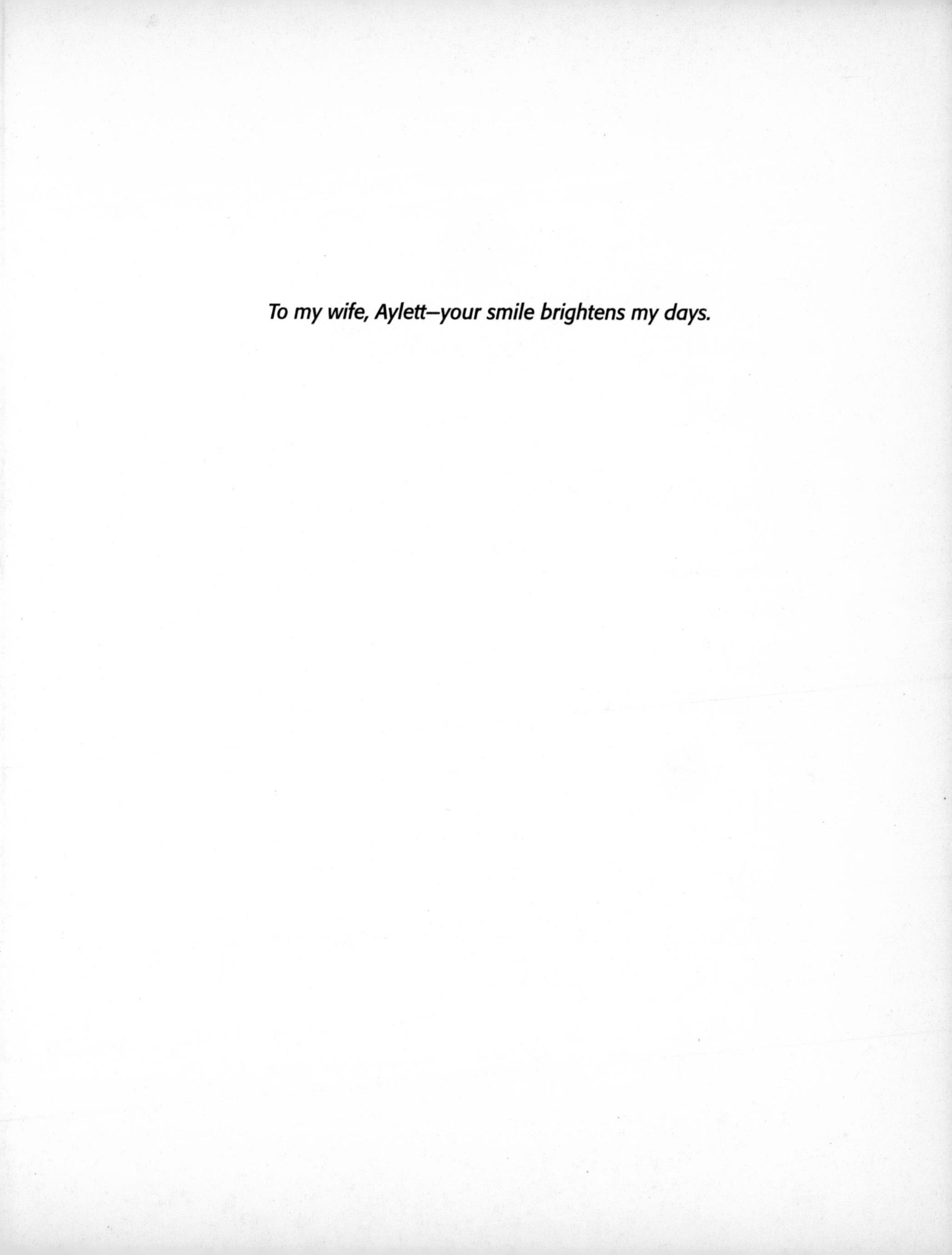

To my wife, Aylett—your smile brightens my days.

Contents

About the Author

Michael D. Thomas is a Software Engineer living in Raleigh, North Carolina. He was lead author for one of the first books on Java, *Java Programming for the Internet* (Ventana, 1996). He also has a long history with XML—he wrote his own XML parser in 1997 as part of a web services app and has used XML on numerous projects over the years. He learned Oracle while working for the company, and has been having adventures with it and other databases ever since. Throughout his career he has worked as both an architect and an engineer on numerous projects using XSQL, XSLT, XML, Java, JSP, JavaScript, PL/SQL, Oracle, and other fun technologies. In 1998, he received the Outstanding Technical Achievement Award from IBM for his Internet integration work using Java, HTTP, XML, and other technologies. He can be reached at `mdthomas@ibiblio.org`.

Introducing Oracle XSQL

Welcome to the exciting world of eXtended Structured Query Language (XSQL) development! What's so exciting? Efficiency and ease of use. XSQL isn't some razzle-dazzle technology to wow your users. It also isn't the latest X standard du jour that no one can stop talking about—until you ask, "But what does it do for me today?" The problem with all of the great stuff out there is that no one technology does it all. A Web server doesn't store all of the company's inventory data. A database, by itself, cannot present its data to its users in an attractive and usable manner. This is where XSQL comes in. XSQL allows you to easily leverage the most robust, mature, and usable technologies in the industry: Standard Query Language (SQL), HyperText Markup Language (HTML), HyperText Transfer Protocol (HTTP), eXtensible Markup Language (XML), Java, and the Oracle relational database management system (RDBMS).

Each of these technologies is arguably the best-of-breed in its space. When it comes to querying relational data, SQL has no competitors. HTML and HTTP are the wonder twins of the Internet. They have their faults, but they also have the ability to evolve. Java has had unparalleled success in the world of enterprise applications and will continue to do so. XML is the standard for structuring data in a platform and application-independent manner. Last but not least, the Oracle RDBMS is the technology, as well as the market, leader in its space.

In the next few hundred pages, XSQL allows you to bring these powerful pieces together. You'll learn how you can use XSQL to instantly present your database data on the Web. You'll develop a complete application with just XSQL and eXtensible

Stylesheet Language Transformation (XSLT). You'll also see how to use XSQL to create graphics on the fly and to render Portable Document Format (PDF) documents based on dynamic data. All the while, the easiest cases require no Java coding at all. You only have to use Java coding for the more complex interactions with the database.

This chapter serves as a general overview to XSQL, as well as the foundation technologies. The first topic covered is an examination of what XSQL solves. This includes some short code examples that illustrate how powerful XSQL can be. The next discussion explores how XSQL relates to other Oracle technologies. You don't have to use XSQL exclusively with Oracle, but XSQL makes a great combination. The chapter ends with some in-depth exploration of XML. XSQL and XSLT are derived from XML, so you need to have a good understanding of XML before diving in.

What XSQL Solves

Before trying to learn any new technology, it is worthwhile to thoroughly understand the problems that the technology solves. In the previous paragraphs, you were promised that XSQL brings technologies together. In this section, you'll see, at a high level, how XSQL delivers on that promise. More important, however, you'll see why the integration of the various technologies is a problem in the first place.

The first step is to understand what the key problems are with Web application development. The marriage of the Web with enterprise applications has its problem spots, just like any marriage. As you'll see, XSQL greatly simplifies a key component of the relationship: database access. This leads to the next discussion: How does the database fit into modern Web application development? As you'll see throughout the book, the Oracle database is great for storing not only relational information, but XML information, also. XML, in turn, offers a lot of solutions to the fundamental problems of Web application development. Because XSQL is fundamentally XML based, it's important to understand how XML provides these solutions. Always nearby XSQL is XSLT. XSLT allows you to transform XML into . . . well, almost anything. In a world of so much technology, the problem of transforming from one data format to another comes up regularly. XSLT solves this problem, and will start the examination in this section. The section ends with an examination of how XSQL bridges the gap between all of these technologies.

The Problems of Web Application Development

This chapter is all about perspective, and nothing gives a better perspective than history. So to begin our discussion of the current state of Web application development, it's worthwhile to first consider the history of the Web itself. In the beginning—way back in 1990—there were just HTML, Uniform Resource Locators (URLs), and HTTP. The real beauty of the system was hyperlinks. Tim Berners-Lee was proposing that you could link documents together—get this—across a network! His paper, "Information Management, A Proposal" from 1990 says it best:

> *Imagine, then, the references in this document, all being associated with the network address of the thing to which they referred, so that while reading this document you could skip to them with a click of the mouse.*

From this concept, the hyperlink as we know it today was born. Now, Tim Berners-Lee wasn't the first to conceive of a hyperlink, but he implemented his system correctly and kept it simple enough so that it could propagate. He was also helped by a couple of other factors. First, the timing was right. The Internet's underlying protocol, Transmission Control Protocol/Internet Protocol (TCP/IP), was well formed and widely used by this time. Second, he invented the system in an academic setting. This is a commonality of many of the great Internet standards. It's easier to freely share a set of protocols through academia than in a commercial landscape. In the early 1990s, it was unheard of for software companies to give away complex software and designs for free.

However, the key reason why the Web grew is that it began as a very simple system. HTTP began as an extremely simple protocol and remains largely so to this day. You send a request and receive a response. It's the server's duty to figure out how to respond, and it's the client's duty to act upon the response. There were only three possible methods for asking: GET, POST, and the rarely used HEAD. This made it easy to develop Web servers. The client only had to understand a handful of possible responses. Likewise, HTML was designed with simplicity in mind. Instead of using the much more powerful but much more complex SGML, Berners-Lee opted for only a subset. Developing servers and clients was so easy, in fact, that much of the early development of the Web was completed by developers and students working in their spare time, or by professionals working on it as a special project. It's telling to note that the two institutions that did so much to give birth to the Web—the Conseil Européen pour la Recherche Nucléaire (CERN) and the National Center for Supercomputing Applications at the University of Illinois at Urbana-Champaign—had no research focus on network computing at the time the Web was invented in their labs!

Because of its simplicity, the Web spread like wildfire. It spread so far that now more than half of the American people have Web access. Most everyone who has a computer on their desk at work has Web access. This pervasiveness makes it an ideal platform for application development. You don't have to worry about installing a software application on everybody's desktop or requiring customers to install software at home. On top of that, you don't have to worry about different platforms. From a logistical standpoint alone, the Web is the obvious platform choice for many applications.

There's only one little problem: The Web was originally intended for simple document sharing! This causes some issues, the most obvious of which derives from the stateless nature of the Web. HTTP originally didn't support cookies, which allow you to bind different HTTP transactions together into user sessions. When you are just sharing static documents, you don't need to tie different HTTP transactions together. The documents always remain the same, so it doesn't matter what documents the user requested previously. However, when your data is dynamic, it often does matter what requests preceded the current one. A shopping cart application is a good example of this. When the user is ready to purchase the items, the Web application has to have tracked what items were selected across several HTTP transactions.

There are several techniques to address this problem, not the least of which is cookies. XSQL fully supports both cookies and servlet sessions. You'll learn about these mechanisms as the book progresses. More to the point, though: the mechanisms for supporting sessions were added to the original HTTP after the initial design, as were JavaScript and the concept of connecting databases to the Web. Perhaps most important, however, is that HTML documents are inadequate for conveying information.

HTML only gives instructions to a Web browser regarding how to display the information. This is a very important function, but it means that you can't interpret the HTML semantically. This is where XML comes in.

It's easy to say that the Web could have been designed better, but hindsight is always 20/20. In truth, the Web is great because it's so easy to extend. Though it was originally intended for static documents, it was easy to add support for images and dynamic data. A Web server doesn't care what kind of information it sends or where it came from. HTTP merely describes the mechanics of transferring the information in a simple and lightweight manner. If the HTML document contains JavaScript, that's fine—it's up to the browser to understand how to use that information.

Likewise, creating database-driven Web pages is just a burden on the server. Web browsers don't know the first thing about interacting with a database. Strictly speaking, an HTTP server process doesn't, either. It just knows to hand off certain URLs to servlets and other server-side modules that interact with the database and produce dynamic results.

This evolution continues today with Web services. HTTP is so simple that you can easily embed simple Web clients in your code. Then, you can grab data from remote machines and use their data in your programs. Because HTTP doesn't care what is sent, you can use XML to structure the data. HTTP is also very loose in what it receives, so you can send data back to the server. Thus, a protocol originally intended to make it easy for physicists to share documents can be used as the backbone for powerful distributed applications.

The process of developing Web applications is maturing. While early Web application developers had to concoct solutions as they encountered a wide variety of problems, a lot of the pioneering is done. The best solutions are being recognized as such and adopted widely. Java and Java Database Connectivity (JDBC) are good examples of this, as are XML and XSLT.

The XSQL framework is yet another evolution in Web development. With XSQL, producing dynamic Web pages that interact with the database is nearly as simple as writing an HTML page itself. In the not-so-distant past, you had to write a module in a language like Java, Perl, or C++ that managed the database connection, executed SQL against the database, and then processed the results. That just got you started. From there, you had to figure out what to do with the results. Because the number and type of results could vary widely for the same module, you had to deal with issues like how many results to put on a page and how to format different types. This model, often called the three-layered model, is illustrated in Figure 1.1.

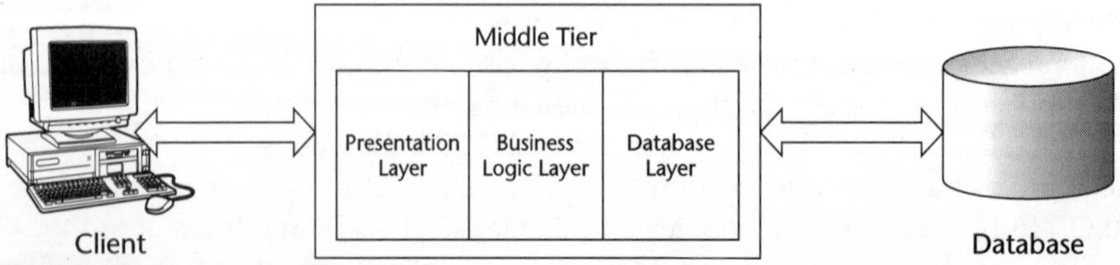

Figure 1.1 The three-layered model.

As already discussed, the user interface (UI) tier only knows how to present the data to the user. The database stores the data, usually for a variety of purposes beyond any one particular application. This leaves a lot of work to be done by that middle layer. A lot of architects like to refer to the middle layer as containing business logic. This euphemism seems to imply that the middle layer is a pristine set of simple, easy rules like "fill the warehouses to 80 percent of capacity" and "offer 10 percent discounts across the board." The client takes care of all the messy UI stuff, while the database does the hard work of managing the data.

When you peel back and examine that middle layer, it usually doesn't look like the drawings on the whiteboard. Instead, you find a lot of hard-coded SQL and UI code deep in the middle layer. Though many application development teams do their best to separate a presentation layer and a database layer, it's hard to define the lines sharply. Even if you use a scripting language like Java Servlet Pages (JSP), the snippets of code usually have dependencies deep in the system. What if the UI designer decides they want a slightly different set of data returned, or they want it ordered in a different way? Then you have to find the SQL statement and change it. That might have repercussions elsewhere in the system. You might have to create a new class. Thus, to make a relatively simple UI change, you are forced to make changes at the database layer. When the system inevitably has to be extended, then you'll probably find very little of your UI code to be truly reusable.

Now, let's assume, for a moment, that a particular application has achieved a good separation between the various layers. Everyone read all of the design pattern books and spent a lot of time at the whiteboard before coding started. They all had enough time to do the separation correctly, and the management or customer understood how important it is. There is still another problem: The output of the system is HTML. What if you want to make the data available to Web services or to a new platform such as wireless? Then you have to port the UI layer to an entirely new type of user interface. Because the code was written with only HTML in mind, you'll probably have to rewrite all of the interface widgets. If the system is perfectly designed, this is a lot of work. Now, imagine if the system isn't perfectly designed.

The Web is the greatest accidental application development platform ever. It started as an internal project at an academic institute in Switzerland and has grown into one of the great technological forces of our time. It has its complexities and intricacies, but it is infinitely adaptable. The key to the success of the Web is to understand it as an evolving technology. The art of developing Web applications is also evolving, and a successful Web application developer is always on the lookout for the next evolution. Now, it's time to see how XSQL greatly simplifies the process of developing for this platform.

XSQL as a Keystone Technology

XSQL is a keystone, rather than a cornerstone, technology. The Oracle RDBMS is a great example of a cornerstone technology. There are many companies whose entire businesses are built around their Oracle databases. Java and HTTP are also cornerstone technologies. However, XSQL is more like the keystone of an arch—the piece that holds the rest of the technologies together in a simple and elegant manner.

To see why, examine what you actually need when developing a database-driven Web application. Clear your mind of all of the three-tier and *n*-tier talk that you've heard. Many database-driven Web pages out there are really just beautified database queries. For these Web pages, the requirements are simple:

- SQL for extracting the data
- A way to produce HTML for presentation

Creating the SQL is simple. If you don't already know it, you'll learn all about it in Chapter 8. The problem is that you have to go from the SQL result set to the HTML markup. In many cases, this is what the entire middle tier in the three-tier model is doing. You start with a result set of some sort, like this:

```
>SELECT ename, job, sal FROM emp
    WHERE deptno=20
    ORDER BY sal;


ENAME   JOB              SAL
------- --------- ----------
SMITH   CLERK            800
ADAMS   CLERK           1100
JONES   MANAGER         2975
SCOTT   ANALYST         3000
FORD    ANALYST         3000
```

This isn't very palatable for the users, so you want it to look prettier. The results are shown in Figure 1.2.

Figure 1.2 Pretty SQL results.

In a case like this, you aren't doing a lot of work on the data. The data is the same, and the results are in the same order. You just want to present the results in a better way. All you need is a way to transform the results that come back from the database into what you want. The ideal situation is shown in Figure 1.3.

This is where XSQL and XSLT come in. XSLT will take an XML document and transform it into whatever you want. It is an open-standards solution to the problem of merging dynamic data with static HTML. This usually means transforming it into HTML, but you aren't limited to just that. For instance, in Chapter 15, you'll see how you can use XSLT to write scripts based on database data. If you know cascading style sheets (CSS), then you have a head start in understanding XSLT. If you are familiar with Server Side Includes, you can consider XSLT as Server Side Includes on steroids. XSLT is almost always used in combination with XSQL in some way. The core architecture is shown in Figure 1.4.

To get a better idea of how SQL, XSQL, and XSLT work together, here is some sample code. These two files are all you need to produce the Web page that was shown previously in Figure 1.2. The first file is the XSQL page. The `<xsql:query>` element, which is called an action, defines the SQL query that you need:

```
<?xml version="1.0"?>
<?xml-stylesheet type="text/xsl" href="emp-intro.xsl"?>
<page xmlns:xsql="urn:oracle-xsql" connection="demo">
  <xsql:query>
    SELECT ename, job, sal FROM emp
     WHERE deptno=20
     ORDER BY sal
  </xsql:query>
</page>
```

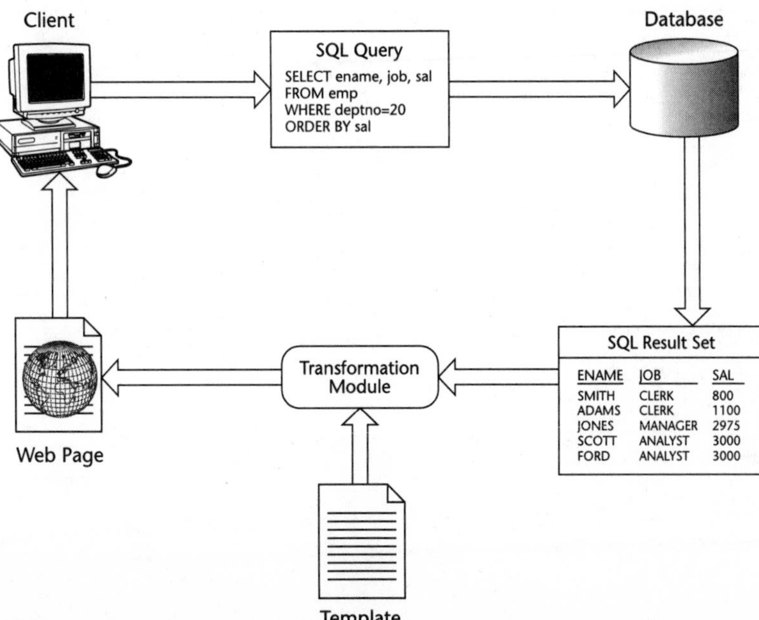

Figure 1.3 Transforming SQL results.

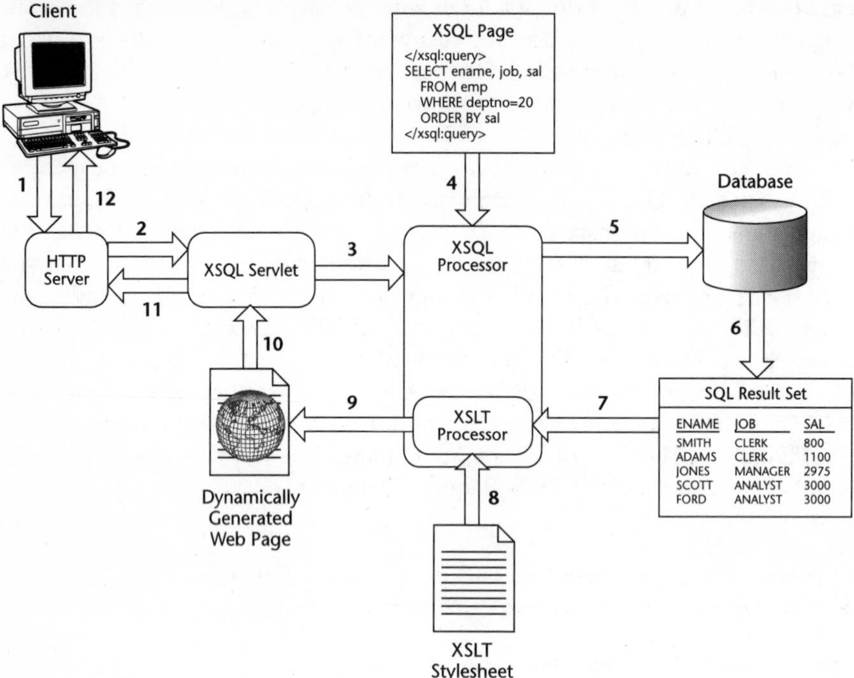

Figure 1.4 Core XSQL architecture.

The XSQL page processor connects to the database, gets the results back, and returns the following XML:

```
<page>
 <ROWSET>
  <ROW num="1">
   <ENAME>SMITH</ENAME>
   <JOB>CLERK</JOB>
   <SAL>800</SAL>
  </ROW>
  <ROW num="2">
   <ENAME>ADAMS</ENAME>
   <JOB>CLERK</JOB>
   <SAL>1100</SAL>
  </ROW>
  <ROW num="3">
   <ENAME>JONES</ENAME>
   <JOB>MANAGER</JOB>
   <SAL>2975</SAL>
  </ROW>
  <ROW num="4">
   <ENAME>SCOTT</ENAME>
   <JOB>ANALYST</JOB>
```

```
      <SAL>3000</SAL>
    </ROW>
    <ROW num="5">
      <ENAME>FORD</ENAME>
      <JOB>ANALYST</JOB>
      <SAL>3000</SAL>
    </ROW>
  </ROWSET>
</page>
```

The second line of the XSQL file links to an XSLT stylesheet. The XSQL page processor tells the XSLT processor to take the XML and transform it according to the stylesheet. Here is the stylesheet that produces the output that you see in Figure 1.2:

```
<?xml version="1.0"?>

<xsl:stylesheet
 version="1.0"
 xmlns:xsl="http://www.w3.org/1999/XSL/Transform">

 <xsl:template match="page">
  <html>
   <head><title>Simple Stylesheet</title></head>
   <body>
    <h1>Employees</h1>

    <table border="1">
     <tr bgcolor="#DDDDDD">
      <td><b>Name</b></td><td><b>Job</b></td><td><b>Salary</b></td>
     </tr>
     <xsl:apply-templates select="ROWSET/ROW"/>
    </table>
    <hr />
   </body>
  </html>
 </xsl:template>

 <xsl:template match="ROWSET/ROW">
  <tr>
   <td>
    <xsl:value-of select="ENAME"/>
   </td>
   <td>
    <xsl:value-of select="JOB"/>
   </td>
   <td>
    <xsl:value-of select="SAL"/>
   </td>
  </tr>
 </xsl:template>

</xsl:stylesheet>
```

You'll learn all about stylesheets in Chapter 13, but you probably want a brief description of what is going on here. The root element of the XML document is called page, so the page template in the stylesheet is processed first. That template is everything from `<xsl:template match="page">` to the next `</xsl:template>` tag. All of the static HTML in the template is written out more or less verbatim. The second template, `ROWSET/ROW`, is called inside the table. It defines how the values for each row in the result set should be displayed. As you can see from the screenshot, this template is called for each row that was returned in the result set. If you change the queries so more rows are returned, they will all be displayed.

If you look at the stylesheet, the majority of the code is HTML. It also falls out very logically—the dynamic data appears amid the static HTML, precisely where you want it to. The principle part of the XSQL page is a SQL query. At the beginning of this section, it was stated that you only really needed a SQL statement and a way to turn the results to HTML. The XSQL solution is very close to this. You will need to learn about XSQL and XSLT, but notice that there has been no mention of Java, JSP, JDBC, business logic, or anything else having to do with the middle tier. XSQL handles all of those details for you.

This takes care of getting data from the database, but what about putting data into it? You can also do that with XSQL. You use a different action, called `<xsql:dml>`. Instead of specifying a select statement, you issue a statement that will modify the data. As you'll see in Chapter 14, you can use it in conjunction with forms to create editors. XSQL also provides you with built-in ways to call stored procedures.

You may be looking at this and thinking, "Simple! . . . but maybe a little too simple . . . ." Of course, the simple architecture isn't going to be good enough for all problems. But that doesn't mean that you can't use XSQL to solve harder problems that involve multiple queries or complex validation before putting data into the database. Luckily, you can easily extend XSQL. Remember the `<xsql:query>` that you saw in the same page? You can write your own special actions that you can use just like that one. The action handler code that processes the action is written in Java. Your action handler code can do whatever it likes, and you can pass to it any type of data you like from the XSQL page. As with the `<xsql:dml>` action, you can also make use of parameters passed on by the user. The only expectation is that the action handler generate XML to be added to the datagram. Then, a stylesheet specified in the XSQL page can be used to convert the datagram for presentation. Figure 1.5 diagrams the XSQL architecture with action handlers.

There is one final trick up XSQL's sleeve. You aren't limited strictly to text data! As you'll see in Chapter 19, you can use serializers to produce images and PDF documents. Once again, XSQL can be easily extended to conquer tough problems. The XSQL architecture with serializers is specified in Figure 1.6. The serializer can be used to control what is written as the final output.

XSQL makes it very easy to create simple database-driven Web pages. For the more complex cases, you can use custom action handlers and serializers to extend the architecture. Your custom code works seamlessly with the rest of XSQL, so you don't give up XSQL's elegance and simplicity—you just augment it. XSQL becomes even more powerful when you use it in conjunction with other Oracle technologies, such as Oracle Text and Oracle XML DB. You'll read more about that in the next section.

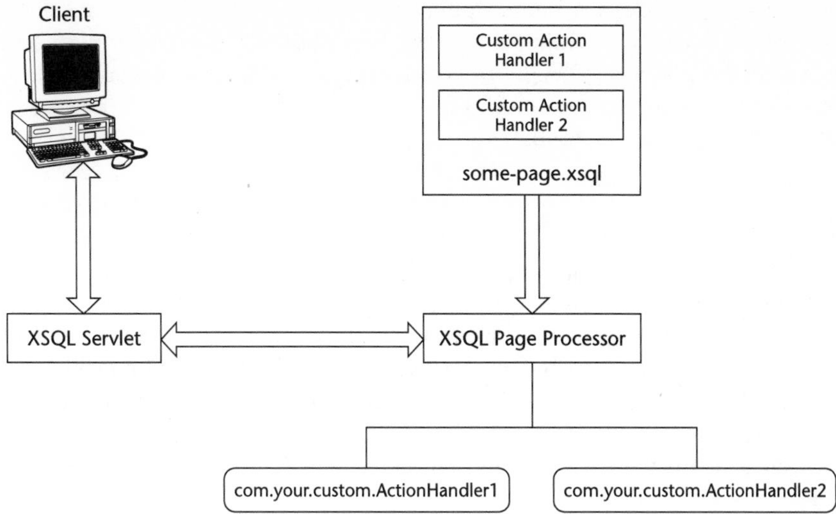

Figure 1.5 XSQL with action handlers.

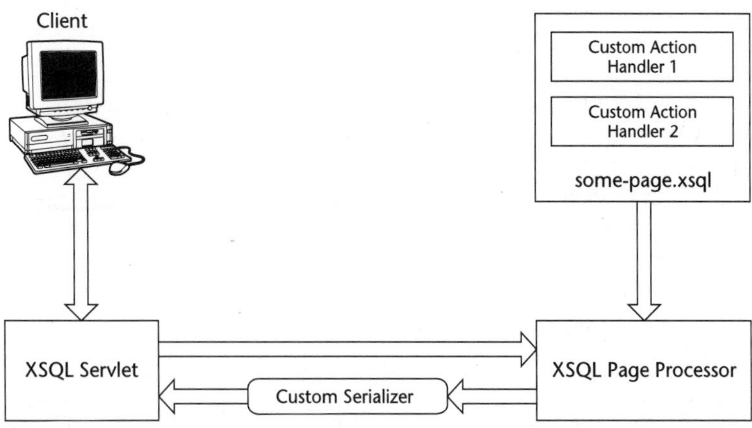

Figure 1.6 XSQL with serializers.

XSQL and Other Oracle Technologies

XSQL can be used with any database that supports JDBC. Being an Oracle product, though, it is optimized for use with the Oracle Server and its family of database technologies. Oracle provides a rich Java application program interface (API) for database access and XML. You'll use these when extending XSQL with action handlers and serializers, and also when using XSQL from inside programs. You can also use Oracle JDeveloper to help you develop your XSQL pages. This section looks at the core technologies and how they relate to XSQL.

Oracle Text

SQL is great when the data is structured, like accounts receivable or inventory. A lot of data, however, is unstructured text. Searching text is different than searching records in a database. When searching text, you want to know if keywords occur in the text and how they occur. SQL, on the other hand, is used mainly to see if a record matches to a particular term. Oracle Text bridges the gap by allowing you to perform complex unstructured text searches inside SQL statements.

Because Oracle Text is tightly integrated with Oracle SQL, you can use it from any other SQL statement in your XSQL pages.

XML Support

XML is a fantastic way to store and transport data. However, it doesn't exist in isolation. If you are writing a program that consumes XML, you need to be able to parse, create, and update XML documents. If you want to store XML, you'll quickly run into problems if you strictly try to store XML as files. Multithreaded applications don't interact well with flat files. What if two users are trying to write to the file at the same time?

Oracle provides a variety of tools to help you in the brave new world of XML. Oracle provides an XML parser and XSLT processor. These are used by the XSQL servlet in the simple model, but you can use them directly in your applications, too. These tools are part of the XML Developer's Kit (XDK), which includes a robust set of classes that allow you to interface with XML in your code. Both the Document Object Model (DOM) and Simple API for XML (SAX) APIs are fully supported. In addition, you get a lot of additional methods to make your life easier. These APIs are covered in depth in Chapter 17.

This takes care of handling XML programmatically, but what about storing documents? New to Oracle 9i, you can store XML documents directly in the database using the XmlType. This is an object type and takes advantage of the object-relational capabilities of Oracle. Once in the database, you can use XPath, the XML search language, to search XML and extract data from inside the documents. The searching of XML is integrated with Oracle Text, so you can do complex text searches on an entire XML document or just certain nodes inside the XML document. All of these capabilities are integrated with Oracle SQL and are accessible from XSQL pages. You'll learn more about this capability in Chapter 11.

Oracle is already the best relational database on the market. Now, it is in step with the latest advances in XML. Not only can you store and search XML inside the database, you can also handle XML programmatically using Oracle-supported APIs. Throughout the book, you'll see how well Oracle is integrated with XML in all of its forms.

Oracle JDeveloper

You can use any development tool you wish to develop XSQL pages, but Oracle JDeveloper offers some advantages. It is a development environment for building all types of Java and Java 2 Enterprise Edition (J2EE) applications with great support for XML. It highlights your text for you, provides easy lookup of Java classes, and checks the syntax of your XML and XSLT documents. In addition, you get the project management capabilities found in most development environments.

Because XSQL pages are also XML documents, the XML syntax checking will keep your documents well formed. JDeveloper also provides specific support for XSQL page development. It will perform XSQL-specific syntax checking and will interactively execute your code. When you get into the development of action handlers and serializers later in the book, you can use it to interactively debug your Java code.

The approach of this book is to be a development tool agnostic. All of the various types of files—Java, XSLT, and XSQL—are all text files that can be developed with any text editor. This said, JDeveloper is tuned for XSQL page development. If you haven't already found a development environment that you like, JDeveloper is an obvious and promising candidate.

Introduction to XML

Now that you have an overview of the XSQL architecture, it is time to explore the nitty-gritty of XSQL. As with any language, you also need to know a bit about the syntax. Because all XSQL documents are also XML documents, the syntax is actually defined by XML. XSLT is also an XML-based language, so the same is true for it. This means that you need to learn a bit of the basics of XML.

XML is a very simple language. Its power lies partly in this simplicity. With XML, you have an easy, industry-standard way to package data. Because XML parsers are prevalent, anyone can parse your XML document and get at your data. Most important, you can design exactly how you want your data structured. Here, you are going to learn the basics of XML. Our aim is to educate you on the structure of XML documents.

The Role of XML

XML is a metalanguage that allows you to define your own markup languages. It is a project of the World Wide Web Consortium (W3C) and is an open standard. An XML document looks a lot like an HTML page, but they serve different purposes. Whereas HTML tells a Web browser how to present data, XML is about structuring data.

XML is best understood as a child of Standard Generalized Markup Language (SGML). SGML is also the parent of HTML, so XML and HTML can be considered cousins, and SGML can be considered the mother tongue. SGML has been in use since the mid-1980s as a way to describe and organize complex documents. Among other things, SGML was used in the documentation of the stealth bomber. A typical SGML project results in the creation of a complex HTML-like language. In fact, HTML is an application of SGML.

Why didn't the Web creators just use SGML? SGML is much too heavyweight for popular use over the Internet. Though the Web would be a richer place if everyone used SGML to create their Web sites, no browser vendors were willing to implement SGML. SGML would also dramatically increase the network burden. Perhaps most important, SGML is complex to learn, whereas HTML is very simple. Without a simple markup language like HTML, the Web probably would have never reached critical mass.

So then, what's wrong with HTML? While SGML is too complex, HTML is a bit too simple for the demands of contemporary Web applications. HTML is intrinsically tied to how documents should look to their users. Though HTML documents are highly structured, they are structured around presentation. Consider the H1 tag. The text contained inside of an H1 tag is usually a headline of some sort, but you don't really know much more about it than that. About all you know is that the Web page author wants that text to stand out.

Along the same lines, consider Web sites that tell you when the Web site was last modified. You can look at a table of contents Web page and it will tell you instantly when the content was last changed. However, there is no way to look at the HTML code and algorithmically determine when it was last updated. Even though HTML documents are highly structured, they aren't semantically structured. There is no way to look at HTML and interpret it as much more than text data.

What would work is the ability to define your own tags somehow; however, HTML doesn't let you do that. The tag set is created by a standards body. Because all of the browser vendors are expected to implement the latest features of HTML, any additional functionality needs to be universally applicable. This is understandable, of course. HTML represents the presentation layer and will never be applicable to the structure of your data. What is needed, then, is a way to structure your data separate from HTML.

This is the value of XML. Instead of confining yourself to HTML, you are able to create your own language for your application. Oracle's canonical schema that you'll learn about in a few pages is an example of this. Oracle developed a way to represent SQL result sets in XML. Once established, XSQL developers can use it to present and manipulate the data. You also have the power to define your own markup language and can do it very quickly. You don't have to write a parser—XML parsers are widely available. Your burden is simply to think about what you need, create an XML schema, and document it. Once created, other people inside and outside of your organization can use it for data interchange.

NOTE Defining your own tags is great, but an XML document isn't instantly useful by itself. While an HTML document is immediately usable by millions of Web browsers worldwide, an XML document isn't. You can create a `<LastUpdated>` tag, but what application will understand it? Thus, XML is primarily used, in conjunction with XSLT, to create HTML and other standardized document types, or by a Web services client that knows the XML schema you are using.

As an XSQL developer, you will be creating your own implicit schemas along the way. However, it is a bit grandiose to think of these as brand new markup languages. In most cases, they are going to be the Oracle canonical representation plus some XML that you add around the edges. Still, this does give you an XML layer to your application that is separate from the actual presentation. In terms of XSQL development, this is the key advantage of XML. You are able to separate your application data from the actual presentation. XSLT yields the actual presentation while you are able to easily repurpose the XML layer.

Well-Formed versus Valid Documents

You may have heard of a document being referred to as valid or well formed. The definition and distinction is important to the discussion here. A well-formed document is simply an XML document that is syntactically correct. A valid document is a well-formed document that also follows the rules of a schema.

Anytime you write XML, it has to be well formed. The need for validity is determined by whether there is a schema associated with your document. On the one hand, if an application is processing the document, it is required to be valid. This makes the job of the application much easier. If the document is unacceptable, the parser will generate an error before the document gets to the application. This greatly reduces the number of error cases that the application must be prepared to handle. Because XSQL documents are fed to an application—the XSQL page processor—they must be valid. They must agree with the schema for XSQL pages.

On the other hand, the XML documents that XSQL generates only need to be valid. This does not mean that it is all free love and long hair. First, you may have a Web service consuming your XML that expects a schema. In most cases, your document is going to be transformed. If your generated XML doesn't come out right, your transformation will be ugly. Fortunately, the XML that XSQL generates is pretty tight. Bad transformations are really only a problem if you get fancy with custom action handlers or include foreign XML.

Document Structure

An XML document is structured like a tree. Trees are some of the most pervasive structures in all of computer science. Probably the most common usage is a file system. Trees are a great elegant structure because they can be used to establish relationships between any set of data. Even a table of data can be easily represented with a tree, as you'll see later in this chapter.

Trees can be generally described with the following rules:

- There can be only one root element.
- The root element is the only element that has no parent.
- Every nonroot element has exactly one parent element.
- Any element can have one or more children elements, or no children at all.

In XML, the parent-child relationships are represented by start and end tags. The following example shows a simple document that contains two child elements.

```
<?xml version="1.0"?>
<Root>
  <ChildElement1 />
  <ChildElement2 />
</Root>
```

This should look very familiar to anyone who has coded HTML. The `<Root>` element looks like a `<UL>` tag, and child elements look like `<LI>` tags. There is a key difference, though. If you look at the child elements, you'll notice that the tag ends with `/>`. This is required in XML so that the parser knows that this element has no children.

The preceding example represents the three tag types in XML: (1) the start tag, (2) the end tag, and (3) the empty element tag. Table 1.1 documents the syntax of these tags. In the "Form" column, the unique syntax requirements for each type of tag are documented. There are also common syntactical requirements that apply to all tags.

As you would expect, start and end tags must be properly nested. A child element must be entirely contained within its parent's start and end tags. The following example demonstrates bad and illegal nesting:

```
<?xml version="1.0" ?>
<Root>
     <Troublemaker>
</Root>
</Troublemaker>
```

Our last structural consideration involves our children elements. In our previous example, there were only two children elements, and each had a different name. This isn't a requirement. You can have many children with the same name. For instance, the XML returned from the database by Oracle will have as many row child elements as there are rows in the result set. Our final example is of a valid document with multiple elements of the same name. Just for fun, this example is also more deeply nested.

```
<?xml version="1.0" ?>
<Root>
    <FirstLevelChild>
          <SecondLevelChild/>
    </FirstLevelChild>
    <RedHeadedStepChild />
    <FirstLevelChild />
    <FirstLevelChild>
        <GrandchildOfRoot>
           <KidsTheseDays />
        </GrandchildOfRoot>
    </FirstLevelChild>
</Root>
```

Table 1.1 XML Tags

TYPE	FORM	EXAMPLE	CONSTRAINTS
Start tag	Must start with <, end with >, not start or end with </ or />.	`<Root>`	Must have a matching end tag of the same name.
End tag	Must start with </, end with >, and not end with />.	`</Root>`	Must have a matching start tag of the same name.
Empty element tag	Must start with <, end with />, and not start with </.	`<Child Element1 />`	

Processing Instructions

You may have noticed that all of our sample documents begin with the same line. This is a processing instruction. Processing instructions give input to the application that is handling the document. The `<?xml version="1.0" ?>` processing instruction is required. It can also have an additional attribute to describe the character encoding of the document. Here is an example that reinforces the default encoding:

```
<?xml version="1.0" encoding="UTF-8" ?>
```

Your documents can have more than one processing instruction. For XSQL pages, your documents will usually have a processing instruction that references an XSLT stylesheet. This will be covered in depth later this chapter.

```
<?xml-stylesheet type="text/xsl" href="emp.xsl"?>
```

Attributes

Attributes are name-value pairs that are associated with an XML element. Most HTML elements also have attributes. The bgcolor attribute of the body element is one of many examples. You can have as many attributes in your element as you wish. However, each attribute name can appear only once for a particular element. Values always have to be quoted with either single or double quotes. Attribute names and values are restricted in that they can only contain some characters. These restrictions are the same as the restrictions on the names of XML elements and are covered in the next section.

Here is an example of an XSQL page where three attributes are used: `<connection>`, `<xmlns:xsql>`, and `<tag-case>`.

```
<?xml version="1.0"?>
<page connection="demo" xmlns:xsql="urn:oracle-xsql">
  <xsql:query tag-case="lower">
     select * from emp
  </xsql:query>
</page>
```

Syntax Nitty-Gritty

You know almost everything that you need to know to create well-formed XML documents. There are a couple of rules that you haven't seen yet, though. This section acts as a review of the rest of the syntax rules. The most common restrictions that you will encounter involve the names of elements and attributes. This is covered first. XML, like most languages, has reserved characters. Sometimes, you'll want to use these, so you'll learn how. One option you'll learn about is the CDATA entity, which allows you to define special sections of character data. The final section here covers XML comments.

There is one instruction that isn't discussed here: `<!DOCTYPE>`. It is used to specify a Document Type Definition (DTD), a type of schema. Before covering the rest of the syntax rules of XML, let's review the syntax rules that have already been covered:

- You must have an XML processing instruction at the top of the document.
- There can be only one root element.
- Start tags must have matching end tags, and vice versa.
- Tags must be nested correctly.
- A particular attribute can appear only once per element.
- Attribute values must be enclosed in single or double quotes.

Element Name and Attribute Restrictions

Element names and attributes share the same restrictions. Both must be composed entirely of the same set of characters. This set consists of all alphanumeric characters, the underscore, and the period. The colon is also valid, but has special meaning—you'll learn more about that when XML namespaces are discussed. A name or attribute can only start with an underscore or a letter. The last restriction is that no name or attribute may begin with the string xml. Case-insensitive Table 1.2 gives examples of legal and illegal strings.

Table 1.2 Example Name/Attribute Strings

STRING	LEGAL?	COMMENT
`howdy`	Yes	All valid characters; doesn't start with a number or xml.
`_howdy123-`	Yes	All valid characters; doesn't start with a number or "xml".
`_123-howdy`	Yes	All valid characters; doesn't start with a number or "xml".
`123howdy`	No	Starts with a number.
`howdy everybody`	No	Contains a space.
`howdy!`	No	! isn't a valid character.
`xml-howdy`	No	Starts with "xml".
`howdy:everyone`	Yes, but . . .	Use of a colon is forbidden, except in conjunction with XML namespaces. This is legal only if you have a namespace called `howdy`.

Special Characters

There are several characters that have special meaning in XML. From time to time, this will pose an inconvenience because you want to use these characters. The full set of special characters is described in Table 1.3.

Table 1.3 Special Characters

CHARACTER	RESTRICTIONS	WORKAROUND
'	Not allowed in attribute values quoted by "	Use &apos.
"	Not allowed in attribute values quoted by '	Use "e.
&	Must always be escaped	Use &.
<	Must always be escaped	Use <.

The most common problem encountered with XSQL is with the < symbol. This symbol is also an operator in SQL, so its special status in XML causes problems. The following XSQL page will produce an error:

```
<?xml version="1.0"?>
<page connection="demo" xmlns:xsql="urn:oracle-xsql">
   <xsql:query>
    select * from emp where sal < 50000
   </xsql:query>
</page>
```

When the XML parser encounters the <, it thinks that it has encountered a new tag. When it encounters the next character, a space, it gives up. There are two workarounds: (1) Use the escape sequence as demonstrated in the following code, or (2) use CDATA, which is covered in the next section.

```
<?xml version="1.0"?>
<page connection="demo" xmlns:xsql="urn:oracle-xsql">
<xsql:query>
    select * from emp where sal &lt; 50000
</xsql:query>
</page>
```

CDATA

The CDATA entity allows you to declare a section of character data off-limits to the XML parser. When the parser encounters the CDATA declaration, it skips all characters inside of it. Here is an example that resolves the earlier problem with the < operator:

```
<?xml version="1.0"?>
<page connection="demo" xmlns:xsql="urn:oracle-xsql">
<xsql:query>
    <![CDATA[
    select * from emp where sal < 50000
    ]]>
</xsql:query>
</page>
```

CDATA entities are useful any time that you have sections that shouldn't be processed because they also take a load of the processor.

Comments

No programming language is complete without comments. The syntax for comments in XML is as follows. It is identical to HTML comments.

```
<!-- An XML Comment -->
```

Namespaces

As discussed earlier, XML allows you to create your own languages. However, what if someone else has developed a schema that you want to use? There is the chance that element names from this other schema will conflict with yours. XML has a solution for this: namespaces. Namespaces allow you to make your elements globally unique. It does this by attaching your element names to a Universal Resource Identifier (URI). A Uniform Resource Locator (URL) is an example of a URI, as is a Uniform Resource Name (URN). Even if you use an extremely common element name in your document, such as name, you can make it globally unique by specifying a URI that you control.

XSQL uses a URN—`<oracle-xsql>`—for its namespace. You may have noticed it in the examples:

```
<page connection="demo" xmlns:xsql="urn:oracle-xsql">
```

The `<xmlns:xsql>` attribute signifies that some children elements of the page element will belong to the XSQL namespace. Namespaces can overlap—in fact, that's the whole point. The following XSQL example shows this. This page uses both the XSQL namespace and the Mike namespace.

```
<?xml version="1.0"?>
<page connection="demo" xmlns:xsql="urn:oracle-xsql"
xmlns:mike="http://www.ibiblio.org/mdthomas">
  <xsql:query>
   select * from emp where ename='SMITH'
  </xsql:query>
  <mike:mikeNode>
     Value
  </mike:mikeNode>
</page>
```

The output of this XSQL is shown above. Notice that the `<xmlns:mike>` attribute is preserved but the `<xmlns:xsql>` namespace isn't. In the output, no member of the XSQL namespace is present. The `<xsql:query>` element was replaced with the results of the query. Because there are no members of the namespace in the document, the XSQL page processor removes the attribute.

Schemas

We spoke earlier about how XML allows you to create your own languages. These languages are formally known as schemas. A schema is a definition of how elements in your XML should relate to one another, what attributes are appropriate, and what values are appropriate for nonempty elements. You can program very successfully in XSQL without ever creating your own schema. At the least, it's important to be conversant about schemas.

The XML documents that you have seen so far are very simple, but XML can be very complex. The purpose of a schema is to rein in that complexity. This makes it easier for applications to be able to consume the XML—they know what they are expecting.

Since we've talked about creating your own languages with XML, perhaps we can extend that analogy. If the elements are the words of our language, the schema is the grammar. It tells the world how the words have to be arranged so that they are meaningful to our applications. You read earlier about valid XML documents. A schema is used to determine that an XML document is valid for that schema's particular set of rules.

As with natural languages, there is a lot that can go into determining that a document is valid. Think about it in terms of plain old English documents, such as this book. On one level, this book is valid if the individual sentences are grammatically correct. The editors have certain requirements about section headings before they will call it valid. The publisher wants the book to be a certain length and of a correct tone and quality before it is considered valid to ship it to the stores. Ultimately, the reader makes the call as to how valid the book is as a resource based on a number of factors.

The validity tests for XML documents can be as multifaceted as this. At the lowest level, a schema can be used to determine if particular nodes have values of the right type. The next step is to determine that the structure is right. Do the children elements belong with their parent? Does the parent have all of the children nodes for it to be valid? Then, you can look at how the different elements relate to each other to make determinations of integrity. From there, the sky is the limit. If you desire, you can pile complex business rules into your schema.

With an idea as to what schemas are about, it's time to focus on how to implement one. This can be as confusing as the complicated schemas we are talking about! There are several different ways to define schemas. These are called schema languages. (Good thing the languages we develop with XML are called schemas, or else they would have to be called language languages!) The original schema language is DTD. In fact, it has its own instruction built in to XML: `<!DOCTYPE>`. Though still widely used, DTDs are becoming unpopular for a number of reasons, including cumbersome syntax and the inability to define data types. The other popular schema languages are XML based. W3C XML Schema is the heir apparent. There are other players, including RELAX NG, Schematron, and Exampletron.

Moving On

In the previous pages, XSQL was covered at a high level. You learned the problems that XSQL addresses and how it integrates the technologies together. The XML basics covered in the previous section will come up again and again throughout the book. Now, it's time to dive into XSQL development. The next couple of chapters cover the installation and setup of XSQL. After you have XSQL installed, you'll be ready to move forward.

CHAPTER

2

Getting Started with XSQL

Now that you have had a glimpse of all the wonderful things that you can do with XSQL, your next step is to get it working and start developing. This chapter focuses on getting it installed on your system, getting the demos up and running, and creating your very first XSQL page. As with any new addition to your system, XSQL introduces a new set of security concerns. Security is best attacked at the time of installation, so you will learn about the security implications of XSQL in this chapter.

NOTE It is important to note that these next few pages aren't meant to be an exhaustive guide on production-ready, optimized Oracle database installations. The rest of the book could be on that! Rather, the aim is to get you up and running quickly. Though the system you install here may not be ready to serve millions of users and complete thousands of transactions a second, you *will* be able to start development. You will also understand how to install XSQL in an existing production system that presumably is capable of handling real-world loads and how to make it secure.

The good news is that XSQL is easy to install, and the security issues raised—though important—are easy to understand and simple to resolve. If you are starting from scratch, you should be able to get up and running in only a few hours. Most of that time will be waiting to click the next button in the Oracle 9i database installation.

If you are on your way to developing production applications with Oracle XSQL, at some point you will need to install the Oracle XDK in a production environment. This makes things a little more complex. For example, maybe you won't be able to use the default Web server that the Oracle Installer will install for you. If you are going against a production database, you will probably have to change the configuration to point at that database.

Although a little more complex, installing XSQL in an existing environment shouldn't cause any loss of hair or even loss of sleep. In the next few pages, you will start by covering the simple case of installing everything from scratch and then pay special attention to issues that arise when installing in an existing environment. The last few pages are spent getting you well versed in the security issues around XSQL so that you can feel safe as you learn about this tool.

Basic Installation

It's time to dive into the installation. Before starting, you will first look at the anatomy of the components, so that you know what you are installing and how the pieces fit together. The next step is to get the files, either from Oracle's Web site or from your Oracle 9i CD. From there, you will see how to install the whole system, including the database and Web server, from scratch. Then you will look at how to integrate with existing environments.

TIP **If you haven't already done so, you should sign up for the Oracle Technology Network Web site (`otn.oracle.com`). Sign-up is free, and you get access to a lot of resources, including downloads of the latest and greatest Oracle technologies.**

Installation Anatomy

Before blindly invoking the installer and pushing buttons, your first step should be conceptual. What are all the pieces that you are installing? Figure 2.1 shows how the pieces fit together from an installation perspective. This isn't an all-inclusive diagram of how a working XSQL system should work. You have a lot more fun stuff to add. For now, this glimpse should be enough so that, in addition to successfully installing XSQL, you will understand what you installed.

Here's some more information about each of the components described in the diagram:

- *Oracle XSQL Servlet*. This is the key piece of the puzzle. Most of this book will focus on the functionality of this servlet.
- *HTTP server*. For the purposes of this discussion, the Web server handles HTTP requests from the client.
- *HTTP client*. For now, this is a Web browser. Later on, you will see how this can also be a Web Services client—instead of a person reading rendered HTML, a piece of software will consume XML data.

- *Servlet container.* A servlet container is a Java Virtual Machine (JVM) that will invoke a servlet in response to a certain HTTP request. A servlet container is usually one part of an application server. Also, J2EE containers superset the functionality of servlet containers—a J2EE-enabled application server like IBM WebSphere, BEA WebLogic, or IPlanet Application Server can be considered a servlet container, just as Tomcat is a servlet container.
- *XSQL files.* These files describe the database queries and are the key pieces that you, as a developer, add to an XSQL system. There are several examples files included in the installation, and you will create your own from scratch before this chapter is finished.
- *JDBC driver.* The XSQL servlet is written in Java, and the JDBC driver is necessary to access the database.
- *Oracle database.* For your purposes, consider this an Oracle 9i database. However, Oracle XSQL isn't limited to only 9i. Older Oracle databases can be used, including Oracle 7.3. Database compatibility is determined by JDBC compatibility. Thus, non-Oracle JDBC-compliant databases can also be integrated with XSQL. This book will focus on XSQL integration with Oracle 9i and how to take advantage of the rich technology available only from Oracle.

You may be looking at the diagram and saying, "Wasn't this supposed to be easy?" Except for the Web browser, all of these components are installed by default. In fact, you don't need to know all of these details to successfully complete a scratch installation. However, this anatomy lesson will become important if you ever have to install XSQL in an existing environment.

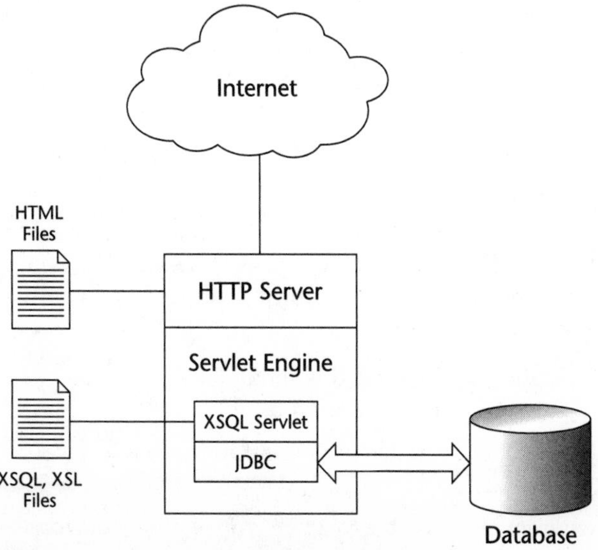

Figure 2.1 Anatomy of an installation.

Scratch XSQL Installation

Now that you've got an idea of what all the different pieces do, you're ready to do your first installation. The good news is that you won't have to make many choices, and the choices are pretty easy. The bad news is that it will take a while to complete. You are going to cover the two common cases: a Unix server installation (Linux, Solaris, etc.) and a Windows server installation (NT, 2000, XP). First, you will look at the prerequisites of a Unix installation. Oracle shouldn't be installed or run as root on a Unix machine. Windows servers don't have the distinction of a powerful root user, so those steps aren't required.

Before beginning the installation, you should make sure that there is no Web server active on port 80. Oracle will install an Apache Web server for you, and the examples can be accessed from this Web server. It is certainly possible to work with an already installed Web server—the next section explores how this works. If you are most interested in getting XSQL to work with existing components, you may want to skip forward to the next section. If you would like to get a XSQL system up and running quickly, just take the Web server down for now. To verify that there is no Web server running, perform `netstat -a -n` and scan the Local Address column for entries ending in :80. If you see any, you have an active Web server that needs to be stopped.

Unix Prerequisites

Before beginning a Unix installation, you need to create a `dba` group and an `oracle id`. The `dba` group allows several users on the system to control the database. The `oracle` user actually owns the database. Depending on your particular system, you may need to tweak the kernel parameters so that the System Global Memory (SGA) structure of the Unix system can be accommodated. In most cases, this step isn't necessary for development systems of adequate hardware that won't be bearing a heavy load. However, you may wish to consult your OS `readme` file on this subject.

After this, your first step is to create the `dba` and `oinstall` groups. This can be completed by the `groupadd` command as root. On Red Hat Linux, this can be as follows. The `-f` flag causes the command to exit with an error if the group already exists:

```
# groupadd -f dba
# groupadd -f oinstall
```

With this step completed, you should add any users to these groups that should be able to perform database administration or installation tasks, respectively. The next step is to create the `oracle` user with the `useradd` utility. After creation, you have several configuration tasks for the `oracle` user:

- Set the `umask` to 022. Depending on the shell, this should be done in the startup file—either the `.profile` or the `.cshrc` file.
- Set the `ORACLE_BASE` environment variable in the startup file to where you want Oracle products to be installed.
- Set the `ORACLE_HOME` environment variable to where you want the database installed. This should probably be a subdirectory of `ORACLE_BASE`.

- Before preceding, either exit the session and reenter it, or refresh the session with the new settings (e.g., `source .cshrc`).

After these steps are complete, you are ready to begin the Oracle installation. Simply cd in to the CD mount point (e.g., `/cdrom`) or the top level of the untarred distribution and execute `runInstaller`. If you are doing the installation remotely, you will not be able to complete the installation from the command line. You'll need X Windows. Make sure that you have X-Server running on your local machine and that the remote machine isn't restricted from your X-Server. Then, set the `DISPLAY` environment variable to your console. If your local machine name is `my.localMachine.com` and the machine where you are installing Oracle is running CSH, the following will work:

```
oracle>setenv DISPLAY my.localMachine.com:0.0
```

If you are going to be working remotely with this machine a lot, you might want to go ahead and add that to the startup script.

Using Oracle Universal Installer

If you are installing on a Windows server, then you start the installer by running `setup.exe`. At this point, the steps precede the same regardless of operating system. This is the beauty of the Universal Installer. You should now have the first screen as shown in Figure 2.2.

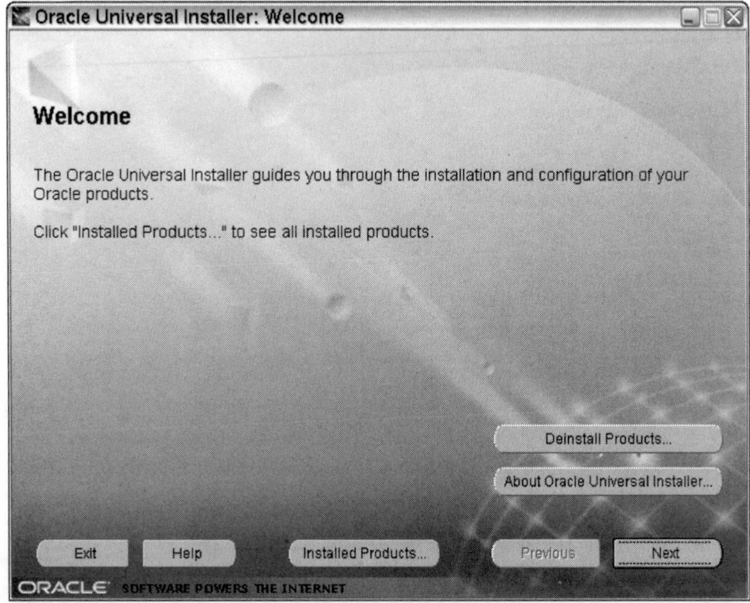

Figure 2.2 Start screen of the Oracle Universal Installer.

Your first step is to click Next. There are really only a couple of choices that need to be made in the next few screens. The default choices should be adequate for creating a development system. The most important choice comes on the File Locations screen (Figure 2.3). Before choosing the location for the Oracle installation, you should make sure that you have enough space on the drive or file system. You should have at least 2 GB free. However, you don't have to plan to have enough space on the given drive or file system for all the data that could possibly be put into your database. As your database grows, you can easily add new data files on other drives or file systems.

The other choice that you will need to make is the System Identifier (SID) of your default Oracle instance. The preferred SID is `ORCL`, and using this name means that the XSQL samples will work upon completion of the installation. If you name it something else, you will need to tweak some settings in the `XSQLConfig.xml` file before the samples will work. The other setting in this screen is the Global Database Name. This should be the full Domain Name Service (DNS) hostname of the machine where you are installing Oracle prefixed by the SID. This isn't the only instance that can be configured on this machine. You can configure as many instances as you would like. If you are experimenting with different configurations, you can keep your experiments largely separate by setting up different instances.

The Summary screen is the last screen that appears before you click Install to start the installation (Figure 2.4). If you took all of the defaults, you should be able to scroll down to the end of the list and see XSQL Servlet as shown. If you choose to do a custom installation, you will need to scrutinize this screen carefully.

Now the installation is ready to begin in earnest. Depending on your system, it will probably take at least a couple of hours to complete. Upon completion, you should be able start the Web server and access the samples at `http://localhost/xsql/`.

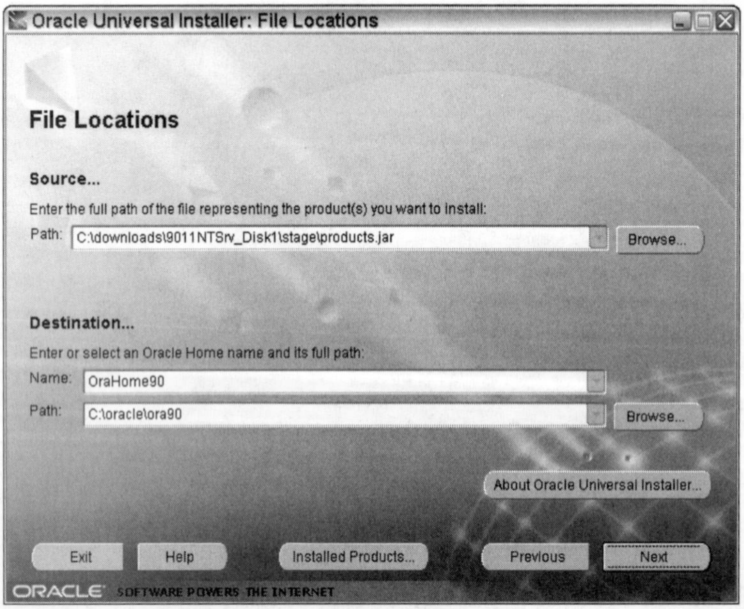

Figure 2.3 Choosing your installation location.

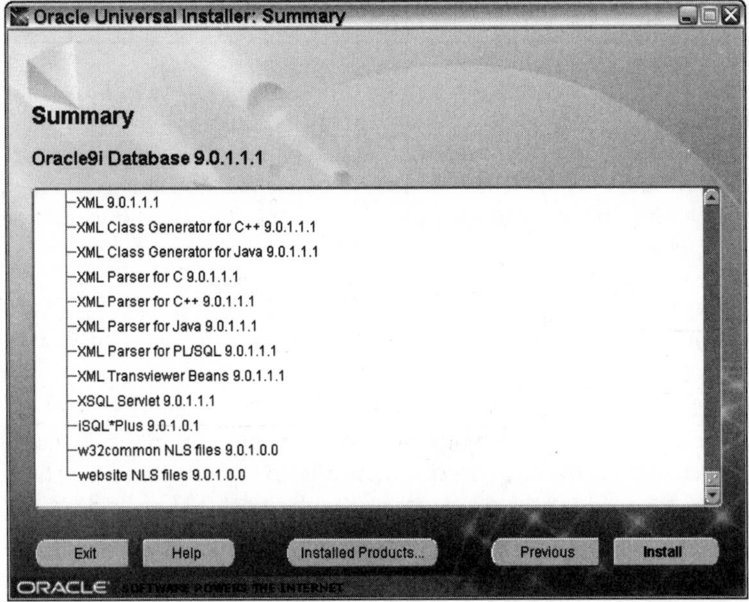

Figure 2.4 Reviewing installation options.

Configuring Java

As you progress through the book, you will program in Java to enhance the core functionality of XSQL. If you haven't already installed Java, you should do so now. Installation of the Java Developer's Kit (JDK) is easy. Just go to `www.javasoft.com`, download the JDK version that you want for your operating system, and install. Be careful, however, which JDK version you download. It should be a supported version listed in the release notes for your version of XSQL. The release notes are available at `http://localhost/xdk/java/xsql/readme.html` after you have completed the installation. This book is based on XSQL version 9.0.1.0.0 and JDK 1.3.

You will also need to modify the `CLASSPATH` before doing Java development. The following Java Archives (JARs) need to be included in the `CLASSPATH`:

- `jlib/sax2.jar`
- `rdbms/jlib/xsu12.jar`
- `lib/xmlparserv2.jar`
- `lib/oraclexsql.jar`
- `jdbc/lib/classes12.jar`

Installing in Existing Environments

It's often easiest and most fun to start from scratch. But in reality, you will probably have to get XSQL working with an existing environment at some point. This section looks at the challenges in linking XSQL to an existing database and application server. There are numerous permutations of Web server and database that you may encounter. This section looks at two specific cases: integration with Microsoft Internet Information Server and Apache Tomcat.

The integration is twofold. On the Web server or application server side, the XSQL servlet must be loaded by a Java servlet engine. Most popular Web servers provide a hook for running servlets, so the real problem is just figuring out how to load servlets contained in JAR files.

On the database side, the XSQL servlet is connected to a JDBC driver. If a JDBC driver is already installed and working with your database, the most you may need to do is to make a couple of changes to the `XSQLConfig.xml` file. In the worst case, you have to install a JDBC driver, but as long as you are working with a post-7.3 Oracle database, you should be able to find one easily. Things get tricky only when you start pointing the XSQL servlet at a non-Oracle database. You'll still probably find a solution, though, because XSQL Servlet links to a JDBC driver, not to any particular database.

Web and Application Server Integration

To function, the XSQL servlet must be able to receive HTTP requests from the Internet. The XSQL servlet doesn't listen to TCP/IP directly. Rather, a component listening to the wire and processing TCP/IP must pass the requests to the XSQL servlet. This request is usually passed via a servlet engine to the servlet. Typically, a servlet engine functions as an extension to the Web server that handles the actual HTTP requests. This means that most any Web server—including Microsoft IIS—can be extended to handle servlets by integrating a servlet engine with it.

NOTE Later in the book, you are going to look at how to integrate Java Server Pages (JSP) with XSQL. Most application servers that support servlets also support JSP. JSP certainly isn't a requirement for working with XSQL, but it is nice in many ways. If you are at the point of making a decision as to which application server to choose, you may want to consider one with strong JSP support.

The next section covers the Web servers that have been tested by Oracle with XSQL. Following that is one example installation using Apache Tomcat.

Servlet Engine Compatibility

You should be able to install XSQL in any environment where you can run Java servlets. In your release notes for XSQL you should find a list of all the servlet engines that have been tested with your version of XSQL. Following is the list from the time of this writing. If your particular servlet engine isn't listed here, all hope is not lost. This list represents only what Oracle pushed through its quality assurance labs. If you have other servlets running, in all likelihood you will be able to get XSQL Servlet running in your system.

These servlet engines were tested and verified with the XSQL 9.0.1.0.0 release:

- Oracle Internet Application Server 8*i*
- Allaire JRun 2.3.3 and 3.0.0
- Apache 1.3.9 with JServ 1.0 and 1.1
- Apache 1.3.9 with Tomcat 3.1 or 3.2 Servlet Engine
- Apache Tomcat 3.1 or 3.2 Web Server + Servlet Engine
- Caucho Resin 1.1
- Java Web Server 2.0
- Weblogic 5.1 Web Server
- NewAtlanta ServletExec 2.2 and 3.0 for IIS/PWS 4.0
- Oracle8*i* Lite Web-to-Go Server
- Oracle8*i* 8.1.7 Oracle Servlet Engine
- Sun JavaServer Web Development Kit (JSWDK) 1.0.1 Web Server

It's important to note that this is a list of the servlet engines, not necessarily Web servers. Your Web server may not be listed here, but a servlet engine that is compatible with your Web server may be. For instance, in the case of Microsoft IIS, you can use ServletExec and JRun because they can be installed on top of IIS.

Installing on a Servlet Engine

Installing the XSQL servlet is much the same as installing any other servlet. The only real differences are that the XSQL servlet will have to make a JDBC connection to the database, and there are some auxiliary packages that the XSQL servlet uses. The implication of the latter is that this is more than a single-class file installation. The JDBC connection complicates matters only if your network topology is complex. For instance, if a firewall is sitting between your database machine and the machine where you are installing XSQL, then you may have some problems getting a connection between the servlet and the database.

The installation of the XSQL servlet is performed in three steps: reconfiguring the servlet engine's `CLASSPATH`, mapping the `.xsql` extension to the servlet, and creating a virtual directory. The release notes that come with XSQL detail the specific steps for a variety of servlet engines. Here, you will detail these steps at a conceptual level.

The first step is to add the necessary XSQL JARs to the servlet engine's `CLASSPATH`. This is necessary so that the servlet engine will be able to load the XSQL servlet and the classes it needs. If you are using a JDBC driver other than the one provided by default, you will also need to add the JDBC driver's class to the `CLASSPATH`. The entries that need to be added to the `CLASSPATH` are:

- jlib/sax2.jar
- rdbms/jlib/xsu12.jar
- lib/xmlparserv2.jar
- lib/oraclexsql.jar
- jdbc/lib/classes12.jar
- xdk/admin

The last entry is necessary so that the XSQL servlet can find its configuration file, XSQLConfig.xml.

The second step is to map the .xsql extension to the XSQL servlet. This tells the servlet engine to hand requests for .xsql pages over to the XSQL servlet. This mapping is usually accomplished as a name/value entry in a configuration file or in an administrative user interface. Here is an example of how to accomplish this for Apache JServ. This entry goes in to the jserv.conf file.

```
ApJServAction .xsql /servlets/oracle.xml.xsql.XSQLServlet
```

The last step is to set up a virtual directory. This isn't completely necessary, but there are many advantages to having your XSQL pages in one area. Also, your demos won't work quite right unless they are inside an /xsql virtual directory. This is usually handled at the Web server level, though Tomcat handles it as part of the configuration of a context. For Tomcat, the context handles both the mapping mentioned previously and the establishment of the virtual URL mapping. On Apache, the virtual directory is configured as follows in the httpd.conf file:

```
Alias /xsql/ "/your-oracle-home/xdk/demo/java/xsql"
```

Configuring the Database

If Oracle 9i has been installed, then in all likelihood XDK, PL/SQL, JDBC, and Text have already been installed. XSQL sits outside of the database, so it isn't necessary that it be installed as part of the database. PL/SQL and Text do need to be installed in the database, but only if you need them. As you'll see in the coming chapters, they provide some very useful functionality. It's very unlikely that PL/SQL is not installed, but your database administrator (DBA) might not have wanted to install Text. If you want to install it now—and your DBA agrees—just install it with the Oracle Universal Installer.

It isn't necessary to use the Oracle JDBC driver. XSQL Servlet is at its best using the latest Oracle JDBC driver, but it is designed to degrade gracefully with other JDBC drivers. Why would you want to use another JDBC driver? Because XSQL isn't Oracle dependent, any database that can be accessed with JDBC can be used with XSQL.

Configuring the Database Connection

Once you have your XSQL servlet working, the XDK is installed, and the JDBC driver is in place, there is only one step left: configuring the database connection. If your database resides on the same machine as your XSQL installation, the SID is `ORCL`, and the `SCOTT/TIGER` demo user is in place, this may already work. Regardless, it is a simple process to get this configured. Then you are on your way!

Moving On

This chapter helped you through an XSQL installation. You should now have XSQL set up and be ready to move forward. The next chapter focuses on getting the demos configured and understanding security issues. From there, you'll be ready to start real development.

Hello, XSQL!

At this point, you have a development environment for XSQL. You've been able to confirm that the simplest demos work. By the end of this section, we are going to have created our first XSQL page. First, you will complete the base installation by installing the rest of the samples. Then, the development environment will be readied by straightening out the Java CLASSPATH. Next, you will create a new Oracle user and a connection definition in the `XSQLConfig.xml` file. Last of all, you will create your very first XSQL page and a XSLT stylesheet to go along with it.

Loading the XSQL Samples

As mentioned before, only a couple of the samples are working so far. The reason that the other samples aren't working is because the sample data hasn't been loaded into our database yet. To get these samples working, you need to run a SQL script. The SQL script, named `install.sql`, is located in `xdk\demo\java\xsql`. Executing this script will run separate scripts for each of the demos.

You run this script using SQL*PLUS as follows:

```
>sqlplus scott/tiger @install.sql
```

If you are working with a database other than the default for your instance of SQL*PLUS, you will need to include that in the connection string. If the database is SAMPLE_DB, this would be as follows:

```
>sqlplus scott/tiger@SAMPLE_DB @install.sql
```

There is one last step to complete for loading the demo data. The doyouxml example includes some XML data that needs to be imported into your database. Change into the doyouxml/ directory, and load this with the import utility as follows:

```
>imp scott/tiger doyouxml.dmp
```

If you are loading into a different database, do this as follows:

```
>imp scott/tiger@SAMPLE_DB doyouxml.dmp
```

With these steps completed, you should be able to view all of the demos. Figure 3.1 shows what the airport code display demo should look like after doing a lookup on Washington.

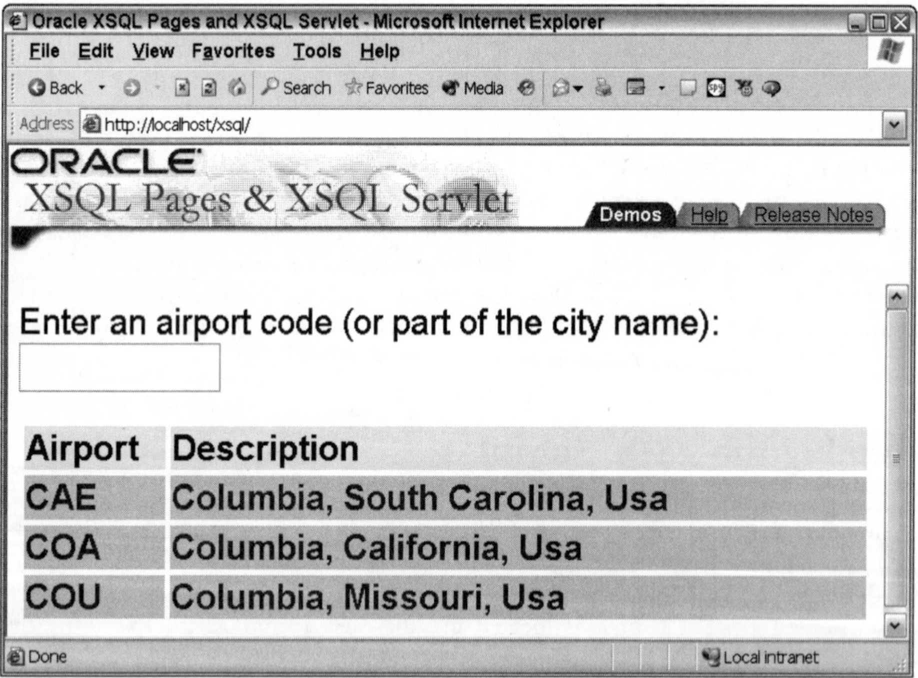

Figure 3.1 Airport code display demo.

Creating a Demo User and Table

Now that the demos provided by Oracle are in place, we are going to get started on the example that we will use for the rest of the book. As discussed in Chapter 1 our sample application is an online catalog. In this section, you will create our example user and a single table using SQL*PLUS. In the next section, you will create a connection definition that accesses the database as this user. From there, you will create your first XSQL application using the data in the table that you create here.

You will create the MOMNPUP user for our client company, Mom N' Pop Retail. Oracle gives you a huge amount of flexibility in creating users. Among other things, you can specify the default tablespace, the temporary tablespace, the quota, the user's profile, and the rollback segment. For this exercise, we will create the user as simply as possible. You should consult your administrator's guide for in-depth information about all of the different options.

Our first step is to log in to the database as SYSTEM. The default password is MANAGER:

```
>sqlplus SYSTEM/MANAGER@ORCL
```

Once you are logged in, you can create a user as follows:

```
SQL> create user MOMNPUP identified by MOMNPUP;
SQL> grant RESOURCE to MOMNPUP;
```

Now that the user is created, log out and log back in as the user:

```
>sqlplus MOMNPUP/MOMNPUP@ORCL
```

The table that you will create is very simple. It will keep information about employees of the company.

```
SQL> create table EMPLOYEE (id NUMBER,
                            lastname VARCHAR2(15),
                            firstname VARCHAR2(15),
                            job VARCHAR2(30));
```

With the following statements, you will create the table and populate two rows of data.

```
SQL> insert into employee (id,lastname,firstname,job) values (1,
'N''Pop','John','Catalog Editor');
SQL> insert into employee (id,lastname,firstname,job) values (2,
'N''Pop','Mom','Boss');
```

TIP **Our task here was easily completed at the command line. However, if you are new to Oracle, you should definitely check out Oracle Enterprise Manager. This is a Graphical User Interface (GUI) that allows you to perform tasks like these with a few mouse clicks. Even better, Enterprise Manager will show you the SQL that it uses to complete the tasks that you define graphically.**

Setting Connection Definitions

Now that you have your MOMNPUP user ready, you need to set up a connection in the `XSQLConfig.xml` file. You can find this file in the `xdk/admin` directory. Once in the file, find the `connectiondefs` node in the XML file. Immediately after this line, just add the following:

```
<connection name="momnpup">
    <username>momnpup</username>
    <password>momnpup</password>
    <dburl>jdbc:oracle:thin:@localhost:1521:ORCL</dburl>
    <driver>oracle.jdbc.driver.OracleDriver</driver>
</connection>
```

If you are going against a database other than ORCL, you will need to replace the SID in the `dburl`.

Your First XSQL Page

You are now about two minutes away from your first XSQL page! The first step is to create a new directory called `momnpup` in `xdk\demo\java\xsql`. In that directory, create the file `simple1.xsql` and enter the following:

```
<?xml version="1.0"?>
<?xml-stylesheet type="text/xsl" href="helloworld.xsl"?>
<page connection="momnpup" xmlns:xsql="urn:oracle-xsql">
<xsql:query>
       SELECT * FROM EMPLOYEE
</xsql:query>
</page>
```

You can access it with the URL `http://localhost/xsql/momnpup/helloworld.xsql`, and there and you should see the code that's shown in Figure 3.2.

Figure 3.2 `helloworld.xsql`.

Your First XSLT Stylesheet

Okay, so maybe your first XSQL experience wasn't that thrilling. XML just isn't that pretty to look at in a browser. This is where XSLT comes in. By creating a stylesheet, you can beautify the XML into presentable HTML. Here you will do a simple example.

Your first step is to create the file named `helloworld.xsl` and put the following text in it:

```
<?xml version="1.0"?>
<xsl:stylesheet xmlns:xsl="http://www.w3.org/1999/XSL/Transform"
version="1.0">
<xsl:import href="../common/rowcol.xsl"/>
  <xsl:template match="page">
    <html>
      <head><link rel="stylesheet" type="text/css"
href="../common/rowcol.css" />
```

```
        </head>
        <body class="page">
          <center></center>
          <xsl:apply-templates select="ROWSET"/>
        </body>
      </html>
    </xsl:template>
  </xsl:stylesheet>
```

You will learn more about XSLT stylesheets in Chapter 13. For now, you should focus on getting the example working. Most important, if you didn't create the example in the xdk/demo/java/xsql directory, this example won't work. The xsl:import element references another stylesheet in the xdk/demo/java/xsql/common directory. A lot of the complex work is done in that stylesheet.

In this file, you can see the basics of how XSLT works. First, notice that the XSL stylesheet is almost entirely HTML. The idea is that the stylesheets describe how the XML elements should be rendered in HTML. If you look back at the XML file, you will see that it has a ROWSET element that contains ROW elements. Now, look at the line <xsl:apply-templates select="ROWSET">. When the XSLT processor encounters this element, it selects the ROWSET element in the XML file and renders it according to the ROWSET template contained in the rowcol.xsl file.

The in-depth discussion is later. Your work isn't finished until you tie the stylesheet to the helloworld.xsql file. You can do this by adding the following as the second line in the helloworld.xsql file:

```
<?xml-stylesheet type="text/xsl" href="helloworld.xsl"?>
```

After saving the file, you should be able to access http://localhost/xsql/momnpup/helloworld.xsql and see the following results as shown in Figure 3.3.

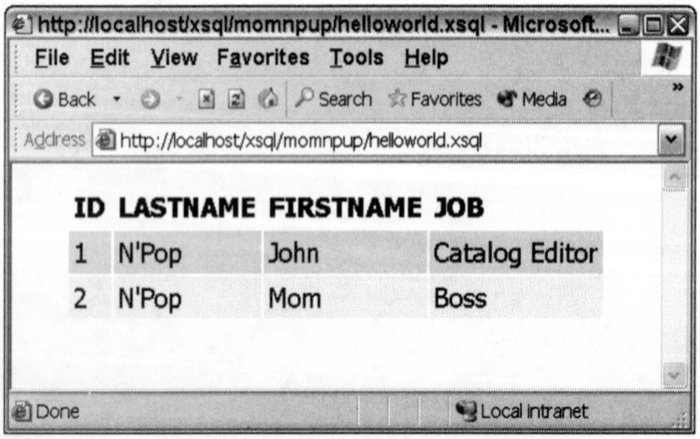

ID	LASTNAME	FIRSTNAME	JOB
1	N'Pop	John	Catalog Editor
2	N'Pop	Mom	Boss

Figure 3.3 Helloworld.xsql **with stylesheet.**

XSQLConfig.xml

At this point, you have at least done a little work in the XSQLConfig.xml file. If your environment was unorthodox, you may have already spent more time with this file than you would like. Now you are going to learn more about this configuration file and the role that it plays. First, you will learn it's overall purpose and place in the XSQL architecture. Then you will look at the individual settings available, one by one.

Because the config file is an XML document, it has a tree structure and resembles a file system. There are top-level elements that contain second-level elements, the second-level elements contain third-level elements, and so forth. XML is ideal for configuration files. It allows related configuration parameters to be grouped together and makes it easy to configure an indeterminate number of the same entities.

For this section, you cover the configuration elements from the top down using a depth-first approach. This means that you will go all the way down one branch of the tree then recurse back up the tree and go all the way down the next branch.

XSQLConfig Element

This is the top-level element that contains all other elements. It is required but has no configuration options.

Servlet Element

This element has several children elements that configure the behavior of the XSQL servlet. The servlet element itself has no configuration options. Table 3.1 shows the two children elements that can be configured.

Table 3.1 Servlet Configuration Elements

ELEMENT NAME	DESCRIPTION	CHILDREN ELEMENTS?	EXAMPLE
output-buffer-size	Size in bytes of the buffered output stream of the servlet. Set to 0 if your servlet engine buffers.	No	<output-buffer-size> 10000</output-buffer-size>
<suppress-mime-charset>	For the given mime type, charset won't be set. Needed for SVG.	Media-type	<suppress-mime-charset><media-type>image/svg+xml</media-type><media-type>image/svg</media-type>

Processor Element

This section covers database caching, file caching, and security-related parameters. The processor element has no configuration options. Table 3.2 details the immediate children that have direct configuration parameters.

Beyond these elements, there are several that are more complex. The first is the stylesheet-pool element. This element defines the characteristics the individual pools, while the stylesheet-cache-size parameter described in Table 3.2 specifies the number of individual pools. Table 3.3 details the options of the children of the stylesheet-pool element. The stylesheet-pool element itself takes no parameters.

Here is an example of the stylesheet-pool element:

```
<stylesheet-pool>
  <initial>1</initial>
  <increment>1</increment>
  <timeout-seconds>60</timeout-seconds>
</stylesheet-pool>
```

Table 3.2 Processor Configuration Elements

ELEMENT NAME	DESCRIPTION	EXAMPLE
`reload-connections-on-error`	If yes, the `XSQLConfig.xml` is reloaded if a connection can't be found in memory. This is useful during development when you might be adding connection definitions, but is inefficient in a production system.	`<reload-connections-on-error>yes</reload-connections-on-error>`
`default-fetch-size`	The default value of the `Row Fetch Size`, the number of rows fetched from the database at a time. Requires the Oracle JDBC Driver.	`<default-fetch-size>50</default-fetch-size>`
`result-cache-size`	The size of the LRU cache of XSQL page fragment results.	`<result-cache-size>50</result-cache-size>`
`page-cache-size`	The size of the LRU cache for XSQL files.	`<page-cache-size>25</page-cache-size>`
`stylesheet-cache-size`	The size of the cache for pools of XSL stylesheet instances. These instances are defined by the stylesheet-pool element.	`<stylesheet-cache-size>25</stylesheet-cache-size>`

Table 3.3 Stylesheet-Pool Elements

ELEMENT NAME	DESCRIPTION
`initial`	The initial size of a pool
`increment`	The size by which the pool should increase when it needs to grow
`timeout-seconds`	The number of seconds of inactivity that will cause a particular stylesheet to be dropped out of the pool

The connection-pool element controls the behavior of the JDBC connections. By pooling the connections, database transactions can complete much more efficiently. Table 3.4 details the options of the children of the connection-pool element. The connection-pool element itself takes no parameters.

The connection-manager element controls the XSQL Configuration Manager Factory class. There is little reason to use a connection manager other than the one that is used by default. If you happen to find a reason to use another one, simply replace the value of the factory element to the fully qualified class name of the factory class you desire. The class must implement the `oracle.xml.xsql.XSQLConnectionManagerFactory` interface.

```
<connection-manager>

<factory>oracle.xml.xsql.XSQLConnectionManagerFactoryImpl</factory>
</connection-manager>
```

The next element to explore is the security element. The configuration elements here will factor heavily into our security discussion at the end of the chapter. Here we detail the various elements and the effect they have. The security element has one child element, `stylesheet`. Neither of these elements have any configuration options. The interesting elements are children of `stylesheet`. All of the following examples should be included between `<security><stylesheet>` and `</stylesheet></security>`.

Table 3.4 Connection-Pool Elements

ELEMENT NAME	DESCRIPTION
`initial`	The initial size of a pool.
`increment`	The size by which the pool should increase when it needs to grow.
`timeout-seconds`	The number of seconds of inactivity that will cause a particular connection to be dropped.
`dump-allowed`	If yes, a browser-based status report of the current state of connections is enabled.

The first element to examine is allow-client-style. When set to "yes," the HTTP client can specify the stylesheet that should be used for transformation, including none. Setting this element to "yes" is slightly helpful during development because you can easily see the raw XML. There is no reason to have it set to "yes" in a production environment. In fact, this configuration caused a security alert in 2001 because it allowed the execution of arbitrary Java code on the server. Here is how you set the allow-client-style element:

```
<defaults>
    <allow-client-style>no</allow-client-style>
</defaults>
```

The next element, trusted-hosts, is related to the allow-client-style element. Generally, stylesheets should be referenced with relative URIs and reside on the same Web server. If, for some reason, you want to access a stylesheet from another Web server, it must be from a trusted host. A trusted host appears as the value of a host element as shown in the following code. It is also possible to trust all hosts by making a <host>*</host> entry, but you really shouldn't do this.

```
<trusted-hosts>
   <host>127.0.0.1</host>
   <host>trustedHost.trustedDomain.com</host>
</trusted-hosts>
```

Http Element

The http element is a very simple element. It allows for the definition of an HTTP proxy server for use by the XSQL servlet. If you are going to grab documents from beyond your firewall and need to use a proxy server to access them, you define it here. Here is an example:

```
<http>
    <proxyhost>your-proxy-server.yourcompany.com</proxyhost>
    <proxyport>80</proxyport>
</http>
```

Connectiondefs Element

The connectiondefs element describes the connections to the database. Each XSQL page specifies the connection that should be used to process the SQL statements contained in that page. The connectiondefs element and the connection element itself has no configuration options. Table 3.5 describes the child elements of the connection element.

Table 3.5 Connection Elements

CHILD ELEMENT	DESCRIPTION
`username`	User name for the connection
`password`	Password for the user name
`dburl`	JDBC URL for the connection
`Driver`	Fully qualified class name for the Oracle driver

Generally, you set up a new connection because you need to access the database as a different user or you need to access a different database. To access as a different user, simply copy and paste a working connection element and change the user name and password. Configuring access to a different database is more complex.

`Actiondefs` Element

The `actiondefs` element configures action handlers that can be called from an XSQL page. You will learn more about action handlers in Chapter 8. Here is an example showing how to configure a new action handler:

```
<action>
<elementname>current-date</elementname>
<handlerclass>
    oracle.xml.xsql.actions.ExampleCurrentDBDateHandler
      </handlerclass>
 </action>
```

`Serializerdefs` Element

The `serializerdefs` element configures serializers that can be called from an XSQL page. You will learn more about serializers in Chapter 19. Here is an example showing how to configure a new serializer:

```
<serializer>
      <name>FOP</name>
      <class>
          oracle.xml.xsql.serializers.XSQLFOPSerializer
      </class>
</serializer>
```

Security Issues

Now that you have a new package installed and understand how it works, it is a good time to consider the security implications. XSQL doesn't introduce grave and complex security concerns. However, it is a new window onto your system from a public network. This gives hackers a new avenue of attack not only on your system but also your entire enterprise. Because XSQL attaches directly to the database, the potential of information compromise is especially high.

We can't promise that reading the next few pages will prevent hackers from penetrating your system. The very nature of Internet security dictates that you have to insulate yourself from vulnerabilities that aren't currently known. What you will learn here is what the current vulnerabilities are and what some past weakness have been. By using these known issues as a case study, we will explore various strategies to protect yourself from XSQL-based attacks.

Known Issues

There are a couple of current and known issues involving XSQL. These are issues, not security holes. A security hole is a flaw in the design and implementation of a product that isn't documented. It gives hackers a secret route to exploit your system. The issues that you are going to learn about here are: the need to protect the `XSQLConfig.xml` file, the problem of SQL poisoning, and the implications of denial-of-service (DOS) attacks. You will also see a true security hole that was found in 2001, which has subsequently been resolved. The ability to pull in stylesheets from other hosts meant that it was possible to execute arbitrary Java code on the Web server machine. Though not a problem now, it is valuable to know how XSQL was compromised in the past so that you can think about the overall architecture in terms of security.

The `XSQLConfig.xml` File

When you are setting up XSQL it is easy to put the `XSQLConfig.xml` file into a directory that is accessible from the Web. This is a big mistake. The `XSQLConfig.xml` file contains all of the information that someone needs to be able to access your database. They have the user name, the password, and even the host and the System Identifier (SID).

After you have the `XSQLConfig.xml` file configured as you like, the file only needs to be readable by the XSQL servlet, or more specifically, by the user that XSQL Servlet runs as. The XSQL servlet is run by the user, which runs the servlet engine. You'll need to consult the documentation of your servlet engine to determine the user. Then you can limit the availability of the file at an operating system level.

Under no circumstances should the `XSQLConfig.xml` reside in a virtual directory or otherwise be publicly available.

SQL Poisoning

One thing that makes XSQL great is that it is very easy to create Web pages that are based on SQL queries. This also is a security issue. As you will learn in detail in Chapter 6, it is easy to plug parameters into your queries. Without jumping ahead too much, let's look at an example of this functionality and then discuss the security ramifications of it:

```
<?xml version="1.0"?>
<xsql:query connection="demo" xmlns:xsql="urn:oracle-xsql">
    SELECT {@field} FROM EMP WHERE ENAME = '{@name}'
</xsql:query>
```

You can use this XSQL page to provide the data of a particular employee by name. The name parameter can be specified in the URL embedded in the query string. If the preceding example is saved as `hack.xsql` into the `momnpup` directory created earlier, you should get the output that is shown in Figure 3.4 when you access `http://localhost/xsql/momnpup/hack.xsql?name=ADAMS&field=job`.

If your users are clever, they can even do their own queries. The URL `http://localhost/xsql/momnpup/hack.xsql?field=ename,job&name=ADAMS'%20OR%20ENAME='ALLEN` can select a couple of employees at once, as shown in Figure 3.5.

However, it is easy to abuse this. In the next example, your user goes from benignly saving himself or herself some time to getting information that he or she shouldn't see. In this example, the hacker uses knowledge of the EMP table combined with a clever "where" clause to get the salaries of all of the workers. The URL used is `http://localhost/xsql/momnpup/hack.xsql?field=ename,sal&name=ADAMS'%20OR%20NOT%20ENAME='ZZZZ`. The result is shown in Figure 3.6.

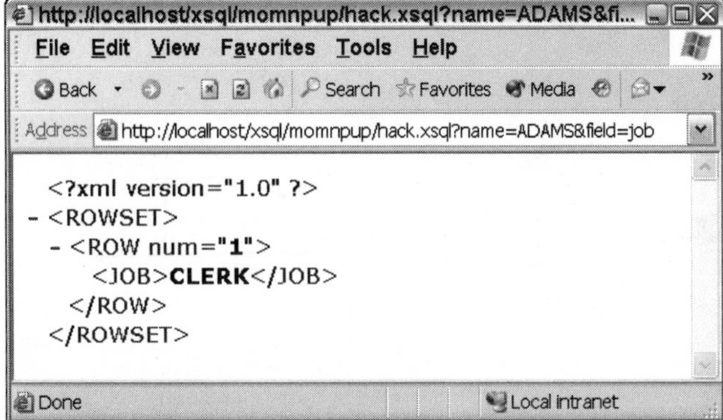

Figure 3.4 Unpoisoned XSQL access.

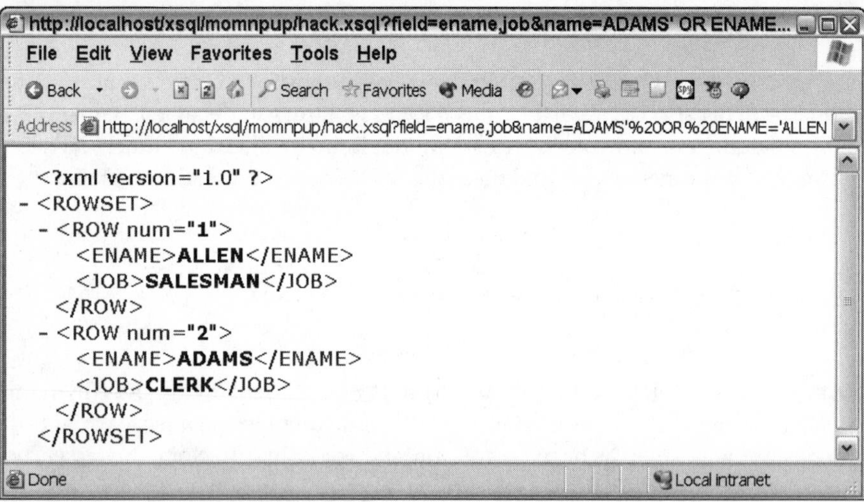

Figure 3.5 Benign SQL poisoning.

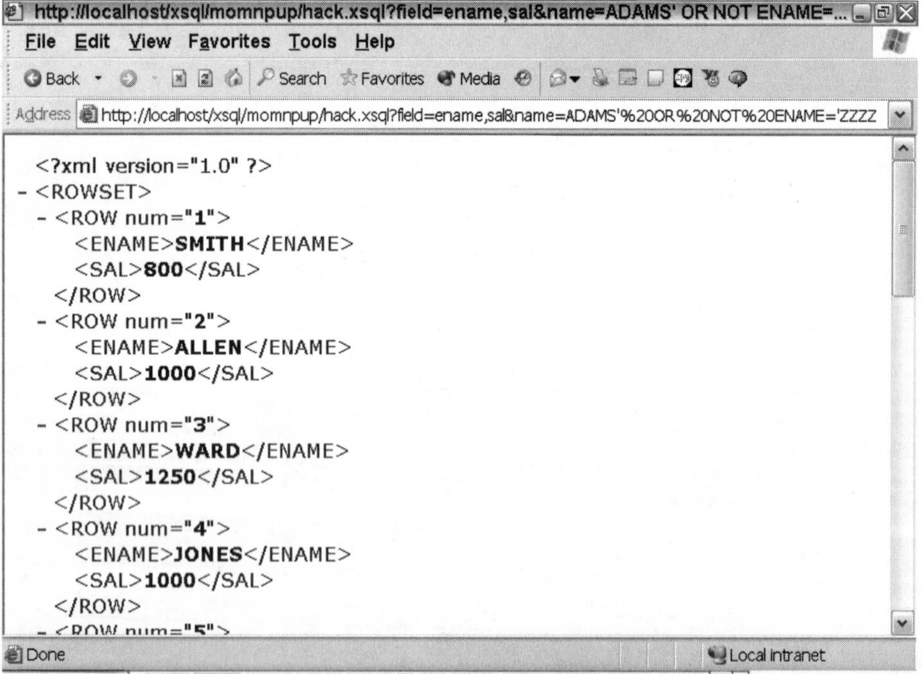

Figure 3.6 Malignant hack.

It's important to note that the programmer that created this code walked right into this kind of attack. By parameterizing too much of the SQL statement, hackers are able to access secret information through a Web browser by coming up with their own SQL statements. Even though this example may look a bit contrived, it's important to note that this is only one example of this type of hack. XSQL yields a great deal of power in this regard, but as you design and implement XSQL pages, you should think about the security implications. In Chapter 6, you will see how to use the flexibility safely.

Denial-of-Service Attacks

The first thing that should be said about denial-of-service (DOS) attacks is that it is hard to prevent them at the application level. The strategy behind DOS attacks is to so overwhelm your servers that it puts you out of business. They don't exploit a particular hole in your application that you can plug. Instead, they attempt to overwhelm your system through a mass of legitimate requests. The best you can do at an application level is attempt to sense that you are being attacked and then try to block the individual attackers, but this is risky. If you try to do this based on IP, for instance, you might find yourself cutting off all AOL users from your system. AOL tends to proxy lots of users through the same IP.

Instead of attempting to block DOS attacks, let's look at how to sustain them and minimize their impact on your operations. You should assume that your firewall engineers will ultimately defeat a DOS attack, after some good sleuthing as to their origins and some cooperative action with the ISPs from where the attacks originated. As an XSQL application developer, your responsibility is to survive the (hopefully temporary) siege.

During a DOS attack, your Web performance to legitimate users will suffer. Stopping that suffering is the responsibility of your security engineers. Because XSQL applications are database driven, your responsibility is to protect the database. DOS attacks have two avenues of attack on your database: (1) resource overload and (2) data overload.

A DOS attack pointing at your database will slow the database down for legitimate users. It could even cripple it. This is unfortunate for your legitimate Web-based users. After all, during the initial siege you can't tell the difference between your legitimate Web-based users and the Web-based hackers. However, it is likely that your database has more than one face. It may have multiple distinct Web faces, and internal users may use non-Web tools to access it.

Therefore, the contingency strategy is to sustain an attack on one front while still operating relatively well on the other fronts. Oracle's distributed database technology is very good at providing this if implemented correctly. While the attack pegs the central processing units (CPUs) on the machines that service the Web, other machines that comprise the same distributed database can serve their users more or less normally. This also makes it easier on everyone if you have to shut down the besieged Web interface for a while.

Along the same lines, you can take a data warehousing approach. In some cases, this can be a little simpler than implementing a full-blown distributed database. If your Web interface mainly provides querying and the data doesn't need to be synchronized in real time with the rest of your operations, you may want to offload the necessary data from your internal operational systems to your dedicated Web interface database. Then if this machine heats up, it doesn't risk interfering with the rest of your operation.

The other problem is data overload. As you will see, your XSQL application can enter and modify information into your database, such as orders and registrations. First, you should consider how to ensure that such information is legitimate and how you would either block illegitimate information or at least be able to back illegitimate information out of the database. However, this is only one side of the problem. The other side is that you can easily fill up all of your drives with bogus data. There are two approaches to this: Either (1) buy more drives or (2) put quotas on how much space your Web interface can generate. After the quota is reached, no more data for that user can be entered. However, that may be preferable to preventing other database applications from working. More information about setting quotas for users can be found in your *Oracle Database Administrator's Guide.*

An Example Security Hole

This section documents a security hole that was found in January 2001 by Georgi Guninski. The hole was patched almost immediately. It is discussed here only for historical reasons. As is discussed in the next section, a lot of security strategy is planning for the security holes that you don't know about or that may not even exist yet. By looking at this one, hopefully you will gain some insight as to what other security holes may exist or come to exist. In the section about `XSQLConfig.xml`, you read about the security element and how it could prevent the client from overriding the prescribed stylesheet for an XSQL page. You also learned about how to restrict absolute URLs to only certain trusted hosts. In January 2001, these settings were not in place as they exist today. By default, stylesheets for any XSQL page could be overridden by the client. This was the basis of the security hole.

A hacker could create an XSL file that referenced arbitrary Java code. Then, he could override the intended stylesheet with this hostile stylesheet from a hostile host. The arbitrary code would execute on the XSQL host.

The immediate workaround was to set the allow-client style to "no" for all publicly available XSQL pages. Now, you can set that as the global default for XSQL pages in the `XSQLConfig.xml` file. Also, you can define which hosts you actually trust. This particular exploit underlies the importance of not trusting all hosts. Even on a default installation, this exploit would not work today.

Thinking about XSQL Security

Now that you've looked at some specific XSQL security issues, you are ready to think about security at an architectural level. Security is best considered at the beginning of an application design. If you wait too late in the game, then your solutions will most likely be reactive Band-Aids. In some cases, the cure will be worse than the disease. The previous section discussed specific known items you should consider immediately. However, your long-term security strategy must allow for security holes and issues that aren't currently known. The goal of this section is to give you some basis to approach security as an important architectural consideration. It will draw on some of the lessons learned in the previous section.

Provide Few Opportunities

The evangelists of a popular operating system like to talk about how long it has been since the default installation was last hacked. Upon examination, it's obvious that the default installation has almost no network services available. Because hack attempts inevitably come across the network, the claim is a bit obtuse. It's somewhat like claiming, "My refrigerator has never been hacked."

If you are going to put an application up on the Internet, you are inevitably vulnerable. However, the claim underlies an important point. The less network services you have running, the less vulnerable you are. Your first step should be to close down all unnecessary network services running on your production machines. This doesn't make your actual application any less vulnerable, but it does increase your overall security.

On this same strategy, there are some XSQL-specific steps that you should take. All those demos install by default. You shouldn't have them on your production machines. They represent a well-known access point that is asking for someone to find a hole. As you trash them, don't forget to remove all of those unnecessary connection elements in your `XSQLConfig.xml` file.

Keep Up-to-Date

A lot of attacks, such as the popular e-mail worms, are exploits of known vulnerabilities. You can save yourself a lot of pain and embarrassment simply by keeping up-to-date. Oracle is highly committed to keeping its customers secure, so you can count on them to be proactive in addressing concerns. Still, someone in your organization will have to watch for the emails and apply the patches. You can also keep an eye on security through some focused Web sites, such as `www.secureroot.com`.

Always Consider Security in Application Design

In the previous section, you read about SQL poisoning. The programmer created an XSQL page that could be easily used to get construct unintended SQL queries. However, the XSQL code was great in one aspect: The code was very reusable.

In the heat of software design, it is easy to overfocus on the concepts taught in beginning computer science classes, such as code reuse. For many of us, those classes were taught at a time when security wasn't such an issue. Applications were written for a defined audience, and in many cases it could be assumed that the applications users had no malice.

Security especially conflicts with reusability. Reusability implicitly means that a module can receive many types of input. However, when Internet users are lent too much transparency to the module, they might reuse your code in ways you don't want them to. You'll learn how to balance XSQL reusability with security in later chapters. However, as a general rule you should consider code security in the same breath as other development concepts such as reusability and encapsulation.

The Multilateral Approach

Many barbarians attacking castles were able to get through the front door, only to receive the hot-oil treatment in the anteroom. Likewise, many organizations such as law firms and ad agencies have Chinese walls so that private client information can't pass from one part of the organization to another. Both of these represent a multilateral approach to security. Lateral transgressions inside and across a system are contained and prevented.

The basic approach is to think, "A hacker gets to this part of my system. Now what damage can he do?" A lot of organizations focus solely on front-end security. If a hacker can break through the front end, internal security is so lax that they can mount a variety of lateral exploits. A common example of the multilateral approach is the demilitarized zone (DMZ): By having two firewalls, a hacker who can break through the front-end has to go through another firewall to reach the organization.

Often, however, a more granular approach is needed at the database level. We touched on some of this in the earlier section about DOS attacks. If someone can get into the database, it is possible that they can use basic SQL commands to compromise a lot of data and inflict a lot of damage. The approach, then, is to assume that a hacker has logged in as any user in your `XSQLConfig.xml` file. What damage can they do? Is there anything you can do to limit the damage?

An easy step in this direction is to have multiple connections configured of varying levels of access. Each user that you create should have only the minimum privileges necessary to perform the tasks necessary for that part of the application. For instance, you can have one user that only knows how to query a set of tables, and another user that only inserts or updates into a particular table. This approach can get complicated quickly. However, creating users and changing the privileges of users is easily done, and the creation of connections in the `XSQLConfig.xml` file is simple. This task can be one of the last completed before putting an application into production.

Moving On

In this chapter, you went from a basic installation of the files to actually seeing XSQL in action. You know how to secure your XSQL applications and how to configure all of the options in the `XSQLConfig.xml` file. Now you're ready to go! The next four chapters cover the workings of XSQL and the details of all of the XSQL features. With this base knowledge, you'll branch out to the other key technologies, starting with Oracle SQL. You'll then learn all about XSLT. The book wraps up by showing you how to extend XSQL with Java. Now that you have a development environment set up, it's time to put XSQL to work!

XSQL Architecture

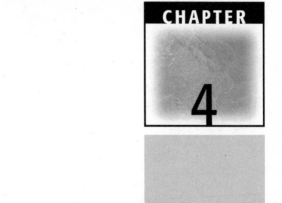

You have already seen a lot of XSQL architecture through the install. In this chapter, you will refine your understanding and explore new parts that you didn't see in the earlier chapter. You'll start with an overview and then dive into the specifics of database access and presentation. From there, you'll explore the concept of actions. For this, you have a head start—you used actions when accessing the database in the last chapter. Then, you'll look at action handlers, which allow you to create your own types of actions. The final concept you'll examine here is serializers.

Overview

In looking at the high-level architecture, the first step is to separate the XSQL servlet from the XSQL page processor. The XSQL servlet calls the XSQL page processor to execute XSQL pages. The XSQL page processor interfaces with the database through JDBC and uses XML SQL to create the XML datagram. The XML processor loads the XSQL page that is specified by the URI used to invoke the XSQL servlet. The XSLT processor loads the XSQL page if it specifies an XSLT stylesheet. After processing, the result is returned to the client via the XSQL servlet and Web server. The high-level view is diagrammed in Figure 4.1.

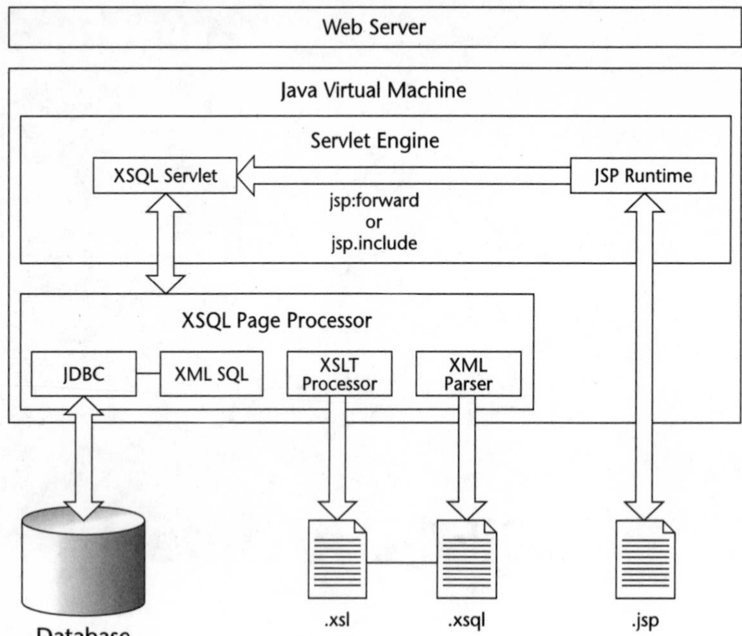

Figure 4.1 High-level view of XSQL.

The JSP runtime is also shown in the diagram. As with any servlet running in the context, you can integrate JSP and XSQL via the `jsp:forward` and `jsp:include` tags. The `jsp:forward` tag tells the XSQL servlet to handle the request, while `jsp:include` can be used to include the XSQL result in the page that JSP produces. If you are using some other kind of scripting language, such as Cold Fusion, or if you are using an active server page (ASP), you should also be able to redirect to an XSQL result by simply redirecting to the XSQL servlet.

For 90 percent (and perhaps all) of your XSQL pages, you'll use the XSQL servlet. However, this isn't the only way to invoke an XSQL page. You can also invoke an XSQL page either by using the XSQL command line utility or programmatically. In such cases, the XSQL servlet isn't involved at all. These components interface directly with the XSQL page processor. They are discussed in more depth later in the chapter.

Now it's time to figure out how all of the pieces fit together. Hopefully you got some hands-on experience with this in the previous chapter. But in the heat of getting everything working, it's sometimes hard to think conceptually. So now, each piece will be examined.

Java Parts

XSQL is written in Java and uses the server-side Java architecture. It isn't strictly necessary to be a Java pro to do great things with XSQL. But understanding the basics of Java architecture can help you in understanding the big picture. This section covers the Java Virtual Machine (JVM), JDBC drivers, servlet engine, and JSP.

Java Virtual Machine

The first step is a quick tour of the JVM. Java knowledge isn't essential for success with XSQL, but it does help. Because the XSQL components are written in Java, understanding Java is important for understanding how the pieces work. Also, Java is the language to use for extending the capabilities of XSQL. Java is a platform-independent language; the key to platform independence is the JVM. As the name implies, the JVM acts as a virtual machine. When you compile source code for platform-dependent languages such as C++, you create a binary file that can be understood and executed only on one platform. It is written in platform-specific machine language. Instead of compiling Java code for a particular operating system and hardware, your compile target will be the language of the JVM. The compiler creates Java bytecode, which is the equivalent of machine language. However, the JVM isn't a machine; it's a piece of software.

The JVM, which is almost always written in C++ itself, is a platform-dependent program. To date, however, JVMs have been written for essentially every platform imaginable—even cell phones. So once you compile your Java code, it can work on a variety of programs. This is the idea of the Write Once, Run Everywhere principle of Java. Critics of Java like to rework this principle as Write Once, Test Everywhere. Theirs is a valid criticism, for there are differences in the different JVMs. You will sometimes encounter platform-dependent bugs. However, the promise of platform independence is fulfilled for the vast majority of Java programs, especially on the server side.

In addition to executing your code, the JVM provides access to system resources and mandates a security policy. System resources include the basics such as keyboard and mouse input and output to a text console or graphics window. The JVM also handles network connections, the reading and writing of files, and the execution of other programs. The JVM also has control over what your program can and cannot do. This control is the idea of a *sandbox*. For instance, Java applets, which execute inside the Web browser, are severely restricted in what they can do. You wouldn't want an applet to erase all of your files or read private information off your hard drive, for instance. Each JVM controls what a program can and can't do through its security manager.

Since its inception, Java has always been considered inefficient. The JVM is a layer that sits between the bytecode and the operating system. There is a translation step required to change your Java bytecode instruction into a machine-language instruction. There is overhead in that. However, modern JVMs contain something that is called a Just in Time (JIT) compiler. When the JIT sees a block of code once, it will compile it into machine language. The next time that block of code is encountered, the JIT will execute it at near-native speeds. Doing so is especially effective on server-side applications that usually consist of the same loops executing repeatedly until the server is shut down.

But these efficiency concerns always compare optimal code. The most optimized Java code won't run as fast as the most optimized C++ code, which means that network drivers, for example, shouldn't be written in Java. Most of the time, however, the code isn't as optimized as you would like to believe. The more valid comparison is between common C++ code and common Java code. It's arguable that common Java code is more efficient than common C++ code. Other areas to consider, beyond speed, are the ease of programming and the maintainability of the code. Java has many advantages over C++ in these areas. In terms of architecture, the most important one is the garbage collector.

The garbage collector is used to manage memory on behalf of your code. In C++, you have to manage your own memory. You have to ask for memory, and when you're done using it, you have to explicitly return it to the operating system. It's very easy for programmers to mismanage memory. When they do, their programs often either crash outright or experience a memory leak. A program-leaking memory will eventually consume all of the system's memory and crash.

The Java garbage collector makes the your life as a programmer easier. You aren't able to explicitly ask for memory; instead, memory is allocated when you need it, upon the creation of objects. Most important, you don't have to explicitly declare when you no longer need the memory you are using. The garbage collector keeps track of the objects that you are using by keeping track of the references to that object. When there are no more references to an object, the garbage collector will mark it for garbage collection. The next time that garbage collection is performed, the memory will return to the operating system.

Driver

Java Database Connectivity (JDBC) is a key piece in server-side Java development. It yields a standard mechanism for accessing SQL databases from Java applications. The XSQL page processor uses JDBC to get to your database. Since the XSQL page processor interfaces with JDBC, you can actually use any database with XSQL for which there is a JDBC driver.

The best driver to use with XSQL is the Oracle Type 4 JDBC driver that installs with Oracle 9i. This driver does a direct connection to the database without any intermediary client interface, and it is superior to the more primitive JDBC drivers that sit on top of Object Database Connectivity (ODBC) and other native libraries. These features lead to less portable architecture and that you inherit any problems of the lower interface.

Servlet Engine

The servlet engine either uses or is run inside a JVM. What defines a servlet engine is its ability to run servlets. Servlets are Java objects that, at their simplest, receive requests from the Web and write output to the Web. Also, they can read and write to the file system, transact with the database, and even make network connections to interact with other services.

In strictly technical terms, a servlet is any Java class that implements the `javax.servlet.Servlet` interface. Most servlets actually implement the `javax.servlet.http.HttpServlet` interface, which is a subinterface of `javax.servlet.Servlet` and is designed for HTTP. This interface is a set of methods (the Java name for subroutines) that define how a servlet will react to a HTTP request. Generally speaking, a Web server receives the HTTP request, determines that it should go in the servlet engine, and hands it off. The servlet engine looks at its configuration information and figures out which servlet should handle it. It then calls the appropriate methods of the `javax.servlet.http.HttpServlet` interface. The servlet does its deeds and then creates a response. The response is written on to the network and handled by the client. In the usual case of a Web browser, the servlet writes HTML that is relayed back to the requesting Web browser that renders it upon receipt.

Servlets are often compared to Common Gateway Interface (CGI) scripts, so-called because they use the common gateway interface to extend a Web server. Instead of just serving files, you could have your Web server execute programs and then serve the output of those programs. However, CGI is very inefficient. The code has to be loaded into memory each time a call is made, a process that can be very taxing on busy servers. Servlets, on the other hand, are already in memory at the time they are called. Because they are Java objects, not separate programs, the servlet engine can interact with them very efficiently.

JSP Runtime

The Java Server Page (JSP) runtime handles requests for JSP pages are similar to PHP, ASP, and Cold Fusion pages. You can mix HTML (or another presentation-level language) with Java code giving you the ability to easily create dynamic pages. It's a much better way than trying to create HTML directly with a servlet. A servlet-to-HTML architecture has, usually, two hard and messy paths. In one path, you end up with a bunch of HTML code inside your servlet code—not fun to write or maintain. In the other path, you leave the HTML outside the servlet and read it in, doing the appropriate gestations in your code to get the output you want. In this case, however, you have to write a parser. This scenario is better than having your servlet junked up with HTML, but using JSP or XSLT is easier.

JSP or XSLT, that is the question! Lots of smart programmers are debating this question. You'll get some perspective on this question later in this chapter. For now, you'll focus on JSP and how JSP integrates with XSQL.

The key requirement is that the JSP page and the XSQL servlet have to live in the same context. The included call may look like a URL, but it isn't quite. The XSQL servlet isn't invoked through the network; rather, the servlet engine calls XSQL servlet directly as if it were called from the Web.

Why are JSP and XSLT sometimes viewed as competitive technologies? Both can merge static HTML with dynamic data to create a dynamic page. How they do this is radically different. XSQL is focused on the XSLT solution, and so is this book. But since you'll be getting so much XSLT in this book, you should know what JSP brings forth. JSP gives you all the power of a procedural, object-oriented language. You can do all the basic programming stuff, such as variables, for loops and conditional expressions. You can even create and manipulate objects. In fact, you could easily write your whole application in JSP! Doing so, however, will lead to some very messy, hard-to-maintain code—one of the biggest complaints with JSP. The generally accepted design pattern for JSP is to have the heavy lifting done by Java classes and then write very minimal scriptlets that get string data from the underlying classes. In this way, you keep the JSP as clean as possible—a very important condition. It is widely agreed that the look and feel of your pages should be cleanly separated from the programming. If your Web designer can't easily make changes to the Web site without consulting a programmer, your site will have lots of maintenance headaches and probably some unhappy staffers.

XSLT is very well tuned for this separation. With XSLT, there is simply no way to code your entire application in the stylesheets. XSLT simply isn't that kind of language; it's a declarative language, like HTML. Since XSLT and JSP are essentially cousins, they fit very well together. However, this relationship is also a weakness of sorts. There are problems that JSP can easily solve that require some stretching with XSLT. Working too hard in XSLT generally means that the problem should have been addressed and solved elsewhere in the architecture. However, architecture is not taught in beginning computer classes; procedural programming, however, is. Thus JSP is appealing because it is more like the programming that people have been taught and are used to.

Ultimately, though, the problem is one of separating presentation from the programming logic. XSLT guarantees this separation in a standardized way. JSP can provide this separation, but the developers and designers working on the system have to learn how this separation is made on a project-by-project basis. Unfortunately, this architectural separation is often marred by late night programming in advance of important deadlines.

There are factors that play heavily in favor of JSP. XSLT, after all, is mated to XML. If you don't come up with an XML document, the XSLT processor isn't going to do a lot with your stylesheet. In some cases, it doesn't make since to translate your data into XML just so you can use XSLT. If all you have is simple string data and you aren't going to do a lot of complex processing, using JSP may be the easiest solution. However, XML is becoming more and more prevalent. This reasoning makes no sense for database-driven applications because of the abundance of tools that translate the results of SQL queries into XML automatically for you.

Faces Of XSQL

When most people think of XSQL, they think of a way to easily create dynamic Web pages. This is what XSQL is best known for. But this functionality, which is provided by the XSQL servlet, is only one way to access the power of XSQL. You can also use the XSQL command line utility, as well as access XSQL programmatically. In the latter case, you embed calls to XSQL inside your Java code. This section looks at each of the ways to call XSQL. Each reaches the XSQL page processor, covered in the next section, differently.

XSQL Command Line Utility

XSQL command line is, as you would expect, a command line tool. It is diagrammed in Figure 4.2. It works much like the XSQL servlet, and it is a Java class, just as the XSQL servlet is. But instead of invoking the XSQL page processor in response to a Web request, you invoke it from the command line. If you specify an XSLT stylesheet in your XSQL page, the datagram will be transformed. The result can then be written back either to the console or to a file.

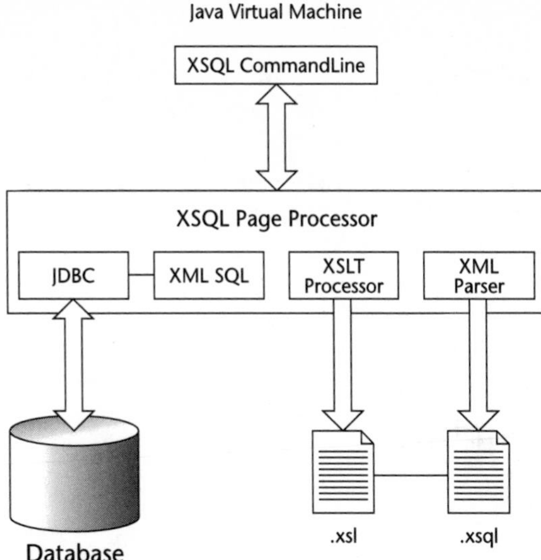

Figure 4.2 XSQL command line utility.

Why would you want to use XSQL from the command line? There are a few good reasons. In a lot of situations, the data in your database may not be changing frequently. In such a case, it may make more sense to generate an HTML page once a day by using XSQL. When your users access the server, they won't create any work for the database. Instead, the Web server just picks up the HTML that has already been created from the file system.

Also, XSQL and XSLT make a good pair for general file processing. In an example given in Chapter 15, you'll learn how to use the XSQL command line for routine tasks like creating SQL scripts. Although you will probably use XSQL most frequently for Web interaction, XSQL certainly isn't limited to that. You can easily make use of the XSQL command line for more general tasks.

XSQLRequest Class

XSQL request, diagrammed in Figure 4.3, is the programmatic interface to XSQL. With it, you can invoke an XSQL page and process the results inside your programs. It works much like the command line utility.

XSQL request has many uses. One is that it gives you a very easy way to invoke SQL queries without burying them in your Java code. Another is that instead of getting a result set back from the database, you get XML. Now, there are many times that you would rather have the result set. However, if you are creating an XML-based application, it would be desirable to already have the data in the correct format. You'll learn more about programmatic invocation and the XSQL request class in Chapter 17.

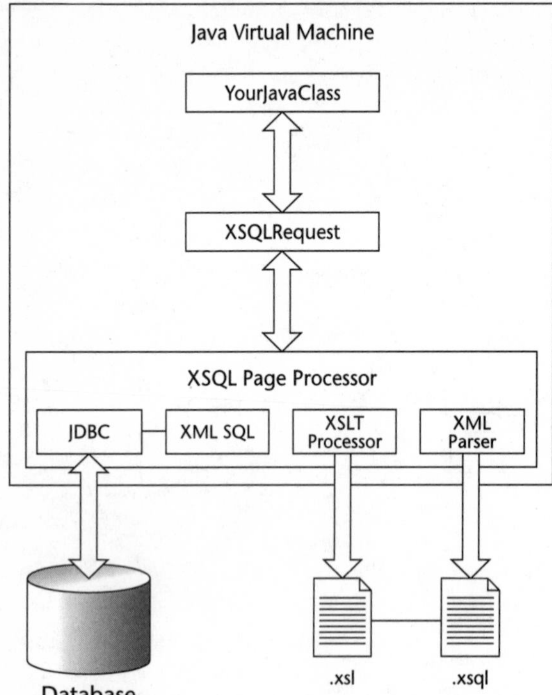

Figure 4.3 XSQL programmatic invocation architecture.

XSQL Servlet

XSQL servlet invokes the XSQL page processor. You will have a lot of interaction with the XSQL servlet. As described in the previous chapter, you must register the XSQL servlet with the servlet engine. There are also two servlet-specific configuration elements: output-buffer-size and suppress-mime-types.

Though XSQL servlet is the Web interface to all XSQL functionality, it itself does little. It receives a request and passes it to the XSQL page processor. The XSQL page processor does the heavy lifting and hands back a result. If you have buffering turned on, the XSQL servlet will buffer the output for you. If the XSQL servlet is configured appropriately, it will suppress the sending of character-encoding information. And that's about it.

It's time to move on to the real player—the XSQL page processor!

XSQL Page Processor

The XSQL page processor, as the name applies, is responsible for processing the XSQL pages. It is the magician of the system. It takes a simple XSQL and a XSLT file, connects to the database, and gives you back something presentable. At the highest level, it performs this function as described in Figure 4.4. This invoker is the XSQL servlet, the XSQL command line, or the XSQL request. At the time of invocation, it is possible to know how the XSQL page processor was invoked. For this discussion, you'll learn how the XSQL page processor behaves regardless of how it is invoked.

The XSQL page processor is already loaded into memory at the time of invocation except when you call it from the command line or make the first call for the instance of the JVM. When the XSQL page processor loads, it reads its `XSQLConfig.xml` file.

At about a 5,000-ft level, the XSQL page processor does the following when invoked:

1. Parses the request from the invoker
2. Selects the XSQL page
3. Processes the actions described in the XSQL page (most of the time by going to the database)
4. Applies an XSLT stylesheet, if one is specified, to the resulting XML datagram
5. Passes the result back to the invoker

But alas, it couldn't possibly be that simple! The engineers at Oracle have always been known to put some brilliant, elegant machinery under the covers. You've already had a glance at some of these widgets. In the previous chapter, you read about all the configuration parameters in the `XSQLConfig.xml` file. In that discussion, you learned about the XSQL page cache, the stylesheet cache, and the database connection pool. Each of these are modules in the XSQL page processor. They ensure that the XSQL page processor can drive your application with high efficiency. Figure 4.5 gives a detailed view. You'll learn about the two caches here; in the next section, you'll learn about the database connection pool.

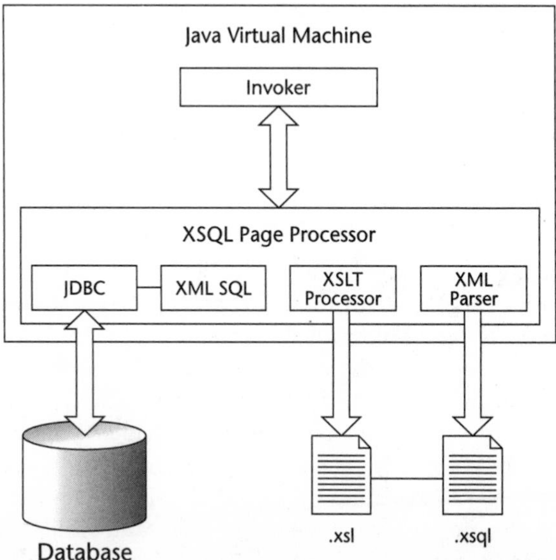

Figure 4.4 High-level diagram of the XSQL page processor.

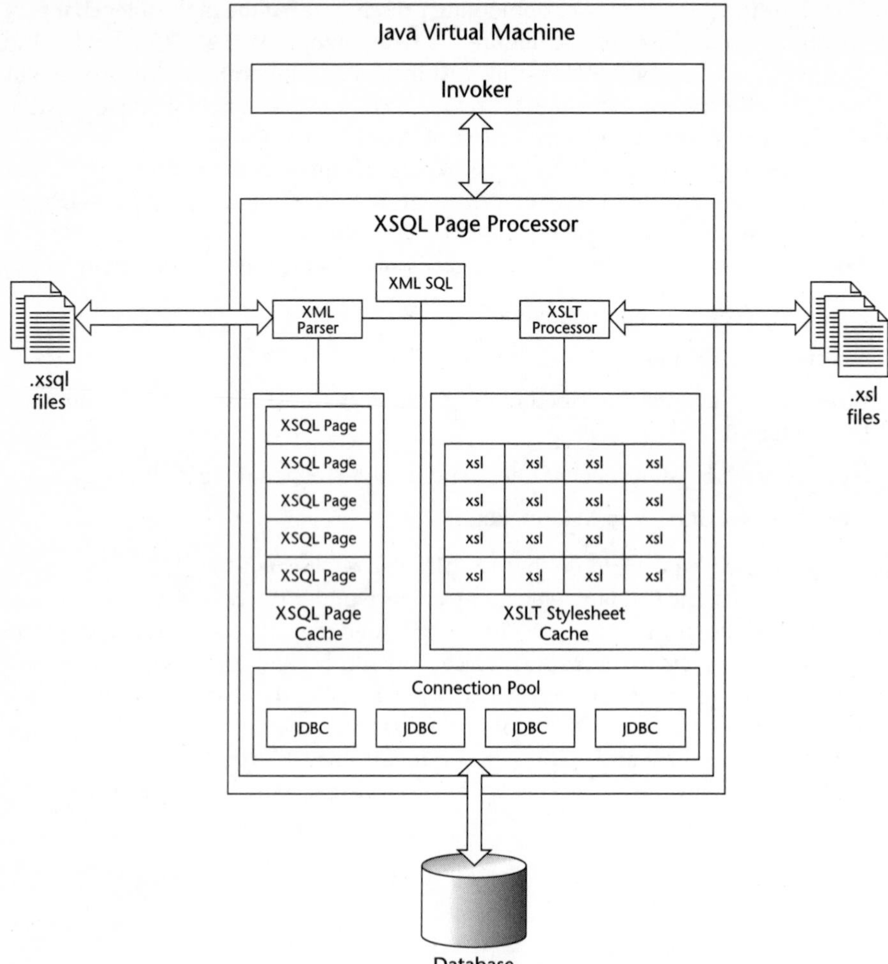

Figure 4.5 The XSQL page processor.

We begin with the XSQL page cache. This is a simple least recently used (LRU) cache. When the cache is full and a page not in the cache gets called, the page in the LRU cache is expelled. The algorithm, an LRU algorithm, is used to determine this action. So, if one page gets hammered a lot, it would probably stay in the cache all the time. The frequently used pages stand at alert, ready to be processed. This saves the XSQL page processor the trouble of loading into memory the most active XSQL pages each time they are called. By using a process described in the previous chapter, you can configure how many pages you want the XSQL page cache to hold. In small sites, you can expect all the XSQL pages to be easily loaded into the cache. If you have performance problems, you may want to bump up the size of the cache. The trade-off is that you will have less memory available for other tasks.

In concept, the stylesheet cache is similar to the XSQL page cache. It caches stylesheets so that the XSQL page processor doesn't have to fetch them from the file system every time. Like the XSQL page cache, it uses an LRU algorithm to determine which stylesheets most greatly need to be in the cache. However, it works quite a bit differently than the XSQL page cache. It is optimized for multithreaded servlet engines.

Why would the two need to work differently? The acts of XSQL page processing and stylesheet processing are quite different. Once an XSQL page is loaded, it can be represented statically in memory. The XSQL page processor can respond to requests by accessing instantiated objects; that is, the XSQL page itself doesn't need to be reparsed in any way on each request.

XSLT is more complex. An XSL stylesheet is merged with the resulting XML in a way described by the stylesheet. As you will see in Chapter 5, the XSLT language isn't trivial. Since the XML is expected to change from one query to the next, there is a lot of processing work that must occur at the time of invocation. On a multithreaded servlet engine, multiple threads could easily process the same XSLT stylesheet at the same time. For caching to be effective, it makes sense that there should be multiple instances of the cached stylesheet. Thus, the stylesheet cache uses an LRU cache in conjunction with pooling.

The LRU cache is a cache of pools. The pool is designed to grow when multiple threads demand the same stylesheet and to contract when activity is slower. When there is a set amount of inactivity (the time-out seconds parameter in the `XSQLConfig.xml` file), a particular stylesheet instance will drop out of the pool. In a busy servlet engine, the individual pools can grow for popular stylesheets so that all threads can have their own instance.

The pooling is one side of the equation; the cache itself is the other side. The LRU cache works essentially the same as the XSQL page cache. Think of it like this: If you configured the stylesheet pool so that it could have, at a maximum, only one stylesheet instance, the XSQL page cache and the stylesheet cache would work exactly the same.

As you can see, the actual processing of XSQL is quite complex. This complexity, however, is hidden from the user. Programmers could work with XSQL for years and never have any reason to know about the details discussed here, but if they encounter performance problems, an understanding of the underlying XSQL architecture would be very useful.

Oracle XML Modules

XSQL is built on top of other XML modules from Oracle. In this section, we look at the different underlying pieces and how they provide the necessary functionality. First, you'll learn more about the Oracle XML parser; then, you'll learn about XML SQL, which transforms SQL results into XML; finally, you'll learn about the XSLT processor, which handles XSLT transformations.

XML Parser

In any XML-based system, sooner or later you are going to run into an XML parser. There is no exception to this rule here. The XSQL page processor makes use of the

Oracle XML parser in a couple of key ways. XSQL pages and XSLT stylesheets are all XML documents, so they need to be parsed. As an XSQL developer, you may never need to use the XML parser. However, if you wish to extend the functionality of XSQL, you may find reason to use the parser directly. You'll learn more about programming with the XML parser in later chapters; here, you'll learn about the architecture of the Oracle XML parser.

XSQL uses the Document Object Model (DOM) functionality of the Oracle XML parser. Like all DOM XML parsers, the Oracle XML parser takes a stream—which may be a file, a string generated internally by an application, or data received over the network—and creates an in-memory representation of the XML. The representation, called a document, looks like a tree and can be traversed and queried to get data out of it. The document can also be added to and otherwise modified. Usually, at some point it is passed along to some other component. It might be written to the file system, sent over the network, or just handed as an argument to another component.

XML SQL

The Oracle XML SQL utility is used by the XSQL page processor in its interaction with the database. This is a stand-alone utility that you can use as part of the Oracle XDK. The use of the utility in conjunction with XSQL pages is transparent. You can be an effective XSQL developer without knowing anything about XML SQL, but for a solid understanding of the overall architecture, it's important that you know how XML SQL fits in.

On queries, XML SQL is used to translate the result set into XML. It produces a canonical XML representation, covered in detail later in this chapter. This representation is based on a standard schema that works for all SQL queries. When working with the output of XSQL, you can assume that the results will come back in this schema. XSQL replaces the query call with these results that XML SQL provides.

XML SQL is also used by XSQL when pushing data to the database by using the `xsql:insert-request`, `xsql:update-request`, `xsql:delete-request`, and `xsql:insert-param` actions. The canonical schema is used for these cases, also. In these situations, the burden is on you to ensure that your data is in the correct format. Doing so is easily accomplished with XSLT stylesheets, as you'll see.

Much of XSQL is based on XML SQL. If you find yourself wanting to get under the hood of XSQL, you'll want to explore the Oracle XML SQL utility. As you'll see in Chapter 18, it is easy to exploit the power of XML SQL from your own custom action handlers.

XSLT Processor

The XSLT processor performs the XSLT transformations. Without the XSLT processor, XSQL is pretty boring, for all you have is an easy way to execute commands against the database and produce XML from SQL statements. The XSLT processor takes the result of the XSQL page processor and transforms it into something usable by the requesting agent.

As an XSQL developer, you have very little direct interaction with the XSLT processor. You tell it what to do with the stylesheet processing instruction that is documented completely later in this chapter. The most significant part of this instruction is the location of the stylesheet. The XSLT processor finds the stylesheet and performs the transformation.

The transformation itself is dictated by the stylesheet, which is written in the XSLT language. This language allows you to describe how you want the source XML to merge with the text in the stylesheet. Usually, the stylesheet contains HTML markup that describes how nodes in your XML should be output. You can, however, output whatever you want.

The XSLT engine is compliant with the World Wide Web Consortium (W3C) XSLT 1.0 Recommendation released in 1999 and, for the moment, acting as the driving standard behind XSLT. You might run across an old stylesheet based on an earlier standard. The processing instruction of the stylesheet should enable you to determine whether that stylesheet is old.

Core XSQL Components

So far in this chapter, you've learned a lot about the technologies that XSQL leverages and the ways to access XSQL functionality. What you haven't learned are the components that XSQL developers work with daily. These components are discussed in this section and revisited throughout the remainder of the book. The first component is the XSQL page, which is the key component of XSQL.

XSQL Pages

These are XML documents that describe what the XSQL page processor should do. We've already described several XSQL pages used for executing SQL queries, as well as those for linking to a stylesheet that transforms the resulting XML.

First, it's important to note that an XSQL page doesn't have to be a file. When in Chapter 17 you learn about embedding the XSQL page processor into your Java code, you'll see that you can construct your XSQL page at runtime. You can also create an XSQL page with another XSQL page, dynamically. To do so, the XSQL page processor requires only that the XSQL page be a valid, well-formed XML document. When XSQL is used programmatically, there is a lot of flexibility in how an XSQL page may originate. When the XSQL servlet is used, however, your XSQL page needs to exist as a file.

An XSQL page itself can contain several different entities. Any nontrivial XSQL page contains one or more actions, which are discussed in the next chapter. The actions tell the XSQL page processor what it should do. You can also link an XSQL page to an XSLT stylesheet. Doing so tells the XSQL page processor to use the specified stylesheet to transform the results. The XSQL page can also specify a serializer, which is discussed in more detail later in this section. You can use a serializer to specify exactly how the data are written to the output.

Actions

XSQL is built around the concept of *actions*, an XML element that defines what you want to do. You have already seen the xsql:query action. This action is, by far, the most popular, but there are others.

The XSQL page processor executes the actions. It takes the resulting XML datagram for a particular query and replaces the original action element with the XML datagram. More than one action can be included in the same page. In the case of multiple actions in a page, you must have a top-level element that contains all the action elements on the page. This is an XML requirement, so if you don't follow this requirement, the document will not be valid XML.

The following code is the first XSQL page that you saw in Chapter 1. It contains one action, the xsql:query action. This action is simply an XML element that belongs to the XSQL namespace.

```
<?xml version="1.0"?>
<?xml-stylesheet type="text/xsl"
                 href="emp-intro.xsl"?>
 <page xmlns:xsql="urn:oracle-xsql"
       connection="demo">
  <xsql:query>
    SELECT ename, job, sal FROM emp
     WHERE deptno=20
     ORDER BY sal
  </xsql:query>
 </page>
```

In Chapter 5, you'll learn more about built-in actions. In Chapter 18, you'll see how you can define your own actions.

Action Handlers

Action handlers handle XSQL actions. In the case of the built-in actions, XSQL implicitly relates a given action to an action handler. When the built-in actions don't provide you with the functionality that you desire, you can create your own custom action handlers. The architecture of action handlers is diagrammed in Figure 4.6. The XSQL page processor knows about the built-in action handlers; for the custom action handlers, you either specify the name of the class in the XSQL page or cite it by a nickname given in the XSQLConfig.xml file.

In Figure 4.6, the some-page.xsql has three actions, including the xsql:query action that you've seen used in the code examples so far. The XSQL page processor handles that action with the built-in action handler called the XSQL query handler. There is a built-in action handler for each action discussed in the next chapter. The two custom action handler classes handle the two custom actions and are loaded into the JVM. A custom action handler can do whatever you want. In Chapter 18 you'll learn more about programming custom action handlers.

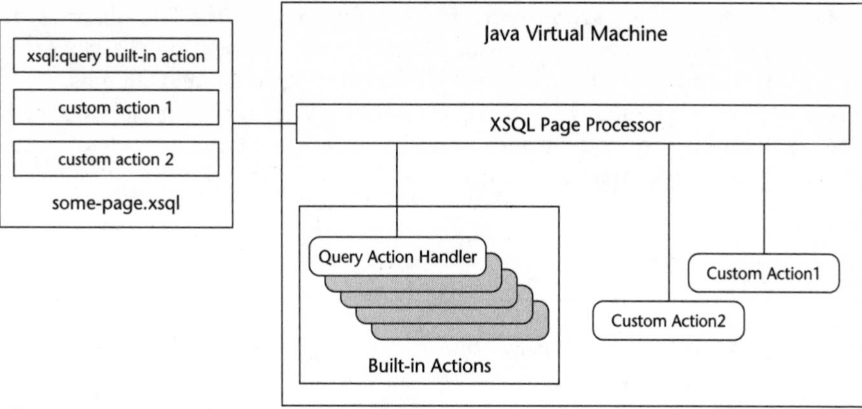

Figure 4.6 Architecture of action handlers.

Serializers

Serialization is the process of writing the end XML document. In our earliest examples in the last chapter, the default serializer wrote XML out to a network stream only, and our browser displayed it. The serializer's job isn't hard: It just takes what the XSQL page processor assembles in memory and writes it to output. Figure 4.7 shows how the serializer fits in.

The architecture of serializers is simpler than that of action handlers. Although you can—and often will—use multiple action handlers in your XSQL page, you can specify only one serializer per XSQL page. In most cases, you won't need to specify a serializer at all.

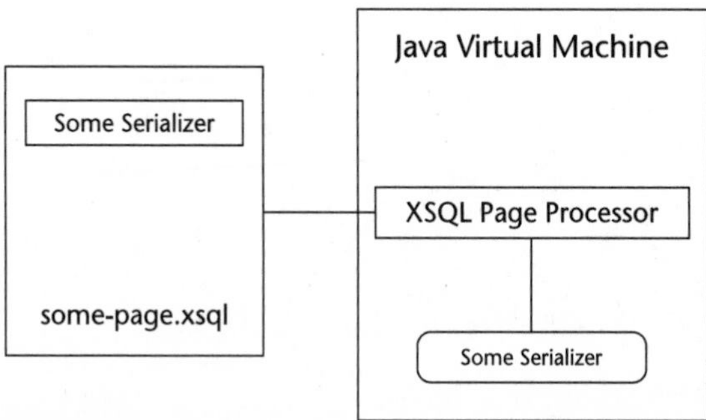

Figure 4.7 The serializer.

There are several built-in action handlers, but the only built-in serializer is the default one. Like action handlers, you can create your own custom serializers, a process you'll learn more about in Chapter 19. Why would you want to? In most cases, you won't need to; the default serializer will do just fine. The primary reason to specify a serializer is to output binary data, such as a PDF or image. Oracle provides a serializer that allows you to use Apache FOP to create dynamic PDFs.

Moving On

This chapter focused on the high-level architecture of XSQL. Chapter 5 discusses XSQL coding; Chapters 6 and 7 show you the ins and outs of how XSQL works. You'll examine the technologies associated with XSQL—first, SQL and other Oracle database technologies, then XSLT. You can use much of the material in Chapters 5 through 7 for building upon, implicitly, the knowledge you've gained from this chapter. By having a good understanding of XSQL architecture, you'll find developing good XSQL-based systems easy.

Writing XSQL Pages

In the previous chapter, you learned about the architecture of XSQL. You looked at a lot of diagrams, but you did not write any code. In this chapter, you start coding. The first step is to flesh out your knowledge of the `xsql:query` action, which you used in previous examples. This is the action used to retrieve data from the database using SQL statements. This is only one of the built-in actions, though. All of them are covered in this chapter. But before going in to the rest of the actions, you will learn about the canonical XSQL schema and date formatting. These two areas apply generally to several of the built-in actions, including `xsql:query`. The chapter ends by describing how to link to XSLT stylesheets.

This chapter provides all of the raw information for using the built-in XSQL actions. A couple of the areas, however, are explored in more detail in later chapters. Passing parameters between pages is very important, and is covered in Chapter 6. The actions that allow you to put information into the database are covered here, but an in-depth discussion of how to modify your database is presented in Chapter 7. You will learn how to create your own custom actions in Chapter 18.

Querying the Database

The `xsql:query` action is used to retrieve information from the database. You have already used it several times. At its simplest, you simply put a SQL statement between the xsql:query tags as shown in the following example. The only requirement is that it be a select statement. If you try to insert a statement that would modify data or administer data objects, the XSQL page processor will reject it.

```
<?xml version="1.0"?>
<xsql:query connection="demo" xmlns:xsql="urn:oracle-xsql">
  SELECT * from emp
</xsql:query>
```

As you have observed earlier, the result set from the query is turned into an XML fragment that replaces the xsql:query element in the output. The names of the XML elements are determined by the query. For our particular example here, the emp table has columns named empno, ename, job, mgr, hiredate, sal, comm, and deptno. For each row, an XML element with the name of the column contains the data for that column. This can be seen in Figure 5.1.

If you don't like the names of the columns, you can alias them using SQL. For instance, you can use SELECT ename as "employee name" so that the XML is returned with employee_name elements instead of ename elements, as in the following example

```
<?xml version="1.0"?>
<xsql:query connection="demo" xmlns:xsql="urn:oracle-xsql">
  SELECT ename as "employee_name" from emp
</xsql:query>
```

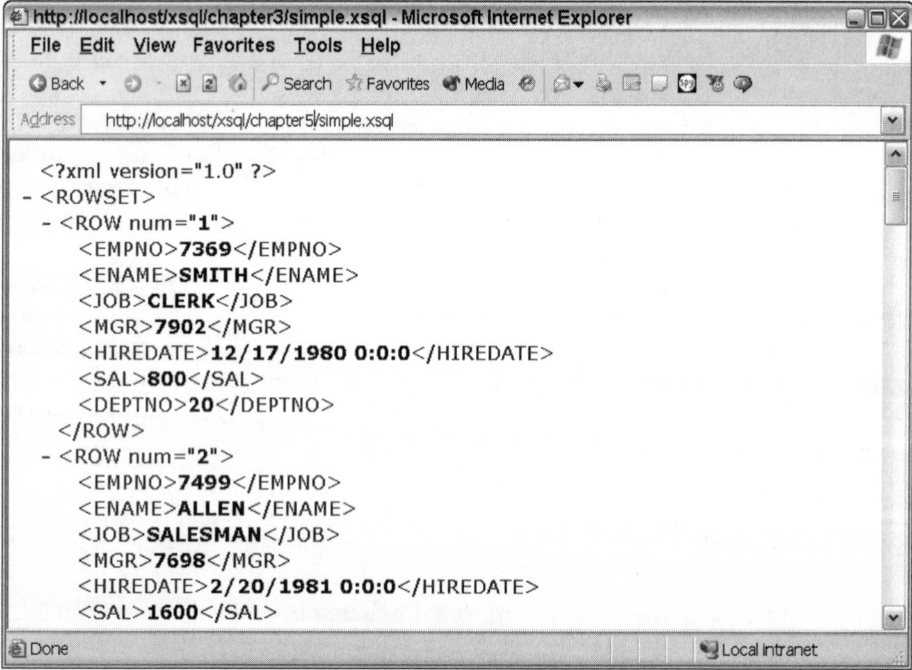

Figure 5.1 Simple xsql:query example.

In some cases, you have to alias the field name. Let's say that, in addition to the name, you want to know the year and month. The simplest SQL for getting that information is:

```
SELECT ename, to_char(hiredate,'YYYY-MON')
  FROM emp
```

But if you put this into your XSQL page, you will get an error. The default name for the second field contains parentheses, which are illegal characters for an XML tag name, so you need to alias the field to something else. Here's how you do it:

```
<?xml version="1.0"?>
<xsql:query connection="demo" xmlns:xsql="urn:oracle-xsql">
  SELECT ename as "employee_name",
         to_char(hiredate,'YYYY-MON') AS "hiredate"
    FROM emp
</xsql:query>
```

This XSQL page will produce the result shown in Figure 5.2.

You will remember from the previous discussion on XML that there are several illegal characters for XML tag names. This means that you cannot arbitrarily alias the field names to anything you want. A common mistake is to try to alias a field to a name that contains a space. This will generate an error message.

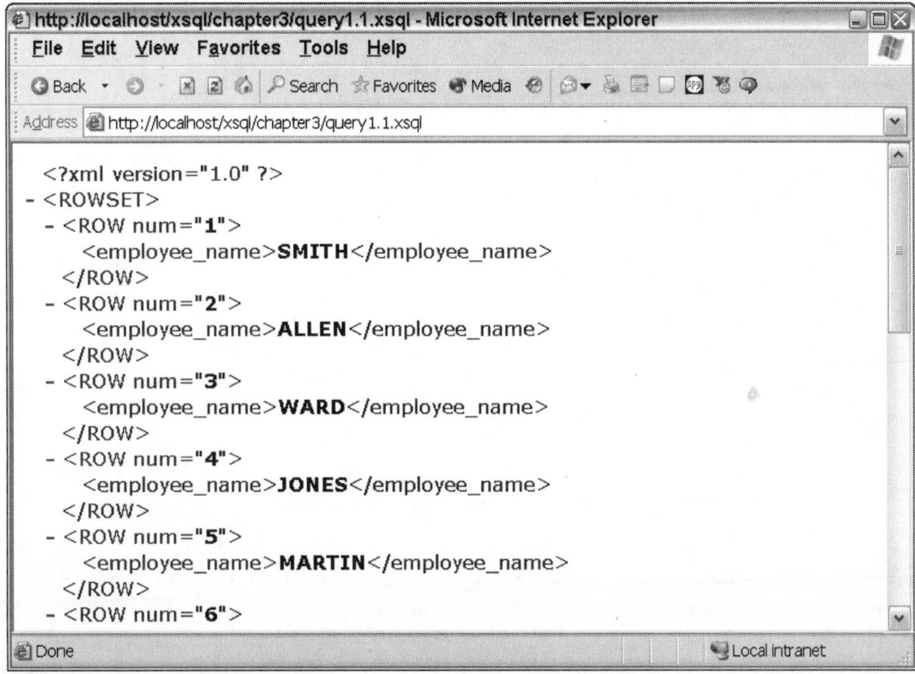

Figure 5.2 Aliasing field names.

NOTE Unless you are a SQL guru, you probably have a lot of questions about specific types of SQL queries. Chapter 8 covers all of SQL from an XSQL perspective. Stay tuned!

You can also control the row and rowset element names. You do this by setting the `row-element` and `rowset-element` attributes of `xsql:query`. Here's how it works:

```
<?xml version="1.0"?>
<xsql:query connection="demo"
            xmlns:xsql="urn:oracle-xsql"
            row-element="EMPLOYEES"
            rowset-element="EMPLOYEE_LIST">
  SELECT * FROM emp
</xsql:query>
```

This will yield the result shown in Figure 5.3.

As you can see, you have a lot of control over the format of the results. In some cases, you have to exercise some control, because the default column name would not be valid XML. Beyond this situation, you will find that you can make the resulting datagram much easier to understand by using SQL aliasing and multiple `xsql:query` actions.

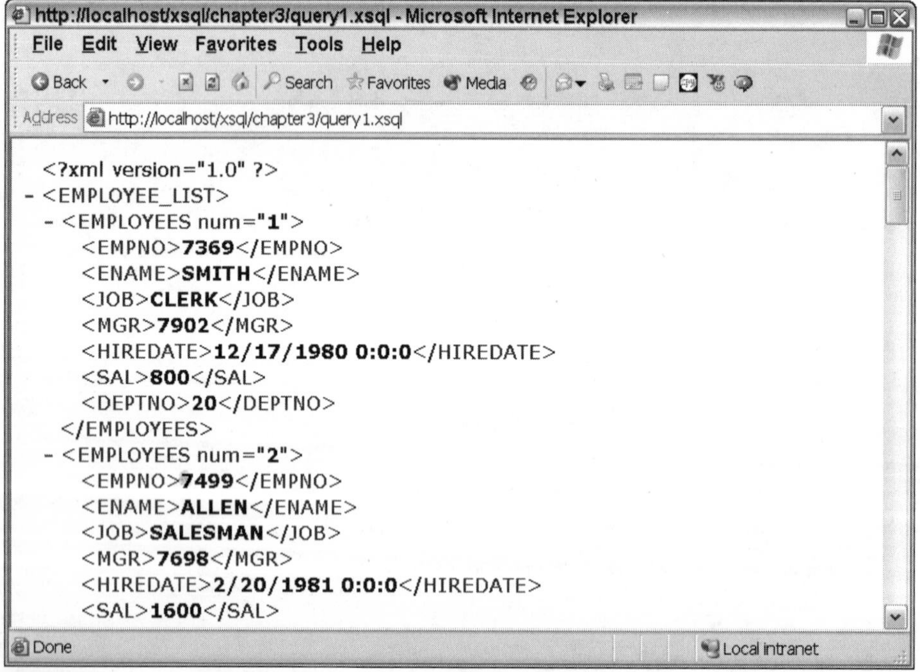

Figure 5.3 Result with custom row and rowset names.

Multiple `xsql:query` Actions

You will often have multiple `xsql:query` actions in the same page. This is shown in the following example. Note that if you have multiple actions, they have to be contained by a root node. This goes back to the earlier discussion about XML. There must be one root node for each document.

```
<?xml version="1.0"?>
<page connection="demo" xmlns:xsql="urn:oracle-xsql">
 <xsql:query>
  select dname from dept where deptno=10
 </xsql:query>
 <xsql:query>
  select ename from emp where deptno=10
 </xsql:query>
</page>
```

When you look at this example, you should see something similar to Figure 5.4. In this screenshot, the operator has scrolled down to where the first query ends and the second query begins.

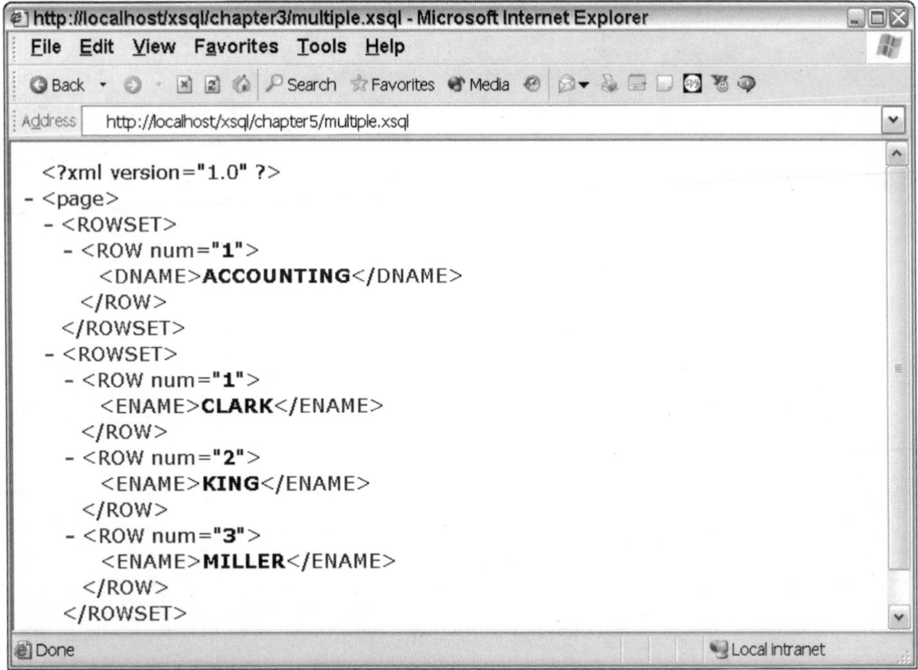

Figure 5.4 Multiple `xsql:query` actions.

In this case it is easy to see, because the two queries pulled from different tables. But what if you had two different queries in the same page that pulled the same fields from the same table? It would be hard to distinguish where one query ended and the other began. Instead, you should enclose each query inside a distinct element, as follows:

```
<?xml version="1.0"?>
<page connection="demo" xmlns:xsql="urn:oracle-xsql">
 <dept-query>
  <xsql:query>
   select dname from dept where deptno=10
  </xsql:query>
 </dept-query>
 <emp-query>
  <xsql:query>
   select ename from emp where deptno=10
  </xsql:query>
 </emp-query>
</page>
```

This produces the results shown in Figure 5.5.

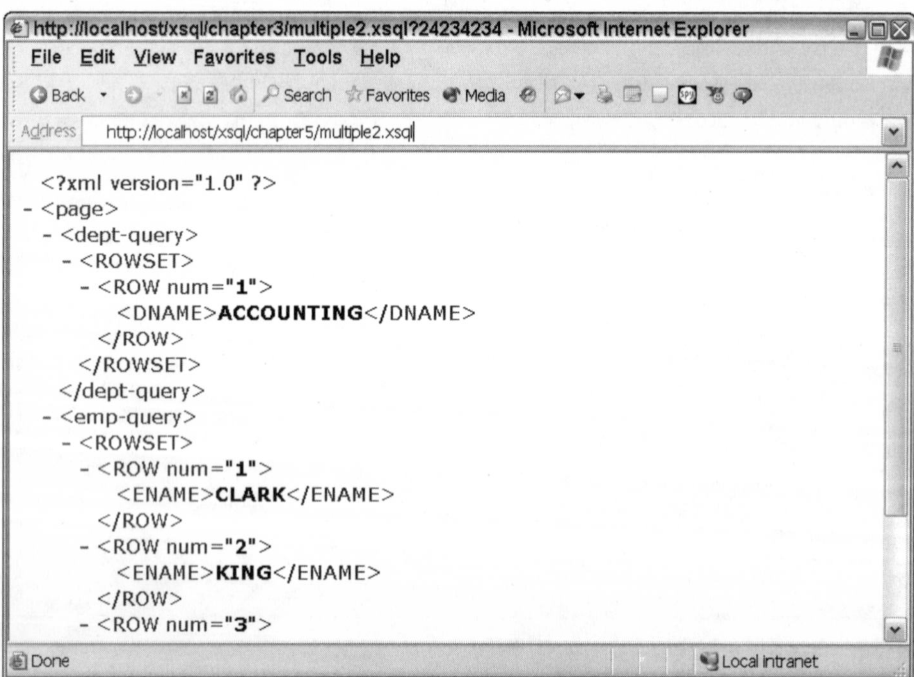

Figure 5.5 Multiple `xsql:query` actions and arbitrary XML.

`xsql:query` Details

The `xsql:query` element has several available attributes. These attributes control how the action behaves. In the coming chapters, you will make use of many of these attributes to access functionality. Here, the attributes are grouped together by the kind of effect they have. The first group includes the XML control attributes. These attributes control how the XML is created, including the date format, the case of the tag names, the presentation of null values, and the grouping tag names provided by default by XSQL. These are all outlined in Table 5.1.

Table 5.1 Presentation Attributes

ATTRIBUTE	DESCRIPTION
`date-format ="string"`	The date format mask to use for dates. Changing this changes how dates are presented in the XML. Any value in the `java.text.SimpleDateFormat` class is available—these are listed in Table 5.2.
`id-attribute="string"`	The attribute name to use instead of the default `num` attribute for the unique identification of rows.
`id-attribute-column="string"`	The name of the column that should provide the unique identifier for the row. For instance, if you want to use the `empno` column to uniquely identify each row, then you would set `id-attribute-column="empno"`. To be useful, the column you use should be unique. By default, the row's position in the result set is used.
`null-indicator="boolean"`	Determines if a column with a null value is represented as an element for a particular row. By default, it is not—in this example, if an employee's commission is set to `null`, then the `<comm>` element simply won't be included in the row. If you set this value to `yes`, then an element will be included with an attribute `NULL="Y"`. The element itself will have no value.
`row-element="string"`	Element name to use instead of `<ROW>` to group a particular row's data.
`rowset-element="string"`	Name of the element that is parent to all the rows. Default is `<ROWSET>`.
`tag-case="string"`	The case of element names—lower or upper. By default, the case matches the field name in the query.

Table 5.2 Pagination Attributes

NAME	DESCRIPTION
`max-rows`	Maximum number of rows to fetch and write to the XML. If `skip-rows` is defined, that number of rows is skipped before fetching either `max-rows` or some number of rows less than `max-rows`. (The latter case would occur if you are at the end of the `result-set`.)
`skip-rows`	Number of rows that to skip before fetching and writing rows from the query in to the XML.

The next group of `xsql:query` attributes helps with the pagination of a large result set. These attributes are described in Table 5.2. You will see more on how to use them to create stateless paging in Chapter 14.

Table 5.3, creatively named "Miscellaneous Attributes," lists the last group of attributes. These attributes couldn't be grouped together any other way.

Table 5.3 Miscellaneous Attributes

ATTRIBUTE NAME	DESCRIPTION
`bind-params="string"`	Ordered list of XSQL parameter names that will bind to JDBC bind variables. More on this later in the chapter.
`error-statement="boolean"`	If set to `no`, the SQL statement that generated the error won't be included in the output. This keeps your users (and possibly hackers) from being able to reverse engineer your database schema. Default is `yes`.
`fetch-size="integer"`	Overrides the `default-fetch-size` configuration in the `XSQLConfig.xml` file.
`include-schema="Boolean"`	If set to `yes`, an inline schema that describes the resulting XML is included. This is useful if your XML is being consumed by an application or tool that needs the schema. Default is `no`.

The `xsql:query` element is one of the key elements for all of XSQL. Hopefully, this section gives you a good basis and can act as a good reference. You will be using the `xsql:query` element, and the lessons learned here, throughout the rest of the book.

xsql:no-rows-query

The `xsql:no-rows-query` element is an element that can only be used as a child of `xsql:query`. It helps with a common situation—your query returns no rows. If your query does not match any rows, then you are not going to get any XML back. If all you want is to display a message such as "No data" when this situation occurs, XSLT can easily accomplish this for you. However, you may want to use an entirely different query.

In such a case, you simply place an `xsql:no-rows-query` element inside the `xsql:query` element as follows. In case your `no-rows-query` statement also fails to return rows, you can nest as many `xsql:no-row-query` elements inside of an `xsql:no-row-query` element as you need.

```
<xsql:query>
    SELECT statement
     <xsql:no-rows-query>
         SELECT statement to use in case of no rows
     </xsql:no-rows-query>
</xsql:query>
```

Canonical Schema

In interacting with the database, XSQL solves a couple of basic problems. It converts SQL results to XML, and it converts XML to SQL. You've seen the conversion of SQL results to XML already with the `xsql:query` action, and you'll see the XML-to-SQL conversion later in this chapter. In both of these cases, data that is usually arranged in a table has to be represented in a tree format. Oracle solves this problem with a canonical schema. This schema is used by `xsql:query` when result sets are presented as XML and is required by the XSQL actions that insert XML documents into database tables as relational data.

The schema uses the following common format for queries and XML insertions, updates, and deletions. In all these cases, you use XSLT transformations to massage the data. For queries, you use an XSLT stylesheet to transform the data to a format that is appropriate. Most often, this means transforming the canonical representation into HTML. When pushing data to the database, you use a stylesheet to transform the data from its original format into the canonical form.

The canonical form can be used to represent all of the Oracle datatypes, including cursors, objects, and collections. But first, say that you have a simple table in the database, which includes the values in Table 5.4.

Table 5.4 Simple Database Table

COLUMN_NAME_1	COLUMN_NAME_2
Value1.1	Value1.2
Value2.1	Value2.2

When you select all of the rows from the table, the canonical representation will appear as follows.

```
<ROWSET>
     <ROW id="1">
        <COLUMN_NAME_1>Value1.1</COLUMN_NAME_1>
        <COLUMN_NAME_2>Value1.2</COLUMN_NAME_2>
     </ROW>
      <ROW id="2">
        <COLUMN_NAME_1>Value2.1</COLUMN_NAME_1>
        <COLUMN_NAME_2>Value2.2</COLUMN_NAME_2>
     </ROW>
</ROWSET>
```

If you add more rows, you will get additional row elements. If you add more columns, you will have additional elements inside each row. The general pattern is that each row is an element that contains each field in that row as child element. In this case, you can assume that the datatypes are strings. In fact, it doesn't matter. Numbers will appear the same way without any signifying formatting. In the canonical form, everything is text. This is also true for dates, although you control how dates are presented and interpreted with the date formats described later in this chapter. As you learned before, you can change the rowset and row element names when using `xsql:query`. But even when these are changed, you have not changed the overall structure of the result datagram.

NOTE It's important to note that the canonical representation is in XML and must follow the rules of XML. This implies that the column names, which vary from query to query, are restricted. They must begin with either a letter or an underscore and can contain only alphanumeric characters along with underscores, hyphens, and periods. This doesn't mean that you have to rename all of the columns in your database. It's easy to alias column names in SQL; this is explained in the xsql:query section of this chapter, as well as in Chapter 8.

If you've been around SQL for a while, you know that not all queries produce such a simple output. You can have cursors that create their own tree structures. In such a case, the form looks like the following example:

```
<ROWSET>
      <ROW id="1">
```

```
        <REGULAR_COLUMN>Regular Value</REGULAR_COLUMN>
        <YOUR_CURSOR_NAME>
             <YOUR_CURSOR_NAME_ROW id="1">
                  <FIELD1>Value For Field #1 of the Cursor</FIELD1>
                  <FIELD2>Value For Field #2 of the Cursor</FIELD2>
             </YOUR_CURSOR_NAME_ROW>
        </YOUR_CURSOR_NAME>
    </ROW>
</ROWSET>
```

As you can see, cursors work quite naturally with the tree structure of XML. The following real-world example demonstrates this more clearly. Here is a SQL query that you can run as the `scott/tiger` user that utilizes cursors. If you aren't familiar with cursors, don't worry—they are covered in Chapter 8.

```
select dname, cursor(select ename from emp b where b.deptno=a.deptno) as
employees from dept a
```

The result of the first two rows of this canonical query is as follows:

```
<ROWSET>
<ROW num="1">
            <DNAME>ACCOUNTING</DNAME>
                  <EMPLOYEES>
                        <EMPLOYEES_ROW num="1">
                              <ENAME>CLARK</ENAME>
                        </EMPLOYEES_ROW>
                        <EMPLOYEES_ROW num="2">
                              <ENAME>KING</ENAME>
                        </EMPLOYEES_ROW>
                        <EMPLOYEES_ROW num="3">
                              <ENAME>MILLER</ENAME>
                        </EMPLOYEES_ROW>
                  </EMPLOYEES>
      </ROW>
      <ROW num="2">
            <DNAME>RESEARCH</DNAME>
                  <EMPLOYEES>
                        <EMPLOYEES_ROW num="1">
                              <ENAME>SMITH</ENAME>
                        </EMPLOYEES_ROW>
                        <EMPLOYEES_ROW num="2">
                              <ENAME>JONES</ENAME>
                        </EMPLOYEES_ROW>
                        <EMPLOYEES_ROW num="3">
                              <ENAME>SCOTT</ENAME>
                        </EMPLOYEES_ROW>
                        <EMPLOYEES_ROW num="4">
                              <ENAME>ADAMS</ENAME>
```

```
                        </EMPLOYEES_ROW>
                 </EMPLOYEES>
      </ROW>
  </ROWSET>
```

Oracle objects and collections also appear as nested structures in the canonical representation. The following example shows a single row with an object and a collection:

```
<ROWSET>
<ROW num="1">
           <YOUR_OBJECT_COLUMN_NAME>
              <ATTRIBUTE1>Value1</ATTRIBUTE1>
              <ATTRIBUTE2>Value2</ATTRIBUTE2>
         </YOUR_OBJECT_COLUMN_NAME>
<YOUR_COLLECTION_NAME>
              <YOUR_COLLECTION_NAME_ITEM>
                  <ATTRIBUTE1>Value1</ATTRIBUTE1>
                        <ATTRIBUTE2>Value2</ATTRIBUTE2>
</YOUR_COLLECTION_NAME_ITEM>
<YOUR_COLLECTION_NAME_ITEM>
                  <ATTRIBUTE1>Value1</ATTRIBUTE1>
                        <ATTRIBUTE2>Value2</ATTRIBUTE2>
</YOUR_COLLECTION_NAME_ITEM>
</YOUR_COLLECTION_NAME>
     </ROW>
</ROWSET>
```

Formatting Dates

Because most applications use dates at some point, it is very important to understand how XSQL works with dates. XSQL uses date formats that act as masks. A date format is a combination of different symbols that represent different parts of the date-time stamp. XSQL uses date formats both when retrieving information from the database and when putting information into it. When retrieving information, XSQL writes the date to output in accordance with the date format. When inputting information, it assumes that dates are in the format specified by the date format.

The characters that represent different parts of the date format are listed in Table 5.5. Padding for variable-length data can be supplied by repeating the symbol. For example, if you want `08` to represent 8 A.M., you put hh in the format string.

Table 5.5 Date Format Symbols

SYMBOL	MEANING	EXAMPLE
G	Era designator	AD
y	Year	1996
MM	Month in year as number	07

Table 5.5 Date Format Symbols *(Continued)*

SYMBOL	MEANING	EXAMPLE
`MMM`	Month in year as word	July
`D`	Day in month	10
`h`	Hour in A.M./P.M. (1-12)	12
`H`	Hour in day (0-23)	0
`m`	Minute in hour	30
`s`	Second in minute	55
`S`	Millisecond	978
`E`	Day in week	Tuesday
`D`	Day in year	189
`F`	Day of week in month	2 (2nd Wed in July)
`W`	Week in year	27
`W`	Week in month	2
`a`	A.M./P.M. marker	PM
`k`	Hour in day (1~24)	24
`K`	Hour in A.M./P.M. (0~11)	0
`z`	Time zone	Pacific Standard Time
'	Escape for text	
''	Single quote	'

Table 5.6 shows a couple of examples of formatting dates.

Table 5.6 Example Date Formats

FORMAT	EXAMPLE
`"MM.dd.yyyy G 'at' hh:mm:ss z"`	05/02/2002 AD at 15:08:56 PDT
`"EEE, MMM d, ''yy"`	Sun, Apr 10, '02
`"hh 'o''clock' a, zzzz"`	12 o'clock PM, Pacific Daylight Time
`"yyyyy.MM.dd HH:mm"`	2002.July.10 23:08

Several of the XSQL built-in actions use date formats. All of them use the same format.

Other Built-in Actions

This section exposes the details of the rest of the XSQL actions. The next two chapters will look more deeply in to several of these actions as you learn about modifying the database and passing parameters. All of these actions work in the same manner as the `xsql:query` action with which you are already familiar. You specify attributes and a value for the action element.

xsql:dml

DML stands for Data Manipulation Language. It means that you are going to change something in the database. The `xsql:dml` element is used for statements of change, including insertions, updates, deletions, and even creation and deletion of database objects. Though you should heed the warning against actually deleting whole tables, the `xsql:dml` element is very useful for processing input to your database. You can also use it to execute PL/SQL blocks.

The following example uses a PL/SQL block to insert two records into the database and commit them. As you will learn in Chapter 9, PL/SQL can be used to do a great variety of tasks. You can call a wide variety of procedures, use conditional logic, and even process results. The example here is very pedestrian, but you will see more complex examples in Chapter 9.

```
<page connection="demo" xmlns:xsql="urn:oracle-xsql">
   <dml>
   <xsql:dml>
      begin
       insert into emp (empno, ename) values (8000,'Joe Schmoe');
       insert into emp (empno, ename) values (8001,'Billy Blue');
       commit;
      end;
   </xsql:dml>
   </dml>
   <query>
   <xsql:query>
       select * from emp
   </xsql:query>
   </query>
</page>
```

When you look at the results of the example, you will see that there is little result that comes back from the `xsql:dml` tag. All that you can expect is either an error message if something goes wrong or an element that tells you the number of rows that are affected. You will learn in Chapter 14 how best to return to the user the status of a DML request

There are a couple of attributes that you can use to configure the behavior of the `xsql:dml` element. They are described in Table 5.7.

Table 5.7 `xsql:dml` Attributes

ATTRIBUTE NAME	DESCRIPTION
`commit="boolean"`	If `yes`, a commitment is issued on the connection after a successful execution of the DML statement. Default is `no`.
`bind-params="string"`	Ordered list of XSQL parameter names that will bind to JDBC bind variables. More on this later in the chapter.
`error-statement="boolean"`	If set to `no`, the SQL statement that generated the error won't be included in the output. This keeps your users (and possibly hackers) from being able to reverse engineer your database schema. Default is `yes`.

xsql:ref-cursor-function

This action interacts with a PL/SQL function. A PL/SQL function returns a value at the end of execution. Some PL/SQL functions return cursors, acting essentially like a result set. The difference is that the PL/SQL function can assemble the cursor by using conditional logic and several SQL statements across a variety of tables. Only PL/SQL functions that return the type `REF CURSOR` can be called from a `xsql:ref-cursor-function` action.

Assume that you have a function whose name is `MyPackage.MyFunction` and that it returns a `REF CURSOR`. You would call it as follows:

```
<?xml version="1.0"?>
<page connection="demo" xmlns:xsql="urn:oracle-xsql">
   <ref-cursor>
   <xsql:ref-cursor-function>
       MyPackage.MyFunction(1)
   </xsql:ref-cursor-function>
   </ref-cursor>
</page>
```

This action works very similarly to the `xsql:query` action, except that it calls a PL/SQL function instead of issuing SQL statements directly. It is little surprise, then, that almost all of the attributes for `xsql:query` work for `xsql:ref-cursor-function`. There is only one exception—the fetch-size attribute can't be applied here.

You will learn more about using PL/SQL in Chapter 9.

xsql:include-owa

It may be the case that you have stored procedures in the database that generate XML. It's quite reasonable that you might want to reuse that logic and have that XML included in your XSQL page. This is the purpose of the `xsql:include-owa` action. There are two standard Oracle Web Agent (OWA) packages (HTP and HTF) that will write to the server-side page buffer. When this action is used, the XSQL page processor executes the PL/SQL block included in the action, assuming that the functions and procedures of the HTP and HTF are being used to write XML to the server-side page buffer. The XSQL page processor then grabs the output out of the page buffer and inserts it in to the outgoing XSQL page. It is the responsibility of the PL/SQL programmer to ensure that the XML is well formed. Here is an example of how to use this action:

```
<xsql:include-owa>
PL/SQL Block using HTP and/or HTF packages to write to server-side page
buffer
</xsql:include-owa>
```

There are a couple of attributes that can be used with the `xsql:include-owa` action. They are described in Table 5.8.

xsql:include-request-params

This action is a utility action designed to make it easier to write XSLT stylesheets. It formats every parameter and its value to XML, including not only form- and URL-based parameters but also session parameters and cookies. The usage is very simple, and there are no optional attributes. Just put the following into your XSQL document:

```
<xsql:include-request-params/>
```

In its place you will get XML back in the following form. If there are no session variables or cookies, those elements will not occur.

```
<request>
   <parameters>
     <ParamName1>value1</ParamName1>
     <ParamName2>value2</ParamName2>
   </parameters>
   <session>
     <SessionVarName1>value1</SessionVarName1>
     <SessionVarName2>value2</SessionVarName2>
    </session>
    <cookies>
     <cookieName1>value1</cookieName1>
     <cookieName2>value2</cookeName2>
    </cookies>
</request>
```

When you look at XSLT in depth in Chapter 13, you will learn more about the usefulness of this action.

Table 5.8 `xsql:include-owa` Attributes

ATTRIBUTE	DESCRIPTION
`bind-params="string"`	Ordered list of XSQL parameter names that will bind to JDBC bind variables. More on this later in the chapter.
`error-statement="boolean"`	If set to `no`, the SQL statement that generated the error won't be included in the output. This keeps your users (and possibly hackers) from being able to reverse engineer your database schema. Default is `yes`.

xsql:include-param

This action allows you to include a single parameter in to your XML datagram. It is essentially a scaled back, specific version of the `xsql:include-request-params` action. It gives you an easy way to make your parameters and their values available to your XSLT stylesheets. Here is the syntax:

```
<xsql:include-param name="paramname"/>
```

The name attribute is required, and there are no optional attributes.

xsql:include-xml

This action allows you to include XML in your datagram from any URL. Relative URLs will point to files in your local Web space, whereas absolute URLs can grab the resource from anywhere on the Web. The XML retrieved must be well formed. Here is how you use it:

```
<xsql:include-xml href="URL"/>
```

The `href` attribute is required, and there are no optional attributes.

xsql:set-page-param

The `xsql:set-page-param` action allows you to set a page-private parameter for the XSQL page. You can set the parameter either as text, as text and other parameter values, or as the result of a SQL statement. There are two different syntaxes for this attribute. The first syntax covers the first two cases:

```
<xsql:set-page-param name="paramname" value="value"/>
```

This will set paramname=value. You may be wondering how you would use this syntax to assign the value of another parameter. You will learn more about this later in the chapter, when you read about passing parameters. For now, here is one example:

```
<xsql:set-page-param name="new-param" value="{@org-param}"/>
```

This will set the value of org-param as the value of new-param.

The other syntax is quite a bit more interesting. With it you can set parameters based on SQL statements. An example follows. The value assigned is that of the first column of the first row. For clarity, it is best to structure your SQL statements so that only one row and one column will be returned.

```
<xsql:set-page-param name="sql-based-param">
SQL statement
</xsql:set-page-param>
```

This action has a couple of attributes, detailed in Table 5.9. The name attribute is required.

xsql:set-session-param

The xsql:set-session-param action allows you to set a parameter on the current browser user's HTTP session. This session is controlled by the Web server, but it generally ends after a time out or when the browser is closed. This action has an effect only when you are using XSQL in conjunction with Java servlets. Nothing happens if the XSQL request object or XSQL command line encounters this action in a page that it is processing.

The syntax behaves very much like the syntax for the xsql:set-page-param action. You can set a parameter's value in two ways. You can set it directly, as follows:

```
<xsql:set-session-param name="paramname" value="value"/>
```

You can also set the parameter's value by issuing a SQL statement. The value assigned is that of the first column of the first row. For clarity, it is best to structure your SQL statements so that only one row and one column will be returned.

Table 5.9 xsql:set-page-param Attributes

ATTRIBUTE NAME	DESCRIPTION
name="string"	Name of the page-private parameter to set.
bind-params="string"	Ordered list of XSQL parameter names that will bind to JDBC bind variables. More on this later in the chapter.
ignore-empty-value="boolean"	If yes, the parameter won't be set if the value that would be assigned is an empty string. Default is no.

```
<xsql:set-session-param name="sql-based-param">
SQL statement
</xsql:set-session-param>
```

The xsql:set-session-param action has several attributes, listed in Table 5.10. The name attribute is required.

xsql:set-cookie

This action sets an HTTP cookie to a specified value. This action has an effect only when you are using XSQL in conjunction with Java servlets. Nothing happens if the XSQL request object or XSQL command line encounters this action in a page that it is processing.

The syntax behaves very much like the syntax for the xsql:set-page-param action. You can set a parameter's value in two ways. You can set it directly, as follows:

```
<xsql:set-cookie name="paramname" value="value"/>
```

You can also set the parameter's value by issuing a SQL statement. The value assigned is that of the first column of the first row. For clarity, it is best to structure your SQL statements so that only one row and one column will be returned.

```
<xsql:set-cookie name="sql-based-param">
SQL statement
</xsql:set-cookie>
```

The xsql:set-cookie action has several attributes, listed in Table 5.11. The name attribute is required.

Table 5.10 xsql:set-session-param Attributes

ATTRIBUTE NAME	DESCRIPTION
name="string"	Name of the session parameter to set.
bind-params="string"	Ordered list of XSQL parameter names that will bind to JDBC bind variables. More on this later in the chapter.
ignore-empty-value="boolean"	If yes, the parameter won't be set if the value that would be assigned is an empty string. Default is no.
only-if-unset="Boolean"	If yes, this parameter will be set only if the parameter doesn't exist in the session. Default is no.

Table 5.11 `xsql:set-cookie` Attributes

ATTRIBUTE NAME	DESCRIPTION
name="string"	Name of the session parameter to set.
bind-params="string"	Ordered list of XSQL parameter names that will bind to JDBC bind variables. More on this later in the chapter.
ignore-empty-value="boolean"	If yes, the parameter won't be set if the value that would be assigned is an empty string. Default is no.
only-if-unset="Boolean"	If yes, this parameter will be set only if the parameter doesn't exist in the session. Default is no.
max-age="integer"	Sets the maximum age of the cookie in seconds. By default, the cookie will expire when the browser session ends.
path="string"	The relative URL path where the cookie value is valid. By default, this is set to the path of the XSQL document. For the cookie to be readable by all pages on your Web server, set path="/".

xsql:set-stylesheet-param

This action allows you to dynamically set a top-level stylesheet parameter that the XSQL page processor should pass on to the XSLT stylesheet. You will learn more about XSLT stylesheet parameters in Chapter 13.

The syntax is similar to that of the `xsql:set-page-param`, `xsql:set-session-param`, and `xsql:set-cookie` actions. To set the stylesheet to a particular value, including possibly another parameter, use:

```
<xsql:set-stylesheet-param name="paramname" value="value"/>
```

You can also set the parameter's value by issuing a SQL statement. The value assigned is that of the first column of the first row. For clarity, it is best to structure your SQL statements so that only one row and one column will be returned.

```
<xsql:set-stylesheet-param name="sql-based-param">
SQL statement
</xsql:set-stylesheet-param>
```

The `xsql:set-stylesheet-param` action has several attributes, listed in Table 5.12. The name attribute is required.

Table 5.12 `xsql:set-session-param` Attributes

ATTRIBUTE NAME	DESCRIPTION
`name="string"`	Name of the session parameter to set.
`bind-params="string"`	Ordered list of XSQL parameter names that will bind to JDBC bind variables. More on this later in the chapter.
`ignore-empty-value="boolean"`	If `yes`, the parameter won't be set if the value that would be assigned is an empty string. Default is `no`.

xsql:action

The `xsql:action` element is used to enable custom action handlers. When this action is processed, a custom action handler of your choosing is invoked. You will learn more about how to write custom action handlers in Chapter 17. The only requirement is that the `xsql:action` element have a handler attribute. Beyond that, it is restricted only by the XML syntax for all elements and the requirements of the custom action handler.

```
<xsql:action handler="somepackage.SomeCustomHandler" param1="value1"
param2="value2">
    <SomeElement>blah</SomeElement>
<SomeOtherElement>foo</SomeOtherElement>
</xsql:action>
```

The custom action handler will consume the containing elements and parameters. As you will learn in Chapter 17, it is very important that custom action handler developers thoroughly document what their action handlers require and can optionally use.

xsql:include-xsql

The `xsql:include-xsql` action can be used to include the results of other XSQL pages in the current XSQL page. This can make your XSQL pages more reusable. The `xsql:include-xsql` action is used as follows:

```
<xsql:include-xsql href="other.xsql"/>
```

The results of the other XSQL page will be included wherever this element is placed in the XSQL document. If the XSQL document is tied to a stylesheet, the stylesheet will be applied before inclusion. The results can also be reparsed. All of the request and session parameters available to the including page will be available to the included page. Table 5.13 lists the optional attributes.

Table 5.13 `xsql:include-xsql` Attributes

ATTRIBUTE NAME	DESCRIPTION
`href="string"`	Relative or absolute URL of the XSQL page that you want to include.
`reparse="Boolean"`	If `yes`, the output of the included XSQL page is reparsed so that the including page can treat the text of the result as elements. Default is `no`.

xsql:insert-request

This action allows you to insert an XML document into the database. There are two ways that data can be inserted: An XML document received over HTTP can be inserted, or the parameters for the XSQL page, including possibly HTML form parameters, can be inserted. In the first case, an XML document is received in the body of a HTTP post request. Either the XML document must be in the canonical `ROWSET/ROW` format, or a stylesheet must be specified to translate the XML document to the canonical form.

In the second case, the parameters included in a request can be inserted. These can include cookies, session parameters, and request parameters. The most common case involves inserting data from HTML forms. If you wish to insert HTML form data, the XSQL page processor will translate the form data to XML, using the `xsql:include-request-params` action. You then translate this XML format to the canonical format with your own XSLT stylesheet.

The use of this action in the insertion of data is further discussed in Chapter 7. The syntax of this action is as follows:

```
<xsql:insert-request table="emp"/>
```

Table 5.14 lists the attributes that can be used in conjunction with this action.

Table 5.14 `insert-request` Attributes

ATTRIBUTE NAME	DESCRIPTION
`table="string"`	The table in which to insert the XML. Views and synonyms are also valid here.
`transform="URL"`	The URL of the XSLT stylesheet that should be used to transform the XML to the canonical `ROWSET/ROW` format.
`columns="string"`	List of one or more column names whose values will be inserted. List should be either space or column delimited. Any columns not listed here will be ignored. If no data for a particular column is present in a `ROW` element, it will be set to `NULL` in the database.

Table 5.14 `insert-request` Attributes *(Continued)*

ATTRIBUTE NAME	DESCRIPTION
`Commit-batch-size="integer"`	Data will be committed after this number of rows are inserted. If 0, no commitments will be issued until after the end of the insertion.
`date-format="string"`	Date format mask to use for dates on this insert. Format mask should match any dates in the XML.

xsql:update-request

This action allows you to update an XML document against the database. There are two ways that data can be updated: An XML document received over HTTP can be updated, or the parameters for the XSQL page, including possibly HTML form parameters, can be updated. In the first case, an XML document is received in the body of a HTTP post request. Either the XML document must be in the canonical `ROWSET/ROW` format, or a stylesheet must be specified to translate the XML document to the canonical form.

In the second case, the parameters included in a request can be updated. These can include cookies, session parameters, and request parameters. The most common case involves updating rows based on data from HTML forms. If you wish to do this, the XSQL page processor will translate the form data to XML using the `xsql:include-request-params` action. You then translate this XML format to the canonical format with your own XSLT stylesheet.

The use of this action in the insertion of data is further discussed in Chapter 7. The syntax of this action is as follows:

```
<xsql:update-request table="emp" columns="sal"/>
```

Table 5.15 lists the attributes that can be used in conjunction with this action.

Table 5.15 `insert-request` Attributes

ATTRIBUTE NAME	DESCRIPTION
`table="string"`	The table in which to insert the XML. Views and synonyms are also valid here.
`transform="URL"`	The URL of the XSLT stylesheet that should be used to transform the XML to the canonical `ROWSET/ROW` format.

(continues)

Table 5.15 `insert-request` Attributes *(Continued)*

ATTRIBUTE NAME	DESCRIPTION
`columns="string"`	List of one or more column names whose values will be inserted. List should be either space or column delimited. Any columns not listed here will be ignored. If no data for a particular column is present in a `ROW` element, it will be set to `NULL` in the database.
`Commit-batch-size="integer"`	Data will be committed after this number of rows are inserted. If 0, no commitments will be issued until after the end of the insertion.
`date-format="string"`	Date format mask to use for dates on this insert. Format mask should match any dates in the XML.

xsql:delete-request

This action allows you to delete data from the database base on an XML document. There are two ways that data can be deleted: An XML document received over HTTP can define the deletion, or the parameters for the XSQL page, including possibly HTML form parameters, can define the deletion. In the first case, an XML document is received in the body of a HTTP post request. Either the XML document must be in the canonical `ROWSET/ROW` format, or a stylesheet must be specified to translate the XML document to the canonical form.

In the second case, the parameters included in a request can define the deletion. These can include cookies, session parameters, and request parameters. The most common case involves data from HTML forms. If you wish to go this route, the XSQL page processor will translate the form data to XML using the `xsql:include-request-params` action. You then translate this XML format to the canonical format with your own XSLT stylesheet.

The use of this action in the deletion of data is further discussed in Chapter 7. The syntax of this action is as follows:

```
<xsql:delete-request table="emp" columns="deptno"/>
```

Table 5.16 lists the attributes that can be used in conjunction with this action.

Table 5.16 `delete-request` Attributes

ATTRIBUTE NAME	DESCRIPTION
`table="string"`	The table in which to insert the XML. Views and synonyms are also valid here.
`transform="URL"`	The URL of the XSLT stylesheet that should be used to transform the XML to the canonical `ROWSET/ROW` format.
`columns="string"`	List of one or more column names whose values will be inserted. List should be either space or column delimited. Any columns not listed here will be ignored. If no data for a particular column is present in a `ROW` element, it will be set to `NULL` in the database.
`Commit-batch-size="integer"`	Data will be committed after this number of rows are inserted. If 0, no commitments will be issued until after the end of the insertion.
`date-format="string"`	Date format mask to use for dates on this insert. Format mask should match any dates in the XML.

xsql:insert-param

The `insert-param` action is used to interpret the value of a particular parameter as a XML document and insert it into the database. The parameter arrives as part of an HTTP request. The syntax is as follows:

```
<xsql:insert-param name="xml-data" table="emp"/>
```

The attributes available are detailed in Table 5.17.

Table 5.17 `xsql:insert-param` Attributes

ATTRIBUTE NAME	DESCRIPTION
`table="string"`	The table in which to insert the XML. Views and synonyms are also valid here.
`transform="URL"`	The URL of the XSLT stylesheet that should be used to transform the XML to the canonical `ROWSET/ROW` format.

(continues)

Table 5.17 `xsql:insert-param` Attributes *(Continued)*

ATTRIBUTE NAME	DESCRIPTION
`columns="string"`	List of one or more column names whose values will be inserted. List should be either space or column delimited. Any columns not listed here will be ignored. If no data for a particular column is present in a `ROW` element, it will be set to `NULL` in the database.
`Commit-batch-size="integer"`	Data will be committed after this number of rows are inserted. If 0, no commitments will be issued until after the end of the insertion.
`date-format="string"`	Date format mask to use for dates on this insert. Format mask should match any dates in the XML.

Linking to XSLT Stylesheets

XSLT stylesheets are a key component of the XSQL architecture. You will rarely use XSQL without an accompanying stylesheet. This section covers the different options available for working with stylesheets in XSQL. The first topic is something that you have already done several times: referencing stylesheets. XSQL also allows you to decide on a stylesheet based on the browser string and defer the transformation to the client.

The stylesheet processing instruction is a standard XML processing instruction. It sits at the top of the page and is enclosed by `<?` and `?>`. Here is the simple usage. This stylesheet processing instruction tells the XSLT processor to apply the `emp.xsl` stylesheet. The type attribute is also required when using XSLT; it must be set to the mime type `text/xsl`.

```
<?xml version="1.0"?>
<?xml-stylesheet type="text/xsl" href="emp.xsl"?>
<page connection="demo" xmlns:xsql="urn:oracle-xsql">
<xsql:query>
       SELECT * FROM EMP
</xsql:query>
</page
```

By default, the XSLT stylesheet is processed on the server. If you want to defer the processing to the client, you can do this by setting the client attribute to `yes`. Some Web browsers, including Internet Explorer 5.0 and 6.0, contain XSLT processors and can perform the transformation at the client. However, it is important to know that you introduce browser-compatibility issues when you defer to the client. In fact, even IE 5.0 and IE 6.0

transform stylesheets differently. The most appropriate reason to defer processing to the client is to offload processing to the clients. Even then, you should do it only if you can mandate what XSLT processors exist on the client, or be prepared to deal with different flavors of processors. Here is an example of deferring the transformation to the client:

```
<?xml version="1.0"?>
<?xml-stylesheet type="text/xsl" href="emp.xsl" client="yes" ?>
<page connection="demo" xmlns:xsql="urn:oracle-xsql">
<xsql:query>
       SELECT * FROM EMP
</xsql:query>
</page>
```

Processing Instruction Details

All of the attributes of the processing instruction are covered in Table 5.18. Because the processing instruction isn't an XML element, these aren't really attributes in the XML sense. Instead, they are referred to as pseudoattributes.

Table 5.18 Pseudoattributes of the Stylesheet Processing Instruction

NAME	DESCRIPTION
`type="string"`	The mime type of the stylesheet. For XSLT stylesheets, this must be `text/xsl`. If the serializer attribute is set, this may be present or absent. If present, the XSLT processor will transform prior to handing control to the serializer.
`Href="URL"`	URL for the stylesheet. If an absolute URL, the host must be one of the trusted hosts listed in the `XSQLConfig.xml` file.
`Media="string"`	If provided, a case-insensitive match on the `User-Agent` string determines if this stylesheet should be used.
`Client="boolean"`	If set to `yes`, the XSLT Processor isn't invoked and the client is expected to perform the transformation.
`Serializer="string"`	Name of a custom serializer to use to output the data. By default, the XML DOM serializer is used when no stylesheet is present, while the XSLT processor's serializer is used if a stylesheet is present. When this attribute is set, the custom serializer is invoked instead of the appropriate default serializer. Valid values are either fully qualified Java class names of custom serializers or the name defined in the `<serializerdefs>` section of the `XSQLConfig.xml` file.

Choosing Stylesheets Based on Client Type

One of the beauties of XSLT is that you can create different faces for different types of browsers. You can have one stylesheet for Netscape, one for Internet Explorer, one for the text-only browser Lynx, and several for the various wireless devices. XSQL provides a simple way to switch the stylesheet based on the type of Web agent making the request. The following example uses one stylesheet for Lynx and another for Microsoft Internet Explorer 5.0.

```
<?xml version="1.0"?>
<?xml-stylesheet type="text/xsl" media="lynx" href="lynx-emp.xsl"
client="yes" ?>
<?xml-stylesheet type="text/xsl" media="msie 5" href="msie-emp.xsl"
client="yes" ?>
<page connection="demo" xmlns:xsql="urn:oracle-xsql">
<xsql:query>
       SELECT * FROM EMP
</xsql:query>
</page>
```

XSQL makes the choice by doing a case-insensitive match on the `User-Agent` string, which a Web agent uses to identify itself. This functionality is convenient in some cases. However, it is generally too limited. The `User-Agent` string has been misused by Web browsers since the mid-1990s; determining the type of requesting agent is more complex than the simple matching that is provided by XSQL.

Moving On

Now you have a working knowledge of all of the XSQL actions. Still, you probably have some unanswered questions about the specifics. The next two chapters delve more deeply into the XSQL parameters and database modification. This will get you squared away with XSQL and then you will be ready to tackle the Oracle database technologies and XSLT. The focus returns to actions in Chapter 18, where you will learn how to create your own custom actions.

CHAPTER 6

XSQL Parameters

HTTP is a stateless protocol—each transaction is separate. This makes HTTP highly efficient and very scalable. However, it has always presented problems for developing applications over the Web. Web developers are always faced with the task of passing parameters between the separate transactions. There is also the issue of abstraction. Anytime you add a layer of abstraction—in this case, XSQL—you need to learn how parameters are treated. Generally, the layer of abstraction makes parameter handling easier. Still, you need to actually learn how it makes it easier and how to access parameters.

XSQL works with four different types of parameters: (1) page-private parameters, (2) stylesheet parameters, (3) session parameters, and (4) cookies. Page-private parameters most resemble typical parameters. The parameters that you used with the `xsql:dml` action in the previous section were typical parameters. Stylesheet parameters are really XSLT creatures—XSLT has its own parameterization system with which you can interact from XSQL. Session parameters belong to a user session. The servlet engine controls the session itself. Cookies are HTTP cookies that you can set directly from XSQL.

WARNING If you are using XSQL from the command line or from your own program, session and cookie parameters won't work. Even if you are using XSQL Servlet, session parameters and cookies aren't guaranteed: Session parameters depend on the configuration of the servlet engine; cookies can only be set if the browser allows them.

Here you'll see all the different types of parameters in action. Your first steps are to learn how to reference parameters and how parameters can be represented in XML. Next, you'll look at page-private parameters, session parameters, followed by cookies. Then, you'll learn how XSQL references all of the different types of parameters and resolves conflicts. From here you are ready to learn how to make your SQL queries more efficient with JDBC bind parameters. Finally, you'll look at integrating your parameters with XSLT stylesheets.

Referencing Parameters

The XSQL page processor parses XSQL pages for parameters by looking for an @ enclosed with curly brackets. When it sees this inside an XSQL page, it will replace the token with the parameter value. This works the same regardless of how the page is invoked. Here, you'll learn how to reference parameters when the HTTP GET and HTTP POST methods are used to invoke the XSQL servlet. The other kinds of invocation—XSQL command line and XSQL request—will be covered later in Chapters 7 and 8, respectively.

The following XSQL page shows examples of parameter references. This example allows you to perform essentially any SQL select statement on any configured database. Be sure to save this file as `very-unsecure.xsql`—you don't want to run it on a production server!

```
<?xml version="1.0"?>
<page xmlns:xsql="urn:oracle-xsql" connection="{@conn}">
  <xsql:query>
     select {@fields} from {@tables}
  </xsql:query>
</page>
```

If you call just the URL by itself, you will get an error message. However, once you put the `conn`, `fields`, and `tables` parameters in the query string, you'll get a result from your database. This URL will fetch all fields and all rows from the emp table that is under the scott user `http://localhost/xsql/ref-params.xsql?conn=demo&fields=*&tables=emp&`.

Figure 6.1 shows the result that you will get for this URI.

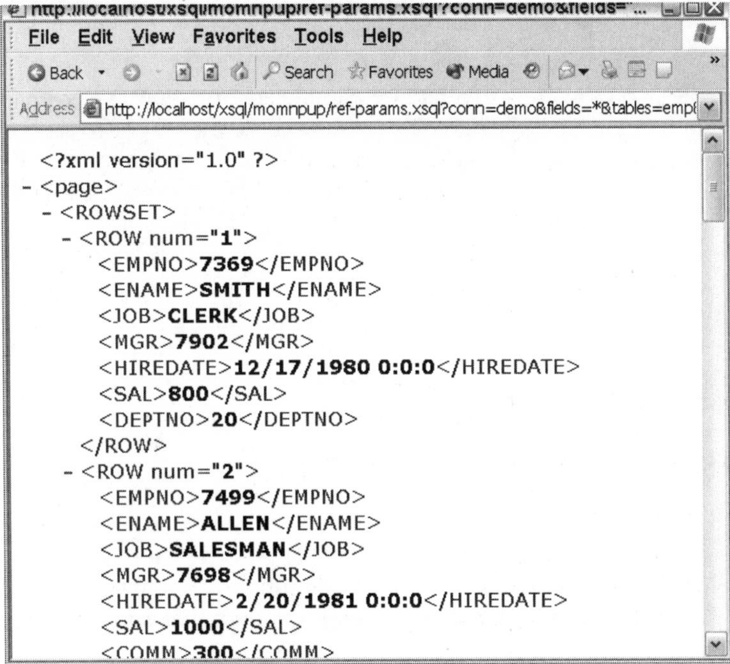

Figure 6.1 XSQL datagram using parameters.

Parameters aren't replaced outside of the XSQL actions. If you modify your XSQL document as shown in the following code, you won't get the values inside the <conn>, <fields>, and <tables> tags. Instead, you'll just get the literal text that you put in.

```
<?xml version="1.0"?>
<page xmlns:xsql="urn:oracle-xsql" connection="{@conn}">
    <xsql:query>
     select {@fields} from {@tables}
  </xsql:query>
  <conn>{@conn}</conn>
  <fields>{@fields}</fields>
  <tables>{@tables}</tables>
</page>
```

Though it would be nice to have this kind of functionality, XSQL has another way to achieve the same result, which is discussed in the next section. You can use the <xsql:include-param> action.

Parameter XML Representation

In the previous examples, you saw how to reference parameters from your XSQL page. But what if you want the parameters to be part of the result? This is the job of two actions: `<xsql:include-request-param>` and `<xsql:include-request-params>`. This action outputs all of the parameters to the XML. Here is an example of `<xsql:include-request-param>`:

```
<?xml version="1.0"?>
<page xmlns:xsql="urn:oracle-xsql">
    <xsql:include-param name="conn" />

    <xsql:include-param name="fields" />

    <xsql:include-param name="tables" />
</page>
```

Now save this as `include-param.xsql`. You can either pass the parameters in on the URL as before or change the action of your `very-unsecure.html` form to `include-params.xsql`. In either case, this page should produce the result shown in Figure 6.2.

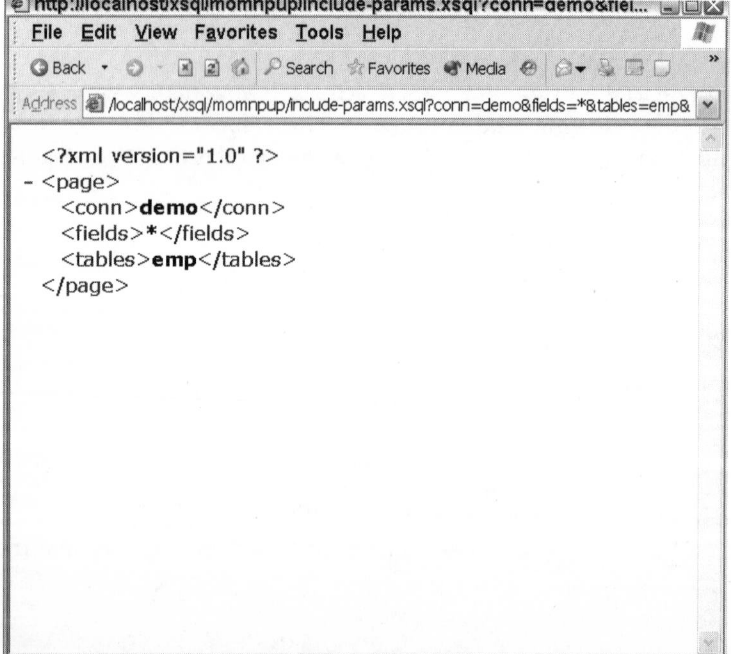

Figure 6.2 XML representation of parameters.

In this case, you have to specify the parameters one at a time. If you know that you want all of the parameters—or, if you want so many parameters that it's easier to just grab all of them—then you can use the `<xsql:include-request params>` action. You can create the following XSQL page as `include-request-params.xsql`. With only one line of code, you'll have every parameter:

```
<?xml version="1.0"?>
<page xmlns:xsql="urn:oracle-xsql">
   <xsql:include-request-params />
</page>
```

The result for this, when you use the same parameters as before, is shown in Figure 6.3.

The XML schema is very simple. Even if there are no parameters at all, you'll always have the following skeleton:

```
<request>
  <parameters>
  </parameters>
  <session>
  </session>
  <cookies>
  </cookies>
</request>
```

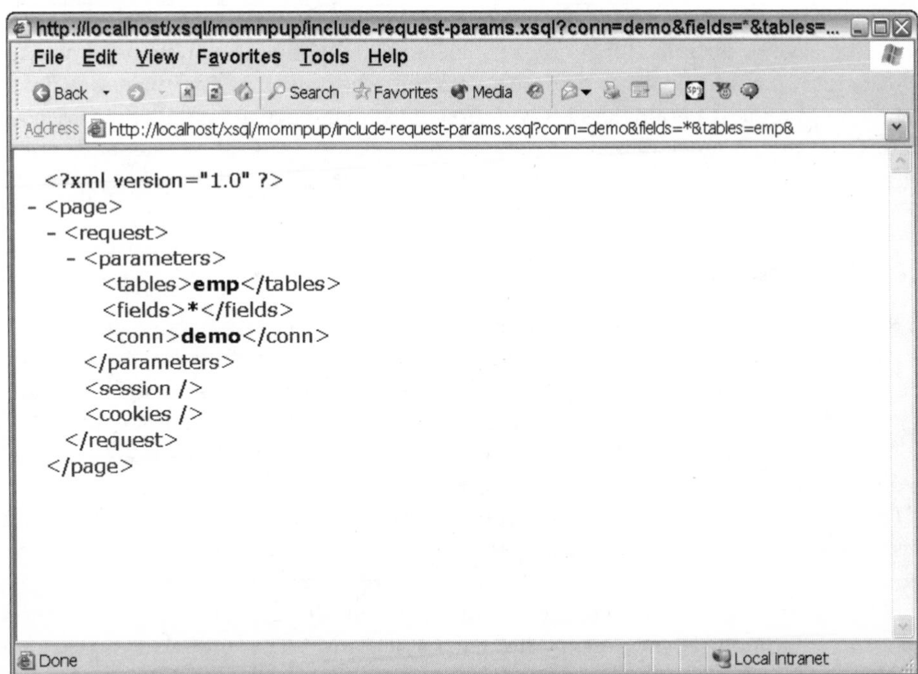

Figure 6.3 Result of `<xsql:include-request-params>`.

The parameters are children of the respective elements. As you can see in the previous example, parameters received from forms are children of the <parameters> element. For each parameter, a child element with the same name as the parameter encloses the parameter's value. This works the same for session parameters and cookies. Here is an example where two of each are set:

```
<request>
  <parameters>
     <param1>param-value1</param1>
     <param2>param-value2</param2>
  </parameters>
  <session>
     <session1>session-value1</session1>
     <session2>session-value2</session2>
  </session>
  <cookies>
     <cookies1>cookies-value1</cookies1>
     <cookies2>cookies-value2</cookies2>
  </cookies>
</request>
```

Parameter Types

There are several different types of parameters in XSQL. So far, you've been dealing with request parameters. This section covers the other types of parameters. A quick definition of request parameters is given first. Next, page-private parameters are covered. These are parameters that are defined inside of a page. Last, session and cookie parameters are covered. These can only be used in conjunction with the XSQL servlet.

Request Parameters

In the previous examples, you used request parameters. Request parameters come in as part of the request. When you are using XSQL in conjunction with the XSQL servlet, they are passed as either an HTTP `GET` or `POST` request. If you are using XSQL from the command line or it is embedded in your code, you can also pass in request parameters. Exactly how you do this is a bit beyond the scope of this chapter, but you'll learn how to do this in Chapters 15 and 17, respectively.

For now, you should focus on how request parameters are used with HTTP. You did this in the earlier example when you accessed the URL `http://localhost/xsql/ref-params.xsql?conn=demo&fields=ename&tables=emp&`.

In this case you are using an HTTP `GET` method to query your data. The `GET` method is the most common HTTP method—it is what you use most any time that you click on a link. The second most common method is `POST`—this is what your HTML forms usually use. You can reference parameters in XSQL with both `GET` and `POST`. For this example, let's say that you want to create a simple form for processing queries. Here is the HTML for the form.

```
<html>
 <body>
<h1>Sample Form </h1>
  <form action="ref-params.xsql" method="post">
   <table border="0">
    <tr>
     <td>Connection:</td>
     <td><input type="text" name="conn" /></td>
    </tr>
    <tr>
     <td>Fields:</td>
     <td><input type="text" name="fields" /></td>
    </tr>
    <tr>
     <td>Tables:</td>
     <td><input type="text" name="tables" /></td>
    </tr>
    <tr>
     <td colspan="2" align="center">
      <input name="submitButton" type="submit" value="Select" />
     </td>
    </tr>
   </table>
  </form>
 </body>
</html>
```

You can now do essentially any `Select` statement with this form. Figure 6.4 shows how to fill out the form so you can query on just the employee names from the emp table.

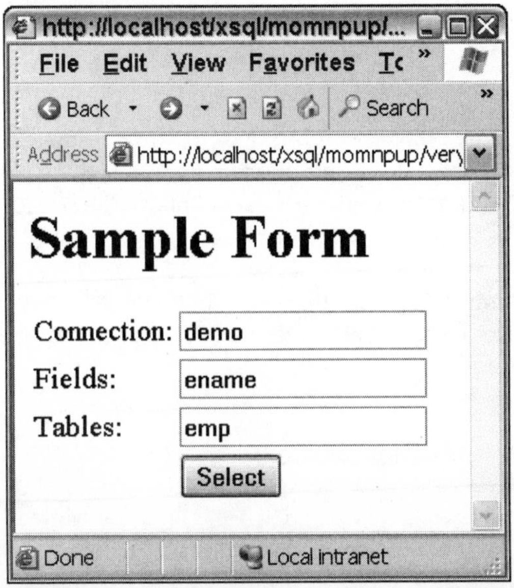

Figure 6.4 Using parameters with an HTML form.

When you click Select, you should get the results shown in Figure 6.4. You would get the exact same results with the URI specified earlier and shown in Figure 6.1.

Page-Private Parameters

You can think of page-private parameters as being local to the page, whereas session parameters and cookie parameters can span multiple page calls. Page-private parameters aren't limited solely to HTTP transactions. The XSQL command line and XSQL request object can also provide page-private parameters. The important characteristic of page-private parameters is that they are gone after the result is returned. Subsequent transactions won't know about the parameters unless they are explicitly passed.

Sometimes, you may wish to set page-private parameters explicitly in your XSQL page. You do this with the `<xsql:set-page-param>` action. It allows you two ways to set parameters. The first way equates a parameter with a string value, whereas the second way allows you to set a parameter based on a SQL query. Examples of both ways to set parameters follow:

```
<?xml version="1.0"?>
<page xmlns:xsql="urn:oracle-xsql" connection="demo">
  <xsql:set-page-param name="ename" value="ADAMS" />
  <xsql:set-page-param name="deptno">
     select deptno from emp where ename='{@ename}'
  </xsql:set-page-param>
  <xsql:include-param name="ename" />
  <xsql:include-param name="deptno" />
  <xsql:query>
     select * from emp where deptno={@deptno}
  </xsql:query>
</page>
```

Session Parameters

So far, all of our examples about parameters have been of page-private parameters. These parameters function much like parameters to scripts. Session parameters, on the other hand, exist across invocations of XSQL. Your servlet engine maintains the session on behalf of the XSQL servlet. This has the implication that only servlets will be able to make use of session parameters.

Setting session parameters is quite simple. You set them just like you set cookie parameters. The following XSQL will set a session parameter named `ename` and one named `deptno`:

```
<?xml version="1.0"?>
<page xmlns:xsql="urn:oracle-xsql" connection="demo">
  <xsql:set-session-param name="ename" value="{@r-p-ename}" />
  <xsql:set-session-param name="deptno">
    select deptno from emp where ename='{@ename}'
  </xsql:set-session-param>
</page>
```

Now, save the file as `set-session-param.xsql`, and access it with the URL `http://localhost/xsql/momnpup/set-session-param.xsql?r-p-ename=ADAMS&`.

If you now go back to the `include-request-params.xsql` page that you created earlier, you'll see the output that is shown in Figure 6.5. These parameters will be part of your session until the session ends. Your servlet engine ultimately controls the session itself. It usually continues until the browser window is closed or until some period of inactivity.

If you know that a given XSQL page will only be called within a session, then you can use session parameters instead of having to deal with the complexities of request parameters or page-private parameters. For instance, let's suppose that you want various kinds of information about a particular employee. You can create a simple form that has an input field named `r-p-ename` and then set its action to the `set-session-param.xsql` page you created previously. Alternatively, you can just use the URL that you just used.

WARNING **Notice that our request parameter,** `r-p-ename`**, and our session parameter,** `ename`**, have different names, though they refer to the same entity. A session parameter can't be assigned the value of a request parameter of the same name. (It is legal for parameters of different types to have the same name—the rules for resolving the naming of conflicts are laid out later in this section.)**

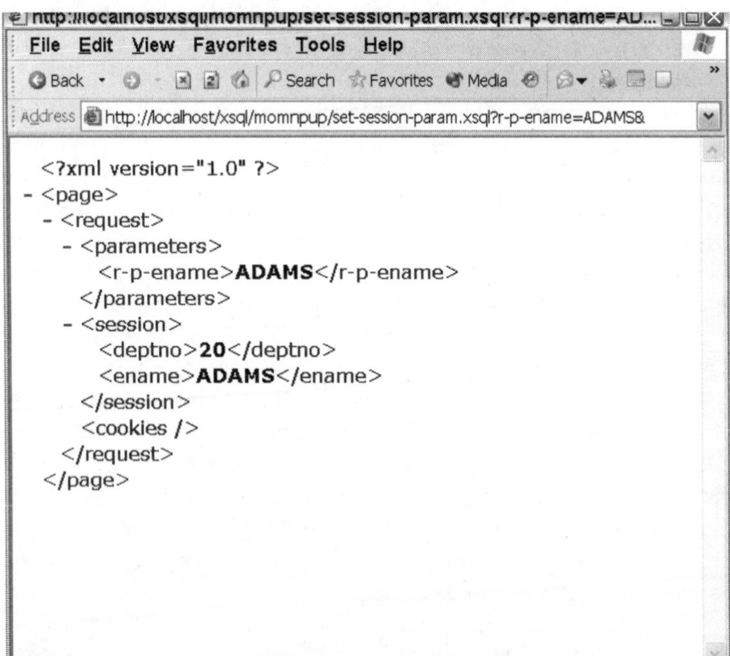

Figure 6.5 Session parameters and `<xsql:include-request-params>`.

Now, the ename and the deptno parameters are set for the entire session. If you want a list of everyone in the department, you can do that with a very simple XSQL page:

```
<?xml version="1.0"?>
<?xml-stylesheet type="text/xsl" ?>
<page xmlns:xsql="urn:oracle-xsql" connection="demo">
  <xsql:query>
     select * from emp where deptno={@deptno}
  </xsql:query>
</page>
```

Cookies

HTTP cookies try to solve a fundamental problem of HTTP. How do you create state when using a stateless protocol? You saw cookies at work in the previous section. If you look back at Figure 6.5, you'll see an entry in the cookies element. This cookie is actually the one that is used by the servlet engine to control the session.

The basic mechanism is that a cookie is set on the Web browser. The cookie itself is really just a string. The Web browser stores that cookie in some way on the local machine. That cookie is passed back on subsequent requests. The browser will only pass a cookie back on requests for which the cookie was specifically meant. This means that if www.yahoo.com sets a cookie, there is no way that the cookie will be passed to your Web application, assuming that your Web application isn't running in the yahoo.com domain. Further, you can restrict cookies so that they are only sent back to certain URLs within your own domain. Cookies can be either session based (i.e., they are erased when the Web browser closes down) or long lived. Long-lived cookies can stay on the browser virtually forever.

When the cookies return, your application is able to assume that the current transaction is originating from the same Web browser as previous transactions. Thus, you are able to maintain state on the server side. This is exactly what the servlet engine does with the cookie that it sets. It attaches all of the session information to that particular cookie on the server side. That single cookie can act as a key to a lot of different information. When you set cookies manually, you can create the same kind of architecture.

This is the way cookies generally work. However, it is very important to understand that the individual users ultimately have control of whether cookies will work this way for them. Users can set their browser so that they don't accept cookies, or don't accept long-lived cookies. They can go in and choose to delete cookies that your application uses. If you depend on cookies for authentication, you may find your users trading their cookies around. When using cookies, it's important to remember that you can't depend fully on their full and appropriate use. Cookies certainly make the developer's life easier. If you can require your users to have cookies enabled on their browser, then you'll have an easier time designing your application. However, if you can't, you need to consider ways that your application will degrade gracefully.

With an understanding of the problems of cookies, let's look at how to use cookies with XSQL. The basic model is the same as with page-private parameters and session parameters, but with some extensions. Let's cover the basics first. The following XSQL page will set the employee name and the department number as cookies:

```
<?xml version="1.0"?>
<page xmlns:xsql="urn:oracle-xsql" connection="demo">
  <xsql:set-cookie name="ename" value="{@r-p-ename}" />
  <xsql:set-cookie name="deptno">
    select deptno from emp where ename='{@ename}'
  </xsql:set-cookie>
  <xsql:include-request-params />
</page>
```

Save this as `set-cookies.xsql`. You can call it with `http://localhost/xsql/momnpup/set-cookie-param.xsql?r-p-ename=SMITH&`. You can then invoke the `include-request-params.xsql` page that you developed previously and see the results that are shown in Figure 6.6.

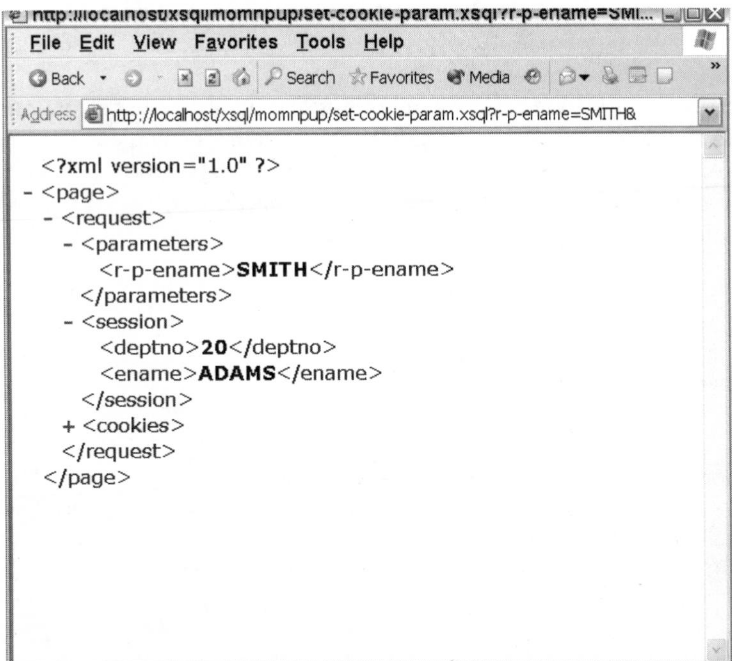

Figure 6.6 Setting cookies with XSQL.

An obvious question is, "Why would I want to set cookies manually instead of just using the session?" In most cases, you wouldn't. Cookies do have one advantage over session parameters: You can request that cookies live past the current session. You are able to do this with the max-age attribute as follows:

```
<?xml version="1.0"?>
<page xmlns:xsql="urn:oracle-xsql" connection="demo">
  <xsql:set-cookie name="long-living-cookie" max-age="999999"
value="To_Life" />
  <xsql:set-cookie name="deptno">
    select deptno from emp where ename='{@ename}'
  </xsql:set-cookie>
  <xsql:include-request-params />
</page>
```

If you invoke this XSQL page, shut down your browser, and then restart it, the cookie will survive. A call to include-request-params.xsql will confirm this. The max-age value is in seconds, so in our example, the cookie will live for about 11 days.

You can also control the URLs to which a cookie should be returned. Previously, you learned that your application isn't going to receive cookies set by www.yahoo.com. In fact, by default, no URL outside of the original directory where XSQL first set the cookie will see it. To demonstrate this, create another directory named test-cookies in the demo directory and copy include-request-params.xsql in it. When you go to http://localhost/test-cookies/include-request-params.xsql, you won't see the long-living cookie. Go back to the original include-request-params.xsql page, and there you will find it.

For many applications, this is too restrictive. If nothing else, it means that all of your application must be in the same directory or subdirectories. Luckily, you can control this behavior very easily. Using the path attribute of the xsql:set-cookie action, you can make the cookie generally available to all of the application. This XSQL page sets another cookie that should be available anywhere on your server:

```
<?xml version="1.0"?>
<page xmlns:xsql="urn:oracle-xsql" connection="demo">
  <xsql:set-cookie name="long-living-remote-cookie" value="To_Life"
path="/" max-age="999999"/>
</page>
```

You can reference cookies just like you can any other parameter by using the {@cookie-name} syntax. You aren't limited solely to parameters set by XSQL. You can reference any cookies that come your way, including cookies set by other applications in your system.

Setting Default Parameters

In the previous section, you learned that you can't depend on cookies always being available. If you can't depend on them, then can you set a default value? Can you set default values for other parameters? You can, and the mechanism is pretty simple.

Let's look back at our very-unsecure.xsql page. For that example, you had to specify three parameters for the action to work at all. This is an ideal case for setting default values. The following XSQL will accomplish this. You should save it as very-unsecure-with-defaults.xsql.

```
<?xml version="1.0"?>
<page fields="*" conn="demo" tables="emp" xmlns:xsql="urn:oracle-xsql"
connection="{@conn}" >
  <xsql:include-request-params />
  <xsql:query>
     select {@fields} from {@tables}
  </xsql:query>
</page>
```

If you execute this page with no arguments, you'll get the same results as before. Attaching arguments will yield different results, of course, providing that the default values are more graceful and reusable. If you only get one parameter, you don't fail entirely.

You can provide multiple default values for the same parameter. This is useful if you have multiple queries in the same XSQL page. The following example sets the default for the max attribute for all queries, while still allowing a lesser default for a couple of queries.

```
<?xml version="1.0"?>
<page max="10" conn="demo" xmlns:xsql="urn:oracle-xsql"
connection="{@conn}" >
  <xsql:query>
     select * from table1
  </xsql:query>
  <xsql:query max="5" max-rows="{@max}">
     select * from table2
  </xsql:query>
  <xsql:query>
     select * from table3
  </xsql:query>
  <xsql:query max="7" max-rows="{@max}">
     select * from table4
  </xsql:query>
  <xsql:query>
     select * from table5
  </xsql:query>
</page>
```

Using Bind Variables

So far, you've been using lexical parameters when you've made references with {@param}. When the XSQL document is parsed, a lexical substitution is made. After this parsing, it's as if all of the parameters were hard-coded. This is fine in a lot of ways, but it isn't optimal for SQL statements. Before explaining why, let's look at how bind variables are used. In this example, you get a list of the employees with a particular job in a particular department.

```
<?xml version="1.0"?>
<page deptno="20" job="CLERK" xmlns:xsql="urn:oracle-xsql"
connection="demo" >
  <xsql:query bind-params="deptno job">
     select * from emp where deptno=? and job=?
  </xsql:query>
</page>
```

Instead of having the parameter reference inside of the SQL, you have question marks. The question marks are replaced, in order, by the values of the parameters listed in the `<bind-params>` attribute. Notice that you don't have to put quotation marks around the question mark for job. This is taken care of for you.

Bind variables make it easier to optimize SQL statements. When you don't use bind variables, the SQL optimizer can only optimize the statements one at a time. The optimizer has no way to know that there are going to be lots of statements of the same basic structure. By using bind parameters, the SQL optimizer can optimize with the expectation that there will be more queries like the first one. In this case, it knows that it will be looking for rows in the emp table with a particular department number and a particular job. By using bind parameters, some optimization work of previous queries from this page can be reused in subsequent pages.

Resolving Conflicting Parameter Names

You may have noticed that the different types of parameters were all resolved with the same syntax. This begs the question: How does XSQL resolve conflicts? What happens if you have a cookie that has the same name as a page-private parameter, a session parameter, and a request parameter? Luckily, the result isn't undefined. The following algorithm, which resolves parameter names, stops when one of the questions is answered yes or is at the last step:

1. Is there a page-private parameter with this name? (If yes, use the value of the page-private parameter.)
2. Is there a cookie with this name? (If yes, use the value of the cookie.)
3. Is there a session parameter with this name? (If yes, use the value of the session parameter.)
4. Is there a request parameter with this name? (If yes, use the value of the request parameter.)
5. Is there a default value provided in the current action element? (If yes, use the default value specified in the current action element.)

6. Is there a default value provided in any ancestor element? (If yes, use the nearest default value specified [e.g., a default value specified in the parent element would be preferred over the default value specified in the grandparent element].)
7. If all answers are no and this is a bind variable, null is assigned.
8. If all answers are no and this is a lexical parameter, the empty string is assigned.

Generally, you want to avoid the last two cases. They'll probably cause errors for SQL statements. Instead, you should provide default values so that your SQL statements will execute. However, in some cases, you may prefer that the SQL statements don't execute and just toss an error. In Chapter 14, you'll learn how to gracefully handle errors from inside your stylesheets.

Stylesheets and Parameters

XSLT stylesheets can have their own parameters. As you'll learn in Chapter 13, these parameters can be used for a variety of reasons. Here, you'll see how you can pass parameters to XSLT stylesheets. When you are doing this, you are communicating with the XSLT processor that the XSQL page processor invokes.

You set XSLT parameters using the `xsql:set-stylesheet-param` action. It works like the other parameter-setting actions that you've seen. You can set a parameter directly or based on a SQL statement. In our example, you'll set a stylesheet with the parameters `ename` and `deptno`.

```
<?xml version="1.0"?>
<?xml-stylesheet type="text/xsl" href="stylesheet-params.xsl"?>
<page xmlns:xsql="urn:oracle-xsql" connection="demo">
  <xsql:set-stylesheet-param name="ename" value="{@ename}" />
  <xsql:set-stylesheet-param name="deptno">
    SELECT deptno
     FROM emp
     WHERE ename='{@ename}'
  </xsql:set-stylesheet-param>
</page>
```

The stylesheet, `stylesheet-params.xsl`, receives the parameters. Stylesheet parameters are covered thoroughly in Chapters 13 and 14, respectively. Here is a simple example for now. The following stylesheet defines the parameters `ename` and `deptno`. They are outputted as part of the output of the transformation. This is what the stylesheet looks like:

```
<?xml version = '1.0'?>
<xsl:stylesheet xmlns:xsl="http://www.w3.org/1999/XSL/Transform"
version="1.0">
```

```
  <xsl:param name="ename"/>
  <xsl:param name="deptno"/>

  <xsl:template match="/page">
   <html>
   <head></head>
   <body>
    <H1>Stylesheet Param Sampler</H1>
    <p>
     <b>Ename: </b><xsl:value-of select="$ename"/>
    </p>
    <p>
     <b>Deptno: </b><xsl:value-of select="$deptno"/>
    </p>
   </body>
   </html>
  </xsl:template>
</xsl:stylesheet>
```

The result of the XSQL page is displayed in Figure 6.7

Figure 6.7 Stylesheet parameters example.

This particular result was produced by setting `ename` equal to `ADAMS` as part of the request. The following request would do it: `http://localhost/xsql/momnpup/stylesheet-params.xsql?ename=ADAMS&`.

There is a lot more that you can do with stylesheet parameters than the simple examples shown here, and you'll learn more about them later in the book. For now, here is a brief description of what is going on. In the stylesheet, the stylesheet parameters `ename` and `deptno` are defined with the `xsl:param` element. The parameter names match exactly the parameters that you set using the `xsql:set-stylesheet-param` element in the XSQL page. Inside the stylesheet, the parameters are referenced by prefixing the name with a $. Because they are specified in an `xsl:value-of` element, the value of the parameter is written to the page.

From this example, you see how you can pass the parameter values directly to your stylesheet for output. There is more that you can do with stylesheet parameters from inside the stylesheet, but that's for later in the book. You'll learn all about that in Chapter 13.

Moving On

Now that you have a strong understanding of how parameters work with XSQL, you are well on your way to building applications with XSQL. Because your applications almost always consist of more than one page, now you will be able to tie your XSQL pages together. The next chapter will complete the discussion of XSQL basics with a look at how to modify the database with XSQL. When you develop an XSQL application in Chapter 14, you'll again look closely at parameter passing and see how it works with a real-world application.

CHAPTER

7

Database Modifications with XSQL

Database-driven Web applications generally have two purposes: accessing the data in the database and adding to or modifying the database in some way. In this chapter, you will learn more about inputting data to the database. The actions that you will use in this section have already been discussed in Chapter 5. The intent here is to move beyond reference and see how the pieces can fit together.

The first step is to review the canonical schema that XSQL uses. You learned about it in Chapter 5. Now you will be using it in a different way—to get data into the database. Next, you will see how to input HTML forms in two different ways—by using `xsql:insert-request`, `xsql:update-request`, and `xsql:delete-request`; and by using `xsql:dml`. Finally, you will learn how to handle XML documents.

Inputting HTML Forms

There is scarcely a Web application that does not have an HTML form. Sooner or later, you will need to have your users fill out some text fields and make some selections. In some cases, the users will just be interacting with your application. Perhaps they will be logging in, or maybe they will be choosing the options of a particular query. In many cases, they will be providing data that will need to be inserted into the database. This process is the focus of this section.

This is not an exhaustive survey. Rather, this section attempts to further explain the concepts behind the data modification actions covered in Chapter 5. You will first learn about the built-in actions for inserting, updating, and deleting data and how to use them with forms. These are good for simple cases, but become difficult to use in complex ones. Thus, you will then learn how to use the `xsql:dml` action for more complex cases.

The example for both of these exercises will be a newsletter service. The example newsletter table has columns for e-mail, name, and organization. To keep everything simple, the table will have no constraints on it. When you begin building real applications, everything necessary for a production application will be considered. The following SQL will create this table. You should create it under the `momnpup` user.

All of the examples that you see here will consist of a single SQL statement per page. However, there is no reason that you could not have more than one per page.

Form Parameters and the Canonical Schema

In Chapter 5, you learned about the canonical schema. It is the default method of returning data when you use `xsql:query`. It also plays a role when inputting data. The built-in actions that allow you to create, modify or delete data in your database also expect it as input. The process works as the reverse of the process that you learned about earlier. Instead of writing a stylesheet that takes XML in the canonical format as input and produces the output that you desire, you have to write a stylesheet that expects the form parameters and writes a document that follows the canonical schema. This difference is diagrammed in Figure 7.1.

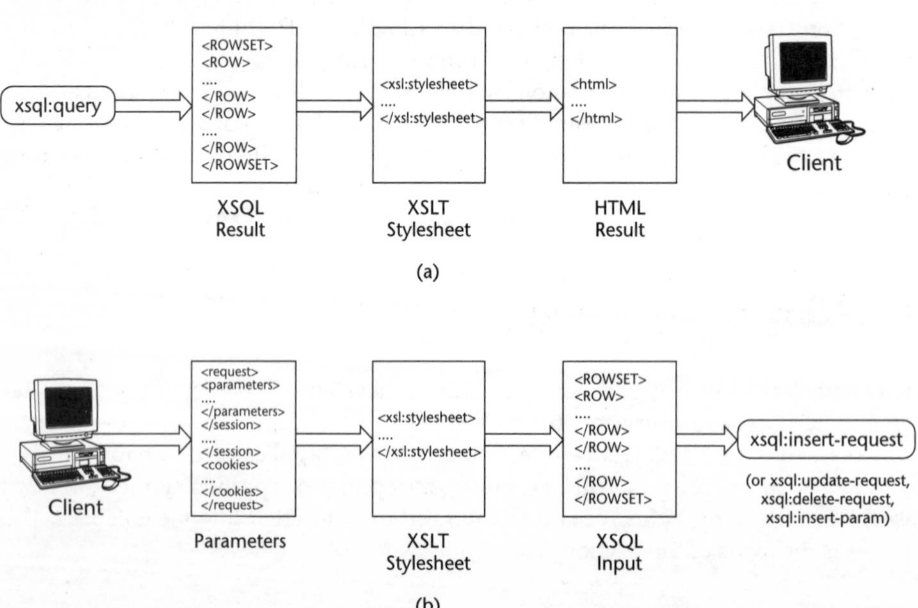

Figure 7.1 The role of the canonical schema on input versus output.

This is probably different from what you have seen before, so here is a full example. Your first step is to create the HTML form. Here is a very simple one that you will use for inserting data into the newsletter table. There are a couple of things to note about this example. First, the action of your form is an XSQL page. You will make this XSQL page next. Most important is the method. As you would expect, it is `post`. To work with XSQL, your form must have a `post` method.

```
<html>       <body>
 <h1>Sign Up For Newsletter</h1>
  <form action="dummy.xsql" method="post">
   <table border="0">
    <tr>
     <td>Name:</td>      <td><input type="text" name="name"/></td>
    </tr>
    <tr>
     <td>Email:</td>
      <td><input type="text" name="email"/></td>
    </tr>
    <tr>
     <td>Organization:</td>
     <td><input type="text" name="org"/></td>
    </tr>
    <tr>
     <td colspan="2" align="center"><input type="submit" value="Sign Me
Up!" /></td>
    </tr>
   </table>
  </form>
 </body>
</html>
```

The next step is to create the XSQL page that will insert the data. However, it is important to understand the overall process. As you probably know, the HTTP POST request passes the form parameters as name-value pairs. XSQL implicitly changes those to a simple XML document. Your stylesheet than transforms the request XML document to the canonical XML form required by the data modification actions.

For now, take one step at a time. The `xsql:include-request-parameters` action shows you what the transformation will look like. The following XSQL page will display the parameters in the XML schema that XSQL uses:

```
<?xml version="1.0"?>
   <xsql:include-request-params />
```

When you save this file as `dummy.xsql` in the `momnpup` directory alongside the `newsletter-insert.html` file, it will produce the output shown in Figure 7.2. You saw this format in Chapter 6. It is the canonical schema. As you look at the output, notice the `<parameters>` element nested inside of the `<request>` element. Each of your form's parameters is represented by an element of the parameter element. Also, notice the `<cookies/>` and `<session/>` elements. There are a couple of cookie elements, but this does not matter. They will not interfere with the insertion or modification of the parameter data.

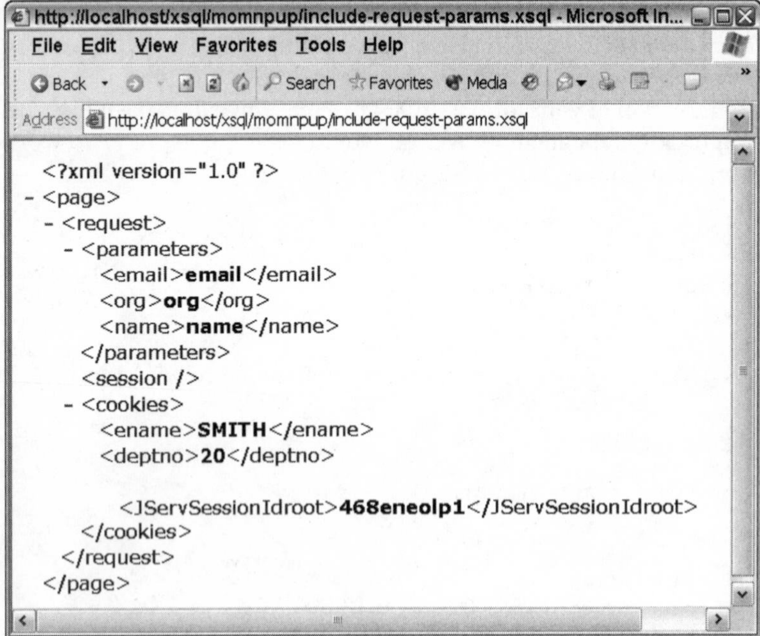

Figure 7.2 Form parameters as XML.

From here, the request needs to be transformed to this format.

```
<ROWSET>
 <ROW>
  <EMAIL>emailValue</EMAIL>
  <NAME>nameValue</NAME>
  <ORGANIZATION>orgValue</ORGANIZATION>
 </ROW>
</ROWSET>
```

This transformation can be completed with the following stylesheet. This is an example of an XML-to-XML transformation. You need not delve into this transformation now. Stylesheets will be covered in depth in Chapter 13.

```
<?xml version = '1.0'?>
<ROWSET xmlns:xsl="http://www.w3.org/1999/XSL/Transform"
xsl:version="1.0">
 <ROW>
  <EMAIL>
```

```
      <xsl:value-of select="/request/parameters/email"/>
   </EMAIL>
   <NAME>
      <xsl:value-of select="/request/parameters/name"/>
   </NAME>
   <ORGANIZATION>
      <xsl:value-of select="/request/parameters/org"/>
   </ORGANIZATION>
  </ROW>
</ROWSET>
```

Using `xsql:insert-request`

Your next step is to create `insert-request.xsql` file. Before creating it, you should go back to the `newsletter-insert.html` file. The action needs to be changed from `dummy.xsql` to `insert-request.xsql`. After that has been changed, you can make the `insert-request.xsql` file as follows:

```
<?xml version="1.0"?>
<page connection="momnpup" xmlns:xsql="urn:oracle-xsql">
   <xsql:insert-request table="newsletter" transform="transform-
request.xsl"/>
</page>
```

When you go back to `newsletter-insert.html` and fill out the form, you should get the result that is shown in Figure 7.3 in your browser. If you login as `momnpup` and `select * from newsletter` you should see the data that you entered into your form.

Figure 7.3 Result of `insert-request` action.

Your users do not need to see the results in this form, of course. If you would just like to say "Thanks," you can do so with this very simple stylesheet. It hides the raw XML.

```
<?xml version="1.0"?>
<xsl:stylesheet xmlns:xsl="http://www.w3.org/1999/XSL/Transform"
version="1.0">
 <xsl:template match="/">
  <html>
    <h1>Thanks!</h1>
  </html>
 </xsl:template>
</xsl:stylesheet>
```

To use the stylesheet, you need to add the following line as the second line in your `insert-request.xsql` file:

```
<?xml-stylesheet type="text/xsl" href="thanks.xsl" ?>
```

Using `xsql:update-request`

The use of `xsql:update-request` is very similar to the use of `xsql:insert-request`. The general process is exactly the same. First, you create your HTML form and set the action to an XSQL page. When the form is submitted, the XSQL servlet will pass the parameters as XML to the XSQL page processor. You need a stylesheet to transform the passed XML to the canonical XML schema.

The key difference really relates to the difference between SQL inserts and updates. An insert adds an entirely new row to your table. An update, on the other hand, modifies an existing row. To perform an update, XSQL needs to know which row (or rows) in the database will be modified. This is done through the `key-columns` attribute of the `xsql:update-request` element. It lists the columns that have to match for a particular row of data to be updated.

First things first. For this example, you can use the exact same form as was used for `xsql:insert-request`. Assume that the e-mail address is staying the same and that the user wants to modify the organization and name. It would be simple enough to populate the fields in the form, but you aren't quite ready to do that yet. For now, life is hard for your users. Here is the modified HTML form that you should save as `newsletter-update.html`:

```
<html>
<body>
  <h1>Sign Up For Newsletter</h1>
  <form action="update-request.xsql" method="post">
   <table border="0">
    <tr>
```

```
      <td>Name:</td>     <td><input type="text" name="name"/></td>
     </tr>
     <tr>
      <td>Email:</td>
      <td><input type="text" name="email"/></td>
     </tr>
     <tr>
      <td>Organization:</td>
      <td><input type="text" name="org"/></td>
     </tr>
     <tr>
      <td colspan="2" align="center">
       <input type="submit" value="Sign Me Up!" />
      </td>
     </tr>
    </table>
   </form>
  </body>
</html>
```

Now you are ready to code your update-request.xsql file. It looks very much like the insert-request.xsql file that you coded before. The difference is the key-columns attribute. This attribute tells XSQL that you want to make changes in any of the rows where the email field matches the e-mail address that is entered.

```
<?xml version="1.0"?>
<?xml-stylesheet type="text/xsl" href="thanks.xsl" ?>
<page connection="momnpup" xmlns:xsql="urn:oracle-xsql">
   <xsql:update-request table="newsletter" key-columns="email"
transform="transform-request.xsl"/>
</page>
```

After saving this file as update-request.xsql, you should get the same "Thanks!" screen when you fill out the form of newsletter-update.html. You can see that this XSQL page is linked to the same thanks.xsl file as the insert -request.xsql file. There is another interesting similarity: Both XSQL pages use the same transform-request.xsl file. You are able to do this because the names of the form parameters are the same for both pages. Coincidence? Somewhat. The lesson to learn here is that with a little discipline, you can save yourself some recoding.

Using xsql:delete-request

The purpose of this request is to remove data from the database. All of the steps are the same as with the xsql:update-request. The main difference is that you only need to submit the data that matches the key-columns that you specify. This data is used to determine which rows should be deleted.

Your first step is to create the HTML form. This is the same form as in the other two examples here, except that only the `email` field is needed. This is the key to tell you when to delete rows.

```
<html>
<body>
  <h1>Sign Up For Newsletter</h1>
   <form action="delete-request.xsql" method="post">
   <table border="0">
    <tr>
     <td>Email:</td>
     <td><input type="text" name="email"/></td>
    </tr>
    <tr>
     <td colspan="2" align="center">
      <input type="submit" value="Delete Me!" />
     </td>
    </tr>
   </table>
  </form>
 </body>
</html>
```

Your next step is to create the `delete-request.xsql` file. It has only one difference from the `update-request.xsql` file. Instead of using the `xsql:update-request` action, the `xsql:delete-request` action is used.

```
<?xml version="1.0"?>
<?xml-stylesheet type="text/xsl" href="thanks.xsl" ?>
<page connection="momnpup" xmlns:xsql="urn:oracle-xsql">
 <xsql:delete-request table="newsletter" key-columns="email"
                          transform="transform-request.xsl"/>
</page>
```

Modifying with `xsql:dml`

Using the built-in actions covered in the preceding section is easy—if your form parameters map easily to the underlying table. However, the required stylesheet complicates things a bit, especially if you are already familiar with SQL. In this section, you will use the `xsql:dml` action to complete the same tasks as in the preceding examples. These examples assume that you have some knowledge of SQL. If you don't, you'll learn all about SQL in Chapter 8.

You can reuse the `newsletter-insert.html` form almost entirely. Only one change is necessary—the action should point at your new `dml-insert.xsql`. Here is line that needs to be changed:

```
<form action="dml-insert.xsql" method="post">
```

Here is the `dml-insert.xsql` file that you need to create. The form parameters are interpolated directly to the SQL statement. This is your first glimpse at parameter handling with XSQL. You will see more of this in the next section of this chapter.

```
<?xml version="1.0"?>
<page connection="momnpup" xmlns:xsql="urn:oracle-xsql">
<xsql:dml>
  BEGIN
   INSERT INTO  newsletter (email,name,organization)
VALUES('{@email}','{@name}','{@org}');
   COMMIT;
  END;
</xsql:dml>
</page>
```

If you are familiar with SQL, this is far simpler than creating a XSLT stylesheet to transform the request XML. If you are not familiar with SQL, then just wait until Chapter 8, you are sure to find the `xsql:dml` action to be the simpler route for your data modification needs. To complete the example, you need to cook up a `dml -update.xsql`. Here it is.

```
<?xml version="1.0"?>

<?xml-stylesheet type="text/xsl" ?>

<page connection="demo" xmlns:xsql="urn:oracle-xsql">


<xsql:update-request table="newsletter" key-columns="email"
transform="include-request.xsl"/>
</page>
```

The last example is deletion. Again, it has the same pattern as the other examples.

```
<?xml version="1.0"?>
<page connection="momnpup" xmlns:xsql="urn:oracle-xsql">
<xsql:dml>
  BEGIN
   UPDATEnewsletter SET
email='{@email}',name='{@name}',organization'{@org}';
   COMMIT;
  END;
</xsql:dml>
</page>
```

Handling XML Documents

In the preceding section, you learned how to use the built-in action handlers with built-in HTML forms. You performed the appropriate action by interpreting an XML document containing the form parameters. In conjunction with HTML forms, their use probably seemed a bit clumsy. However, in conjunction with Web services and browsers capable of sending XML, their use is easier and starts to make more sense. You will see how this works in this section. In addition to seeing how the `xsql:insert-request`, `xsql:update-request`, and `xsql:delete-request` actions work with XML documents, you will learn about the `xsql:insert-request-parameter` action. This action is used when a parameter has, as its value, an XML document.

Handling Posted XML

Before beginning with the `xsql:insert-request` action, your first step is to understand how XML is posted. The action itself works the same—you specify the table and a stylesheet to transform the XML to the canonical form. What works differently is how the data arrives. With HTML forms, the key-value pairs arrive contained in the XML request element. In this case, the XML document arrives within the XML request.

To understand the difference, it is important to understand what an HTTP `POST` looks like. When you hit Submit on an HTML form, your Web browser starts an HTTP transaction. There isn't much mysterious about the transaction. In plain text, it sends the following message to the Web server:

```
POST /xsql/insert-request.xsql HTTP/1.0
User-Agent: Mozilla/4.7 (X11; Linux)
Accept: */*
Content-length: 41
Content-type: application/x-www-form-urlencoded
email=someEmail&name=someName&org=someOrg
```

The XSQL servlet receives the parameters and does the translation to XML. The data is inserted, and a result is returned. That is the complete HTTP transaction. If you can type fast enough, you can actually manually execute the exact same insertion that your Web browser performs when you fill out the form. Just enter `telnet localhost 80` and start typing!

The case you are working at here is one in which you are receiving an XML document directly as part of the body of the HTTP `POST` request. In this case the transaction looks like the preceding request. The difference is that the XML is already formatted—the XSQL servlet doesn't need to conjure up XML out of a list of name-value pairs. As you will see, from here you simply have to transform the XML to the canonical format.

If you have been doing Web work for a while, you may be asking yourself: "The old way of submitting forms is great. Why should I bother with this new way?" There are a few reasons why posting XML in this manner is important. First, a lot of work often goes into transforming name-value pairs to a more usable data structure. In a lot of cases, the problem is figuring out how the different name-value pairs are related to each other. XML is simply a more powerful way to represent data than simple name-value pairs. The second most important reason is that a lot of Web services applications work on this principle. The XML is passed from a machine to your application over HTTP, and then you handle the XML. You will learn more about this in Chapter 16.

NOTE **You have probably heard a lot about Web services and a lot about Simple Object Access Protocol (SOAP). Per the preceding description, you can consider any two applications communicating over HTTP to be a Web service. They tend to exchange XML because it is the best format for the job. SOAP is a protocol that encapsulates this basic architecture. You'll learn more about Web services in Chapter 16.**

At present, not all Web browsers will allow you to submit XML in HTTP `POST` requests. Microsoft Internet Explorer will, so it is required for these examples. The first step is to construct the HTML form. Note that it invokes a Javascript function on submit.

```
<HTML>
 <BODY>
  <SCRIPT>
function PostOrder (xmldoc)
  {
     var xmlhttp = new ActiveXObject ("Microsoft.XMLHTTP");
     xmlhttp.open("POST", "insert-request-xml.xsql",false);
     xmlhttp.send(xmldoc);
     return xmlhttp;
  }
function submitInfo(){
 var xmldoc  = new ActiveXObject ("Microsoft.XMLDOM");
 xmldoc.async = false;
 xmldoc.loadXML(xmldocText.value);
 var response = PostOrder(xmldoc);
 document.write(response.responseText);
 window.location.reload( false );
}

   </SCRIPT>
   <b>Type in an XML Document to Post:<b><br>
     <TEXTAREA rows="12" style="width:100%" cols="70" NAME="xmldocText">
      <request>
       <parameters>
        <email>email10</email>
        <name>name10</name>
        <org>org10</org>
       </parameters>
      </request>
</TEXTAREA>

    <P>
    <INPUT TYPE="button" Value="Post XML Document"
onclick="submitInfo()">
  </BODY>
</HTML>
```

When the form is loaded in the browser, it looks like a normal form, as shown in Figure 7.4. It behaves differently, though. The `Microsoft.XMLHTTP` ActiveX object is created to handle the transaction. In the present case, all of the data from the `textarea` element is simply passed along. However, you aren't limited to only text areas. You can have any HTML form elements and then just assemble them into the XML document as you like.

For this first example, you are using the exact same XML schema that you had to use in the preceding form examples. This makes the `insert-request.xsql` document very simple. Note that it uses the exact same stylesheet as was used in the earlier example.

```
<?xml version="1.0"?>
<?xml-stylesheet type="text/xsl" href="thanks.xsl" ?>
<page connection="momnpup" xmlns:xsql="urn:oracle-xsql">
  <xsql:insert-request table="newsletter" transform="insert-
request.xsl"/>
</page>
```

This XML schema is overkill, though. The request and parameters elements are unnecessary for the purposes of this example. Instead, you can simplify the schema so that it looks like the following code. (At this point, you might also want to delete or modify the default for the text area in the HTML page.)

```
<newsletter-member>
   <email>email value</email>
   <name>name value</name>
   <org>org value</org>
</newsletter-member>
```

Your new, simpler XML schema means that you need a new stylesheet. The stylesheet that follows will do the trick. The only change required in the XSQL document is the `transform` attribute. That should be set to `xml-transform.xsl` or whatever name you choose.

```
<?xml version = '1.0'?>
<ROWSET xmlns:xsl="http://www.w3.org/1999/XSL/Transform"
xsl:version="1.0">
 <ROW>
  <email>
    <xsl:value-of select="/newsletter-member/email"/>
  </email>
  <name>
    <xsl:value-of select="/newsletter-member/name"/>
  </name>
  <organization>
    <xsl:value-of select="/newsletter-member/org"/>
  </organization>
 </ROW>
</ROWSET>
```

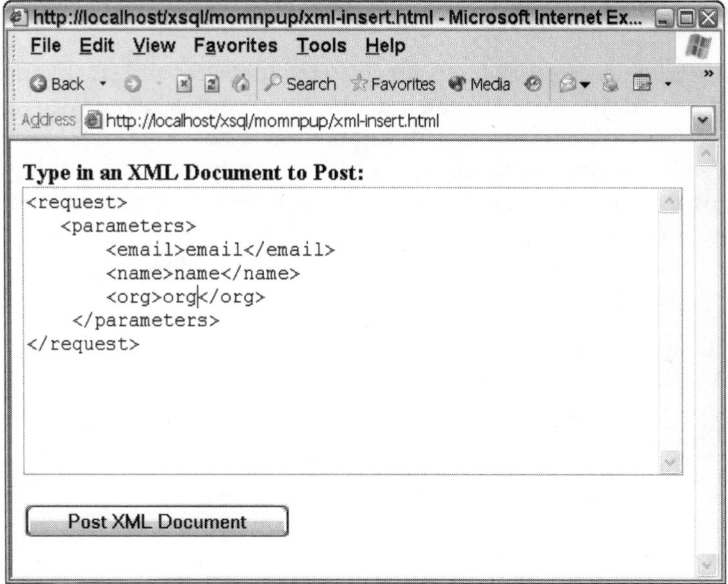

Figure 7.4 XML-enabled form.

From here, updates and deletions can be created with the same steps. Your XML schema hasn't changed, so you don't need to create a new stylesheet. All that is needed is to create the `update-request-xml.xsql` and `delete-request-xml.xsql` files. Here is the `update-request-xml.xsql` file:

```
<?xml version="1.0"?>
<?xml-stylesheet type="text/xsl" href="thanks.xsl" ?>
<page connection="momnpup" xmlns:xsql="urn:oracle-xsql">
  <xsql:update-request table="newsletter" key-columns="email"
transform="xml-transform.xsl"/>
</page>
```

Here is the `delete-request-xml.sql` file:

```
<?xml version="1.0"?>
<?xml-stylesheet type="text/xsl" href="thanks.xsl" ?>
<page connection="momnpup" xmlns:xsql="urn:oracle-xsql">
  <xsql:delete-request table="newsletter" key-columns="email"
transform="xml-transform.xsl"/>
</page>
```

Handling XML Parameters

XSQL also makes it possible to insert XML documents that are values of HTML form parameters. This is different from the work you did with HTML forms before. As with the examples with posted XML documents, you can use any schema that you want. Unlike with the posted XML documents, this works with any Web browser.

The first step is to create the HTML form. This one looks like the last one, but without any Javascript and ActiveX:

```
<HTML>
  <BODY>
    <b>Type in an XML Document to Post:<b>
    <br>
     <FORM action="" method="POST">
     <TEXTAREA rows="12" style="width:100%" cols="70" NAME="xmldocText">

      <ROWSET>
       <ROW>
        <EMAIL>email</EMAIL>
        <NAME>name</NAME>
        <ORGANIZATION>org</ORGANIZATION>
       </ROW>
      </ROWSET>
     </TEXTAREA>
     <P>
      <INPUT TYPE="submit" Value="Post XML Document">
    </FORM>
  </BODY>
</HTML>
```

The next step is to create the XSQL page. It looks exactly like the `insert-request-xml.xsql` page, except that you use the `xsql:insert-param` action. The only difference between the `xsql:insert-param` action and the `xsql:insert-request` action is that you must specify the parameter element with the `xsql:insert-param` action. The value of that parameter will be treated as an XML document.

```
<?xml version="1.0"?>
<?xml-stylesheet type="text/xsl" href="thanks.xsl" ?>
<page connection="momnpup" xmlns:xsql="urn:oracle-xsql">
 <xsql:insert-param name="xmldocText" table="newsletter"/>
</page>
```

In this example, the input is not transformed. As you can see in the default value for `xmldocText`, the input is expected to be in the canonical schema format. If you expect the data to be in a different format, you will need to transform it. You do this just as you do with the `xsql:insert-request` action—by specifying a stylesheet with the `transform` attribute:

```
<xsql:insert-param table="newsletter"_transform="insert-request.xsl"/>
```

You probably won't expect the user to enter an XML parameter correctly, as in this example. Instead, you could use this action in conjunction with Javascript to assemble one or several XML documents. Then you would use the `xsql:insert-param` action to get the data into the database.

Inserting XML as XML

The final case is the simplest. What if you have an XML document that you want to store in the database as XML? Instead of dividing it up into different columns and so forth, you just want to put the entire document in as text and be able to retrieve it as such. This is easy and can be done with `xsql:dml`. You will use the following HTML page:

```
<HTML>
  <BODY>
    <FORM action="" method="POST">

    <b>Document name:</b>
    <br>
    <input type="text" name="name" />

    <b>Type in an XML Document to Post:</b>
    <br>
     <TEXTAREA rows="12" style="width:100%" cols="70" NAME="xmldocText">

       <newsletter-member>
          <email>email13</email>
          <name>name13</name>
          <org>org13</org>
       </newsletter-member>

     </TEXTAREA>
    <P>
     <INPUT TYPE="submit" Value="Post XML Document">
    </FORM>
  </BODY>
</HTML>
```

Your parameter that has the XML is `xmldocText`. To insert it into the database, just use the `xsql:dml` action.

Moving On

This chapter showed you how you could move beyond just querying data in your database. Now you can create, modify, and delete data. This competes your knowledge of how XSQL pages work out-of-the box. From here, the book proceeds to look deeply at the other technologies that are used in conjunction with XSQL. Oracle SQL and related database technologies are covered first, followed by XSLT. At the end of the book, you'll return to XSQL to see how it can be extended with action handlers and serializers.

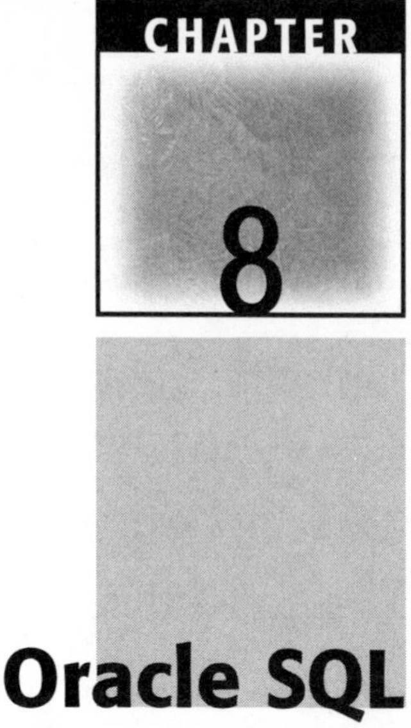

Oracle SQL

The key of any XSQL system is the Oracle database. This chapter covers how to access and input data in Oracle, focusing on SQL, the predominant language for Oracle. However, SQL isn't procedural, so there's a lot you can't do with it. You fill in the gap with PL/SQL. Oracle Text, which allows you to store, search, and retrieve text data and XML, is also covered here. It gives you a powerful way to search text and serves as a great basis for search engines. Chapter 11 covers the XMLType, which allows you to store and retrieve full and partial XML documents.

SQL Syntax

This section outlines the basics of SQL syntax. Real-life examples are used to explain select statements and make them easier to understand. This section is meant to serve as both a quick reference and an introduction to terms that you will be learning later.

Case Sensitivity

SQL is, except for string literals, a case-insensitive language. What this means is that it doesn't matter whether you use `SELECT` or `select`, `emp` or `EMP`, and so on. However, anything in quotes is case-sensitive, as are the strings stored in the database. Thus, these three statements are equivalent:

```
SELECT * FROM EMP WHERE ENAME='ADAMS'
SELECT * FROM emp WHERE ename='ADAMS'
SeLEcT * fROm eMP wHErE eNaME='ADAMS'
```

But these two statements are not:

```
SELECT * FROM EMP WHERE ENAME='ADAMS'
SELECT * FROM EMP WHERE ENAME='adams'
```

If you wish to perform a case-insensitive query, you can do so with the `UPPER` function:

```
SELECT * FROM EMP WHERE UPPER(ENAME)=UPPER('adams')
```

This and the other functions are covered in detail later in the chapter.

Lexical Conventions

An SQL statement is a combination of alphanumeric characters, whitespace, and the following special characters:

```
* @ ! < > _ - , . ? = | $ # () + ' "
```

Some programming languages make special use of certain whitespace characters, such as tabs and line feeds. Thankfully, SQL isn't such a language. All the whitespace characters—spaces, tabs, and carriage returns—are completely interchangeable and repeatable. You can have as much space of any type anywhere space is allowed. Comments are also completely interchangeable with a single space character and can appear anywhere that you desire. These two factors make the following two statements completely equivalent:

```
SELECT ename, sal, bonus, deptno FROM emp WHERE sal > 1000

SELECT ename, sal, bonus, deptno /*The fields I want */
   FROM emp
   WHERE sal > 1000
```

String literals are enclosed in single quotes, such as 'brother's keeper'. If you wish to have a single quote inside of a string literal, simply put two quotes next to each other. Double quotes allow you to have the equivalent of string literals inside of string literals that you pass to functions. They should be used with column aliases containing spaces or special characters.

Data Types

SQL has many built-in data types, and you can also create your own. A data type is a fixed set of properties that a value is guaranteed to have. If a column is declared with a NUMBER data type, you know that you will get a number back and you are only allowed to put a NUMBER in. The most common data types are NUMBER, VARCHAR2, and DATE. Most data types are used to define the type of data in the columns of your database. Also, SQL functions return their results in a particular data type, and they can take parameters only of particular data types.

The data types can be broken into several categories: string types, number types, date types, large-object types, and raw types. Although the purposes of the first three are pretty obvious, the last two might not be. The large object types give you the ability to store large amounts of data—up to 4 GB. The raw types are used when you don't want Oracle to perform implicit character conversions. The following paragraphs outline each of the different groups of data types.

String Types

The string types—CHAR, NCHAR, VARCHAR2, and NVARCHAR2—are used to store character data with a maximum length of either 2,000 or 4,000 bytes. Generally, VARCHAR2 is used because the strings are variable-length. CHAR and NCHAR are fixed-length and should only be used if you know in advance that all data will be of a particular length. Table 8.1 describes all string types.

Number Types

The number type is used to define both integer and floating-point numbers. It takes the following form:

```
NUMBER(p,s)
```

Table 8.1 String Types

TYPE	DESCRIPTION	MAXIMUM SIZE
CHAR(n)	Fixed-length string	2,000 bytes
NCHAR(n)	Fixed-length string in a national character language-supported character set, which may consist of multibyte characters	2,000 bytes
VARCHAR2(n)	Variable-length string	4,000 bytes
NVARCHAR2(n)	Variable-length string in a national character language- supported character set, which may consist of multibyte characters	4,000 bytes

The p argument, which is required, is the *precision*. It represents the number of digits left of the decimal place and can range from 1 to 38. The s argument, which is optional and defaults to 0, is the *scale*. It can range from (-84 to +127. A negative number given for the scale is rounded to the specified number of places to the left of the decimal place.

The data types in Table 8.2 are also recognized so that Oracle SQL is compatible with the American National Standards Institute (ANSI) SQL. However, all of these are aliases to the number type.

Date Types

The date types represent dates and times. In many cases, you use them in conjunction with the date functions discussed later in the chapter. The date types present a particular problem—unlike numbers and strings, there are many ways to format dates. To interpret dates correctly, you use date-format masks, discussed in their own section in this chapter. The basic DATE type is used in most cases; the other types provide for special needs. All are described in Table 8.3.

Large-Object Types

The large-object types are used to store objects of up to 4 GB. They work great for unstructured text documents, movies, and audio files. The internal data types are BLOB, CLOB, and NCLOB. These data types are stored in the Oracle database itself. The BFILE data type points to a file outside the database.

Table 8.2 Other Number Types

TYPE	DEFINITION
DECIMAL(p,s)	NUMBER(p,s). This can specify only fixed-point numbers.
DOUBLE PRECISION	NUMBER. The precision is 126.
FLOAT(b)	NUMBER. The binary precision is specified by the argument.
INT	NUMBER(38).
INTEGER	NUMBER(38).
NUMERIC(p,s)	NUMBER(p,s).
REAL	FLOAT(63).
SMALLINT	NUMBER(38).

Table 8.3 Date Types

TYPE	DESCRIPTION
DATE	Describes a date and time between January 1, 4712 B.C. and December 31, 9999 A.D.
TIMESTAMP(p)	A date with the ability to store fractional seconds as specified by the argument p, which must be between 0 and 9. The default is 6.
TIMESTAMP(p) WITH TIME ZONE	Same as timestamp, but the timezone offset is also stored.
TIMESTAMP(p) WITH LOCAL TIME ZONE	Same as timestamp but normalized to the database's timezone upon storage and translated to the session timezone upon retrieval.
INTERVAL YEAR(year_p) TO MONTH	Stores a period of time in years and month. The argument year_p is the number of digits in the year field, which must be between 0 and 9 and defaults to 2.
INTERVAL DAY(day_p) TO SECOND (fractional_second_p)	Stores a period of time in days, hours, minutes, seconds, and fractional seconds. The argument day_p is the maximum number of digits in the day field and the argument fractional_second_p is the number of fractional second digits. Both must be between 0 and 9, and the defaults are 2 and 6, respectively.

WARNING **The LONG type was the first attempt to allow storage of large amounts of data in a table, but you should use the newer types described here instead. The LONG type stores a smaller amount of data, and you can only have one LONG per table. Oracle plans to desupport creation of the LONG data type and the LONG RAW data types. Neither should be created, and exisitng columns of these types should be converted.**

Table 8.4 defines the various data types. At any time you suspect that you might have to store more than 4,000 bytes worth of data, you should use one of the data types, all variable-length, that are outlined in Table 8.4.

Table 8.4 Large-Object Types

DATA TYPE	DESCRIPTION
`BLOB`	A binary large object.
`CLOB`	A character large object containing single-byte characters.
`NCLOB`	A character large object storing Unicode characters. Characters may be multibyte, depending on the national character set.
`BFILE`	A pointer to an externally stored file.

Raw Types

The raw data type are used to store binary data. Unlike character data, Oracle won't convert raw data when moving it between the user session and the database, the latter possibly having different character sets. Also, raw data is imported and exported without conversion. The raw type is a variable-length column, like `VARCHAR2`, with a maximum size of 2,000 bytes.

Other Types

There are several other data types that are available in a default Oracle install. PL/SQL has data types that allow you to store data sets. These types—varray and nested tables—are discussed in the PL/SQL section of this chapter. Also, two types are used to describe the position of data—`REF`, `ROWID`, and `UROWID`—.

You can also create your own types by defining object types. In addition to the built-in types, Oracle provides several object types. The XMLType is an example of one and is specifically covered at the end of this chapter. The following is a list of some other Oracle-provided key object types.

XMLType. Used to store XML data

"Any" Types. Used when the data type isn't known or when maximum flexibility is wanted

URI Types. Used to describe URIs

Spatial Types. Used to store spatial information (e.g., geographical coordinates)

Media Types. Used to store and easily manipulate audio, video, image, and other media data

Table 8.5 Arithmetic and Concatenation Operators

OPERATOR	DESCRIPTION	EXAMPLE
+	Addition of the operands.	`a+b`
-	Subtract the second operand from the first, or negate a sole operand.	`a(b; (a`
*	Multiply the first operand by the second.	`a*b`
/	Divide the first operand by the second.	`a/b`

Operators

Oracle operators are used in expressions to either compare two operands or evaluate two operands and return a result. Relationship comparison operators, set comparison operators, logical operators, set operators, and wildcard operators are covered later in the chapter when the select statement is discussed. The remaining operators are the arithmetic operators and the concatenation operators, described in Table 8.5. As you've seen, the * can be used to select all fields from a table.

SQL Expressions

An expression is essentially anything that results in a single value. It can include function calls, operators, literal values, columns, and even an SQL statement. Different types of expressions are required in different parts of SQL. Table 8.6 defines the different Oracle expressions.

Table 8.6 Expressions

TYPE	DESCRIPTION	EXAMPLES
Simple	A column, psuedocolumn, literal, sequence value, or NULL	`emp.ename 'hello' 40 NULL`
Compound expressions	Any combination of other expressions.	`40*4 emp.ename || emp.deptno sal*1.1 upper(emp.ename)`

(continues)

Table 8.6 Expressions *(Continued)*

TYPE	DESCRIPTION	EXAMPLES
CURSOR expressions	Describes a cursor that will be returned as a nested field in a select statement. The inner select statement, along with the CURSOR keyword, is a CURSOR expression	`CURSOR(SELECT ename, sal FROM emp e WHERE e.deptno= d.deptno) FROM dept d,emp m WHERE d.deptno= m.deptno AND m.job='MANAGER';`
Datetime expressions	A datetime column, function expression or compound expression that yields a datetime value.	`emp.hiredate to_date ('05/31/2002', 'DD/MM/YYYY')`
Function expressions	The result of any built-in SQL function or user-defined function.	`to_date('05/28/2002') upper('adams')`
INTERVAL expressions	Anything, such as date arithmetic or certain date functions, that yields the interval date types.	`(SYSTIMESTAMP - hiredate) DAY TO SECOND`
Object access expressions	An expression that accesses a member of an object.	`sys.XMLtype .createXML(text) .extract('/article /subject')`
Scalar subquery expressions	An expression that shouldn't return more than one row. If more than one row is returned, it is an error.	
Expression lists	A combination of other expressions.	`ename, sal, comm`

In addition to these expressions, there are two types that are specific to PL/SQL—case expressions and type constructor expressions. Many of these expression descriptions include SQL that you have not yet encountered in this book. You'll notice, as you progress through this chapter, that some of the same examples are used. For now, it's important to know only that there are many types of expressions and that not all are interchangeable—you cannot put any type of expression into all parts of SQL statements that require expressions.

Describing Tables

Often, you need to determine what the columns and data types of a table are. You can do so by using the describe statement, which works as follows:

```
DESC emp;
```

This will provide the following information about the emp table:

```
Name                                       Null?    Type
 ----------------------------------------- -------- --------------------
 EMPNO                                      NOT NULL NUMBER(4)
 ENAME                                               VARCHAR2(10)
 JOB                                                 VARCHAR2(9)
 MGR                                                 NUMBER(4)
 HIREDATE                                            DATE
 SAL                                                 NUMBER(7,2)
 COMM                                                NUMBER(7,2)
 DEPTNO                                              NUMBER(2)
```

The describe command is very useful for finding out information about a particular object. However, it isn't useful for finding out how objects relate to one another, for which you need the data dictionary. Appendix A includes pointers to online information about the data dictionary.

Select Queries

The `select` statement is by far the most used statement in all of SQL. You've seen it a lot already—we couldn't have gotten even this far without using lots of examples. So far, your use has been simple, but here in this section its full power is revealed. As you might expect, the `select` statement can be quite complicated. With an understanding of the purposes of the basic component pieces, you'll learn the specifics of each.

You've seen this statement a lot so far. It returns everything in the emp table.

```
SELECT * FROM emp
```

A couple of times, you've used a `select` statement that has a `where` clause, such as the following:

```
SELECT ename,sal FROM emp WHERE sal > 1000
```

This statement returns just the names of employees with salaries greater than 1,000. This example has all the component parts. Here's a translation of this select statement in plain English:

`SELECT` the data I want `FROM` one or more data sources `WHERE` these conditions are met

The first component—"the data I want"—is `called` the elements clause. In our first statement, you used the wildcard operator to say that you wanted all the fields for all the rows, where as in the second statement you asked only for two specific fields. The second component is the target—it tells the database what objects will be involved. The last component, the `where` clause, is optional, as is demonstrated in the first statement above. However, you'll almost always use it in real-life code.

The first topic covered will actually be the second component—the `target`. You need to know a little bit about this before you can fully understand the `element` expression, which is covered secondly. The section that follows is about the `where` clause.

Target Clause

The target clause is typically a comma-delimited list of tables, but it can also contain a couple other types of objects. First you'll learn what else can be in the list. Then, since you have experience with select statements involving only one table, you'll learn what happens when there is more than one object, as well as take your first look at joins. Finally, you'll learn table aliasing and when it is used.

Types of Target Objects

So far, you've only seen tables used as target objects. However, tables can also contain snapshots and views, which you haven't learned about yet. A view acts like a table but is actually a window—or "view"—onto the content of one or more tables. A snapshot is a view that refreshes periodically. Usually, a snapshot is used when there is a table that you want on a remote database; however, going across the network on every query is too costly. For now, just be aware that `select` statements can select from more than just tables. Their syntax for using views and snapshots in the target is exactly the same as it is for tables, so you won't have to relearn anything.

Multiple Target Objects and Joins

When you have more than one target object involved, you have what is known as a *join*. The join is the fundamental piece of all of relational databases and allows you to arbitrarily map the data of one table with that of another. A simple example, found at the end of this section, is mapping an employee's name in the `emp` table to the department's name in the `dept` table. Before looking at that, it is important to understand what is happening beneath the surface.

When more than one target object is listed in the target clause, the database does a Cartesian product between the two tables. A Cartesian product is the mapping of each member of one set with each member of another set. This is best illustrated by example. Try the following SQL statement:

```
SELECT ename, dname FROM emp,dept
```

Notice that there is a lot of repeated data in the result. Also notice the number of rows returned: 56. The emp table has 15 rows, while the dept table has 4. The number of rows you got back is 14 multiplied by 4, or 56. If you look at the data, you'll see that for each employee, each department is listed. That result is a Cartesian product between ename and dname.

You're probably wondering, "Why would I ever want a result like that?" You really don't. However, what you are seeing here is the foundation operation of a relational database, the join. You have taken two different sets of data and multiplied them so that every permutation is available to you. You then use the where clause to choose just the data you want. Without getting too far ahead of yourself, here is a simple example:

```
SELECT ename, dname
  FROM emp,dept
  WHERE dept.deptno=emp.deptno
```

Now you have only 14 rows, each having the correct department name for the employee. You've joined two different entities from two different tables—ename and dname.

You can have any number of objects that you desire in your list. The Cartesian product works the same way. For instance, if you add the bonus table to your target as shown in the following select statement—and the bonus table has 3 rows—then you will get 168 rows: $14 \times 4 \times 3 = 168$. If the bonus table has 0 rows, which is the default, you'll get 0 rows: $14 \times 4 \times 0 = 0$.

```
SELECT * FROM emp,dept,bonus
```

Target Aliasing

In the previous example, you referenced the deptno columns by specifying the table and the column name. Aliasing allows you to declare that you want an object to be known by a different name in the SQL statement. Here is an example:

```
SELECT ename, dname, a.deptno,b.deptno FROM emp a,dept b
```

Why would you want to do this? Three reasons. First, it can make your SQL more readable. Second, you need to alias if you use subqueries or cursors. Third, it allows you to perform self-joins. This is where you join a table to itself. Here is an example with the dept table. The dept table has 4 rows, and your query will return $4 \times 4 = 16$ rows.

```
SELECT a.deptno,b.deptno FROM dept a,dept b
```

Self-joins are important for a table in which one column references another. A common use is to represent a tree structure in the table Here's how you might use this technique to store the nodes of an XML document in a table. To simplify the example, we have ignored attributes, processing instructions, and text nodes. Your table might look similar to Table 8.7.

To get the names of the child and its parent, you can execute the following self-join. It will not select the root node, since the root node has no parent listed in the table.

```
SELECT child.name, parent.name
   FROM xml_test child,xml_test parent
   WHERE child.parent_id=node.node_id
```

Subqueries as Targets

When you use an object as a `target`, all the data in the object is a candidate to be returned. Oracle also gives you the ability to use queries as targets. A query is just a `select` statement, most likely with a limiting `where` condition. Here is an example in which you use a query as `target` so that you return employees with salaries greater than 1,300.

```
SELECT ename,dname FROM
     dept,
     (SELECT * FROM emp WHERE sal > 1300) filtered_emp
   WHERE filtered_emp.deptno=dept.deptno;
```

Often, a subquery isn't necessary. As you'll see when you read about the `where` clause, this result set can be produced more simply with a `where` condition. Alternatively, if you do a query on this subquery a lot, you can create a view.

Table 8.7 XML Structure in a Database Table

NODE_ID	PARENT	NAME
1	0	Root
2	1	Daughter1
3	2	GrandDaughter1
4	2	GrandDaughter2
5	1	Daughter2

Elements Clause

The `elements` clause describes what you want from your targets. It contains one or more *expressions,* which are typically column names. However, they can be any valid Oracle expression, including functions. You can alias the expressions so that the field is listed differently in the output. Doing so is very important in terms of XSQL, so we'll pay special attention to it. In many cases, XSQL requires expressions to be aliased. Also covered here is the `DISTINCT` keyword. It allows you to get only the unique rows in the result set.

Element Expressions

An expression, in terms of the `elements` clause, is any one of the following:

- An unambiguous column name of any object listed in the target clause
- A function
- A number or quoted string

It's most important to note that the column name is unambiguous. In many cases, the same column, such as `deptno`, will exist multiple times in the tables that you are using. In such a case, you have to declare which column you mean. You do so by prefixing the object name onto the column—`emp.deptno` or `dept.deptno`. Here is an example that uses each of the different types of expressions:

```
SELECT  'howdy' AS "howdy",to_char(hiredate,'yyyy'),5,ename FROM emp
```

By default, only the column names can possibly be valid XML names. You must use aliasing for other types of expressions, which is covered in detail in the "Expression Aliasing" section. Here is how to make our example work in XSQL:

```
<?xml version="1.0"?>
<page connection="demo" xmlns:xsql="urn:oracle-xsql">
<xsql:query>
   SELECT
     ename,
     'howdy' AS "howdy",
     1 AS "number",
     TO_CHAR(hiredate) AS "hiredate"
   FROM emp
</xsql:query>
</page>
```

The result of this query is shown in Figure 8.1.

The usefulness of string and number expressions in XSQL is a bit dubious, but it is a good technique to know. For one thing, it automatically creates an XML element for you. If you need to create XML elements for use with action handlers, you can use this technique to have the element ready to go. Then, all you have to do is set the value and the attributes. As you'll also see when you learn about the special dual table, you can also use this technique to grab parameter names and put them into an XML element of your choosing.

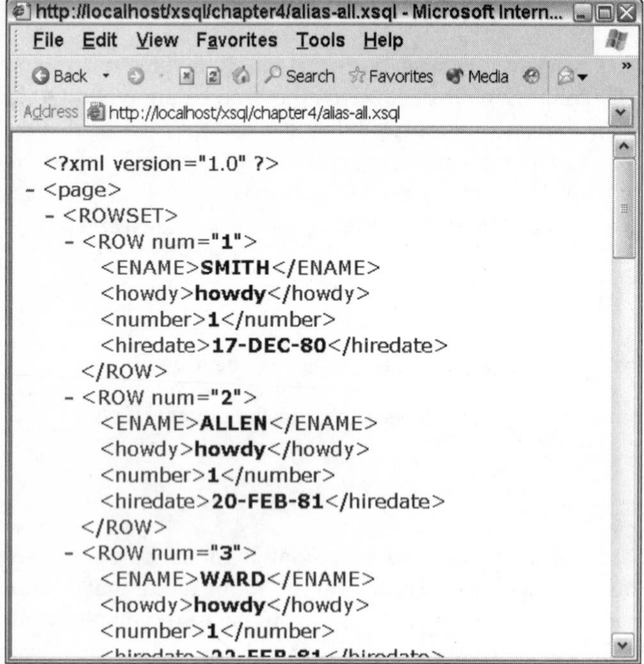

Figure 8.1 SELECT statement with all expression types.

Expression Aliasing

You've already seen a lot of basic `elements` clauses. You can use the wildcard character to fetch all the fields for each row, or you can name each row explicitly. Here are two SQL statements that produce the same result:

```
SELECT * FROM dept
SELECT deptno,dname,loc FROM dept;
```

As you know from the last chapter, the XML elements for each piece of data take the name of the column. You can alter the name of the column by using aliasing. For instance, you might want the element names `Department_Number`, `Department_Name`, and `Location` in your XML. You would alias these names as follows by using the `AS` keyword:

```
<?xml version="1.0"?>
<page connection="demo" xmlns:xsql="urn:oracle-xsql" >
 <xsql:query>
   SELECT
```

```
      deptno AS Department_Number,
      dname AS Department_Name,
      loc AS Location
    FROM dept
  </xsql:query>
 </page>
```

Your results will come back as shown in Figure 8.2.

But wait! All the columns are uppercase, following from the simple fact that SQL is case-insensitive. The fix is to use quotation marks:

```
<?xml version="1.0"?>
<page connection="demo" xmlns:xsql="urn:oracle-xsql" >
<xsql:query>
   SELECT
     deptno AS "Department_Number",
     dname AS "Department_Name",
     loc AS "Location"
   FROM dept
</xsql:query>
</page>
```

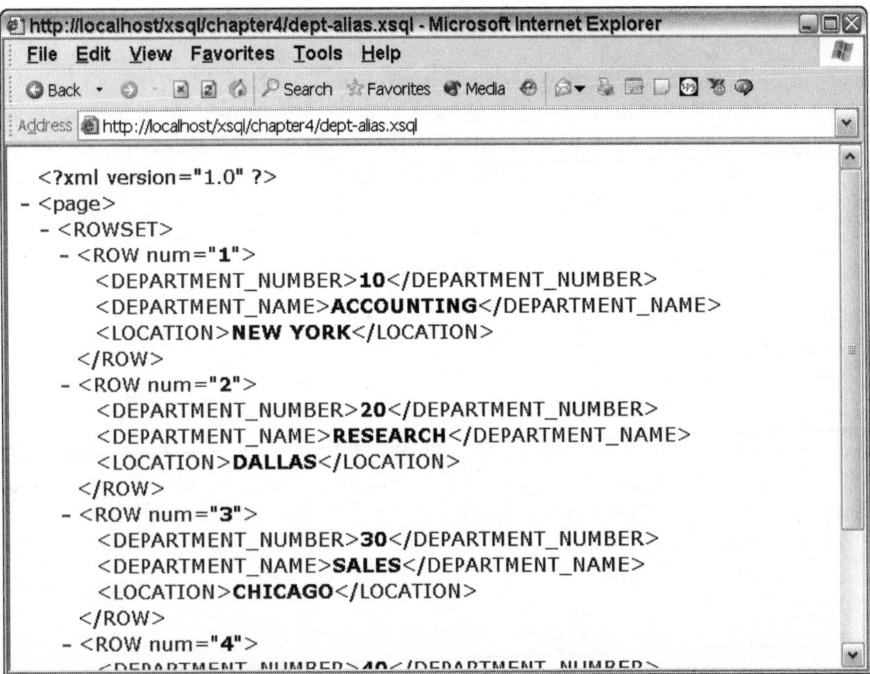

Figure 8.2 Aliasing.

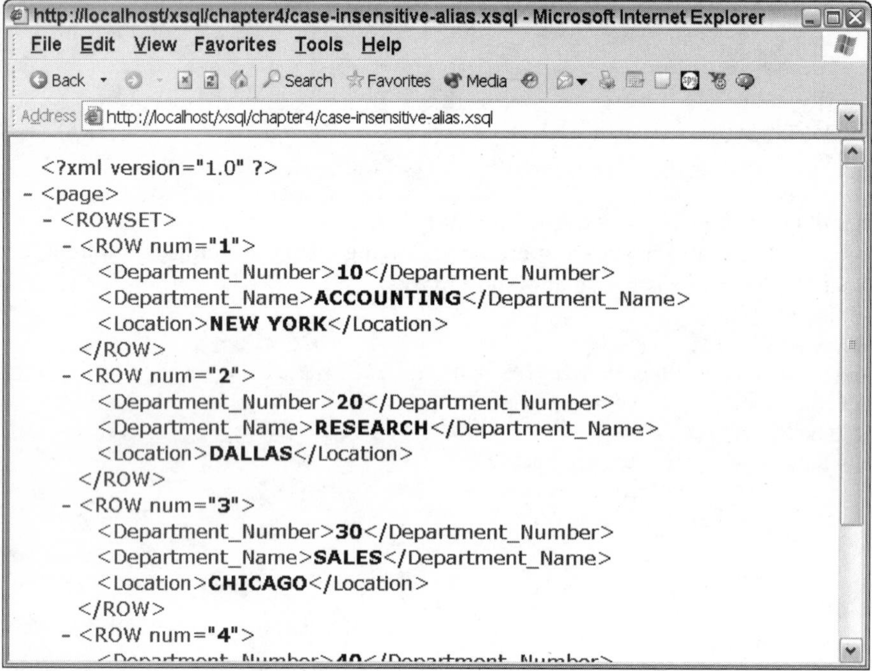

Figure 8.3 Case-sensitive aliasing.

This will yield the desired result, as seen in Figure 8.3.

In conjunction with XSQL, aliasing is often required. When functions are used, the default expression name isn't a valid XML element name. Consider the following example where you want to know in which year each employee was hired:

```
<?xml version="1.0"?>
<page connection="demo" xmlns:xsql="urn:oracle-xsql" >
<xsql:query>
  SELECT ename,to_char(HIREDATE,'yyyy') FROM emp
</xsql:query>
</page>
```

If you try to load this page in your browser, you will get an error. However, if you run it in SQL*Plus, the query runs fine. The problem is that parentheses and single quotes aren't allowed in XML names. Thus, you have to alias the second expression to something valid, as follows:

```
<?xml version="1.0"?>
<page connection="demo" xmlns:xsql="urn:oracle-xsql" >
<xsql:query>
  SELECT
     ename AS "Employee Name",
     to char(HIREDATE,'yyyy') AS "Hire Date"
  FROM emp
```

```
</xsql:query>
</page>
```

Then you'll get the desired result, as shown in Figure 8.4.

The obvious corollary to this discussion is that you can't choose an alias that isn't a valid XML name. The most common instance in which this issue arises is an alias with spaces. XSQL won't accept such queries because the column name violates the rules of XML element names.

`Distinct` Keyword

Sometimes, you want to know only what the unique members of a set are. For instance, you might want to know only those years in which any hiring was done. With what you know so far, you would do the following:

```
SELECT to_char(HIREDATE,'yyyy') AS "Hire_Date" FROM emp
```

But then you'd have to go through all of the rows and eliminate those entries that are repeats. Instead, you just use the `DISTINCT` keyword. It does this work for you. Here's how it works:

```
SELECT DISTINCT to_char(HIREDATE,'yyyy') AS "Hire_Date" FROM emp
```

You can also use the `UNIQUE` keyword to do this—they are synonyms.

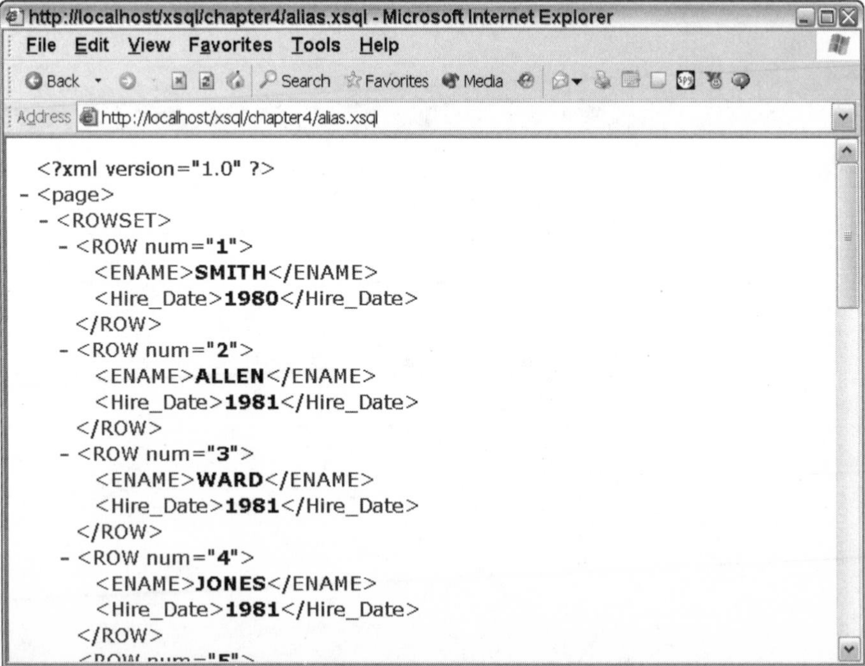

Figure 8.4 Aliasing SQL functions.

`Where` Clause

The real work of any select statement is done in the `where` clause. In fact, you couldn't even get through our discussions of the other two clauses without using the `where` clause a couple of times! Even a fairly modest production database has thousands, if not millions, of pieces of data. The rest of the select statement is used to get the data, while the `where` clause is the tool to filter it. First, you'll look at how the `where` clause works. Next, you'll examine joins, which are among the key components of the RDBMS architecture, more deeply. Finally, you'll see some complex `where` clauses.

How the `Where` Clause Works

The `where` clause is a condition expression that evaluates either true, false, or NULL. If the expression evaluates to true, the row will be returned. In form, the expression is mostly identical to the Boolean conditions of any programming language. However the NULL evaluation is often tricky. You'll look at this closely when you reach the discussion of the `NOT` operator in the next section. In most cases, NULL acts like false, but it is important to understand the distinction.

You can think of the `where` clause as a test that is applied to each row returned by the `target` clause. If the row passes, it will be included in the result set; if it doesn't, it will be excluded. Here's a simple example of this idea:

```
SELECT ename
    FROM emp
    WHERE sal < 1500
    ORDER BY ename
```

Table 8.8 Simple `Where` Clause

ename	sal	sal < 1500?
ADAMS	1100	TRUE
ALLEN	1600	FALSE
BLAKE	2850	FALSE
CLARK	2450	FALSE
FORD	3000	FALSE
JAMES	950	TRUE
JONES	2975	FALSE
KING	5000	FALSE

Table 8.8 Simple `Where` Clause *(Continued)*

ename	sal	sal < 1500?
MARTIN	1250	FALSE
MILLER	1300	TRUE
SCOTT	3000	FALSE
SMITH	800	TRUE
TURNER	1500	FALSE
WARD	1250	TRUE

You can consider the `where` clause filtering as listed in Table 8.8. The six rows selected are the six for which the expression evaluates to true. The `where` clause doesn't limit you to just one test. You can combine tests with boolean operators. Consider this query in which the salary test is set differently for different departments:

```
SELECT ename FROM emp
  WHERE (deptno=10 AND sal < 1500)
         OR
        (deptno=20 AND sal < 2000)
         OR
        (deptno=40 AND sal < 3000)
  ORDER BY ename
```

This yields the following matrix, as listed in Table 8.9:

Table 8.9 Salary Range Based on Departments

ename	deptno	sal	deptno=10 and sal<1500?, deptno=20 and sal<2000?, deptno=40 and sal<3000?
ADAMS	20	1100	FALSE, TRUE, FALSE
ALLEN	30	1600	FALSE, FALSE, FALSE
BLAKE	30	2850	FALSE, FALSE, FALSE
CLARK	10	2450	FALSE, FALSE, FALSE
FORD	20	3000	FALSE, FALSE, FALSE
JAMES	30	950	FALSE, FALSE, FALSE

(continues)

Table 8.9 Salary Range Based on Departments *(Continued)*

ename	deptno	sal	deptno=10 and sal<1500?, deptno=20 and sal<2000?, deptno=40 and sal<3000?
JONES	20	2975	FALSE, FALSE, FALSE
KING	10	5000	FALSE, FALSE, FALSE
MARTIN	30	1250	FALSE, FALSE, FALSE
MILLER	10	1300	TRUE, FALSE, FALSE
SCOTT	20	3000	FALSE, FALSE, FALSE
SMITH	20	800	FALSE, TRUE, FALSE
TURNER	30	1500	FALSE, FALSE, FALSE
WARD	30	1250	FALSE, FALSE, FALSE

Because of the structure of the statement, only one of the conditions needs to be met for the statement to evaluate to true. Notice that none of the employees in department 30 makes it to the result set. There is no way for them to evaluate to true. The following statement will see employees of department 30 in the result set, because some of them have commissions greater than 500.

```
SELECT  ename, deptno, sal FROM emp
WHERE
 (
  (deptno=10 and sal < 1500)
   OR
  (deptno=20 and sal < 2000)
   OR
  (deptno=40 and sal < 3000)
 )
  OR
 comm<1400
      ORDER BY ename
```

Notice that Turner, who has a commission of 0, is in the result set for this query. This is to be expected, for 0 is less than 1400. But do a quick `SELECT * FROM emp` and you'll notice that there are a lot of employees for whom no commission is specified. The value for their commission is `NULL`, not 0. The value `NULL` has no numeric value, so it will never evaluate to true in a range condition such as `comm` < 1,400. If you want to get all the employees who have no commission or a commission less than 1,400, you can do the following:

```
SELECT  ename, deptno, sal FROM emp
WHERE
 (
  (deptno=10 AND sal < 1500)
   OR
  (deptno=20 AND sal < 2000)
   OR
  (deptno=40 AND sal < 3000)
 )
  OR
 (comm<1400 OR comm IS NULL)
      ORDER BY ename
```

Comparison Operators

So far, you've seen only five operators used—`AND`, `OR`, `NOT`, =, and <. The first three are logical operators; the last two are comparison operators. As you might expect, there are other operators available for you. Here you'll examine all the operators that exist.

The operators you use most often are the relationship comparison operators. These are the operators that you first learned about in math class. The key difference is that they work against more than just numbers. You can also use them with dates and strings. For instance, the following query,

```
SELECT ename FROM emp WHERE ename > 'MARTIN'
```

will return all the rows that are alphanumerically greater than '`MARTIN'`. The same is true for dates. The following query will return all of the employees hired after 1982:

```
SELECT * FROM emp WHERE to_date('1982','yyyy') < hiredate
```

Table 8.10 Relationship Comparison Operators

PURPOSE	OPERATORS	EXAMPLE
Equality	=	`SELECT * FROM emp WHERE sal=3000`
Inequality	!=, ^=, <>	`SELECT * FROM emp WHERE sal!=3000`
Less than	<	`SELECT * FROM emp WHERE sal < 3000`
Greater than	>	`SELECT * FROM emp WHERE sal > 3000`
Less than or equal to	<=, !>	`SELECT * FROM emp WHERE sal <=3000`
Greater than or equal to	>=, !<	`SELECT * FROM emp WHERE sal >=3000`
Between	BETWEEN	`SELECT * FROM emp WHERE sal BETWEEN 2000 and 3000`
Not between	BETWEEN	`SELECT * FROM emp WHERE sal NOT BETWEEN 2000 and 3000`

All the relationship comparison operators are listed in Table 8.10. They are listed by what they do, because several of them do the same thing. In those cases, the operator that you'll see used in this book is listed first.

If either operand is null, the expression will always evaluate to NULL. Here are some examples to prove this point. They also backup our claim that NULL is not 0. Neither query returns rows.

```
SELECT * FROM emp WHERE NULL > -200
SELECT * FROM emp WHERE NULL=0
```

Table 8.11 lists the two operators that allow you to compare values to NULL.

Table 8.11 Null Comparison Operators

OPERATOR	DESCRIPTION	EXAMPLE
IS NULL	The operand is NULL	`select * from emp where comm IS NULL`
IS NOT	The operand isn't NULL	`select * from emp where comm IS NOT NULL`

String-Matching Operators

It is possible to do wildcard matching in SQL. The like and not-like operators provide this functionality. Wildcard matching differs from the text searching made possible with Oracle Text, which you'll learn about later. While not as powerful, the like and not-like operators work against any column and don't carry the overhead of Oracle Text. Both operators work the same way. Consider the following queries. The first returns employees who have an A in their name; the second returns employees who don't have an A in their name.

```
SELECT ename FROM emp WHERE ename LIKE '%A%'
SELECT ename FROM emp WHERE ename NOT LIKE '%A%'
```

In the following queries, there are two wildcard characters: the % (matching zero or more characters) and the _ (matching one character). The first query returns employees who have the letter A as the second character in their names; the second query returns employees who have E as the second-to-last character; and the third query returns employees who have N as the third-to-last character:

```
SELECT ename FROM emp WHERE ename LIKE '_A%'
SELECT ename FROM emp WHERE ename LIKE '%E_'
SELECT ename FROM emp WHERE ename LIKE '%N__'
```

If there is no wildcard character at the beginning, the string matches only those characters that start with the string you specify. The same is true at the end of the string. Although there are many employees who have A's and S's in their names, the following statement matches only Adams:

```
SELECT ename FROM emp WHERE ename LIKE 'A%S'
```

It isn't necessary to use wildcard characters in a wildcard expression. However, if you aren't wildcarding, you probably should be using the = operator.

Logical Operators

There are three types of logical operators: AND, OR, and NOT. You've seen AND and OR in action. NOT is fairly intuitive when NULL isn't involved. Here is an example that lists everyone not in department 10. The parentheses aren't required, but as always they're a nice touch. Frankly, it's hard to overuse parentheses.

```
SELECT * FROM emp WHERE NOT (deptno=10);
```

The use of NOT in conjunction with NULL values is a bit nonintuitive. It's important to remember that NOT always works in conjunction with a relationship comparison operator. If an operand in the subordinate expression is NULL, the expression will evaluate to NULL. The important thing to realize is that the inverse of NULL is NULL. (This is different from true and false, which are inverses of each other.) So, when you apply NOT to a NULL condition, it will still be NULL. Here is an example:

```
SELECT * FROM emp WHERE NOT comm=500
```

Although there are many people without commissions, they aren't listed in the results. For those people, the query evaluates as "select * from emp where NOT (NULL)". On the other hand, the query for those people who have commissions that aren't equal to 500 evaluates as "select from emp where NOT (false)". In the latter case, the where clause evaluates to true because false is the inverse of true, whereas the former statement evaluates to NULL, which is not true. If you want to get all the people who don't have commissions of 500, you would do it as follows:

```
SELECT * FROM emp WHERE NOT (comm=500) OR (comm IS NULL)
```

The AND and OR operators have their own ways of dealing with NULL for the same reasons. If both operands are NULL, then the expression is NULL. Applying NOT to it won't make it true. Cases where only one operand is NULL are more interesting. Consider the following two examples:

```
SELECT ename FROM emp WHERE (sal=2975 or comm=500)
SELECT ename FROM emp WHERE (sal=2975 and comm=500)
```

In the database, Ward has a commission of 500, while Jones has a salary of 2,975. The first query returns both Ward and Jones, while the second query returns no rows.

This is completely expected behavior. Now, this is what happens when you apply NOT:

```
SELECT ename FROM emp WHERE NOT (sal=2975 OR comm=500)
```

This returns only three rows—those who have commissions that aren't 500 and that don't have salaries that are 2,975. You know that commission either has a value or is NULL and that everyone has a salary. This means that the first operand of OR can evaluate to either true or false, while the second operand can evaluate to true, false, or NULL.

From this, you can deduce how the OR operator behaves when it is confronted with an operand that has a NULL value. Since employees without commissions didn't show up in our result here, you know the following:

- If one operand is NULL and the other TRUE, an OR expression will evaluate to TRUE.
- If one operand is NULL and the other FALSE, an OR expression will evaluate to NULL.

The second observation is the nonintuitive one. It seems that when you imply a NOT, you should get the inverse set—all the rows the query didn't return without NOT. This isn't the case, however. Instead, you only got the other employees who have commissions. For those employees, the original query evaluated to false; now it evaluates to true. For the other employees—those without commissions—the original query evaluated to NULL. Since the inverse of NULL is NULL, those rows don't show up when you apply NOT.

Here's the second case:

```
SELECT ename FROM emp WHERE NOT (sal=2975 and comm=500)
```

The original query returned no rows, so now you can expect to get all rows. But someone is missing—Jones! Jones is our employee with a salary of 2,975 and no commission. From this, you can deduce the following about AND statements:

- When one operand is NULL and one is true, the expression will evaluate to NULL.
- When one operand is NULL and one false, the expression will evaluate to false.

This behavior may seem incredibly counterintuitive. The best way to think about it by considering the overall structure of the language. Consider the following two statements:

```
SELECT ename,comm,sal FROM emp WHERE NOT (5=5 AND comm=500)
```

5 always equals 5, so this statement is really just the following:

```
SELECT ename,comm,sal FROM emp WHERE NOT (comm=500)
```

As you've already learned, this statement should only display employees with commissions that aren't 500. If the preceding rules weren't in place as they exist, these last two statements wouldn't return the same result. Logically, they should. Putting a truism in a statement—or not having a truism—shouldn't affect the end result.

By now, you're probably thinking, "Isn't there an easier way?" The treatment of NULLs has been debated ever since SQL started. The truth is that you have to distinguish between NULL values and conditions that are false. If you just treat as false any condition in which a NULL is an operand, in your applications you'll end up doing a lot of work sorting out what is NULL and what is false. In practice, the theory here is that you don't generally want NULL conditions grouped in with false conditions. If the inverse theory were used—you do want NULL conditions grouped in with false conditions—we'd be talking about what steps are needed to keep them separate.

This discussion has been somewhat long-winded and theoretical. If your brain is hurting a bit, Table 8.12 should help. If in doubt, just look up how the expression is supposed to behave and remember the following rules of thumb:

- That NULL isn't FALSE
- That the inverse of NULL isn't TRUE

Table 8.12 lists the logical operators. The first and second operands are always interchangeable for `AND` and `OR`, while `NOT` only has one operand.

Table 8.12 Logical Operators

OPERAND 1	OPERATOR	OPERAND 2	EVALUATION
TRUE	AND	TRUE	TRUE
FALSE	AND	TRUE	FALSE
FALSE	AND	FALSE	FALSE
TRUE	AND	NULL	NULL
FALSE	AND	NULL	FALSE
NULL	AND	NULL	NULL

(continues)

Table 8.12 Logical Operators *(Continued)*

OPERAND 1	OPERATOR	OPERAND 2	EVALUATION
TRUE	OR	TRUE	TRUE
TRUE	OR	FALSE	TRUE
FALSE	OR	FALSE	FALSE
TRUE	OR	NULL	TRUE
FALSE	OR	NULL	NULL
NULL	OR	NULL	NULL
	NOT	TRUE	FALSE
	NOT	FALSE	TRUE
	NOT	NULL	NULL

Joins Examined

In the discussion on targets, you learned that when you list more than one object in the table you get the Cartesian product of the objects. This is almost never what you want. Instead, you would want to use the `where` clause to limit the rows that are returned. Here's a statement that gives you the Cartesian product. Consider the following statement:

```
SELECT emp.ename,emp.deptno,dept.deptno,dept.dname
   FROM emp,dept
   WHERE ename='ADAMS'
```

This will return the results listed in Table 8.13.

The `where` clause trims the emp table down to just the one row, but it doesn't trim the `dept` table. The following join table does the trick:

```
SELECT emp.ename,emp.deptno,dept.deptno,dept.dname
   FROM emp,dept
   WHERE ename='ADAMS' AND emp.deptno=dept.deptno
```

Table 8.13 Cartesian Product for Adams

ename	emp.deptno	dept.deptno	dname
ADAMS	20	10	ACCOUNTING
ADAMS	20	20	RESEARCH
ADAMS	20	30	SALES
ADAMS	20	40	OPERATIONS

Now you will get only one row. It tells you to which department Adams belongs, as listed in Table 8.14.

In practice, you'd probably never include both `emp.deptno` and `dept.deptno`. This example, however, shows you how joins work. When you say `ename='ADAMS'`, it will filter on all the rows of the Cartesian product of `emp` and `dept`. The join expression—`emp.deptno=dept.deptno`—is simply doing the exact same thing. The assumption is that between the tables and signified by the deptno columns is a *foreign key relationship*. Figure 8.5 illustrates this relationship for the emp.deptno and dept.deptno tables.

More than one join can exist in one `SELECT` statement. The same principles apply when there are multiple joins. When there are multiple targets, the database combines them to make a Cartesian product. At that point, the combination looks like a table, albeit one with a lot of repeated data. You use any number of join conditions to reduce the Cartesian product to the rows that you want.

Table 8.14 Adams Query with a Join

ename	emp.deptno	dept.deptno	dname
ADAMS	20	20	RESEARCH

If an employee's department number is set to NULL, that employee won't be returned. This makes sense, for the join—`emp.deptno=dept.deptno`—evaluates to NULL for that employee. However, it's quite common that you might want the rows to be included even if one of the columns of your join is NULL. For instance, what if an employee has just been hired and hasn't been assigned to a department yet? In such a case, you use an *outer join*. Here's an example:

```
SELECT ename,emp.deptno
   FROM emp,dept
   WHERE emp.deptno=dept.deptno(+)
```

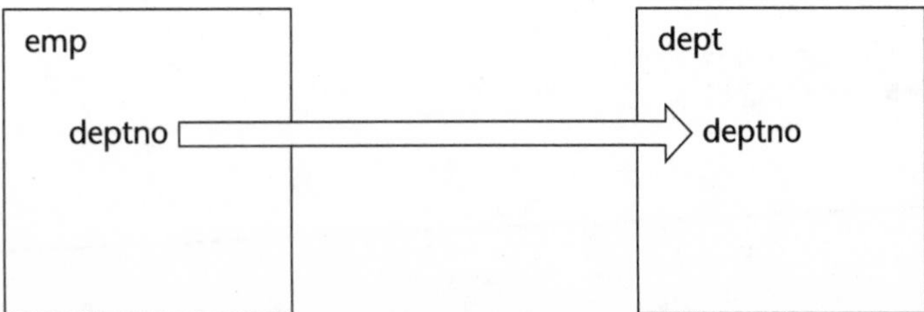

Figure 8.5 Foreign Key Relationship.

The (+) signifies that you want the preceding join to evaluate as true if the first column is null.

`Order By` Clause

When you use the `order by` clause, you tell the database that you want your data ordered in a certain way. This clause tends to be very important with XSQL. Since you can translate your result XML directly into the HTML that you present, you can easily get your data sorted correctly just by using a `where` clause in your SQL. The `order by` clause works very simply. Here's an example:

```
SELECT job,ename
  FROM emp
  ORDER BY job
```

An ascending sort results, as shown in Figure 8.6. You can also perform a descending sort by using the `desc` keyword:

```
SELECT job,ename
  FROM emp ORDER BY job DESC
```

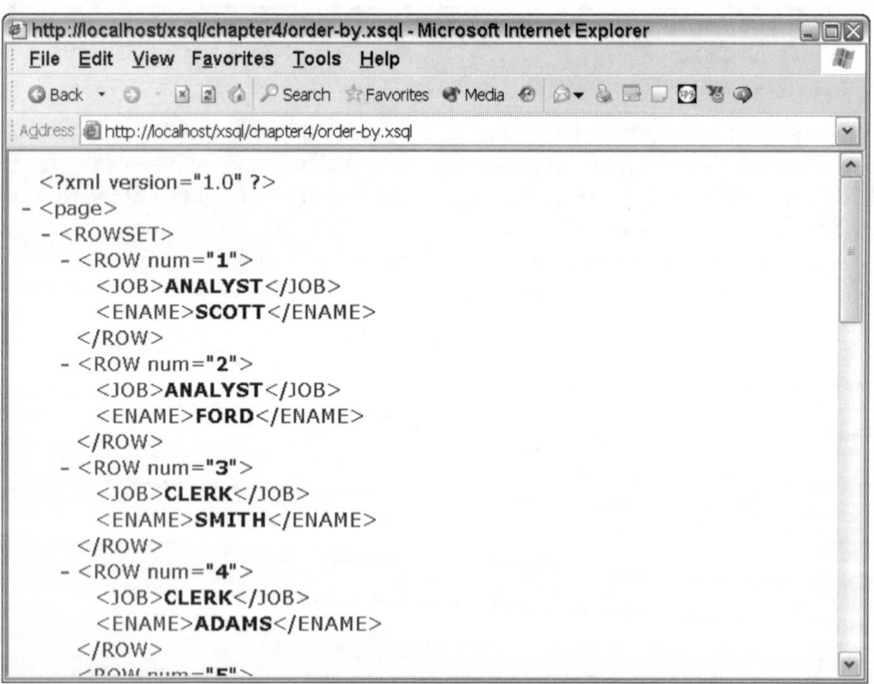

Figure 8.6 Default `order by`.

Secondary sorts are easy to perform too; just separate your sorts with commas. Here's an example in which the jobs are sorted first, with the secondary sort on name. You can have as many sorts as you like. It's a good idea to have a sort clause for each element expression. The `ASC` in the example specifies an ascending sort. It is the default, and although it isn't strictly needed, it does make your SQL statement clearer.

```
SELECT job,ename
  FROM emp
  ORDER BY job DESC, ename ASC
```

One final note: In the preceding examples, our sort keys have also been fields you wish to return. This condition doesn't have to be the case, however. In the following statement, you sort by salary even though the salary isn't in the output:

```
SELECT job,ename
   FROM emp
   ORDER BY sal DESC
```

NULL values are sorted before other values for descending sorts and after other values for ascending sorts.

Working with Sets

`Select` statements returns sets of rows, so sometimes you will want to do set operations on them. For example, you might want to write a `where` clause that checks to see whether a value is included in a set of values, or you might wish to take two SQL statements and find their intersection—that is, those rows common to both results. SQL has two classes of set operations: the set comparison operators, used in `where` clauses, and the set operators, used for performing operations between select statements.

SQL has five set comparison operators, listed in Table 8.15. They greatly simplify some SQL statements that would otherwise require a complex expression of `OR`s, `AND`s, and `NOT`s. As with other comparison operators, if the operand is NULL, the expression will evaluate to NULL.

The set operators operate on two different result sets of two different SQL statements. The following is an example of one of the operators, `UNION`. It gives all the department names and employee names in a single query.

```
SELECT ename
  FROM emp
  UNION
    SELECT dname
      FROM dept
```

For set operators to work, the same number and type of fields must be in each select statement. Table 8.16 lists all of the set operators.

Table 8.15 Set Comparison Operators

OPERATOR	DESCRIPTION	EXAMPLE
`IN`	Tests if an operand belongs to the specified set.	`SELECT ename FROM emp WHERE sal IN (800,950,1100)`
`NOT IN`	Tests if an operand doesn't belong to the specified set.	`SELECT ename FROM emp WHERE sal NOT IN (800,950,1100)`
`ANY`	Used in conjunction with a relationship comparison operator. Determines if the specified relationship is true for any of the values.	`SELECT ename FROM emp WHERE sal > ANY (800,950,1100)`
`SOME`	Used in conjunction with a relationship comparison operator. Determines if the specified relationship is true for one or more of the values.	`SELECT ename FROM emp WHERE sal > SOME (800,950,1100)`
`ALL`	Used in conjunction with a relationship comparison operator. Determines if the specified relationship is true for all of the values.	`SELECT ename FROM emp WHERE sal > ALL (800,950,1100)`

The Imaginary Dual Table

Oracle provides the dual table, an imaginary table used largely for allowing you to perform functions. For instance, if you want to use a `select` statement to get the current date, you could do so as follows:

```
SELECT sysdate FROM dual
```

Table 8.16 Set Operators

OPERATOR	DESCRIPTION
`UNION`	All unique rows of both queries are returned.
`UNION ALL`	All rows of both queries are returned.
`MINUS`	Eliminates rows that appear in the second query from the rows returned in the first query.
`INTERSECT`	Returns only the rows that are common to both queries.

Of course, to do this from XSQL requires that you perform the following:

```
<?xml version="1.0"?>
<page connection="demo" xmlns:xsql="urn:oracle-xsql">
<xsql:query>
   SELECT sysdate AS "Date" FROM dual
</xsql:query>
</page>
```

You can also use the dual table to include parameters in the result set:

```
<?xml version="1.0"?>
<page connection="demo" xmlns:xsql="urn:oracle-xsql">
<xsql:query>
   select '{@param}' AS "ParamName" FROM dual
</xsql:query>
</page>
```

Managing Tables

The `select` statement is the tool used for getting data out of the database. The flip side of select is getting data in to the database. Before you can do that, however, you must have places to put the data. The construction of the database is the job of Data Definition Language (DDL) statements, which create, modify, or delete objects in the Oracle database. This section covers the part of DDL that pertains to the most popular and useful type of object, tables.

There are a lot of things to consider when managing your table. At the highest level, you must decide what data you want in the table. You think about this based on how you want this table to fit in to the rest of your application. But there are lots of system level attributes to consider, also. Ultimately, you'll want to work with your DBA on a lot of these parameters. Here, you'll get a gentle introduction.

Creating Tables

There are many options in creating tables. In this section, first you'll examine the simplest way to create a table; then you'll examine some of the more useful aspects of table creation. A lot of the options presented here concern how the table is stored. Finally, you'll learn how to create an exact copy of another table. The following SQL will create a table for customer orders. You'll use this table in later examples, so you should create it under the `momnpop id`.

```
CREATE TABLE customer (
   custid     NUMBER(8),
   fname      VARCHAR2(30),
   lname      VARCHAR2(30),
   address1           VARCHAR2(50),
```

```
    address2            VARCHAR2(50),
    state               VARCHAR(5),
    zip                 VARCHAR(10),
    country             VARCHAR(5)
);
```

If you now do a `desc customer`, you'll see that your table is in place. There are, however, a few problems that you will run into immediately. First, the `custid` will be used to identify your customers uniquely. You don't want someone using the same customer identification (id) twice. There is an easy way to prevent this from happening—just issue the following command:

TIP **To get rid of the old table, just issue the command** `DROP TABLE customer;`

```
CREATE TABLE customer (
    custid    NUMBER(4) PRIMARY KEY,
    fname     VARCHAR2(30),
    lname     VARCHAR2(30),
    address1  VARCHAR2(50),
    address2  VARCHAR2(50),
    state     VARCHAR(5),
    zip       VARCHAR(10),
    country   VARCHAR(5)
);
```

The database will now automatically prevent anyone from reusing the same `custid`. Your next problem concerns the country column. Because most of your customers are in the United States, you will want to set USA as the default value. If the value of the country column isn't explicitly defined in an `insert` statement, it will be `USA`. The first sentence asks that you set USA as the default value; the second sentence (as well as first sentence following the display code below) says that if you don't explicitly define (set?) the default value, it will be USA. You can define the default value with the following code:

```
CREATE TABLE customer (
    custid    NUMBER(4) PRIMARY KEY,
    fname     VARCHAR2(30),
    lname     VARCHAR2(30),
    email       VARCHAR2(30),
    address1  VARCHAR2(50),
    address2  VARCHAR2(50),
    state     VARCHAR(5),
    zip       VARCHAR(10),
    country   VARCHAR(5) DEFAULT 'USA'
);
```

Now, one thing you do want your user to define is his or her last name. If you don't define the last name, the row will be completely useless. You can require that the last name be defined as follows:

```
CREATE TABLE customer (
   custid    NUMBER(4) PRIMARY KEY,
   fname     VARCHAR2(30),
   lname     VARCHAR2(30) NOT NULL,
   email        VARCHAR2(30),
   address1  VARCHAR2(50),
   address2  VARCHAR2(50),
   state     VARCHAR(5),
   zip       VARCHAR(10),
   country   VARCHAR(5) DEFAULT 'USA'
);
```

NOTE The NOT NULL and PRIMARY KEY are examples of *constraints*, which you will learn more about later in the chapter. The best time to create them is along with the table, so a couple are introduced here. You'll see all of them in a little while.

Your next problem is that you want the table to live on a particular tablespace. You expect to get a lot of customers, so you want this table to be on your new terabyte drive. Here's how you would do that, assuming the tablespace is named `cust_tablespace`:

```
CREATE TABLE customer (
   custid    NUMBER(4) PRIMARY KEY,
   fname     VARCHAR2(30),
   lname     VARCHAR2(30) NOT NULL,
   email        VARCHAR2(30),
   address1  VARCHAR2(50),
   address2  VARCHAR2(50),
   state     VARCHAR(5),
   zip       VARCHAR(10),
   country   VARCHAR(5) DEFAULT 'USA'
   )
   TABLESPACE cust_tablespace;
```

NOTE There are many other storage options for your table that allow you to fine-tune how your data is stored. They require a deep understanding of the Oracle architecture to be used properly. These options are beyond the scope of this text and aren't covered here.

Let's say that you want to base your table on data that already exists in the system. By using the `AS` keyword, you can create a new table based on the following select statement, and the table will automatically populate. Notice that you use the aliasing you learned earlier to change the `empno` column name to `EMPID`.

```
CREATE TABLE empdept
    AS SELECT empnoAS"EMPID",ename,dname
      FROM emp,dept
      WHERE emp.deptno=dept.deptno;
```

The last topic for this section concerns *temporary tables,* used for storing data on a per-session basis. The data you put in can be seen only by your session, at the end of which the data goes away. Other sessions can use the same temporary table at the same time and your session won't see their data. Temporary tables are often used in complex queries for which you need to grab a subset of data. They have limited usefulness in conjunction with XSQL pages because of the short duration of an XSQL session. However, there may be some situations in which you'll find it much easier and efficient to process a subset from a temporary table rather than to repeatedly requery the database or load the data set into memory. Here is how a temporary table is created:

```
CREATE GLOBAL TEMPORARY TABLE temptable (
    temp_col1 VARCHAR2(20),
    temp_col2 VARCHAR2(20)
    );
```

Altering Tables

The `alter table` statement allows you to change aspects in a table that has already been created. In many cases, you can make changes to a table that already has data in it. This section looks at how the `alter table` statement works, what it is usually used for, and what it can't be used for. Before beginning the discussion, it's important to note that you can modify the storage characteristics of tables. These characteristics won't be itemized here, but most can be altered at any time. In this section, most of the emphasis is on working with columns, but it also covers moving a table to a new tablespace. Some discussion of constraints is given, but the "Constraints" section provides the greatest discussion of that topic.

Working with Columns

The `alter table` statement works almost exactly like the `create table` statement; it shares most of the same keywords and syntax. However, to use the `alter table` statement with columns is troublesome when you work with existing columns that are already populated with data. It is far simpler to add a column to a table. Here's an example that uses the `emp` table you created previously. It adds to the table a `home_phone` column.

```
ALTER TABLE emp ADD
  (home_phone VARCHAR2(10));
```

The good news is that adding a basic column is easy. It's even easy to add a column that has a default value, as follows:

```
ALTER TABLE emp ADD
  (benefits VARCHAR2(20) DEFAULT 'STANDARD HEALTH');
```

But if your table already has data in it, things get more complex. For instance, what if you want to create a column as `NOT NULL`? Each row has to have a value. As shown in the following, the syntax is simple enough:

```
ALTER TABLE emp ADD
  (home_zip VARCHAR2(10) NOT NULL);
```

If you run this against the `emp` table, which has data in it, you will get the following error message:

```
ORA-01758: table must be empty to add mandatory (NOT NULL) column
```

The problem is that at the time you add the column, all the data is null. The `NOT NULL` constraint couldn't possibly be satisfied. You have several alternatives:

- Set a default value for the column, such as `ALTER TABLE emp ADD (home_zip VARCHAR2(10) NOT NULL DEFAULT '27607');`
- Remove all the data and alter the column
- Create the column without the NOT NULL constraint, add the data, and apply the NOT NULL constraint afterwards.

The second option leads directly to the discussion about altering existing columns. To make these alterations, you would use the `modify` keyword and a similar expression that you would use if you were creating the column from scratch.

```
ALTER TABLE emp ADD (
  home_zip VARCHAR2(10));
```

. . . add the data home zip data.

```
ALTER TABLE emp MODIFY (
    home_zip NOT NULL);
```

You don't need to include anything about the data type, since that would remain the same. However, if you want to change the data type, you can. But there are restrictions. Anything goes if the column has no data in it. If you want, you can even change the data type entirely from `varchar2` to `date`, `date` to `number`, `number` to `varchar2`, and so on. If, however, there is any data in the column, this kind of modification isn't allowed.

Table 8.17 lists the rules for modifying columns that already contain data.

Table 8.17 Modifying Columns Containing Data

ACTION	DESCRIPTION	OKAY?	EXAMPLE
Assigning default value	Using the `DEFAULT` keyword to specify a default value for the column. The default value will only be used moving forward; null and other values already in the system will remain the same.	Always	`ALTER TABLE emp MODIFY (home_zip DEFAULT 27609)`
Widening strings	Increasing the number of characters allowed.	Always	`ALTER TABLE emp MODIFY (home_zip VARCHAR2(12))`
Narrowing strings	Decreasing the number of characters allowed. Oracle won't do this if it would require any existing string to be shortened.	Only to longest string length	`ALTER TABLE emp MODIFY (ename VARCHAR2(7));`
Increasing scale For numbers	Increasing the number of digits to the left of the decimal point.	Always	`ALTER TABLE emp MODIFY (empno NUMBER(6,0))`
Increasing precision For numbers	Increasing the number of digits to the right of the decimal point.	Always	`ALTER TABLE emp MODIFY (empno NUMBER(8,2))`
Decreasing scale and precision For numbers	Shrinking the size of a number column on either the left or right of the column.	No	

Our last topic for this section concerns dropping a column altogether, the ultimate modification. This can be accomplished by way of the `drop column` clause. If there is data in the column, it will be deleted.

```
alter table emp drop column home_zip;
```

Dropping Tables

Dropping tables is the process of removing a table and all of its data from your database. To drop a table, you need the `drop table` privilege for the table. Also, you need to be very careful; if you are having a bad day, you might end up inadvertently dropping the incorrect table.

There are two ways to drop tables. The following way you've already seen:

```
DROP TABLE table_to_drop;
```

Often when trying to drop a table, you will encounter the following error message:

```
ORA-02449: unique/primary keys in table referenced by foreign keys
```

You get this error message because foreign key constraints are being used. You learn more about foreign key constraints later; for now, it's important to know only that there are rows in other tables that reference keys in this table. If you just go and drop this table, those other tables will be very, very upset. Thus, Oracle doesn't allow you to do it. Here are ways around this problem:

- Getting rid of the foreign key constraints; then dropping the table
- Deleting the data that references this table
- Dropping this table and all the tables with references to it

The first two options will be examined in the foreign constraints discussion. The last option is a bit draconian and risky: You delete the `table_to_drop` table and recursively drop all tables that have a reference to it. Oracle will drop the tables with references to your target table, and if it finds that it can't drop a table because another table has a reference to it, it will go and find that table and then drop that one too. It's like a scorched-earth campaign against the `ORA-02449` error. Use with care.

```
DROP TABLE table_to_drop CASCADE CONSTRAINTS;
```

Adding and Modifying Data

Now that you've created some tables, you are ready to put data in them. Data is added to tables by way of the `insert` statement, existing data is changed by way of the `update` statement, and data is removed by way of the `delete` statement. The customer table created earlier for examples is used for discussing all these statements. Before these statements are discussed, sequences are introduced. Sequences solve a fundamental problem—that of creating unique keys for your tables. But before you read about any of these topics, you need to learn about Oracle transactions.

When you add and modify data, you use the `xsql:dml` action. This action isn't limited to only one SQL statement the way that the `xsql:select` action is. Even though our examples here use one statement only, you can combine as many statements as you like between the `begin` and `end` statements inside the `xsql:dml` element.

Transactions

A transaction is one or more SQL statements executing against the database. They are very important when you work with Data Manipulation Language (DML) statements because you often want all of the statements to succeed or fail as a group. A classic example is a banking transaction in which $100 is transferred from a savings to a checking account. This transaction really involves three steps:

1. Subtract $100 from savings.
2. Add $100 to checking.
3. Record the transaction in the transaction log.

If any of the preceding statements fail individually, you will have problems. If the customer doesn't have $100 in savings, you will hand him or her free money to put into their checking account. If a problem occurs in adding the money to checking, you will have an upset customer. If you can't log the transaction, you will have bookkeeping problems in the future.

Oracle addresses this problem with the `commit`, `rollback`, and `savepoint` statements. No data is saved permanently to the database until a `commit` is issued. The `commit` is the end of the transaction, and the first SQL statement issued—either in a session or after a `commit`—is the beginning of the session.

If you run into trouble halfway through a transaction, you can issue a `rollback` to tell Oracle to ignore all the statements that have been executed so far in the transaction. The database is rolled back to the state that it was in before the start of the transaction.

You can also specify a `savepoint`, which is an intermediate commit. At the time you issue a `savepoint`, no data is permanently written to the database; instead, you have a point to roll back to other than the beginning of the transaction. This can save time and horsepower, because you don't have to repeat all of the work that was done before you issue the `savepoint`, which is presumably okay.

Sequences

Earlier, you created a table with a primary key. The purpose of the primary key is to uniquely identify each row in your table. Each time you insert a new row, you need to create a new, unique key. You know that Oracle won't let you insert a nonunique key, but how do you generate a new key? Finding the last key used is one strategy, but what if multiple sessions are creating new keys at the same time?

Fortunately, there is an easy solution—a sequence. An Oracle sequence generates a sequence of numbers. The numbers are guaranteed to be unique. Each time a call is made, the next number in the sequence is returned. Here is a simple sequence:

```
create sequence my_seq;
```

To use the sequence to generate ids, you can use the dual table as follows:

```
<?xml version="1.0"?>
<page connection="demo" xmlns:xsql="urn:oracle-xsql">
<xsql:query>
```

```
    SELECT my_seq.nextval FROM dual
  </xsql:query>
  </page>
```

If you are interested in getting the last value that was selected—known as the current value—you can do that as follows:

```
SELECT my_seq.currval FROM dual
```

Each time you reload the page, you will get a new sequence number. By default, a sequence starts at 1, increments by 1, has no `max` value (other than 10^27), will never cycle back to where it started, will cache 20 numbers at a time, and does not guarantee that numbers will be generated in the order of the request. All these options can be tweaked, as listed in Table 8.18.

Table 8.18 Sequence Options

KEYWORD	DESCRIPTION	EXAMPLE
`INCREMENT BY`	Value to increment by between calls. Can be negative.	`create sequence my_seq increment by 2`
`START WITH`	The first sequence number to be generated. Defaults to `MINVALUE` for ascending sequences and `MAXVALUE` for descending sequences.	`create sequence my_seq start with 10`
`MAXVALUE`	The largest value possible for the sequence. Default is `10^27`.	`create sequence my_seq MAXVALUE 9999`
`MINVALUE`	The smallest value possible for the sequence. Default is `1`.	`create sequence my_seq MINVALUE 20`
`CYCLE`	The sequence will cycle when either `MINVALUE` or `MAXVALUE` is reached.	`create sequence my_seq CYCLE`
`CACHE`	Number of numbers that will be kept in cache. Unused numbers are lost when the database shuts down.	`Create sequence my_seq CACHE 100`
`ORDER`	The sequence will guarantee that numbers are returned in the order that requests were received.	`CREATE SEQUENCE my_seq ORDER`

Often, developers make the assumption that if they always use the sequence there will be no holes in their list of ids. For instance, if you always use the a sequence that increments by 1 for your order table and you have 1,000 orders, the numbers 1 to 1,000 will be your keys. There are several reasons why this may not be the case. First, if the database is shutdown any unused ids left in the cache are lost. Second, if a transaction has to be rolled back before completion and a call to your sequence is made, that particular id will be lost. Thus, you can be certain that all your ids are unique, but you can't be certain that they are all sequential.

Sequences can be altered with the `ALTER SEQUENCE` statement and the keywords documented above. Sequences can be dropped using the `DROP SEQUENCE` statement:

```
DROP SEQUENCE my_seq;
```

`Insert` Statements

The `insert` statement is one of the simplest statements in all of SQL. You specify the table, the columns you wish to insert, and the data. Here is an example where you insert a new customer order from XSQL:

```
<?xml version="1.0"?>
<page connection="momnpop" xmlns:xsql="urn:oracle-xsql">
<xsql:dml>
   BEGIN
     INSERT INTO customer (custid,lname,email)
      VALUES (my_seq.nextval,'SMITH','smith@ibiblio.org');
   commit;
   END;
</xsql:dml>
</page>
```

You specify the columns that you wish to insert, then the values. The one additional feature to cover for now is the use of subqueries. Imagine that you wish to insert all the data generated by a particular `select` statement. You could select the data, store it somewhere, and insert each row one at a time. Luckily, SQL makes it far easier than that. You can embed the `select` statement directly into your `insert` statement. Here's how:

```
INSERT INTO emp (SELECT * FROM scott.emp);
```

The only other SQL options beyond this involve partitions and subpartitions. You can explicitly specify the partition or subpartition of your table into which you wish to insert the data. Except for a couple of PL/SQL specific options that you will see later in the book, that is it.

NOTE **In your travels, you may have seen an `Insert` statement without the columns specified. This only works when you are inserting a value into every column of the table. In general, this is a bad idea. It is hard to tell which values match up with which columns from just looking at the SQL, and if columns are ever added or dropped, your SQL statement won't work any more.**

If there are constraints on your table, it's possible to write an `insert` statement that will generate an error. Our customer table, for instance, requires a unique, nonnull key for `custid`. If you don't insert a `custid` value, you'll get an error message like this one:

```
ORA-01400: cannot insert NULL into ("MOMNPOP"."CUSTOMER"."CUSTID") ORA-
06512: at line 2
```

Generally, you should be able to structure your `insert` statements to avoid errors. However, errors are always a possibility, if for no other reason than the database being full. In Chapter 14, you'll learn how to build your applications around the need to handle errors like this.

`Update` Statements

`Update` statements are a little trickier than `insert` statements. As with `insert` statements, you can use a subquery to specify the value you wish to insert. More important, you almost always use a `where` clause to specify the rows you wish to update.

The following `update` statement will win you a lot of fans, because it gives all the employees a 10 percent raise:

```
UPDATE emp SET sal=sal*1.1;
```

If you want only to give the clerks a raise, you can do so as follows:

```
UPDATE emp SET sal=sal*1.1 WHERE job='CLERK';
```

If you want to set the value of the column based on an SQL statement, you can do so as follows. (This gives everyone in `emp4` the same salary as Adams in `emp`.)

```
UPDATE emp4 SET sal=(SELECT sal FROM emp WHERE ename='ADAMS');
```

Often, an `update` statement follows a `select` statement on the same table. You base your update on the data retrieved from the `select` statement. But what if someone else changes the data in the table between the time that you select it and the time that you update it? To remedy this problem, you can append `FOR UPDATE` to your `select` statements, thereby locking the rows in the table returned by the `select` statement.

`Delete` and `Truncate` Statements

Deleting is always dangerous, and SQL is no exception. SQL gives you two flavors—dangerous and really dangerous. The merely dangerous way uses the `delete` statement. Here's an example that gets rid of all of the clerks from the `emp` table:

```
DELETE FROM emp WHERE job='CLERK';
```

Subqueries can also be used as `targets`:

```
DELETE FROM (SELECT * FROM emp WHERE sal>500) WHERE job='CLERK';
```

The real danger in the `delete` statement is getting the `where` clause wrong or accidentally forgetting it. The following `delete` statement gets rid of all the rows in your table:

```
DELETE FROM emp;
```

Oracle also gives you the `truncate` statement to get rid of all the data in your table. The `truncate` statement deletes all the data quickly—there is no way to roll back a `truncate`. Only use when you know that you want all the data gone and when time is of the essence:

```
TRUNCATE emp;
```

The following version automatically deallocates all storage associated with the table:

```
TRUNCATE emp DROP STORAGE;
```

Views

In the "Select Statement" section, you joined the `emp` and the `dept` tables many times. If you find yourself using the same join over and over again, you might want to create a view. A view is defined by an SQL statement and acts just like a table. When you issue a `select` statement on the view, it will essentially translate the view by using the SQL for which the view was defined and then return the results. When you insert or update the view, it will insert or update the underlying tables.

Creating and Altering Views

Creating a view is almost as simple as writing a `select` statement. Here is an example where you create a view that pulls the employee name and department name together:

```
CREATE VIEW emp_dept_name
    AS
```

```
SELECT ename,dname
  FROM emp,dept
  WHERE emp.deptno=dept.deptno;
```

This view has two columns, ename and dname. The options for altering a view are exactly the same as those for creating one. Usually, views are created as follows. If you want to modify a view, you have to specify CREATE OR REPLACE; REPLACE isn't a keyword by itself.

```
CREATE OR REPLACE VIEW emp_dept_name
    AS
   SELECT ename,dname
     FROM emp,dept
     WHERE emp.deptno=dept.deptno;
```

There are other keywords, detailed in Table 8.19, that you can use when creating views. All are pretty straightforward, with the possible exception of WITH CHECK OPTION. Examples are provided in the "Using Views" section.

Table 8.19 View Creation Keywords

KEYWORD	DESCRIPTION	EXAMPLE
FORCE	Forces the creation of the view even if the base tables don't exist.	CREATE OR REPLACE FORCE VIEW emp_dept_name AS SELECT ename,dname FROM emp,dept WHERE emp.deptno=dept.deptno;
WITH CHECK OPTION	Data being inserted or updated must meet the criteria set forth in the where clause of the view definition. This means that data won't be permitted that wouldn't be returned by the select statement defining the view.	CREATE OR REPLACE FORCE VIEW emp_dept_name AS SELECT ename,dname FROM emp,dept WHERE emp.deptno=dept.deptno WITH CHECK OPTION;
CONSTRAINT	Provides an explicit name for the constraint that is created automatically when CHECK OPTION is used.	CREATE OR REPLACE FORCE VIEW emp_dept_name AS SELECT ename,dname FROM emp,dept WHERE emp.deptno=dept.deptno WITH CHECK OPTION CONSTRAINT emp_dept_name_constraint;

If the underlying tables change, you should recompile your view. You do that as follows:

```
ALTER VIEW emp_dept_name COMPILE;
```

To get rid of a view altogether, just drop it:

```
DROP VIEW emp_dept_name;
```

Using Views

The whole point of views is that they resemble tables, so using them isn't hard at all. Here's how you select data from the `emp_dept_name` view:

```
SELECT * FROM emp_dept_name
```

Inserts also work the same, but with a caveat: If the underlying tables have constraints that can't be satisfied by the view, then the insert will fail. The `emp_dept_name` view is an example of this. The `emp` and the `dept` tables have primary key and not null constraints. The pertinent columns aren't part of this view, so any attempt to insert into this view will fail.

Updates have a somewhat similar problem with views. For example, define a view as follows:

```
CREATE OR REPLACE VIEW emp_view
    AS
   SELECT * FROM emp WHERE sal>1300;
```

You won't get any updates with a query like the following, because there are no rows with a `sal` of less than 1,000 in the database:

```
UPDATE emp_view SET sal=sal*1.1 WHERE sal<1000;
```

However, you are able to remove rows from the view by making changes so that the rows won't be selected by the view's select statement. After running this statement, you won't have any rows in your view.

```
UPDATE emp_view SET sal=1000;
```

You may want to prevent such modifications. To do so, use the `WITH CHECK OPTION` keyword as follows:

```
CREATE OR REPLACE VIEW emp_view
    AS
   SELECT * FROM emp WHERE sal>1300
    WITH CHECK OPTION;
```

Constraints

At this point, you are ready to be a pretty productive SQL coder. You have learned how to read data out of the database, how to administer your objects, and how to manage the data in your objects. With just this knowledge, you could do lots of fine work with SQL. But before writing tons of SQL, it's important that you understand and use constraints. Their purpose is to keep you from shooting yourself in the foot. When you define constraints, you restrict the kind of data that can go into your database columns. This restriction makes it much easier for you to write applications, because it enables you to make assumptions about the data.

Types of Constraints

With any database, there are implicit expectations of the data. For instance, you expect that each employee has a unique id and that each belongs to a known department. Constraints give you a way of ensuring that the data is correct when it goes into the database. This keeps you and others from having to do a lot of error handling when the data is fetched. Table 8.20 lists the constraints in order from simplest to the most complex.

Multiple constraints are allowed, though it is redundant to define a not null or unique constraint where a primary key constraint has already been defined. If multiple check constraints are used, they must all evaluate to true for the data to be entered. If two check constraints contradict each other, no data will ever be input into your table.

Table 8.20 Types of Constraints

CONSTRAINT	DESCRIPTION
`NOT NULL`	A column isn't allowed to have NULL values.
`UNIQUE`	All nonnull values in the column (or columns) must be unique.
`PRIMARY KEY`	A column (or columns) must be both unique and nonnull. Only one primary key is allowed per table.
`CHECK`	A Boolean expression is used to determine if the row that is to be input should be allowed.
`FOREIGN KEY`	An input value must also be a value of another column in another table.
`PL/SQL triggers`	PL/SQL triggers are subprograms that give you procedural control over the values that are to be input into a table.

The unique and primary key constraints allow you to define uniqueness based on more than one column. For instance, you can store the area code in one column and the local phone number in another. You can then use a composite unique constraint to ensure that the same phone number isn't entered twice while still able to easily query based on the area code.

A foreign key constraint is used to enforce *referential integrity*. Referential integrity means that the relationship of data between tables has integrity. Generally, referential integrity is expected to exist between columns used frequently in joins. A foreign key constraint is enforced between the `dept` and `emp` tables that you have seen in the examples. You can't enter just any `deptno` into the `emp` table; it must be a `deptno` that appears in the `dept` table. Also, you can't delete a row in the `dept` table if the `deptno` is in use by rows in the `emp` table.

In referential integrity terms, the `dept` table is the parent table and the `emp` table is the child table. A foreign key constraint is defined on a column of the child table (e.g., `emp.deptno`) and points to a column of the parent table (e.g., `dept.deptno`). The column on the child table is called the foreign key; the column on the parent table, the referenced key. Table 8.21 lists the foreign key restraints and shows how actions are constrained once a foreign key constraint is in place. Compound foreign key constraints are allowed where both the foreign key and the referenced key are composites of several columns.

Table 8.21 Foreign Key Constraints

ACTION	ALLOWED WHEN . . .
Selects	Always allowed.
Inserts into parent table	Always allowed.
Inserts into child table	Only if the foreign key matches the referenced key in the parent table or if the values for one or more of the foreign key composite parts are null.
Updates on parent table	Not allowed if referenced key in the parent table is changed and the original value exists in the foreign key of the child table.
Updates on child table	Allowed only if the value in the referencing columns remains the same, is changed to a value that also exists in the referenced key, or is changed to null.
Deletes on the child table	Always allowed.
Deletes on the parent table	Allowed only if the value in the referenced key doesn't exist in any referencing key and an `on delete` clause isn't specified for the foreign key constraint. To force deletion of the parent row and all referencing children rows, you can use the cascade constraints option of delete.

As you can see from Table 8.21, nulls are allowed on either side of a foreign key constraint. Generally, though, a NOT NULL constraint is applied on the columns comprising both the foreign keys and the referenced keys. Also, the referenced key usually has a `unique` constraint, and it is typical for the primary key for a table to have one or more foreign key constraints referencing it.

Using Constraints

Although constraints are used by the database during DML operations, as a user you don't see them except when they occur in error messages. You implement constraints at the time you create tables or, possibly, by altering an existing table. It's better to implement constraints at the time that you create a table, because you can't apply a constraint to a table with data that already violates it.

You can create constraints in two ways: with names and without names. Creating constraints without names is a little simpler, but creating constraints with names can make the constraints easier to manage. The following example creates one of each type of constraint:

```
CREATE TABLE customer (
   custid    NUMBER(4) PRIMARY KEY,
   fname     VARCHAR2(30),
   lname     VARCHAR2(30) NOT NULL,
   age       NUMBER(3) CHECK (age>18),
   email     VARCHAR2(30) UNIQUE,
   address1   VARCHAR2(50),
   address2   VARCHAR2(50),
   state      VARCHAR(5),
   zip        VARCHAR(10),
   country    VARCHAR(5),
   salesrepid NUMBER(4) REFERENCES salesrep(repid)
);
```

To specify more than one constraint on a column, just enter more than one declaration. You don't have to use commas to separate the constraints. If you are going to create composite constraints, this type of declaration won't work. Instead, you would need to specify the constraint by using the constraint clause given in this example to create a composite primary key constraint. To name a constraint, you follow a column name with the keyword constraint, the name, and the constraint definition.

```
CREATE TABLE phone_bank (
  area_code NUMBER(3),
  local_number NUMBER(7),
  custid NUMBER(4) CONSTRAINT customer_fk REFERENCES customer(custid),
  CONSTRAINT composite_pk PRIMARY KEY (area_code,local_number))
  ;
```

As described earlier, foreign key constraints can affect the ability to delete rows in the parent table. You can use the `on delete` clause of the foreign key constraint to specify what should happen in the child table upon the occurrence of deletes in the parent table. Here is an example:

```
CREATE TABLE phone_bank (
  area_code NUMBER(3),
  local_number NUMBER(7),
  custid NUMBER(4) CONSTRAINT customer_fk REFERENCES customer(custid) ON
DELETE set null,
  CONSTRAINT composite_pk PRIMARY KEY (area_code,local_number))
  ;
```

In this case, a deletion of the parent customer will cause the `custid` to be set to null. Your other option for the `on delete` clause is cascade, which if a customer is deleted will cause all of that customer's phone numbers to be deleted in the `phone_bank` table.

If you need to remove a constraint, you would use the drop constraint statement:

```
ALTER TABLE phonebank
  DROP CONSTRAINT constraint_name;
```

If you created a named constraint, this should be pretty easy. If you didn't, you'll need to use the data dictionary to figure out the name that was created for the constraint. For primary and unique constraints, you can remove a constraint either with the word `primary` or based on the constraint's definition.

Date Formatting

Oracle stores dates in an internal format that isn't very useful to you. By default, dates are converted to a character representation that uses the default date format on the application that makes the SQL call. For example, the default date format for XSQL is different from the default date format for SQL*PLUS. However, if you explicitly specify a date format, you should make it be the same regardless of the client that is executing the SQL.

This section shows how date formatting works with SQL. Before it explores the specifics of date formatting, it discusses the differences between SQL*PLUS and XSQL.

XSQL Dates versus Oracle Dates

SQL*PLUS uses the default date format of the database, while XSQL uses the default date format of the JDBC driver. Thus, executing this statement from SQL*PLUS,

```
SELECT sysdate AS cur_date FROM dual
```

will probably result in a date like this one:

```
18.May-02
```

The following XSQL, which uses the same SQL query, returns a different result.

```
<?xml version="1.0"?>
<page connection="demo" xmlns:xsql="urn:oracle-xsql">
<xsql:query>
   SELECT sysdate AS "Date" FROM dual
</xsql:query>
</page>
```

The result is shown in Figure 8.7.

If you specify your own date using the `to_char` function, then you'll get the same date returned in both XSQL and SQL*PLUS. Here is an example:

```
SELECT to_char(sysdate,'YYYY-MM-DD HH24:MI:SS') AS date_str FROM dual
```

In this statement, the date data type is translated to a string explicitly using a date-format mask. Since the SQL client is given a string, instead of a date, it presents the string exactly as you described.

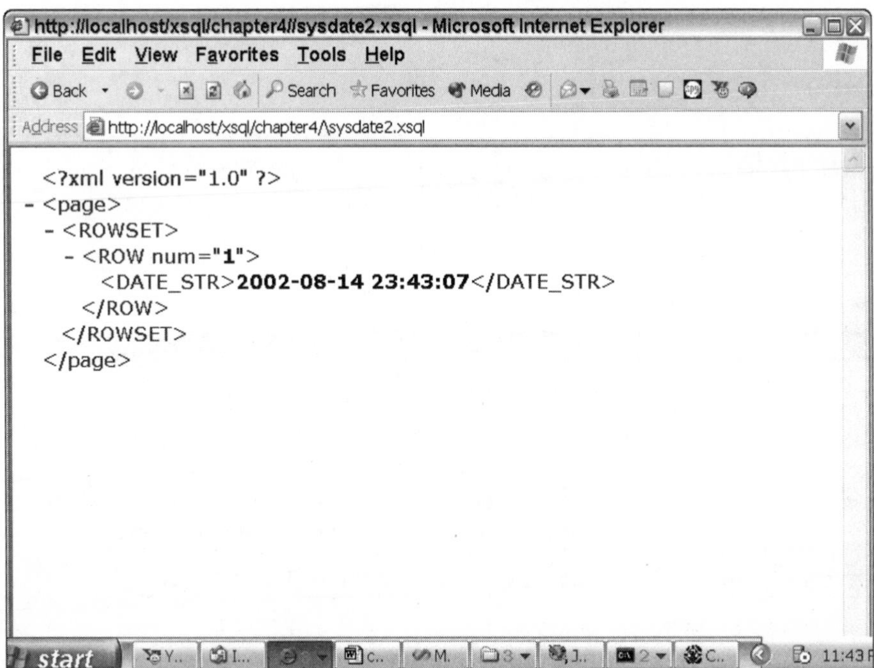

Figure 8.7 Sysdate with XSQL.

Table 8.22 Date-Format Examples

SQL	RESULT
`SELECT to_char(current_timestamp, 'YYYY-MM-DD HH24:MI:SS.FF') AS date_str FROM dual`	2002-05-19 01:01:07.000001
`SELECT to_char (sysdate,'"year": YYYY') AS date_str FROM dual`	year: 2002
`SELECT to_char (sysdate,'DAY, MONTH DD, YYYY AD') AS date_str FROM dual`	SUNDAY, MAY 19, 2002 AD

NOTE **You can change the default date format by editing the `init.ora` file or by using the ALTER SESSION statement to change it for a particular SQL session. Altering the session is generally impractical for XSQL and can't be done from the xsql:query action. If you change the date format in the `init.ora` file, then the default date format will be changed for everyone on your database. This may be ill-advised if your database has other applications.**

Date-Format Elements

An SQL date format mask is made up of elements that are replaced by the appropriate value from the date in the output. Table 8.22 lists some examples of date formats. Table 8.23 lists all the elements that you can use in date formats.

Table 8.23 Date-Format Elements

ELEMENT	DESCRIPTION
`-/,.;:`	These punctuation marks can appear anywhere in the format mask. They will be included verbatim in the output.
`"text"`	Quoted text can be included anywhere in the format mask. It will be included verbatim in the output.
AD, A.D., BC, or B.C.	Outputs if the date is A.D. or B.C.
AM, A.M., PM, or P.M.	Outputs if the time is A.M. or P.M.
CC	Century number.
SCC	Century number with B.C. dates represented by a negative number.

Table 8.23 *(Continued)*

ELEMENT	DESCRIPTION
D	Numerical day of the week. Sunday is 1 and Saturday is 7.
DAY	Full name of the day (e.g., Sunday).
DD	Day of the month.
DDD	Day of the year.
DY	Abbreviated day (e.g., Sun).
E	Abbreviated era name (only valid for Japanese Imperial, Republic of China Official, and Thai Buddha calendars).
EE	Full era name (only valid for Japanese Imperial, Republic of China Official, and Thai Buddha calendars).
FF	Fractional seconds.
HH, HH12	Hour of the day on a 12-hour clock.
HH24	Hour of the day on a 24-hour clock.
IW	Week of the year.
I	One-digit year.
IY	Two-digit year.
IYY	Three-digit year.
IYYY	Four-digit year.
J	Julian day or days since the last day of the year 4713 B.C. Day is January 1, 4712 B.C.
MI	Minute.
MM	Month number. 1 is January and 12 is December.
MON	Three-letter month abbreviation.
MONTH	Full month name (e.g., January)
Q	Quarter of the year (e.g., quarter 1 is January to March).
RM	Month number is given in Roman numerals.
RR	Last two digits of the year, when used with TO_CHAR.
RRRR	Last four digits of the year, when used with TO_CHAR.
SS	TSecond.

(continues)

Table 8.23 Date-Format Elements *(Continued)*

ELEMENT	DESCRIPTION
SSSSS	Seconds since midnight.
TZD	Daylight saving time information.
TZH	Timezone hour.
TZM	Timezone minute.
TZR	Timezone region information.
WW	Week of the year.
W	Week of the month, with week one starting on the first of the month.
YEAR	Year spelled out in words.
SYEAR	Like YEAR, with a negative sign in front if it is a B.C. year.
X	Local radix character.
Y	One-digit year.
YY	Two-digit year.
YYY	Three-digit year.
YYYY	Four-digit year.
SYYYY	Like YYYY, with a negative sign in front if it is a B.C. year.

SQL Functions

Oracle has a vast array of built-in functions that you can use in your SQL statements. You've already seen examples of some of the functions, such as `to_date` and `to_char`. Here, you'll see all the functions broken down by type. Covered first are aggregate functions. These functions, such as `max`, take a data set and aggregate it in to one value. The numeric functions allow you to do math in your SQL; the character functions, to manipulate and get information on strings; the date functions, to provide operations on dates. There is also a set of conversion functions, as well as—inevitably—the miscellaneous functions.

WARNING **As discussed previously, the default element name for functions will usually be an illegal XSQL name. When using with select statements, you must alias your function names to legal XML element names or XSQL will choke on your query.**

These functions are Oracle expressions and can be used anywhere an Oracle expression can be used. For instance, you can use them in the elements clause or the where clause of a select statement or in the values clauses of insert and update statements.

Using Aggregate Functions

Aggregate functions summarize data. However, since they return only one value, they aren't strictly compatible with other elements in a `select` statement. The lack of compatibility has a couple of implications. The first implication is solved by the `GROUP BY` and `HAVING` clauses, which allow you to group the elements before you apply aggregate functions. Aggregate functions also allow you to use the `DISTINCT` keyword. From this keyword, you can access the actual functions themselves. Before beginning, it's good to know how the aggregate functions deal with NULL values. NULL values are ignored.

GROUP BY Clauses

`Group by` clauses make your aggregate functions more valuable. With a single statement, you can get separate aggregates across your data. To get a breakdown of job-based salary, you would use the `GROUP BY` function as follows:

```
SELECT job,max(sal) AS max_sal FROM emp GROUP BY job
```

Table 8.24 lists the resulting output.

You can use `GROUP BY` in conjunction with joins and have multiple `group by` expressions, as follows:

```
SELECT job,dname,max(sal) AS max_sal
    FROM emp,dept
    WHERE emp.deptno=dept.deptno
    GROUP BY job,dname
```

Table 8.25 lists the results.

Table 8.24 `Group By` Job

JOB	max_sal
ANALYST	3000
CLERK	1300
MANAGER	2975
PRESIDENT	5000
SALESMAN	1600

Table 8.25 Group By Job and Department Name

JOB	DEPARTMENT NAME	max_sal
ANALYST	RESEARCH	3000
CLERK	ACCOUNTING	1300
CLERK	RESEARCH	1100
CLERK	SALES	950
MANAGER	ACCOUNTING	2450
MANAGER	RESEARCH	2975
MANAGER	SALES	2850
PRESIDENT	ACCOUNTING	5000
SALESMAN	SALES	1600

The GROUP BY clause can be used in conjunction with the HAVING clause to restrict the end output. It works a lot like the where clause, except that it works to exclude the rows based on the value of the aggregate. Here's an example in which you get only the job and department name pairs where the max_sal is greater than 2,500:

```
SELECT job,dname,max(sal)
    FROM emp,dept
    WHERE emp.deptno=dept.deptno
    GROUP BY job,dname
     HAVING max(sal)>2500
```

Aggregate Functions and DISTINCT Keyword

Earlier, you learned that the DISTINCT keyword returns only the distinct values for a column. What if you want an aggregate function to work only on distinct values? You can do that by simply specifying DISTINCT when calling the function. Here is an example that gives you the count of distinct jobs in the emp table:

```
SELECT count(distinct job) AS distinct_job,
       count(job) AS job
   FROM emp
```

Table 8.26 lists the results.

Table 8.26 Distinct Values and Aggregates

Distinct_job	JOB
5	14

Avg

The AVG function averages all the values in its domain of rows. If a GROUP BY clause is used, the function will be performed once for each value or unique sets of values specified by the GROUP BY clause. AVG works on numeric values only.

The following are some examples of the AVG function.

```
SELECT avg(sal) AS avg_sal FROM emp
```

```
SELECT DISTINCT avg(DISTINCT sal) AS avg_distinct_sal FROM emp
```

Table 8.27 lists the results.

Table 8.27 avg(sal) and avg(distinct sal) **Results**

avg_sal	avg_distinct_sal
2073.21429	2064.58333

```
SELECT job, avg(sal) AS avg_sal
   FROM emp
   GROUP BY job
```

Table 8.28 lists the results.

Table 8.28 **Grouped** All **and** Distinct **Results**

JOB	AVG_SAL
ANALYST	3000
CLERK	1037.5
MANAGER	2758.33333
PRESIDENT	5000
SALESMAN	1400

```
UPDATE dummy_emp
     SET sal=(SELECT avg(sal)
               FROM emp)
     WHERE dummy_emp.ename='ADAMS';
```

Count

The count function counts all the specified values in its domain of rows. If a GROUP BY clause is used, the function will be performed once for each value or unique sets of values specified by the GROUP BY clause. Count works on any data type.

The following are some examples and their results.

```
SELECT count(ename) AS count_ename FROM emp
```

Table 8.29 lists the results.

Table 8.29 COUNT(ename) **Results**

count_ename
14

```
SELECT deptno, count(DISTINCT job) AS count_job
   FROM emp
   GROUP BY deptno
```

Table 8.30 lists the results.

Table 8.30 Grouped Results

DEPTNO	count_job
10	3
20	3
30	3

Max

The max function averages all the values in its domain of rows. If a GROUP BY clause is used, the function will be performed once for each value or unique sets of values specified by the GROUP BY clause. Max works on numeric values only.

The following are some examples.

```
SELECT max(sal) AS max_sal FROM emp
```

Table 8.31 lists the results.

Table 8.31 `max(sal)` **Results**

max_sal
5000

```
SELECT job, max(sal) AS max_sal
   FROM emp
   GROUP BY job
```

Table 8.32 lists the results.

Table 8.32 Grouped `All` and `Distinct` Results

JOB	AVG_SAL
ANALYST	3000
CLERK	1300
MANAGER	2975
PRESIDENT	5000
SALESMAN	1600

```
UPDATE dummy_emp
    SET sal=(SELECT max(sal)
              FROM emp)
    WHERE dummy_emp.ename='ADAMS';
```

Min

The `min` function averages all the values in its domain of rows. If a `GROUP BY` clause is used, the function will be performed once for each value or unique sets of values specified by the `GROUP BY` clause. `Min` works on numeric values only.

The following are some examples and their results.

```
SELECT min(sal) AS min_sal FROM emp
```

Table 8.33 lists the results.

Table 8.33 `min(sal)` **Results**

min_sal
800

```
SELECT job, max(sal) AS max_sal
   FROM emp
   GROUP BY job
```

Table 8.34 lists the results.

Table 8.34 Grouped `All` and `Distinct` Results

JOB	AVG_SAL
ANALYST	3000
CLERK	800
MANAGER	2450
PRESIDENT	5000
SALESMAN	1250

```
UPDATE dummy_emp
    SET sal=(SELECT min(sal)
              FROM emp)
    WHERE dummy_emp.ename='ADAMS';
```

Stddev

The `stddev` function averages all the values in its domain of rows. If a `GROUP BY` clause is used, the function will be performed once for each value or unique sets of values specified by the `GROUP BY` clause. `Stddev` works on numeric values only.

The following are some examples.

```
SELECT stddev(sal) AS stddev_sal FROM emp
```

Table 8.35 lists the results.

Table 8.35 `stddev(sal)` **Results**

stddev_sal
1182.50322

```
SELECT stddev(DISTINCT sal) AS stddev_sal FROM emp
```

Table 8.36 lists the results.

Table 8.36 `max(sal)` **Results**

stddev_sal
1229.95096

```
SELECT job, stddev(sal) AS stddev_sal
   FROM emp
   GROUP BY job
```

Table 8.37 lists the results.

Table 8.37 **Grouped** `All` **and** `Distinct` **Results**

JOB	AVG_SAL
ANALYST	0
CLERK	213.600094
MANAGER	274.241378
PRESIDENT	0
SALESMAN	177.951304

```
UPDATE dummy_emp
    SET sal=(SELECT stddev(sal)
              FROM emp)
    WHERE dummy_emp.ename='ADAMS';
```

Sum

The sum function averages all the values in its domain of rows. If a GROUP BY clause is used, the function will be performed once for each value or unique sets of values specified by the GROUP BY clause. Sum works on numeric values only.

The following are some examples.

```
SELECT sum(sal) AS stddev_sal FROM emp
```

Table 8.38 lists the results.

Table 8.38 sum(sal) Results

sum_sal
29025

```
SELECT stddev(DISTINCT sal) AS stddev_sal FROM emp
```

Table 8.39 lists the results.

Table 8.39 Distinct sum(sal) Results

stddev_sal
24775

```
SELECT job, sum(sal) AS sum_sal
   FROM emp
   GROUP BY job
```

Table 8.40 lists the results.

Table 8.40 Grouped All and Distinct Results

JOB	SUM_SAL
ANALYST	6000
CLERK	4150
MANAGER	8275

Table 8.40 Grouped `All` and `Distinct` Results *(Continued)*

JOB	SUM_SAL
PRESIDENT	5000
SALESMAN	560

```
UPDATE dummy_emp
    SET sal=(SELECT sum(sal)
             FROM emp)
    WHERE dummy_emp.ename='ADAMS';
```

Variance

The `variance` function averages all the values in its domain of rows. If a `GROUP BY` clause is used, the function will be performed once for each value or unique sets of values specified by the `GROUP BY` clause. `Variance` works on numeric values only.

The following are some examples:

```
SELECT variance(sal) AS var_sal FROM emp
```

Table 8.41 lists the results.

Table 8.41 `variance(sal)` Results

var_sal
1398313.87

```
SELECT variance(DISTINCT sal) AS var_sal FROM emp
```

Table 8.42 lists the results.

Table 8.42 `Distinct variance(sal)` Results

var_sal
1512779.36

```
SELECT job, variance(sal) AS var_sal
   FROM emp
   GROUP BY job
```

Table 8.43 lists the results.

Table 8.43 Grouped `All` and `Distinct` Results

JOB	SUM_SAL
ANALYST	0
CLERK	45625
MANAGER	75208.3333
PRESIDENT	0
SALESMAN	31666.6667

```
UPDATE dummy_emp
    SET sal=(SELECT variance(sal)
              FROM emp)
    WHERE dummy_emp.ename='ADAMS';
```

General-Purpose Numeric Functions

The following text describes the various general-purpose numeric functions, which take numeric values and perform operations on them.

Abs

`Abs` returns the absolute value of a number. Returns are NULL if given a null value.

```
SELECT abs(10) AS positive,abs(-10) AS negative FROM dual
```

Table 8.44 lists the results.

Table 8.44 Results of `Abs`

positive	negative
10	10

Bin_to_num

Bin_to_num converts a bit vector to a number.

```
SELECT bin_to_num(1,1,1,1) AS fifteen,
       bin_to_num(1,0,0,1) AS nine,
       bin_to_num(0,1,0,1) AS five,
       bin_to_num(0,0,0,1) AS one
  FROM dual
```

Table 8.45 lists the results.

Table 8.45 Bin_to_num **Results**

FIFTEEN	NINE	FIVE	ONE
15	9	5	1

Ceil

Ceil returns the next greatest integer or, if the number is an integer, the integer itself.

```
SELECT ceil(1) AS integer_num,
       ceil(1.1) AS rational,
       ceil(-2.1) AS neg_rational
  FROM dual
```

Table 8.46 lists the results.

Table 8.46 **Results of** Ceil

integer_num	rational	neg_rational
1	2	-2

Floor

Floor returns the next lower integer or, if the number is an integer, the integer itself.

```
SELECT floor(1) AS integer_num,
       floor(2.1) AS rational,
       floor(-2.1) AS neg_rational
  FROM dual
```

Table 8.47 lists the results.

Table 8.47 Results of `Floor`

integer_num	rational	neg_rational
1	2	-3

Greatest

The `greatest` function returns the greatest number in its parameter list. Numbers and dates can be intermixed in the parameter list, but dates use the default date mask. It's best to convert dates to strings first with the `to_char` function.

```
SELECT greatest(deptno,21) FROM dept
```

Table 8.48 lists the results.

Table 8.48 `Greatest` Results

GREATEST_NUM
21
21
30
40

Least

The `least` function returns the least number in its parameter list. Numbers and dates can be intermixed in the parameter list, but dates use the default date mask. It's best to convert dates to strings first with the `to_char` function.

```
SELECT least(deptno,21) FROM dept
```

Table 8.49 lists the results.

Table 8.49 `Least` **Results**

LEAST_NUM
10
20
21
21

Mod

`Mod` returns the modulo of two numbers—the remainder after the first number is divided by the second.

```
SELECT mod(4,3) AS r_4_mod_3,
       mod(8,3) AS r_5_mod_3,
       mod(12,3) AS r_6_mod_3
    FROM dual
```

Table 8.50 lists the results.

Table 8.50 `Mod` **Results**

R_4_MOD_3	R_8_MOD_3	R_12_MOD_3
1	2	0

Power

`Power` returns the first number raised to the power of the second number.

```
SELECT power(10,2) AS r_10_power_2,
       power(10,-2) AS r_10_power_2_neg
    FROM dual
```

Table 8.51 lists the results.

Table 8.51 Power Results

R_10_POWER_2	R_10_POWER_2_NEG
100	.01

Round

Round will round the value to the specific number of decimal places. By default, the number is rounded to the closest integer. If a negative argument is given, the number will be rounded to a place to the left of the decimal place.

```
SELECT round(555.555) AS DEFAULT,
       round(555.555,2) AS TWO_PLACES,
       round(555.555,-2) AS NEG_TWO_PLACES
    FROM dual
```

Table 8.52 lists the results.

Table 8.52 Round Results

DEFAULT	TWO_PLACES	NEG_TWO_PLACES
556	555.56	600

Sign

Sign is used to determine whether the value is positive or negative. It returns 1, 0, or -1, depending on whether the number is positive, zero, or negative.

```
SELECT sign(60) AS positive,
       sign(0) AS zero,
       sign(-77.77) AS negative
    FROM dual
```

Table 8.53 lists the results.

Table 8.53 Sign Results

positive	zero	negative
1	0	-1

Sqrt

`Sqrt` provides the square root of a number. Negative numbers aren't allowed:

```
SELECT sqrt(100) AS square_root
    FROM dual
```

Table 8.54 lists the results.

Table 8.54 `Sqrt` Results

square_root
10

Trunc

`Trunc` truncates a number to the specified number of decimal places. If the number is negative, the truncation begins on the left side of the decimal point.

```
SELECT trunc(555.555) AS default,
       trunc(555.555,2) AS two_right,
       trunc(555.555,-2) AS two_left
   FROM dual
```

Table 8.55 lists the results.

Table 8.55 `Trunc` Results

DEFAULT	TWO_RIGHT	TWO_LEFT
555	555.55	500

Logarithmic and Trigonometric Functions

Table 8.56 lists the trigonometric functions that are available. All these examples return NULL if NULL is passed to them. All angles for the trigonometric functions are expressed in radians.

Table 8.56 Trigonometric Functions

FUNCTION	DESCRIPTION
`ACOS(x)`	Arc cosine
`ASIN(x)`	Arc sine
`ATAN(x)`	Arc tangent
`ATAN2(n,m)`	Arc tangent of n/m
`COS(x)`	Cosine of the angle
`COSH(x)`	Hyperbolic cosine of an angle
`SIN(x)`	Sine
`TAN(x)`	Tangent
`TANH(x)`	Hyperbolic tangent of the angle

Table 8.57 lists the logarithmic functions.

Table 8.57 `Logarithmic` Functions

FUNCTION	DESCRIPTION
`EXP(x)`	The value of the constant e raised to the power of x.
`LN(x)`	The natural logarithm of a x.
`LOG(m,n)`	The base m logarithm of the number n.

Character Functions

The following text describes the various character functions, which work with strings.

Ascii

The `ascii` function returns the numeric value of the first character of the parameter. The value returned is based on the character set of the database and is only an `ascii` value if a 7-bit `ascii` value is in use.

```
SELECT ascii('a') AS lower_a,
       ascii('A') AS upper_a,
       ascii('z') AS lower_z,
```

```
      ascii('Z') AS upper_z,
      ascii('0') AS zero,
      ascii('9') AS nine
   FROM DUAL
```

Table 8.58 lists the results.

Table 8.58 `ASCII` **Results**

LOWER_A	UPPER_A	LOWER_Z	UPPER_Z	ZERO	NINE
97	65	122	90	48	57

Bitand

The `bitand` function performs a bitwise 'and' between the two arguments. The operation examines the numbers in binary form and sets the 1 bit in the output only if both numbers have a 1 bit in that particular position. Table 8.59 shows how the `bitand` function computes the values seen in SQL.

Table 8.59 `Bitand` **Computations**

1 **AND** 3	127 **AND** 128	16 **AND** 63
1=01	127=01111111	16=10000
3=11	128=10000000	63=111111
1 bitand 3 = 01=1	127 bitand 128=0	16 bitand 63=10000=16

```
SELECT bitand (1,3) AS num_1_3,
       bitand(127,128) AS num_127_128,
       bitand(16,63) AS num_16_63,
    FROM dual
```

Table 8.60 lists the results.

Table 8.60 `Bitand` **Results**

NUM_1_3	NUM_127_128	NUM_16_63
1	0	16

Chr

The chr function returns the character associated with the number in the database's character set. If USING NCHAR_CS is specified, it would use the database's national character set.

```
SELECT chr(65) SIXTY_FIVE ,
       chr(65 USING NCHAR_CS) SIXTY_FIVE_NATIONAL
   FROM DUAL
```

Table 8.61 lists the results.

Table 8.61 Chr Results

SIXTY_FIVE	SIXTY_FIVE_NATIONAL
A	A

Concat

The concat function is equivalent to the || operator. It merges two strings.

```
SELECT concat(job,concat('-',ename)) AS concat_str
   FROM emp
   WHERE deptno=10
```

Table 8.62 lists the results.

Table 8.62 Concat Results

CONCAT_STR
MANAGER-CLARK
PRESIDENT-KING
CLERK-MILLER

Greatest

The greatest function returns the alphanumerically greatest string in its parameter list. Numbers and dates can be intermixed in the parameter list, but dates use the default date mask. It's best to convert dates to strings first with the to_char function.

```
SELECT greatest('MAZE1',ename,job,dname,'MAZE2') AS greatest_str
   FROM emp,dept
   WHERE emp.deptno=dept.deptno
     AND emp.deptno=10
```

Table 8.63 lists the results.

Table 8.63 `Greatest` Result

GREATEST_STR
MAZE2
PRESIDENT
MILLER

Initcap

The `initcap` function capitalizes the first letter and lowercases all other letters.

```
SELECT INITCAP('mIXeD CaSE') AS initcap_str FROM DUAL
```

Table 8.64 lists the results.

Table 8.64 `Initcap` Results

INITCAP_STR
Mixed case

Instr

The `instr` function, which can be translated to mean "in string," searches the first string for the second string and returns the position. You can specify where to start searching in the string and which occurrence to find.

```
SELECT instr('tripper','rip') AS rip_pos,
       instr('tripper','trip') AS trip_pos,
       instr('tripper','per') AS rep_pos,
       instr('tripper','xxx') AS xxx_pos
  FROM dual
```

Table 8.65 lists the results.

Table 8.65 `Instr` Simple Results

RIP_POS	TRIP_POS	REP_POS	XXX_POS
2	1	5	0

```
SELECT instr('00-11-00-11-00-11','00',2) AS start_1,
       instr('00-11-00-11-00-11','00',2,2) AS start_2_get_2
   FROM dual
```

Table 8.66 lists the results.

Table 8.66 `Instr` **Position and Instance Results**

START_1	START_2_GET_2
7	13

Instrb

The `instrb` function provides the same functionality of `instr` but returns the byte position. This is advantageous when multibyte character sets are used. It searches the first string for the second string and returns the position. You can specify where to start searching in the string and which occurrence to find.

```
SELECT instr('tripper','rip') AS rip_pos,
       instr('tripper','trip') AS trip_pos,
       instr('tripper','per') AS rep_pos,
       instr('tripper','xxx') AS xxx_pos
   FROM dual
```

Table 8.67 lists the results.

Table 8.67 `Instr` **Simple Results**

RIP_POS	TRIP_POS	REP_POS	XXX_POS
2	1	5	0

```
SELECT instr('00-11-00-11-00-11','00',2) AS start_1,
       instr('00-11-00-11-00-11','00',2,2) AS start_2_get_2
   FROM dual
```

Table 8.68 lists the results.

Table 8.68 `Instr` **Position and Instance Results**

START_1	START_2_GET_2
7	13

Least

The `least` function returns the alphanumerically least string in its parameter list. Numbers and dates can be intermixed in the parameter list, but dates use the default date mask. It's best to convert dates to strings first with the `to_char` function.

```
SELECT least('DOH1',ename,job,'DOH2') AS least_str
   FROM emp,dept
   WHERE emp.deptno=dept.deptno
     AND emp.deptno=10
```

Table 8.69 lists the results.

Table 8.69 `Least` Results

LEAST_STR
CLARK
DOH1
CLERK

Length

The `length` function returns the number of characters in the string.

```
SELECT dname,length(dname) AS length FROM dept
```

Table 8.70 lists the results.

Table 8.70 `Length` Results

DNAME	LENGTH
ACCOUNTING	10
RESEARCH	8
SALES	5
OPERATIONS	10

Lengthb

The `lengthb` function returns the number of bytes in the string. This function is advantageous when multibyte character sets are used.

```
SELECT dname,length(dname) AS length FROM dept
```

Table 8.71 lists the results.

Table 8.71 `Length` **Results**

DNAME	LENGTH
ACCOUNTING	10
RESEARCH	8
SALES	5
OPERATIONS	10

Lower

The `lower` function changes all letters to lowercase.

```
SELECT lower('mIXeD CaSE') AS lower_str FROM DUAL
```

Table 8.72 lists the results.

Table 8.72 `Initcap` **Results**

INITCAP_STR
mixed case

Lpad

The `lpad` function guarantees the length of the string by prefixing characters or truncating. By default, spaces are the `pad` character, but this can be specified.

```
SELECT dname,
       lpad(dname,8) AS space_pad,
       lpad(dname,8,'-') AS dash_pad
   FROM dept
```

Table 8.73 lists the results.

Table 8.73 Lpad Results

DNAME	SPACE_PAD	DASH_PAD
ACCOUNTING	ACCOUNTI	ACCOUNTI
RESEARCH	RESEARCH	RESEARCH
SALES	SALES	SALES
OPERATIONS	OPERATIO	OPERATIO

Ltrim

The ltrim trims characters from the left side. By default, spaces are trimmed, but the strings to trim can be specified.

```
SELECT ltrim('   string') AS trim_str,
       ltrim('####string','#') AS single_char_trim,
       ltrim('/**string','*/') AS multi_char_trim
FROM dual
```

Table 8.74 lists the results.

Table 8.74 Ltrim Results

TRIM_STR	SINGLE_CHAR_TRIM	MULTI_CHAR_TRIM
string	string	string

Nls_initcap

The nls_initcap function capitalizes the first letter and lowercases all other letters, based on the national character set.

```
SELECT nls_initcap('mIXeD CaSE') AS initcap_str FROM DUAL
```

Table 8.75 lists the results.

Table 8.75 Initcap Results

INITCAP_STR
Mixed case

Nls_lower

The `nls_lower` function changes all letters to lowercase, based on the national character set.

```
SELECT nls_lower('mIXeD CaSE') AS lower_str FROM DUAL
```

Table 8.76 lists the results.

Table 8.76 `Initcap` Results

INITCAP_STR
mixed case

Nls_upper

The `nls_upper` function changes all letters to lowercase.

```
SELECT nls_upper('mIXeD CaSE') AS upper_str FROM DUAL
```

Table 8.77 lists the results.

Table 8.77 `Upper` Results

UPPER_STR
MIXED CASE

Nls_sort

The `nls_sort` function returns the byte sequence used to sort a string.

Replace

The `replace` function replaces one substring with another in your string.

```
SELECT replace('good or bad','or','and') replace_str FROM dual
```

Table 8.78 lists the results.

Table 8.78 `Replace` **Results**

REPLACE_STR
good and bad

Rpad

The `rpad` function guarantees the length of the string by suffixing characters or truncating. By default, spaces are the `pad` character, but this character can be specified.

```
SELECT dname,
       rpad(dname,8) AS space_pad,
       rpad(dname,8,'-') AS dash_pad
   FROM dept
```

Table 8.79 lists the results.

Table 8.79 `Rpad` **Results**

DNAME	SPACE_PAD	DASH_PAD
ACCOUNTING	ACCOUNTI	ACCOUNTI
RESEARCH	RESEARCH	RESEARCH
SALES	SALES	SALES---
OPERATIONS	OPERATIO	OPERATIO

Rtrim

The `rtrim` function trims characters from the right side. By default, spaces are trimmed, but the characters to trim can be specified.

```
SELECT ltrim('string   ') AS trim_str,
       ltrim('string####','#') AS single_char_trim,
       ltrim('string**/','/*') AS multi_char_trim
FROM dual
```

Table 8.80 lists the results.

Table 8.80 `Ltrim` **Results**

TRIM_STR	SINGLE_CHAR_TRIM	MULTI_CHAR_TRIM
string	string	string

Soundex

`Soundex` is used to derive a phonetic pronunciation of the input string. It is used to help in cases where a string may not be spelled exactly right. The first letter is retained, all vowels *h* and *y* are dropped, and the remaining letters are encoded.

```
SELECT soundex(dname) AS soundex_dname FROM dept
```

Table 8.81 lists the result.

Table 8.81 `Soundex` **Results**

SOUNDEX_DNAME
A253
R262
S420
O163

Substr

The `substr` function returns a substring of the given string. The second parameter, if positive, is the character position where your desired substring starts. If negative, the position is an offset from the end of the string. By default, the string ends at the end of the string. If the third parameter is passed, it will specify the length of the string to extract.

```
SELECT substr(dname,4) AS dname_4,
       substr(dname,-4) AS dname_neg4,
       substr(dname,2,3) AS dname_2_3,
       substr(dname,-3,2) AS dname_neg3_2
FROM dept
```

Table 8.82 lists the results.

Table 8.82 `Substr` **Results**

DNAME_4	DNAME_NEG4		DNAME_2_3
OUNTING	TING	CCO	IN
EARCH	ARCH	ESE	RC
ES	ALES	ALE	LE
RATIONS	IONS	PER	ON

Substrb

The `substrb` function returns a substring of the given string where the parameters refer to a byte position. It differs from substr only when a multibyte character set is used. The second parameter, if positive, is the byte position where your desired substring starts. If negative, the position is an offset from the end of the string. By default, the string ends at the end of the string. If the third parameter is passed, it will specify the length of the string in bytes to extract.

```
SELECT substrb(dname,4) AS dname_4,
       substrb(dname,-4) AS dname_neg4,
       substrb(dname,2,3) AS dname_2_3,
       substrb(dname,-3,2) AS dname_neg3_2
FROM dept
```

Table 8.83 lists the results.

Table 8.83 `Substrb` **Results**

DNAME_4	DNAME_NEG4	DNAME_2_3	DNAME_NEG3_2
OUNTING	TING	CCO	IN
EARCH	ARCH	ESE	RC
ES	ALES	ALE	LE
RATIONS	IONS	PER	ON

Translate

The `translate` function changes one set of characters to another in the given string.

```
SELECT translate(dname,'AEIOU','12345') AS trans_str

   FROM dept
```

Table 8.84 lists the results.

Table 8.84 `Translate` **Results**

TRANS_STR
1CC45NT3NG
R2S21RCH
S1L2S
4P2R1T34NS

Trim

The `trim`function trims characters from the left side. By default, spaces are trimmed, but the strings to trim can be specified.

```
SELECT trim('   string   ') AS space_trim,
       trim('*' FROM '****string****') AS trim_char
       trim(LEADING '*' FROM '****string****') AS lead_trim,
       trim(TRAILING '*' FROM '****string****') AS trail_trim
FROM dual
```

Table 8.85 lists the results.

Table 8.85 `Ltrim` **Results**

SPACE_TRIM	LEAD_TRIM	TRAIL_TRIM	TRIM_CHAR
string	string	string****	****string

Upper

The `upper` function changes all letters to lowercase.

```
SELECT upper('mIXeD CaSE') AS upper_str FROM DUAL
```

Table 8.86 lists the results.

Table 8.86 `Upper` Results

UPPER_STR
MIXED CASE

Date Functions

Date functions allow you to manipulate dates in SQL. They are some of the most widely used functions in SQL. With these functions you can get the current time, do arithmetic on dates, and convert between time zones. The date formats used in this section were covered in the "Date Format Elements" section.

Add_months

The `add_months` function adds months to a particular date. The date is kept unless it is too large for the new month. In that case, the last date of the last month is used instead.

```
SELECT
   to_date('01-31','MM-DD') AS jan_str,
   add_months(to_date('01-31','MM-DD'),1) AS feb_str,
   add_months(to_date('01-31','MM-DD'),2) AS mar_str,
   add_months(to_date('01-31','MM-DD'),3) AS apr_str
  FROM dual
```

Table 8.87 lists the results.

Table 8.87 `Add_months` Results

JAN_STR	FEB_STR	MAR_STR	APR_STR
31-JAN-02	28-FEB-02	31-MAR-02	30-APR-02

Current_timestamp

The `current_timestamp` function returns the current timestamp from the table with a `TIMESTAMP WITH A TIMEZONE` data type.

```
SELECT to_char(current_timestamp,'YYYY-MM-DD HH24:MM:SS.FF') AS date_str

   FROM dual
```

Table 8.88 lists the results.

Table 8.88 `Sysdate` Results

DATE_STR
2002-05-19 01:05:00.000001

Dbtimezone

The `dbtimezone` function returns the timezone of the database:

```
SELECT dbtimezone AS tz FROM dual
```

Table 8.89 lists the results.

Table 8.89 `Dbtimezone` Results

TZ
-5:00

Extract

The `extract` function extracts the specified part (year, month, day, hour, minute, second, `timezone_hour`, `timezone_minute`, `timezone_region`, and `timezone_abbr`) from the date.

```
SELECT hiredate, extract(YEAR FROM hiredate) AS year
FROM emp
WHERE deptno=10
```

Table 8.90 lists the results.

Table 8.90 `Extract` Results

HIREDATE	YEAR
09-JUN-81	1981
17-NOV-81	1981
23-JAN-82	1982

Greatest

The `greatest` function returns the greatest number in its parameter list. Numbers and dates can be intermixed in the parameter list, but dates use the default date mask. It's best to convert dates to strings first with the `to_char` function.

```
SELECT
  greatest(hiredate,to_date('16-NOV-1981','DD-MON-YYYY')) AS
greatest_date
  FROM emp WHERE deptno=10;
```

Table 8.91 lists the results.

Table 8.91 `Greatest` Results

GREATEST_DATE
16-NOV-81
17-NOV-81
23-JAN-82

Last_day

The `last_day` function returns the last day of the month in which the specified date falls.

```
SELECT hiredate,last_day(hiredate) AS last
   FROM emp
   WHERE deptno=10
```

Table 8.92 lists the results.

Table 8.92 `Last_day` Results

HIREDATE	LAST
09-JUN-81	30-JUN-81
17-NOV-81	30-NOV-81
23-JAN-82	31-JAN-82

Least

The `greatest` function returns the least number in its parameter list. Numbers and dates can be intermixed in the parameter list, but dates use the default date mask. It's best to convert dates to strings first with the `to_char` function.

```
SELECT
  least(hiredate,to_date('16-NOV-1981','DD-MON-YYYY')) AS least_date
  FROM emp WHERE deptno=10;
```

Table 8.93 lists the results.

Table 8.93 `Least` Results

LEAST_DATE
09-JUN-81
16-NOV-81
16-NOV-81

Local_timestamp

The `local_timestamp` function returns the timestamp in the local timezone as a timestamp data type. This function is sometimes preferable to `current_timestamp`, because the latter returns the timestamp with the timezonedata type.

```
SELECT to_char(localtimestamp,'YYYY-MM-DD HH24:MI:SSXFF') AS time

  FROM dual
```

Table 8.94 lists the results.

Table 8.94 `Local_timestamp` Results

TIME
2002-05-19 01:34:21.000001

Months_between

The `months_between` function returns the number of months between two dates. Integers are only returned if both dates have the same day of the month or if both dates fall on the last day of their respective months. A negative number is returned if the first argument precedes the second argument. You can use the `abs` function to always get a positive number.

```
SELECT months_between(to_date('01-16','MM-DD'),to_date('08.16','MM-DD'))
        AS btwn_1,
       months_between(to_date('08.16','MM-DD'),to_date('01-16','MM-DD'))
        AS btwn_2,
       months_between(to_date('01-16','MM-DD'),to_date('08.31','MM-DD'))
        AS btwn_3,
       months_between(to_date('02-28','MM-DD'),to_date('08.31','MM-DD'))
        AS btwn_4
  FROM dual;
```

Table 8.95 lists the results.

Table 8.95 `Months_between` **Results**

BTWN_1	BTWN_2	BTWN_3	BTWN_4
-7	7	-7.483871	-6

New_time

The `new_time` function converts a time from one timezone to another.

```
SELECT to_char(
         new_time(to_date('08:00','HH24:MI'),'EST','GMT'),
         'HH24:MI') AS new_time_str
    FROM dual
```

Table 8.96 lists the results.

Table 8.96 `New_time` **Results**

NEW_TIME_STR
13:00

Next_day

The `next_day` function returns the date after a given date that falls on the given day of the week. If the given date falls on the given day of the week, the date one week hence is returned. This can be fixed by always subtracting 1 from the date.

```
SELECT ename,
       deptno,
       to_char(hiredate,'DY, MON-DD') AS hire_date,
       next_day(hiredate,'Fri') AS next_fri_1,
       next_day(hiredate-1,'Fri') AS next_fri_2
```

```
FROM emp
WHERE deptno=30
```

Table 8.97 lists the results.

Table 8.97 `Next_day` **Results**

	HIRE_DATE	NEXT_FRI_1	NEXT_FRI_2
ALLEN	FRI, FEB-20	27-FEB-81	20-FEB-81
WARD	SUN, FEB-22	27-FEB-81	27-FEB-81
MARTIN	MON, SEP-28	02-OCT-81	02-OCT-81
BLAKE	FRI, MAY-01	08-MAY-81	01-MAY-81
TURNER	TUE, SEP-08	11-SEP-81	11-SEP-81
JAMES	THU, DEC-03	04-DEC-81	04-DEC-81

Numtodsinterval

The `numtodsinterval` function converts the parameter to an interval day to second interval. The string argument specifies the unit and can be one of `SECOND`, `MINUTE`, `HOUR`, or `DAY`.

```
SELECT hiredate,
       hiredate+numtodsinterval(100,'day') AS days,
       hiredate+numtodsinterval(1000,'hour') AS hours,
       hiredate+numtodsinterval(10000,'minute') AS minutes,
       hiredate+numtodsinterval(100000,'second') AS seconds
FROM emp
WHERE deptno=10
```

Table 8.98 lists the results.

Table 8.98 `Numtodsinterval` **Results**

HIREDATE	DAYS	HOURS	MINUTES	SECONDS
09-JUN-81	17-SEP-81	20-JUL-81	15-JUN-81	10-JUN-81
17-NOV-81	25-FEB-82	28-DEC-81	23-NOV-81	18-NOV-81
23-JAN-82	03-MAY-82	5-MAR-82	29-JAN-82	24-JAN-82

Numtoyminterval

The numtoyminterval function converts the parameter and interval year to month interval. The string argument specifies the unit and can be either MONTH or YEAR.

```
SELECT hiredate,
       hiredate+numtoyminterval(1,'year') AS years,
       hiredate+numtoyminterval(10,'month') AS months
FROM emp
WHERE deptno=10
```

Table 8.99 lists the results.

Table 8.99 Numtoyminterval **Results**

HIREDATE	YEARS	MONTHS
09-JUN-81	09-JUN-82	09-APR-82
17-NOV-81	17-NOV-82	17-SEP-82
23-JAN-82	23-JAN-83	23-NOV-82

Round

The round function rounds a datetime value to the nearest unit specified by the format. By default, the date is rounded to the precision of the default format.

```
SELECT to_char(round(sysdate,'HH'),'YYYY-MM-DD HH24:MI') AS hour,
       to_char(round(sysdate,'MM'), 'YYYY-MM-DD HH24:MI') AS month,
       to_char(round(sysdate,'YYYY'), 'YYYY-MM-DD HH24:MI') AS year,
       to_char(round(sysdate,'CC'), 'YYYY-MM-DD HH24:MI') AS century
     FROM dual
```

Table 8.100 lists the results.

Table 8.100 Round **Results**

HOUR	MONTH	YEAR	CENTURY
2002-05-18 22:00	2002-06-01 00:00	2002-01-01 00:00	2001-01-01 00:00

Sessiontimezone

The sessiontimezone function returns the timezone setting for the current session.

```
SELECT sessiontimezone FROM dual
```

Table 8.101 lists the results.

Table 8.101 Sessiontimezone **Results**

SESSIONTIMEZONE
-04:00

Sys_extract_utc

The sys_extract_utc function extracts the universal coordinated time (UTC), also known as Greenwich mean time (GMT), from the timestamp.

```
SELECT sys_extract_utc(systimestamp) AS utc FROM dual
```

Table 8.102 lists the results.

Table 8.102 Sys_extract_utc **Results**

UTC
19-MAY-02 06.02.58.000001 AM

Sysdate

The sysdate function returns the system date from the dual table.

```
SELECT to_char(sysdate,'YYYY-MM-DD HH24:MM:SS') date_str

   FROM dual
```

Table 8.103 lists the results.

Table 8.103 Sysdate **Results**

DATE_STR
2002-05-19 01:05:46

Systimestamp

The `systimestamp` function returns the system date and time, including fractional seconds and timezone information.

```
SELECT systimestamp FROM dual
```

Table 8.104 lists the results.

Table 8.104 `Systimestamp` **Results**

SYSTIMESTAMP
19-MAY-02 02.07.45.000000 AM -04:00

Trunc

The `trunc` function works much like `round`, except that it truncates the date to the next lowest value. By default, the date is truncated to the precision of the default format.

```
SELECT to_char(trunc(sysdate,'HH'),'YYYY-MM-DD HH24:MI') AS hour,
       to_char(trunc(sysdate,'MM'), 'YYYY-MM-DD HH24:MI') AS month,
       to_char(trunc(sysdate,'YYYY'), 'YYYY-MM-DD HH24:MI') AS year,
       to_char(trunc(sysdate,'CC'), 'YYYY-MM-DD HH24:MI') AS century
     FROM dual
```

Table 8.105 lists the results.

Table 8.105 `Trunc` **Results**

HOUR	MONTH	YEAR	CENTURY
2002-05-18 22:00	2002-05-01 00:00	2002-01-01 00:00	2001-01-01 00:00

Conversion Functions

Conversion functions allow you to convert data between data types. You've already used the `to_date` and `to_char` functions extensively. Table 8.106 lists the simple conversion functions. The `to_char` function is examined as it pertains to numbers. (The `to_char` function, as it pertains to dates, and the `to_date` function are not discussed further here. For more information, read the "Date Formats" section in this chapter.) More complex conversion functions are also discussed.

Table 8.106 Simple Conversion Functions

FUNCTION	DESCRIPTION
`Asciistr`	Returns the ASCII string. Non-ASCII characters are converted to their Unicode (UTF-16) binary code value.
`Chartorowid`	Changes a string to a row id.
`Compose`	Returns a fully normalized Unicode string.
`Hextoraw`	Converts a hexadecimal number to a raw value.
`Rawtohex`	Converts a raw value to a hexadecimal number.
`Rowidtochar`	Converts a row id to a string.
`To_char`	Converts argument to a string.
`To_clob`	Converts argument to a `CLOB`.
`To_date`	Converts argument to a date.
`To_dsinterval`	Converts argument to a day-second interval.
`To_lob`	Converts argument to a `LOB`.
`To_multi_byte`	Converts a single character to a multibyte character.
`To_nchar`	Identical to `to_char`, except that it converts to the national character set.
`To_nclob`	Converts to the national character set.
`To_number`	Converts string to number. Generally not used, because Oracle automatically performs the conversion.
`To_singlebyte`	Converts a multibyte character to single byte if possible.
`To_yminterval`	Converts argument to a year-month interval.

When used with dates, the `to_char` function takes the same format as that described in the "Date Formatting" section. When the `to_char` function is passed a number, it must decide how to appropriately output the string. It does this by using a format mask similar to the date format mask you learned about earlier. The most important element is the number 9. It represents a significant digit, and the number of 9's represents the number of significant digits that you want displayed. Table 8.107 lists the number-format elements.

Table 8.107 Number-Format Elements

ELEMENT	DESCRIPTION
A significant digit	
A padding zero. Usually appears on the left.	
`$`	Places a dollar sign in the output.
`,`	Places a comma in the output.
`.`	Places a period in the output.
`B`	Zero values are displayed as blanks.
`MI`	Negative sign for negative values.
`S`	Forces the sign of the number to be displayed.
`PR`	Places negative values to be displayed in angle brackets.
`D`	TDecimal point.
`G`	Group separator.
`C`	The International Organization for Standardization (ISO) currency indicator.
`L`	Local currency indicator.
`V`	Scaled values.
`RN`	Displays value in Roman numerals.

Convert

The `convert` function converts one character set to another. If a character doesn't exist in the destination character set, a replacement character appears.

```
SELECT CONVERT('Ä Ê Í Õ Ø A B C D E ', 'US7ASCII', 'WE8ISO8859P1') AS convert_str

   FROM DUAL
```

Table 8.108 lists the results.

Table 8.108 `Convert` **Results**

CONVERT_STR
A E I ? ? A B C D E ?

Decompose

The `decompose` function returns a Unicode string after decomposition.

```
SELECT decompose('Châteaux') AS decompose_str FROM dual
```

Table 8.109 lists the results:

Table 8.109 `Decompose` **Results**

DECOMPOSE_STR
Châteaux

Translate

The `translate` function translates strings to either the database character set or the national character set.

```
SELECT translate('text' USING char_cs) AS str FROM dual
```

Table 8.110 lists the results.

Table 8.110 `Translate` **Results**

STR
text

Unistr

The `unistr` function returns a string in the database Unicode character set.

```
SELECT UNISTR('\00D6') AS str FROM dual
```

Table 8.111 lists the results.

Table 8.111 `Unistr` Results

STR
ö

Miscellaneous Functions

The remaining functions don't fit easily into the other categories. The most important functions to the XSQL developer are `decode`, which allows you to write conditional logic into your SQL functions, and `nvl`, which allows you to substitute a value when NULL is encountered.

Table 8.112 lists the functions.

Table 8.112 Miscelleneous Functions

NAME	DESCRIPTION
`Bfilename`	Returns a `bfilename` based on a specified directory.
`Coalesce`	Returns the first nonnull expression in list of arguments, which are expressions.
`Decode`	Compares an expression to any number of search values that are mated to results. The result is returned for the first search value to match. If none match, a default value will be returned.
`Dump`	Returns a dump of internal information for the given expression.
`Empty_blob`	Returns an empty `BLOB`.
`Empty_clob`	Returns an empty `CLOB`.
`Nls_charset_decl_len`	Returns the declaration width of an `NCHAR` column.
`Nls_charset_id`	Returns a character set id number for a character name.
`Nls_charset_name`	Returns a character set name for a character set id.
`Nullif`	Returns null if two expressions are equal, the first expression otherwise.
`Nvl`	If an argument is null, replace it with the given value.

(continues)

Table 8.112 Miscelleneous Functions *(Continued)*

NAME	DESCRIPTION
`Nvl2`	If the first expression isn't null, return the second. If the first expression is null, return the third.
`Sys_guid`	Returns a system global unique identifier.
`Uid`	Returns the user id of the user who logged on.
`User`	Returns the user name of the user who logged on.
`Vsize`	Returns the number of bytes in the internal representation of the given expression.

Moving On

In the previous chapters, you saw examples of some SQL in the code. This chapter helped to fill out your understanding and showed you the ins and outs of SQL. The next three chapters delve more deeply into the Oracle database technologies. The technologies described are by no means an inclusive representation of the entire Oracle database; rather, they are the technologies that you'll find most useful in conjunction with XSQL.

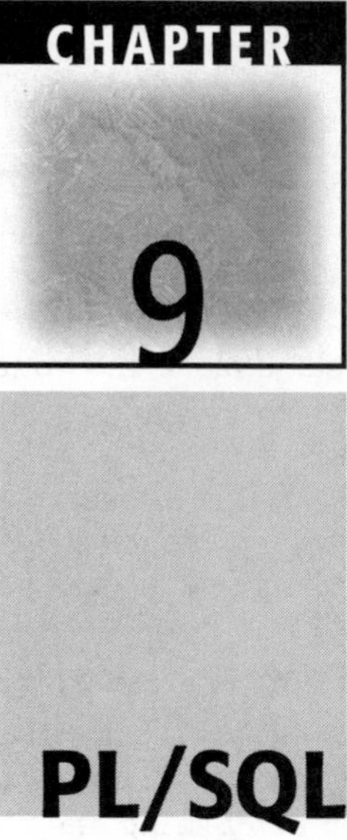

CHAPTER 9

PL/SQL

PL/SQL stands for the *procedural language extensions to SQL*. It gives you a new level of power when working with the database. Instead of being limited to the functions provided by SQL, you can write your own. You can also use all of the basics of procedural programming: loops, conditional statements, variables, and encapsulation.

The PL/SQL code that you will be creating here is stored in the database. Unlike code that executes at the client, server-side PL/SQL doesn't incur the costs of network roundtrips. Calls to PL/SQL can be integrated closely with SQL. Likewise, PL/SQL can be used from XSQL and can be a valuable tool for you as you develop your XSQL applications. This section outlines how to create PL/SQL code and the different options that are available.

Hello, PL/SQL!

Your first step is to create a simple PL/SQL function and execute it from an XSQL page. Your function will simply return the string "Hello, PL/SQL!" when called. As with all PL/SQL code, you should create it in its own file and then load the file using SQL*PLUS. By doing it this way, if you need to change the code later, it will be easy to do so.

TIP **If you get a message that you have received compilation errors, you can use the** `SHOW ERRORS` **command from SQL*PLUS to see what those errors are.**

For this example, you'll create a package. A package is a set of functions, parameters, and variables. The definition looks a bit like a class, but PL/SQL isn't an object-oriented language. Rather, the PL/SQL package is just an encapsulation mechanism. For this example, our package contains just one sub-routine. Your subroutines can be stand-alone, but your code will be better organized and more reusable if you always use packages.

```
CREATE OR REPLACE PACKAGE hello_pkg AS
   FUNCTION hello_plsql (param NUMBER) RETURN VARCHAR2;
END hello_pkg;
```

Your next step is to create the body of your package. This includes the actual code of your `hello_plsql`. As is befitting a first try, our code is simple. It takes the `param`, assumes that it is the empno for a row in the emp table, looks up the salary, and appends it to the string `"hello pl/sql:."` If the parameter passed doesn't match an empno in the database, then the string `"invalid param"` is returned.

```
CREATE OR REPLACE PACKAGE BODY hello_pkg AS    -- package body header
   FUNCTION hello_plsql (param NUMBER)         -- function header
   RETURN VARCHAR2 IS
       hello_str VARCHAR2(20);
       sal_val NUMBER(7,2);                    -- declaration block
   BEGIN
     hello_str:='hello pl/sql ';               -- set the string
     SELECT sal INTO sal_val                   -- SELECT statement.
        FROM emp                               -- INTO is used to set
        WHERE param=empno;                     -- the sal_val variable
     IF sal_val=NULL THEN                      -- conditional statement.
        sal_val:=-1;
     END IF;
     hello_str:=hello_str || sal_val;          -- combining the strings
     RETURN hello_str;
   EXCEPTION                                  -- if the SELECT statement
      WHEN NO_DATA_FOUND THEN                  -- returned nothing,
        RETURN 'invalid param';                -- this code executes.
   END;
END hello_pkg
```

With this package successfully compiled, you can invoke the function just like you invoked a lot of the SQL functions. Just select it as a pseudocolumn from the dual table. Just pass to it an employee ID that you know is valid, such as 7900.

```
SELECT hello_pkg.hello_plsql(7900) AS hello_plsql FROM dual
```

You should get the following result:

```
hello pl/sql 950
```

Of course, you aren't limited to only using this function with the dual table. You can use this function anywhere that functions are permitted. In this example, the function is called as an element in the `SELECT` statement of the `emp` table.

```
SELECT hello_pkg.hello_plsql(empno) AS hello_plsql FROM emp WHERE
deptno=10
```

In this case, the function is called for each row in `emp` where `deptno` is equal to ten. The result of this statement should look like this:

```
hello pl/sql 2450
hello pl/sql 5000
hello pl/sql 1300
```

Your final step is to use this example in an XSQL page. Your XML page will look like this:

```
<?xml version="1.0"?>
<page connection="demo" xmlns:xsql="urn:oracle-xsql">
<xsql:query>
   SELECT hello_pkg.hello_plsql(empno) AS hello_plsql
     FROM emp
     WHERE deptno=10
</xsql:query>
</page>
```

This should produce output as seen in Figure 9.1.

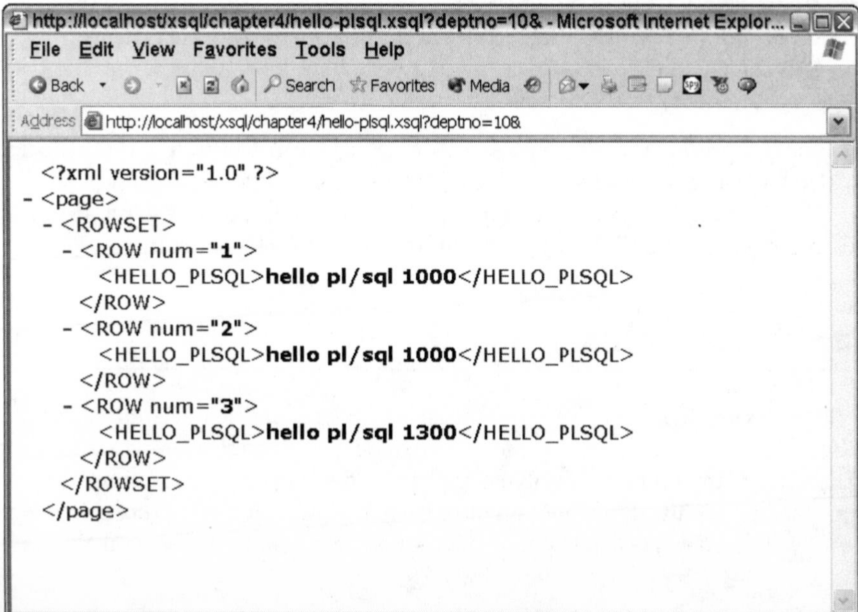

Figure 9.1 XSQL and the `hello_plsql` function.

Structure

The preceding example gave you a taste of PL/SQL code. Now you will step back and look at how PL/SQL is structured. Because you created a named function inside of a package in the first example, you have already seen most of the structural components that PL/SQL code can have. In these pages, you'll learn the names for the parts that you have already learned and see what the other pieces are.

PL/SQL code is defined as blocks. The individual statements (such as control statements, SQL statements, variable declarations, and variable assignments) are included in these blocks.

Block header. This block formally names and contains another block. In our `hello_plsql` function, the line beginning with `FUNCTION hello_plsql` and ending in a semicolon was a block header. It contained a declaration block and an execution block. Likewise, the package declaration is another block header that contains all of the blocks in our sample code. Block headers are optional. If there is a block header, the code that it contains is a named block; in the absence of a block header, the code is an anonymous block. Named blocks are generally preferable because they are easier to reuse.

Declaration section. The declaration section declares the variables that you want to use. It is also optional—there are many times that you don't need to declare variables. Our `hello_plsql` function had a declaration block consisting of one line: `sal_val NUMBER(7,2);`. Any variable used in the execution section must be declared in the declaration section.

Execution section. The execution section is the meat of your code. All of the code between the `BEGIN` statement and the `EXCEPTION` statement belongs to the execution block.

Exception section. The exception block handles errors that are encountered in the execution block. In the case of `hello_plsql`, it handles the case where the `SELECT` statement returns no rows.

These blocks represent the core basics of PL/SQL code. In addition to these blocks, you can also have a package specification, which was the first statement that you executed. It declares the package to the world and declares what is in it. Now that you know the basic parts of PL/SQL, you can start examining each part in turn.

Declaring Variables

As described earlier, all of your variables must be declared in the declaration section. (This differs from C++ and Java, in which you can declare variables anywhere in your code.) There are many types of variables that can be declared. Many are simple scalar data types that are identical to what you have seen in SQL. You'll learn those first. You can also have record variables that are data structures containing several different variables of possibly different types. As you would expect from any decent programming language, PL/SQL has arrays. Perhaps most important, PL/SQL has cursors. A cursor contains the results of a SQL `SELECT` statement. By using a cursor, your SQL code can easily iterate over data in your database.

Scalar Variable Declarations

Scalar variable declarations take the following form:

```
name [CONSTANT] type [NOT NULL] [:=|DEFAULT  initial_value]
```

Using the `CONSTANT` keyword declares that the variable is a constant—the value can't be changed. `NOT NULL` declares that the variable can never be set to a `NULL` value. Both of these keywords require that the initial value be set—either the assignment operator or the `DEFAULT` keyword can be used. Of course, you don't have to declare a variable to be `NOT NULL` or `CONSTANT` if you simply want to set an initial value, and you aren't required to set an initial value at all. You've already seen the easiest way to declare a variable in the `hello_plsql` example. In that code, you declared a scalar variable of type `NUMBER(7,2)` with the following line:

```
sal_val NUMBER(7,2);
```

This is the simplest scalar variable declaration. You give the variable name followed by the type. Perhaps more useful, though, is referencing an existing database column:

```
sal_val emp.empno%TYPE;
```

This declaration tells PL/SQL that you want the variable to take the type of the `empno` column in the `emp` table. If you know that you are going to be using the variable to set data from a specific column (as you did in our example), you should do it this way. First, if the underlying table changes, you don't have to modify your code. Second, it becomes obvious to anyone reading your code that the variable is related to that particular column.

The following lines show examples of all of the remaining permutations of declaring scalar variables:

```
dummy_1 emp.empno%TYPE :=7900;
dummy_2 NUMBER(7,2) :=7900;
dummy_3 emp.empno%TYPE NOT NULL :=7900;
dummy_4 NUMBER(7,2) NOT NULL :=7900;
dummy_5 CONSTANT emp.empno%TYPE :=7900;
dummy_6 CONSTANT NUMBER(7,2) :=7900;
```

Though you should declare variables based on a database column whenever practical, there are many cases in which this isn't done. The following tables list all of the data types that you can use when you are explicitly declaring the types of your variables.

First, look at the numeric data types in Table 9.1. Many equate with each other. This is for compatibility with other vendors' systems. You shouldn't skip around between equivalent data types—simply pick one that you like and stick to it. This will make your code easier to read.

Table 9.1 PL/SQL Numeric Data Types

TYPE	BASE TYPE	DESCRIPTION
DEC	NUMBER	Equivalent to NUMBER.
DECIMAL	NUMBER	Equivalent to NUMBER.
DOUBLE PRECISION	NUMBER	Equivalent to NUMBER.
FLOAT	NUMBER	Equivalent to NUMBER.
INTEGER	NUMBER	A number restricted to 38 digits with no fractional part (nothing to the right of the decimal point).
INT	NUMBER	Equivalent to INTEGER.
NATURAL	BINARY INTEGER	BINARY INTEGER restricted to nonnegative values but can be NULL.
NATURALN	BINARY INTEGER	BINARY INTEGER restricted to nonnegative and can't be NULL.
NUMBER		The internal Oracle NUMBER data type.
NUMERIC	NUMBER	Synonym for NUMBER.
PLS_INTEGER		Stores signed integers between -2,147,483,647 and 2,147,483,647. Faster than NUMBER.
POSITIVE	BINARY INTEGER	BINARY INTEGER restricted to nonnegative values but can be NULL.
POSITIVEN	BINARY INTEGER	BINARY INTEGER restricted to nonnegative values and can't be NULL.
REAL	NUMBER	Equivalent to NUMBER.
SIGNTYPE	BINARY INTEGER	Restricted to the values -1, 0, and 1.
SMALLINT	NUMBER	Equivalent to INTEGER.

Record Declarations

A record type in PL/SQL is a complex type that allows you to store a number of different variables in the same bundle. The variables themselves are declared similarly to scalar variables, but without the CONSTANT and NOT NULL keywords and without a way to specify initial values:

```
variable_name type_name;
```

The complexity comes in declaring record types. The easiest way to declare a record type is to base it on a database table. If you are going to use your records to store rows of data from a database table, this is the most elegant way to do it, also. The form for this declaration is as follows:

```
variable_name table_name%ROWTYPE;
```

Here's how you would declare a record variable that represents a row of the emp database:

```
emp_rec emp%ROWTYPE;
```

If you need to explicitly define your record type, you do it using the following form. All PL/SQL types are available for use in a record type. When declaring the type, you can use the NOT NULL keyword and specify a default value. Unlike with scalar variables, these settings will pertain to all variable instances that use the particular type.

```
TYPE record_type IS RECORD (
       variable_name type [NOT NULL] [:=|DEFAULT initial_value]
      [,variable_name type [NOT NULL] [:=|DEFAULT initial_value]
      ...]
      )
```

For example, this code defines a record that contains four variables, uses the NOT NULL keyword, and sets initial values:

```
TYPE dummy_rec IS RECORD (
     num_var NUMBER(6),
     char_var VARCHAR2(10),
     num_var2 NUMBER(6) :=8,
     char_var3 VARCHAR2(10) NOT NULL :='howdy'
  );
```

You use records by referencing their parts using the . operator. The following example of an anonymous block shows you how to do this and also includes our other examples in this section.

```
SET SERVEROUTPUT ON
DECLARE
  emp_var emp%ROWTYPE;
  TYPE dummy_rec IS RECORD (
```

```
      num_var NUMBER(6),
      char_var VARCHAR2(10),
      num_var2 NUMBER(6) :=8,
      char_var3 VARCHAR2(10) NOT NULL :='howdy'
   );
   dummy_var dummy_rec;
BEGIN
   dummy_var.num_var:=5;
   SELECT * INTO emp_var FROM emp WHERE ename='ADAMS';
   DBMS_OUTPUT.PUT_LINE('emp_var='||emp_var.empno);
END;
```

Cursors

Cursors are perhaps the most exciting feature in all of PL/SQL. You declare a cursor with a SELECT statement, and it holds all of the results of that SELECT statement. Cursor declarations use the following syntax:

```
CURSOR variable_name IS
SELECT statement
[FOR UPDATE [OF column [,column...]] [NOWAIT]];
```

The following cursor grabs all of the employees with salaries greater than sal_param. The sal_param variable must already have been declared before the cursor declaration. Generally, you also want it to have a value. Thus, parameters passed into a function are often used in a cursor definition.

```
CURSOR emp_cursor IS
   SELECT * FROM emp
   WHERE sal>sal_param;
```

Our discussion of cursors will pick up again in the execution block section.

Array Structures

PL/SQL has two arraylike structures: INDEX BY tables and varrays. varrays act most like the arrays of other programming languages, whereas associative arrays are like hash tables and the INDEX BY tables in Perl. You use a varray to access your objects by number, while you use an INDEX BY table to access your objects by name. You'll learn about declaring both types in this section, starting with INDEX BY tables.

To use an INDEX BY table, you must first declare an INDEX BY table type. By specifying an index type of VARCHAR2, the INDEX BY table works much like a Perl INDEX BY table or hash table. You can link the records you put into the INDEX BY table to a string value.

```
TYPE type_name IS TABLE OF
   type
   INDEX BY [BINARY_INTEGER | PLS_INTEGER | VARCHAR2(size_limit)];
```

Here is an example of a declaration of an INDEX BY table and the instantiation of an actual index:

```
TYPE ibt_emp_type IS TABLE OF emp%rowtype INDEX BY BINARY INTEGER;
emp_idx ibt_emp_type;
```

WARNING
The VARCHAR2 option of the INDEX BY clause is only available in Oracle 9.2 and higher.

Here is an example of a declaration of a varray and its instantiation:

```
TYPE v_emp_type IS VARRAY (1000) OF emp%rowtype;
emp_varray v_emp_type;
```

You access both varrays and INDEX BY tables with the same syntax:

```
emp_varray(1):=emp_var;
emp_idx(1):=emp_var;
```

Both have several methods in common that can be used to perform the same actions. They are accessed using the . operator and are outlined in Table 9.2.

Table 9.3 lists the methods that only exist for varrays.

Table 9.2 Varray and INDEX BY Table Shared Methods

METHOD	DESCRIPTION
COUNT	Returns the number of rows in the table.
DELETE	Deletes all of the rows in the table.
DELETE(x)	Deletes the row with key *x*.
DELETE(x,y)	Deletes all rows with keys between *x* and *y*, inclusive.
FIRST	Returns the row with the lowest key.
LAST	Returns the row with the highest key.
NEXT(x)	Returns the next row after row *x*.
PRIOR(x)	Returns the row prior to row *x*.

Table 9.3 `Varray`-Only Methods

METHOD	DESCRIPTION
`EXISTS(x)`	Returns true if there is an entry at *x*; otherwise, it returns false.
`TRIM`	Deletes the entry with the highest index value.
`TRIM(y)`	Deletes the highest *y* entries.
`EXTEND`	Adds one entry to the table, assuming that it won't make the table larger than its maximum.
`EXTEND(x)`	Adds one entry to the table, assuming that it won't make the table larger than its maximum.
`EXTEND(x,y)`	Repeats entry *y x* times and adds them to the table, assuming that it won't make the table larger than its maximum.
`LIMIT`	Returns the maximum size for the array.

PL/SQL Blocks and the Execution Section

The execution section of your code performs some action. It begins with a `BEGIN` statement and ends with an `END;` statement. It can contain multiple nested blocks—other sections of code delineated by `BEGIN` and `END` statements—as well as SQL statements, procedure calls, and control statements. Each block must have at least one valid statement of some type.

The full syntax diagram of execution sections follows, with an example that uses each type of statement. The various types of statements are covered in the next few pages, as well as PL/SQL expressions.

```
BEGIN
    {assignment                       |
     control_structure                |
     exception_section                |
     PL/SQL_block                     |
     Procedure_call                   |
     SQL statement
    };
    [{assignment_statement            |
      control_structure               |
      exception_section               |
      PL/SQL_block                    |
      Procedure_call                  |
      SQL statement
    };
    . . .]
END;
```

Here is code that uses each of these types:

```
DECLARE                                          -- Declaration Section
  dummy_num  emp.sal%TYPE;
  dummy_str  VARCHAR2(15);

BEGIN                                            -- Top level begin
 dummy_num:=0;                                   -- Assignment
 BEGIN                                           -- Nested PL/SQL_Block

  SELECT sal                                     -- SQL
    INTO dummy_num
  FROM emp
  WHERE ename='ADAMS';

  IF dummy_num=0 THEN                            -- Control Structure
    DBMS_OUTPUT.PUT_LINE('volunteer!');          -- Procedure call
  END IF;
  EXCEPTION                                      -- Exception Section
    WHEN NO_DATA_FOUND THEN
     BEGIN
      DBMS_OUTPUT.PUT_LINE('Sorry, no data');
     END;
   END;
   dummy_str:='salary: '||dummy_num;             -- Assignment
   DBMS_OUTPUT.PUT_LINE(dummy_str);              -- Procedure call
END;
```

SQL Statements in PL/SQL

PL/SQL is tightly integrated with SQL, more so than most all other languages. Because SQL statements can be used inline with your code, your PL/SQL can be exceptionally easy to read. This contrasts with other languages, such as Java and C++, which must pass SQL strings to subroutines and gather the results of SQL statements in data structures. This leads to an abundance of plumbing and can make database interaction code cumbersome to write.

The SQL statements that you see appear to be nearly identical to the Oracle SQL that you've seen elsewhere in the table, but there are some important differences. Not all of SQL can be used in PL/SQL. Second, the SQL statements you use in PL/SQL—most significantly the `SELECT` statement—can be extended to allow tighter interaction.

First, it's important to understand what SQL is allowed in PL/SQL. Data Definition Language (DDL) statements, such as `CREATE TABLE`, `ALTER SESSION`, and `CREATE FUNCTION`, are not allowed in PL/SQL. Only DML statements are allowed. Table 9.4 lists the SQL statements that you can use in your PL/SQL code, along with any additional features.

Table 9.4 SQL Allowed In PL/SQL

STATEMENTS	ADDITIONAL FEATURES
`COMMIT`	
`DELETE`	PL/SQL expressions can be used in `where` clause; integration with open cursors.
`INSERT`	PL/SQL expressions can be used.
`LOCK TABLE`	
`SAVEPOINT`	
`ROLLBACK`	
`SELECT`	PL/SQL expressions can be used in the `where` clause; `INTO` keyword can be used for variable assignment.
`SET CONSTRAINTS`	
`SET ROLE`	
`SET TRANSACTION`	
`UPDATE`	PL/SQL expressions can be used in the `where` clause; integration with open cursors.

Table 9.4 summarizes the additional features that can be used for each statement. However, these aren't quite all of the key differences between standard SQL and SQL as it's used in a PL/SQL program. The following list enumerates these key differences:

- SQL statements don't write output to the screen or other output device. If you want to do this, use the `DBMS_OUTPUT` package.
- PL/SQL expressions (and hence, PL/SQL variables) can be used anywhere that SQL expressions can be used. Usually, they are used in the `WHERE` clauses.
- Select statements in the execution section, and use the `INTO` keyword to assign the fields to a variable.
- `DELETE` and `UPDATE` statements are integrated with cursors using the `CURRENT OF` keyword. This integration allows you to specify that a `DELETE` or `UPDATE` should occur on the current row of an open cursor. Examples of these statements will be given in the next section, "Control Structures," when cursors are examined.

Control Structures

PL/SQL has three types of control structures: (1) conditional, (2) iterative, and (3) sequential. A conditional control structure is the typical IF-THEN-ELSE code, while an iterative control structure is best known as a loop. The sequential control structures, which are either a NULL statement or a GOTO, have little practical benefit to the production PL/SQL developer. They will be mostly dismissed last. Our first discussion here pertains to conditional control structures, and then the iterative control structures are covered.

Conditional Control Structures

The conditional control structures work much like other popular programming languages. You have an IF structure and the CASE structure. You'll look at both, starting with IF. The only difference with which you may not be familiar is the ELSIF keyword, which means "else if". The syntax for control structures follows.

```
IF expression THEN
    statement;
    [statement; . . .]
[ELSIF expression THEN
    statement;
    [statement; . . .]
. . .
[ELSE
    statement;
    [statement; . . .]
]
END IF;
```

The conditional control structure must begin with an IF, end with an END IF, and have at least one statement. You can have as many ELSIF blocks as you like, or none at all. You don't have to have an ELSE block, or you can have only one, and it must follow any ELSIF blocks that you might have. Here is an example that uses all parts.

```
SET SERVEROUTPUT ON
DECLARE
   dummy_rec emp%ROWTYPE;
   BEGIN
        SELECT * INTO dummy_rec FROM emp WHERE ename='ADAMS';
        IF dummy_rec.sal>1300 THEN
            DBMS_OUTPUT.PUT_LINE('They are rich!');
            IF dummy_rec.comm>0 THEN
              DBMS_OUTPUT.PUT_LINE('And they get a commission!');
            END IF;
```

```
        ELSIF dummy_rec.sal>500 THEN
            DBMS_OUTPUT.PUT_LINE('Not so rich.');
            DBMS_OUTPUT.PUT_LINE('Maybe a performance review?');
        ELSE
            DBMS_OUTPUT.PUT_LINE('Living wage, please');
            DBMS_OUTPUT.PUT_LINE('It is no longer the eighties');
        END IF;
    END;
```

The CASE structure is similar to the IF structure. It is more convenient when all of your logic involves the same value. You declare the variable with which you are working once and then set up a series of blocks that execute when the variable has a particular value. Here is the syntax:

```
CASE variable
   {WHEN value THEN
        statement;
        [statement; . . .]
   }
   [WHEN value THEN
        statement;
        [statement; . . .]

   ]
   [ELSE
        statement;
        [statement; . . .]
   ]
END CASE;
```

The following is an example that deals with multiple cases. Notice that you are free to mix IF statements with CASE statements.

```
SET SERVEROUTPUT ON
DECLARE
   dummy_rec  emp%ROWTYPE;
   BEGIN
        SELECT * INTO dummy_rec FROM emp WHERE ename='ALLEN';
        CASE dummy_rec.deptno
         WHEN 30 THEN
            DBMS_OUTPUT.PUT_LINE('sales');
            IF dummy_rec.comm>0 THEN
              DBMS_OUTPUT.PUT_LINE('They get a commission!');
            END IF;
         WHEN 10 THEN
            DBMS_OUTPUT.PUT_LINE('accounting');
            DBMS_OUTPUT.PUT_LINE('May be an auditor.');
         ELSE
```

```
        DBMS_OUTPUT.PUT_LINE('Not accounting or sales');
    END CASE;
END;
```

There are two remaining tales to be told concerning CASE structures. First, if you do not specify an ELSE statement and no WHEN statement is satisfactory, PL/SQL will raise a CASE_NOT_FOUND exception. Second, PL/SQL also supports a variation on the CASE structure, called a searched-case statement, where you don't specify a variable on the CASE line and, instead, have a conditional expression with the WHEN statements.

Iterative Control Structures

Iterative control structures are known commonly as loops. PL/SQL provides three: LOOP, WHILE LOOP, and FOR LOOP. Each loop can be exited at any time by using an EXIT or EXIT WHEN statement. A LOOP is the most basic form—anything that can be done with a WHILE LOOP or a FOR LOOP can be done with a LOOP. You can also use a LOOP in conjunction with a cursor—this is covered later in the section "Cursors." The syntax for these LOOP types is as follows:

```
{LOOP                                           |
 WHILE condition LOOP                           |
 FOR counter IN [REVERSE] start..end LOOP
}
  {statement  | EXIT | EXIT WHEN condition ;}
  [statement; . . .]
  [EXIT;] . . .
  [EXIT WHEN;] . . .
 END LOOP;
```

As with all PL/SQL blocks, you have to have at least one statement. If you are using a WHILE or FOR LOOP, you can put the EXIT condition at the top of LOOP, whereas with a LOOP, you have to specify the EXIT condition explicitly. You can always have more than one EXIT condition. The EXIT WHEN keyword gives you an easy way to do this. Instead of saying "if some condition then exit," you just say "exit when condition."

Here are examples of each type of loop, starting with the basic LOOP. Each example does the same thing: It prints out the numbers one through ten and then exits.

```
SET SERVEROUTPUT ON
DECLARE
  dummy_var NUMBER(2);
BEGIN
   dummy_var:=1;
   LOOP
     DBMS_OUTPUT.PUT_LINE('dummy_var: '||dummy_var);
     EXIT WHEN dummy_var>=15;
     dummy_var:=dummy_var+1;
   END LOOP;
END;
```

The WHILE LOOP moves the EXIT condition to the top of the loop:

```
SET SERVEROUTPUT ON
DECLARE
  dummy_var NUMBER(2);
BEGIN
   dummy_var:=1;
   WHILE dummy_var<=15 LOOP
     DBMS_OUTPUT.PUT_LINE('dummy_var: '||dummy_var);
     dummy_var:=dummy_var+1;
   END LOOP;
END;
```

The FOR LOOP is most convenient for this kind of loop. It handles the counting for you. You are also guaranteed that the FOR LOOP will exit—PL/SQL won't let you assign to the counter while the loop is in progress.

```
SET SERVEROUTPUT ON
BEGIN
   FOR dummy_var IN 1..15 LOOP
     DBMS_OUTPUT.PUT_LINE('dummy_var: '||dummy_var);
   END LOOP;
END;
```

Sequential Control Structures

The sequential control structures are the GOTO and the NULL statements. You shouldn't use GOTO statements in your code, even if it is really complicated. Instead, you should try to simplify your code and probably write some subroutines. If you really, really have to write a GOTO, here is how you do it:

```
statement
statement
GOTO goto_target
statement
statement
statement
<<goto_target>>
statement you want to go to
```

The NULL statement does nothing. It is convenient as a placeholder and generally should be removed after development. During development, you might need it because of PL/SQL's requirement that each block have at least one valid statement. If you have constructed a complicated series of `IF-THEN-ELSE` statements, you might find that you don't want a particular block to do anything. However, your PL/SQL won't execute without a valid statement. Instead of disturbing the overall structure of your code, you can just throw in a `NULL` statement. In this way, you meet both goals— The code will run, and the problem block won't do anything. Here's an example:

```
IF a < b THEN
   NULL;
END IF;
```

Cursors

Earlier in this chapter, in the section entitled "Declaring Variables," you got your first glimpse of cursors. Now you get to see them in action. A cursor allows you to programmatically move through the results of a SQL query. Here is an example:

```
SET SERVEROUTPUT ON
DECLARE
  CURSOR emp_cursor IS
     SELECT *
     FROM emp;
  emp_rec emp%ROWTYPE;
BEGIN
   FOR emp_rec IN emp_cursor LOOP
     DBMS_OUTPUT.PUT_LINE(emp_rec.ename);
   END LOOP;

END;
```

This code will print each employee's name. Of course, you can do anything you want with the data that is captured in the `emp_rec` variable. Before going any further, you should know the syntax of the `FOR IN LOOP`. Notice that you can define the cursor in the `LOOP` with the `SELECT` statement. It's generally better to define it as a variable, though, so that your code is more readable.

```
FOR {scalar_variable . . . | record }
 IN {cursor_name | (SELECT_statement) } LOOP
  {statement;}
  [statement; . . .]
END LOOP;
```

You are also not restricted to using the FOR IN LOOP as shown here. You can open and close the cursor explicitly and fetch the records. Here is some sample code that does the same thing using this methodology:

```
SET SERVEROUTPUT ON
DECLARE
  CURSOR emp_cursor IS
     SELECT *
     FROM emp;
  emp_rec emp%ROWTYPE;
BEGIN
   OPEN emp_cursor;
   LOOP
     FETCH emp_cursor INTO emp_rec;
     EXIT WHEN emp_cursor%NOTFOUND;
     DBMS_OUTPUT.PUT_LINE(emp_rec.ename);
   END LOOP;
   CLOSE emp_cursor;
END;
```

This introduces three new keywords: (1) OPEN, (2) CLOSE, and (3) FETCH. OPEN and CLOSE are both simple—you just follow them with a cursor name. FETCH is only slightly more complex. You can follow it with one or more variables instead of a record.

Notice how the EXIT condition works in this case. There is a cursor attribute, NOTFOUND, that evaluates as true when the cursor returns some data. There are a total of four attributes for cursors, which are described Table 9.5.

You can use cursors with UPDATE and DELETE statements, also. By specifying CURRENT OF in the where clause, the update statement will work against the last row fetched from the specified cursor. This assumes that there is nothing else in the WHERE clause that will cause the update to skip that particular row. The following sample code, which works against a copy of emp called dummy_emp, shows how this works. The same syntax works for a DELETE statement.

```
SET SERVEROUTPUT ON
DECLARE
  CURSOR emp_cursor IS
     SELECT * FROM dummy_emp FOR UPDATE OF sal;
  emp_rec dummy_emp%ROWTYPE;
BEGIN
   OPEN emp_cursor;
   LOOP
     FETCH emp_cursor INTO emp_rec;
     EXIT WHEN emp_cursor%NOTFOUND;
     UPDATE dummy_emp SET sal=emp_rec.sal+100 WHERE CURRENT OF
emp_cursor;
   END LOOP;
   CLOSE emp_cursor;
END;
```

Table 9.5 Cursor Attributes

ATTRIBUTE	DESCRIPTION
%FOUND	True if the previous fetch returned a row.
%NOTFOUND	True if the previous fetch didn't return a row.
%ISOPEN	True if the cursor is open.
%ROWCOUNT	Number of rows returned by the cursor so far.

You can also return a cursor from a function. XSQL has special support for this with the REF-CURSOR-FUNCTION action. The idea is that instead of returning just a single point of data, you return an indeterminate number of rows—just like a SELECT statement. What is different is that you can use all of the power of PL/SQL to determine the data that you wish to return. Here is a simple example that allows you to control whether to get the salaries that are greater than or less than the given value:

```
CREATE OR REPLACE PACKAGE ref_cursor_example IS
   TYPE emp_sal_cursor_type IS REF CURSOR;
   FUNCTION return_cursor(comp_sal NUMBER,op VARCHAR2) RETURN
emp_sal_cursor_type;
END;

CREATE OR REPLACE PACKAGE BODY ref_cursor_example IS
   FUNCTION return_cursor(comp_sal NUMBER, op VARCHAR2) RETURN
emp_sal_cursor_type IS
      emp_sal_cursor emp_sal_cursor_type;
   BEGIN
     IF op='greater' THEN
      OPEN emp_sal_cursor FOR SELECT * FROM emp WHERE sal>comp_sal;
     ELSE
       OPEN emp_sal_cursor FOR SELECT * FROM emp WHERE sal<=comp_sal;
     END IF;
     RETURN emp_sal_cursor;
    END;
END;
```

You can access this function directly using the XSQL REF-CURSOR-FUNCTION action:

```
<?xml version="1.0"?>
<page connection="demo" xmlns:xsql="urn:oracle-xsql">
  <xsql:ref-cursor-function>
      ref_cursor_example.return_cursor(1200,'greater')
  </xsql:ref-cursor-function>
</page>
```

Packages

A package is a way to group your PL/SQL types, items, procedures, and functions together. Type definitions, such as records and cursors, can be defined once for all of your subroutines. You can declare variables at a package level that all of the procedures and functions can share. However, all procedures and functions share the exact same copy of the variables—if it is changed by a subroutine, all subroutines will see the same change (i.e., they aren't like the instance variables of object-oriented languages).

As you saw in the `hello_pkg` example earlier, a package definition has two parts: (1) a package specification and (2) a package body. If you want a subroutine, type, or variable to be publicly available beyond your package, you must include it in the package specification. Private items that are only available to the package code should only be defined in the package body.

The following specification extends our earlier example to include a public variable, `pub_var`.

```
CREATE OR REPLACE PACKAGE hello_pkg AS
   pub_var  NUMBER(6):=0;
   FUNCTION hello_plsql (param NUMBER) RETURN VARCHAR2;
END hello_pkg;
```

This package body includes a private variable, `priv_var`, and a private procedure, `priv_proc`.

```
CREATE OR REPLACE PACKAGE BODY hello_pkg AS    -- package body header
   priv_var NUMBER(6);

   PROCEDURE priv_proc IS
    BEGIN
     priv_var:=priv_var+1;
    END;

   FUNCTION hello_plsql (param NUMBER)
    RETURN VARCHAR2 IS
       hello_str VARCHAR2(20);
       sal_val NUMBER(7,2);
   BEGIN
     priv_proc;
     pub_var:=pub_var+1;
     -- other function code
   END;
END hello_pkg;
```

Because package level variables are shared by all of the executing subroutines, their usefulness is limited. However, it is quite useful to define types, such as records and cursors, once for a set of different subroutines and to group related subroutines together. Though you can create functions and procedures as separate entities, it is advisable to consider creating a package instead.

Procedures and Functions

You've now seen the three ways to write PL/SQL code for execution: (1) functions, (2) anonymous blocks, and (3) procedures. This section looks specifically at subprograms: procedures and functions. There is only one key difference between procedures and functions: A procedure doesn't return a value, whereas a function does. (Thus, a procedure is like a void method in Java or a void function in C++.) Procedures and functions are alike except for this difference.

In our examples thus far, you have created procedures and functions as part of packages. You can also create subprograms as stand-alone objects with the `CREATE OR REPLACE PROCEDURE` and `CREATE OR REPLACE FUNCTION` statements. Here are examples creating stand-alone subprograms:

```
CREATE OR REPLACE FUNCTION simple_func (param NUMBER)
   RETURN VARCHAR2 IS
       hello_str VARCHAR2(20);
       func_var NUMBER(7,2);
   BEGIN
     func_var:=param+1;
     RETURN 'hello '|| func_var;
   END;

CREATE OR REPLACE PROCEDURE priv_proc (param NUMBER) IS
    proc_var NUMBER(7,2);
    BEGIN
     proc_var:=param+1;
     DBMS_OUTPUT.PUT_LINE('hello'||proc_var);
    END;
```

The declaration section is implicit—it's between the `IS` and the `BEGIN` keywords. The `BEGIN` and `END` keywords contain the execution block, which you learned about previously, and can optionally have an `EXCEPTION` block. To fill out a basic understanding of PL/SQL subprograms, you need to understand how parameters are passed to PL/SQL subprograms. Parameters can be passed as `IN`, `OUT`, `IN OUT`, and `NO COPY`. These options are outlined in Table 9.6. Among other things, they affect whether a parameter is passed by reference or by value. When passing by value, a copy is made. Changes to the parameter won't be seen outside the subprogram. When passing by reference, a reference to the actual parameter is passed. If you modify the parameter inside your subprogram, it will be modified in the code that called your subprogram.

Table 9.6 Parameter Options

OPTION	DESCRIPTION
`IN`	A parameter is an input parameter. Inside the subprogram the parameter acts as a constant. It is always passed by reference.
`OUT`	A parameter is an output parameter. Inside the subprogram the parameter acts as a variable. Changes made to the variable inside the subprogram will be seen by the code calling the subprogram. By default, it is passed by value. *Not allowed directly with XSQL.*
`IN OUT`	A parameter is both an input and output parameter. It acts as an initialized value. By default it is passed by value. *Not allowed directly with XSQL.*
`NOCOPY`	A compiler hint used to make PL/SQL more efficient. When used in conjunction with `OUT` and `IN OUT`, it tells PL/SQL that the parameter *may* be passed by reference instead of by value. It has no effect when used with `IN`. In certain cases, PL/SQL will pass by value in spite of the `NOCOPY` hint.

You can't call procedures and functions with `OUT` parameters with XSQL directly when there is no place to which you can return the variable. For instance, you can call such subprograms from inside an `xsql:dml` anonymous block, but not as a single procedure or function call in `xsql:dummy` or `xsql:include-owa`. If you have a procedure or function that you need to use that has `OUT` parameters, the workaround is to write a wrapper function or procedure. If you need data that is returned via an `OUT` parameter, you can write a function that returns the value, or use `xsql:include-owa` to write it back to the page. If you don't need the data returned by the `OUT` parameter, you can simply disregard it in your wrapper function. In general, you'll want to write wrapper functions, unless you are using `xsql:include-owa`.

By default, parameters are passed as `IN` parameters. The following example shows how to specify each type:

```
CREATE OR REPLACE PROCEDURE priv_proc (defaultInParam NUMBER,
                                       inParam IN NUMBER,
                                       inOutParam IN OUT NUMBER,
                                       outParam OUT NUMBER,
                                       noCopyParam IN OUT NOCOPY NUMBER)
 IS
   -- declaration
  BEGIN
   -- execution
  END;
```

There is one point left to be covered regarding parameters and PL/SQL. You will occasionally see a subprogram called as follows:

```
update_emp(emp_number=>7790,sal=>5000,name=>'EDWARDS');
```

This is named notation as opposed to positional notation. Positional notation might look like this instead, assuming that the order of parameters in the `update_emp` definition is `name`, `emp_number`, and `sal`.

```
update_emp('EDWARDS',7790,5000);
```

Positional notation is typical of many popular programming languages. However, named notation is self-documenting, easier to read, and easier to get right. You can more easily avoid the classic problem of interchanging variables of the same type. For instance, if 7,790 and 5,000 were interchanged in our example, the wrong employee might get an unexpected raise!

Exceptions

PL/SQL uses exception handling to help you deal with unexpected conditions. Exceptions don't bugproof your code, but they do make it easier to make your code bulletproof. Instead of having to use extensive logic to make sure that your code doesn't crash, you can use exception handlers to define what should happen if something does go wrong. PL/SQL comes with several built-in exceptions, which are tied to Oracle error codes. You can also define your own exceptions and raise exceptions from within your execution block. This section covers all of these aspects of exceptions.

First, a more extensive example using exceptions is needed. So far, you've had exception sections that only handle one exception. This example shows how you can use the exception section to handle multiple exceptions.

```
CREATE OR REPLACE PROCEDURE print_high_sal(sal_var IN OUT emp.sal%TYPE)
IS
    BEGIN
    SELECT sal INTO sal_var FROM emp WHERE sal>sal_var;
    DBMS_OUTPUT.PUT_LINE('sal_var'||sal_var);
    EXCEPTION
        WHEN NO_DATA_FOUND THEN
            DBMS_OUTPUT.PUT_LINE('no data');
        WHEN TOO_MANY_ROWS THEN
            DBMS_OUTPUT.PUT_LINE('too many rows');
        WHEN OTHERS THEN
            DBMS_OUTPUT.PUT_LINE('unknown error');
  END;
```

There are several things that can go wrong. First, our `SELECT` statement might not return any rows. If that happens, the `NO_DATA_FOUND` exception is raised and handled. The opposite might occur, in which more than one row is returned. In that case, the `TOO_MANY_ROWS` exception handler will execute. If anything else goes wrong, the `OTHERS` handler kicks in.

When an exception is raised, execution immediately either switches to the applicable exception handler, or PL/SQL exits with an error message. If you are writing a function, you should return a value in all of your exception handlers. Using the `OTHERS` exception handler always guarantees that your code will exit gracefully.

Except the `OTHERS` handler, all of the built-in exception handlers are tied to an Oracle error code. Table 9.7 lists all of them.

In addition to these exceptions, you can declare your own. You do this in the `DECLARE` section as follows:

```
DECLARE
  obsolete_exception EXCEPTION;
  PRAGMA EXCEPTION_INIT (obsolete_exception,-3007);
  my_exception EXCEPTION;
  BEGIN
    -- code
  EXCEPTION
    WHEN obsolete_exception THEN
       DBMS_OUTPUT.PUT_LINE('obsolete feature used');
    WHEN my_exeception THEN
       DBMS_OUTPUT.PUT_LINE('my_exception was raised');
  END;
```

The exception `obsolete_exception` is tied to ORA-03007, "obsolete feature." (The actual error number is almost always the negative of the number in the name of the error.) If the ORA-03007 error occurs, then the handler will print out the message. The story is different for `my_exception`. Because `my_exception` isn't tied to an error message, it has to be raised explicitly. You do this with the `raise` keyword as follows. Typically, you would raise an exception from within a control structure because something didn't go as planned:

```
BEGIN
  statement
  statement
  RAISE my_exception;
  statement
  statement
EXCEPTION
  WHEN my_exeception THEN
    DBMS_OUTPUT.PUT_LINE('my_exception was raised');
END;
```

Triggers

If you want to execute a procedure or function, you have to call it explicitly. For instance, you called the `hello_pkg.hello_plsql` function by selecting it from the dual table. Triggers, on the other hand, respond to events. Triggers are tied to inserts, updates, and deletions of particular tables. The syntax for creating triggers is as follows:

Table 9.7 Built-in Exceptions

NAME	DESCRIPTION
ACCESS_INTO_NULL	An assignment was attempted to an attribute of an uninitialized object.
CASE_NOT_FOUND	No cases were met in a CASE statement that didn't have a ELSE clause.
COLLECTION_IS_NULL	A collection method other than EXISTS was called on a collection that hasn't been initialized.
CURSOR_ALREADY_OPEN	OPEN was called on a cursor that is already open.
DUP_VAL_ON_INDEX	A unique column constraint was violated.
INVALID_CURSOR	An illegal cursor operation was attempted.
INVALID_NUMBER	An invalid string-to-number conversion was attempted in a SQL statement.
NO_DATA_FOUND	A SELECT INTO statement returns no rows.
PROGRAM_ERROR	Internal PL/SQL error.
ROWTYPE_MISMATCH	The host cursor variable and PL/SQL cursor variable involved in an assignment have incompatible return types. For example, when an open host cursor variable is passed to a stored subprogram, the return types of the actual and formal parameters must be compatible.
SELF_IS_NULL	Access of a member method of an uninitialized object was attempted.
STORAGE_ERROR	A memory error occurred.
SUBSCRIPT_BEYOND_COUNT	An attempt was made to access a collection with a number larger than the size of the collection.
SUBSCRIPT_OUTSIDE_LIMIT	An attempt was made to access a collection with a number outside the legal range.
SYS_INVALID_ROWID	A ROWID conversion failed because the string doesn't represent a valid ROWID.
TIMEOUT_ON_RESOURCE	A time-out occurs while Oracle is waiting for a resource.
TOO_MANY_ROWS	A SELECT INTO statement returns more than one row.
VALUE_ERROR	An arithmetic, conversion, truncation, or size-constraint error occurred.
ZERO_DIVIDE	An attempt was made to divide a number by zero.

```
CREATE [OR REPLACE] TRIGGER [schema.]trigger_name
  {BEFORE | AFTER  | INSTEAD OF}
  {INSERT | DELETE | UPDATE [OF {column} [,column . . .]]}
  [OR {INSERT | DELETE | UPDATE [OF {column} [,column . . .]]}. . .]
  ON [schema.]{table | view}
  [REFERENCING [OLD AS old] [NEW AS new]]
  [FOR EACH ROW [WHEN condition]]
  BEGIN
    pl_sql code
  END;
```

By default, a trigger executes once per statement. You determine whether it should execute before, after, or instead of the declaration. However, insert, update, and delete statements can result in more than one record being affected by a single statement. If you wish to have the trigger fire for each row that is affected, you can designate this by using the `FOR EACH ROW` keyword and optionally specifying a condition. Inside the trigger, you can simultaneously have old and new data. Old data is whatever was there before, and new data is what is on its way in. By default, you reference old data as "old" and new data as "new." If you wish, you can change this in the referencing clause.

Reference Cursors

Earlier, you learned that a function returns some variable of some type. What can be very interesting is returning a cursor. Also, XSQL has special support for this with the `ref-cursor-function` action. The idea is that instead of returning just a single point of data, you return an indeterminate number of rows—just like a `SELECT` statement. What is different is that you can use all of the power of PL/SQL to determine the data that you wish to return. Here is a simple example that allows you to control whether to get the salaries that are greater than or less than the given value:

```
CREATE OR REPLACE PACKAGE ref_cursor_example IS
   TYPE emp_sal_cursor_type IS REF CURSOR;
   FUNCTION return_cursor(comp_sal NUMBER,op VARCHAR2) RETURN
emp_sal_cursor_type;
END;

CREATE OR REPLACE PACKAGE BODY ref_cursor_example IS
   FUNCTION return_cursor(comp_sal NUMBER, op VARCHAR2) RETURN
emp_sal_cursor_type IS
      emp_sal_cursor emp_sal_cursor_type;
   BEGIN
     IF op='greater' THEN
      OPEN emp_sal_cursor FOR SELECT * FROM emp WHERE sal>comp_sal;
     ELSE
       OPEN emp_sal_cursor FOR SELECT * FROM emp WHERE sal<=comp_sal;
     END IF;
     RETURN emp_sal_cursor;
    END;
END;
```

You can access this function directly using the XSQL `ref-cursor-function` action:

```
<?xml version="1.0"?>
<page connection="demo" xmlns:xsql="urn:oracle-xsql">
  <xsql:ref-cursor-function>
      ref_cursor_example.return_cursor(1200)
  </xsql:ref-cursor-function>
</page>
```

PL/SQL and XSQL

Now that you have the basics of PL/SQL down, it is time to discuss how XSQL and PL/SQL work together. All of the aspects that you have learned can at least be used indirectly from an XSQL call. This list looks at how to directly integrate PL/SQL and XSQL.

Anonymous blocks and the `dml` action. The `dml` action can contain a PL/SQL anonymous block, complete with a declaration section and an exception section. However, you can't write output to the XML document.

Functions and the query action. As seen at the beginning of this section with the `hello_plsql` function, you can call a pl/sql function from a `SELECT` statement in a query action.

Function and Procedure output through the `include-owa` action. You can return XML by writing it to the buffer using the htp and htf packages. This will be explored in Chapter 11.

In addition, database triggers are called any time you fire them by executing a statement to which they are tied. PL/SQL subprograms are a powerful server-side ally to XSQL. XSQL doesn't give you much in the way of conditional logic, but PL/SQL gives you a great deal. Plus, you don't have to make network round trips to the database to process queries.

Moving On

At this point, you know how to use both Oracle SQL and its procedural counterpart, PL/SQL. You should have a solid understanding of how you use these technologies with XSQL. In Chapters 10 ("Using Oracle Text") and 11 ("Retrieving XML"), you'll see how to use Oracle to do specialized text searching and retrieving and managing XML. Then, you'll complete your base knowledge by learning XSLT.

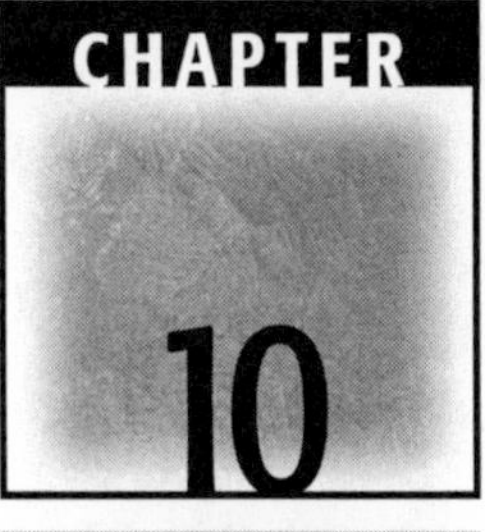

CHAPTER 10

Using Oracle Text

Oracle Text is a powerful technology that allows you to perform complex searches on unstructured text data. It's like the wildcard searching you learned about with the `SELECT` statement, but much better. In addition to being able to doing simple wildcard searches, you can:

- Rank your searches
- Do proximity searches, which are searches that require words to be close together
- Stem your search terms to include all variations of a word (e.g., hike, hikes, hiking, hiked)

This section will work through several of these examples. To complete these examples, you need to set up a table that has an indexed column. Oracle Text will work against any of the following data types: `VARCHAR2`, `CLOB`, `BLOB`, `CHAR`, `BFILE`, and `XMLType`. For the lessons here, you'll use a simple table with a `VARCHAR2` column containing our small documents. Here's what you do:

- `CREATE TABLE docs_table (id number primary key, doc_name VARCHAR2(10),text VARCHAR2(2000));`
- `INSERT INTO docs_table (id,doc_name,text) VALUES (1,'About HTML','HTML is a presentation markup language that allows you to make beautiful documents');`

- `INSERT INTO docs_table (id,doc_name,text) VALUES (2,'About XML','XML is a language where you are allowed to make beautiful languages');`
- `INSERT INTO docs_table (id,doc_name,text) VALUES (3,'allow doc','An allowance was made so that beautiful presents can be given to the language department');`
- `ALTER INDEX docs_index REBUILD;`
- `COMMIT;`

Simple Keyword Searching

Now that you have your table indexed and your minidocs in place, it is time to do some searching. You search with the `contains` clause as follows:

```
SELECT doc_name FROM docs_table WHERE contains(text,'language')>0
```

You specify the column in which you wish to search first, followed by the terms as a string argument. You can use the operators `AND`, `NOT`, and `OR`, along with parentheses in order to do Boolean searches. Here is an example:

```
SELECT doc_name
   FROM docs_table
   WHERE contains(text,'(presentation OR language) AND (HTML not
XML)')>0;
```

You may have noticed that `contains` returns a number. The number is the score. Oracle ranks the results, and you can structure your queries so that you only get higher-ranking results. You can also access the score directly by using the score operator and labelling your queries. Here is an example:

```
SELECT doc_name,score(1) AS text_score FROM docs_table WHERE
    contains(text,'language',1)>0 ORDER BY score(1) DESC;
```

Though there isn't much difference in the scoring with our small sample data, you can see that the `allow doc` scores higher. This is because the word `language` appears twice in the `allow doc`. The scoring algorithm is too complex to detail here, but it is structured so that a higher-scoring document contains proportionally more occurrences of the search term or terms than the other documents in the set. Table 10.1 lists the results.

Table 10.1 Scoring Results

DOC_NAME	TEXT_SCORE
allow doc	9
HTML doc	4
XML doc	4

As you may have guessed, you could have gotten only the `allow doc` if you had said `contains(text,'language',1)>4`. You can also establish a threshold inside of the search expression itself. Here is an example that will select only `allow doc` and `XML doc` because of a threshold applied to the term `'language'`:

```
SELECT doc_name,score(1)
 FROM docs_table
 WHERE contains(text,'language>4 OR XML',1)>0 ORDER BY score(1) DESC;
```

Stemming, Fuzzy, Wildcard, and Soundex Searching

The scoring algorithm alone makes Oracle Text much more impressive than plain SQL wildcard searching. But wait, there's more! First, you can do wildcard searching exactly as it is done in SQL. Just use the _ character to represent a single character and the % character to represent any number of characters. More interesting, however, are the expansion operators. You can use the expansion operators so that related terms are also searched. You can expand the term to include words with a common root, words that sound similar, and words that are spelled similarly. Table 10.2 lists the three types of operators.

Table 10.2 Expansion Operators

OPERATOR	EXAMPLE	DESCRIPTION
STEM	$allow	All words that share the same root are included in the search.
SOUNDEX	!effect	All words that sound the same are included in the search.
FUZZY	?success	All words with similar spellings are included in the search. This is useful when there are a lot of misspellings in the documents.

Here is an example using the stemming operator. If you perform the following query, you get no rows returned. This is to be expected because the word `allow` doesn't occur in any of our documents.

```
SELECT doc_name,score(1)
  FROM docs_table
  WHERE contains(text,'allow',1)>0 ORDER BY score(1) DESC
```

However, the words `allowed` and `allows` do occur, and they share the same root, `allow`. If you perform the following query, you will get `XML doc` and `HTML doc`. Notice that you won't get the `allow doc`, even though it contains the word `allowance`. Though `allowance` and `allow` start with the same letters, they don't share the same root.

```
SELECT doc_name,score(1)
   FROM docs_table
   WHERE contains(text,'$allow',1)>0
   ORDER BY score(1) DESC;
```

In this case, `allow` is the root. However, you don't have to give the root word for this query to work. For instance, the following query returns the same results because `allowed` and `allows` have the same root as `allowing`.

```
SELECT doc_name,score(1)
   FROM docs_table
   WHERE contains(text,'$allowing',1)>0
   ORDER BY score(1) DESC
```

Searching within XML Documents

Oracle Text can also be used to perform searches within sections of a document stored in the database. This includes HTML documents and other non-XML documents. You can also do searches on terms within the same sentence or paragraph. For this section, though, you are going to learn specifically about using Oracle Text to search XML documents. All of the other rules of searching that you have learned apply. You are still searching unstructured text. If you have an XML document in the text column of the `docs_table`, you can search in the exact same way that you search any document. The key advantage that you will learn about here is how to restrict those unstructured searches to particular XML elements within the document.

Some assembly is required. As a first step, let's create a couple of new XML documents and insert them into the table. These statements should do the trick:

```
INSERT INTO docs_table (id,doc_name,text) VALUES (3,'doc2',
'<article>
 <subject>networking</subject>
```

```
 <title>Networking Basics</title>
 <body> People didn't notice the first fax machine. The second
infinitely increased the value of both. </body>
</article>'
);
INSERT INTO docs_table (id,doc_name,text) VALUES (4,'doc3','
<article>
 <subject>software</subject>
 <reference>Mythical Man Month, Dr. Fred Brooks</reference>
 <title>Brook''s Law</title>
 <body>Putting more people on a late software project makes it
later.</body>
</article>'
);
COMMIT;
```

Next, you need to re-create the index so that Oracle is able to search on the XML documents. You'll notice that this creation is different from the first time the index was created. To make the document searchable by section, you first have to create a section group. For XML documents, the easiest and most powerful way to do this is to create a section group of type PATH_SECTION_GROUP. There are other ways to create section groups that give you much more granular control over what is a valid section. You can also make HTML documents searchable by using the HTML_SECTION_GROUP. Information on these other types can be found in the "Oracle Text Reference" at Oracle's techweb Web site.

```
DROP INDEX docs_index;
EXEC CTX_DDL.CREATE_SECTION_GROUP('sample_group','PATH_SECTION_GROUP');
CREATE INDEX docs_index ON docs_table(text)
    INDEXTYPE IS ctxsys.context
    PARAMETERS('section group sample_group');
```

Now that you have created the index, you are ready to start searching. The following query will return both documents:

```
SELECT id,doc_name
    FROM docs_table
    WHERE contains(text,'people WITHIN body')>0
```

This search looks only at the text between the <body> and </body> tags of the documents. However, this might be too limited for you. What if your XML documents are allowed to have body tags at multiple levels in your document? For such a case, you can use the INPATH operator instead. This allows you to examine a particular element in the document by its path. Here is an example:

```
SELECT id,doc_name
   FROM docs_table
   WHERE contains(text,'people INPATH (/article/body)')>0;
```

You can use its companion, HASPATH, to only return articles that have a certain path. For instance, only one of our documents has the element reference. Here's how you would use HASPATH so that only those documents having a reference element will be returned:

```
SELECT id,doc_name
   FROM docs_table
   WHERE contains(text,'HASPATH (/article/reference)')>0;
```

Both of these operators use a specialized minilanguage to describe paths. It is quite like XPath, which you will learn about in Chapter 11, "Retrieving XML," but different. Table 10.3 describes the operators and gives examples of how they work.

Table 10.3 Path Syntax

OPERATOR	DESCRIPTION	EXAMPLE
//	Signifies that the element can exist at any lower level in the document.	people INPATH (//body) foo INPATH (grandparent// great-grandchild)
*	Wildcard operator. Effectively skips a level in the tree.	foo INPATH (/level_1/*/ level_2)
A[B])	Evaluates element A if and only if it has a child named B. In the example, foo would be searched out of element A.	foo (INPATH /A[B]0
@attrib	Refers to an attribute. In the example, foo is only searched in elements named element1 that have an attribute ele1_attrib1.	foo INPATH (element1[@ ele1_attrib1])
=, !=	Can be used in comparison operations for attributes.	foo INPATH (element1 [ele_attrib1="value1"])
AND, OR, NOT	Boolean operators can be used inside the brackets to create Boolean expressions.	foo INPATH (A[@attrib="value" OR B]

Other Features

This section has given you a taste of what Oracle Text can do. There are many features that aren't covered here. Though you should be able to get pretty far with just the items in the previous pages, it's important to know what else is available. Here is a 50,000-foot view of some other important aspects of Oracle Text:

Theme searching. If your language is English or French, you can search documents based on what they are about. Oracle classifies documents into themes such as politics. You can search on politics and documents that don't contain the word "politics" but are about politics will be returned.

Searching on other formatted documents. In our examples, our documents were simple text or XML. You can also insert and query more complex formatted documents (e.g., Microsoft Word).

Thesaurus capabilities. You can use a thesaurus to expand searches to include synonyms of search terms.

Proximity searching. You can search and require that terms must be within a certain distance of each other by using the `NEAR` operator.

Stopword lists. A stopword list contains common words, (e.g., "this" or "that,") that shouldn't be indexed. You can add your own words to the stopword list.

As you learn more about Oracle Text, hopefully you'll get the chance to explore some of these areas. From an XSQL perspective, nothing in this list changes how you should write your code. Rather, these items give you a way to extend on the back end.

Moving On

This chapter focused on Oracle Text, which you can use to create robust search engines using XSQL. You'll see an example of how to build a search engine in Chapter 14, "Building XSQL Web Applications." Oracle Text works with text that is stored in the database. In Chapter 11, "Retrieving XML," you'll see how you can work with XML that is stored in the database.

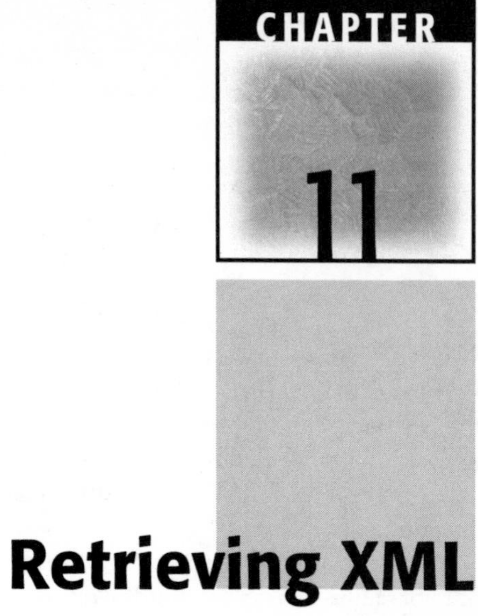

Retrieving XML

Oracle can store any media type in the database—XML is no exception. In the previous pages, you saw how to query against XML documents stored in the database. This section examines how to return XML—as opposed to strings—into your XSQL. The first tool you'll examine is the `xsql:include-owa` action, which allows you to write XML into the XSQL result. Next, you'll learn about the XMLGEN utility. It essentially allows you to do what XSQL does—generate XML based on a SQL query. The difference is that you can generate XML from inside a PL/SQL procedure. The last section covers a new feature of Oracle 9i—the XMLType. This allows you to easily store and query XML documents stored in Oracle. Before beginning the lessons, it's important to understand what is hard about retrieving XML with XSQL. The first section covers these difficulties.

What's So Hard?

In the previous section on Oracle Text, you saw that it is quite easy to store XML in the table. Just insert it like any other text. The size of our test documents was limited, but that is easily remedied—just use a CLOB type and you can store gigabytes of XML. You might be wondering, "Can't you just select the text?"

Well, you can, but not with the `xsql:query` action. Consider the following XSQL:

```
<?xml version="1.0"?>
<page connection="demo" xmlns:xsql="urn:oracle-xsql">
 <xsql:query>
   SELECT text
   FROM docs_table
   WHERE contains(text,'software INPATH (/article/body)')>0
 </xsql:query>
</page>
```

It will execute easily enough and return the result shown in Figure 11.1.

It looks like XML, so what's the problem? Upon closer examination, you'll see that the XML returned by the query isn't XML at all! Notice that Internet Explorer didn't render it with the customary colored tags. When you look at the source, you'll see that all of the essential XML characters have been escaped and replaced with their URL-encoded equivalents.

What a shame! In the context of this example, it seems that you have uncovered a horrible failing of XSQL. But it isn't, really. XSQL's default behavior is to assume that XML isn't being returned. Thus, it's proper and required to escape the special XML characters. As you'll see, the workarounds are pretty easy. In this chapter, you'll learn about the PL/SQL-based workaround. You can also retrieve XML with the help of custom XSQL action handlers, as you'll see in Chapter 18, "Custom Action Handlers."

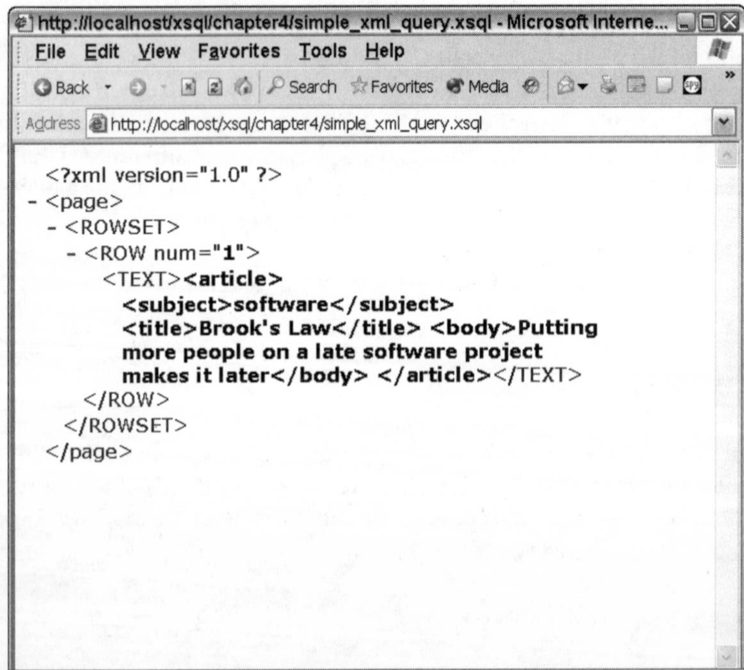

Figure 11.1 Result of retrieving XML with `xsql:query`.

Creating XML with `xsql:include-owa`

In Chapter 5, "Writing XSQL Pages," you learned that you could use the `xsql:include-owa` to include XML of your own choosing in your result. At that point, PL/SQL hadn't been covered, so you couldn't explore this action in detail. Now you can. Here you'll learn how to use the `htp.print PL/SQL` procedure to write XML of your own choosing to the XSQL datagram.

First, however, you need to cover a little background. Oracle provides two packages, (1) `htp` and (2) `htf`, that have a series of procedures and functions, respectively. The original purpose of these was to allow PL/SQL developers to easily create Web applications. For each HTML element there is both a wrapper procedure and wrapper function. This XSQL executes the wrapper procedure for the italic tag.

```
<?xml version="1.0"?>
<page connection="demo" xmlns:xsql="urn:oracle-xsql">
<xsql:include-owa>
  htp.italic(htf.bold('hello'));
  </xsql:include-owa>
</page>
```

This will produce the output seen in Figure 11.2. The <I> tags are included in our XML result, and the angle brackets weren't replaced with < and >. How do the `htp` and `htf` procedures escape escaping? The procedures in the `htp` package write to the server-side page buffer.

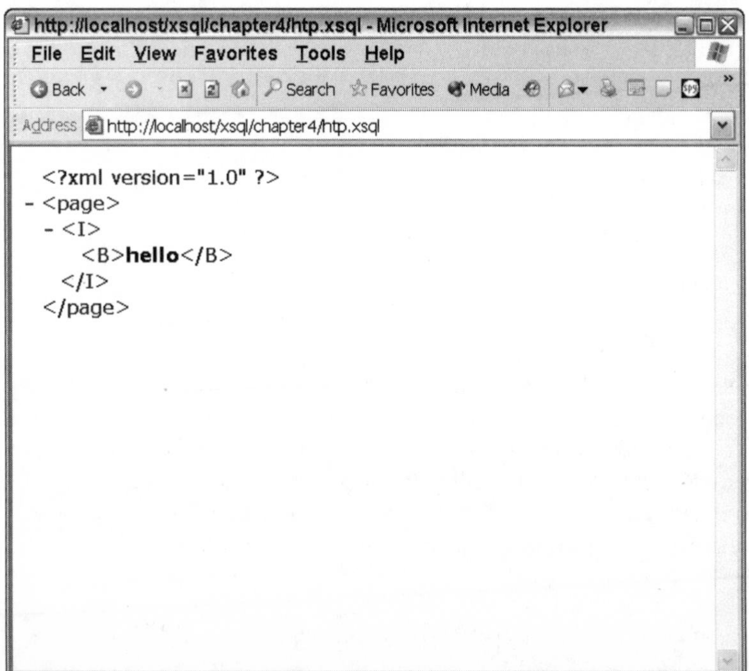

Figure 11.2 Result of `htp.italic` and `htf.bold`.

Here's how the `htp` procedures and `htf` functions are able to get the angle brackets all the way through to the browser:

- The `htf` functions wrapper their argument with the appropriate tags and return the resultant string. In this case, `hello` is wrappered and `<b>hello</b>` is returned.
- The `htp` procedures also wrapper their argument. In this case, the wrappering produces `<i><b>hello</b></i>`.
- Instead of returning anything, the `htp` procedures write their result to the server-side page buffer.
- The `xsql:include-owa` action reads the contents of the server-side page buffer and writes those to the output without escaping the reserved XML characters.

In all likelihood, you don't have any interest in using the `htp` and `htf` subprograms to generate HTML for your XSQL. (If you do have a strong interest in creating such an architecture, consider taking a head-clearing walk. There be dragons!) From an XSQL standpoint, there is really one subprogram of interest—`htp.print`.

The `htp.prn` procedure allows you to print an arbitrary string to the server-side page buffer without a trailing carriage return. (If you want a trailing carriage return, use `htp.print`.) You aren't limited solely to HTML tags, and all of the angle brackets will stay intact. The following procedure works this magic:

```
CREATE OR REPLACE PROCEDURE get_doc_xml IS
   doc_xml docs_table.text%TYPE;
   CURSOR doc_cursor IS
  SELECT text FROM docs_table WHERE
     contains(text,'software INPATH (/article/body)')>0;
  BEGIN
    htp.prn('<article-set>');
    OPEN doc_cursor;
     LOOP
      FETCH doc_cursor INTO doc_xml;
      EXIT WHEN doc_cursor%NOTFOUND;
      htp.prn(doc_xml);
     END LOOP;
     htp.print('</article-set>');
   END;
```

The procedure selects the articles that have the word "software" inside the body element of the XML documents. Before looping through the cursor, a start tag for the root element is printed to the buffer. This is required because the `xsql:include-owa` will return an error if the XML that you write isn't well formed. In the loop itself, each document is written to the buffer and the loop exits at the end of the cursor. The final step is to close the root element. The procedure can be called with the following XSQL:

```
<?xml version="1.0"?>
<page connection="demo" xmlns:xsql="urn:oracle-xsql">
<xsql:include-owa>
```

```
    get_doc_xml;
    </xsql:include-owa>
</page>
```

The result is an XML document that contains two XML documents stored in the database, as shown in Figure 11.3.

In our example, the query was hard coded. As you learned earlier, however, you can easily make the queries completely dynamic and based on user input.

Generating XML from PL/SQL

From the previous section, you saw how to write a particular data field as XML. Of course, you can use the same methodology to create quite complex XML documents and write them to the XSQL output. If you want to do this, there are a couple of PL/SQL packages that can help you. These are discussed in this section. They allow you to do exactly what XSQL does, but from inside a procedure. This raises the obvious and valid architectural question: Why would you want to generate XML from inside PL/SQL for consumption by XSQL? We'll look at these valid concerns after learning a bit about the helper code available. Oracle 9i users can use the `DBMS_QUERY` package, while Oracle 8i users can use the `XMLGEN` package.

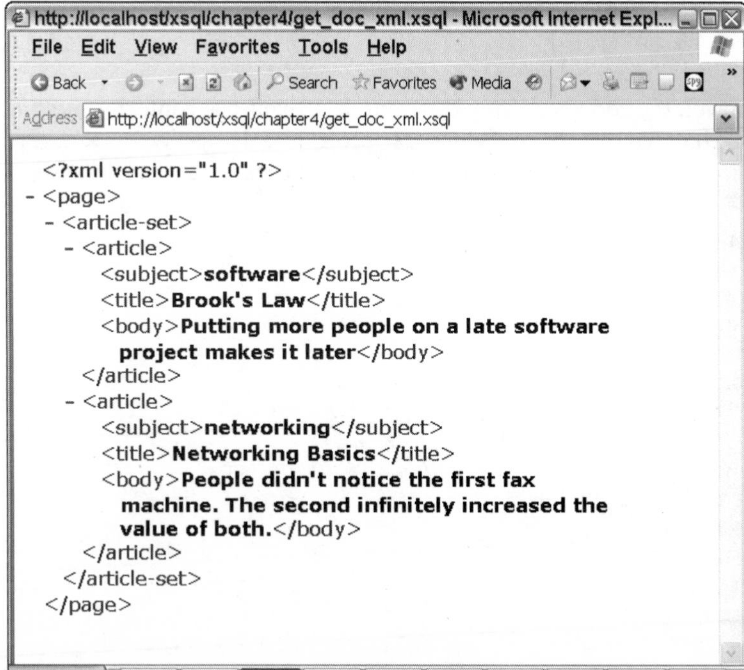

Figure 11.3 XML documents in XSQL results.

For Oracle 9i, the DBMS_QUERY package will XML-ify a query into a CLOB variable. You then break the CLOB into strings that can be passed to the http.prn procedure.

```
CREATE OR REPLACE PROCEDURE use_dbms_xmlgen IS
  ctx dbms_xmlgen.ctxhandle;
  result_clob CLOB;
  output_var VARCHAR2(4000);
  offset_var INTEGER :=1;
  buf_size INTEGER:=4000;
BEGIN
  ctx:=dbms_xmlgen.newContext('SELECT * FROM emp');
  result_clob:=dbms_xmlgen.getXML(ctx);
  WHILE offset_var < dbms_lob.getlength(result_clob) LOOP
    DBMS_LOB.READ(result_clob,buf_size,offset_var,output_var);
    htp.prn(output_var);
    offset_var:=offset_var+4000;
  END LOOP;
END;
```

You call this procedure with the following XSQL:

```
<?xml version="1.0"?>
<page connection="demo" xmlns:xsql="urn:oracle-xsql">
  <xsql:include-owa>
    use_dbms_xmlgen;
  </xsql:include-owa>
</page>
```

At the Oracle 8i level, the code is slightly different: It doesn't use contexts, and the SQL statement can be handed directly to the getXML procedure. However, the XMLGEN package has been deprecated. Oracle 9i users should use the DBMS_XMLGEN package instead.

```
CREATE OR REPLACE use_xmlgen IS
 result_clob CLOB;
 output_var VARCHAR2(4000);
 offset_var INTEGER :=1;
 buf_size INTEGER:=4000;
BEGIN
  result_clob:=xmlgen.getXML('SELECT * FROM emp');
  WHILE offset_var < dbms_lob.getlength(result_clob) LOOP
    DBMS_LOB.READ(result_clob,buf_size,offset_var,output_var);
    htp.prn(output_var);
    offset_var:=offset_var+4000;
  END LOOP;
END;
```

In both of these cases, your result is going to look exactly the same as if you executed the SQL using the `xsql:query` element. The XML generated using these APIs is also in the canonical format.

So, for these simple examples, you've done a lot of work in order to do what XSQL does anyway! In general, if you can get the same result using a straight XSQL query, then you probably should. Of course, with this methodology you can apply a lot of procedural logic, as you did with reference cursors a few pages ago. But then, you can probably accomplish the same logic using the `xsql:ref-cursor-function` action. It works great any time you wish to procedurally create the SQL statement whose results you want in XML. And again, if you can get the same result using `xsql:ref-cursor-function`, then you should employ that action instead.

There are some cases where you will find use for the `DBMS_XMLGEN` (or `XMLGEN`) packages at the PL/SQL level. The key advantage is that you can assemble your XML at a very atomic level and have great control over it. You can dynamically select exactly the XML elements you wish to put into the output and base those decisions on any data you can access in the database. If you need to grab a couple of rows from the database, you can put them into the output with the `htp.prn` procedure discussed earlier.

However, it's important to remember that the `DBMS_XMLGEN` (or `XMLGEN`) packages used in this way are just one tool in your toolbox. You should probably keep it in the bottom of your toolbox and reach for `xsql:query` and `xsql:ref-cursor-function`. Also, you should understand action handlers before basing too much code on this approach. An action handler can also give you fine-grained control over the XML, as well as give you more precise ways of handling elements than the approach described here.

XMLType

In our earlier example with Oracle Text, you stored the XML as a simple string. Oracle 9i users can also store documents using the `XMLType`. The `XMLType` gives you much more power over your XML than you have with simple strings. There are two ways to use `XMLType`: (1) You can create an `XMLType` object at runtime based on a string or clob, or (2) you can create a column in the database of `XMLType`. Having an `XMLType` as a column is more efficient, so you'll learn about this method first. However, it's often impractical to do this, especially if you are working with existing database schemas. You'll see how to construct and use the `XMLType` dynamically, also. This section concludes by detailing all the procedures and functions you can use in conjunction with `XMLType`.

Here is how you get started. Your first step is to create a table that has an `XMLType` column. You can do that as follows:

```
CREATE TABLE XMLType_table(
  ID  NUMBER,
  DOC_NAME VARCHAR2(20),
  xml_doc SYS.XMLTYPE);
```

Now you want to put some data in to your table. The only difference between this insert and the plain-text insert is the call to `sys.XMLType.createXML`. This changes the string data into the `XMLType`.

```
INSERT INTO XMLType_table (id,doc_name,xml_doc) VALUES (1,'doc1',
sys.XMLType.createXML('<article>
 <subject>networking</subject>
 <title>Networking Basics</title>
 <body> People didn''t notice the first fax machine. The second
infinitely increased the value of both. </body>
</article>')
);

INSERT INTO XMLType_table(id,doc_name,xml_doc) VALUES (2,'doc2',
sys.XMLType.createXML('<article>
 <subject>software</subject>
 <reference>Mythical Man Month, Dr. Fred Brooks</reference>
 <title>Brook''s Law</title>
 <body>Putting more people on a late software project makes it
later.</body>
</article>')
);
```

As before, you have to create an index on your column, and you'll have to update it every time that you update the data. However, you don't have to create a section group first. Oracle already knows it's dealing with XML.

```
CREATE INDEX XMLType_index ON XMLType_table(xml_doc)
    INDEXTYPE IS ctxsys.context;
```

At this point, you can do all of the types of searches that you did earlier with Oracle Text. Here is one example:

```
SELECT xml_doc
   FROM XMLType_table
   WHERE contains(xml_doc,'people INPATH (/article/body)')>0;
```

Using the `xsql:include-owa` action, you can also use the `htp.prn` technique to push the document into the XSQL output. In this particular case, the documents are less than 4,000 characters, so you can use the `getStringVal` function. However, if the documents are larger, a runtime error would be generated. If there may be documents longer than 4,000 characters, you would have to iterate through a `CLOB`, as you did in the previous section.

```
CREATE OR REPLACE get_XMLType_xml IS
  xml_doc_str VARCHAR2(4000);
  CURSOR doc_cursor IS
```

```
      SELECT a.xml_doc.getStringVal()
       FROM XMLType_table a
       WHERE CONTAINS(xml_doc,'people INPATH (/article/body)')>0;
      BEGIN
       htp.print('<article-set>');
      OPEN doc_cursor;
      LOOP
       FETCH doc_cursor INTO xml_doc_str;
       EXIT WHEN doc_cursor%NOTFOUND;
       htp.prn(xml_doc_str);
      END LOOP;
      htp.print('</article-set>');
   END;
```

At this point, you haven't done anything more than you did when the XML was just plain text. The following example takes you into new territory. The `extract` function allows you to pull just the nodes you want from the document. By simply altering our cursor statement as follows:

```
   CURSOR doc_cursor IS
      SELECT a.xml_doc.extract('/article/subject').getStringVal()
       FROM XMLType_table a
       WHERE CONTAINS(xml_doc,'people INPATH (/article/body)')>0;
```

you can get a result that just returns the subject nodes. But the `getStringVal` is still limited to 4,000 characters. If the node that you're extracting (including the text, all the children, and all of the tags) contains more than 4,000 characters of data, a runtime error will be raised.

With this simple `SELECT` statement you are solving a complex problem very elegantly. The relational model is great at storing structured data, such as a company's payroll or accounts receivable, but has a hard time with unstructured document data. XML is great for formatting documents, but it is complex to store and search across sets of XML documents. By storing XML documents in the Oracle database, you get all of the benefits of the relational model plus the backup, recovery, and performance afforded by Oracle. By using Oracle Text in conjunction with the `XMLType`, you can easily search the documents and extract the nodes that you want. You'll be seeing more of this lucrative combination in Chapter 14, "Building XSQL Web Applications," when you build your first XSQL application from scratch.

NOTE The `extract` function, along with several other functions and procedures of `XMLType`, uses XPath to search the document. You'll learn more about XPath in the next chapters.

In this case, you had `XMLType` set up at the database level. You can also instantiate `XMLType` at runtime. In the following example, you return to the `docs_table` used in the original examples of Oracle Text. In that table, the XML is stored simply as a

VARCHAR2. If you want to use the procedures and functions of XMLType with that XML, you can do so by using the following createXML function:

```
SELECT
sys.XMLType.createXML(text).extract('/article/subject').getStringVal()
 AS subject_node
  FROM docs_table
  WHERE CONTAINS(text,'people INPATH (/article/body)')>0;
```

By replacing the SELECT statement in the cursor definition in the createXML function can take either a string or a CLOB as its argument. However, as before, the get StringVal is still limited to 4,000 characters, and a runtime error will be generated if your extraction is more than that.

In the preceding examples, you've seen three of the subprograms available to XML Type: (1) createXML, (2) extract, and (3) getStringVal. Table 11.1 describes the member functions that are available to you. The member functions can be called on an xMLType object, while the static functions can be called at any time.

As with all functions, they can be compounded. This is most useful with the extract function. You can extract a subset of the document—which could possibly only be one node—and then perform further functions on it. This is typically how getNumberVal and getStringVal are used.

Table 11.1 XMLType Functions

FUNCTION	DESCRIPTION
sys.XMLType.createXML (input IN CLOB) RETURN sys.XMLType	Static function creates XMLType object from a CLOB.
Sys.XMLType.createXML (input IN varchar2) RETURN sys.XMLType	Static function creates XMLType object from a string.
existsNode(xpathExpr IN varchar2) RETURN number	Evaluates the XPath expression on the given document and returns 1 if there are any nodes that match, 0 if none.
extract(xpathExpr IN varchar2) RETURN sys.XMLType	Evaluates the XPath expression and returns the node that it describes, or NULL.
getNumberVal() RETURN number	Returns the value of a text node as a number. The text of the node must describe a number.
getStringVal() RETURN number	Returns the value of a node as a string. If the string is more than 4,000 characters in length, an error will be raised at runtime.
isFragment() RETURN number	Returns 1 if the XMLType object is a fragment, 0 if it is well formed.

Moving On

This chapter showed you how you can access XML in your database. Now, the coverage of the Oracle database is complete. You've learned the basics of Oracle SQL, PL/SQL, Text, and now XML retrieval and how to use these technologies with XSQL. Now that you've mastered data retrieval, the next step is to learn about presentation of your data. The next few chapters cover XSLT.

CHAPTER 12

XSLT

This chapter covers one of the most exciting XML standards, XSLT. An XSLT processor takes an XML document and an XSLT stylesheet as input and produces whatever the stylesheet tells it to. This can be HTML, XML, some other markup language, text, or anything else that you can imagine. This chapter walks you through XSLT, starting with a conceptual overview. XSLT isn't your typical programming language, and a lot of procedural programmers dive in a little too quickly. Hopefully, the first section will help you avoid that fate.

The next section looks at how to create stylesheets using your current Web skills. Generally, stylesheets are designed to template Web pages, and they include a lot of HTML in them. However, XSLT stylesheets have to be well-formed XML documents, and traditional HTML is not. XHTML is a standard that makes HTML XML-compliant. Though stylesheets aren't required to be XHTML, you can use the XHTML standard as a way to make old HTML XML-compliant and in the creation of new Web documents.

In the next chapter, you get in to the heart of XSLT. The first step is to look at all of the different elements of XSLT. These elements merge your source XML with the templates in your stylesheet. Next, XPath is covered, which is the language that allows you to navigate the input XML tree. We wrap up with an overview of the XSLT and XPath functions available to you.

Getting Started with XSLT

After you've learned a couple of programming languages, they tend to blend together. Java is like C, but with objects. XML is like HTML. PL/SQL is a procedural language like Pascal, but is tightly integrated with SQL. However, though it might be easy to make the transition from, say, C++ to Java, the transition to XSLT can be tough. It's not that XSLT is a hard language—it is quite simple and elegant. Rather, the beginning XSLT developer needs to have the right mind-set when approaching it. It's not only a question of what XSLT can and can't do, it's what your XSLT stylesheets *should* and *should not* do.

This section considers XSLT on a conceptual level. The first step is to understand the goals that XSLT was designed to accomplish. Next, you'll learn about the push and pull models, which are two different ways to think about how XSLT interacts with XML. Our final discussion concerns the process of creating stylesheets and how this affects the way you think about your XSLT code.

The Place of XSLT

XSLT is a standards-based way to separate the problems of Web design from the problems of application development. Instead of having to train Web designers a different way to "design around" the logic for each project—something necessary when scripting languages are involved—XSLT provides a standard way that can be learned once by all and easily used across multiple projects. However, as with all new paradigms, there is some learning-curve pain both for designers and programmers.

Web interface designers are used to the problem. They design a Web page based on static data and hand it over to the developers. The developers mangle it for a while and integrate it with the back end. At some point, there is some kind of problem. The designer is shown a problem that needs to be fixed on the Web page, which, in the browser, looks remarkably like the page they had recently handed over to the developers. The code itself, however, is most certainly not. In the original code is a mishmash of new elements: maybe PHP: Hypertext Preprocessor (PHP), maybe active server page (ASP), maybe Java Server Page (JSP). To fix the design problem, they not only have to manipulate the markup, they also have to work correctly with whatever scripting language is involved.

In some ways, XSLT is yet another scripting language du jour. The key difference is that it is built for this particular problem, and XSLT skills can be used over a variety of projects. When scripting languages are involved, the interface designers have to relearn the new widgets for each project. The problem is always, "How are we getting the data?" In an XSLT world, you know how you are getting the information—it's coming as XML. Then, the challenge is designing and communicating how that XML is being provided. For XSQL developers, this is especially easy because the XML is always passed in a standard way.

The problem for developers is twofold. First, the data has to be passed as XML. Generally, this isn't too difficult, and it is usually trivial when using XSQL because the XML is created in the same way by default. Second, the real issue for developers is learni how to use XSLT in the best way

XSLT has some of the facets of procedural programming, such as loops and cond tional processing. However, it is much more closely akin to HTML than it is to a procedural language. If you try to use it like a procedural language, then you are likely to get into trouble. Your code will be messy and difficult to maintain. Though a little spaghetti code is a fact of life on development projects, it's especially defeating in the case of XSLT. A primary purpose of XSLT is to make it easy to separate application development from front-end design. However, if messy code is interjected into front-end markup, then that purpose has been subverted.

As you learn XSLT, it's important to keep the readability and reuse goals in mind. XSLT isn't a particularly modular language, but with the right approach you can reuse code. Most important, however, you should work with your teammates to ensure that the XSLT is maintainable. In practice, this often means looking beyond the first tools that you would use as a procedural programmer, such as iteration, variables, and conditional processing.

The most powerful tool in the XSLT arsenal is XPath, the language for locating nodes in an XML tree. You'll find that you can accomplish a lot with this simple language in a situation in which you would normally require a lot of loops and if statements. A good rule of thumb is to try to separate the interface problems so that you use loops as little as possible. This will force you to use templates and to make better use of XPath. In the end, you'll have more modular stylesheets that are more usable by the rest of your team.

Push and Pull

Now that you have a feeling for how XSLT integrates with the overall process, it's time to think about how to use XSLT in relation to XML. There are two primary ways to think about this: (1) push and (2) pull. In the push model, you think of XML as a document, whereas with the pull model you think of XML as a data structure. XSLT itself doesn't change based on the approach, and the two approaches are interchangeable. However, it's important to understand the different paradigms and how you can use them to achieve your goals.

Let's start with the push model, which should be very familiar to those that have developed HTML with cascading stylesheet (CSS). When you use CSS, you have styles that are applied to HTML. In the end, you have your original HTML document beautified by the CSS code. The analogy in XSLT is that you have templates that are applied to XML. The structure of the XML document, such as the ordering of nodes, is largely maintained. What the XSLT processor does is apply stylesheet templates to the various XML nodes to produce the output. This approach is diagrammed in Figure 12.1.

In the push model, the XML document is the driving force. In the pull model, the XSLT stylesheet is the driver. Instead of pushing XML nodes through templates, the stylesheet pulls data out of the XML document. Thus, the XML document acts really more like a data structure. The form of the document is largely dictated by the stylesheet. This approach is diagrammed in Figure 12.2.

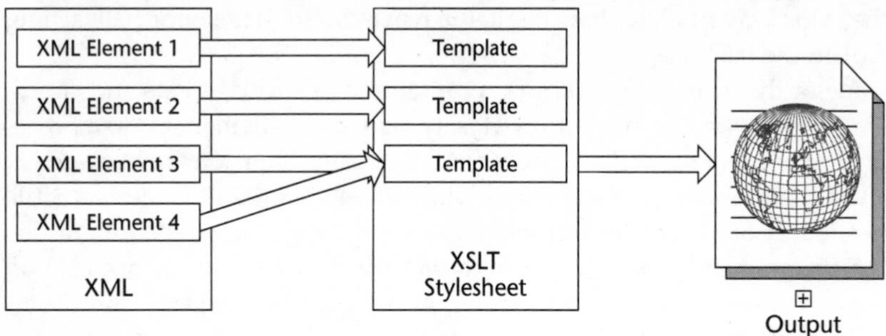

Figure 12.1 The push model.

An XSLT stylesheet is typically a compromise between the push and the pull models. In general, the push model is simpler and more elegant. It requires less heavy lifting inside the stylesheet, and thus the stylesheet is more understandable and maintainable. However, you are at the mercy of the XML input. In the case of XSQL, this means that you are at the mercy of the canonical XML datagram. In spite of this, you still have a lot of control that you can exercise to keep your stylesheets clean and elegant.

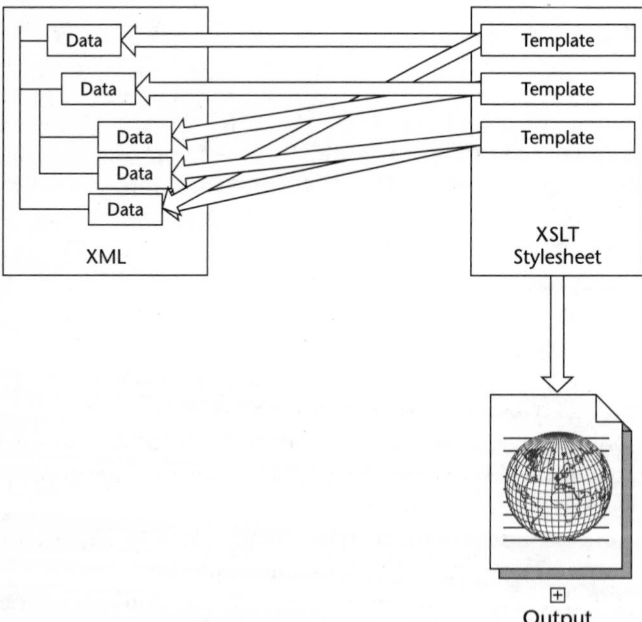

Figure 12.2 The pull model.

This starts by wisely constructing your SQL queries. If the SQL in your XSQL closely resembles how the data should appear in the output page, then you will have an easier time coding your XSLT. For instance, you can use an order by clause in the SQL queries instead of sorting the data in the stylesheet. You can use cursor subqueries that produce XML that is deeper than that achieved with simple queries. In some cases, you may actually find it easier, and possibly more efficient, to do two queries that fetch the same data in different ways. This might keep you from having to pull data out of a result tree into a very different format.

XHTML and Stylesheet Creation

First, XHTML isn't some extreme HTML used for dangerous, risk-taking Web sites that do a lot of bungee jumping and mountain biking. Nor is it HTML with marital problems. XHTML is simply an XML-compliant version of HTML. Because both originated from the same mother tongue, SGML, XML, and HTML are closely related. The angle brackets of XML are very familiar to anyone that has coded a Web page. In fact, many HTML pages out there today are valid XML documents.

The problem is that HTML is a little out-of-sync with XML. Because an XSLT processor requires that a stylesheet be a valid XML document, this makes creating stylesheets out of any given HTML document you have lying around a little tricky. XHTML resolves the discrepancies between XML and HTML.

Your stylesheets don't have to be in compliance with XHTML. In fact, a valid XHTML document can't be a stylesheet—you have to remove the `DOCTYPE` declaration first. So why worry with XHTML? XHTML solves a problem that you have to solve anyway—making HTML valid XML. Instead of reinventing the wheel, you can leverage the research that has gone into XHTML. By making your documents XML compliant in the manner that XHTML does, you are in sync with an important emerging standard. This will have many benefits: Your transitioned stylesheets will probably be able to leverage future XHTML-compatible tools, and you'll be in greater compliance with future Web browsers and other Web agents.

At its strictest, XHTML is a bit out of compliance with early HTML specifications. However, modern Web browsers accept XHTML, and Web browsers have always been designed to be very tolerant when processing markup. Part of our discussion in this section will focus on how to ensure compatibility with older browsers while remaining compliant with XHTML.

TIP **If you find that you have some problems with older browsers, you can direct the XSLT processor to output HTML by using the `<xsl:output>` element described later in this chapter. It will change non-HTML-compliant XHTML tags to the equivalent HTML tags, resolving the XHTML problems with older browsers.**

This section will act as a primer on XHTML. It doesn't fully lay out the specification, because if you already know HTML, you don't really need to see it. Rather, the focus is on how to make HTML documents into XHTML documents that can be used with XSLT. The first section looks at the specific changes that you need to make to existing HTML documents to make them XHTML compliant. Our discussion on XHTML ends by looking at some foolproof ways to make your HTML documents XHTML compliant and ready for stylesheet action.

XHTML Defined

A document is an XHTML document if it is well-formed XML and is valid against one of the XHTML document type definitions (DTDs). When transitioning HTML documents to XHTML, you must make a document well-formed XML. Because certain tags in HTML aren't valid XML elements, part of this step is modifying these tags. The documents also must be valid, so you have to choose the appropriate DTD for your case. As is the case with all valid documents, your XHTML document must agree with the structure outlined by those DTDs. This section outlines each of these constraints.

First, let's look at making your HTML well formed in accordance with the guidelines of XHTML. The requirements are as follows:

All tags must be properly nested. Because Web browsers tend to be very forgiving, there is a lot of HTML out there that isn't properly nested. Fixing those cases is really just an issue of making a document HTML compliant.

All tag names must be lowercase. HTML is case insensitive; however, XML is case sensitive. XHTML requires all of its tags to be lowercase.

All attribute values must be quoted. HTML allows attribute values to be unquoted as long as the value doesn't contain spaces. XML forbids this.

Script should be encapsulated as CDATA. Though not strictly required, XML will try to escape special characters (e.g., `&` and <) that often occur in scripts. This is easily avoided by escaping the entire section as CDATA.

Minimized attributes aren't allowed. A minimized attribute is an attribute that doesn't have a value. The checked attribute of the input element and the noshade attribute of hr are common examples. These attributes must be given some value.

Dangling open tags aren't allowed. HTML allows dangling open tags (`<p>` and `<img>`. XML requires all elements to be closed—a start tag must have a matching end tag, or the element must have the form of an empty element.

The last requirement opens the door to some complexities. To achieve XML compliance, you can either change the danglers to empty tags or give them matching end tags. Most browsers will accept either strategy, although some will have trouble with the latter. XHTML defines specifically which tags should be empty elements, as listed in Table 12.1.

Table 12.1 XHTML Empty Elements

XHTML ELEMENT	INSTEAD OF HTML ELEMENT . . .
`<area />`	`<area>`
`<base />`	`<base>`
`<basefront />`	`<basefront>`
` `	` `
`<hr />`	`<hr>`
`<img />`	`<img>`

The space after the element name is deliberate. It helps XHTML to be compatible with older browsers. All other elements should be closed with a matching tag (e.g., <p> and </p>).

Minimized attributes also change in XHTML. XML doesn't allow you to have dangling attributes without a value. Table 12.2 lists the affected attributes and how they should be translated into XHTML.

Table 12.2 Minimized Attributes in XHTML

HTML MINIMIZED ATTRIBUTE	XHTML ATTRIBUTE
checked	checked="checked"
compact	compact="compact"
declare	declare="declare"
defer	defer="defer"
disabled	disabled="disabled"
ismap	ismap="ismap"
multiple	multiple="multiple"
noresize	noresize="noresize"
noshade	noshade="noshade"
nowrap	nowrap="nowrap"
readonly	readonly="readonly"
selected	selected="selected"

After observing these rules, you have a well-formed document. This is all that you need to use your HTML as an XSLT stylesheet. To go ahead and make your document XHTML, it must validate against one of the XHTML DTDs that are listed in Table 12.3. This involves putting a `DOCTYPE`declaration at the top of your file. When you transition your XHTML to an XSLT stylesheet, you will need to remove the `DOCTYPE` declaration.

Generally, you are going to want to use the `Transitional` DTD. You declare this by using the following at the top of your document:

```
<!DOCTYPE html PUBLIC "-//W3C//DTD XHTML 1.0 Transitional//EN"
"http://www.w3.org/TR/xhtml1/DTD/xhtml1-transitional.dtd">
```

If you use frames and you want your frameset page to be XHTML, you need to use the following `DOCTYPE` declaration:

```
<!DOCTYPE html PUBLIC "-//W3C//DTD XHTML 1.0 Frameset//EN"
"http://www.w3.org/TR/xhtml1/DTD/xhtml1-frameset.dtd">
```

If you wish to use the `Strict` DTD, this is the declaration that you want:

```
<!DOCTYPE html PUBLIC "-//W3C//DTD XHTML 1.0 Strict//EN"
"http://www.w3.org/TR/xhtml1/DTD/strict.dtd">
```

The key requirement that both the `Transitional` and `Strict` DTDs enforce is that a head section is required. Even if it is empty, you still have to have it. The strict DTD goes a bit further on a couple of points: It is much stricter about structure and doesn't allow deprecated attributes.

Table 12.3 XHTML DTDs

DTD	DESCRIPTION
`Transitional`	Probably your best bet. It is loose and allows you to create code that is largely compatible with older HTML standards.
`Strict`	This DTD enforces all of XHTML rules, especially pertaining to how documents must be structured. Its use could cause backward compatibility problems for older browsers.
`Frameset`	The `frameset` DTD is used on pages that describe framesets.

When using the `Strict` DTD, you will probably run into the structural requirements when a child element of the body tag isn't a block element. Only block elements can be direct children of the body element. The following are block elements:

HEADING ELEMENTS

`<h1>`

`<h2>`

`<h3>`

`<h4>`

`<h5>`

`<h6>`

LIST ELEMENTS

`<ul>`

`<ol>`

`<dl>`

BLOCKTEXT ELEMENTS

`<pre>`

`<hr>`

`<blockquote>`

`<address>`

`<div>`

`<table>`

`<fieldset>`

`<ins>`

`<del>`

`<script>`

`<noscript>`

The other implication of this is that text can't dangle inside the body tag. It must be enclosed in something—usually a `<p>` element. The `Strict` DTD also forbids the use of deprecated attributes. This is more troubling, because you lose compatibility with older browsers because of this. The structural requirements lead to better HTML, but using the `Strict` DTD works against good, open site design because it takes away older features from you. Generally, the `Transitional` DTD is preferred.

A Simple XHTML Transformation

This section defines precisely what XHTML is and how it relates to traditional HTML. The first step is to look at a typical legal HTML document that isn't XML compliant. Then, you'll make it XML compliant by transitioning it to XHTML. This section concludes with a review that spells out the key rules that define XHTML.

To begin, please consider the following HTML document:

```
<html>
    <body>
       <H1>Hello!</H1>
       <p>
       <IMG SRC=blah.gif ID=my_picture>
       <br>
       Hi! This is my home page. I want to tell you a few things.
       <p>
       <ul>
         <li>I like playing on the Internet
         <li>I just want to dance!
         <li>I wok in the would
       </UL
      That's about all <br>
      I have for now. <BR>
      <p>
      Maybe I'll have <br>
      more to say     <Br>
      later.          <bR>
      <Hr>
      <b><i>Later!</B></I>
    </boDY>
</HTML>
```

This HTML is quite ugly, but it will work in most all Web browsers. However, it doesn't stand a chance of being a valid stylesheet and is a long way from being valid XHTML. Let's examine the worst offense first:

```
<b><i>Later!</B></I>
```

The tags aren't properly nested. As you learned in Chapter 3, "Hello, XSQL!", the tags have to be properly nested for an XML document to be well formed. The first step is therefore to straighten that out. This yields the following:

```
<b><i>Later!</B></I>
```

However, you still aren't out of the woods. XML, unlike HTML, is case sensitive. These tags aren't a well-formed fragment, because the closing tags are capitalized, whereas the opening tags aren't. This line needs to be fixed to be:

```
<b><i>Later!</b></i>
```

Our document has this case mismatch with almost all of the opening and closing tags. Going through and making the end tags match all of the start tags fixes most of this problem. However, the one set of tags that already match have their own problem:

```
<H1>Hello!</H1>
```

XHTML requires that all element names be in lower case. Thus, this needs to be changed to:

```
<h1>Hello!</h1>
```

Now, all of the start tags have matching end tags, and all of the tag names are lowercase. However, our document still isn't well formed. Our document includes several common HTML tags—`<img>`, `<p>`, `<hr>`, `<br>`, and `<li>`—that are illegal in XML. They have the form of the start tag, but they don't have a matching end tag. They should either have an end tag or take the form of an empty tag. XHTML requires that the `<img>`, `<hr>`, and `<br>` tags should be empty tags, while `<p>` and `<li>` should be closed with `</p>` and `</li>`, respectively.

These aren't the only tags in traditional HTML that aren't XML compliant. Table 12.1 describes how to handle the remaining tags that either should be empty or should be closed. But before exploring that, you are only a couple steps away from having an XHTML document. Our next problem deals with attributes. Attributes must be quoted, and the attribute names must be lowercase. This yields the following:

```
<img src="blah.gif" name="my_picture" />
```

You need one other fix on the `img` element: The `name` attribute used by `a`, `applet`, `frame`, `iframe`, `img`, and `map` is deprecated in XHTML and replaced by the `id` attribute. The easiest way to fix this and to maintain compatibility is to specify the `id` attribute and the `name` attribute. Also, the `alt` attribute is required in XHTML.

```
<img src="blah.gif"
     name="my_picture"
     id="my_picture"
     alt="blah blah blah"/>
```

There is one fix left. The `hr` tag has a minimized attribute, `"no_shade"`. Such attributes aren't allowed in XML, because attributes must have a value. The `<hr>` tag should be changed to:

```
<hr noshade="noshade"/>
```

Now you have completed the transformation of the document to XHTML. Here is the final product. It validates against the `Transitional` XHTML DTD.

```
<?xml version="1.0" encoding="UTF-8" ?>
<!DOCTYPE HTML PUBLIC "-//W3C//DTD HTML 4.01 Transitional//EN">
<html>
```

```
    <head>
       <title>Hello!</title>
     </head>
     <body>
       <h1>Hello!</h1>
        <p>
        <img src="blah.gif" id="my_picture" name="my_picture" alt="blah
blah blah"/>
        <br/>
        Hi! This is my home page. I want to tell you a few things.
        </p>
        <ul>
          <li>I like playing on the Internet</li>
          <li>I just want to dance!</li>
          <li>I wok in the would</li>
        </ul>
       <p>
         That's about all <br/>
         I have for now. <br/>
       </p>
       <hr noshade="noshade" />
       <p>
         <b><i>Later!</i></b>
       </p>
   </body>
</html>
```

If you want compliance with strict XHTML, then you simply need to remove the deprecated attributes and add the namespace attribute to the HTML element. The following file is in compliance with `Strict` XHTML.

```
<?xml version="1.0" encoding="UTF-8"?>
<!DOCTYPE html
PUBLIC "-//W3C//DTD XHTML 1.0 Strict//EN"
"http://www.w3.org/TR/xhtml1/DTD/xhtml1-strict.dtd">

<html xmlns="http://www.w3.org/1999/xhtml" xml:lang="en" lang="en">
    <head>
       <title>Hello!</title>
     </head>
     <body>
       <h1>Hello!</h1>
       <p>
        <img src="blah.gif" id="my_picture" alt="blah blah blah"/>
        <br/>

        Hi! This is my home page. I want to tell you a few things.
        </p>
        <ul>
          <li>I like playing on the Internet</li>
          <li>I just want to dance!</li>
```

```
            <li>I wok in the would</li>
        </ul>
        <p>
         That's about all <br/>
         I have for now. <br/>
        </p>
        <hr/>
        <p>
         <b><i>Later!</i></b>
        </p>
    </body>
</html>
```

Compliance with `Transitional` XHTML is more than enough to ensure compatibility with XSLT. The advantage of `Strict` compliance is that you are fully compatible with the latest version of XHTML. However, there is a price for this compatibility: Because you aren't allowed to use deprecated attributes, you lose some backward compatibility.

Tips and Tricks of Migrating HTML

If you have a lot of old HTML that you want to make into stylesheets, you may be bracing yourself for a daunting task. Not to worry—there are many ways to make the transition easy. First and foremost, your stylesheets don't have to be fully XHTML compliant. They just have to be XML compliant. Because you have to do some work anyway, there is a strong argument that you might as well bring them fully up-to-date and make them XHTML compliant. Our first tip shows you how to bring your old HTML into XML compliance by just using the XSLT processor. From there, some XHTML tools and validators will be discussed.

Your first step should be to get Dave Ragget's Tidy utility. It will automatically convert most HTML, even really messy HTML, to well-formed XML. You can locate the utility by going to either of these URIs:

`http://www.w3.org/People/Raggett/tidy/`

`http://tidy.sourceforge.net/`

After installation you can run the tool as follows:

```
Tidy —output-xhtml yes —indent yes MyOld.html > LikeNew.xhtml
```

You can then run a document through the validator at `validator.w3.org`. Simply put the file on a public Web site, navigate to `validator.w3.org`, and type in the URI. You should have one of the XHTML DTDs in place to make sure it is valid XHTML.

From there, your next step is to transition it to a stylesheet. Here is the process:

1. Get rid of any `DOCTYPE` instructions.
2. Add `xsl:version="1.0"` as an attribute/value pair to the html element.
3. Save the file as a stylesheet with the `.xsl` extension.
4. Create a dummy XSQL file that references the stylesheet.

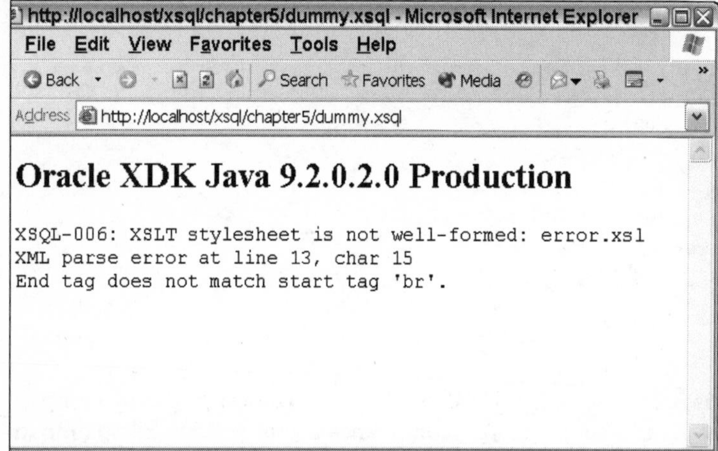

Figure 12.3 XSLT error.

The dummy XSQL file doesn't need to contain any actual SQL queries. In fact, it should be as simple as possible. This is just a way to check and make sure that the Oracle XSLT Processor likes your file. The following will do great:

```
<?xml version="1.0"?>
<?xml-stylesheet type="text/xsl" href="my_stylesheet.xsl"?>
<page>
</page>
```

If your file is okay, the XSLT processor is just going to display the page to the browser. After all, there is no actual XSLT code that needs to be processed. However, if there is a problem with your stylesheet, then the translator will report an error back to you. Figure 12.3 shows an example.

The error was generated by using the original ugly HTML example that appeared previously. If nothing else, you can use the XSLT processor to iteratively fix your HTML, line by line.

Moving On

This chapter gave you a high-level overview of XSLT, which should have complemented the earlier examples that used XSLT. Chapter 13, "XSLT In-Depth," covers the details of coding XSLT. Because XSLT controls how your XSQL application looks, it's an important part of your overall code. You'll see this in Chapter 14, "Building XSQL Web Applications," when you create your own application. A lot of the overall code is XSLT stylesheets.

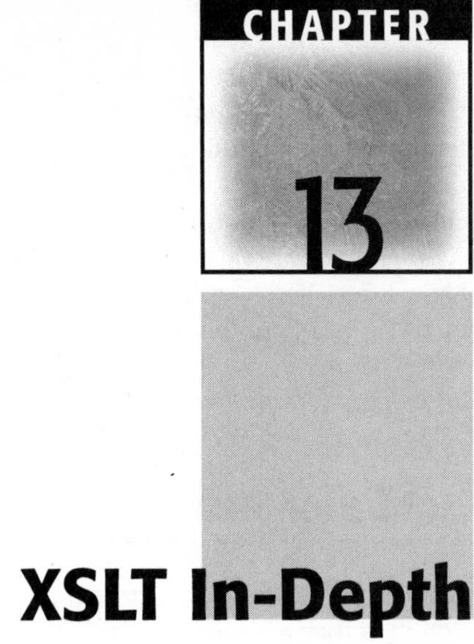

XSLT In-Depth

This section details all the elements in XSLT based on what they do. It is meant as a tutorial on the first reading and then a quick reference after that. It starts with the root element and then introduces all the elements, including their syntax and examples. The following XSQL is used for all the examples in this section. It produces the data for the employees in the emp table. To use the examples in this section, be sure to change href to whatever name you give the stylesheet.

```
<?xml version="1.0"?>
<?xml-stylesheet type="text/xsl" href="some-stylesheet.xsl"?>
<page connection="demo" xmlns:xsql="urn:oracle-xsql">
  <xsql:query>
    SELECT * from emp
  </xsql:query>
</page>
```

At this point in your reading, it is assumed that you know how XSLT stylesheets fit in with the rest of the XSQL framework. In general, a datagram is returned from the database and in the canonical format, and you use an XSLT stylesheet to transform it into something useful to the client. With certain actions—xsql:insert-request, xsql:update-request, xsql:delete-request, and xsql:insert-param—you can also transform the input using an XSLT stylesheet. From there, you'll learn about the selection of values from the inputted XML document.

This chapter looks at all the details of using XSLT stylesheets. You'll learn about all the XSLT elements, as well as XPath, which allows you to search locate nodes in the inputted XML document. The first discussion concerns the root element; the next discussion shows you how to control the output with the `xsl:output` element. From there, you get into the core of XSLT—templates. You can't really write a simple example without using templates, so you've seen them before. In Chapter 14, you'll get a chance to apply your knowledge learned here to a real-world application. Also in that chapter, you'll see how to iterate through sets of nodes and how to use conditional logic. From there, you'll learn about the rest of the XSLT elements, in addition to how to create XML entities and handle special cases with text, how to number elements, how to deal with variables and parameters, how to reuse stylesheets, how to `sor`, and how to handle whitespace. The chapter concludes by looking at whitespace.

Root Element

A stylesheet is an XML document; thus it requires a root element. The XSLT specification says that the root element should be either `xsl:stylesheet` or its synonym, `xsl:transform`. In practice, the Oracle XSLT processor will accept any element as the root element as long as the attributes required of the `xsl:stylesheet` element are attributes of the root. This section looks at the syntax of the root element and provides examples.

xsl:stylesheet Syntax

The `xsl:stylesheet` element can only be the root element of an XSLT stylesheet. It is completely synonymous with the `xsl:transform` element. Its attributes describe the stylesheet to the XSLT processor. You can optionally use the `html` element as the root and simply add these stylesheet attributes to the `html` element. The syntax of the `xsl:stylesheet` element is below. A stylesheet element is required to be the root element and only one stylesheet element is permitted per stylesheet.

```
<xsl:stylesheet
      version = "version_number"
      xmlns:xsl = "namespace_URI"
      id = "id"
      extension-element-prefixes="extension_prefix_list"
      exclude-result-prefixes="exclude_prefix_list">
    any xml
</xsl:stylesheet>
```

Table 13.1 lists the attributes.

Table 13.1 `xsl:stylesheet` Attributes

ATTRIBUTE	DESCRIPTION
`Version`	The version of the stylesheet, which should be 1.0. If it is greater than 1.0, forwards-compatible processing will be enabled. This means that the XSLT processor must process the stylesheet with the expectation that new features of XSLT are being used that the processor doesn't know about.
`Xmlns:xsl`	The namespace for the stylesheet. The URL listed should be the namespace. It is not strictly required, though highly recommended.
`Id`	An identifier for the stylesheet.
`Extension-element-prefixes`	Whitespace-delimited list of namespace prefixes of extension elements used in the stylesheet.
`Exclude-result-prefixes`	Whitespace-delimited list of namespace prefixes that should be excluded from the output.

The root element can't have a parent, but it can have the child elements listed in Table 13.2. Any `xsl:include` or `xsl:import` child elements must precede all other child elements.

Table 13.2 Children of the Root Element

CHILD	ELEMENT
`xsl`	`import`
`xsl`	`include`
`xsl`	`attribute-set`
`xsl`	`decimal-format`

(continues)

Table 13.2 Children of the Root Element *(Continued)*

CHILD	ELEMENT
xsl	key
xsl	namespace-alias
xsl	param
xsl:preserve	space
xsl:strip	space
xsl	output
xsl	template
xsl	variable

Examples

Examples are provided of the `xsl:stylesheet` and `xsl:transform` elements acting as root, as well as the use of an arbitrary root element. The basic stylesheet element looks like this:

```
<xsl:stylesheet
    xmlns:xsl = "http://www.w3.org/1999/XSL/Transform"
    version = "1.0" >
 . . . XSLT code and other XML

</xsl:stylesheet>
```

You might occasionally run across a stylesheet that has a root element like this:

```
<xsl:transform
    xmlns:xsl = "http://www.w3.org/1999/XSL/Transform"
    version = "1.0" >
 . . . XSLT code and other XML

</xsl:transform>
```

The XSLT specification defines the `xsl:transform` element as completely synonymous with the `xsl:stylesheet` element. All processors should allow this behavior.

The following example makes use of the other two attributes—extension-element-prefixes and exclude-element-prefixes.

```
<xsl:stylesheet
    xmlns:xsl = "http://www.w3.org/1999/XSL/Transform"
    version = "1.0"
    extension-element-prefixes=""
    exclude-element-prefixes="">
       XSLT code and other XML

</xsl:stylesheet>
```

Controlling the Output

The output of the XSLT processor can be fine-tuned with the xsl:output element. The xsl:output element is used to communicate directions to the processor about how to produce the output. By default, XML is produced with a mime-type text/xml. The xsl:output element can tell the processor that you wish to have HTML outputted and a mime-type text/html. Though this won't make much difference for modern browsers, it can make your code more compatible with older browsers that predate XML. This section details the syntax of the xsl:output element and provides examples of its use.

xsl:output Syntax

The syntax of the xsl:output element, followed by a table describing the attributes, is given here. As you can see from the syntax diagram, all the attributes are optional. If all the attributes are omitted, the xsl:output element will have no effect.

```
<xsl:output
    method = "xml" | "html" | "text" | "other"
    version = "version_number"
    encoding = "char_encoding"
    omit-xml-declaration = "yes" | "no"
    standalone = "yes" | "no"
    doctype-public = "public_identifier"
    doctype-system = "system_identifier"
    cdate-section-elements = "elements_list"
    indent = "yes" | "no"
    media-type = "mime-type" />
```

The attributes are described in Table 13.3.

It is a top-level element and can only appear as the child of the root element. It can't have children.

Table 13.3 `xsl:output` Attributes

ATTRIBUTE	DESCRIPTION
`method`	Indicates how the output should look and defaults to `xml`. If set to text, non-XML-compliant HTML tags, such ` ` and `<hr>`, will be converted to their original HTML form from their XHTML equivalents, ` ` and `<hr/>`. If set to text, all the XML markup will be excluded from the output.
`version`	Provides a version number for the output. This attribute is ignored by most XSLT processors.
`encoding`	The character encoding that should be used for the output, such as `ISO-8859-1`, `UTF-16`, and `UTF-8`.
`omit-xml-declaration`	If set to `"yes"`, the xml declaration will be omitted from the document.
`standalone`	Sets the value for the stand-alone attribute of the XML declaration.
`doctype-public`	Outputs the value as a public identifier for the document within a DTD.
`doctype-system`	Outputs the value as a system identifier for the document within a DTD.
`cdata-section-elements`	A list of element names that shouldn't have their values altered in any way. Generally, these elements contain characters such as < that are generally URL-encoded.
`indent`	If set to `"yes"`, the XSLT Processor can beautify the output by indenting the XML elements.
`media-type`	The mime-type output. Its default value is `text/xml` for the XML method, `text/html` for the HTML method, and `text/plain` for the text method.

Examples

The most common use of the output element is to choose whether `xml`, `text`, or `html` is output. If you select HTML, XHTML tags such as `<br />` will be converted back to their early HTML form (e.g., `<br>`). This output element will tell the processor to do the following:

```
<xsl:output method = "html" />
```

You can also request that all XML tags be stripped entirely, leaving only the text between the tags. This output method produces text only. It also outputs the text in the iso-8859-1 character set:

```
<xsl:output method = "text" encoding="iso-8859-1"/>
```

The method is global—it changes the way your entire document is output. The cdata-section-elements attribute works on specific elements. It will wrapper any text as a cdata element. This action can be quite useful if an output is to be consumed by an application that will interpret it as XML.

```
<xsl:output method="xml" cdata-section-elements="little_script
funny_element" indent="yes"/>
```

By default, the output method is XML. This doesn't mean that Web browsers won't understand your result; rather, it just means the original XML structure of the document is maintained. Regardless of whether it's interpreted as HTML, you can make the XML prettier by using the indent attribute, as follows:

```
<xsl:output method="ml" indent="yes"/>
```

Let's say that you don't want the output to be understood as some other mime -type, such as Rich Text Format (RTF). You can do this by setting the media-type. In such a case, you might not want the XML declaration to be at the top of the output. This output element takes care of both concerns:

```
<xsl:output method="text" media-type="application/rtf" omit-xml
-declaration="yes"/>
```

The remaining attributes are used to specify XML instructions. Here is an example that uses all three of the remaining attributes:

```
<xsl:output method="xml"
     doctype-public="-//MDT"
     doctype-system="http://www.ibiblio.org/mdthomas"
     standalone="no"/>
```

It yields the following at the top of the document:

```
<?xml version = '1.0' encoding = 'UTF-8' standalone = 'no'?>
<!DOCTYPE html PUBLIC "-//MDT" "http://www.ibiblio.org/mdthomas">
```

Templates

Templates are the key to XSLT. Without at least one of the elements presented here, your stylesheet isn't going to output much from your XML document. The xsl:

template element defines a template, while the apply-template and call-template elements declare where in the stylesheet a template should be invoked.

xsl:template Syntax

The syntax for the xsl:template element, follows, and Table 13.4 describes this element's attributes. It is key to all of XSLT, and it occurs in most XSLT stylesheets. It describes templates that are used to process XML nodes.

```
<xsl:template
  match = "pattern"
  name = "name"
  priority = "number"
  mode = "qname">
. . .
</xsl:template>
```

Table 13.5 lists the parent-child relationships.

No attribute is actually required for the xsl:template element, but generally the match attribute is present. Rarely, the match attribute will be absent, but the name attribute will be present. Without either the match or the name attribute, the template can never be used.

Table 13.4 xsl:template Attributes

ATTRIBUTE	DESCRIPTION
match	The value for this attribute is a pattern that is used to match xml nodes to this template. If more than one template matches a node, XSLT will pick the best template based on the rules described below.
name	This attribute is used to name a template. It is needed only if you wish to use the call-template element with this element.
priority	In cases where more than one template matches and has the same specificity, you should set a priority value to declare which template should be selected.
mode	A mode can be used to specify different templates with the same pattern. The mode is specified on the call to the template.

Table 13.5 Parent-Child Relationships

MAY BE A CHILD OF . . .	MAY BE A PARENT OF . . .
root element	xsl: apply imports
	xsl: apply templates
	xsl: attribute
	xsl: call template
	xsl: choose
	xsl: comment
	xsl: copy
	xsl: copy of
	xsl: element
	xsl: fallback
	xsl: for each
	xsl: if
	xsl: message
	xsl: number
	xsl: processing instruction
	xsl: text
	xsl: value of
	xsl: variable

A value for the match attribute should be written in the abbreviated XPath syntax. You'll learn everything about XPath and the abbreviated XPath syntax later in this chapter. Typically, the patterns used to describe a template are straightforward descriptions of the position of nodes in the document hierarchy. For instance, `"/"` references the root element; the `"/page/rowset/row/*"` references all the the children of row elements. In terms of XSQL, this constitutes all the data fields.

It is possible for more than one template to match a given node in an XML document and for the XSLT processor to choose between multiple templates. It chooses by first looking at the specificity of the various templates. A more specific template is one that more closely describes an XML node and is given more precedence over a less specific template. For instance, if there are two templates with the patterns, `"/page/rowset/row/*"` and `"/page/rowset/row/dept"`, the second template would be applied to the nodes `"/page/rowset/row/dept"`. In cases where multiple templates have the same level of specificity, you would need to use the priority attribute to declare which template should be preferred. If you don't, the XSLT processor can consider it an error. If the processor doesn't consider it an error, the last template to appear in the document is chosen.

The mode attribute simply gives you a way of labeling a template. If you have two different templates but with the same pattern, you can give them different modes. When you invoke the template, either through `apply-templates` or `call-template`, you can specify the mode that you desire. The processor will select the templates of the specified mode. In the absence of a mode attribute in the calling element, XSLT decides on the template based on the rules of specificity and priority described previously.

`xsl:apply-templates` Syntax

The syntax for the `xsl:apply-templates` element follows, and Table 13.6 describes this element's attributes. It directs the XSLT processor to apply templates for a specified set of nodes. By default, the set of nodes comprises the children of the specified node.

```
<xsl:apply-templates
  select = "XPath_expression"
  mode = "mode">
. . .
</xsl:apply-templates>

<xsl:apply-templates
  select = "XPath_expression"
  mode = "mode"/>
```

Table 13.7 lists the parent-child relationships.

If no template is defined for a node, `xsl:apply-templates` grabs the value of the node and applies no formatting of any kind. This is the default template. In such a case, `xsl:apply-templates` is equivalent to the default behavior of `xsl:value-of`. These two elements will be compared further in the next section.

Table 13.6 `xsl:apply-templates` Attributes

ATTRIBUTE	DESCRIPTION
`select`	An `XPath` expression that describes the XML nodes that should have their templates applied. By default, all the children should have their templates applied.
`mode`	Only those templates with a mode attribute of the same value are applied.

Table 13.7 Parent-Child Relationships

CAN BE A CHILD OF . . .	CAN BE A PARENT OF . . .
xsl: attribute	
xsl: comment	
xsl: copy	
xsl: element	
xsl: fallback	
xsl: for-each	
xsl: if	
xsl: message	
xsl: otherwise	
xsl: param	
xsl: processing-instruction	
xsl: template	
xsl: variable	
xsl: when	
xsl: sort	
xsl: with-param	

xsl:call-template

A template can be invoked much like a subroutine with the `xsl:call-template` element. Generally, this element is used in conjunction with one or more `with-params` elements.

```
<xsl:call-template
  name = "template_name">
. . .
</xsl:call-template>

<xsl:call-template
  name = "template_name"/>
```

The only parameter, `name`, is the name of the template that you wish to call. It is specified by that template's name attribute. Table 13.8 lists the parent-child relationships.

Table 13.8 Parent-Child Relationships

CAN BE A CHILD OF . . .	CAN BE A PARENT OF . . .
xsl: attribute	
xsl: comment	
xsl: copy	
xsl: element	
xsl: fallback	
xsl: for-each	
xsl: if	
xsl: message	
xsl: otherwise	
xsl: param	
xsl: processing-instruction	
xsl: template	
xsl: variable	
xsl: when	
xsl: with-param	

When the template is called, the context node isn't changed. Thus, any relative references inside the template won't work. A template referenced by `apply-templates` can assume that the context node has switched to the XML node that matches the template. However, this condition isn't true for `xsl:call-template`. Instead, the references in templates invoked by `xsl:call-template` should be absolute or involve parameters that are passed in.

Examples

The simplest stylesheet that draws data from the source XML use a single `apply -template` call:

```
<?xml version="1.0"?>
<html xmlns:xsl="http://www.w3.org/1999/XSL/Transform" xsl:version="1.0"
>
  <head></head>
  <body>
```

```
    <p>
    <xsl:apply-templates/>
    </p>
   </body>
 </html>
```

This will output the values of all of the text nodes in the XML document. This is rarely what you want, of course, but this example and the next one lend some insight in to how apply-templates works. In this example, only the values for the ENAME elements are returned. If there is no template associated with a particular node, an `apply-templates` simply grabs the text of that node.

```
<?xml version="1.0"?>
<html xmlns:xsl="http://www.w3.org/1999/XSL/Transform" xsl:version="1.0"
>
 <head></head>
  <body>
   <xsl:apply-templates select="/page/ROWSET/ROW/ENAME"/>
  </body>
</html>
```

In the next example, you actually get something that looks nice. You define a template that describes how you want the ENAME nodes to be presented. For this example, they are in boldface and have been included as a list item. The bulleted list is defined around the `apply-templates` element that is inside the page-level template.

```
<?xml version="1.0"?>

<xsl:stylesheet
 version="1.0"
 xmlns:xsl="http://www.w3.org/1999/XSL/Transform">

  <xsl:template match="page">
    <html>
      <head><title>Simple Stylesheet</title></head>
      <body>
        <h1>Simple Stylesheet</h1>
         <ul>
          <xsl:apply-templates select="ROWSET/ROW/ENAME"/>
         </ul>
      </body>
    </html>
  </xsl:template>

  <xsl:template match="ENAME">
      <li><b><xsl:apply-templates/></b></li>
  </xsl:template>

 </xsl:stylesheet>
```

Unlike our previous examples, you are now using a template element. This element must be defined at the top level—a direct child of the root. For this reason, all the HTML code should be included in a template. If you don't include all this code, the XSLT processor won't find it. Generally, a template that matches the root of your XSQL document includes scripts, as well as a head section and any header and footer information

The next example includes the remaining data from the query. Instead of a bulleted list, the data is nicely formatted in a table. It also uses a `call-template` element to put a standard break wherever necessary.

```
<?xml version="1.0"?>
<xsl:stylesheet
 version="1.0"
 xmlns:xsl="http://www.w3.org/1999/XSL/Transform">

  <xsl:template match="page">
    <html>
      <head><title>Simple Stylesheet</title></head>
      <body>
        <h1>Simple Stylesheet</h1>
          <table border="0">
            <th></th><th>Name</th><th>Job</th><th>Salary</th>
            <xsl:apply-templates select="ROWSET/*"/>
          </table>
      </body>
    </html>
  </xsl:template>

  <xsl:template match="ROW">
    <tr>
     <td><xsl:apply-templates select="@num"/></td>
     <td><xsl:apply-templates select="ENAME"/></td>
     <td><xsl:apply-templates select="JOB"/></td>
     <td><xsl:apply-templates select="SAL"/></td>
     <xsl:call-template name="break"/>
    </tr>
  </xsl:template>

<xsl:template name="break">
   <tr><td height="4" colspan="4"><hr/></td></tr>
</xsl:template>

<xsl:template match="JOB | SAL">
      <xsl:apply-templates/>
  </xsl:template>

  <xsl:template match="ENAME">
      <b><xsl:apply-templates/></b>
  </xsl:template>

 </xsl:stylesheet>
```

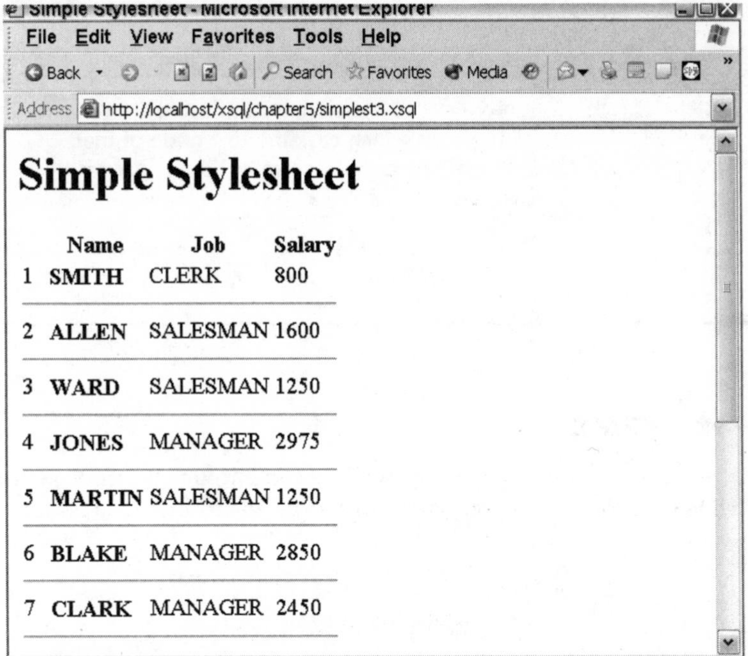

Figure 13.1 Output of stylesheet.

The template produces the output seen in Figure 13.1. The `JOB` and `SAL` elements share a template, while ENAME gets its own. The only named template, break, is referenced by `xsl:call-template`. (In practice, `xsl:call-template` is used in conjunction with parameters. Examples are found later in this chapter.) Also, notice that the `num` attribute from the `ROW` element is in our output. This was accomplished with `<xsl:apply-templates select="@num"/>`. Templates work against nodes, not elements, so you can use these template elements in conjunction with attributes.

This example is a classic example of a `push` stylesheet. In the coming section on loops, you'll see how to get the same output by taking a pull approach.

Value Selection

You can't write a meaningful template without selecting values from the source XML at some point. Previously, to perform this task you used the `xsl:apply-templates` element. It was a rather blunt instrument, though. The `value-of` element introduced here gives you better control. This section shows you the syntax of this element and works though some examples.

Table 13.9 `xsl:value-of` Attributes

ATTRIBUTE	DESCRIPTION
select	Any XPath expression. It can describe an element, in which case the text node of that value will be copied, or an attribute, in which case the attribute's value will be copied.
disable-output-escaping	If set to "yes", XML special characters such as & and < won't be escaped. By default, this is set to "no".

xsl:value-of Syntax

The `xsl:value-of` element copies text from the XML document to the output. Generally, the text copied is value of a node, though it can also be an attribute of a node.

```
<xsl:value-of
  select = "XPath-expression"
  disable-output-escaping = "yes" | "no"./>
```

Table 13.9 lists the attributes. Table 13.10 lists the parent-child relationships.

Table 13.10 Parent-Child Relationships

CAN BE A CHILD OF . . .	CAN BE A PARENT OF . . .
xsl attribute	
xsl comment	
xsl copy	
xsl element	
xsl fallback	
xsl for-each	
xsl if	
xsl message	
xsl otherwise	
xsl param	
xsl processing-instruction	
xsl template	
xsl variable	
xsl:when	

Examples

If there is no template associated with a particular node, `xsl:apply-templates` will provide the same functionality by default. However, it's better to use `xsl:value-of` for a couple of reasons. First, `xsl:apply-templates` will apply any template that matches, which may not be what you want. There often might be a matching template, but you really just want the value. Also, with `xsl:value-of`, you can disable `output` escaping. The first example shows the places in our earlier stylesheet where `xsl:value-of` should be used instead of `xsl:apply-templates`.

```
<xsl:stylesheet
 version="1.0"
 xmlns:xsl="http://www.w3.org/1999/XSL/Transform">

  <xsl:template match="page">
    <html>
      <head><title>Simple Stylesheet</title></head>
      <body>
        <h1>Simple Stylesheet</h1>
        <table border="0">
           <th></th><th>Name</th><th>Job</th><th>Salary</th>
           <xsl:apply-templates select="ROWSET/*"/>
         </table>
      </body>
    </html>
  </xsl:template>

  <xsl:template match="ROW">
   <tr>
    <td><xsl:value-of select="@num"/></td>
    <td><xsl:apply-templates select="ENAME"/></td>
    <td><xsl:apply-templates select="JOB"/></td>
    <td><xsl:apply-templates select="SAL"/></td>
    <xsl:call-template name="break"/>
   </tr>
  </xsl:template>

  <xsl:template name="break">
   <tr><td height="4" colspan="4"><hr/></td></tr>
  </xsl:template>

  <xsl:template match="JOB | SAL">
   <xsl:value-of select="."/>
  </xsl:template>

  <xsl:template match="ENAME">
   <b><xsl:value-of select="."/></b>
  </xsl:template>
</xsl:stylesheet>
```

The `xsl:value-of` element also gives you the ability to disable output escaping. If you know that your query is going to return special characters, such as & and <, and you don't want them to be escaped, set `disable-output-escaping="yes"`. Here is an example XSQL page that returns an &:

```
<?xml version="1.0"?>
<?xml-stylesheet type="text/xsl" href="value-of.xsl"?>
<page connection="demo" xmlns:xsql="urn:oracle-xsql">
  <xsql:query>
    select chr('38') AS ampersand from dual
  </xsql:query>
</page>
```

The ASCII code for the ampersand is 38, so this query will return a single ampersand character. The following stylesheet demonstrates the difference between the default behavior and the behavior when `disable-output-escaping` is set to `"yes"`.

```
<xsl:stylesheet
 version="1.0"
 xmlns:xsl="http://www.w3.org/1999/XSL/Transform">

  <xsl:template match="page">
   <html>
    <head><title>Value-of Escape Example</title></head>
    <body>
     <h1>Value-of Escape Example</h1>
     <ul>
      <li>Default: <xsl:value-of select="."/></li>
      <li>Output Escaping disabled: <xsl:value-of select="." disable-
output-escaping="yes"/></li>
     </ul>
    </body>
   </html>
  </xsl:template>
</xsl:stylesheet>
```

Upon invoking the XSQL page through a browser, you'll probably see an ampersand in both cases. But if you look at the source of the resultant HTML page, you'll see that the first ampersand is `&` the second, `&`.

Iteration

XSLT allows you to loop through a set of nodes with the `xsl:for-each` element. On each iteration, the `context-node` changes to the next node in the set. Within the loop, you can do a series of operations on the `context-node`, such as selecting data. Many of the same goals that can be met with the `xsl:for-each` element can also be met with the `xsl:apply-templates` element. Iteration is more familiar to a procedural programmer than the tree-based recursive approach that `xsl:apply-templates` entails. However, looping can lead to difficult-to-reuse XSLT code.

Xsl:for-each Syntax

The xsl:for-each element declares the beginning of a loop. The loop iterates over all the nodes in the node set described by the value of the select attribute, which is an XPath-expression.

```
<xsl:for-each
  select = "XPath_expression">
  any XML
</xsl:for-each>
```

The sole attribute—select—describes a node set over which the iteration should occur. Table 13.11 lists the parent-child relationships.

Table 13.11 Parent-Child Relationships

CAN BE A CHILD OF . . .	CAN BE A PARENT OF . . .
xsl:attribute	xsl:apply-imports
xsl:comment	xsl:apply-templates
xsl:copy	xsl:attribute
xsl:element	xsl:call-template
xsl:fallback	xsl:choose
xsl:for-each	xsl:comment
xsl:if	xsl:copy
xsl:message	xsl:copy-of
xsl:otherwise	xsl:element
xsl:param	xsl:fallback
xsl:processing-instruction	xsl:for-each
xsl:template	xsl:if
xsl:variable	xsl:message
xsl:when	xsl:number
	xsl:processing-instruction
	xsl:sort
	xsl:text
	xsl:value-of
	xsl:variable

The `for-each` element can be used almost anywhere in XSLT except as a top-level element. One `xsl:for-each` element can be nested inside another element, and multiple levels of nesting are permitted.

Examples

In our example of `xsl:apply-templates` and `xsl:value-of`, you saw how to create a stylesheet by matching templates to nodes and then using `xsl:apply-templates` to match the input XML nodes with the templates in the stylesheet. This is the push approach described earlier. For this example, you'll see how to get the same stylesheet using iteration instead.

```
<xsl:stylesheet
 version="1.0"
 xmlns:xsl="http://www.w3.org/1999/XSL/Transform">
  <xsl:template match="page">
    <html>
      <head><title>Simple Stylesheet</title></head>
      <body>
        <h1>Simple Stylesheet</h1>
        <table border="0">
           <th></th><th>Name</th><th>Job</th><th>Salary</th>
            <xsl:for-each select="ROWSET/ROW">
              <tr>
               <td><xsl:value-of select="@num"/></td>
               <td><b><xsl:value-of select="ENAME"/></b></td>
               <td><xsl:value-of select="JOB"/></td>
               <td><xsl:value-of select="SAL"/></td>
               <xsl:call-template select="break"/>
              </tr>
            </xsl:for-each>
          </table>
      </body>
    </html>
  </xsl:template>

  <xsl:template name="break">
   <tr><td height="4" colspan="4"><hr/></td></tr>
  </xsl:template>

</xsl:stylesheet>
```

In this example, the formatting of the individual data elements is done within the elements. If you wish, you can still use templates in conjunction with an `xsl:for-each` loop:

```
<xsl:stylesheet
 version="1.0"
 xmlns:xsl="http://www.w3.org/1999/XSL/Transform">
```

```
  <xsl:template match="page">
    <html>
      <head><title>Simple Stylesheet</title></head>
      <body>
        <h1>Simple Stylesheet</h1>
        <table border="0">
           <th></th><th>Name</th><th>Job</th><th>Salary</th>

   <xsl:for-each select="ROWSET/ROW">
   <tr>
    <td><xsl:value-of select="@num"/></td>
    <td><xsl:apply-templates select="ENAME"/></td>
    <td><xsl:apply-templates select="JOB"/></td>
    <td><xsl:apply-templates select="SAL"/></td>
    <xsl:call-template name="break"/>
   </tr>
  </xsl:for-each>
   </table>
  </body>
 </html>
</xsl:template>

  <xsl:template name="break">
   <tr><td height="4" colspan="4"><hr/></td></tr>
  </xsl:template>

  <xsl:template match="JOB | SAL">
   <xsl:value-of select="."/>
  </xsl:template>

  <xsl:template match="ENAME">
   <b><xsl:value-of select="."/></b>
  </xsl:template>
</xsl:stylesheet>
```

In this case, the three `apply-templates` elements are applied to each `ROW` element that iterates through the list. Likewise, any of those templates could have its own `for-each` element inside of it.

Conditional Logic

As with most computer programming languages, you can use conditional logic to decide what the output should be based on the input. You have the `xsl:if` element and the `xsl:choose/xsl:when/xsl:otherwise` elements at your disposal. These last three elements are grouped together because they are used collectively for `if-else-if-else` processing. However, the `xsl:if` element adds a set of actions only if its condition is true. Unlike most programming languages, it can't be used in conjunction with an `else` or `else if` construct. This section looks at the syntax of these four elements and provides examples of how to use them in templates. Before you cover the element syntax, you need to understand a `boolean` expression as it is defined by XSLT.

`boolean` Expressions

Used by conditional logic elements. `boolean` expressions evaluate how XSLT should proceed. If the expression evaluates to true, the XSLT inside the element will be output and the other text output as appropriate. If the expression evaluates to false, the element will be skipped. XSLT determines truth and falseness by evaluating the expression and then using the rules of the XPath `boolean()`function on the results. These boil down to the following:

If the expression evaluates to a `boolean` expression, that value will be used to determine truth and falseness. This is the simplest case.

If the expression evaluates to a number, it will be true if it is neither 0 nor `NotANumber`.

If the expression evaluates to a node set, it will be true if it isn't empty.

If the expression evaluates to a string, it will be true if it isn't empty.

You'll be learning more about XPath as you progress through the chapter. XPath provides a variety of functions that can be used not only for `boolean` expressions but for all types of expressions.

`xsl:if` Syntax

The `xsl:if` element allows you to conditionally include the contents of the element.

```
<xsl:if
  test = "boolean_expression">
  XML
  XSLT Template Elements
</xsl:if>
```

It has one attribute, `test`, which is a `boolean` expression that evaluates to either true or false. As discussed in an earlier section, this doesn't mean that the expression must evaluate to either true or false. If it evaluates to a node set, a number, or a string, the rules described in the earlier section on `boolean` expressions will apply. Table 13.12 lists the parent-child relationships.

If the `boolean` expression evaluates to true, any text or XML contained in the element will be output after any XSLT elements have been evaluated. There is no `"else"` element that can be used with `xsl:if`. If you need to do compound conditional processing, you should use the `xsl:choose` element instead.

Table 13.12 Parent-Child Relationships

CAN BE A CHILD OF . . .	CAN BE A PARENT OF . . .
xsl:attribute	xsl:apply-imports
xsl:comment	xsl:apply-templates
xsl:copy	xsl:attribute
xsl:element	xsl:call-template
xsl:fallback	xsl:choose
xsl:for-each	xsl:comment
xsl:if	xsl:copy
xsl:message	xsl:copy-of
xsl:otherwise	xsl:element
xsl:param	xsl:fallback
xsl:processing-instruction	xsl:for-each
xsl:template	xsl:if
xsl:variable	xsl:message
xsl:when	xsl:number
	xsl:processing-instruction
	xsl:text
	xsl:value-of
	xsl:variable

Xsl:choose, xsl:when, and xsl:otherwise Syntax

The xsl:choose provides conditional processing similar to the xsl:if element. However, xsl:choose gives you the ability to select one of many possible alternatives delineated with the xsl:when element. You can also provide a catchall if none of the alternative conditions is met with the xsl:otherwise element. The syntax is as follows:

```
<xsl:choose>
   <xsl:when test="boolean_expression">
      XML text
      Template XSLT Elements
   </xsl:when>
```

```
   . . .
   <xsl:otherwise>
      XML text
      Template XSLT Elements
   </xsl:otherwise>
</xsl:choose>
```

The xsl-when has one attribute, test, which is a boolean expression that evaluates to either true or false. As discussed in an earlier section, this doesn't mean that the expression must evaluate to either true or false. If it evaluates to a node set, a number, or a string, the rules described in the earlier section on boolean expressions will apply.

The only valid parent for xsl:when or xsl:otherwise is xsl:choose. Children of xsl:choose must be xsl:when or xsl:otherwise. Table 13.13 details the parent-child relationships of the triumvirate.

The otherwise element is never required to be a child of xsl:choose. When it is used, it acts like an else clause in an if-then-else structure. If no when condition is met, the default otherwise element is applied. You can include as many xsl:when elements as you want.

Table 13.13 Parent-Child Relationships for xsl:choose/xsl:when/xsl:otherwise

VALID PARENTS OF XSL:CHOOSE	VALID CHILDREN OF XSL:WHEN
xsl:attribute	xsl:apply-imports
xsl:comment	xsl:apply-templates
xsl:copy	xsl:attribute
xsl:element	xsl:call-template
xsl:fallback	xsl:choose
xsl:for-each	xsl:comment
xsl:if	xsl:copy
xsl:message	xsl:copy-of
xsl:otherwise	xsl:element
xsl:param	xsl:fallback
xsl:processing-instruction	xsl:for-each
xsl:template	xsl:if
xsl:variable	xsl:message

Table 13.13 *(Continued)*

VALID PARENTS OF XSL:CHOOSE	VALID CHILDREN OF XSL:WHEN
xsl:when	xsl:number
	xsl:processing-instruction
	xsl:text
	xsl:value-of
	xsl:variable

Examples

These examples cover the two different conditional structures provided by XSLT. The `xsl:if` element only has an effect when the condition is met, while the `xsl:choose` structure can affect a variety of different behaviors based on a number of different conditions. Thus, the `xsl:choose` structure tends to be more interesting and useful. The first stylesheet performs a simple test on the salary node and only displays those with a salary higher than 1,000.

```
<xsl:stylesheet
 version="1.0"
 xmlns:xsl="http://www.w3.org/1999/XSL/Transform">

  <xsl:template match="page">
    <html>
      <head><title>Simple Stylesheet</title></head>
      <body>
        <h1>Simple Stylesheet</h1>
        <table border="1">
           <th></th><th>Name</th><th>Job</th><th>Salary</th>
           <xsl:for-each select="ROWSET/ROW">
             <xsl:if test="number(SAL)>1000">
              <xsl:apply-templates select="."/>
             </xsl:if>
           </xsl:for-each>
         </table>
      </body>
    </html>
  </xsl:template>

  <xsl:template match="ROW">
   <tr>
```

```
      <td><xsl:value-of select="@num"/></td>
      <td><xsl:apply-templates select="ENAME"/></td>
      <td><xsl:apply-templates select="JOB"/></td>
      <td><xsl:apply-templates select="SAL"/></td>
     </tr>
    </xsl:template>

    <xsl:template match="JOB | SAL">
     <xsl:value-of select="."/>
    </xsl:template>

    <xsl:template match="ENAME">
     <b><xsl:value-of select="."/></b>
    </xsl:template>
  </xsl:stylesheet>
```

The choose structure allows you to specify alternatives when a specific condition isn't met. This stylesheet displays all employees and highlights those that have a salary over 1,000. It also makes use of the mode attribute of the `apply-templates` and `template elements`.

```
  <xsl:stylesheet
   version="1.0"
   xmlns:xsl="http://www.w3.org/1999/XSL/Transform">

    <xsl:template match="page">
      <html>
        <head><title>Simple Stylesheet</title></head>
        <body>
          <h1>Simple Stylesheet</h1>
          <table border="0">
             <th></th><th>Name</th><th>Job</th><th>Salary</th>
             <xsl:for-each select="ROWSET/ROW">
              <xsl:choose>
               <xsl:when test="number(SAL)>2000">
               <xsl:apply-templates select="." mode="dark"/>
               </xsl:when>
               <xsl:otherwise>
                <xsl:apply-templates select="." mode="light"/>
               </xsl:otherwise>
              </xsl:choose>
             </xsl:for-each>
           </table>
        </body>
```

```
    </html>
  </xsl:template>

  <xsl:template match="ROW" mode="dark">
   <tr bgcolor="gray">
    <td><xsl:value-of select="@num"/></td>
    <td><xsl:apply-templates select="ENAME"/></td>
    <td><xsl:apply-templates select="JOB"/></td>
    <td><xsl:apply-templates select="SAL"/></td>
   </tr>
  </xsl:template>

  <xsl:template match="ROW" mode="light">
   <tr>
    <td><xsl:value-of select="@num"/></td>
    <td>
    <xsl:if test="number(SAL) &lt;= 1100">
      <i>poor </i>
    </xsl:if>
    <xsl:apply-templates select="ENAME"/>

    </td>
    <td><xsl:apply-templates select="JOB"/></td>
    <td><xsl:apply-templates select="SAL"/></td>
   </tr>
  </xsl:template>

  <xsl:template match="JOB | SAL">
   <xsl:value-of select="."/>
  </xsl:template>

  <xsl:template match="ENAME">
   <b><xsl:value-of select="."/></b>
  </xsl:template>
</xsl:stylesheet>
```

The output of this template is shown in Figure 13.2. For this example, two templates are used with two different modes—`light` and `dark`. The `xsl:choose` structure decides which mode to use based on salary. Doing it this way is a bit redundant since there is only one attribute to change. However, outputting data inside `xml` elements, such as attributes, is a little tricky. You'll learn more in the next section.

Also, note that an `xsl:if` element is used inside the `light` template. If the `sal` is less than 1,000, the word `"poor"` will be added. Note that `"<"` had to be used instead of `"<"`, because `"<"`is reserved in XML.

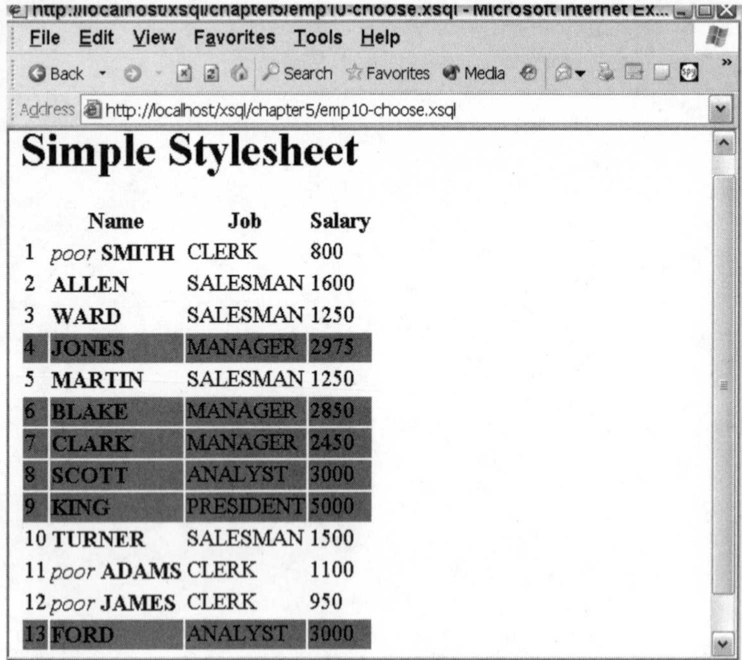

Figure 13.2 Conditional processing example.

Working with XML Entities and Text

Often, you will want to create an `xml` entity, such as text or an attribute or element, in the output. Since XSLT is based on XML, doing so can be a bit tricky. If you just start writing out angle brackets, they will be escaped and you'll have to work around that. Luckily, XSLT provides a series of elements dedicated to outputted XML entities.

The first set of elements discussed allows you to construct elements inside your stylesheets. These elements are used quite often to create elements and set attributes.

Often, you will want to use XSLT to set an attribute inside an element. Common examples include setting the `href` attribute in an element and setting the `src` attribute in an `img` element. Since XSLT is based on XML, you can't put the xsl:value-of element inside of an XML element. Thus, you use these XSL elements to tell the XSLT Processor to create elements and set attributes.

xsl:element, xsl:attribute, and xsl:attribute-set Syntax

The xsl:element is used to create XML elements in the output. Of course, XHTML elements can also be created. A common use is to set the URL value for a link or img tag. The syntax for the xsl:element tag is as follows:

```
<xsl:element
  name = "xml_element_name"
  namespace ="namespace_URI"
  use-attribute-sets = "attribute_set_names">
  xsl:attribute elements
  template xslt elements, other xml, and text
</xsl:element>
```

Any xsl:attribute element defines an attribute for the element and. Anything else between the start and end xsl:element tags will appear as the value in the outputted element. The attributes for the xsl:element element are described in Table 13.14.

Table 13.15 lists the parent-child relationships.

Table 13.14 xsl:element Attributes

ATTRIBUTE	DESCRIPTION
Name	The name that the outputted element should have (i.e., "img" or "a").
Namespace	Associates the namespace at the given URI with the element.
Use-attribute-sets	A whitespace separated list of xsl:attribute-set elements. Each attribute-set element declares a set of attributes that will be included in the outputted element.

Table 13.15 Parent-Child Relationships

CAN BE A CHILD OF . . .	CAN BE A PARENT OF . . .
xsl:copy	xsl:apply-imports
xsl:element	xsl:apply-templates
xsl:fallback	xsl:attribute
xsl:for-each	xsl:call-template
xsl:if	xsl:choose
xsl:message	xsl:comment
xsl:otherwise	xsl:copy
xsl:param	xsl:copy-of
xsl:template	xsl:element
xsl:variable	xsl:fallback
xsl:when	xsl:for-each
	xsl:if
	xsl:message
	xsl:number
	xsl:processing-instruction
	xsl:text
	xsl:value-of
	xsl:variable

Typically, `xsl:element` is used in conjunction with `xsl:attribute` to create a new element. Any XSLT inside the `xsl:element` element is evaluated and set as the value of the created element.

`xsl:attribute` Syntax

The `xsl:attribute` element defines an attribute-value pair for its parent node. Its syntax is as follows:

```
<xsl:attribute
  name ="attribute_name"
  namespace ="namespace_name">
  attribute_value
</xsl:attribute>
```

Table 13.16 lists the attributes.

Table 13.16 `xsl:attribute` Attributes

ATTRIBUTE	DESCRIPTION
`name`	Name for the attribute. Should be the name you want the attribute to have in the output.
`namespace`	Namespace URI for this attribute.

Table 13.17 lists the parent-child relationships.

The `xsl:attribute` should be placed immediately after its parent. If it isn't parented by `xsl:element`, `xsl:attribute-set`, or `xsl:copy`, a new attribute will be created on the context node.

Table 13.17 Parent-Child Relationships

CAN BE A CHILD OF . . .	CAN BE A PARENT OF . . .
`xsl:attribute-set`	`xsl:apply-imports`
`xsl:copy`	`xsl:apply-templates`
`xsl:element`	`xsl:call-template`
`xsl:fallback`	`xsl:choose`
`xsl:for-each`	`xsl:copy`
`xsl:if`	`xsl:copy`
`xsl:message`	`xsl:copy-of`
`xsl:otherwise`	`xsl:fallback`
`xsl:param`	`xsl:for-each`
`xsl:template`	`xsl:if`
`xsl:variable`	`xsl:message`
`xsl:when`	`xsl:message`
	`xsl:number`
	`xsl:text`
	`xsl:value-of`
	`xsl:variable`

Table 13.18 `xsl:attribute-set` Attributes

ATTRIBUTE	DESCRIPTION
name	The name for the attribute set.
use-attribute-set	A whitespace-delimited list of other attribute sets.

`xsl:attribute-set` Syntax

The `xsl:attribute-set` element allows you to define a static set of elements that can be reused. This keeps you from having to repeatedly define the exact same set of `xsl:attribute` elements. The syntax is as follows:

```
<xsl:attribute-set
  name = "set_name"
  use-attribute-sets = "attribute_set_names">
  xsl:attribute elements
</xsl:attribute-set>
```

Table 13.18 lists the attributes.

The only valid parent for `xsl:attribute-set` elements is the root element. The only valid child is `xsl:attribute`.

Element Creation Examples

The following stylesheet illustrates a typical situation where you wish to create a new element. The stylesheet creates a bulleted list of employee names, as you did in an earlier example. This time, you set hyperlinks around the employee name, presumably to a page where you can edit the employee records or something similar.

```
<?xml version="1.0"?>
<xsl:stylesheet
 version="1.0"
 xmlns:xsl="http://www.w3.org/1999/XSL/Transform">

  <xsl:template match="page">
    <html>
      <head><title>Simple Stylesheet</title></head>
      <body>
        <h1>Simple Stylesheet</h1>
        <ul>
         <xsl:apply-templates select="ROWSET/ROW"/>
        </ul>
      </body>
    </html>
  </xsl:template>
```

```
<xsl:template match="ROW">
 <li><b>
  <xsl:element name="a">
   <xsl:attribute name="href">editEmployee?<xsl:value-of
select="EMPNO"/></xsl:attribute>
   <xsl:attribute name="rel">next</xsl:attribute>
   <xsl:attribute name="rev">prev</xsl:attribute>
   <xsl:value-of select="ENAME"/>
  </xsl:element>
 </b></li>
</xsl:template>

</xsl:stylesheet>
```

In this example, the `rel` and the `rev` elements don't take dynamic inputs. They are ideal candidates to be an `attribute-set`. Then, if you need to reuse the same set of attributes somewhere else in your document, you'll have a better mechanism than copy and paste. The first step is to set up the `attribute-set` element:

```
<xsl:attribute-set name="empEditorLink">
  <xsl:attribute name="rel">next</xsl:attribute>
  <xsl:attribute name="rev">prev</xsl:attribute>
</xsl:attribute-set>
```

You'll need to define the `attribute-set` as a child of the root element, since it is the only valid parent for an `xsl:attribute-set` element. Now, you can recreate the `row` template as follows:

```
<xsl:template match="ROW">
      <li><b>
      <xsl:element name="a" use-attribute-sets="empEditorLink">
        <xsl:attribute name="href">editEmployee?<xsl:value-of
select="EMPNO"/></xsl:attribute>
        <xsl:value-of select="ENAME"/>
      </xsl:element>
      </b></li>
  </xsl:template>
```

The `attribute` element can also be used to create attributes on any arbitrary element in your stylesheet. This is a different way to accomplish the same goal of setting attributes. Instead of creating a new element, the attribute is set on the existing XML element.

```
<xsl:template match="ROW">
 <li><b>
   <a>
     <xsl:attribute name="href">editEmployee?<xsl:value-of
select="EMPNO"/></xsl:attribute>
        <xsl:value-of select="ENAME"/>
   </a>
 </b></li>
</xsl:template>
```

`xsl:text` Syntax

The `xsl:text` element is used to insert text verbatim into the document:

```
<xsl:text
  disable-output-escaping = "yes" | "no">
  string data
</xsl:text>
```

By default, special XML characters will be escaped. By setting `disable-output-escaping` to `"yes"`, they will not be. Table 13.19 lists the parent-child relationships.

Table 13.19 Parent-Child Relationships

CAN BE A CHILD OF . . .	CAN BE A PARENT OF . . .
xsl:attribute	
xsl:comment	
xsl:copy	
xsl:element	
xsl:fallback	
xsl:for-each	
xsl:if	
xsl:message	
xsl:otherwise	
xsl:param	
xsl:processing-instruction	
xsl:template	
xsl:variable	
xsl:when	

Generally, `xsl:text` is used to include arbitrary amounts of whitespace in the end document. With the `disable-output-escaping` attribute set to yes, you can also use it to create XML tags in the text. However, you have to use the escaped characters inside the `xml:text` tag:

```
<pre>
  <xsl:text>

     W  o  w ! ! ! !   W  h  i  t  e  s  p  a  c  e ! ! !

     Default tag: &lt;aTag/&gt;

   </xsl:text>
   <xsl:text disable-output-escaping="yes">
     disable-output-escaping tag:  &lt;aTag/&gt;
   </xsl:text>
</pre>
```

`xsl:comment` Syntax

The `xsl:comment` element generates an XML comment in the output:

```
<xsl:comment>
  XSLT and XML
</xsl:comment>
```

Table 13.20 lists the parent-child relationships.

Table 13.20 Parent-Child Relationships

CAN BE A CHILD OF . . .	CAN BE A PARENT OF . . .
xsl:copy	xsl:apply-imports
xsl:element	xsl:apply-templates
xsl:fallback	xsl:call-templates
xsl:for-each	xsl:choose

(continues)

Table 13.20 Parent-Child Relationships *(Continued)*

CAN BE A CHILD OF . . .	CAN BE A PARENT OF . . .
xsl:if	xsl:copy
xsl:message	xsl:copy-of
xsl:otherwise	xsl:fallback
xsl:param	xsl:for-each
xsl:template	xsl:if
xsl:variable	xsl:message
xsl:when	xsl:number
	xsl:text
	xsl:value-of
	xsl:variable

The `start` tag is replaced with <!– and the end tag is replaced with –>. Here is an example:

```
<xsl:comment> This is my comment. </xsl:comment>
```

`xsl:copy` Syntax

The `xsl:copy` element allows you to copy the current node. It won't copy the attributes or child elements.

```
<xsl:copy
  use-attribute-sets = "attribute_set_list">
</xsl:copy>
```

The sole attribute, `use-attribute-sets`, is set to a whitespace-delimited list of attribute set names. These are merged and the attributes are set on the merged node. You call also use the attribute element to accomplish the same thing. Table 13.21 lists the parent-child relationships.

Table 13.21 Parent-Child Relationships

CAN BE A CHILD OF . . .	CAN BE A PARENT OF . . .
xsl:comment	xsl:apply-imports
xsl:copy	xsl:apply-templates
xsl:element	xsl:attribute
xsl:fallback	xsl:call-template
xsl:for-each	xsl:choose
xsl:if	xsl:comment
xsl:message	xsl:copy
xsl:otherwise	xsl:copy-of
xsl:param	xsl:element
xsl:processing-instruction	xsl:fallback
xsl:template	xsl:for-each
xsl:variable	xsl:if
xsl:when	xsl:message
	xsl:number
	xsl:processing-instruction
	xsl:text
	xsl:value-of
	xsl:variable

The following example uses the `xsl:copy` element to copy only those rows of the clerk employees:

```
<?xml version="1.0"?>

<xsl:stylesheet
 version="1.0"
 xmlns:xsl="http://www.w3.org/1999/XSL/Transform">

  <xsl:template match="page">
  <xsl:element name="ROWSET">
   <xsl:apply-templates select="ROWSET/ROW"/>
  </xsl:element>
  </xsl:template>
```

```
<xsl:template match="ROW">

    <xsl:if test="JOB='CLERK'">

        <xsl:copy>
            <xsl:for-each select="@*">
              <xsl:copy/>
            </xsl:for-each>
            <xsl:apply-templates select="ENAME | SAL"/>
        </xsl:copy>

    </xsl:if>
</xsl:template>

<xsl:template match="ENAME | SAL">
    <xsl:copy>
        <xsl:value-of select="."/>
    </xsl:copy>
</xsl:template>
</xsl:stylesheet>
```

xsl:copy-of Syntax

The xsl:copy-of element allows you to copy the tree fragment specified by the select attribute:

```
<xsl:copy-of
  select = "XPath_expression" />
```

The single attribute, select, is an expression that should evaluate to a node set. The members of the node set and their children will be copied. Table 13.22 lists the parent-child relationships.

Table 13.22 Parent-Child Relationships

CAN BE A CHILD OF . . .	CAN BE A PARENT OF . . .
xsl:attribute	
xsl:comment	
xsl:copy	
xsl:element	
xsl:fallback	
xsl:for-each	
xsl:if	

Table 13.22 *(Continued)*

CAN BE A CHILD OF . . .	CAN BE A PARENT OF . . .
xsl:if	
xsl:message	
xsl:otherwise	
xsl:param	
xsl:processing-instruction	
xsl:template	
xsl:variable	
xsl:when	

Here is a simple example that creates a new XML document containing only those employees who are clerks:

```
<?xml version="1.0"?>

<xsl:stylesheet
 version="1.0"
 xmlns:xsl="http://www.w3.org/1999/XSL/Transform">

 <xsl:template match="page">
  <xsl:apply-templates select="ROWSET/ROW"/>
 </xsl:template>

 <xsl:template match="ROW">
  <xsl:if test="JOB='CLERK'">
    <xsl:copy-of select="."/>
   </xsl:if>
 </xsl:template>

</xsl:stylesheet>
```

xsl:namespace-alias Syntax

The xsl:namespace-alias allows you translate one namespace in the input to another namespace in the output:

```
<xsl:namespace-alias
  stylesheet-prefix = "prefix" | "#default"
  result-prefix = "prefix" | "#default" />
```

Table 13.23 lists the attributes.

Table 13.23 `xsl:namespace-alias` Attributes

ATTRIBUTE	DESCRIPTION
`stylesheet-prefix`	The prefix of the namespace that should be translated in the output.
`result-prefix`	The prefix that should replace the prefix described by the stylesheet-prefix attribute.

If the string `"#default"` is used for either attribute, it would represent the default namespace. This is either no namespace declared by `xmlns` or no namespace at all.

The `xsl:namespace-alias` element must be the child of the root element and may not have child elements.

Your stylesheets can have multiple `xsl:namespace-alias` elements. However, it is an error to have multiple `xsl:namespace-alias` elements that have the same `stylesheet-prefix`, and it may produce conflicts to have multiple `xsl:namespace-alias` elements that have the same `result-prefix` elements.

`xsl:processing-instruction` Syntax

The `xsl:processing-instruction` allows you to specify an `xml` processing instruction. It can't be used to specify the `xml` declaration; for that, you can use the `xsl:output` element.

```
<xsl:processing-instruction
  name = "processing_instruction_name">
  xslt template elements and other text & xml
</xsl:processing-instruction>
```

The `name` attribute specifies the name of the processing instruction. Table 13.24 lists the parent-child relationships.

Table 13.24 Parent-Child Relationships

CAN BE A CHILD OF . . .	CAN BE A PARENT OF . . .
`xsl:copy`	`xsl:apply-imports`
`xsl:element`	`xsl:apply-templates`
`xsl:fallback`	`xsl:call-template`
`xsl:for-each`	`xsl:choose`

Table 13.24 *(Continued)*

CAN BE A CHILD OF . . .	CAN BE A PARENT OF . . .
xsl:if	xsl:copy
xsl:message	xsl:copy-of
xsl:otherwise	xsl:fallback
xsl:param	xsl:for-each
xsl:template	xsl:if
xsl:variable	xsl:message
xsl:when	xsl:text
	xsl:value-of
	xsl:variable

The value of the `xsl:processing-instruction` becomes the string value included in the processing instruction. Any template elements between the `start` and `end` tags will be evaluated. Here is an example in which you specify that the output uses a particular stylesheet:

```
<xsl:processing-instruction name="xml-stylesheet">
type="text/xml" href="someStylesheet.xsl"
</xsl:processing-instruction>
```

This `xsl:processing-instruction` would produce the following processing instruction in the output:

```
<?xml-stylesheet type="text/xml" href="someStylesheet.xsl"?>
```

An `xsl:processing-instruction` element must evaluate to a valid XML processing instruction.

Numbering Elements

There are two XSLT elements that concern numbering. The first, `xsl:number`, is used to provide a formatted number that details the position of a node in a node list. The second, `xsl:decimal-format`, is used in conjunction with the `format-number` function that will be covered in the "XPath" section.

xsl:number

The xsl:number element inserts a formatted number into the output. Typically, this element is used to provide numbering for a set of XML elements in the source document.

```
<xsl:number
  level = "single" | "multiple" | "any"
  count = "pattern"
  from = "pattern"
  value = "number_expression"
  format = "format_mask"
  lang = "nmtoken"
  letter-value = { "alphabetic" | "traditional" }
  grouping-separator = "char"
  grouping-size = "number" />
```

The attributes of elements control how the numbering is done. By default, the number element produces the next number in sequence each time the XSLT processor encounters the particular element. The attributes enhance this basic behavior. Table 13.25 lists the attributes.

Table 13.25 xsl:number **Attributes**

ATTRIBUTE	DESCRIPTION
level	If set to single, only the nodes in a node set will be numbered; if set to multiple, the counting crosses node sets will be numbered. Any level is used for multiple layered counting.
count	A pattern that describes which patterns should be counted.
from	A pattern that specifies where counting should start.
value	If present, the expression will be evaluated and the result placed into the output as the number. By default, the value that the xsl:number element outputs is determined by context. More information on this below.
format	Specifies the format mask for the outputted number.
lang	Specifies the language to use in determining the sequence when alphabetic characters are used in the numbering.

Table 13.25 *(Continued)*

ATTRIBUTE	DESCRIPTION
`letter-value`	Used to remove ambiguities, in many languages, of alphabetic lettering. By default, traditional is specified. This means that a format of I starts the roman numeral sequence I, II, III, and so on. Specifying alphabetic starts the sequence I, J, K, and so on.
`grouping-separator`	Specifies the character that separates digits. In English this is customarily a comma, but in some other languages this is a space. The default is a comma.
`grouping-size`	Specifies the size of groups separated by the grouping separator. By default, this is 3.

Table 13.26 lists the parent-child relationships.

Table 13.26 Parent-Child Relationships

CAN BE A CHILD OF . . .	CAN BE A PARENT OF . . .
`xsl:attribute`	
`xsl:comment`	
`xsl:copy`	
`xsl:element`	
`xsl:fallback`	
`xsl:for-each`	
`xsl:if`	
`xsl:message`	
`xsl:otherwise`	
`xsl:param`	
`xsl:processing-instruction`	
`xsl:template`	
`xsl:variable`	
`xsl:when`	

`xsl:decimal-format` Syntax

The `xsl:decimal-format` element is used in conjunction with the `format-number()` function. It defines a named decimal format that can be referenced by the `format-number()` function when it translates floating-point numbers for output.

```
<xsl:decimal-format

  name = "decimal_format_name"
  decimal-separator = "decimal_separator"
  grouping-separator = "grouping_separator"
  infinity = "infinity_string"
  minus-sign = "minus_char"
  NaN = "NaN_string"
  percent = "percent_char"
  per-mille = "per_mille"
  zero-digit = "zero_digit"
  digit = "digit"
  pattern-separator = "pattern_separator" />
```

Table 13.27 describes the syntax.

This element can only be a child of the root element and can't have any children.

Table 13.27 `xsl:decimal-format` Syntax

ATTRIBUTE	DESCRIPTION
`Name`	The string by which this decimal format can be referenced in the format-number-function call.
`decimal-separator`	Separates the integer part from the fractional part. `"."` is the default.
`grouping-separator`	Separates groups of digits. `","` is the default.
`infinity`	String that represents infinity. `"Infinity"` is the default.
`minus-sign`	Prefixes negative numbers. `"-"`is the default.
`NaN`	Represents "not a number". `"NaN"` is the default.
`Percent`	Represents percent. `"%"` is the default.
`per-mille`	Represents per mille. `#x2030` is the default.
`Zero-digit`	Represents zero in the format pattern used by format-number(). `"0"` is the default.
`Digit`	Represent digits in the format pattern used by format-number(). `"#"` is the default.
`Pattern-separator`	Separates positive and negative subpatterns in the format pattern. `";"`is the default.

Variables and Parameters

XSLT allows you to make your templates more modular by using variables and parameters. Parameters behave more like the parameters that you use in other languages, while variables behave more like constants. The `xsl:param` and `xsl:variable` elements represent parameters and variables, respectively. The `xsl:with-param` element is used to pass parameters to a template. This section covers these three elements and provides examples of how variables and parameters can be used.

`xsl:variable` Syntax

An `xsl:variable` actually behaves like a constant—once its value is set, it can't be changed:

```
<xsl:variable
   name="variable_name">
      . . .
</xsl:variable>

<xsl:variable
   name="variable_name"
   select="expression"/>
```

The `name` attribute is the name of the variable. If the `select` attribute is specified, the result of the expression will be the value for the `param`, and the `xsl:param` element should have the empty-element form. Table 13.28 lists the parent-child relationships.

Table 13.28 Parent-Child Relationships

CAN BE A CHILD OF . . .	CAN BE A PARENT OF . . .
xsl:attribute	xsl:apply-imports
xsl:comment	xsl:apply-templates
xsl:copy	xsl:attribute
xsl:element	xsl:call-template
xsl:fallback	xsl:choose
xsl:for-each	xsl:comment
xsl:if	xsl:copy
xsl:message	xsl:copy-of
xsl:otherwise	xsl:element
xsl:param	xsl:fallback

(continues)

Table 13.28 Parent-Child Relationships *(Continued)*

CAN BE A CHILD OF . . .	CAN BE A PARENT OF . . .
xsl:processing-instruction	xsl:for-each
xsl:stylesheet	xsl:if
xsl:template	xsl:message
xsl:transform	xsl:number
xsl:variable	xsl:processing-instruction
xsl:when	xsl:text
	xsl:value-of
	xsl:variables

`variable` Examples

The `xsl:variable` is typically used to grab information from the source XML that will be reused repeatedly throughout the stylesheet or to store information. Once you grab the information, you can use it again and again by referencing the variable name with a $ prefix, as in `$variable_name`. A variable's value is set as part of its definition, making it quite different from the variables you use in other programming languages. Those variables must be defined and their value must be changed many times over the life of the programs in which they are found. In this way, variables act like constants.

You can define a variable either at the stylesheet level or at the template-body level. When a variable is defined at the stylesheet level, it has global scope—you can use it anywhere in the document. When it is defined at the template-body level, it can be used only if it is referenced in following siblings or descendants of following siblings. This is similar to how local variables work in procedural languages—they aren't available outside of the subroutine. In other words, they aren't available outside the element in which they are created, and they are available only inside the element after they have been declared.

Variables at different levels of scope can have the same name. If there are conflicts, the most narrowly scoped variable takes precedence. For instance, the variable `row_num` defined inside of a template preempts the variable `row_num` defined at the stylesheet level.

```
<xsl:stylesheet
 version="1.0"
 xmlns:xsl="http://www.w3.org/1999/XSL/Transform">
  <xsl:variable name="row_num" select="0"/>
  <xsl:template match="page">
```

```
    <html>
      <head><title>Simple Stylesheet</title></head>
      <body>
        <h1>Simple Stylesheet</h1>
        <table border="0">

            <th align="left">Name</th>
            <th align="left">@num</th>
            <th align="left">global variable</th>
            <th align="left">local variable</th>

             <xsl:for-each select="ROWSET/ROW">
               <tr>
                <td align="left" width="200">
                    <xsl:value-of select="ENAME"/>
                </td>
                <td align="left" width="200">
                    <xsl:value-of select="@num"/>
                </td>
                <td align="left" width="200">
                   <xsl:value-of select="$row_num"/>
                </td>
                <xsl:variable name="row_num" select="@num"/>
                <td align="left" width="200">
                   <xsl:value-of select="$row_num"/>
                </td>
               </tr>
             </xsl:for-each>

          </table>
       </body>
    </html>
  </xsl:template>
</xsl:stylesheet>
```

The results of this example are shown in Figure 13.3. The first time `$row_num` is referenced, it takes the value of the stylesheet-level `row_num` variable because no template-body-level `$row_num` exists at that point. The second time it is referenced, it takes the value of the attribute `"num"` of the current row.

The output seems to contradict something you may have read about XSLT—that you can set the value of a variable only once. After all, the local variable `row_num` seems to have been set 14 times! This doesn't make the previous statement false, however. It's more precise to say that a variable's value is set upon its definition. When `xsl:variable` seems to be changing, it is really just being redefined. If the `xsl:variable` element—and thus its value definition—is evaluated more than once, the variable may have different values on each instantiation. This is the case here.

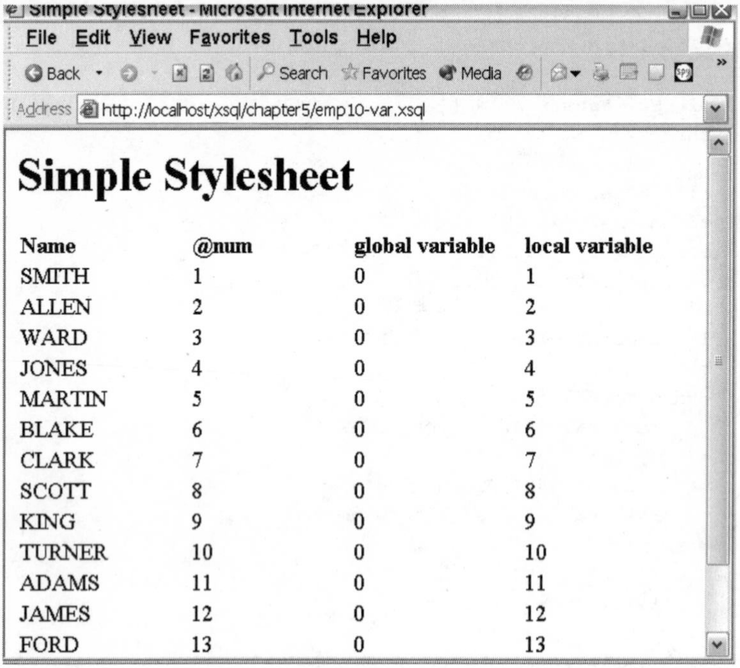
Simple Stylesheet - Microsoft Internet Explorer
File Edit View Favorites Tools Help
Back Search Favorites Media
Address http://localhost/xsql/chapter5/emp10-var.xsql
Simple Stylesheet
Name @num global variable local variable
SMITH 1 0 1
ALLEN 2 0 2
WARD 3 0 3
JONES 4 0 4
MARTIN 5 0 5
BLAKE 6 0 6
CLARK 7 0 7
SCOTT 8 0 8
KING 9 0 9
TURNER 10 0 10
ADAMS 11 0 11
JAMES 12 0 12
FORD 13 0 13

Figure 13.3 Using `variables`.

In this example, the variable took a string value. Variables can also take a number, a `boolean`, or a node-set value. Because they can take a node-set value, variables are often used to store the context node at any particular time during processing. In the following example, variables are used to capture the context node at three different levels—before going into the outer `for-each` loop, before going into the inner `for-each` loop, and at the lowest level of the document.

```
<xsl:stylesheet
 version="1.0"
 xmlns:xsl="http://www.w3.org/1999/XSL/Transform">

  <xsl:template match="page">
    <html>
      <head><title>Simple Stylesheet</title></head>
      <body>
        <h1>Simple Stylesheet</h1>
        <table border="0">
         <th>Top level Node</th>
         <th>Mid Node</th>
         <th>Lowest Node</th>
```

```
        <xsl:variable name="top_node" select="."/>
        <xsl:for-each select="ROWSET/ROW">
         <xsl:variable name="mid_node" select="."/>
         <xsl:for-each select="*">
          <xsl:variable name="low_node" select="."/>
          <tr>
           <td><xsl:value-of select="name($top_node)"/></td>
           <td><xsl:value-of select="name($mid_node)"/></td>
           <td><xsl:value-of select="name($low_node)"/></td>
          </tr>
         </xsl:for-each>
        </xsl:for-each>
       </table>
      </body>
    </html>
  </xsl:template>

</xsl:stylesheet>
```

This example makes use of the name function, which you'll learn more about later in this chapter.

`xsl:param` Syntax

The `xsl:param` and `xsl:variable` elements are closely related and share essentially the same syntax:

```
<xsl:param
   name="param_name">
     . . .
</xsl:param>

<xsl:param
   name="param_name"
   select="expression"/>
```

The name attribute is the name of the parameter. If the `select` attribute is specified, the result of the expression will be the value for the `param`, and the `xsl:param` element should have the empty-element form.

```
<xsl:variable
   name="variable_name"
   select="expression">
  . . .
</xsl:variable>
```

Table 13.29 lists the parent-child relationships.

Table 13.29 Parent-Child Relationships

CAN BE A CHILD OF . . .	CAN BE A PARENT OF . . .
root element	xsl:apply-imports
xsl:template	xsl:apply-templates
xsl:attribute	
xsl:call-template	
xsl:choose	
xsl:comment	
xsl:copy	
xsl:copy-of	
xsl:element	
xsl:fallback	
xsl:for-each	
xsl:if	
xsl:message	
xsl:number	
xsl:processing-instruction	
xsl:text	
xsl:value-of	
xsl:variable	

xsl:with-param Syntax

The xsl:with-param element is used in conjunction with the xsl:apply-templates and xsl:call-template elements to pass parameters to a template. The template should have a xsl:template of the same name already defined inside the template.

```
<xsl:with-param
   name="param-name">
. . .
</xsl:with-param>

<xsl:with-param
   name="param-name"
   select="expression"/>
```

Name is a required attribute. If select is an attribute, then the element should have the empty-element form. Table 13.30 lists the parent-child relationships.

Table 13.30 Parent-Child Relationships

CAN BE A CHILD OF . . .	CAN BE A PARENT OF . . .
`xsl:apply-templates`	`xsl:apply-imports`
`xsl:call-template`	`xsl:apply-templates`
`xsl:attribute`	
`xsl:call-template`	
`xsl:choose`	
`xsl:comment`	
`xsl:copy`	
`xsl:copy-of`	
`xsl:element`	
`xsl:fallback`	
`xsl:for-each`	
`xsl:if`	
`xsl:message`	
`xsl:number`	
`xsl:processing-instruction`	
`xsl:text`	
`xsl:value-of`	
`xsl:variable`	

`Parameter` Examples

Parameters perform like variables in many cases, but they are used mainly to pass arguments to templates. You use `xsl:with-param` with the `xsl:apply-templates` and `xsl:call-template` elements to pass the chosen argument. Inside the template, you have an `xsl:parameter` element that receives the parameter. The `xsl:with-param` element that is used to pass an argument into a template must have the same name as the corresponding `xsl:parameter` element inside the template. If the `xsl:with-param` doesn't match any `xsl:parameter` elements inside the target template, it would be simply ignored. For an `xsl:parameter` element, you can also provide a default value to use in case no `xsl:with-param` element is included in the call.

In an earlier example, you highlighted the high-salary employees to demonstrate the conditional processing of XSLT. In that case, there were two entirely different templates that did essentially the same thing and differed only in color. The following example shows how you can make your code cleaner by using parameters. It also reworks the call template so that it alternates on every other color.

```
<xsl:stylesheet
 version="1.0"
 xmlns:xsl="http://www.w3.org/1999/XSL/Transform">

  <xsl:template match="page">
    <xsl:processing-instruction name="xml-stylesheet">type="text/xml"
href="someStylesheet.xsl"</xsl:processing-instruction>

    <html>
      <head><title>Simple Stylesheet</title></head>
      <body>
        <h1>Simple Stylesheet</h1>

        <table border="0">
           <th></th><th>Name</th><th>Job</th><th>Salary</th>
           <xsl:for-each select="ROWSET/ROW">
            <xsl:choose>
             <xsl:when test="number(SAL)>2000">
             <xsl:apply-templates select=".">
               <xsl:with-param name="bgcolor">gray</xsl:with-param>
             </xsl:apply-templates>
             </xsl:when>
             <xsl:otherwise>
              <xsl:apply-templates select="."/>
             </xsl:otherwise>
            </xsl:choose>
           </xsl:for-each>
         </table>
      </body>
    </html>
  </xsl:template>

  <xsl:template match="ROW">
   <xsl:param name="bgcolor">white</xsl:param>
   <tr>
    <xsl:attribute name="bgcolor">
      <xsl:value-of select="$bgcolor"/>
    </xsl:attribute>
    <td><xsl:value-of select="@num"/></td>
    <td><xsl:apply-templates select="ENAME"/></td>
    <td><xsl:apply-templates select="JOB"/></td>
    <td><xsl:apply-templates select="SAL"/></td>
   </tr>

   <xsl:choose>
    <xsl:when test="@num mod 2 = 1">
     <xsl:call-template name="break">
      <xsl:with-param name="break_color">red</xsl:with-param>
```

```
      </xsl:call-template>
    </xsl:when>
    <xsl:otherwise>
      <xsl:call-template name="break"/>
    </xsl:otherwise>
   </xsl:choose>

  </xsl:template>

  <xsl:template name="break">
   <xsl:param name="break_color">blue</xsl:param>
   <tr><td height="4" colspan="4">
     <xsl:attribute name="bgcolor">
       <xsl:value-of select="$break_color"/>
     </xsl:attribute>
    </td>
   </tr>
  </xsl:template>

  <xsl:template match="JOB | SAL">
   <xsl:value-of select="."/>
  </xsl:template>

  <xsl:template match="ENAME">
   <b><xsl:value-of select="."/></b>
  </xsl:template>
</xsl:stylesheet>
```

Reusing Stylesheets

As you develop stylesheets, you'll probably find yourself addressing some of the same problems over and over again. If you start looking at XSLT with the eye of an experienced programmer, you'll probably wonder whether there is any way to modularize and reuse your code. There is. The `xsl:include` and `xsl:import` elements allow you to use XSLT that is defined in other stylesheets. These elements, combined with variables and parameters, allow you to reuse individual templates and declarations.

When you use the `xsl:include` element, it's as if you've copied and pasted another stylesheet exactly where the `xsl:include` element is placed. In the case of name conflicts, the order of precedence of XSLT determines which element should be used based on the element's position in the document after the `include`. (In other words, the fact that the template was included from another stylesheet makes no difference when determining which element to use.)

The `xsl:import` element works differently. In the case of conflicts, the elements in the importing stylesheet always take precedence over the elements in the imported stylesheet. If you specifically want to use a template in an imported stylesheet, you must use the `xsl:apply-imports` element.

`xsl:include` and `xsl:import` Syntax

These two elements share almost the exact same syntax:

```
<xsl:import href="address" />
<xsl:include href="address" />
```

The `href` attribute specifies the URI of the stylesheet that you wish to import or include, respectively. They can be the children of the top-level element only, and they can have no children. If they are used, they must be the first children of the root element. Specifically, no child element of the root can precede `xsl:import` except `xsl:include`, and no child element of the root can precede `xsl:include` except `xsl:import`.

`xsl:apply-imports`

This element is used to override the default behavior of XSLT concerning imported stylesheets. By default, an imported stylesheet template is used only if there are no templates of the same name defined in the main stylesheet. With `xsl:apply-imports`, you can specifically request that an imported template be applied from within a template of the same name.

```
<xsl:apply-imports/>
```

This element can't have children, and the only valid parent is `xsl:template`.

Sorting

XSLT gives you a mechanism for sorting data. Of course, you can also sort at the SQL level. Generally speaking, it is more efficient to sort at the SQL level than at the XSLT level. There will be cases, though, in which you will need to sort by using XSLT. This section defines the syntax for the `xsl:sort` element and gives examples of it's use.

`xsl:sort` Syntax

The `xsl:sort` element changes the default sorting. By default, elements are presented in document order. However the elements are sequenced in the document in the order in which they are output. The `xsl:sort` element allows the order to be changed to some other kind of sorting, typically alphabetic or numeric and based on some property of the elements to be sorted.

```
<xsl:sort
  select = "sort_expression"
  lang = ""
  data-type = "text" | "number" | "other_processor_supported_type"
  order = "ascending" | "descending"
  case-order = "upper-first" | "lower-first"  />
```

Table 13.31 lists the attributes.

Table 13.31 `xsl:sort` Attributes

ATTRIBUTE	NAME
`select`	The expression that is evaluated for each node. Results of evaluations determine sort order.
`lang`	RFC 1766 language code for the language used in determining order. The default is the system language.
`data-type`	When set to "number", sorting is done numerically (2 precedes 100). When set to "text", sorting is done alphanumerically (100 precedes 2). Any other types must be supported by the XSLT processor. The default is `"text"`.
`order`	Determines the direction of the sort. The default is `"ascending"`.
`case-order`	Determines whether lowercase letters precede uppercase letters or vice versa. Default is language-dependent. In English, uppercase precedes lowercase.

Examples

The most important thing to remember when using the `xsl:sort` element is that numeric sorts aren't the same as alphanumeric sorts. Since the number 1 precedes the number 2, 1,000 will precede 2 in an alphanumeric sort. In the following example in which a sort is done by salary, the data type is set to number. In a numeric sort, of course, 1,000 follows 2. This sort is also a multiple key sort because two different sort elements are specified.

```
<xsl:stylesheet
 version="1.0"
 xmlns:xsl="http://www.w3.org/1999/XSL/Transform">

  <xsl:template match="page">
    <html>
      <head><title>Simple Stylesheet</title></head>
      <body>
        <h1>Simple Stylesheet</h1>
        <table border="0">
           <th></th><th>Name</th><th>Job</th><th>Salary</th>
            <xsl:for-each select="ROWSET/ROW">
              <xsl:sort select="JOB"/>
              <xsl:sort select="SAL"
                        order="descending"
                        data-type="number"/>
```

```
                <tr>
                 <td><xsl:value-of select="@num"/></td>
                 <td><b><xsl:value-of select="ENAME"/></b></td>
                 <td><xsl:value-of select="JOB"/></td>
                 <td><xsl:value-of select="SAL"/></td>
                </tr>
              </xsl:for-each>
           </table>
        </body>
      </html>
    </xsl:template>

  </xsl:stylesheet>
```

Whitespace Handling

You can define how whitespace should be handled for elements by using the `xsl:preserve-whitespace` and `xsl:strip-whitespace` elements. The `xsl:preserve-whitespace` and `xsl:strip-whitespace` elements are closely related and share essentially the same syntax. Both are top-level elements without children, and both must be children of the root element.

```
<xsl:preserve-whitespace elements="element_list" />

<xsl:strip-whitespace elements="element_list" />
```

The `elements` attribute is set to a whitespace-delimited list of element names. For `xsl:preserve-whitespace`, all whitespace between the `start` and `end` tags for those elements is preserved. For the `xsl:strip-whitespace`, all whitespace between the start and end tags for those elements is deleted.

Miscelleneous Elements

These last two elements don't fit in particularly well anywhere else. The first, `xsl:key`, defines search patterns for elements and is used in conjunction with the `key()` function discussed later. The second, `xsl:message`, provides a way to send messages to the XSLT processor, while the third is used with XSLT extensions.

xsl:key Syntax

The `xsl:key` element creates identifiers for elements. A key allows you to easily select one or more elements based on the value of an attribute or the value of the element. It is a top-level element that can be a child of the root element only, and it has no children.

Table 13.32 `xsl:key` Attributes

ATTRIBUTE	DESCRIPTION
Name	The name for the key.
`match`	The `XPath` pattern describing a set of elements to match against.
`use`	The expression describing an attribute or node of target elements. Used by the key function to evaluate whether or not an element should be included in the return node set.

There may be more than one key element per stylesheet, but they should all have unique names. A key is used in conjunction with the `key()` function.

```
<xsl:key
  name = "key_name"
  match = "nodeset_pattern"
  use = "node_expression" />
```

Table 13.32 lists the attributes.

xsl:message

The `xsl:message` element method provides a mechanism to communicate messages to the XSLT processor. What the XSLT processor does with these messages is processor-dependent.

```
<xsl:message
   terminate = "yes" | "no">
  message
</xsl:message>
```

If `terminate` is set to `"yes"`, the XSLT processor should stop processing. By default, it is set to `"no"`.

xsl:fallback

The `xsl:fallback` element works with extension elements that aren't defined in XSLT 1.0. It defines what to do if an extension that you are trying to use is unknown or unavailable to the XSLT processor.

```
<xsl:fallback>
  Template XSLT
</xsl:fallback>
```

The `xsl:fallback` element should be an immediate child of the extension element that might not be supported.

XPath

XPath is a language designed to locate nodes in an XML document. The simple paths and expressions that you've used thus far are all examples of XPath in action. In many cases, its syntax is similar to that used by file systems. This isn't coincidental—both XML documents and file systems are tree-based. However, XPath goes a bit beyond the simple path notation you've seen so far. It has, for example, its own data types and built-in functions. It also has a rich tool set of axes and predicates; the axes allow you to navigate and grab nodes across the XML tree, and the predicates allow you to filter the nodes that you grab.

This section covers XPath by looking first at the different data types that XPath supports. Then you'll learn formally about expressions and paths, with which, from the previous section, you already have experience. This section concludes with a discussion of axes and predicates. The built-in functions are discussed in the final section of this chapter.

Expressions and Data Types

XPath is a simple language, the key, omnipresent component of which is the *expression*. An XPath expression is simply some combination of the XPath language elements—operators, paths, variables, predicates, function calls, names, and/or literals. Basically, any time that you write XPath you write an XPath expression.

An XPath expression is evaluated to a data type. XPath has four data types: node sets, Booleans, numbers, and strings. They are collectively known as objects. Generally, these types can interchange with one another—for instance, it's not an error to pass a node set to a string function. It just interprets the string value of the first node as a string. Let's look at each of these data types in detail.

A node set is one or more nodes. An XPath expression such as `"ROWSET/ROW/*"` returns a node set. Any kind of expression that is meant to return a node set is called a *location path*. Creating a location path is a lot of the work that you do in XPath, and it is covered specifically in later sections of this chapter. The key to constructing good location paths is to understand how to use the axes.

You may have noticed that there isn't a data type for just a single node. This is by design: instead of creating a separate data type, XPath keeps it simple by treating single nodes and sets of node the same. Functions that expect to deal with a single node—`string()` and `number()`, for example—simply take the first node in the node set. As a developer, the burden is on you to make sure that the first node is the one that you want processed.

The XPath number data type is generally used for pedestrian activities such as counting the number of nodes in a node set. Though not a mathematically strong language, XPath does give the ability to do the following mathematical operations:

- Addition (+)
- Subtraction (()

- Multiplication (*)
- Division (div)
- Modulus (mod)

There are several other mathematical functions, covered later in this chapter, that you can use.

XPath strings are composed of Unicode characters by default. Since XPath is a text-focused language, a lot of the work that you do deals with strings. The core functions include several string functions that give you a rich set of functionality. With a little work, you can do a lot of parsing and chopping of strings.

An XPath boolean value is either true or false, and boolean expressions, covered earlier when you learned about conditional processing, evaluate to either true or false.

Location Paths

A location path is an expression that returns a node set. Location paths make XPath powerful, but they also make the language complex. A location path describes one or more nodes, where a node is the root node, an element, an attribute, a comment, a namespace declaration, a processing instruction or some text.

A location path can be either relative or absolute. It is absolute if it begins with a '/'. As with absolute file paths and URLs, an absolute location path starts at the top of the tree. A relative path starts with the context node. Unlike with URLs embedded in Web pages, there is no rule of thumb that says that you should always use relative URLs. In many cases, you should use them, but absolute paths can be invaluable in grabbing data from distant parts of the tree.

Any location path is composed of location steps. Location steps can have three parts—an axis, a node test, and a predicate. They take the following form:

```
axis::node-test[predicate]
```

This form probably looks unfamiliar to you, and you may be unconvinced that this was the same language that you were using earlier. A couple of explanations are in order. First, the predicate isn't required. Second, the child axis is the default axis, which means that a statement such as:

```
ROWSET/ROW
```

translates to:

```
child::ROWSET/child::ROW
```

Following this syntax, ROWSET and ROW are node tests. A node test is a node name, the element wildcard (*), the attribute wildcard (@*), or a node-test function. If a node name is used, only nodes of that name are selected. If the element wildcard character is used, any element will match, while the attribute wildcard will match only attribute nodes. Table 13.33 lists the available node-test functions.

Table 13.33 Node-Test Functions

FUNCTION	DESCRIPTION
`node()`	Returns true on any type of node
`comment()`	Returns true for `comment` nodes
`Processing-instruction()`	Returns true for `processing-instruction` nodes
`Text()`	Returns true for `text` nodes

Unlike with file systems, the wildcard can be used to skip levels of the tree. The following location paths select, regardless of who the parent is, any grandchild of the context node named `ENAME`.

```
*/ENAME
child::*/child::ENAME
```

The last piece in the puzzle is the predicate. The predicate, which is optional, is a way to filter down the node set achieved by the axis and the node test. Ultimately, it is a `boolean` expression much like those discussed earlier. If the expression is true, the node will be included in the resultant node set. There is one twist, however. If a number is given in the predicate itself, it will not follow the rules set out earlier. Rather, it will evaluate to true for that particular node in the node set. So the following location path:

```
ROWSET/ROW[3]
```

actually translates to:

```
ROWSET/ROW[position()=3]
```

The position function is invoked on each `ROW` node, and only the third one will be returned.

Axes

The XPath class is built around the concept of axes. You can think of an axis as a way to define a relationship between two nodes. For any given two nodes and any given axis, the two nodes are either both on the axis or not. Since XML describes trees, the axes that XPath defines describe tree-based relationships. For instance, one popular axis is the descendant axis of a particular node. Node B is on the descendant axis of node A if it or any of its ancestors is a child of node A. Algorithmically, you can consider the descendant axis this way:

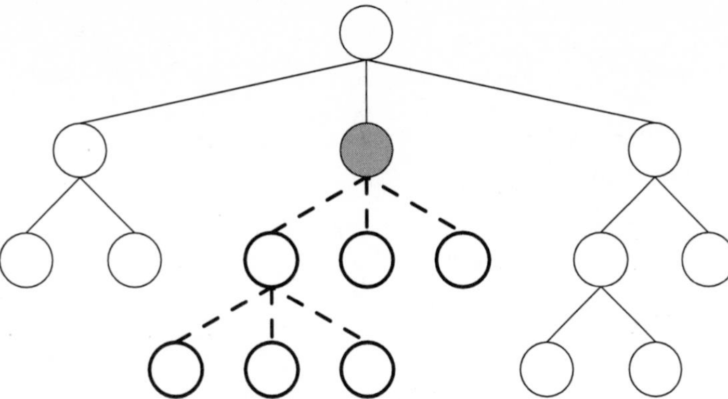

Figure 13.4 Descendant axis of a node.

1. Ask node B, "Who is your parent?"
2. Ask the parent, "Who is your parent?"
3. Continue until the answer is "node A" or you reach the root node.
4. If your algorithm stops on node A, node B would be node A's descendant axis; if your algorithm stops at the root node and the root node is not node A, node B would not be the descendant's axis.

If you are more of a visual thinker than an algorithmic thinker, Figure 13.4 illustrates the same concept. All the nodes denoted with bold circles are on the descendant axis of the node A.

This section covers all of the axes in XPath, starting with the most popular. A diagrams like Figure 13.4 is provided for each axis involving elements. Before moving on, it's important to make a couple of notes about the diagrams. This particular axis includes the node from which the axis is defined. However, this is not always the case. Thus, the reference element of the axis is delineated with a ring. A square inside the ring means that the reference element is not a member of the axis. Additionally, there are several axes—the sibling axes—that don't follow the structural connections that XML defines. Thus, the axes are defined with thick dotted lines, whereas the structure is defined with solid lines.

`self (.)`

The `self` axis describes the reference element itself. It has (and always has) one member only, the reference element. It can be abbreviated with the symbol "." and is shown in Figure 13.5.

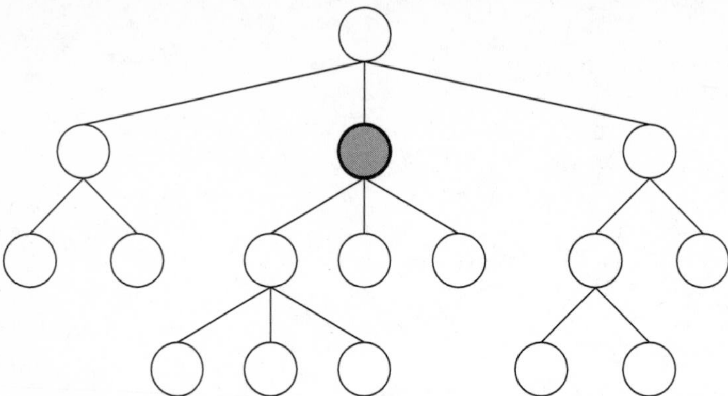

Figure 13.5 `Self` axis.

`descendant-or-self (//)`

The `descendant-or-self` axis includes the reference element and all of its descendants. It always has at least one element, the reference element. It can be abbreviated with the "`//`" symbol and is shown in Figure 13.6.

`parent (..)`

The `parent` axis includes, at most, one element, the parent of the context element. If the context element is the root element, this axis will be empty; otherwise, the axis will have one member only. It can be abbreviated with the symbol and is shown in Figure 13.7.

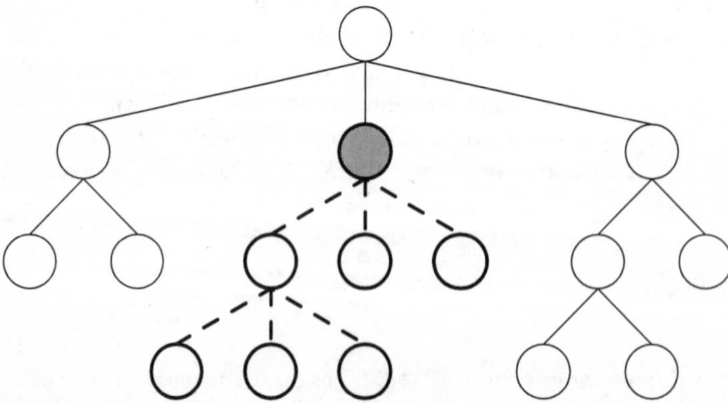

Figure 13.6 `Descendant-or-self` axis.

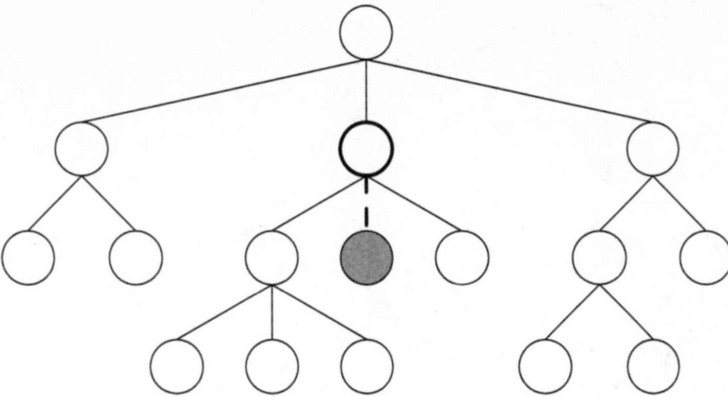

Figure 13.7 `Parent` **axis.**

`attribute (@)`

The `attribute` axis includes the attributes of the given element. As discussed earlier, attributes are considered nodes. This is the one XPath axis that works with nonelement nodes. It can be abbreviated with the `"@"` symbol.

`child`

The `child` axis, which may be empty, includes all the immediate children of the context element. It doesn't include the context element, as shown in Figure 13.8.

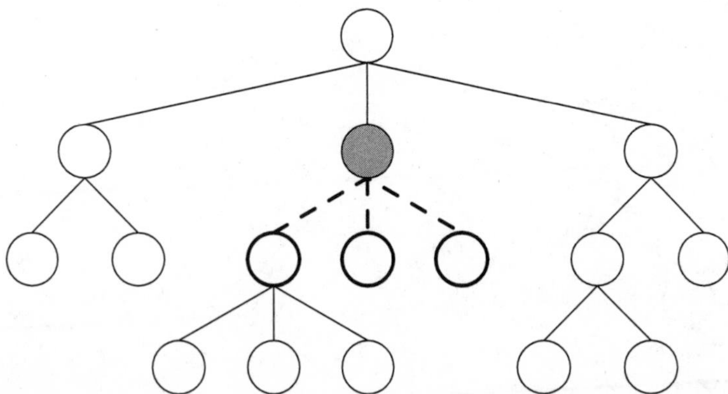

Figure 13.8 `Child` **axis.**

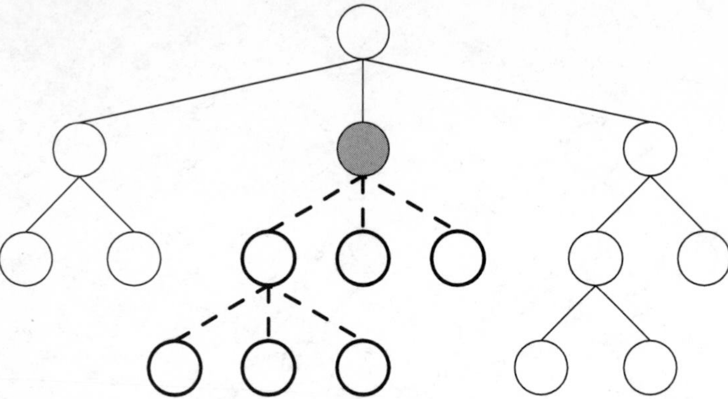

Figure 13.9 `Descendant` axis.

`descendant`

The `descendant` axis, which may be empty, includes all the descendants of the context element but does not include the context element itself. For elements without children elements, this axis will be empty, as shown in Figure 13.9.

`ancestor`

The `ancestor` axis, which may be empty, includes all the ancestors of the context element but does not include the context element itself. This axis is empty for the root element and has at least one member for all other elements, as shown in Figure 13.10.

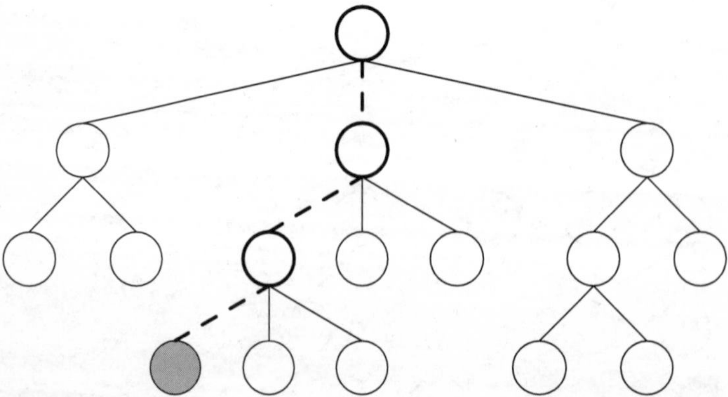

Figure 13.10 `Ancestor` axis.

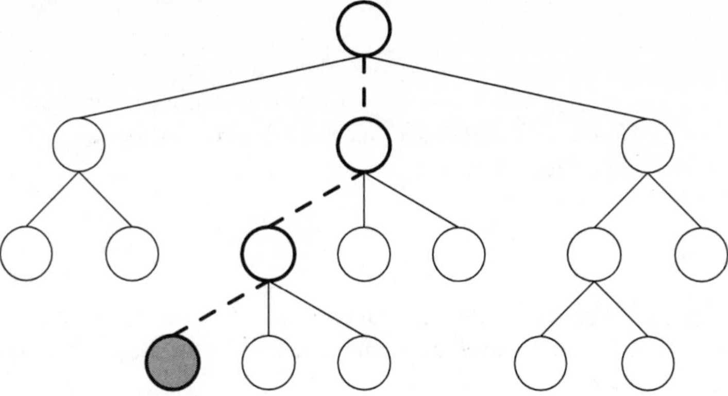

Figure 13.11 `Ancestor-or-self` axis.

`ancestor-or-self`

The `ancestor-or-self` axis includes all of the ancestors of the context element and the context element itself. It always has at least one member, the context element. All elements except the root element will have at least two members on this axis, as shown in Figure 13.11.

`following-sibling`

The `following-sibling` axis includes, at most, one element—the next sibling in document order. If it exists, the only member of this axis is the next element with the same parent. Figure 13.12 assumes that the elements on the left of the document precede the elements on the right.

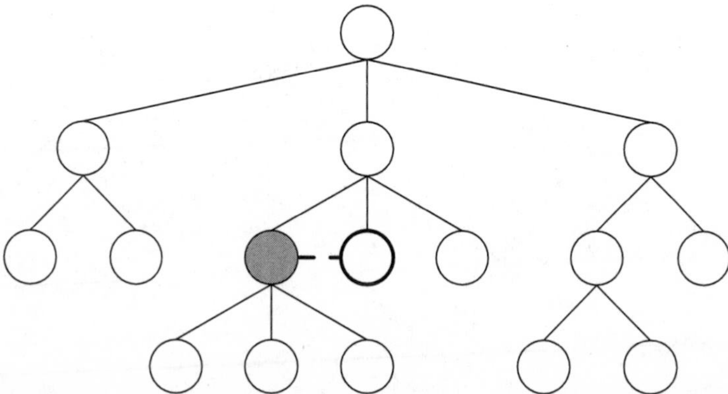

Figure 13.12 `Following-sibling.`

`preceding-sibling`

The `preceding-sibling` axis includes, at most, one element—the previous sibling in document order. If it exists, the only member of this axis is the first preceding element with the same parent. Figure 13.13 assumes that the elements on the left of the document precede the elements on the right.

`following`

The following axis, which might be empty, includes all elements that follow the context element in the document. It does not include the context element, nor does it include any ancestor of the context element.

`preceding`

The preceding axis which might be empty, includes all elements that precede the context element in the document. It doesn't include the context element.

`namespace`

The `namespace` axis includes all elements in the same namespace (as defined by xmlns) as the context node. It will always include the context element, and it may include nothing but the context element.

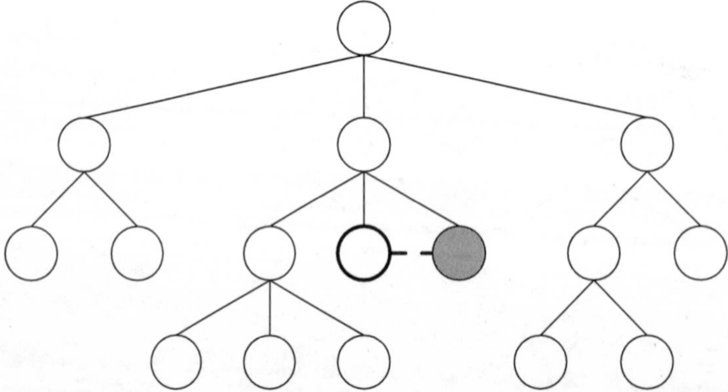

Figure 13.13 Preceding-sibling.

XPath and XSLT Functions

The following functions can be used anywhere in a stylesheet. Most are defined as part of XPath proper, while some were added solely for XSLT. The XSLT-specific functions are covered first, followed by the `node-set`, `string`, `boolean`, and `number` functions.

XSLT Specific Functions

current

The `current` function returns the `current` node.

```
node-set current()
```

document

The `document` function returns one or more external documents as node sets.

```
node-set document(uri, base-uri)
```

```
node-set document(node-set_as_uri, node-set_as_base-uri)
```

Table 13.34 lists the parameters.

format-number

The `format-number` function converts a number to a string in accordance with the specified format.

```
string format-number(num, format_str, decimal_format_name)
```

Table 13.35 lists the parameters.

Table 13.34 `document` Parameters

ARGUMENT	DESCRIPTION
`uri`	The URI of the external document.
`base-uri`	The base URI used to resolve URIs found in the external document.
`node-set_as_uri`	A set of URIs for documents to load. The value of each node is a URI.
`node-set_as_base-uri`	A set of base URIs corresponding to the documents listed in the first argument.

Table 13.35 `format-number` Parameters

ARGUMENT	DESCRIPTION
`num`	The number you wish to format.
`format_str`	The format mask that should be used to format string.
`decimal_format_name`	Optional—the name of a decimal-format element that describes how to format decimals.

generate-id

The `generate-id` function generates a unique identifier for a given node.

```
string generate-id(node_set_to_id)
string generate-id()
```

Table 13.36 lists the parameters.

The function will return a string that can be used as a valid XML name. The XSLT processor must create different identifiers for each node in the document. On a particular transformation, the processor must produce the same id for the same node across multiple calls to `generate-id`. However, the XSLT processor is not required to generate the same id for the same id across separate transformations.

key

The `key` function is used in conjunction with an `xsl:key` element to look up values according to the algorithm that the `key` element describes and using the second parameter as input.

```
node-set key(key_name,node_set_to_evaluate)
node-set key(key_name,string_value)
node-set key(key_name,object_value)
```

Table 13.37 lists the parameters.

Table 13.36 `generate-id` Parameters

ARGUMENT	DESCRIPTION
`node-set`	Optional—a node set in which only the first node is evaluated. If the node set contains more than one node, only a unique identifier will be generated for the first node of the node set, as determined by document order. If the argument is omitted, a unique id is generated for the context node.

Table 13.37 key Parameters

ARGUMENT	DESCRIPTION
key_name	Name of the xsl:key element to use.
node_set_to_evaluate	Each node in the node set evaluated to a string. The result is the node set that would be accumulated by individually calling the key function on each string node value for each node in the node set.
string_value	The string used in the evaluation.
object_value	The object translated to a string as if by a call to the string() function. The effect is that of calling the function with string_value as the second argument.

As you will recall from the earlier discussion on the xsl:key element, keys are a way of defining a search in XSLT. When you set up the xsl:key element, all you have to do is use the key function to get a set of values that you want to pass in a parameter. The key function uses the following algorithm to determine the nodes that should be included in the result, assuming a string is passed as the second parameter of the key function.

1. The value of the match attribute and the value of the use attribute of the specified xsl:key element are retrieved.
2. The node set specified by the match value is loaded from the XML source document.
3. The first node in the node set is pulled.
4. The use attribute is evaluated against the first node to produce a value.
5. The value is compared to the string passed to the key function.
6. If the two are equal, the node will be included in the result node set.
7. The previous four steps are repeated for each node in the node set.
8. The result node set is returned.

In the case where a set of nodes is passed to the key element, the foregoing algorithm is repeated for the value of each node in the node set. The result is a set of unique nodes produced by all the evaluations. In the case where some other object is passed to the key function, it is translated to a string as if by the string function and then the same algorithm is returned.

system-property

The system-property asks the XSLT processor to return a system property.

```
object system-property(property_name)
```

Table 13.38 lists the parameters.

Table 13.38 system-property Parameters

ARGUMENT	DESCRIPTION
property_name	The name of the property you desire.

There are only three properties that an XSLT processor is required to return:

xsl:vendor. The vendor that provides the XSLT processor.

xsl:vendor-url. The URL of the vendor.

xsl:version. The version of XSLT implemented by the XSLT processor.

A given XSLT processor may (or may not) return other properties.

unparsed-entity-uri

The unparsed-entity-uri returns an unparsed entity URI from the source document type definition (DTD). If doesn't exist, the empty string will be returned.

```
string unparsed-entity-uri(entity_name)
```

Table 13.39 lists the parameters.

Table 13.39 unparsed-entity-uri Parameters

ARGUMENT	DESCRIPTION
entity_name	The name of the entity that has the URI you desire.

Node-Set Functions

count

The count function returns the number of nodes contained in a node set.

```
number count(node_set_to_count)
```

Table 13.40 lists the parameters.

Table 13.40 `count` Parameters

ARGUMENT	DESCRIPTION
`node_set_to_count`	The node set that you wish to count.

id

The `id` function selects an element by its unique XML id.

```
node-set id(string_list_of_ids)
node-set id(node_set_to_evaluate)
node-set id(object_to_evaluate)
```

Table 13.41 lists the parameters. The id for the nodes is specified by the source XML DTD. If the DTD doesn't exist or doesn't specify a default, no nodes will be returned.

last

The `last` function returns the size of a node set. When used in a predicate, the size of the predicate's node set is returned. When used by itself, the size of the context node-set is returned.

```
number last()
```

Table 13.41 id Parameters

ARGUMENT	DESCRIPTION
`String_list_of_ids`	A whitespace-delimited list of ids.
`Node_set_to_evaluate`	A set of nodes in which the values are evaluated as a list of ids.
`Object_to_evaluate`	An object that is converted to a string as if by a call to the string function and then read as a whitespace-delimited list of ids.

local-name

The local-name function returns the local name of a node—the name without any namespace prefixes.

```
string local-name()
string local-name(node_set_to_evaluate)
```

If node_set_to_evaluate has more than one node, only the first node in document order will be processed. If no argument is passed, the context node will be evaluated.

Name

The name function returns the fully qualified name of a node, including any namespace prefix.

```
string local-name (node_set_to_evaluate)
string local-name ()
```

If node_set_to_evaluate has more than one node, only the first node in document order will be processed. If no argument is passed, the context node will be evaluated.

namespace-uri

The namespace-uri function returns the namespace URI of a node.

```
string namespace-uri (node_set_to_evaluate)
string namespace-uri ()
```

If node_set_to_evaluate has more than one node, only the first node in document order will be processed. If no argument is passed, the context node will be evaluated.

position

The position function returns the position of the context node within the current context.

```
number position()
```

String Functions

concat

The concat function concatenates the argument strings.

```
string concat(string1, string2, string3 . . .)
```

At least two arguments are required.

contains

The contains function determines whether a string contains a substring.

```
boolean contains(superstring, substring)
```

normalize-space

The normalize-space function strips a string of leading and trailing whitespace and replaces any sequences of whitespace characters with a single whitespace character.

```
string normalize-space(string_to_normalize)
string normalize-space()
```

If the argument is omitted, the context node will be converted to a string.

starts-with

The starts-with function returns true if a string starts with a given string.

```
boolean starts-with(superstring, prefixstring)
```

Table 13.42 lists the parameters.

Table 13.42 starts-with Parameters

ARGUMENT	DESCRIPTION
superstring	The target string.
prefixstring	The prefix string that the target string may or may not start with.

string

The string function converts an object to a string.

```
string string(node_set_to_convert)
string string(number_to_convert)
string string(boolean_to_convert)
string string(string_to_convert)
string string(object_to_convert)
string string()
```

Table 13.43 lists the parameters.

string-length

The string-length function returns the number of characters in a string.

```
number string-length(target_string)
number string-length()
```

If a string is passed to the function, its length will be returned; otherwise, the string value of the context node is returned.

Table 13.43 string Parameters

ARGUMENT	DESCRIPTION
node_set_to_convert	The string value is returned to the first node in document order of the node set.
number_to_convert	A number is converted as normal, with the following exceptions: an infinite number, which is returned as the string "Infinity" or "-Infinity", and "not a number", which is returned as "NaN".
boolean_to_convert	If true, the string "true" is returned. If false, the string "false" is returned.
string_to_convert	If a string is passed, it will be returned without modification.
object_to_convert	If some other type of object is passed, its conversion will be object-dependent and not defined by XPath.

Substring

The `substring` function returns a substring of a string.

```
string substring(superstring, beginning_pos, end_pos)
string substring(superstring, beginning_pos)
```

Table 13.44 lists the arguments.

The numbering of characters is different than it is in Java and ECMAScript, where the position of the first character is 0. For this function, the first character is at position 1 and the last character's position is equivalent to the length of the string. If you pass 0 as the second argument, it will resolve as 1. If you pass a noninteger, it will be rounded to an integer and the integer will be evaluated. The function will return the empty string if the arguments don't make sense, because the third argument is less than the second argument, an argument is negative, an argument is infinity, or an argument is `NotANumber`.

substring-before

The `substring-before` function returns a substring of a string that precedes a given token. It can be used to tokenize a string based on a delimiter.

```
string substring-before(superstring, delimiter_string)
```

Table 13.45 lists the arguments.

If the superstring doesn't contain the `delimiter_string`, the empty string will be returned. The delimiter will not be included in the returned string.

Table 13.44 `Substring` Arguments

ARGUMENT	DESCRIPTION
superstring	The string from which the substring is pulled.
beginning_pos	The position of the first character of the substring, where the first character is numbered as 1.
end_pos	If present, the position of the last character of the desired substring. If not present, the last character of the substring is the last character of the superstring.

Table 13.45 Substring-before Arguments

ARGUMENT	DESCRIPTION
superstring	The string from which the substring is pulled.
delimiter_string	The delimiter that should mark the end of the substring that you desire.

substring-after

The substring-after function returns a substring of a string that follows a given token. It can be used to tokenize a string based on a delimiter.

```
string substring-after(superstring, delimiter_string)
```

Table 13.46 lists the arguments.

If the superstring doesn't contain the delimiter_string, the empty string will be returned. The delimiter will not be included in the returned string.

translate

The translate function translates the target_string by interchanging characters of the base_string with characters of the source_string. The function can also be used to remove characters from the target_string.

```
string translate(target_string, base_string, source_string)
```

Table 13.47 lists the arguments.

Each character in the base_string that has a character in the source_string at the same position is replaced in the target_string. If the source_string is shorter than the base_string (or empty), the trailing characters (or all the characters) in the base_string are eliminated from the target_string.

Table 13.46 Substring-after Arguments

ARGUMENT	DESCRIPTION
superstring	The string from which the substring is pulled.
delimiter_string	The delimiter that should precede the substring that you desire.

Table 13.47 `translate` Arguments

ARGUMENT	DESCRIPTION
`target_string`	The string to be translated.
`base_string`	The base_string, which contains the list of characters that should be translated.
`source_string`	The source_string, which is the source of characters that should replace the base-string characters.

`boolean` Functions

The following functions return true and false. They have theoretical importance, but probably the only one you will regularly use is the not function.

boolean

The `boolean` function returns a `boolean` value based on the argument

```
boolean boolean(node-set)
boolean boolean(string)
boolean boolean(number)
boolean boolean(boolean)
boolean boolean(object)
```

Table 13.48 lists the arguments.

Table 13.48 `boolean` Arguments

ARGUMENT	DESCRIPTION
`node-set`	True if the node set is not empty.
`string`	True if the length is greater than 0.
`number`	True if it isn't 0 or `NotANumber`.
`boolean`	True if true.
`object`	The `boolean` value of objects of a type other than the basic type is dependent on that type and isn't defined by `XPath`.

false

The false function returns false.

```
boolean false()
```

lang

The lang function determines whether a particular lang is the language or whether a sublanguage specified by the argument is the same as the context node.

```
boolean lang(lang_string)
```

The lang value of the context node is determined by the xml:lang attribute of the context node or the xml:lang attribute of the nearest ancestor that has an xml:lang attribute. If no xml:lang attribute can be found, the function returns false.

not

The not function inverses the boolean value of its argument. True returns false and false returns true.

```
boolean not(boolean_value)
```

true

The true function returns true.

```
boolean true()
```

Number Functions

ceiling

The ceiling function returns the next highest integer compared to the number _argument or the number_argument itself if it is an integer.

```
number ceiling(number_argument)
```

floor

The floor function returns the next-lowest integer compared to the number_argument or the number_argument itself if it is an integer.

number

The number function converts its argument to a number.

```
number number(node_set_as_single_node)
number number(string)
number number(number)
number number(boolean)
number number(object)
```

Table 13.49 lists the arguments.

round

The round function rounds a number to the nearest integer or returns a number if it is an integer, a positive infinity, a negative infinity, or a NotANumber.

```
number round(number)
```

sum

The sum function converts the string value of each node in a node set to a number, adds them, and returns the result.

```
number sum(node-set)
```

Table 13.49 number Arguments

ARGUMENT	DESCRIPTION
Node_set_as_single_node	If a node set is passed, the first node in document order is converted to a string; then the string is converted to a number.
string	A string that represents a number is converted to a number. If the string can't be interpreted as a number, then NotANumber will be returned.
boolean	True is converted to 1 and false is converted to 0.
object	An object of a type other than the basic type is converted in a way that is dependent on that type and not defined by XPath.

Moving On

This chapter covered all the details of XSLT. At this point, you now have learned all the core technologies that you need for developing XSQL applications. In the next chapter, you'll put XSLT, SQL, and XSQL to use when you develop a real-world application.

CHAPTER

14

Building XSQL Web Applications

You've covered a lot of ground in the past few chapters. You've seen all of the syntax and elements for XSQL, a large percentage of SQL and PL/SQL, and you've learned XSLT. You know all the parts—now it is time to put them together. This chapter focuses on using the knowledge that you've acquired to efficiently create XSQL applications.

The first step is to examine how to create an architecture of XSQL applications. We've touched on this subject before, but this time you can focus on how to make specific architectural decisions, such as "Should I sort in SQL or in XSLT?" We'll also discuss how Java action handlers come into play. Though you haven't learned those at an implementation level yet, it is important to understand the opportunities that they make available to you. Often, action handlers can greatly simplify a task that would be quite hard to accomplish in SQL and PL/SQL.

From here, you'll walk through the process of designing and implementing a simple application—an online product catalog for the Mom N' Pup store. It has two parts: (1) a public part that allows you to browse and search the catalog, and (2) a simple data editor that allows you to input new entries. This example will be used to demonstrate a process for designing an XSQL application architecture followed by the core code for the public catalog part of the application. Based on this core code, you'll extend the application to include pagination, where large queries are separated into more manageable pages. Then, you'll develop the data editor, and that application will be used to show how to integrate XSLT and JavaScript. The chapter ends by looking at how to handle errors.

Application Architecture

XSQL is more of a framework than a language. It allows you to easily leverage the power of the database and XSLT. If your database is well suited to your application, you can have a simple query-only application in place in a matter of minutes and hours instead of days and weeks. For applications that are more complex, you can extend the basic model with action handlers and PL/SQL procedures. Even then, you'll still hopefully find yourself writing far less code than you would in a traditional *n*-tier development model.

"Hopefully" is the key word here. The chief challenge of XSQL development isn't to figure out how to manipulate strings or write the most efficient loops in XSQL—you can't do those things in XSQL anyway! Rather, it is to make the best decisions regarding where to put the logic. This section looks in detail at this question. Because each of the individual technologies is so powerful, a lot of the decisions are trade-offs. For instance, both XPath and SQL are searching languages—when should you use each? Should you extend the framework with stored procedures or Java action handlers?

NOTE In Chapter 9, "PL/SQL," you learned about PL/SQL stored procedures. You can also create stored procedures in Java. This, of course, means yet another decision: Should you write stored procedures in Java or PL/SQL? This discussion focuses on stored procedures of either language as a building block and considers how they relate to the other building blocks.

Your first step is to examine the simple XSQL model that uses only SQL and XSLT. From there you'll look at how to consider how stored procedures and action handlers fit in. Then, we'll talk about the various ways to extend the simple model. Before launching into the various architectures, you may wish to review the high-level architecture figures earlier in the book that describe the various components. In this section, you'll see how to think about the different components in terms of application development.

The real challenge facing us: Which component should do what? There are no absolute answers, but the next few pages should give you some guidelines for examining this question. The way you answer this question will have a lot to do with your preferences and the preferences of your team and management. For instance, if you're a Java guru, you may find that action handlers are the primary building blocks for your solutions. If your management prefers to have everything in PL/SQL, then you'll find that many of the action handler duties can be handled in PL/SQL stored procedures. Perhaps the best way to approach this section is by focusing on the parts that you don't know so well. You may find that you can more efficiently handle a task with PL/SQL in spite of being a Java master or that you can win over your team of Java action handlers and change the policy.

The Simple XSQL Architecture

The challenge for a lot of individual Web pages is straightforward: Display the data that resides in the database in an intuitive, pleasing manner to your audience. If you then consider that a lot of pages are simply static, you'll find that a large majority of your pages can be handled solely with the XSQL query action and XSLT stylesheets. Even as you move into the Web services arena, the same premise holds true. Instead of pretty HTML, you use XSQL and XSLT to create XML that can be consumed by the Web service client.

At some point, you'll want to gather information from your audience. Maybe you want their feedback or you want to get some basic information from them. Maybe a Web service client wishes to provide you with data. In many of these cases, the simple `xsql:dml` action will handle your needs.

In these cases, you are basically providing a pretty front end to SQL. The stylesheets handle the transformations and create the user interface. The challenges of storing and retrieving the data are left to the database.

Query pages are represented by one or more `SELECT` statements, and input pages are represented by one or more DML statements, using either the `xsql:dml`, `xsql:insert-request`, `xsql:update-request`, or `xsql:delete-request` actions. These last three actions assume that the data is going to be provided as XML. Though you can use them in conjunction with traditional Web sites, they are generally more useful in Web services. For now, let's focus only on the `xsql:query` and `xsql:dml` actions.

On the surface, the `xsql:dml` appears more flexible. You can put any number of statements that you wish into the action, whereas the `xsql:query` action is restricted to one `SELECT` statement. This restriction seems quite limiting at first, and it might make you doubt the earlier claim that a large majority of database-driven Web pages can be developed with the simple XSQL architecture. To back up that claim, consider a couple of points:

- You can have more than one `xsql:query` action per page.
- You have access to all of the built-in SQL functions and PL/SQL functions.
- You can use the searching capabilities of Oracle Text inside SQL queries.
- You can use cursors inside `SELECT` statements to provide a deeper result set of data.

All of these combine to give your `xsql:query` actions a lot of power. Your stylesheets don't care how many `xsql:query` actions you have in a page—they just translate the XML. There are lots of SQL functions and Oracle-provided PL/SQL functions that can help you process the data in the database and provide better data in the output. Perhaps most important, you can use cursors inside a SQL statement so that the result is multileveled. These are especially useful to XSLT stylesheets.

You can't do everything with a `SELECT` statement or two, but you can do a lot. Two obvious cases in which you need to move beyond the `xsql:query` action are (1) when you need to perform intermediate queries in which one query dictates how another should be formed, and (2) when you need to return XML from the database into your document. There are certainly others. For example, you may find that it is easier to maintain an action handler or stored procedure that makes multiple SQL queries, even though the result could be produced with a single, very complex `SELECT` statement.

Let's turn our attention to the Data Manipulation Language (DML) statements. As mentioned in Chapter 7, "Database Modifications with XSQL," the `xsql:dml` action actually contains an anonymous PL/SQL block. This means that you can put any number of statements in the action and can even use conditional processing and variables. The real drawback with the `xsql:dml` action is that you can't provide good feedback to the user. You can put data in, but you can really only communicate back to the user whether it was successful. Often, you want more granularity than that. You can place an `xsql:query` statement after the `xsql:dml` statement, but this doesn't give you a lot of control. The `xsql:dml` action runs out of runway when you wish to provide precise feedback regarding what happened while you were modifying the data.

These distinctions may seem hopelessly abstract at this point. As you work through this chapter and develop a sample application, they should start to make more sense. In advance of that, the next section outlines a design process that can help you to detect when you need to move beyond the simple architecture.

Process for Developing Your Architecture

At its most sublime, the actual coding process is mostly typing. Your design is well thought out; the test cases are already developed, and the end result should pass them; and the pieces of the architecture will work together. All that is left is to type in the necessary computer code and fix the odd, misplaced semicolon. Such is the dream. For this section, we refuse to be cynical and claim that such a heavenly state can be achieved. The means that are necessary for enjoying a good development cycle is a good process.

Oh, process! That thing that is supposedly intrinsic to around 80 percent of the most boring meetings. Many a developer have daydreamed through such a meeting waiting to return to cranking code. The meetings themselves tend to instill in us a code-first, ask-questions-later attitude. But as scarred as all of our experiences are with processes and architecture, they become more important in the world of frameworks. Those that are quick to hack are quite likely to lose out on the key benefits of the overall system.

Before proceeding with our section, which frighteningly includes both the words "process" and "architecture," it's important for you to clear your head for a moment. To paraphrase Obi-Wan Kenobi of *Star Wars*, "These are not the processes you are looking for." Nor is the process that is allowed here the best one for all of your projects. For instance, this one assumes that you already have a database developed, which may not always be the case.

This process functions most like an algorithm. If your system can be built using the simple XSQL architecture, then you'll be able to complete your implementation with this process. If it cannot, you will realize it early on and well before you've gone down the wrong path. Let's look at the process first, and then we'll examine how to tell if you need to move beyond the basic architecture.

1. Develop the requirements for the system, and/or pester the appropriate person to actually write the requirements down.
2. Develop a site map of the interface and possibly a mockup.
3. Identify the places where you need to retrieve dynamic data and user input.
4. Identify the database tables, views, and other objects that relate to each item found in step 3, or design the database if one doesn't exist.
5. Create the SQL `SELECT` statements that you need for the queries.
6. Create the DML statements that you need to input data.
7. Identify when parameters are going to need to be passed from one page to another and the best way for doing that (e.g., cookies, page parameters).
8. Create XSQL pages for each page in your site map, encapsulating the SQL from steps 5 and 6 in XSQL actions.
9. Tie the XSQL pages together so that parameters are passed appropriately.
10. Develop the core XSLT stylesheets using live data from the database.
11. Develop the error handling stylesheets.

In 11 fairly easy steps, you've created your Web application! This does assume, of course that your problems could be solved with the simple architecture. However, you should be able to determine if the simple architecture will suffice on or before step 6 and before you do any real work. Let's look at how to tell if the application isn't going to fit the simple architecture and the steps to get around the problem:

1. *Develop the requirements for the system, and/or pester the appropriate person to actually write down the requirements.* With any luck, you'll be able to get past this step. Unfortunately, many projects fail because the basic design of the system is never formalized. Some would argue that success here requires a full-blown functional specification and technical specification with lots of diagrams. In reality, there certainly are projects that are small and simple enough in scope not to require such formalism. Even then, however, the process of writing down a couple of paragraphs can reveal certain types of problems early on. It's also helpful when the project goes sideways and everyone wants to claim that such and such a feature was required from the very beginning. Of course, XSQL doesn't require such a document, but in spite of this, its power shouldn't be underestimated.
2. *Develop a site map of the interface and possibly a mockup.* Your first red flag may appear during this step. If your application requires user authentication, then the simple XSQL architecture may not work for you. You may be able to handle this at the Web server or authentication level. For instance, if the Web server won't open a URL except for authenticated users, you can use the simple XSQL

architecture for the pages themselves. However, if you wish to implement complex rules for your users, you may find that you need an action handler to take care of this.

3. *Identify the places where you need to retrieve dynamic data and user input.* This step, in and of itself, shouldn't present any problems. It is important to complete this step without thinking too hard about the database, XSQL, and other implementation issues. The remaining steps will flesh out the specifics of your application's architecture.

4. *Identify the database tables, views, and other objects that relate to each item found in step 3, or design the database if one doesn't exist.* First, if you are creating the database as part of your development effort, then you'll need to design the database now. A section further in this chapter covers this topic extensively. If this application is going to be built on top of a database that already exists, then you'll need to acquire documentation on the underlying database. After discovering that no one has documented the database, you should needle the database administrator (DBA) to tell you which tables you'll need and how they relate to each other. If you plan on putting data into the database, then you'll want to be very sure that you aren't going to corrupt the data or interfere with other applications that use the database.

   Whether the database exists or not, an obvious problem may crop up here. What if your application gets data from places other than the database, or what if it gets data from multiple databases? If you are getting data from a nondatabase data source, such as a Lightweight Directory Access Protocol (LDAP) server, then XSQL may not be useful to you. In such a case, your first step is to investigate whether you can get your data as XML by calling a URI. If you can, you might be able to use the `xsql:include-xml` action inside your XSQL pages. You simply hand it a URI, and the XML that is retrieved is placed into the XSQL output. Then your stylesheet just needs to be able to transform it appropriately.

   If you find that your nondatabase data source won't return good XML to you, you'll probably need to create an action handler. Inside the action handler, you can reach out to the data source by whatever means necessary. If the data source is an operating system file, you can read it. If the data source is reached by a URI or by some other kind of network connection, you can write code to reach it over the network. If you need to reach the resource through a C Application Programmer's Interface (API), you can use the Java Native Interface (JNI). As long as you can reach the data source through Java code and you can get the data quickly, you'll be able to reach it from the action handler. Also, if the data that you are trying to reach doesn't change much over time, you might find it easier just to create a table in your database for it. Then you can grab the data with a simple XSQL query. Instead of creating an action handler, you just need to create a script to load the data as needed into your table.

   What if you have more than one database that you need to access? First, it doesn't matter if the databases are Oracle or not—they just have to be reachable by Java Database Connectivity (JDBC). The problem is that any given XSQL page can only connect to one particular database. There are two ways to address this. First, you can use the `xsql:include-xsql` action to include the results from another XSQL page. Your main page can attach to one database while the page or pages you specify in each `xsql:include-xsql` action can attach to other databases.

It is also possible to link the databases together at the database level. This is especially easy if all of the databases are Oracle. You create a distributed database that is composed of several databases but appears to your SQL statements to be one.

5. *Create the SQL* `SELECT` *statements that you need to create the dynamic data parts.* For this step, your goal is to make sure that you can construct SQL `SELECT` statements to grab the different dynamic parts that you've constructed. Remember that you can embed parameter and cookie values into your `SELECT` statements. You should watch out for cases in which you want to perform completely different SQL statements based on different parameters or where you actually need to execute multiple SQL statements to get the desired result. In either of these cases, an action handler or a stored procedure is probably in order.

   If you need to execute multiple SQL statements, a stored procedure will be more efficient. Before going that route, however, you may want to investigate a little further and make sure that multiple SQL statements are really necessary. Often, you can accomplish what you need to do with a single SQL statement by using a complex where clause, aggregate functions, cursors, and unions. Writing good SQL for XSQL is covered later in this chapter.

   Though it is more efficient to handle multiple SQL statements inside a stored procedure, an action handler can make a great traffic cop. If you have several complex forms tied together and each step depends on a previous step, then you can use an action handler to decide on the correct next action by looking at the current parameters and a possible user session.

   When it looks like your problems won't be solved with simple SQL statements, there are no hard and fast rules about whether you should use an action handler or a stored procedure. In most cases, the answer is application dependent. At this point, it is best to make a note of those situations that are more complex. Before making any decisions, you should learn more about writing action handlers by reading Chapter 18, "Custom Action Handlers," and review the stored-procedure discussions in Chapter 9. From there, you should look for similarities in the different cases. It's quite likely that you'll be able to solve multiple problems with a single stored procedure or action handler.

6. *Create the DML statements that you need to input data.* The simple architecture will be adequate if you have a couple of values that need to go straight into the database without any processing and you only need to know that the transaction succeeded. However, if you need to base what is inputted on variables in the form, you'll need an action handler. For example, if a radio button setting determines how the data should be interpreted, you should use an action handler to do the interpretation. You may find a stored procedure helpful, but an action handler affords a lot more flexibility.

7. *Identify which pages need to be tied together and whether you need parameters to pass from one page to another or you need cookie-based sessions.* XSQL supports the basic methods of passing parameters used by HTTP-based applications. You can set cookies on the browser, and you can process and pass GET and POST parameters. Thus, you can handle forms, parameters passed in the query string, and the getting and setting of cookies. In the simple architecture, you can pass any parameter and cookie value to the `xsql:query` and `xsql:dml` actions. However, if you want to do a complex interaction (e.g., performing one query based on one parameter value but a different based on another parameter value), you'll probably want to consider writing an action handler or creating a stored procedure for that purpose.

   Cookies deserve special consideration. Cookies are usually used as a way to bind different HTTP transactions together into a session. Because the cookie value returns on subsequent calls to the server, you can assume that the same user (or at least the same Web browser) is reconnecting. The cookie may contain meaningful data, or it may just contain a pointer to data that is stored on the server.

   The latter architecture tends to be more flexible—only one cookie needs to be set. In fact, Java servlets use this architecture so that you never have to set a cookie at all. From an action handler, you can use this servlet session architecture. Instead of setting and managing cookies directly, the servlet container takes care of the plumbing. Because the database is readily accessible, you can even store the session data in the database and reapply it to a session when the user returns, as discussed in Chapter 6 ("XSQL Parameters"). You can also assign and read cookies from inside an XSQL page. Cookies can play a role in a simple XSQL architecture. With some clever SQL statements and maybe a stored procedure or two, you can have something that looks a lot like the session object available via an action handler. The question is: Is that worth the effort? If you find that your application needs session capabilities, you'll find it easier to use an action handler to handle them.

8. *Create the XSQL pages, encapsulating the SQL from steps 6 and 7 in XSQL actions.* This doesn't necessarily result in a single XSQL page for each page of the site map. If you have a dynamic data area that is repeated throughout the site, you can create a single XSQL page for it and include it in other XSQL pages.

9. *Develop the core XSLT stylesheets using live data from the database.* Now that the XSQL is developed, you can write your XSLT that produces the presentation layer. As with the XSQL pages, you should be on the lookout for code reuse. Rather than developing the same stylesheet several times, you can develop it once and either include or import it from other stylesheets. You'll see an example of this later in this chapter.

   You'll also need to consider the roles of cascading stylesheets (CSS) and JavaScript in your Web site. When used with the Web, an XSLT transformation creates HTML for consumption by a Web browser. If you wish, the provided HTML can contain CSS and JavaScript. There is nothing inherent in XSLT that prohibits the use of JavaScript or CSS in any way. CSS and JavaScript is just text, after all. For instance, you could even use XSLT to dynamically create CSS styles and JavaScript code.

Generally, however, you want your CSS styles and JavaScript code to be static—debugging can be quite hard if the code itself is generated on the fly! Your CSS styles should be separated into a separate file for use by the entire site. You should try to do this as possible for JavaScript functions, too, though it can be harder for JavaScript. Because many functions are specific to particular forms and page elements, it's fine to keep those close to the elements with which they deal.

The real issues with CSS and JavaScript involve how styles and functions should be referenced and invoked from stylesheet templates. This subject is covered in detail later in this chapter.

10. *Tie the XSQL pages together so that parameters are passed appropriately.* At this point, you may run into some of the same difficulties described in step 5. You may discover that you are better off using a servlet session instead of handling all of the parameters manually.

11. *Develop the error handling stylesheets.* Your last step is to develop the stylesheets that handle errors. You'll learn more about this later in this chapter. It is basically a two-step process: (1) Determine what errors could occur; (2) determine how you want to inform the user about them. It is also helpful to develop a generic error handling template that simply displays a message.

Through this process, you've seen that there are many problems that the simple XSQL architecture can't solve. However, as you'll see throughout the rest of the book, the problems can be solved with a variety of different strategies. The art of XSQL development is choosing how to extend XSQL. The choice of how to extend is addressed specifically further in the next section and will enter into our discussions for the rest of the book.

Extension Options

In the previous section, you saw how to develop the architecture of your application. There are many times when you need to extend beyond the simple architecture. There are four ways to extend XSQL: (1) Write an action handler; (2) write a stored procedure; (3) invoke XSQL programmatically; and (4) write an XSLT extension. You've already learned about stored procedures in Chapter 9. This section looks at how to view each of these options in terms of the overall design of your application. You'll start with stored procedures, and then continue into the subjects that you haven't covered in depth.

Stored Procedures

You learned a lot about PL/SQL stored procedures in Chapter 9. This discussion centers not on the mechanics but on the concepts. Instead of worrying with how you would implement a particular functionality with a stored procedure, the question here is what you can do with a stored procedure and if it is best to use a stored procedure for a particular purpose. For this discussion, it doesn't matter if you are using PL/SQL for your stored procedures or Java.

There are two key advantages of stored procedures: you can integrate very easily with SQL and your code runs inside the database. As is so often the case, the latter advantage can also be a disadvantage, depending on your system configuration. Likewise, the tight integration can mean that you have limited access to other system resources beyond the database.

First, let's look at the advantages. With PL/SQL, SQL is built directly into the language. The results of SQL statements can be stored in variables and processed further. With Java stored procedures, you use SQLJ to accomplish the same goal. This tight integration makes it far easier to develop database-intensive code than using JDBC from an action handler.

The other key advantage of stored procedures is that they are executed inside of the database. This means that you don't suffer network round trips. When you call SQL from an action handler or other client program, each SQL query means a trip across the network and the return of a possibly large data set. Stored procedures aren't necessarily the solution to all of your performance worries, but you will at least be able to save some load on your network and the requisite time required in transferring data.

However, stored procedures are limited in dealing with resources beyond the database. If you need to deal with nondatabase data, such as files or other servers, then stored procedures won't be much help. This underlies the key point about stored procedures: They are extremely special-purpose.

NOTE If you wish to use database-stored XML in conjunction with XSQL, you can use either stored procedures or action handlers. If you choose stored procedures, you'll use the `xsql:include-owa` **action and the** `htp` **and** `htf` **packages, as discussed in Chapter 9. Special care must be taken if your XML document or fragment is longer than 4,000 characters.**

Perhaps the best way to think about stored procedures is as extensions to SQL. If you find yourself needing data from your database and SQL is too simple for your task, a stored procedure is a natural alternative. You'll find that they are easy to write and use. However, if you find yourself doing more typical, less database-intensive tasks, you should probably be using action handlers.

Action Handlers

Action handlers are the key to the programming unit for the entire XSQL framework. Because you haven't actually created an action handler yet, they may be hard to grasp. The easiest way to think about them is to remember that all of the actions you've been using, such as `xsql:query` and `xsql:dml`, use action handlers. When you write your own action handlers, you can solve the same class of problems solved by the built-in actions that you've been using all along. You can query the database, put data into the database, run stored subprograms or most anything else.

Most important, you can invoke the built-in action handlers in your action handlers. If you want to do multiple SQL calls, just call the `xsql:query` action handlers multiple times. If you want to input data, do a query, and then input more data, you can do that with very little new code.

The built-in action handlers can take values and attributes of the invoking element as inputs. Your action handlers can do this, also. Additionally, you can also access the data that came with the HTTP request. Your action handler is responsible for passing an XML element back to the XSQL servlet, which inserts it into the output.

With an action handler, you can do anything that you'd like to do with a stored subprogram. As covered earlier, there are advantages to coding the most database-intensive parts of your application as storedsubprograms. The stored subprograms that you create can be used in conjunction with any action handler made. Action handlers and stored subprograms are in no way mutually exclusive.

In Chapter 18, you'll implement your own action handlers. If you've written servlets or CGI programs, you'll probably be impressed by the simplicity and power that action handlers can give you. The details of the underlying HTTP protocol are available, but you don't have to manage everything about the transaction. You can easily query the database but still do anything else that a servlet can do. You can also pare down or augment the XML before returning it. As you work through this chapter, you may find the XSQL built-in actions to be limiting. As you'll see, though, action handlers can overcome these limitations and then some.

Programmatic Invocation

So far, the XSQL page has functioned as the key to the entire application. It drives the action. But you can also invoke an XSQL page from inside of an application written in Java. You create an instance of the XSQL page processor, and it loads a specified XSQL page. If you've defined action handlers and serializers in the XSQL page, it invokes those. If your XSQL page needs parameters, you can set the parameters before page processing. When the page processing is done, you can do whatever you wish with the output. You could even interpret it as XSQL and pass it back to the XSQL page processor for more processing.

There are several advantages of programmatic invocations. First and foremost, you have complete control. You can decide, at runtime, the XSQL page that you wish to use. You could even create the XSQL page at runtime if you'd like. When the page processor completes its job with the XSQL page, you can do what you wish with the results. If you are invoking the XSQL page processor from inside a servlet, you can modify the results before sending them onto the Web. Or, you can do something else with the results entirely.

The programmatic API gives you all the power you need to do anything that you want with XSQL. You aren't limited to just Web applications or the input-output model that you've been using thus far. Instead, you can think of programmatic invocation as a general way to fetch and input data with the SQL defined externally. As a bonus, you get the results of SQL back as XML. You can even perform XSLT transformations inside your programs if you want.

Power always comes with a price, though. The danger with using the programmatic APIs is that your overall architectures can become muddled. A chief advantage of a framework is that everyone knows where all the moving pieces are. It's easier to bring new developers onto a project because the architecture itself is standardized. They don't have to relearn what all the pieces are and how they fit together. Of course, not all problems fit nicely into a framework. Programmatic invocation allows you to mold the framework any which way that you desire. However, if you don't carefully consider how best to use the programmatic APIs, you can end up losing a lot of the benefits of the framework itself. A minimalist approach is often beneficial. In Chapter 17, "XSQL Beyond Web Browsing," you'll see the details of programmatic invocation, and you'll see how to use it to augment the basic XSQL architecture.

Stylesheet Extensions

Our last topic is stylesheet extensions. The Oracle XSLT processor allows you to call Java methods from inside a stylesheet. You do this by declaring the Java class that you wish to use and then calling the method inside a value-of element. The most palatable uses involve simple conversions using static methods. For instance, you could change a number into a binary number.

There are a number of reasons why stylesheet extensions are bad and are best avoided. First, they haven't been formally standardized. If you ever find that you wish to use a different XSLT processor with your stylesheets, they may not work. Also, they tend to make your stylesheets harder to understand. At the very least, someone looking at your stylesheets will need to defer to the documentation of the method just to understand what you are trying to do. If you develop a stylesheet extension habit, your stylesheets can start to look more like scripts instead of templates.

The problems that extensions solve can always be solved elsewhere in your architecture. A stylesheet extension takes as input a particular piece of data from the input XML document. The most that it can reasonably do is modify that string. Earlier in this section, we used the example of changing a decimal number to a binary number. Another example is rewriting the value as uppercase. Sometimes, these are necessary manipulations. However, you can always do them in an action handler before the XML reaches the XSLT processor.

Extending the Interface with JavaScript and CSS

HTML started as a very simple markup language; however, as the Web progressed through the 1990s, Web browsers began to support a variety of new standards to extend the capabilities of Web pages. The good news is that all of these standards (e.g., applets, plug-ins, JavaScript, CSS) are compatible with XSLT. The Web browser doesn't know that XSLT was used to produce a Web page—it just knows how to render HTML. The issue, then, isn't how to use JavaScript and CSS with XSLT, but how best to use them.

CSS styles and JavaScript code are just another type of text that Web browsers know how to interpret. For instance, you could even use XSLT to dynamically create CSS styles and JavaScript code. Generally, however, you want your CSS styles and JavaScript code to be static—debugging can be quite hard if the code itself is generated on the fly!

Practically, debugging is the best thing to keep in mind when extending HTML with CSS and JavaScript. If something goes wrong, or something needs to be modified or extended later, how hard is it going to be? Technically, the key issue is escaping the reserved XML characters when creating JavaScript on the fly. JavaScript also introduces another conceptual issue: How do you make methods that can be called from inside templates that may be applied numerous times?

Let's consider CSS, as JavaScript is covered in detail later in this chapter. Your CSS rules should be in a separate file for use by the entire site. This is a generally accepted best practice whether XSLT is used or not. It's especially important when used with XSLT. Stylesheet bugs tend to occur because templates aren't applying properly to the XML elements in the input document. If you are creating CSS rules inside a particular stylesheet, you are adding yet another moving part to your code. It's far better to define the CSS rules in a separate CSS file. Then only the selectors reside inside a stylesheet template.

This approach assumes that you aren't dynamically generating CSS rules. What if you store a user's preferred colors in the database? Even in such a case, there is still a strong argument for setting up the set of possible CSS rules in the CSS file and then using XSLT to dynamically select the right style. However, if the best option really is dynamic rule generation, you certainly can do that with XSLT. You can either dynamically generate the CSS file itself using XSQL, or you can generate the rules inside the templates of an XSLT stylesheet.

Extension at the Database Level

In the previous section, we discussed how to extend the simple architecture at the interface level. You can also extend the architecture at the other end—at the database level. You'll learn more about the ins and outs of designing databases from scratch in the next section. Rather, extending the database means that you have options at the database level to ease the implementation of your application. Specifically, you can database views, and triggers can make your job easier. The details of these were covered in Chapter 8, "Oracle SQL." Here, they are considered as valuable pieces in the overall puzzle.

First, let's consider views. If you find that the SQL statements that you formulated in steps 5 and 6 are overly complex, you may be able to simplify them greatly by creating views. Views don't have an operational impact on your database. Even if the underlying tables are off-limits to change because they are in use by other applications, a view can be created without any impact. They sit as a window on top of the tables. If you find yourself wishing, "If only I had a table like . . .," or "if only these two tables were combined like . . .," then you should look to create a view.

If you are inputting data, you may find triggers useful. You can set a trigger to execute whenever some action is performed on the database. For instance, a trigger set on Table A could be set to perform updates on Table B whenever an update is called on Table A. However, triggers are intrusive on an existing database. If another application is already using a particular table, that application will also cause the trigger to fire. This might make you very unpopular with the owner of that application.

Developing a new application against an existing database can be challenging. Though you don't have to do the work of designing a new database, you lose certain freedoms also. If you find that your application isn't meshing well with the existing database, you might want to look into augmenting the database with new tables.

A Sample Application

Our sample application is an online catalog for the Mom N' Pup retailer. In the course of developing this application, we'll run into some issues that are best resolved with action handlers and a programmatic approach. For now, we'll follow roughly the design process that we laid out in the previous section. Much of the remainder of our discussion in this chapter will revolve around our development. In this section, we'll develop the site map for the application and implement the database schema.

The Requirements

The first step in our process is to state the requirements for the application. The customer wants an online catalog that will be available over the Web. They currently don't have a database, so they'll need to have one built to contain the data. They want the users to either browse based on product category or perform searches based on the descriptions. In addition, they want to be able to edit the prices of products through a Web interface. At a high level, the requirements are as follows:

- Web-based online catalog, browsable by product category and searchable by keywords
- Database to store data
- Edit function for prices

In addition to these requirements, they are also throwing a couple of curve balls. First, they want some products to belong to more than one product category. For instance, hand soap could be used in the kitchen or in the bathroom. They want hand soap products to appear under both kitchen supplies and bathroom supplies, though for internal purposes it should be stored under only under one product category. They've browsed some other product sites and don't like it when too many product titles are loaded at the same time. Instead, they want the results of a query to be separated across several pages.

Mom N' Pup also runs specials from time to time. They want the home page to have a list of specials on the right-hand side of the home page. Clicking on the ad will take the shopper directly to the product page for the particular product. The specials should also be configurable through a Web-based interface.

The customer is also aware that the Web is an evolving medium, and they want to be sure that their catalog will be usable via different types of interfaces. They require that a demo version of the catalog is available through Wireless Application Protocol (WAP) that allows browsing of products only. They figure if the application design allows for this, then they'll be ready for any type of interface. This leaves us with our secondary requirements:

- Products can appear as members of multiple product categories.
- Product listings should paginate.
- Ads for specials should be listed.
- Specials should be configurable through a Web interface.

Now at this point, the imaginary customer would sign an imaginary contract drawn up by imaginary lawyers. Luckily for us, this step isn't necessary. If this were a real project, we'd also need to examine issues such as where the site is going to be hosted, how the data is going to be loaded, and how the database is going to be backed up and, in case of a failure, restored. These issues are largely beyond the scope of this book, so we'll punt those. Instead, we'll begin with the development work starting with the user interface design.

Application Interface Design

In keeping with the process developed earlier, the first step is to lay out the design of the interfaces. You may have noticed that this doesn't have to be the next step. If we wanted, we could work from the other direction and start dealing with the database first. However, starting with the interface is better. All applications, even Web services applications, have users. If the user experience isn't good, the application will ultimately fail. By starting on the interface, you increase the chances of success. The code and the database are molded around the interface instead of the other way around.

The logical place to start is the home page of the application. From the requirements, we know that users should be able to browse by product category and perform text searches. The customer also wants a set of ads to appear on the right-hand side of the browser window. A quick mockup looks like Figure 14.1.

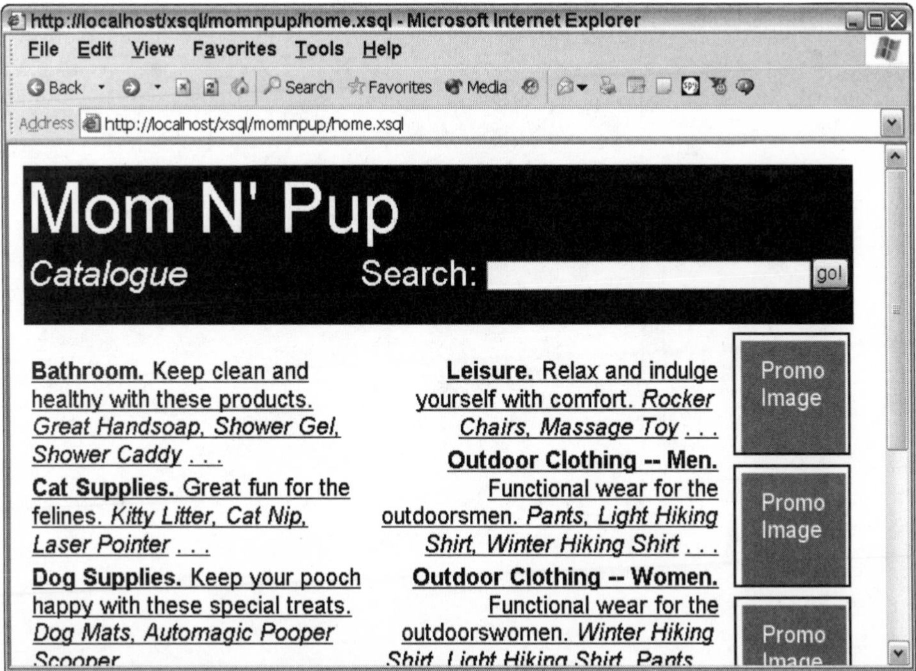

Figure 14.1 HTML mockup of the home page.

With this as a starting point, the rest of the site can be formulated. The primary goal of the site is to drive people to product-specific pages. Each product needs to have its own page with descriptions and pricing information. It can be reached through one or more product category pages, a search result page, or the ad. The primary site navigation is diagrammed in Figure 14.2.

If you stopped here, you would have a functional application, but not that pleasing of a user experience. Once users start to drill down, they wouldn't have any way to navigate back to the home page or across the site. Users need some sort of navigational elements to help them move around the site. The proposed resolution is to have a navigational tool bar across the top and a listing of product categories along the left-hand side. These navigational elements will appear in all of the subordinate pages—the product pages, the search result pages, and the product category pages. A mockup of a product page is diagrammed in Figure 14.3.

We have two mockups left to complete—the search results page and the product category page. Both are very similar in nature—they list products. The search results page is simpler in nature and is displayed in Figure 14.4. It lists the products based on their names, and the links lead to the respective product pages.

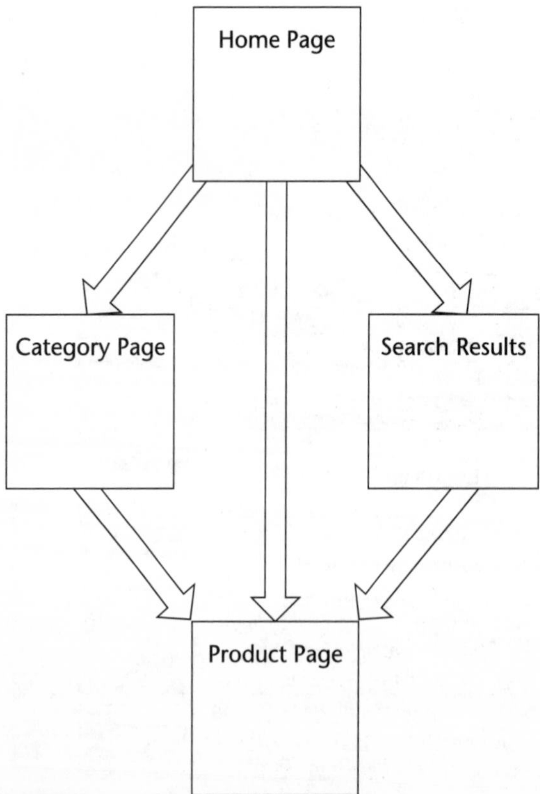

Figure 14.2 Primary site navigation.

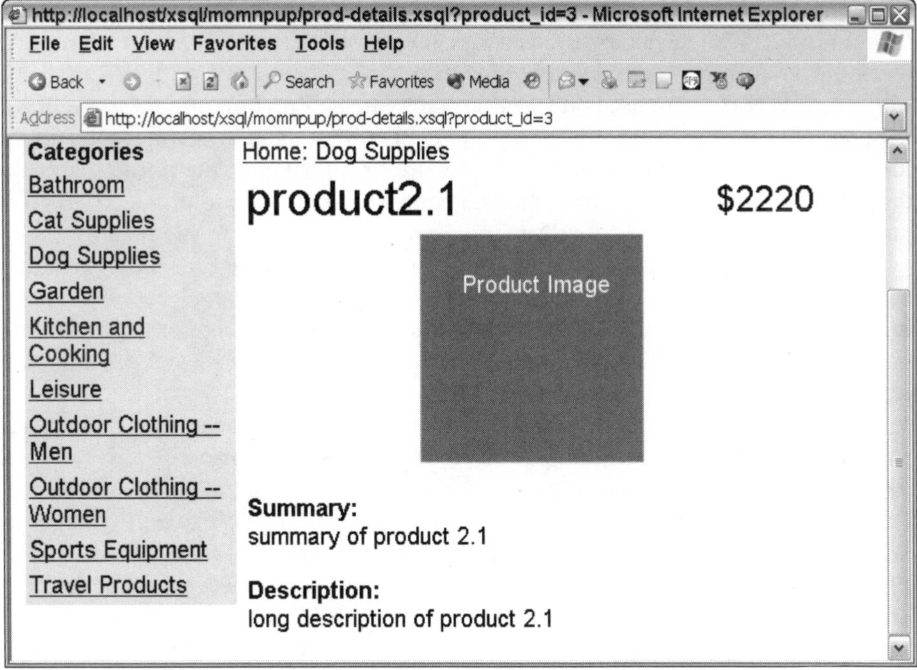

Figure 14.3 Product page.

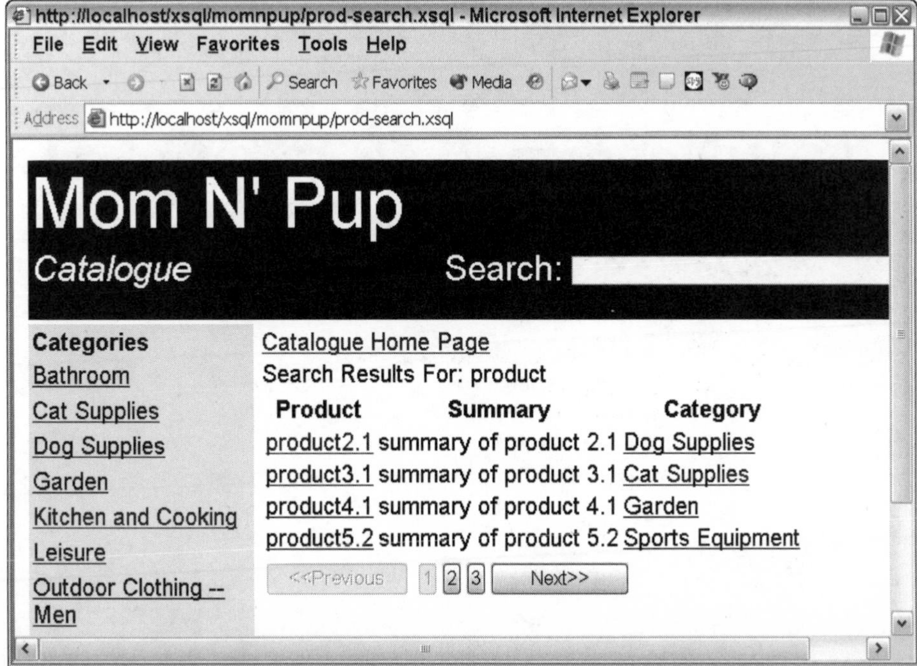

Figure 14.4 Search results page.

Our last page to design is the product category page. The main difference is that all of these products are related by product category, and the product category name and description should appear at the top of the page. It is pictured in Figure 14.5.

In these last two examples, you'll notice that there are Previous and Next buttons at the bottom of the pages. These meet requirements for pagination of the results. In the mockup, Previous is grayed out because we are presumably at the beginning of the search results. If we are at the end, the Next link should be grayed out. If a particular search doesn't return enough results to require pagination, neither should appear.

This takes care of the public catalog. Now, attention is needed for the price editor and the promotion editor. The customer wants to be able to change the prices of the items easily and to change multiple items at the same time. The editor page itself can appear similar to Figure 14.6. The top search field allows users to search for the products that they wish to edit.

At this point in the process, we would ask our customer to review our mockups in order to ensure that we are heading in the right direction. This is another advantage of starting with the interface—your customer can see it and understand it. An E-R diagram isn't nearly as exciting to most customers as a couple of Web pages tied together that kind of look like they work. This is also the time when the requirements can be clarified and possibly expanded. (Just make sure that if the project expands, the price also expands.)

In our case, Mom N' Pup is delighted with our work and are already hailing us as geniuses! (Hey, we might as well make the most out of our imaginary customers. They are much more malleable than the real ones.)

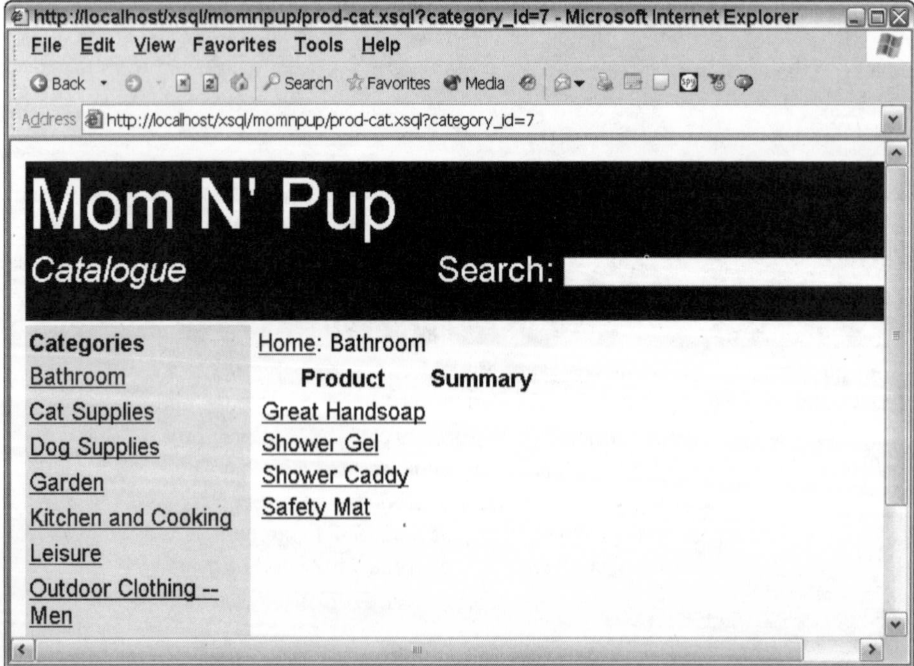

Figure 14.5 Product category page.

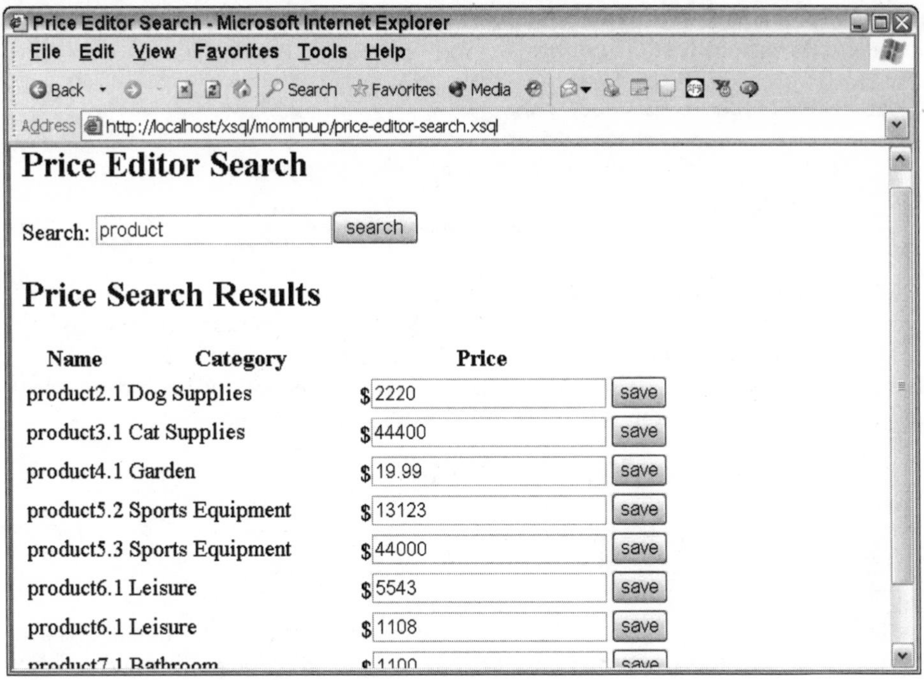

Figure 14.6 Price editor page.

Database Requirements

At this point, you've moved through steps 1 and 2 in our process. You have the requirements and you've developed an interface. The next step is to formulate the database requirements. To do this, you need to examine the interface design and identify the areas of your interface that interact with your database. With the areas identified, you can come up with pseudo-SQL statements that you will need for the required functionality.

First, a word is needed about our pseudo-SQL. This isn't yet another new-fangled language you have to learn. It's just a way to describe the data that is needed from the database in plain English. Because we don't have a database yet, we don't have to be syntactically correct. Even if we did have a database, this method is a good way to quickly determine the requirements without getting mired in the workings of the actual database. For our pseudo-SQL, we deliberately leave the tables out of the picture for now and focus on the pieces of data that are needed. Determining which fields should live in which tables is a task that will be addressed in the database design phase.

To find these database-related areas, we need only to examine the mockups formulated in the previous section. Let's start with the home page described in Figure 14.1. There are two dynamic data areas: (1) the listing of product categories and (2) the promotions. Our interface design puts usability limits on the number of each of these, but they can't be static. They should be generated from the database. Here's a pseudo-SQL statement for the product categories:

```
SELECT the product category name,
       the product category description,
       the product category identifier
FOR all of the product categories
IN alphabetic ORDER OF the product category name
```

Our statement retrieves the data that is seen on the screen as well as the product category identifier. The product category identifier will be embedded in the link. This illustrates an important point of this exercise. You need to look not only at what is displayed in the mockups, but also at data points that are needed for behind-the-scenes work. The next pseudo-SQL statement also illustrates this point:

```
SELECT the URL for the promotion image,
       the product id that the promotion should link to,
       the slot for the promotion
FOR each of the promotions that should be displayed
```

There is one database-related area left on the home page: the search field. It is actually a simple static form, but it will need to be linked to an XSQL page that can handle the form. For talking purposes, let's name the form handler `textSearch.xsql`. The `textSearch.xsql` page will need to have its own SQL statement based on the following:

```
SELECT the product id,
       the product name,
       the product summary,
FOR all of the products that meet the search criteria
IN ORDER OF the most relevant searches first
```

When the Search button is pressed, the search results page will be displayed. The dynamic data area for that page is furnished with the preceding SQL statement. When users click on a product, they need to be taken to the product page. The product ID can be embedded in the link to handle this. The link will be to `product_details.xsql`, and this XSQL page should contain a query like this:

```
SELECT the product name,
       the product summary,
       the product price,
       the complete product description,
FOR one particular product
```

This covers our search functionality, and this same query can be used when users click on a promotion and when they select a product from the product category page. Now, let's back up and cover the browsing functionality. Our product category names will be linked to the product category pages. As with the search results, we can assume that the type_id for a product category will be embedded in the links that will be generated for the home page. They'll be handled by an XSQL page that you will call product_type.xsql. It needs a SQL statement to select the products. It should look something like this:

```
SELECT the product id,
       the product name,
       the product summary,
FOR all of the products in a particular category
IN alphabetic ORDER OF the product name
```

The queries that have been developed thus far cover nearly all of the primary functionality of the application. Now we have to flesh out the navigational aspects. The first step is the listing of product categories that appear on the left side of the subordinate pages. This one is similar to our earlier query for the home page, except we need less information:

```
SELECT product category name,
       product category id
FOR all of the product categories
IN alphabetic ORDER OF the product category name
```

We also have a horizontal navigational element across the top of the page. It contains a text search field along with a link to the home page and the product category. The home page link is always the same. The category link is a bit trickier. We could write a query that pulls the primary category for the displayed product. Remember, though, that one of our requirements is to be able to assign multiple categories to a product. The product category that is returned by the query may not be the category that the user used to navigate to this page. Thus, we shouldn't formulate a query for this information. Rather, we need to pass the category ID as a parameter.

Our analysis for the public part of the application is now complete. The price editor part of the application is covered separately later in the chapter.

Database Design

In the previous section, we identified all of the areas in our application that should interact with the database. We have a good idea of the kind of database that is needed. Now the trick is to put the database together. Before plunging in, the requirements should be revisited. The customer will be providing XML for the product descriptions, and we've determined that it makes the most sense to store the XML documents in the database. We also know that there is a many-to-many relationship between the product categories and the products. A single product can belong to multiple product categories, and of course, a single product category can have multiple products.

With these requirements in mind, we can consider the key question in database design: Should the database be normalized or denormalized? Per our earlier discussion, you know that denormalization is best reserved for data warehousing-type applications. If this were an extremely large product catalog, then a denormalized database may be necessary. However, once you go the route of optimizing for performance, you risk making a database that is hard to extend for other applications that might come along. Because our product catalog isn't going to contain hundreds of thousands of items, the normalization approach is best. Besides, it's far easier to make a denormalized database based on a normalized one than to try to go the other way.

Now it's time to look back at the pseudo-SQL developed earlier and determine the necessary fields. Each field should be grouped with an entity.

PRODUCT

Product identifier

Product price

Product name

Product summary

Primary product category

Complete product description

PRODUCT CATEGORY

Product category identifier

Product category name

Product category description

PROMOTION

Promotion slot

Product ID for the promotion

URL of the promotional image

Promotion status

The next step is to make sure that our entities are in the third normal form, described earlier in this chapter. You can determine this by stepping through first, second, and third normal forms. The first normal form says that there shouldn't be multiple columns for the same field. This doesn't look to be a problem for any of our entities. If the product category had columns for each product in the category, we would be in violation of the first normal form. Usually, developers are instinctively in compliance with first normal form. However, if you find yourself putting a comma-delimited list in a column, then you are in violation of the first normal form. You should take whatever data that you are listing and make a table for it.

Next, we need to see if we are in compliance with the second normal form. The rule for the second normal form states that you need to have a primary key, and the nonkey fields need to be dependent on it. The product and the product category entities meet this test—you can use the product identifier and product category identifier as the primary keys. However, the promotion entity isn't as straightforward. You could use either promotion slot or product id as a primary key, but this is a bit limiting. What if you want to tie multiple promotions to a single product? What if you want to tie multiple promotions to a particular slot and rotate them? It is best to modify the promotion entity so that it has a promotion ID that is independent of the other entities:

PROMOTION

Promotion ID

Promotion slot

Product ID for the promotion

URL of the promotional image

Promotion status

Last, you need to check to make sure that all of the entities are in third normal form. The question is: Are there any nonkey columns dependent on other nonkey columns? There are not. If we had combined the product and the product category tables, then there would be a problem. The product category name and description would be dependent on each other. The purpose of third normal form is to make sure that tables shouldn't be split up.

Now that the database is normalized, it's time to set up the relationships between the different entities. There are three relationships: (1) promotion to product, (2) product to primary product category, and (3) multiple product categories to product. The promotion-to-product relationship is easiest. Per the requirements, it is a one-to-one relationship, but there is no harm in making it a many-to-one relationship. This yields the ERD for these two entities, as shown in Figure 14.7.

In terms of our fields, the product ID for the promotion field in the promotion entity can be tied to the product identifier field in the product entity. When you implement the database, you can create a foreign key constraint between these two columns.

The primary product category to product relationship looks basically the same. Every product needs to have a product category to which it belongs. The diagram for this relationship is shown in Figure 14.8.

Figure 14.7 ERD for promotion and product.

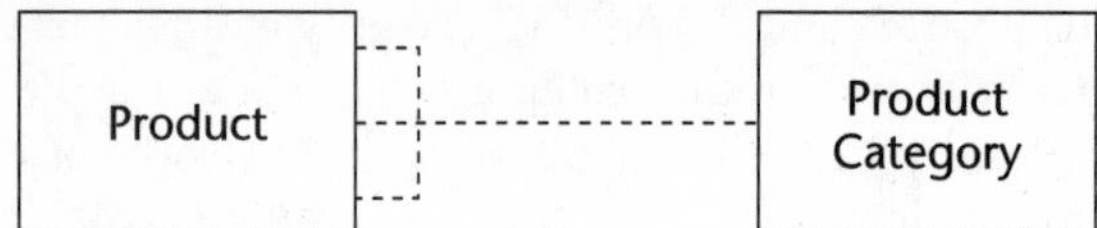

Figure 14.8 ERD for primary product category and product.

Our last relationship is more complex. For browsing purposes, the customer wants some products to appear in multiple product categories. This will make some products easier to find. At the database level, though, it means that we need to define a many-to-many relationship between the product table and the product category table. Drawing the ERD is easy—it is shown in Figure 14.9. However, actually implementing the relationship isn't as simple.

The problem is that you need a list of the different product categories to which a product should belong. However, as you know from the normalization discussion, you can't store the list in the product entity. To do so violates the first normal form, and the list would be hard to maintain. Likewise, you can't store a list of all of the products for a product category in the product category entity. The best solution is to create a join entity that resolves the many-to-many relationship:

PRODUCT CATEGORY JOINER

Product ID

Product category ID

You may look at this entity and say, "But wait! There is no primary key." This is a good case for a composite primary key. When implemented, the composite primary key constraint will disallow a row that is exactly like an existing row, making a separate primary key redundant. A foreign key constraint will exist between the product ID in the joiner table and the product ID in the product table, as well as between the product category identifiers in the joiner table and the product category table. With the fourth entity in place, our complete ERD appears in Figure 14.10. The field names have been changed to valid database names, and the primary keys have been noted.

If you have a tool such as Oracle Designer, you can plug in the ERD and it will generate a script for you that will create all of the tables. In the next section, we'll translate the ERD by hand to come up with our database.

Figure 14.9 ERD for many-to-many product category to products.

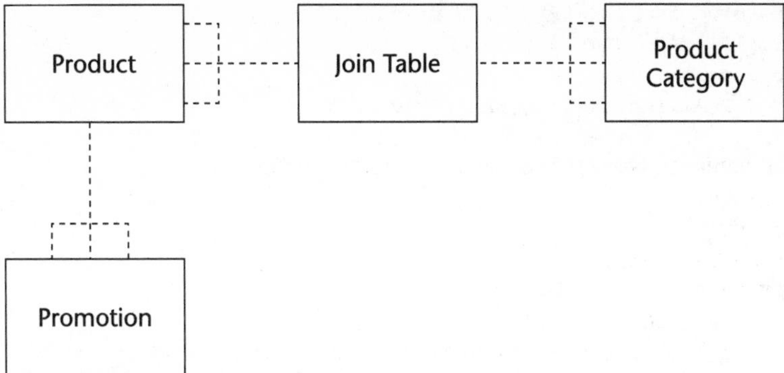

Figure 14.10 The complete ERD.

Database Implementation

Now you get to write your first real code. In this section the design starts to become reality. You'll create the four tables along with their constraints. You'll also create three sequences for use by the tables. Any time you create a database, it is a good idea to put all the commands into a script. If you ever have to recreate the database, then you can just rerun the script.

The first step is choosing the order in which the tables should be created. When creating a database, it's best to first create the tables that don't define foreign key constraints. Then when you create the tables that do define foreign key constraints, the tables they reference already exist. This keeps you from having to define foreign key constraints separately. By examining the ERD, the order of table creation should be:

1. product_category
2. product
3. promotion
4. product_category_joiner

The creation of these tables is as follows:

```
CREATE TABLE product_category
  (id NUMBER CONSTRAINT product_category_primary_key PRIMARY KEY,
  name VARCHAR2(100),
  description VARCHAR2(1000));
CREATE TABLE product(
  id  NUMBER CONSTRAINT product_pk PRIMARY KEY,
  name VARCHAR2(100),
  price NUMBER,
  category_id NUMBER
```

```
      CONSTRAINT prod_cat_fk REFERENCES product_category(id),
   doc SYS.XMLTYPE);
CREATE TABLE promotion
   (id NUMBER CONSTRAINT promotion_pk PRIMARY KEY,
    slot NUMBER,
    product_id NUMBER CONSTRAINT product_fk REFERENCES product(id),
    url VARCHAR2(200),
    status varchar2(10));
CREATE TABLE prod_cat_joiner
   (product_id NUMBER,
    product_cat_id NUMBER,
    CONSTRAINT prod_cat_joiner_pk PRIMARY KEY (product_id,product_cat_id)
    );
```

The tables are created. Now you need to create sequences for the `product_category`, `product`, and `promotion` tables. These sequences will be used to generate the next primary key for these tables:

```
CREATE SEQUENCE product_seq;
CREATE SEQUENCE prod_cat_seq;
CREATE SEQUENCE promotion_seq;
```

The final step is to create an index for the doc column of the `product` table. This step is best performed after data is loaded into the table. It's also important to remember to reindex the table after new data is added. The command for creating the index is:

```
CREATE INDEX product_doc_index ON product(doc)
     INDEXTYPE IS ctxsys.context;
```

Now your database is complete. There's no need to waste the space here loading the database. You can download the scripts for that from the Web site described in the introduction.

Writing the SQL

The next step is to create the SQL statements that you'll need. You can start this with the home page by looking back at the pseudo-SQL. The two pseudo-SQL statements were:

```
SELECT the product category name,
       the product category description,
       the product category identifier
FOR all of the product categories
IN alphabetic ORDER OF the product category name
SELECT the URL for the promotion image,
       the product id that the promotion should link to
FOR each of the promotions that should be displayed
```

```
IN ORDER OF the slot they should occupy
In real SQL, they become:
SELECT id,name,description
   FROM product_category
   ORDER BY name
SELECT url,product_id
   FROM promotion
   WHERE status='ACTIVE'
   ORDER BY slot
```

The next SQL statement to write is for the text search capability. You'll use the Oracle text that you learned about in Chapter 8 for this. Our pseudo-SQL was:

```
SELECT the product id,
       the product name,
       the product summary,
FOR all of the products that meet the search criteria
IN ORDER OF the most relevant searches first
Our actual SQL is:
SELECT id, name, a.doc.extract('/doc/summary').getStringVal() AS summary
  FROM product a
  WHERE contains(doc,'{@terms}')>0
  ORDER BY contains(doc,'{@terms}')
```

This leads to the product details page. For this page we wanted:

```
SELECT the product name,
       the product summary,
       the product price,
       the complete product description,
FOR one particular product
```

This one is a little more complex. We want to return all of the XML doc for a particular product. As you learned in Chapter 11, "Retrieving XML," you can't just push the XML back as a string because the markup would be escaped. You need to use the `htp` and `htf` packages in conjunction with `xsql:include-owa` element get the XML into the XSQL output. There are two ways to do this. If you are certain that the document contains less than 4,000 characters, you can do it with the following procedure:

```
CREATE OR REPLACE PROCEDURE get_product_xml(product_id NUMBER) IS
 output_var VARCHAR2(4000);
BEGIN
  SELECT a.doc.getStringVal() INTO output_var
    FROM product a
    WHERE a.id=product_id;
  htp.prn(output_var);
END;
```

If there is any chance that you are going to have more than 4,000 characters in your document, then you need to use CLOB as the data type for output_var. However, htp.prn won't take a CLOB as a parameter. You can still get the data to the output using the following technique:

```
CREATE OR REPLACE PROCEDURE get_product_xml(product_id NUMBER) IS
 ctx dbms_xmlgen.ctxhandle;
 output_var CLOB;
 output_str VARCHAR2(4000);
 offset_var INTEGER:=1;
 buf_size INTEGER:=4000;
BEGIN
  SELECT a.doc.getStringVal() INTO output_var
    FROM product a
    WHERE a.id=product_id;
  WHILE offset_var < dbms_lob.getLength(output_var) LOOP
      DBMS_LOB.READ(output_var,buf_size,offset_var,output_str);
      htp.prn(output_str);
      offset_var:=offset_var+buf_size;
  END LOOP;
END;
```

The second procedure is certainly safer. Even if you can require that an XML document that you are using contains under 4,000 characters, you still need to make sure that larger documents don't make it into the database. If they do, then you risk generating errors at runtime.

Back to the product details query. In the pseudo-SQL, we had only one query. When implementing the query, it should be broken into two: (1) a procedure call using the xsql:include-owa action and (2) a SELECT statement for the other data. The SELECT statement looks like the following:

```
SELECT id,name,price
   FROM product
   WHERE id={product_id}
```

The text search query was a bit challenging because of the need for a procedure. The next query is also interesting because we must handle the many-to-many relationship between product categories and products. Our pseudo-SQL looked like this:

```
SELECT the product id,
       the product name,
       the product summary,
FOR all of the products in a particular category
IN alphabetic ORDER OF the product name
```

The actual SQL must involve the joiner table because a particular product may belong to more than one category for the purposes of browsing. Here is how to write the SQL:

```
SELECT p.id AS product_id,
       p.name AS product_name,
       p.doc.extract('/doc/summary/text()').getStringVal() AS summary
  FROM product p,prod_cat_joiner pcj
  WHERE pcj.product_cat_id={@category_id} AND p.id=pcj.product_id
```

If a user was limited to finding a product in only one product category, the `SELECT` statement would just look up that ID in the product table. If the query needs to join the `product_category` and the `product` tables, you would join on the category ID of those two tables. You'll see an example of this when you implement the price editor.

```
SELECT p.name,
       pc.name
  FROM product p, prod_cat_joiner pcj, product_category pc
  WHERE p.id=pcj.product_id
        AND
        pcj.product_cat_id=pc.id
        AND
        pc.id={@category_id};
```

The next SQL needed is for the navigational item on the left side of the subordinate pages. The pseudo-SQL looked like this:

```
SELECT product category name,
       product category id
FOR all of the product categories
IN alphabetic ORDER OF the product category name
```

The actual SQL is nearly the same:

```
SELECT id,name,description
   FROM product_category
   ORDER BY name
```

As mentioned before, the name of the product category that appears at the top of the details page is tricky. Because you can get to a product from multiple product categories, you can't simply look up the correct product category based on the product ID. Instead, you have to pass the product category ID as a parameter to the product details page. From the product details XSQL, you can access the product category name with the simple `SELECT` statement:

```
SELECT name
  FROM product_category WHERE id={@category_Id}
```

The remaining SQL statements are used with the edit functionality. The first step is to locate the products in which the editor is interested, as described by the pseudo-SQL:

```
SELECT the product id,
       the product price,
       the product name
FOR all products matching a search criteria
IN alphabetic ORDER OF the product name
```

In the case of editing, you don't want the search query to generate too many false positives, so you can use a SQL statement that just searches against the name:

```
SELECT p.name AS product_name,
          pc.name AS product_cat_name,
          p.price
     FROM product p, prod_cat_joiner pcj, product_category pc
     WHERE p.id=pcj.product_id
        AND
        pcj.product_cat_id=pc.id
        AND
        p.name like '%{@terms}%'
```

After someone selects a product, then they will need to get the product information based on the product ID. They can do this with this SQL:

```
SELECT id, name, price
    FROM product
    WHERE id={@product_id}
```

This leaves one final SQL statement: the update statement required for our price editor. The pseudo-SQL looked like this:

```
UPDATE the product price
FOR one particular product
```

The SQL for this is as follows:

```
UPDATE product
  SET price={@new_price}
  WHERE id={@product_id}
```

Now you have all of your SQL statements necessary for the application. If your application were a sandwich, you would have both pieces of bread. You know from the mockups what the application should look like, and now you have the database along with all of the SQL. The last step is the meat of the application: You create the XSQL pages along with the XSLT.

Integrating XSQL with XSLT

Now you'll bridge the gap between the database that you developed and the mockup HTML for the sample application. The deep technical details of XSQL and XSLT have already been covered in previous chapters. The discussion here focuses on how to bring the two together in a real-world application.

The emphasis here is on making both your XSQL and your XSLT as modular as possible. This makes it easier to maintain and reuse. To accomplish this, the `xsql:include-xsql` action, and `xsl:import` and `xsl:include` elements are used. There is sometimes a trade-off between modularity and performance. The caches that the XSQL processor uses make the performance impact minimal. Also, we will not be applying stylesheets to the XSQL that is included before its insertion into the called XSQL page. Thus, we will still be doing only one XSLT transformation per request.

In the first section, the development of our sample application is continued with the creation of the XSQL pages. Then, the mockup is reexamined and those pages are developed as XSLT pages. The final section reviews the general lessons of making the site come together.

We do not attack stateless paging in this section, which is a requirement for the text search and product category list pages. These are addressed in a later section. Likewise, the error handling pages are addressed later in this chapter.

Making the XSQL Pages

All of the XSQL actions and attributes that you'll be using in this section are covered in Chapter 7, "Database Modifications with XSQL." What you'll see here is how to leverage what you have already learned for a real application. You'll see how to use the `xsql:include-xsql` action to pull pages together. We'll also start using bind variables in the SQL so that our database interactions are more efficient. Because our XSQL is getting more complex, it's also important to mind the XML that is being produced. Instead of relying on the default XSQL datagrams, you'll tune the element names used to write the XSQL so that the end results will be easier for your stylesheets to manage.

When we developed the SQL, we started with the home page and worked down. We'll use a different approach to develop the XSQL. We'll start with the XSQL pages that can be reused and build those first. Then we'll pull those pages into our other pages using the `xsql:include-xsql` action. The first step is to create the product category navigational page. A first cut of it looks like this:

```
<?xml version="1.0"?>
<xsql:query connection="momnpup" xmlns:xsql="urn:oracle-xsql">
       SELECT id,name FROM product_category
</xsql:query>
```

This looks just like all of the other XSQL that you've seen as you've learned the basics of XSQL. But now, you are developing not just a single XSQL page but a series of XSQL pages. XSLT tends to work best on well-thought-out and well-organized XML input documents. Because you are including this page within other XSQL documents, you will have multiple rowset and rowelements relating to completely different data. Using the rowset-element and the row-element parameters, you can better organize your data:

```
<?xml version="1.0"?>
<xsql:query
    connection="momnpup"
    xmlns:xsql="urn:oracle-xsql"
    rowset-element="PRODUCT_CATEGORIES"
    row-element="CATEGORY">
       SELECT * FROM product_category
</xsql:query>
```

The next page to complete is the promotion page. It is only used once in our site, but it has the aspect of its own element. Using the same technique as before, you can create it so that it can fit anywhere in the site.

```
<?xml version="1.0"?>
<xsql:query
    connection="momnpup"
    xmlns:xsql="urn:oracle-xsql"
    rowset-element="PROMOS"
    row-element="PROMO">
  SELECT url,product_id
   FROM promotion
   WHERE status='ACTIVE'
   ORDER BY slot
</xsql:query>
```

Now you can start with the development of the home page. The home page has the two queries: (1) product categories with their descriptions and (2) the promo page. You'll include the preceding promo page, so this leaves only one query that will be in the page.

```
<?xml version="1.0"?>
<home connection="momnpup"
    xmlns:xsql="urn:oracle-xsql">
  <xsql:query rowset-element="PRODUCT_CATEGORIES"
    row-element="CATEGORY">
   SELECT id,name,description FROM product_category
  </xsql:query>
  <xsql:include-xsql href="promo.xsql"/>
</home>
```

The next page is the product list page. Using the SQL developed earlier, it appears as follows:

```
<?xml version="1.0"?>
<cat-list connection="momnpup"
    xmlns:xsql="urn:oracle-xsql">
 <xsql:include-xsql href="cat-nav.xsql"/>
 <xsql:query rowset-element="PRODUCTS"
    row-element="PRODUCT">
   SELECT p.id AS product_id,
       p.name AS product_name,
       p.doc.extract('/product/summary/text()').getStringVal() AS
summary
  FROM product p,prod_cat_joiner pcj
  WHERE pcj.product_cat_id={@category_id} AND p.id=pcj.product_id
 </xsql:query>
</cat-list>
```

We can improve on this a bit. When developing the SQL, we used the standard parameter interpolation syntax. However, as discussed in Chapter 8, it is more efficient to use bind parameters. Here is the revised SQL using bind parameters. It also sets a default parameter for `category_id` in case the page is called without the `category_id` parameter.

```
<?xml version="1.0"?>
<cat-list connection="momnpup"
    xmlns:xsql="urn:oracle-xsql">
 <xsql:include-xsql href="cat-nav.xsql"/>
 <xsql:query rowset-element="PRODUCTS"
    row-element="PRODUCT"
     category_id="0"
    bind-params="category_id">
   SELECT p.id AS product_id,
       p.name AS product_name,
       p.doc.extract('/product/summary/text()').getStringVal() AS
summary
  FROM product p,prod_cat_joiner pcj
  WHERE pcj.product_cat_id=? AND p.id=pcj.product_id
 </xsql:query>
</cat-list>
```

Now you're down to the product details page. The following XSQL page gets the information about a particular product using two different actions. A query gets the id, name, and price while the xsql:include-owa action is used to return the XML document using the get_product_xml procedure used earlier.

```
<?xml version="1.0"?>
<prod-details connection="momnpup"
    xmlns:xsql="urn:oracle-xsql">
 <xsql:include-xsql href="cat-nav.xsql"/>
 <xsql:query rowset-element="PRODUCT-SET"
    row-element="DETAILS"
    product_id="0"
    bind-params="product_id">
   SELECT id,name,price FROM product WHERE id=?
 </xsql:query>
 <xsql:include-owa product_id="0" bind-params="product_id" >
    get_product_xml(?);
 </xsql:include-owa>
</prod-details>
```

The last page for the public interface is the search results page. It uses the query developed earlier and, like our other subordinate pages, includes the navigational element on the left.

```
<?xml version="1.0"?>
<prod-search connection="momnpup"
    xmlns:xsql="urn:oracle-xsql">
 <xsql:include-xsql href="cat-nav.xsql"/>
 <xsql:query rowset-element="PRODUCT_SEARCH"
    row-element="PRODUCT">
       SELECT id, name,
a.doc.extract('/product/summary/text()').getStringVal() AS summary
  FROM product a
  WHERE contains(doc,'{@search_terms}')>0
  ORDER BY contains(doc,'{@search_terms}')
 </xsql:query>
</prod-search>
```

You have three XSQL pages for the price editor interface. The first displays the necessary information in response to a lookup:

```
<?xml version="1.0"?>
<prod-search connection="momnpup"
    xmlns:xsql="urn:oracle-xsql">
 <xsql:query rowset-element="PRICE_EDITOR_SEARCH"
    row-element="PRICE_EDITOR_PRODUCT">
   SELECT p.name AS product_name,
          pc.name AS product_cat_name,
          p.price
     FROM product p, prod_cat_joiner pcj, product_category pc
     WHERE p.id=pcj.product_id
        AND
        pcj.product_cat_id=pc.id
```

```
        AND
        p.name like '%{@terms}%'
 </xsql:query>
</prod-search>
```

Your second XSQL page is very similar to the product details page. The information for this page will be used to fill the values for the fields of a particular editor.

```
<xsql:query connection="momnpup"
    xmlns:xsql="urn:oracle-xsql"
    rowset-element="PRODUCT-SET"
    row-element="DETAILS"
    product_id="0"
    bind-params="product_id">
   SELECT id,name,price FROM product WHERE id=?
 </xsql:query>
```

The last page to create is the page that handles the price change:

```
<price-editor xmlns:xsql="urn:oracle-xsql" connection="momnpup">
 <update>
  <xsql:dml commit="yes"
    product_id="0"
    bind-params="new_price product_id">
  UPDATE product
   SET price=?
   WHERE id=?
  </xsql:dml>
 </update>
 <xsql:dml>COMMIT</xsql:dml>
  <xsql:include-xsql href="edit-prod-details.xsql"/>
</price-editor>
```

Now you have all of your XSQL pages created. You can test them using URLs to make sure that you are getting the results you want back. In the next section, the stylesheets are created to transform the raw data into something useful for your users.

Writing the Stylesheets

Earlier in this chapter, you developed the mock Web site. In the previous section, you got the XSQL setup to pull the data from the database. Now you pull the two together using XSLT stylesheets. The elements you'll use were all covered earlier in this chapter. What you'll see here is how to fit the pieces together in a real application. As with the preceding XSQL pages, you'll see how to reuse and nest stylesheets. You'll also see techniques that are specific to XSQL.

You'll start at the top of the site and develop the home page. Then you'll handle the two product listing pages—the search results page and the product-by-category page. This section also includes the development of the product category navigational menu. The last page of the public interface is the product details page, and then the two stylesheets for the price editor will be developed. Two points of functionality are covered in later sections of this chapter: (1) the stateless paging of product result sets and (2) parameter passing. In reality, you'll probably want to solve those problems at the same time as the stylesheet problems that you'll be solving here. However, from a discussion standpoint, it is far easier to cover those topics in their own sections.

NOTE Before going any further, there is one fact of XSQL of which you should be aware. Regardless of how you set the `rowset` and `row element` names in your XSQL, they will be uppercase in your output. In the preceding examples they were always set uppercase, so you won't notice the difference. Because XML is case sensitive, though, it's important to be aware of this before you start writing stylesheet code. If you specify lowercase `rowset` and `row element` names in your XSQL and then write your stylesheets expecting those, your stylesheets won't work. The solution is simple—just uppercase the element names in your stylesheet expressions.

First on the hit list is the home page. As with all of the XSQL pages, your first step is to link to the stylesheet in your XSQL. For **`home.xsql`**, you should add the following as the second line:

```
<?xml-stylesheet type="text/xsl" href="home2.xsl"?>
```

Now it's time to create the stylesheet itself. The following code is the top of the document and the main template that is invoked for the top-level element, `"home"`. There are other templates to add, so you don't have a closing stylesheet tag yet.

```
<?xml version = '1.0'?>
<xsl:stylesheet xmlns:xsl="http://www.w3.org/1999/XSL/Transform"
version="1.0">
<xsl:include href="banner.xsl"/>
<xsl:template match="/home">
 <html>
  <head>
    <link rel="stylesheet" type="text/css" name="catalogue"
href="catalogue.css">
    </link>
  </head>
  <body>
    <table width="800" border="0">
     <tr><td colspan="2" height="100">
      <!-- banner table -->
      <xsl:call-template name="banner"/>
     </td></tr>
     <tr>
      <td width="600">
       <!--product category table -->
       <xsl:apply-templates select="PRODUCT_CATEGORIES"/>
      </td>
      <td valign="top" width="200">
```

```
        <!--promotion table-->
        <xsl:apply-templates select="PROMOS"/>
       </td>
      </tr>
     </table>
   </body>
  </html>
 </xsl:template>
```

As promised, there are no problems integrating CSS with XSLT. We'll use references to CSS styles throughout the code examples. Working down through the example, the next thing to notice is the `xsl:include` of `banner.xsl`. The `banner.xsl` stylesheet contains a single template-named banner. It is called with an `xsl:call-template` element. Notice that no parameters are passed to it. Here we are using XSLT for a simple purpose—HTML reuse. By separating the banner into its own file, it can be called from all of our files. If we want to change it, we can change it once, and it will be changed throughout the site. The fact that it doesn't actually interpolate any of the inputted XML data doesn't actually matter. Here is the `banner.xsl` stylesheet:

```
<?xml version = '1.0'?>
<xsl:stylesheet xmlns:xsl="http://www.w3.org/1999/XSL/Transform"
version="1.0">
 <xsl:template name="banner">
  <table width="100%" height="100" class="banner-style" border="0">
   <tr>
    <td colspan="2">
      <span class="banner-title">
       Mom N' Pup
      </span>
    </td>
   </tr>
   <tr>
    <td align="left" valign="top">
      <i>
       <span class="banner-subtitle">
        Catalogue
       </span>
      </i>
    </td>
    <td align="right" valign="top">
    <form action="prod-search.xsql" method="post">
     <span class="banner-subtitle">
      Search: <input name="search_terms" size="30"></input>
      <input type="submit" value="go!"></input>
     </span>
    </form>
    </td>
   </tr>
  </table>
 </xsl:template>
</xsl:stylesheet>
```

The banner code itself isn't particularly interesting. There aren't even any XSLT elements besides `xsl:stylesheet` and `xsl:template`. It could, of course, contain any XSLT elements. However, because `xsl:call-template` is used to invoke the template, you don't know what the context node will be, and thus your XPath expressions should be absolute. As discussed in Chapter 13, you can pass parameters to a template that is invoked with `xsl:call-template` and have functionality similar to a subroutine.

The one thing to note in the `banner.xsl` is the search field. It links to the `prod-search.xsql` page using a post query. You'll develop that stylesheet in another couple of pages. For now, it's time to round out the `home.xsl` stylesheet that we started earlier. Looking at the top-level template for `home.xsql`, you can see that two other templates are invoked with `apply-templates`. These templates in turn invoke their own templates. Let's start with the `"PROMOS"` template and its associated template:

```
<xsl:template match="PROMOS">
 <table border="0">
  <xsl:apply-templates select="PROMO"/>
 </table>
</xsl:template>
<xsl:template match="PROMO">
 <tr>
  <td width="200" height="100">
   <a>
    <xsl:attribute name="href">prod-details.xsql?product_id=<xsl:value-
of select="PRODUCT_ID"/></xsl:attribute>
    <img width="200" height="100">
     <xsl:attribute name="src">
      <xsl:value-of select="URL"/>
     </xsl:attribute>
    </img>
   </a>
  </td>
 </tr>
</xsl:template>
```

Looking back at `promo.xsql`, you'll see that it pulls two pieces of data on the promo: (1) the product ID and (2) the URL for the promo image. The image is assumed to be 200 x 100. A link is set around the image so that when you click on the image you are taken to the product details page.

This template has the first of many uses of the `xsl:attribute` element to set the value of an HTML attribute. You can't use an XSLT element inside of an XML element, like `<a>`, so you have to set the attribute separately. You may notice that the `xsl:attribute` code isn't nicely tabbed like the rest of the example. This is purposeful; If you put the `xsl:value-of` element on its own line, then there will be white space inside of your attribute value. You should always keep all of an `xsl:attribute` element on one line.

The `"PRODUCT CATEGORIES"` template is the most complex in our entire application. There are several challenges. First, the categories are separated into columns with the first categories appearing in the left-hand column and the later categories appearing in the right-hand column. This is more complex than listing the columns in a left-to-right ordering. To solve this, we have two separate tables nested into a higher-level table consisting of only two cells. The `xsl:apply-templates` is called first on all categories that are in the first half of the result set, and then a separate `xsl:apply -templates` is called on all categories in the second half of the result set. If there is an odd number of categories, the right-hand column will have the extra.

```
<xsl:template match="PRODUCT_CATEGORIES">
 <table border="0">
  <tr>
   <td valign="top">
    <!-- left hand table -->
    <table valign="top" width="300" border="0">
     <xsl:apply-templates select="CATEGORY[position() &lt;= (last() div
2) ]"/>
    </table>
   </td>
   <td valign="top">
    <!-- right hand table -->
    <table valign="top" width="300" border="0">
     <xsl:apply-templates select="CATEGORY[position()>(last() div 2) ]">
      <xsl:with-param name="align-val">right</xsl:with-param>
     </xsl:apply-templates>
    </table>
   </td>
  </tr>
 </table>
</xsl:template>
```

Notice that a parameter is passed for the right-hand categories. This is because the mockup requires that the text in the left-hand column be left-adjusted, and the text in the right-hand column be right-adjusted. You could develop two templates—one for each column—but most all of the code would be redundant. Instead, you simply pass a parameter and set the `"align"` attribute based on the parameter. Because the default value of the parameter is “left”, it isn’t necessary to pass a parameter for the preceding left-hand `apply-templates`. Here is the `"CATEGORY"` template that is invoked.

```
<xsl:template match="CATEGORY">
  <xsl:param name="align-val">left</xsl:param>
  <tr>
   <td>
    <xsl:attribute name="align"><xsl:value-of select="$align-
val"/></xsl:attribute>
     <span class="category">
      <a>
       <xsl:attribute name="href">prod-cat.xsql?category_id=<xsl:value-
of select="ID"/></xsl:attribute>
       <!-- product name -->
```

```
        <b><xsl:value-of select="NAME"/>. </b>
        <!-- product description -->
        <xsl:value-of select="DESCRIPTION"/>.
      </a>
      <i><xsl:apply-templates select="PRODUCTS"/></i>
     <a>
       <xsl:attribute name="href">prod-cat.xsql?category_id=<xsl:value-of
select="ID"/></xsl:attribute>
       . . .
      </a>
     </span>
    </td>
  </tr>
</xsl:template>
```

For this template you pull the text values for the name and description elements for the category and link them to the product category page. You also have to list the first products in the category. The template for this follows. It solves two problems. First, only the first three elements are pulled while the rest are ignored. Second, commas are only inserted between elements 1 and 2 and elements 2 and 3. This is a common problem in XSLT and is easily solved with an `xsl:if` element along with the `position` and `last` functions. The individual product names are linked to the product pages.

```
<xsl:template match="PRODUCTS">
 <xsl:for-each select="PRODUCTS_ROW[position() &lt;= 3]">
  <a>
   <xsl:attribute name="href">prod-details.xsql?product_id=<xsl:value-of
select="./ID"/></xsl:attribute>
   <xsl:value-of select="./NAME"/>
   <xsl:if test="position() &lt; last()">, </xsl:if>
  </a>
 </xsl:for-each>
</xsl:template>
</xsl:stylesheet>
```

The last tag is the close of our stylesheet for the `home.xsql`. You'll now have a home page that looks like Figure 14.1 that appeared earlier in this chapter, but now all of the data is database driven. What's really neat is that all of the links and search functionality work. You still get back the ugly XML, but you are getting back actual data from the database. Now, it's time to make the rest of the application pretty.

The search results page and the product category page present essentially the same set of challenges. We might as well start with the product category page. On the left of the page is the category directory. As with the banner template, the template for the category directory will be separated into its own file. The main stylesheet along with the stylesheet header is as follows:

```
<?xml version = '1.0'?>
<xsl:stylesheet xmlns:xsl="http://www.w3.org/1999/XSL/Transform"
version="1.0">
<xsl:include href="banner.xsl"/>
<xsl:include href="cat-nav.xsl"/>
<xsl:template match="/prod-cat">
 <html>
  <head>
    <link rel="stylesheet" type="text/css" name="catalogue"
href="catalogue.css">
    </link>
  </head>
  <body>
    <table width="800" border="0">
     <tr><td colspan="2" height="100">
      <!-- banner table -->
      <xsl:call-template name="banner"/>
     </td></tr>
     <tr>
      <td width="200">
       <!--product category list -->
       <xsl:apply-templates select="product_categories"/>
      </td>
      <td valign="top" width="600">
       <table>
        <tr><td>
        <a href="home.xsql">Home</a>:
         <xsl:value-of select="//CATEGORY_NAME"/>
        </td></tr>
        <tr><td>
       <!--search results-->
       <xsl:apply-templates select="PRODUCTS"/>
       </td></tr>
       </table>
      </td>
     </tr>
    </table>
  </body>
 </html>
</xsl:template>
```

First, notice that the top-level template references a different element than home.xsl. The top-level home.xsql page outputs "home" as the top-level element, whereas the top-level element here is "prod-cat". By having a different root element for each XSQL page, you are able to build distinct templates for the different types of data. If you ever need to intermingle the templates, it will be easier to do so.

As with the home page, the banner template is invoked to create the banner at the top of the page. The product-categories template is in the cat-nav.xsl stylesheet covered later. It handles the directory listing on the left-hand side of the page.

From there, the template precedes simply. The category name is pulled from the XML, and then the template for the set of products is invoked. For the category name we use the // to mean "child-or-descendant". Because this axis appears at the beginning of the expression, it means child or descendent of root. This syntax is a little dangerous because it assumes that there is only one element of that name in the entire XML document. In our case we know for certain that there is only one CATEGORY_NAME, so it's okay. The alternative would be to spell out multiple layers in order to access this one data point. XSQL always expects there to be more than one row, so the XML is always structured that way. However, if there really is only one row, it's just another layer of elements that needs to be navigated. Used with caution, the child-or-descendant axis can make your code a little more readable when you are only pulling one row of data.

The products template and its child template, called "PRODUCT", follow. These are fairly straightforward. For each product in the result set, the product name and summary are listed. The product names are linked to the respective product details pages. As this is the end of the stylesheet, the end tag is also included.

```
<xsl:template match="PRODUCTS">
 <table class="search-results" width="100%">
  <th><span class="search-results">Product</span></th><th>Summary</th>
  <xsl:apply-templates select="PRODUCT"/>
 </table>
</xsl:template>
<xsl:template match="PRODUCT">
 <tr>
  <td>
   <a>
    <xsl:attribute name="href">prod-details.xsql?product_id=<xsl:value-
of select="PRODUCT_ID"/></xsl:attribute>
    <xsl:value-of select="PRODUCT_NAME"/>
   </a>
  </td>
  <td><xsl:value-of select="SUMMARY"/></td>
 </tr>
</xsl:template>
</xsl:stylesheet>
```

Before moving onto the product search page, we need to back up and do the category navigation page. It is a straightforward stylesheet that matches up with the cat-nav.xsql page. The cat-nav.xsql page furnishes the XML as a top-level element, and the cat-nav.xsl page takes that XML and formats into a list of linked category names.

```
<?xml version = '1.0'?>
<xsl:stylesheet xmlns:xsl="http://www.w3.org/1999/XSL/Transform"
version="1.0">
 <xsl:template match="product_categories">
```

```
  <table valign="top" width="100%" height="100%" class="cat-directory"
border="0">
   <tr><td><b>Categories</b></td></tr>
    <xsl:apply-templates select="category"/>
  </table>
 </xsl:template>
 <xsl:template match="category">
  <tr>
   <td>
    <a>
     <xsl:attribute name="href">prod-cat.xsql?category_id=<xsl:value-of
select="ID"/></xsl:attribute>
     <xsl:value-of select="NAME"/>
    </a>
   </td>
  </tr>
  <tr>
   <td height="10%"> </td>
  </tr>
 </xsl:template>
</xsl:stylesheet>
```

On to the search results page! The search results page is very similar to the product category page and its full display follows. The one difference is that the linked category name for a product is included in the results. The primary category for the product is used.

```
<?xml version = '1.0'?>
<xsl:stylesheet xmlns:xsl="http://www.w3.org/1999/XSL/Transform"
version="1.0">
<xsl:include href="banner.xsl"/>
<xsl:include href="cat-nav.xsl"/>
<xsl:template match="/prod-search">
 <html>
  <head>
    <link rel="stylesheet" type="text/css" name="catalogue"
href="catalogue.css">
    </link>
  </head>
  <body>
    <table width="800" border="0">
     <tr><td colspan="2" height="100">
      <!-- banner table -->
      <xsl:call-template name="banner"/>
     </td></tr>
     <tr>
      <td width="200">
       <!--product category list -->
       <xsl:apply-templates select="product_categories"/>
      </td>
      <td valign="top" width="600">
```

```
        <table>
         <tr><td><a href="home.xsql">Catalogue Home Page</a></td></tr>
         <tr><td>Search Results For: </td></tr>
         <tr><td>
        <!--search results-->
        <xsl:apply-templates select="PRODUCT_SEARCH"/>
        </td></tr>
        </table>
       </td>
      </tr>
     </table>
   </body>
  </html>
 </xsl:template>
 <xsl:template match="PRODUCT_SEARCH">
  <table class="search-results"  height="100%" width="100%">
    <th><span class="search-
results">Product</span></th><th>Summary</th><th>Category</th>
    <xsl:apply-templates select="PRODUCT"/>
  </table>
 </xsl:template>
  <xsl:template match="PRODUCT">
   <tr>
    <td>
     <a>
      <xsl:attribute name="href">prod-details.xsql?product_id=<xsl:value-
of select="PRODUCT_ID"/></xsl:attribute>
     <xsl:value-of select="PRODUCT_NAME"/>
     </a>
    </td>
    <td><xsl:value-of select="SUMMARY"/></td>
    <td>
     <a>
     <xsl:attribute name="href">prod-cat.xsql?category_id=<xsl:value-of
select="CATEGORY_ID"/></xsl:attribute>
    <xsl:value-of select="CATEGORY"/>
    </a>
    </td>
   </tr>
  </xsl:template>
</xsl:stylesheet>
```

Now it's time to finish the application by creating the product details stylesheet. It includes the `cat-nav.xsl` and the `banner.xsl` as with the two previous stylesheets. It also has a couple of tricks up its sleeve. The other stylesheets dealt with pretty standard entities—names and short sentences. This page must render images of varying sizes and XML documents of varying content. Though it is a little complex, the `prod-details.xsl` stylesheet handles it all with elegance and shows you how powerful XSLT can be. Here are the headers and the main template:

```
<?xml version = '1.0'?>
<xsl:stylesheet xmlns:xsl="http://www.w3.org/1999/XSL/Transform"
version="1.0">
<xsl:include href="banner.xsl"/>
<xsl:include href="cat-nav.xsl"/>
<xsl:include href="product-xml.xsl"/>
<xsl:template match="/prod-details">
 <html>
  <head>
   <link rel="stylesheet" type="text/css" name="catalogue"
href="catalogue.css">
   </link>
  </head>
  <body>
   <table width="800" border="0">
    <tr><td colspan="2" height="100">
     <!-- banner table -->
     <xsl:call-template name="banner"/>
    </td></tr>
    <tr>
     <td width="200">
      <!--product category list -->
      <xsl:apply-templates select="product_categories"/>
     </td>
     <td valign="top" width="600">
      <table>
       <tr><td>
        <a href="home.xsql">Home</a>:
        <a href="#">
         Category
        </a>
       </td></tr>
       <tr><td>
        <table width="600">
         <!--product details -->
         <xsl:apply-templates select="PRODUCT-SET/DETAILS"/>
        </table>
       </td></tr>
      </table>
     </td>
    </tr>
   </table>
  </body>
 </html>
</xsl:template>
```

This template calls three templates. The first two are the old friends, banner and product categories. The meat of the work is done in the `"PRODUCT-SET/DETAILS"` template. Before examining that template, please note that one of our missing pieces of functionality is on this page. The category from which this product was reached (or the primary category if it was reached through a promo or the search engine) is missing. This will be covered in the next discussion. For now, let's look at the key template for this page. The code follows:

```
<xsl:template match="PRODUCT-SET/DETAILS">
 <tr>
  <td align="left">
   <span class="product-name">
    <xsl:value-of select="NAME"/>
   </span>
  </td>
  <td align="right">
   <span class="product-price">
    $<xsl:value-of select="PRICE"/>
   </span>
  </td>
 </tr>
 <tr><td colspan="2">
  <xsl:choose>
   <xsl:when test="WIDTH>100">
    <xsl:apply-templates select="IMAGE_URL">
     <xsl:with-param name="align-var">top</xsl:with-param>
    </xsl:apply-templates>
   </xsl:when>
   <xsl:otherwise>
    <xsl:apply-templates select="IMAGE_URL"/>
   </xsl:otherwise>
  </xsl:choose>
  <xsl:apply-templates select="//product/*"/>
 </td></tr>
</xsl:template>
```

The first thing to note is the match for this template. All of our other templates matched an element one level down, but this one goes two levels down. The data we want is two levels down, so we just skip a level. Once in the `DETAILS` element, we have a couple of jobs to do. The name and the price need to be displayed at the top level. Underneath that, an image needs to be displayed along with XML elements of the product document.

The image is our first challenge because it can vary in size. If it is less than 300 pixels wide, then the text should be on the left. If it is over 300 pixels wide, then the text should be underneath. An `xsl:choose` element is used to set a parameter to affect the appropriate behavior. After the image is set up, the XML document from our database is processed. Before getting to that, let's look at the `IMAGE_URL` template.

```
<xsl:template match="IMAGE_URL">
  <xsl:param name="align-var">right</xsl:param>
  <xsl:if test="$align-var='top'">
    <xsl:text disable-output-escaping="yes">&lt;center&gt;</xsl:text>
```

```
    </xsl:if>
    <img>
     <xsl:attribute name="align"><xsl:value-of select="$align-
  var"></xsl:value-of></xsl:attribute>
     <xsl:attribute name="height"><xsl:value-of
  select="../HEIGHT"/></xsl:attribute>
     <xsl:attribute name="width"><xsl:value-of
  select="../WIDTH"/></xsl:attribute>
     <xsl:attribute name="src"><xsl:value-of select="."/></xsl:attribute>
    </img>
    <xsl:if test="$align-var='top'">
      <xsl:text disable-output-escaping="yes">&lt;/center&gt;</xsl:text>
    </xsl:if>
   </xsl:template>
```

Most of the code in this template sets up the `img` element. The `align` attribute is set by the `align-var` variable that is passed in, or is set to `"right"` if no variable is passed in. The width, height, and src attributes are also set. In the case where the image should appear at top, it should be centered. The `xsl:if` element is used to determine when the beginning center tag and the closing center tag should be used.

This is a ticklish case because we run into the old problem of inserting XML elements into the document. If we tried to do:

```
<xsl:if test="$align-var='top'">
 <center>
</xsl:if>
```

then our document isn't valid XML, and the stylesheet processor will reject it. We could do:

```
<xsl:choose>
 <xsl:when test="$align-var='top'">
  <center>
  . . . bunch o' code
  </center>
 </xsl:when>
 <xsl:otherwise>
  . . . same bunch o' code
 </xsl:otherwise>
</xsl:choose>
```

but then we have a lot of redundant code. The workaround is to use the `xsl:text` element with disable-output-escaping on. The burden is on us to make sure that the end result is well-formed XML.

The last set of templates is in its own separate file. They don't have to be, but it allows our overall code to be a little neater. These templates match against the XML elements in the XML product document. The idea is that the elements of the XML document can vary from product to product. Clothing has sizes, but soccer goals don't. We could do a lot of logical processing to handle all of the different permutations. Or, we can take an XML push approach. Before explaining further, let's look at the code:

```
<?xml version = '1.0'?>
<xsl:stylesheet xmlns:xsl="http://www.w3.org/1999/XSL/Transform"
version="1.0">
 <xsl:template match="summary">
  <p class="product-summary">
   <b>Summary:</b>
   <br/>
   <xsl:value-of select="."/>
  </p>
 </xsl:template>
 <xsl:template match="description">
  <p class="product-description">
   <b>Description:</b>
   <br/>
   <xsl:value-of select="."/>
  </p>
 </xsl:template>
 <xsl:template match="dimensions">
  <p class="product-dimensions">
   <b>Dimensions:</b>
   <br/>
   <xsl:value-of select="long-val"/> <xsl:value-of select="long-unit"/>
long
   <xsl:value-of select="wide-val"/> <xsl:value-of select="wide-unit"/>
wide
   <xsl:value-of select="tall-val"/> <xsl:value-of select="tall-unit"/>
tall   </p>
 </xsl:template>
 <xsl:template match="clothing-size-list">
   <p class="clothing-size">
    Sizes:
    <xsl:for-each select="size">
      <xsl:value-of select="."/>
      <xsl:if test="position()<last()">,</xsl:if>
    </xsl:for-each>
   </p>
 </xsl:template>
 <xsl:template match="*"></xsl:template>
</xsl:stylesheet>
```

So far, all of our templates have been used. In the case of these product-specific XML documents that are being passed to us, some of the templates won't be used. We can assume that summary and description will be present for all of the items. However, you wouldn't provide dimensions for a sweater, and you wouldn't provide the clothing size for a dresser. Instead, the XML elements in a product's document are matched to the appropriate templates. If a new product comes along whose XML document has a new element, you simply write up a template for it and put it in this document. You set up a style for it to be consistent with the rest of the templates, and you're done. If you have elements that you don't want displayed, they won't be because of the wildcard element at the bottom.

What this approach doesn't allow for is the complete reformatting of a page based on the XML document. Also, the elements will be displayed in document order. If the summary in a particular document appears at the bottom of an XML document in the database, it will appear at the bottom of the page in our application. If you can't depend on the order, you can simply use individual `xml:apply-templates` to force the order. Then you are back to requiring foreknowledge of all the XML documents' structures and you lose the flexibility of our looser approach.

The public application is mostly complete. You can browse to your heart's content. If you stick new data into the database, then it should immediately appear in the application. The following sections in this chapter, "Passing Parameters," "Stateless Paging," and "Error Handling," will fullfill the rest of the requirements for the public application.

Passing Parameters

HTTP was originally designed as a stateless protocol. An HTTP transaction performs a single action, such as getting a file or posting HTML form data, and then it ends. This is both a great strength and a great weakness. Because the transactions end immediately after the data is delivered back to the client, HTTP is very lightweight on the network. Your HTTP-based applications can easily scale to large numbers of users because very few transactions are alive at any given point in time.

When developing applications, though, the stateless nature of HTTP comes at a cost. You have data on one page that needs to be passed to another page. A lot of the challenge of Web development is figuring out the best way to pass information between two completely different transactions. The facilities that XSQL has for this were discussed in detail in Chapter 9. Now you'll see how these can be applied in the real world. In this section, you'll mend up some of the holes of our application, and you'll learn some new lessons. You'll immediately apply those lessons in this chapter—first, when you solve the pagination problems, and then when you develop the price editor part of the sample application.

For now, you'll focus on the techniques of passing parameters. The first technique is the simplest: You simply pass your parameter as part of an already existing SQL query. Then you'll look at the other two important techniques to setting parameters: (1) setting stylesheet parameters and (2) using hidden-form variables. Later in this chapter, you'll also see how to set parameter values directly into JavaScript.

Passing Using SQL

The simplest way to move your parameters along to the next page of your application is to have them hitch a ride. An XSQL page usually has at least one `xsql:query`, and it often involves the very data that you wish to pass along to the next page. We already used this technique on the product category page with the following XSQL on the `prod-cat.xsql`:

```
<xsql:query rowset-elements="CATEGORY_ROWSET"
    row-element="CATEGORY_ROW"
    category_id="0"
    bind-params="category_id">
  SELECT id AS category_id,
         name AS category_name
    FROM product_category WHERE id=?
</xsql:query>
```

If you look back at that page, you'll see that it makes perfect sense to pull the category name. We need it to display at the top of the page. But why pull the ID for the category? It doesn't need to be displayed anywhere. The reason is that it needs to be passed to the `prod-details.xsql` page because the selected category name needs to be displayed on the next page. Because the name will also be linked back to the product home page, the ID needs to be passed. This allows you to change the product template of the `prod_cat.xsl` stylesheet as follows:

```
<xsl:template match="PRODUCT">
  <tr>
   <td>
    <a>
     <xsl:attribute name="href">prod-details.xsql?product_id=<xsl:value-
of select="PRODUCT_ID"/>&amp;category_id=<xsl:value-of
select="//CATEGORY_ID"/>&amp;</xsl:attribute>
    <xsl:value-of select="PRODUCT_NAME"/>
    </a>
   </td>
   <td><xsl:value-of select="SUMMARY"/></td>
  </tr>
 </xsl:template>
```

Now, you're passing the parameter in the simplest way possible: embedded in a hyperlink. On the product details page, the following code changes so that you get the name and link to the category at the top of the page:

```
<tr><td>
 <a href="home.xsql">Home</a>:
 <a>
  <xsl:attribute name="href">prod-cat.xsql?category_id=<xsl:value-of
select="//CATEGORY_ID"/>&amp;</xsl:attribute>
  <xsl:value-of select="//CATEGORY_NAME"/>
 </a>
</td></tr>
```

You certainly don't have to have a SQL statement for your parameters to latch on to. Before worrying with how to pass a parameter on from a page, however, you should take a close look at the where clauses of the SQL statements already on that page. It's the nature of database applications that the parameters you want to pass are already being used in a where clause. In such cases, the simplest solution is to also specify them as a field that is returned.

Setting Stylesheet Parameters

In the preceding example, you may have noticed that there was only one CATEGORY_ID and one CATEGORY_NAME in our example. We used the child-or-descendant axis to access these single values. As discussed earlier, this is somewhat dangerous. Wouldn't it be easier just to reference them as a parameter? That is what stylesheet parameters are all about.

You learned in the last chapter that you can use parameters in conjunction with templates. When you invoke a template, you can pass a parameter to it, as you saw earlier in this chapter. You can also set parameters at the top level and then set them at the time the stylesheet is loaded by the XSLT processor. Let's look at this in the context of another lingering problem that we have with our sample application: The search terms need to appear at the top of the search results page.

A quick review of the search functionality may be needed. The prod-search.xsql page performs the search based on the search_terms parameter passed to it from the search form. The search results are rendered by the prod-search.xsl stylesheet. What you need to do is to pass the search terms to the stylesheet so that the user can see what they just searched on.

If you look back at the SQL in the prod-search.xsql page, you'll see that the search terms could hitch a ride over to the page quite easily. For this example, however, let's use a different approach. Using the xsql:set-stylesheet-param action, you can make the search terms available as an easy-to-use stylesheet parameter. In prod-search.xsql, you add the following line anywhere in the page:

```
<xsql:set-stylesheet-param name="search_terms" value="{@search_terms}"/>
```

On the prod-search.xsl stylesheet, you need to add the following line. The xsl:param should be a direct child of the root stylesheet element:

```
<xsl:param name="search_terms"></xsl:param>
```

Further down in the stylesheet, you add the following code in order to get the search terms:

```
<tr>
 <td>
   Search Results For: <xsl:value-of select="$search_terms"/>
 </td>
</tr>
```

As was covered in previous chapters, you can also set the value of stylesheet parameters based on SQL statements. They still can only hold a single value, though—if your SQL statement returns multiple rows and columns, all but the first row and first column are ignored.

Stylesheet parameters are ideal for when you have just a couple of pieces of information that need to be passed onto the next page. You can easily reference the values by using the $ operator. If they need to be passed onto another page, it is easy to embed them in a link or put them in a form parameter. You'll be making more use of stylesheet parameters when you build the price editor.

Using Other XSQL Parameters

You'll remember from previous chapters that there a couple of other types of parameters: page-private parameters, session parameters, and cookie parameters. These are beyond the parameters that arrive as part of the HTTP request. Page-private parameters are a mechanism that is used inside an XSQL page and isn't of interest to us here. Cookies and session parameters can be of great interest to us.

Cookies and session parameters give you much better persistence. As long as the user allows it, you can store a cookie on their machine for as long as you like. If you have a particular value that needs to be stored for the duration of the user's session, then you can do that by setting a session parameter. You don't have to pass it from one page to another.

Let's look at how you would use a session parameter or a cookie to solve the problem of referencing the category name. In the `prod-cat.xsql` file, you add the following actions:

```
<xsql:set-session-param name="category_name_sess"
  category_id="0"
  bind-params="category_id">
  SELECT name FROM product_category WHERE id=?
 </xsql:set-session-param>
 <xsql:set-cookie name="category_name_cookie"
  category_id="0"
  bind-params="category_id">
  SELECT name FROM product_category WHERE id=?
 </xsql:set-cookie>
```

Unlike in the earlier solution, you don't need to make any modifications to the `prod-cat.xsl` stylesheet. With the previous approach, parameters are passed by embedding them in the HTTP request. In the preceding case, they were passed in the URL. In the case where a `POST` request is used, you can pass them as hidden-form variables. In these cases the parameters sit outside of the request. The cookie lives on the user's browser and is sent back to the server on each request, based on the domain parameter of the `xsql:set-cookie` action. The session parameter actually lives on the server but is tied to a cookie on the user's browser. In either case, all you have to do is ask for them when you need them. You can do this regardless of where you are in the application. This is how you would get those values to pop up on the product details page. First, put the following anywhere in your `prod-details.xsql` page:

```
<xsql:include-param name="category_name_cookie"/>
<xsql:include-param name="category_name_sess"/>
```

The values will be placed in XML elements in the output named `category_name_cookie` and `category_name_sess`, respectively. You can grab them using the following code in your XSLT stylesheet:

```
category_name_cookie: <xsl:value-of select="//category_name_cookie"/>
category_name_sess: <xsl:value-of select="//category_name_sess"/>
```

You may look at this code and think, "That looks simple. Why not do that all the time?" There are a couple of problems with this approach. First, both session and cookie parameters assume that the user will accept cookies from you. A lot of applications assume this—there's no big whoop in requiring this from your users.

The second problem requires more consideration. Sessions and cookies behave like global variables in procedural programming. Global variables are generally frowned upon—it's hard making sure that all of the different modules are setting and unsetting them as expected. In fact, our solution has such a problem. If someone goes to a product category page and then doesn't go on to a product details page, the category name is still set. If they then access the page from a different route (e.g., through a promo or through a search), the category name is still set. Then you have a different kind of problem.

In the previous example, you dealt with cookies and session parameters whose names you know. It is sometimes good to deal with parameters more generally. For instance, you may want to pass all of the parameters to a servlet and let the servlet figure out what to do with them. The following example shows you an easy way to deal with all of the parameters without knowing any of their names at development time. To demonstrate this, you first need an XSQL page that sets some parameters, though it doesn't matter what their names are:

```
<?xml version="1.0"?>
<?xml-stylesheet type="text/xsl" href="params.xsl"?>
<page xmlns:xsql="urn:oracle-xsql" connection="demo">
  <xsql:set-cookie name="long-living-cookie" max-age="999999"
value="To_Life" />
  <xsql:set-cookie name="cookie-deptno">
    select deptno from emp where ename='{@ename}'
  </xsql:set-cookie>
  <xsql:set-session-param name="session-sal">
    select sal from emp where ename='{@ename}'
  </xsql:set-session-param>
  <xsql:include-request-params />
</page>
```

Now you want to be able to access all of these values in a stylesheet. Here's a simple stylesheet that will display all of your values:

```
<?xml version = '1.0'?>
<xsl:stylesheet xmlns:xsl="http://www.w3.org/1999/XSL/Transform"
version="1.0">
<xsl:template match="/page">
 <html>
```

```
    <head></head>
    <body>
     <xsl:apply-templates/>
    </body>
  </html>
</xsl:template>
<xsl:template match="request">
    <b>Request:</b>
    <xsl:apply-templates select="*"/>
  </xsl:template>
<xsl:template match="session">
    <b>Session:</b>
     <xsl:apply-templates select="*"/>
  </xsl:template>
  <xsl:template match="cookies">
  <b>Cookies:</b>
    <xsl:apply-templates select="*"/>
  </xsl:template>
<xsl:template match="*">
    <p>
    Name: <xsl:value-of select="name(.)"/>
    Value: <xsl:value-of select="."/>
    </p>
  </xsl:template>
</xsl:stylesheet>
```

This will give you a listing of all of the parameters, regardless of their names. Example output for this is shown in Figure 14.11.

From here, it is a simple matter to create a set of hidden-form parameters that hold these values. Then you can use easily pass the values on as form submissions, or use them in JavaScript. Here is how you do it:

```
<xsl:template match="*">
   <input type="hidden">
     <xsl:attribute name="name"><xsl:value-of
select="name(.)"/></xsl:attribute>
     <xsl:attribute name="value"><xsl:value-of
select="."/></xsl:attribute>
   </input>
```

You'll see more examples of hidden-form variables and the role they can play in JavaScript and XSLT integration when you work with the price editor later in the chapter.

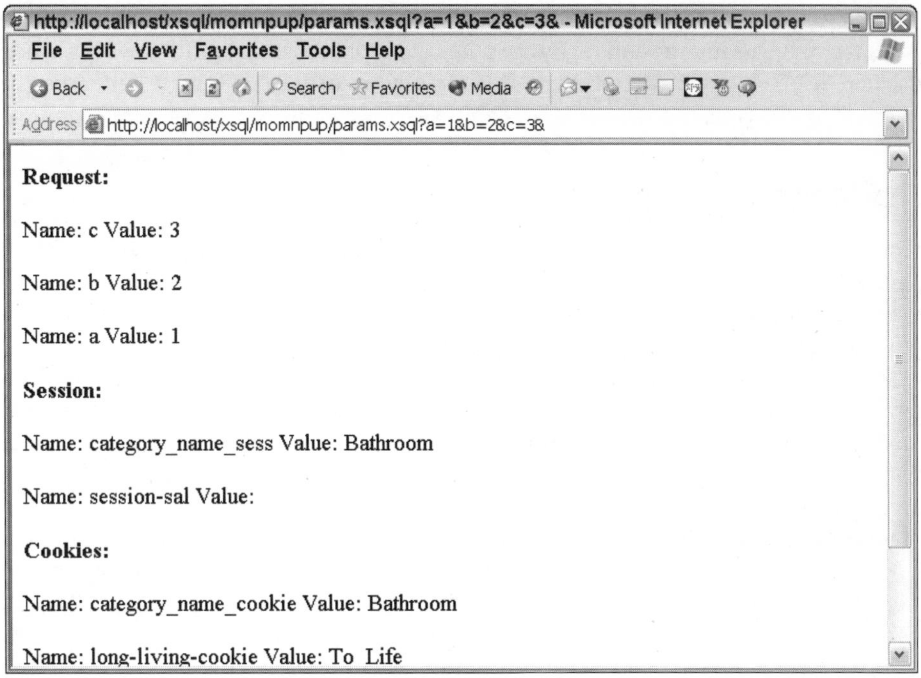
http://localhost/xsql/momnpup/params.xsql?a=1&b=2&c=3& - Microsoft Internet Explorer
File Edit View Favorites Tools Help
Back Search Favorites Media
Address http://localhost/xsql/momnpup/params.xsql?a=1&b=2&c=3&
Request:
Name: c Value: 3
Name: b Value: 2
Name: a Value: 1
Session:
Name: category_name_sess Value: Bathroom
Name: session-sal Value:
Cookies:
Name: category_name_cookie Value: Bathroom
Name: long-living-cookie Value: To Life

Figure 14.11 Output of all parameters.

Stateless Paging

So far, the product catalog doesn't have a lot of data in it. A list of all of the products in the catalog probably still wouldn't necessitate a scroll bar in the browser window. However, what if your queries could easily return thousands of rows? Even if your queries are just returning tens of rows, you want your users to be able to navigate through them in a reasonable manner. This is where paging comes in. Instead of showing all of the results on one page, you see just a set of results, and then you can navigate forward and backward to other sets of results. This section looks at the challenges of pagination from a high level and then shows you how to apply paging to the search screen of the catalog application.

The solution that will be provided here is a pure XSQL/XSLT solution. The example uses a recursive technique and really stretches the capabilities of XSLT. However, when you find yourself stretching too hard, it is often good to ask, "Is there a better way to do this?" In this case, the answer is probably yes.

Challenges of Pagination

Paging offers a simple solution to a common problem. What do you do when you get a lot of results back in your search? You don't want to try to force them all into one browser window. For particularly big searches the browser might run out of memory first. Instead, you want to separate the queries over pages.

The next question is: How do you separate a query into a lot of different pages? You definitely don't want to keep a connection to the database server open. It doesn't scale. You'll be keeping connections open for indefinite periods of time for all of the users that come to the site. Besides, there isn't a way to do it without a custom action handler, anyway. Temporary tables are also a generally bad idea for this kind of thing. You might be able to cobble a solution to the problem, but you'll create big development headaches for yourself. Not to mention, you'll need some multiple of storage space to keep all of the pages of results for the queries. As you get more queries, you'll need more storage space.

Fortunately, the `xsql:query` action offers an easy solution. You use the `max-rows` and `skip-rows` attributes to describe your pages of a query. The `max-rows` attribute sets the size of the page—how many rows you want the query to return. The `skip-rows` attribute specifies where in the query result set you should start—the position of the page.

This does mean, of course, that you will be doing the same query for each page. This may seem expensive and redundant, but it is Oracle's job to optimize queries and make subsequent requests speedy. Besides, you simply can't reasonably keep the database connection open, and even if you tried to hack together a solution with temporary tables, you still would be doing a query for every page.

Pure XSQL Stateless Paging

Now it's time to attack stateless paging. As with most of the problems in this chapter, it is both an XSQL and an XSLT problem. The XSQL code is fairly straightforward. You need to set the `skip-rows` and `max-rows` attributes on the query and get the total number of rows from the database. Then, you need to pass the information on the stylesheet by setting stylesheet parameters. Not hard. The XSLT gets a bit more complex. Because you don't know how many pages you are going to have, you have to calculate that using XSLT. This requires a recursive template. You'll probably either love this technique or hate it. In either case, it is an interesting exercise in how you can solve problems in XSLT that are usually solved in XSLT. First things first, starting with the XSQL. You'll need to change your query to use `skip-rows` and `max-rows` as follows:

```
<xsql:query rowset-element="PRODUCT_SEARCH"
    row-element="PRODUCT"
    max-rows="{@max-rows}"
    skip-rows="{@skip-rows}">
       SELECT p.id AS product_id,
              p.name AS product_name,
              p.doc.extract('/product/summary/text()').getStringVal() AS
summary,
              pc.id AS category_id,
              pc.name AS category
  FROM product p, product_category pc
  WHERE contains(doc,'{@search_terms}')>0
    AND pc.id=p.category_id
  ORDER BY contains(doc,'{@search_terms}')
 </xsql:query>
```

This introduces a new parameter: `skip-rows`. `Skip-rows`, which is where a given page should start, will be passed as part of the request. `Max-rows`, which is the maximum number of records that should be displayed for all of the pages, is really more of a constant. It is made a parameter here so that if you wanted to dynamically change it, you could. Maybe you let your users select how big they want their pages to be. For this example, we set the value of this parameter inside the XSQL page with an `xsql:set-page-param` action:

```
<xsql:set-page-param name="max-rows" value="4"/>
```

The `skip-rows` parameter still needs to be defined. It should be passed in on all requests, including the initial search. This means you need to make a change in the `banner.xsl` page where the search query form is defined. The new form should look like this:

```
<form action="prod-search.xsql" method="post">
 <span class="banner-subtitle">
  Search: <input name="search_terms" size="30"/>
  <input type="hidden" name="skip-rows" value="0"/>
  <input type="submit" value="go!"></input>
 </span>
</form>
```

Now your query will work for the first page. Regardless of the search, you should get at most four results. The next challenge is giving the user a way to navigate to the other results. This is where the real XSLT adventures start. All of these modifications will take place in prod-search.xslt. Your first step is to create top-level parameters so you can receive the values that you set in prod-search.xsql:

```
<xsl:param name="search_terms"></xsl:param>
<xsl:param name="row-count"></xsl:param>
<xsl:param name="skip-rows"></xsl:param>
<xsl:param name="max-rows"></xsl:param>
```

Now you need to create a template that recreates the initial form using all hidden parameters:

```
<xsl:template name="paging-form">
  <xsl:param name="new-skip-rows"></xsl:param>
  <xsl:param name="button-text"></xsl:param>
  <form method="post" action="prod-search.xsql">
   <input type="hidden" name="skip-rows">
    <xsl:attribute name="value"><xsl:value-of select="number($new-skip-
rows)"/></xsl:attribute>
   </input>
   <input type="hidden" name="search_terms">
    <xsl:attribute name="value"><xsl:value-of
select="$search_terms"/></xsl:attribute>
   </input>
   <input type="submit">
    <xsl:attribute name="value"><xsl:value-of select="$button-
text"/></xsl:attribute>
    <xsl:if test="$new-skip-rows=-1">
     <xsl:attribute name="disabled">yes</xsl:attribute>
    </xsl:if>
   </input>
  </form>
 </xsl:template>
```

You call this template with two parameters, new-skip-rows and button-text. The new-skip-rows parameter specifies the position in the query that the user should go to on pressing the form's Submit button. The button-text parameter specifies the text for the button. If the new_skip_rows parameter is set to -1, then the Form button is disabled.

You can get around the need to use a Form button with a little JavaScript, but it's difficult to get around the need to use a form. The query needs to be a POST query because search_terms may have spaces and other funny characters in it. If you tried to pass it as part of a query string, the link would break. In the next section, you'll see a way to encode values using XSLT extensions.

Now that you have your form, you need to link it to some navigational elements. We'll start simply with just Previous and Next buttons. The problem here is determining what the Previous and Next pages are and whether it is valid to enable the buttons.

If you are at the beginning of the result set, then you shouldn't display a Previous button; if you are at the end of a result set, you shouldn't display a Next button. Here is the code that calculates the value of `skip-rows` for Previous and Next and determines whether the buttons should be disabled:

```
<xsl:template name="paging">
  <table><tr><td>
   <xsl:choose>
    <xsl:when test="number($skip-rows)-number($max-rows)&gt;=0">
     <xsl:call-template name="paging-form">
      <xsl:with-param name="new-skip-rows"><xsl:value-of
select="number($skip-rows)-number($max-rows)"/></xsl:with-param>
      <xsl:with-param name="button-text">&lt;&lt;Previous</xsl:with-
param>
     </xsl:call-template>
    </xsl:when>
    <xsl:otherwise>
     <xsl:call-template name="paging-form">
      <xsl:with-param name="new-skip-rows">-1</xsl:with-param>
      <xsl:with-param name="button-text">&lt;&lt;Previous</xsl:with-
param>
     </xsl:call-template>
    </xsl:otherwise>
   </xsl:choose>
  </td>
  <td>
   <xsl:choose>
    <xsl:when test="number($skip-rows)+number($max-rows)&lt;number($row-
count)">
     <xsl:call-template name="paging-form">
      <xsl:with-param name="new-skip-rows"><xsl:value-of select="$skip-
rows+$max-rows"/></xsl:with-param>
      <xsl:with-param name="button-text">   Next&gt;&gt;   </xsl:with-
param>
     </xsl:call-template>
    </xsl:when>
    <xsl:otherwise>
     <xsl:call-template name="paging-form">
      <xsl:with-param name="new-skip-rows">-1</xsl:with-param>
      <xsl:with-param name="button-text">   Next&gt;&gt;   </xsl:with-
param>
     </xsl:call-template>
    </xsl:otherwise>
   </xsl:choose>
  </td></tr></table>
 </xsl:template>
```

As you can see, you basically repeat the same code for the Previous and the Next buttons. The only differences are the test conditions and the value that you pass to the paging-form template. This yields the results that are shown in Figure 14.12.

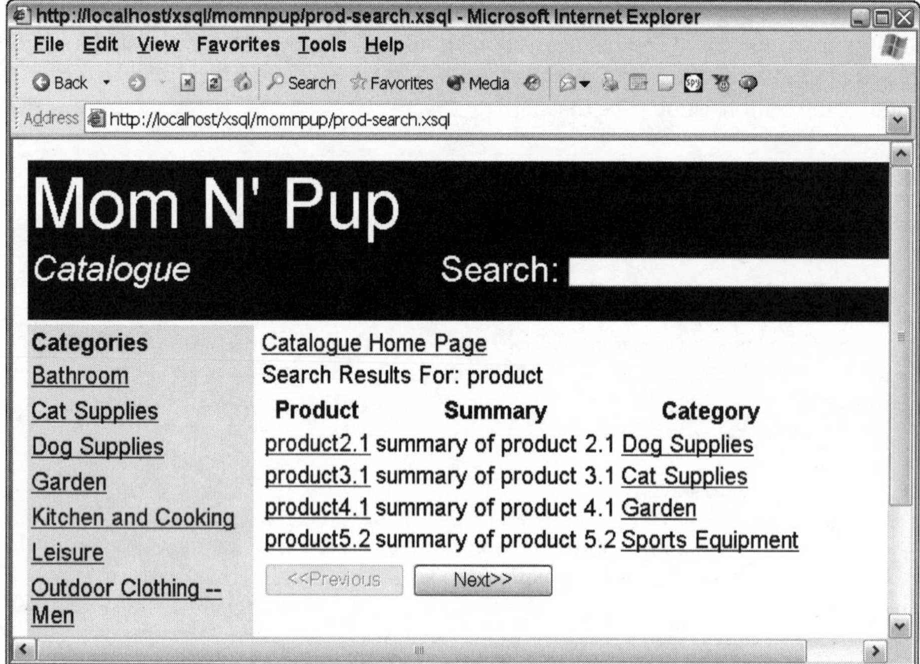

Figure 14.12 Stateless paging with Previous and Next buttons.

Now it's time to spice up the navigation a bit. Instead of just being able to navigate to the Previous or Next page, we want to be able to navigate to any page in our results. The buttons taking us to those results will live between the Previous and Next buttons. The first step is to add the following code right in the middle of the preceding paging code. It should exist between the two cells where the Previous and Next buttons live:

```
<td>
 <xsl:call-template name="paging-list"/>
</td>
```

The final step is the creation of the `paging-list` template. The challenge is that you have to somehow create buttons for an indeterminate number of pages. You'll do this using recursion—you'll invoke the template from inside the template. Before looking at that, though, let's look at the basic stuff. The start of the template does the basic mechanics of translating a page number into a `skip-rows` parameter and a button name. The `paging-form` template is used to actually create the form and the button.

```
<xsl:template name="paging-list">
 <xsl:param name="counter">0</xsl:param>
  <td>
```

```
    <xsl:choose>
     <xsl:when test="number($counter)*number($max-rows)!=number($skip-
rows)">
      <xsl:call-template name="paging-form">
       <xsl:with-param name="new-skip-rows"><xsl:value-of
select="number($counter)*number($max-rows)"/></xsl:with-param>
       <xsl:with-param name="button-text"><xsl:value-of
select="number($counter)+1"/></xsl:with-param>
      </xsl:call-template>
     </xsl:when>
      <xsl:otherwise>
       <xsl:call-template name="paging-form">
        <xsl:with-param name="new-skip-rows">-1</xsl:with-param>
        <xsl:with-param name="button-text"><xsl:value-of
select="number($counter)+1"/></xsl:with-param>
       </xsl:call-template>
      </xsl:otherwise>
     </xsl:choose>
    </td>
```

This code is very similar to the code for the Previous and Next buttons. It determines what the `new-skip-rows` value should be and dynamically determines the name of the button based on the counter. It also disables the button when it isn't appropriate to use it. In this case, the button for the current page is disabled.

If we stopped right here, you would have a single button for the first page. To get buttons for all the pages, you need to recursively call the template. The following code takes care of this. You first have to determine when the template should be invoked. Then, you determine what the new counter value should be. The following code completes the template:

```
 <xsl:if test="number($counter+1)*number($max-rows)&lt;number($row-
count)">
   <xsl:call-template name="paging-list">
    <xsl:with-param name="counter"><xsl:value-of
select="number($counter)+1"/></xsl:with-param>
   </xsl:call-template>
  </xsl:if>
</xsl:template>
```

With all recursion there is the risk of an infinite loop, so it's important that you ensure that the recursion will stop. This is a combination of controlling when the template will be invoked and passing to it parameters so that it will violate that criteria at some point. The output of this particular template is shown in Figure 14.13.

Now you've seen the way to handle stateless paging without the use of an action handler. You've also gotten to see XSLT recursion in action. You can do a lot of neat stuff with recursion, but it can lead to confusing and hard to maintain code. When you find yourself using recursion in XSLT, it's a good time to ask yourself if what you are doing can be better accomplished with an action handler.

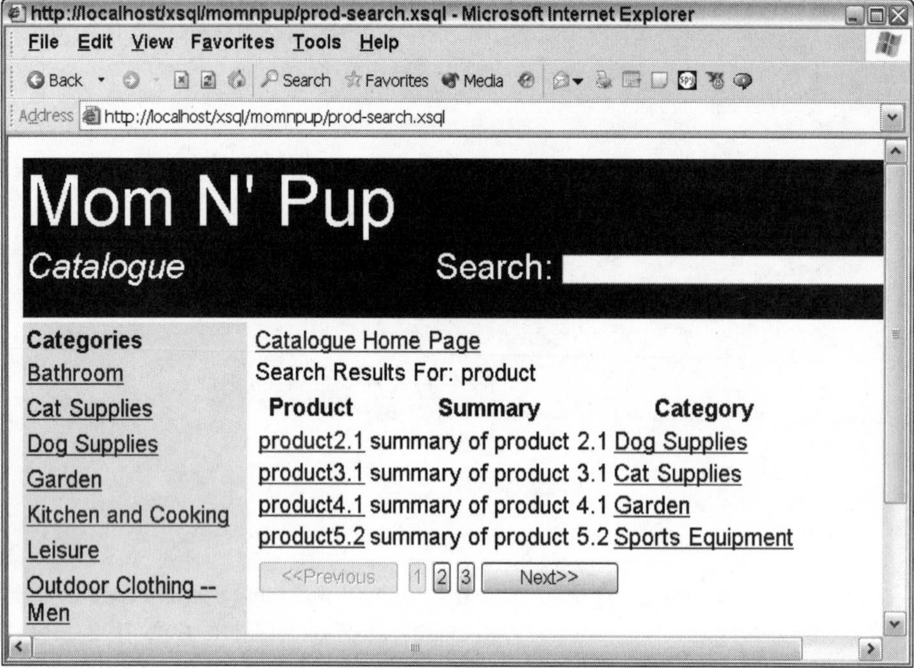

Figure 14.13 Stateless paging with page list.

XSQL Data Editor

One of our requirements was to give the customer a way to edit prices on the Web. This moves us away from the simple publishing of data. In this section, you'll design a simple editor that uses the `xsql:dml` action and an update statement to change data already in the database. The first step is to look at how to design an XSQL editor. Then, you'll develop the XSQL and the XSLT. JavaScript is heavily used in this example, so some of the editor functionality will be covered in the next section.

As with everything in this chapter, we're using a pure XSQL approach. But while a pure XSQL approach can cover a lot of applications that simply publish data, it comes up short a lot more often when inputting data. This will be covered in more detail in Chapter 18.

Editor Architecture

There are a lot of ways to design Web-based editors. In all cases, you have at least one component that actually processes the data into the database. The other components surround this action. There's usually a component that locates the data to be edited, and then there is an HTML form that actually allows the editing of data itself. In cases in which you are inserting new data, the HTML form is blank and is linked to a component that inserts data into the database.

For this example, we're going for a simple interface. Instead of having multiple pages through which a user has to navigate, there is a single interface. Figure 14.14 shows what the finished product will look like. The same interface is reloaded any time you save a record.

The editor consists of three XSQL pages and a single stylesheet. The stylesheet consists of one search form and a separate form for each record returned in the search. One XSQL page, `price-editor-query.xsql`, is used to find the records that the user wishes to edit and is included in the other two XSQL pages. The `price-editor-search.xsql` is invoked when the user searches for items to edit, while the `price-editor-update.xsql` actually updates the items in the database. After updating the items in the database, the same query is performed again and the results are reloaded. Both of the top-level stylesheets are linked to the same stylesheet, `price-editor.xsl`. The diagram appears in Figure 14.15.

This is certainly not the only way to implement an editor in XSQL. A simpler architecture is to have three pages: (1) search, (2) details, and (3) update. However, because we're pretty familiar with XSQL and XSLT by now, this architecture presents some interesting challenges. At the end of the day, it should be more appeasing to the user, too.

Figure 14.14 The price editor.

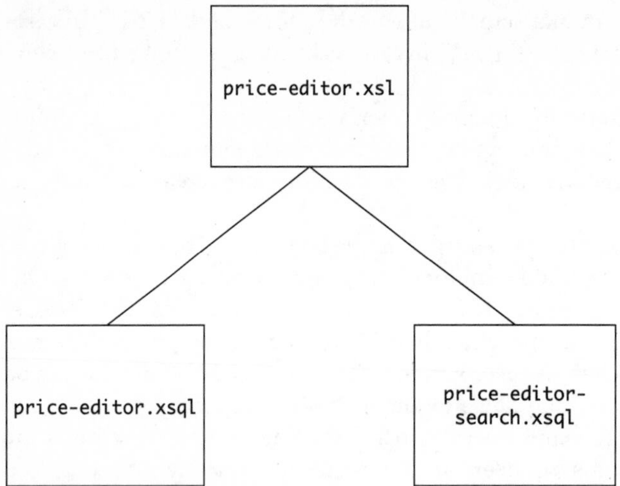

Figure 14.15 Editor architecture.

XSQL Development

As in the previous section, it's a good idea to develop the XSQL before the XSLT stylesheets. By doing things in this order you can develop against live data. For this example you have three XSQL pages to develop. It's best to start with `price -editor-query.xsql` because it is included by the other two. It does a wildcard search against the product name:

```
<?xml version="1.0"?>
<xsql:query
    connection="momnpup"
    xmlns:xsql="urn:oracle-xsql"
    rowset-element="PRICE_EDITOR_QUERY"
    row-element="PRICE_EDITOR_PRODUCT">
     SELECT p.id AS product_id,
          p.name AS product_name,
          pc.name AS product_cat_name,
          p.price AS product_price
     FROM product p, product_category pc
     WHERE pc.id=p.category_id
        AND
        p.name like '%{@terms}%'
        AND
        length('{@terms}')>0
</xsql:query>
```

The second XSQL page is the page that is called after the user enters a search term. It essentially wrappers the `price-editor-query.xsql` page and also passes the term parameter to the stylesheet:

```
<?xml version="1.0"?>
<?xml-stylesheet type="text/xsl" href="price-editor.xsl"?>
<prod-search connection="momnpup"
    xmlns:xsql="urn:oracle-xsql">
 <xsql:set-stylesheet-param name="terms" value="{@terms}"/>
 <xsql:include-xsql href="price-editor-query.xsql"/>
</prod-search>
```

The last XSQL page is responsible for updating the database. After updating the database, it repeats the earlier query so that you can edit more prices that are part of the same query.

```
<?xml version="1.0"?>
<?xml-stylesheet type="text/xsl" href="price-editor.xsl"?>
<price-update xmlns:xsql="urn:oracle-xsql" connection="momnpup">
 <update-results>
  <xsql:dml commit="yes"
    product_id="0"
    bind-params="new_price product_id">
  UPDATE product
   SET price=?
   WHERE id=?
  </xsql:dml>
 </update-results>
 <xsql:dml>COMMIT</xsql:dml>
 <xsql:set-stylesheet-param name="terms"
                            value="{@terms}"/>
 <xsql:set-stylesheet-param name="updated_product"
                            value="{@product_name}"/>
 <xsql:include-xsql href="price-editor-query.xsql"/>
</price-update>
```

This XSQL page takes `new_price` and `product_id` as parameters for the update statement and also needs the terms query in order to requery the database.

Developing the XSQL Interface

The XSLT development consists entirely of developing one file: `price-editor.xsl`. This might seem a little wacky, except when you look at the XML output for the two top-level XSQL pages. The XML schema is almost exactly the same because the majority of the data returned is the results of the search. Two pages have two different stylesheets, which would result in some amount of redundant code.

The first step is to handle the two different top-level elements. This is accomplished by using an `'or'` operator in the select XPath expression at the top level of the stylesheet. It will match on documents with either `prod-search` or `price-update` as their root element. It would be possible to give both XSQL pages the same root element, but it isn't a good practice. Though very similar, the two different XML schemas are distinct.

```
<?xml version = '1.0'?>
<xsl:stylesheet xmlns:xsl="http://www.w3.org/1999/XSL/Transform"
version="1.0">
 <xsl:param name="terms"></xsl:param>
 <xsl:param name="updated_product"></xsl:param>
 <xsl:template match="/prod-search | /price-update">
  <html>
   <head>
    <title>Price Editor Search</title>
    <SCRIPT LANGUAGE="JavaScript">
      <![CDATA[
       <!--
        // The Javascript code. Covered in next section
     -->
    ]]>
    </SCRIPT>
   </head>
```

The head contains a large section of JavaScript that is omitted for now. The next section of the chapter looks in depth at the JavaScript from this example. The rest of the root template follows:

```
   <body onLoad="onLoadMethod()">
    <xsl:apply-templates select="update-results/xsql-status"/>
    <h2>Price Editor Search</h2>
    <form action="price-editor-search.xsql" method="POST">
     Search:
     <input type="text" name="terms">
      <xsl:attribute name="value"><xsl:value-of
select="$terms"/></xsl:attribute>
     </input>
     <input type="submit" value="search">
     </input>
    </form>
    <h2>Price Search Results</h2>
    <p>
      <xsl:apply-templates select="PRICE_EDITOR_QUERY"/>
    </p>
   </body>
  </html>
 </xsl:template>
```

The body has three parts. The first is xsl:apply-templates, which provides the status of a price update. If the price-editor-search.xsql page invoked the stylesheet, then the update-results element won't be present in the inputted XML. The second part of the page is the search form that feeds the price-editor-search.xsql page. The search field has as a default value the last search term. The final section are the results of the previous search results.

In this scheme, a query is launched against the database on the user's first visit to the editor per session. Because the search term is blank, the first query will always return zero rows. However, it does seem a bit wasteful to run a query when you don't expect to get any data. At the same time, though, it's redundant to create a separate static HTML page that will basically be a copy of the stylesheet. There is an easy workaround for this. Simply create a dummy XSQL page like the one that follows, which is saved as price-editor.xsql.

```
<?xml version="1.0"?>
<?xml-stylesheet type="text/xsl" href="price-editor.xsl"?>
<price-editor-dummy xmlns:xsql="urn:oracle-xsql">
</price-editor-dummy>
```

When called, it doesn't even make a connection to the database. You need to make a change in the stylesheet so that the top template will match against price-editor-dummy:

```
<xsl:template match="/prod-search | /price-update | /price-editor-
dummy">
```

When you call price-editor.xsql, the interface is rendered but there is no database impact at all. If you want to change the look and feel of the HTML, you only have to recode in one place.

Now it's time to complete the rest of the stylesheet. The PRICE_EDITOR_QUERY template is first. It sets up the table where the search results are displayed.

```
<xsl:template match="PRICE_EDITOR_QUERY">
 <table>
  <th>Name</th><th>Category</th><th>Price</th>
   <xsl:apply-templates select="PRICE_EDITOR_PRODUCT"/>
 </table>
</xsl:template>
```

The real work is done in the PRICE_EDITOR_PRODUCT template. There is one PRICE_EDITOR_PRODUCT element for each row returned. Each element is transformed into a form that links to the price-editor-update.xsql page.

```
<xsl:template match="PRICE_EDITOR_PRODUCT">
 <form action="price-editor-update.xsql" method="post" onsubmit="return
submitForm(this)">
  <xsl:attribute name="name">edit_product_<xsl:value-of
```

```
select="PRODUCT_ID"/></xsl:attribute>
  <input type="hidden" name="product_id">
   <xsl:attribute name="value"><xsl:value-of
select="PRODUCT_ID"/></xsl:attribute>
  </input>
  <input type="hidden" name="terms">
   <xsl:attribute name="value"><xsl:value-of
select="$terms"/></xsl:attribute>
  </input>
  <input type="hidden" name="original_price">
   <xsl:attribute name="value"><xsl:value-of
select="PRODUCT_PRICE"/></xsl:attribute>
  </input>
  <input type="hidden" name="product_name">
   <xsl:attribute name="value"><xsl:value-of
select="PRODUCT_NAME"/></xsl:attribute>
  </input>
```

The first part of this preceding template sets up some hidden form parameters. The first two, `product-id` and `terms`, are required by the `price-editor-update.xsql` script. The others are used by the JavaScript validation scripts. The remaining code of the template displays the name, category, and form elements as follows:

```
  <tr>
   <td>
    <xsl:value-of select="PRODUCT_NAME"/>
   </td>
   <td>
    <xsl:value-of select="PRODUCT_CAT_NAME"/>
   </td>
   <td>
    $<input type="text" name="new_price">
      <xsl:attribute name="value"><xsl:value-of
select="PRODUCT_PRICE"/></xsl:attribute>
      <xsl:attribute
name="onChange">validatePrice(this,&quot;<xsl:value-of
select="PRODUCT_NAME"/>&quot;)</xsl:attribute>
     </input>
   </td>
   <td>
    <input type="submit" value="save"></input>
   </td>
  </tr>
 </form>
</xsl:template>
```

When you search on the results, you get a form for each product returned in the search. Each form is linked to the `price-editor-update.xsql` page. When you hit save for the row, the `product_id`, `terms`, and `new_price` are passed to `price-editor-update.xsql`. The stylesheet is applied to the result of `price-editor-update.xsql`, which includes the status of the update itself. The last template formats the status that is returned:

```
<xsl:template match="xsql-status">
 <b>
   <xsl:value-of select="@rows"/> row updated for <xsl:value-of
select="$updated_product"/>.
 </b>
</xsl:template>
```

Your editor is complete now. There are some calls to JavaScript, but they aren't strictly necessary for a working editor. If someone entered an incorrect value, then Oracle would generate an error. You can handle the error with the techniques discussed in the last section of this chapter on error handling. However, the validation does make your editor better. It gives immediate feedback to the user about his or her incorrect data entry. The JavaScript validation is covered in our next discussion.

Javascript and XSQL Development

Web development is a mingling of a lot of different standards. Because the standards are more or less open, they have to work together to survive and prosper. Sometimes, however, the actual point of integration between two of these standards can be a little tricky.

JavaScript is completely accessible and usable in your XSQL applications. If you store your JavaScript in an external file, then you'll have no problems at all. If you put JavaScript inside an XSLT stylesheet, there are a couple of syntax tricks that you have to understand. These are covered in the first discussion. We then examine how you can set JavaScript variables with values returned by XSQL.

JavaScript and XSLT Integration

As much as possible, JavaScript methods should also be separated into their own `.js` file. This is especially important because of the special XML characters that JavaScript methods contain. But there are good reasons to include JavaScript in a stylesheet. Here's how we included JavaScript in the stylesheet for the price editor:

```
<![CDATA[
       <!--
      var lockUI="no";
      function lockCheck() {
       if (lockUI=="yes") {
        alert('Updating the database. Please wait.');
        this.focus();
        }
```

```
        }
        function validatePrice(callingElement,product_name) {
         var validChars="0123456789.";
         valid="yes";
         for (var i=0;i<callingElement.value.length;i++) {
          if (validChars.indexOf(callingElement.value.substring(i,i+1))==-
1) {
           valid="no";
           break;
           }
          }
          var decimalPos=callingElement.value.indexOf(".");
          if (decimalPos!=-1 && decimalPos!=callingElement.value.length-3)
{
           valid="no";
          }
          if (valid=="no") {
           alert('The price for '+product_name+' is invalid.\n Valid
examples: 33.33, 20');
           callingElement.value=callingElement.form.original_price.value;
          return false;
          } else {
           return true;
          }
         }
        function submitForm(theForm) {
         if (validatePrice(theForm.new_price,theForm.product_name.value))
{
          lockUI="yes";
          return true;
         } else {
          return false;
         }
        }
       -->
      ]]>
     </SCRIPT>
```

You could also use `xsl:text` to accomplish what CDATA accomplishes. In either case, it's important that the HTML comment strings are inside the text block. If not, the XSLT processor will consider all of your code to be a comment and ignore all of it.

You can escape all of the special XML characters in your JavaScript on a character-by-character basis. For instance, if you have the following line of code:

```
if (str && i < str.length)
```

you can escape the special characters like this:

```
if (str &amp;&amp; i &lt; str.length)
```

However, you probably should always have code that has these special operators enclosed in a CDATA section. The only reason not to include the JavaScript in a CDATA section is because you wish to perform XSLT transformations on it. Because the special characters are operators, this means that you are trying to write your JavaScript on the fly. This is not such a good idea. There may be a case for excluding blocks of code because you know you won't need them based on the input XML, but you should definitely do that at a method level and encapsulate the entire methods inside of templates.

Javascript and XSQL Data

Now that you know how to get your code into a stylesheet, it's time to examine how to integrate your JavaScript with your XSQL data. You do this by using XSLT to transform your data into a format that JavaScript can use. There are three ways to do this: (1) placing JavaScript method arguments, (2) setting hidden-form parameters, and (3) setting JavaScript variables directly. The first two methods were used in the price editor JavaScript, and we'll cook up an example for the last method.

In the `PRICE_EDITOR_PRODUCT` template, the following code set the product name as an argument for the `validatePrice` method. This is a very easy solution to implement. It's easy and clean and you don't have to worry with any of the escape character problems described earlier. On the coding side, you just have to think about mating your JavaScript methods to particular templates, which is probably a good idea anyway.

```
     $<input type="text" name="new_price">
       <xsl:attribute name="value"><xsl:value-of
select="PRODUCT_PRICE"/></xsl:attribute>
       <xsl:attribute
name="onChange">validatePrice(this,&quot;<xsl:value-of
select="PRODUCT_NAME"/>&quot;)</xsl:attribute>
      </input>
```

A problem with this is that you can end up with awfully long method signatures, and you can end up putting the exact same data into the output over and over. The hidden-form parameter technique alleviates these problems. This technique was used inside the `validatePrice` method to reset the value to the original price. The hidden-form variable is set inside the template as follows:

```
<input type="hidden" name="original_price">
 <xsl:attribute name="value"><xsl:value-of
select="PRODUCT_PRICE"/></xsl:attribute>
</input>
```

You can then reference the value through the back door. You reference the form variable of the input element that was passed in to reference the hidden variable:

```
callingElement.value=callingElement.form.original_price.value;
```

You may not always have a form element convenient for doing this. Then, you'll have to reference the hidden-form parameter absolutely. If you are going to generate multiple forms, you should name them reasonable things so that you can reference them. We do that for the template forms:

```
<form action="price-editor-update.xsql" method="post" onsubmit="return
submitForm(this)">
   <xsl:attribute name="name">edit_product_<xsl:value-of
select="PRODUCT_ID"/></xsl:attribute>
```

You can also set data directly as JavaScript variables. You can do this either globally or inside JavaScript methods. You have to break out of any CDATA section that you are in, and then you can use any XSLT elements that you wish. Here is an example:

```
   var numProducts=<xsl:value-of
select="count(//PRICE_EDITOR_QUERY/PRICE_EDITOR_PRODUCT)"/>;
   var firstProductName='<xsl:value-of
select="//PRICE_EDITOR_QUERY/PRICE_EDITOR_PRODUCT/PRODUCT_NAME[position(
)=1]"/>';
   var firstProductPrice='<xsl:value-of
select="//PRICE_EDITOR_QUERY/PRICE_EDITOR_PRODUCT/PRODUCT_PRICE[position
()=1]"/>';
   var productPriceArray=[
       <xsl:for-each
select="//PRICE_EDITOR_QUERY/PRICE_EDITOR_PRODUCT/PRODUCT_NAME">
         "<xsl:value-of select="."/>"
         <xsl:if test="position()!=last()">,</xsl:if>
       </xsl:for-each>];
<xsl:for-each select="//PRICE_EDITOR_QUERY/PRICE_EDITOR_PRODUCT">
   var productPrice<xsl:value-of select="PRODUCT_ID"/>=<xsl:value-of
select="PRODUCT_PRICE"/>;
 </xsl:for-each>
```

This last technique should be used sparingly. Though you are only setting data, you are dynamically writing code. It can be tough to debug in such an environment. Using hidden-form variables gives you a cleaner separation between the dynamic part of the page and the JavaScript, which should be as static as possible. At the same time, it may be easier overall on your application to use this technique.

Error Handling

Errors are tough to avoid. It's rare that an application of any complexity doesn't have some errors at some point. The trick is to be prepared for them and handle them in a reasonable manner. In an XSQL application, the source of errors is the actions. This section looks at how to use XSQL's own built-in error handling to present useful error messages. The first section looks at how XSQL processes errors. Then, we'll develop an XSLT template for translating the errors into a nice format. The final section looks at some various strategies for handling errors in your application.

XSQL Errors

When an XSQL action has a problem, it creates an `xsql-error` element. Inside the `xsql-error` element is data about the error that was generated. The format is as follows:

```
<xsql-error code="code" action="action">
 <statement>SQL statement that caused the error</statement>
 <message>error message</message>
</xsql-error>
```

You can suppress the inclusion of the SQL statement by setting `error-statement` to false in the action. You should get the other items regardless. The code is the Oracle code for the error, while the action is the type of action that caused the message. The error message is the standard message returned by Oracle that you would also get from executing the SQL from SQL*Plus.

An error is easy to generate in our application. Just do a search on the character `'`. This throws Oracle for a loop because this character is placed inside of a SQL statement in the wrong place. If you comment out the stylesheet reference in the `prod-search.xsql`, you should get the XML as a result of this search, as shown in Figure 14.16.

You'll develop a search action handler in the next section to handle this kind of incorrect search more gracefully. For now, we'll use it as an easy way to generate an error.

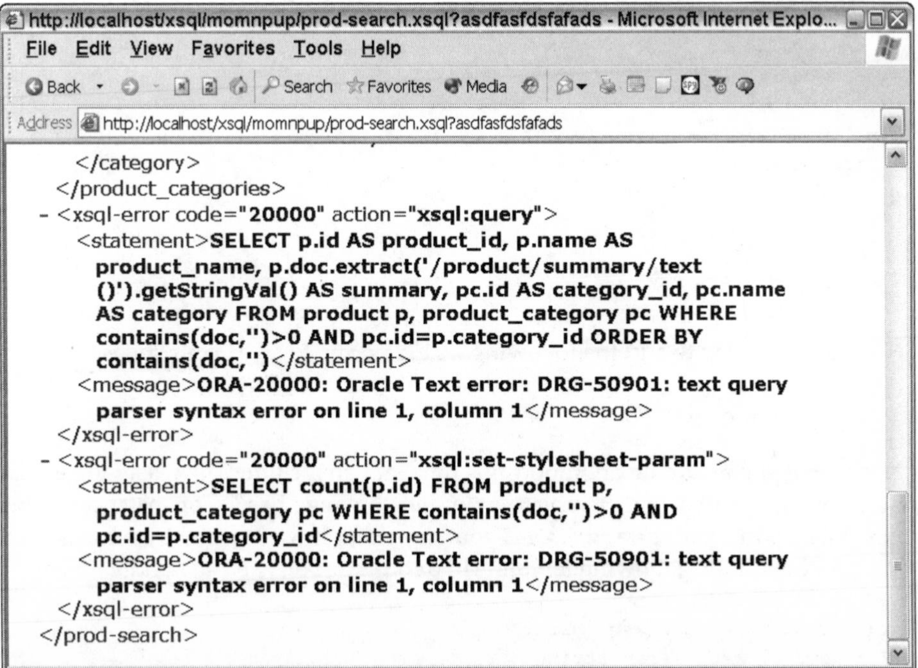

Figure 14.16 XSQL errors in XML output.

An XSQL Error Template

Developing an error handling template is just like developing any other template. Here you'll develop a stylesheet that can be imported into other stylesheets so that you can use the same error handling routines throughout your application. Then you'll look at ways to override the basic error handling stylesheet for specific cases. Here is the error handling stylesheet itself:

```
<?xml version = '1.0'?>
<xsl:stylesheet xmlns:xsl="http://www.w3.org/1999/XSL/Transform"
version="1.0">
 <xsl:template match="xsql-error">
  <xsl:param name="error-mesg">Error!</xsl:param>
  <p>
   <table border="1">
    <tr><td><h3><xsl:value-of select="$error-mesg"/></h3></td></tr>
    <tr><td>
     <b>XSQL Action Handler:</b> <xsl:value-of select="@action"/>
    </td></tr>
    <tr><td>
     <b>Code:</b> <xsl:value-of select="@code"/>
    </td></tr>
    <xsl:apply-templates/>
   </table>
  </p>
 </xsl:template>
 <xsl:template match="message">
  <tr><td><b>Message: </b>
   <xsl:value-of select="."/>
  </td></tr>
 </xsl:template>
 <xsl:template match="statement">
  <tr><td><b>Statement: </b>
   <xsl:value-of select="."/>
  </td></tr>
 </xsl:template>
</xsl:stylesheet>
```

Now you just need to add the following `xsl:import` to all of your stylesheets:

```
<xsl:import href="xsql-error.xsl"/>
```

Notice that you are doing an import this time, not an include. The reasoning is that you can override the default template on a page-by-page basis. For instance, if this error comes up in `prod-search.xsl`, you know that it was caused by a bad search string. You can put the following template in `prod-search.xsl` to handle the error:

```
<xsl:template match="xsql-error">
 Fix your broken search string!
 <xsl:apply-imports/>
</xsl:template>
```

This will give the error and then invoke the template that resides in the `xsql-error.xsl` stylesheet. It is also possible to give more refined messages based on the error code that was returned. This one interprets the error based on the error code that was returned:

```
<xsl:template match="xsql-error[@code=911]">
 Hey! Don't use single quotes in your searches. They aren't allowed.
</xsl:template>
```

Because you know what the error is, you don't need to trouble the user with all of the error code stuff and Oracle messages. This is easily suppressed—just don't use the `xsl:apply-imports` element.

Ways to Handle Errors

If you follow just the preceding instructions, then the error messages will appear wherever the query results were supposed to appear. This may be the behavior that you desire—or maybe not. This section looks at two other ways of handling errors. The first handles errors globally. If any error occurs, then an error page is shown detailing all of the errors instead of having error messages inside of the interface. The second method examines how to deal with errors at a more granular level. You can choose what to do with errors inside the templates that would otherwise handle the results.

First, let's look at how the errors are displayed by default. In Figure 14.17, the error message pops up exactly where the query should be.

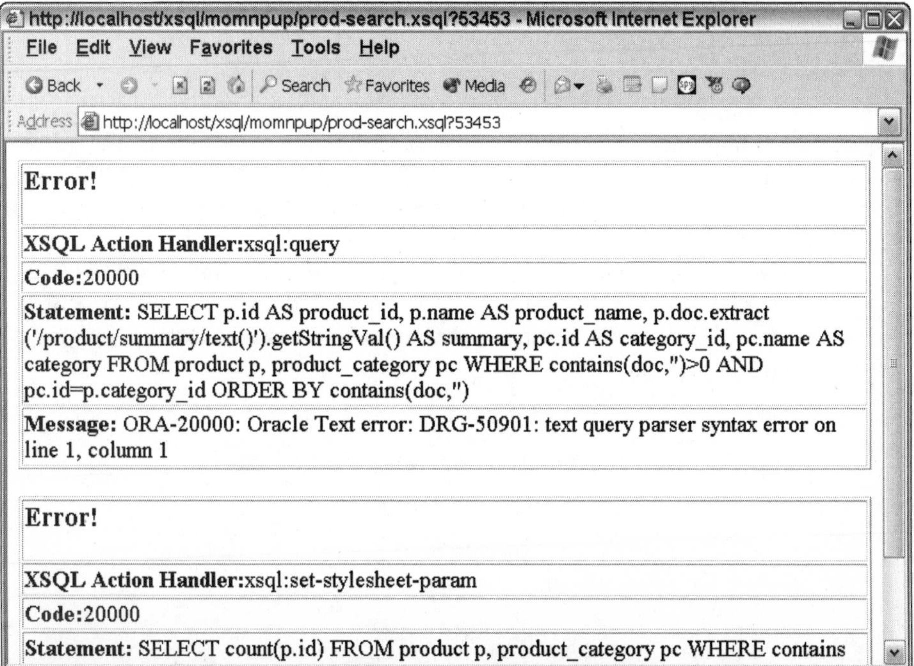

Figure 14.17 Default behavior with error handling template.

What if you want only an error page if any error occurs? You can do that by using the following template that matches at the root of the stylesheet:

```
<xsl:template match="/">
 <xsl:choose>
  <xsl:when test="count(//xsql-error)>0">
   <html>
   <head></head>
   <body>
   <xsl:apply-templates select="//xsql-error"/>
   </body>
   </html>
  </xsl:when>
  <xsl:otherwise>
   <xsl:apply-templates select="/prod-search"/>
  </xsl:otherwise>
 </xsl:choose>
</xsl:template>
```

In this previous example, the node-set `//xsql-error` was used to determine if there were any errors. You can use the same kind of technique inside your templates. You can use `xsl:if` and `xsl:choose` elements to determine if there are errors on a template-by-template basis. Then you can decide what should be done in those cases.

All of these strategies have their own pluses and minuses, and a lot of it depends on what your application requires. Regardless, some kind of error handling is important. By using some of the techniques outlined here, you should be able to make error handling an easy (and error-free!) part of your application.

Moving On

This chapter brought together all of the concepts of the previous chapters. In addition to writing XSQL pages, you also developed XSLT code and used SQL, Oracle Text, and the Oracle XML functionality. You should be able to use this chapter as a basis for developing your own XSQL applications. The next chapters move beyond the core of XSQL, and show you how to use it in new ways and extend the framework. The next two chapters show you how to use XSQL from the command line and how to use XSQL with Web services. Then, for the last three chapters of the book, you'll see how to use XSQL in conjunction with Java.

Command Line Utility

The command line utility gives you the ability to access most of the functionality of XSQL from the command line. You pass the URL of an XSQL page and, optionally, an output file and its parameters to the command line utility. It gives you back the results of processing the XSQL page. Since it isn't servlet-based, you can't make use of session parameters or cookies, but you can pass request-level parameters if you'd like.

The first section covers how to use the command line utility first. The next section provides two examples to demonstrate the command line utility. One example shows how to create a newsletter; the other, shows to send a newsletter with a simple shell script.

Using the Command Line Utility

The command line utility exists as the `oracle.xml.xsql.XSQLCommandLine` class. The syntax for the call is as follows:

```
>java oracle.xml.xsql.XSQLCommandLine xsqlpage [out] [param1=val1 . . .]
```

The `xsqlpage` argument is the URL for the XSQL page that you wish to process. You don't have to have a Web server running to use the command line tool, though. You can use the `file:///` protocol to use local files. The out argument is an optional argument for an output file. If you specify it, the output will be written to the file.

The other arguments are parameters that you wish to pass to the XSQL page. These arguments will function just like request parameters passed in the query string of HTTP GETrequests. Action handlers that reference the servlet environment beyond simple request parameters won't work properly.

Oracle also provides a batch file so that you don't have to type out the full class name. It resides in the bin directory of your XSQL distribution or the bin directory of your Oracle distribution if you installed it in conjunction with your Oracle server. You use it as follows:

```
>xsql xsqlpage [out] [param1=val1 . . .]
```

Before using the command line tool, you'll need a `XSQLConfig.xml` file in the classpath that you are running from. The classpath exists as an environment variable, so just look at it to see where all it points to. You may also have to add the following jar files to the classpath before the command line utility will work.

- `jlib/sax2.jar`
- `rdbms/jlib/xsu12.jar`
- `lib/xmlparserv2.jar`
- `lib/oraclexsql.jar`
- `jdbc/lib/classes12.jar`

You may be tempted to use the command line tool with XSQL pages that are part of an online application. You probably won't have a lot of success calling them with the HTTP protocol, like this:

```
>xsql http://localhost/xsql/momnpup/home.xsql
```

By the time the response comes back, a stylesheet will have already been applied. What you get back isn't the original XSQL page but an HTML page. The command line tool can't make any sense out of it, so you get a weird error like this:

```
Oracle XSQL Command Line Page Processor 9.0.1.1.0 (Prod)
XSQL-005: XSQL page is not well-formed.
XML parse error at line 5, char 10
End tag does not match start tag 'link'.
```

You won't find any `link` tag on page 5 of your XSQL page. You need only call the XSQL page with a file URL, make a copy of the XSQL page without reference to the stylesheet, or set the `xml-stylesheet` parameter to `none` if this is allowed by your setup.

So, what if you want the command line tool to apply a stylesheet to my results? You do this by passing it a `xml-stylesheet` parameter. The command line parameter has three such parameters, as described in Table 15.1.

Table 15.1 Built-in Command Line Parameters

PARAMETER	MEANING
`xml-stylesheet`	The stylesheet's URL or a URL relative to the XSQL page's URL. If set to none, no stylesheet is applied.
`posted-xml`	Optional XML document to be posted to the request. Used in conjunction with the XML handlers to input data.
`useragent`	The user agent to pass to the page. Useful if you choose stylesheets based on the `user agent` string in your XSQL page.

Text Example

So far, you have been very focused on developing applications for the Web. The purpose of this chapter is, in part, to look beyond the Web and examine how else XSQL can be used. In this example, you'll use XSQL to generate a plain-text file. Instead of making a Web page, you'll make one of those goofy email newsletters that likes to refer to you by name. Here's how you do it:

```
<?xml version = '1.0'?>
<xsl:stylesheet xmlns:xsl="http://www.w3.org/1999/XSL/Transform"
version="1.0">
 <xsl:output method="text"/>
 <xsl:template match="/ROWSET/ROW">

  Hi <xsl:value-of select="NAME"/>,

  It is your lucky day! Nothing could be better for you
  and everyone else there at <xsl:value-of select="ORGANIZATION"/>.

  We're talking deals. Good ones! Not like that stuff
  you see in all that spam. Oh, no! This is the real
  thing. Just between you and me, <xsl:value-of select="NAME"/>,
  This could very well be the best thing that ever happened to you.

  So come on by, and we'll figure it out, or your name isn't
  <xsl:value-of select="NAME"/>.

  Cheers!

 </xsl:template>
</xsl:stylesheet>
```

Now you need an XSQL page that will create the email for a particular email address. Here's one:

```
<?xml version="1.0"?>
<xsql:query connection="momnpup"
    xmlns:xsql="urn:oracle-xsql">
 SELECT * FROM newsletter WHERE email='{@email}'

</xsql:query>
```

The following command line pulls the pieces together. It specifies that the `newsletter.xsl` stylesheet should be used and that the email parameter should be passed.

```
>xsql file:///java/xsql/newsletter.xsql xml-
stylesheet=file:///java/xsql/newsletter.xsl email=test2@momnpup.com
```

In this example, the output writes to the console. If you would prefer to write it to a file, you need only specify that file as the second parameter:

```
>xsql file:///java/xsql/newsletter.xsql newsletter.out xml-
stylesheet=file:///java/xsql/newsletter.xsl email=test2@momnpup.com
```

In the next section, you'll use this code as part of a script.

Script Writing

By using the XSQL file from the preceding section, you can generate a newsletter itself. To actually send it, you just have to pass the newsletter to some kind of mail-handling program to get it out to the right recipients. In this example, you'll write a simple script that can be used on Unix with the mail utility. It will send out a batch of newsletters based on a particular XSQL page. Of course, the scripts that you can write with XSQL are pretty unlimited. You can even write SQL scripts based on your XSQL output. This script is mainly intended to get your imagination going about the kind of scripts that are possible.

The first step is to figure out how to send the newsletter to a single address. This is rather simple:

```
 >xsql file:///java/xsql/newsletter.xsql newsletter.out xml-
stylesheet=file:///java/xsql/newsletter.xsl email=test2@momnpup.com |
mail -t test2@momnpup.com
```

To do the mailing, you need an XSQL page that captures all the addresses in the newsletter table. The following XSQL page will do the trick:

```
<?xml version="1.0"?>
```

```
<xsql:query connection="momnpup"
    xmlns:xsql="urn:oracle-xsql">
 SELECT email FROM newsletter
</xsql:query>
```

Now you need a stylesheet that creates one of the foregoing mailer commands for each of the email addresses, such as the following:

```
<?xml version = '1.0'?>
<xsl:stylesheet xmlns:xsl="http://www.w3.org/1999/XSL/Transform"
version="1.0">
 <xsl:output method="text"/>
 <xsl:template match="/">
#/bin/sh
 <xsl:apply-templates select="ROWSET/ROW"/>
 </xsl:template>

 <xsl:template match="ROW">
 java oracle.xml.xsql.XSQLCommandLine file:///java/xsql/newsletter.xsql
xml-stylesheet=file:///java/xsql/newsletter.xsl email=<xsl:value-of
select="EMAIL"/>|mail -t <xsl:value-of select="EMAIL"/> -s "Newsletter"

 </xsl:template>
</xsl:stylesheet>
```

This stylesheet creates a separate command for each newsletter. When the script runs, a newsletter will be generated and then piped to the mail command.

```
 $xsql file:///java/xsql/mailer.xsql xml-stylesheet=mailer.xsl >
mailer.sh
```

After creation, the script will look something like this:

```
#/bin/sh

 java oracle.xml.xsql.XSQLCommandLine file:///java/xsql/newsletter.xsql
xml-stylesheet=file:///java/xsql/newsletter.xsl email=test1@momnpup.com |
mail -t test1@momnpup.com -s "Newsletter"


 java oracle.xml.xsql.XSQLCommandLine file:///java/xsql/newsletter.xsql
xml-stylesheet=file:///java/xsql/newsletter.xsl email=test2@momnpup.com |
mail -t test2@momnpup.com -s "Newsletter"
```

The command line tool gives you a simple but powerful means of creating all kinds of scripts. If you need data out of the database to be in your scripts, you can use XSQL to help create the scripts. A lot of the same lessons from the earlier JavaScript discussion apply. Most important, however, is not to get too fancy. If you find that you are using stylesheets to greatly modify the logic of the stylesheet, you may be creating a beast that no one can maintain.

Creating Static Web Pages

In the catalog application developed in the last chapter, a lot of the pages will come up the same each time. Pages containing product descriptions and category lists probably aren't going to change much. Instead of querying the database each time that a user hits the site, you could generate all the static pages at midnight and then just link to the static pages. This approach won't necessarily work for all the pages in an application; for example, it cannot be applied to the search results page in the product catalog application. In this example, you'll see how to create all the product details pages using a script.

Before going down this path, it's important to note that the links in the application would have to change to use the product details page. Right now, XSLT statements like the following are used throughout the application:

```
<a>
 <xsl:attribute name="href">prod-details.xsql?product_id=<xsl:value-of
select="PRODUCT_ID"/></xsl:attribute>
 <xsl:value-of select="PRODUCT_NAME"/>
</a>
```

You don't want to link to the XSQL page, because it will query the database. Instead, you want to link to a static page. The first step is to determine where you will keep the static pages and how you will name them. For this example, each details page will have a name like `prod-details-1.html`, where 1 is the id for the product. They'll live in the `/momnpup` virtual directory. Thus, this particular link should look like the following:

```
<a>
 <xsl:attribute name="href">/momnpup/prod-details-<xsl:value-of
select="PRODUCT_ID"/>.html</xsl:attribute>
 <xsl:value-of select="PRODUCT_NAME"/>
</a>
```

The next step is to figure out how to create a single page. The following will create the HTML for a single page:

```
prompt>xsql file:///java/xsql/momnpup/prod-details.xsql prod-details-
4.html product_id=4
```

Now you just use XSQL to generate a script for the entire site. Here is what the XSQL looks like:

```
<?xml version="1.0"?>
<xsql:query connection="momnpup"
    xmlns:xsql="urn:oracle-xsql">
 SELECT id FROM product
</xsql:query>
```

Next, you need a stylesheet that will actually create the script:

```
<?xml version = '1.0'?>
<xsl:stylesheet xmlns:xsl="http://www.w3.org/1999/XSL/Transform"
version="1.0">
 <xsl:output method="text"/>
 <xsl:template match="/">
  <xsl:apply-templates select="ROWSET/ROW"/>
 </xsl:template>

 <xsl:template match="ROW">
java oracle.xml.xsql.XSQLCommandLine file:///java/xsql/momnpup/prod-
details.xsql new/prod-details-<xsl:value-of select="PRODUCT_ID"/> xml-
stylesheet=file:///java/xsql/newsletter.xsl product_id=<xsl:value-of
select="PRODUCT_ID"/>
 </xsl:template>

</xsl:stylesheet>
```

You generate the script as follows. You only have to generate the script if new products have been inserted into or deleted from the database since the last time that you ran the script. If the set of products is the same, then you can use the last script that you created.

```
>xsql file:///java/xsql/details-pages-script.xsql details-script.bat
xml-stylesheet=file:///java/xsql/details-pages-script.xsl
```

XSQL and XSLT are useful in a command line environment. The command line tool gives you an easy way to access the database and get data into the scripts.

Moving On

This chapter showed you how you can use XSQL as a command line tool. The XSQL command line utility is a good way for you to easily access the database. This is only one way that you can use XSQL beyond Web publishing. The next chapter shows how you can create Web services with XSQL; Chapter 17 shows you how to use XSQL from inside your Java applications.

Web Services with XSQL

Web services mean different things to different people. Some will have you believe that you need a certain server to provide Web services, while others say that they have to involve certain protocols, such as ebXML, Simple Object Access Protocol (SOAP), or Universal Description, Discovery, and Integration (UDDI). This chapter defines Web services as a way to interface two applications with each other via the Web by using XML. The first section looks at the architecture of Web services and how XSQL fits in.

Before diving into this discussion, it is important to put the subject in context with the other beasts that roam the Web services world. The model of Web services presented here comprises very simple, easy-to-use architecture. You'll learn how to set up a couple of XSQL pages so that you can provide database data to other applications, and you'll also see how to receive information to place in your own applications. Although it's exciting, the SOAP standard moves far beyond the simple interchange of data. SOAP provides a lightweight mechanism for allowing objects, such as JavaBeans or Component Object Model (COM): objects, to interact with each other. Toward this end, the SOAP standard provides transaction and data-type support. If you are trying to create a true distributed application, SOAP would be a much better starting point than the XSQL-based Web services model that you will learn here.

NOTE XSQL uses DOM, which you'll learn more about in the next chapter. DOM requires that all the data be loaded into memory before it is sent to the client. If you try using XSQL with Web services that transfer a lot of data, you'll need more memory on the server side.

SOAP does come with its own overhead and learning curve. For SOAP to be used, both client and server applications must have SOAP processors, and if development needs to be done, developers must be familiar with SOAP. Presented here is a simple lightweight model that is easily accomplished. It introduces you to the Web services fundamentals on which SOAP is based, so if you need to move on you'll be ready.

Architecture

In the traditional world of the Web, you have a Web browser request a Web page. The HTML page is downloaded in some manner that is pleasing to the user. In an XML- and HTTP-based Web services model, an application makes a request of your Web server. The application expects XML as a result. The XML should be understandable to the requesting application. Generally, this means that it is valid in accordance with a defined schema. The application on the other end may also send XML to be processed by your XSQL application as well as standard HTTP parameters. Before processing the sent XML, XSQL must have the data in the canonical schema described in Chapter 5. The basic Web services architecture is diagrammed in Figure 16.1.

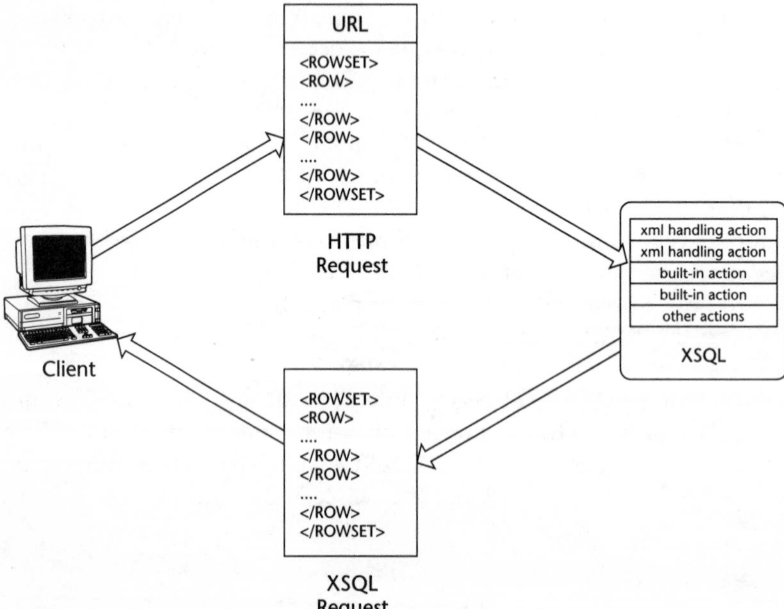

Figure 16.1 Basic Web services architecture.

The Web services application probably isn't going to want the XML data it receives to be in the canonical Oracle schema. Likewise, it probably won't want to post data in that same canonical schema. This is where XSLT comes in to play. You use separate XSLT stylesheets to transform data on the way into and on the way out of the XSQL application. This process is diagrammed in Figure 16.2. To transform the input, you can use a stylesheet with any of the XML handling actions documented in Chapters 5 and 7, and your custom actions can also be written so that they transform input. The other built-in actions cannot transform or use XML input.

In both cases, you perform XML-to-XML transformations, which are covered in the next section. The application can also send standard HTTP parameters to your XSQL app. Your application can interpret them just as they are interpreted for Web browser-based applications. An XSQL Web services application works very much like a traditional Web application, with the following key differences:

- Instead of transforming to HTML, you transform to some particular XML schema. This isn't necessarily easier or more difficult. If the Web services application works with a simple schema, it could be easier. But while HTML is always the same, XML schemas will probably change from application to application.
- You'll probably need to process XML as part of the request. In Chapter 7, you learned how to process XML that comes in as part of the request, but you rarely receive XML from the request in the traditional Web world. Few of the browsers even support sending XML, and it rarely accomplishes something that can't be accomplished with plain HTTP parameters. In the Web services world, however, it's very likely that a Web services application will send XML data along with the request. This means that you will be using the XML-handling actions a lot more often. You learned about these in Chapter 5; later in this section, we'll put them into context.
- Error handling is more constrained. In Chapter 14, you learned about XSQL error handling, and various methods of how to handle errors were suggested. But ultimately, you weren't particularly constrained in how the errors were handled; you just had to communicate that something had gone wrong and possibly how it went wrong. As your approach met the requirements of the application, you had a lot of freedom in precisely how you presented the error to the user. In Web services, error handling must be much more precise. Humans are pretty flexible in how they understand things, but applications aren't. Error handling should be part of the Web service application's schema, and you'll have to follow the rules of that schema when errors occur.

These points not withstanding, the lessons you've learned so far apply. You use the same actions and have to make the same decisions as to when to use action handlers and stored procedures. You should still try to modularize your XSQL and your XSLT as much as possible. In general, developing Web services is like developing traditional Web applications, except you'll probably get more input in the request. You output some particular flavor of XML rather than HTML, and the user is much stricter about what you send.

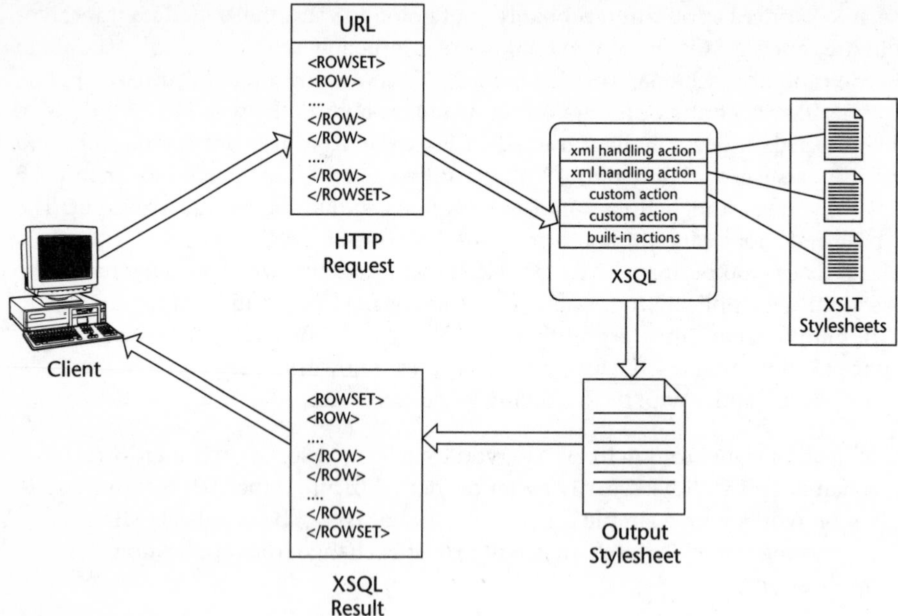

Figure 16.2 Web services with XSLT.

Now it's time to think a bit more deeply about Web services architectures. In Chapter 14, you saw how multiple pages make up an application. The same can be true of a Web services system. The Web services consumer makes an initial call of some sort, followed by subsequent calls. The consumer may make use of data collected in the previous calls, or maybe not. Although you may need to have a good understanding of how the system makes use of the data it receives, you don't have to worry with passing parameters in the same ways that you did in Chapter 14.

In the traditional Web, you can think of a Web browser as a Web services consumer. It makes the request, then processes the data it gets back. The difference is that you know (more or less) how it is going to process the data. You know that if you want the hyperlinks to come back to the application with a particular argument, you'll have to write the hyperlinks that way when you write out the page. You also know that you can set cookies and thus also use session parameters as long as the user hasn't turned cookies off.

In the Web services world, you don't know what the Web services consumer looks like. But generally, you can be guaranteed that it is well tuned for the purposes of the application. If it needs to make another request, it will probably put the request together based on the XML data that it downloaded. You probably don't need to put together the hyperlinks on the server side.

Of course, as soon as you read this you'll hear that the Web services consumer that you are going to be working with requires exactly this. But unlike Web browsers, they don't have to. While Web browsers are always more or less fixed in their functionality, Web services consumers vary greatly in how they behave. And while Web browsers are always black boxes that you must conform to, you will often have a role in designing and developing the Web services consumers.

Web services consumers vary. In terms of XSQL, perhaps the most important way they vary is how they interact with the XSQL provider over a series of differing HTTP transactions. The consumer can use either multiple URLs—one for each type of transaction—or a single URL that multiplexes types of transactions (see Figure 16.3).

In this case, you have a different XSQL page for each type of request. In terms of XSQL, this is really what you want. The XSQL transforms the incoming data; then it passes it to one of the XML handling actions for processing into the database. The alternative is the multiplex architecture, as shown in Figure 16.4.

The idea here is that the Web services provider determines the appropriate response by examining the XML that comes in as part of the request. The problem with this approach is that you simply don't get the chance to do this in the simple XSQL architecture. To make these kinds of decisions, you have to have an action handler process the XML. In such a case, it becomes questionable what benefit you would get from using XSQL at all.

Now that you have an understanding of how Web services architectures are put together, the next discussion looks at how to create a simple Web services consumer.

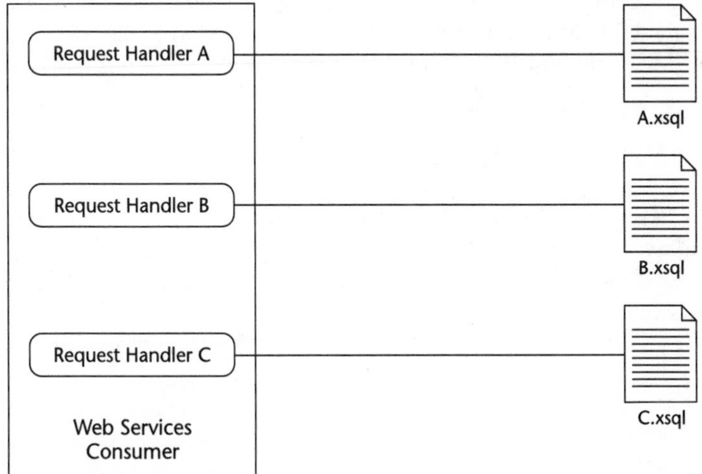

Figure 16.3 Multiple URL architecture.

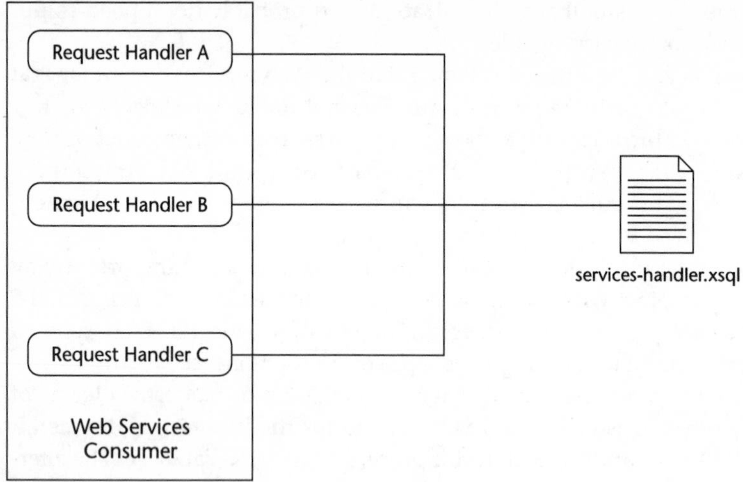

Figure 16.4 Mulitplex architecture.

A Simple Web Services Consumer

To lend the discussion some context, let's use an example of a Web services consumer in Java. The consumer runs from the command line. You point theconsumer at the URL of a Web service. It calls the URL and prints the result of the transaction to the console. You can optionally include documents that you want to post to the service. It is used as follows:

```
java SimpleServicesApp url [xml_file] [param1=val1] . . .
```

The consumer doesn't accomplish any grand business objective. But you will see how to perform, from a Java application, basic communication with a Web server by using a main method and a couple of supporting methods. Here is the main method and the requisite imports and class definition:

```
import java.io.Reader;
import java.io.Writer;
import java.io.FileReader;
import java.io.BufferedReader;
import java.io.BufferedWriter;
import java.io.PrintWriter;
import java.io.InputStreamReader;
import java.io.FileInputStream;
import java.io.OutputStream;
import java.io.IOException;
import java.io.FileNotFoundException;
```

```
import java.net.URL;
import java.net.URLConnection;
import java.net.MalformedURLException;
import java.net.URLEncoder;

import java.util.Hashtable;
import java.util.Enumeration;

public class SimpleServicesApp {

 static String errMesg="";

 String xmlFile=null;
 URL target;
 Hashtable params=new Hashtable();

 public static void main( String[] args) throws Exception {

  SimpleServicesApp app=new SimpleServicesApp();

  if (!app.setParams(args)) {
   app.writeError(errMesg);
  }

  System.out.println("Opening Service"+args[0]);

  app.invokeWebService(System.out);

 }
```

The default constructor is used for this class. The rest of the code is in the setParams and invokeWebService methods. The setParams loads the first parameter as the URL; it then loads the rest of the optional parameters. If the second parameter doesn't have an equals sign, it will be treated as a filename. The file is loaded and sent along with the HTTP request. Here's how the parameters are set:

```
 boolean setParams(String[] args) throws Exception {

   try {
    target=new URL(args[0]);
   } catch (MalformedURLException e) {
    errMesg="Invalid URL";
    return false;
   }

   int paramPos=1;

   if (args.length>1 && args[1].indexOf("=")==-1) {
    xmlFile=args[1];
    paramPos++;
   }
```

```
    while (paramPos<args.length) {

     String paramStr=args[paramPos];
     int eqPos=paramStr.indexOf("=");

     String fileName=null;

     String key=paramStr.substring(0,eqPos);
     String val=paramStr.substring(eqPos+1,paramStr.length());

     val=URLEncoder.encode(val);
     params.put(key,val);
     paramPos++;

    }
    return true;
   }
```

The HTTP transaction takes place in the `invokeWebService` method. First, the XML file is opened if an argument for one was provided. Then, the `URLConnection` is instantiated and the request, including any XML, is sent to the HTTP server. A reader for the response is created, and the data is written to the out stream.

```
  void invokeWebService(OutputStream out)
          throws IOException,
                 FileNotFoundException {

     // Make a reader for the XML file if necessary
     BufferedReader xmlInputReader=null;
     if (xmlFile!=null) {
      xmlInputReader=new BufferedReader(new FileReader(xmlFile));
     }


    // Open a connection the Web server, setting content type
    // if XML is going to be sent
    URLConnection conn = target.openConnection();
    if (xmlFile!=null) {
     conn.setRequestProperty("Content-Type","text/xml");
    }
    conn.setDoOutput(true);

    // Make a writer for the connection and send the data

    PrintWriter targetWriter = new PrintWriter(conn.getOutputStream());
    setRequestData(targetWriter,params,xmlInputReader);
    targetWriter.close();
```

```
  // Make a reader for the connection and read the data

  BufferedReader targetReader = new BufferedReader(
    new InputStreamReader(conn.getInputStream()));


  //Write the data to the stream

  String inputLine;

  while ((inputLine = targetReader.readLine()) != null) {
   System.out.println(inputLine);
  }

  targetReader.close();

 }
```

This looks like any stateless HTTP client written in Java, except for the `Content-Type` setting. This setting is required when you send XML. The actual transmission of the XML is done in `setRequestData`, which is given as follows. Also, the setting sends any parameters and values along after it URL-encodes them.

```
void setRequestData(PrintWriter outWriter, Hashtable params, Reader
xmlReader)
   throws IOException {

  Enumeration e=params.keys();

  System.out.println("params: "+params);

  while (e.hasMoreElements()) {

   String key=(String)e.nextElement();
   String val=(String)params.get(key);

   outWriter.println(key+"="+val);
  }

  if (xmlReader!=null) {

   for (int c=xmlReader.read();c!=-1;c=xmlReader.read()) {
    outWriter.write(c);
   }
  }
 }
```

There is only one method left to document—the `writeError`. This is a simple utility method for writing out any errors. Since it is the last method, this code snippet also contains the closing brace for the class:

```
void writeError(String mesg) {
  System.out.println("An error occurred");
  System.out.println(mesg);
 }
}
```

Now you can put this code to use. In Chapter 7, you used a table called newsletter to study the XML handling actions. In this example, you use the command line tool to input some rows into the table. Here is the XSQL that will exist on the Web server side; the filename is `insert-to-newsletter-plain.xsql`:

```
<?xml version="1.0"?>
<page connection="momnpup" xmlns:xsql="urn:oracle-xsql">
 <xsql:insert-request table="newsletter"/>
</page>
```

As discussed in Chapter 7, the `xsql:insert-request` action assumes that there is an XML document in the canonical `rowset` schema contained in the HTTP request. Our `SimpleServicesApp` will load a file and embed the XML in the request. Here is what the file looks like, which we'll call `newsletter.xml`:

```
<?xml version = '1.0'?>
<ROWSET>
 <ROW num="1">
  <NAME>test name2</NAME>
  <EMAIL>test1@momnpup.com</EMAIL>
 </ROW>
 <ROW num="2">
  <NAME>test name2</NAME>
  <EMAIL>test2@momnpup.com</EMAIL>
 </ROW>
</ROWSET>
```

You invoke the `SimpleServicesApp` as follows:

```
prompt> java SimpleServicesApp http://localhost/xsql/momnpup/insert-
request.xsql newsletter.xml
```

When the request arrives at the HTTP server, it looks like this:

```
POST /xsql/momnpup/insert-request.xsql HTTP/1.1
Content-Type: text/xml
User-Agent: Java1.3.1_02
Host: localhost
Accept: text/html, image/gif, image/jpeg, *; q=.2, */*; q=.2
Connection: keep-alive
```

```
Content-length: 226

<?xml version = '1.0'?>
<ROWSET>
 <ROW num="1">
  <NAME>test name2</NAME>
  <EMAIL>test1@momnpup.com</EMAIL>
 </ROW>
 <ROW num="2">
  <NAME>test name2</NAME>
  <EMAIL>test2@momnpup.com</EMAIL>
 </ROW>
</ROWSET>
```

There are two differences between this and a standard post. First, the `Content -Type` is set to `text/xml`. The second difference is more obvious. Instead of having a list of name-value pairs in the body of the request, you have the XML document contained in `newsletter.xml`.

XSQL processes the data into the database and then returns the result. In this case, the result looks like this:

```
Opening http://localhost/xsql/momnpup/insert-request.xsql
<?xml version = '1.0'?>
<page>
<xsql-status action="xsql:insert-request" rows="2"/>
</page>
```

The result isn't transformed, so you get a plain `xsql-status` message. Likewise, you had to have your input in the plain-vanilla canonical format as well. If you are forced to deal with the XML like this, your Web services wouldn't be very flexible. As with the application development discussed in Chapter 14, the secret lies with XSLT.

The remaining sections focus on how you can use XSLT to create truly independent Web services.

XML-to-XML Transformations

In most examples given in earlier chapters, the target of the transformation is HTML. The HTTP client makes a request and the XSQL application transforms XML to HTML by using XSLT. In this section, you'll see how to transform into XML, which is required by most Web services consumers. Your stylesheet starts with XML in the canonical Oracle format and then transforms that into another XML document. Consequently, the Web services consumer takes the outputted XML document. This discussion looks at the specifics on how to perform XML transformations.

The XSLT stylesheet is referenced in the XSQL page exactly as it is in other cases. The key syntax difference is to use the `xsl:output` element so that XML is sent to the consumer.

```
<xsl:output method="xml"/>
```

This should be an immediate child of the root element of your stylesheet. Depending on the requirements of your Web services consumer, you may also need to use some of the other attributes of the `xsl:output` element. The most commonly used are `encoding`, `doctype-public`, and `doctype-system`. All of these are covered in Chapter 14, so here we'll just look at them in terms of how they apply to Web services.

The `encoding` attribute controls what character encoding the XSLT processor will use when it sends the output to the Web services consumer. If your Web services consumer expects a particular character encoding, then you'll need to set it in the `xsl:output` element. Otherwise, you may encounter some very difficult-to-solve errors.

The `doctype-public` and `doctype-system` attributes concern DTDs. You haven't seen DTDs actually used yet because Web browsers don't need them. But in Web services, you will usually have some kind of schema definition. The consumer may just assume that it always receives valid XML, but more likely it wants to have the schema referenced in the document. The `doctype-public` and `doctype-system` attributes take care of this when you use the DTD schema language. If you need to have a DTD in your document that looks like the following,

```
<!DOCTYPE mydef PUBLIC "-//SOME_DEF//DTD MYDEF 1.1//EN"

     "http://www.momnpup/DTD/my_def.xml">
```

you can create it by using the following `xsl:output element`:

```
<xsl:output method="xml"
      doctype-public="-//SOME_DEF//DTD MYDEF 1.1//EN"
      doctype-system=" http://momnpup.com/DTD/my_def.xml">
```

If you use an XML-based schema language, such as W3C's XML Schema, you can set the schema as you would any other XML data. In the case of XML Schema, you would include only the following as static text in your stylesheet:

```
<root
  xmlns="http://momnpup/ns/my_namespace"
  xmlns:xsi="http://www.w3.org/2001/XMLSchema-instance"
  xsi:schemaLocation="http://momnpup.com/xsd file:my_def.xsd">
```

From here, your stylesheet transformations will be just like the transformations that you've been doing all along. Instead of conforming to HTML, you conform to the rules of the Web consumer's expected schema. This usually means that you make a lot of use of the `xsl:element` and `xsl:attribute` elements.You'll start with the simple XSQL tricks; then you'll look at the XSLT techniques. For this example, imagine that the Web services consumer expects a document like the following when it requests a list of products:

```
<PRODUCTS>
   <PRODUCT>
```

```
      <PRODUCT_ID>3</PRODUCT_ID>
      <PRODUCT_NAME>Step Ladder</PRODUCT_NAME>
      <PRODUCT_PRICE>30.00</PRODUCT_PRICE>
   </PRODUCT>
   <PRODUCT>
      <PRODUCT_ID>4</PRODUCT_ID>
      <PRODUCT_NAME>Coffee Mug</PRODUCT_NAME>
      <PRODUCT_PRICE>20.00</PRODUCT_PRICE>
   </PRODUCT>
</PRODUCTS>
```

Here's the query that gets the data:

```
SELECT id,
       name,
       price
    FROM product
```

Unfortunately, this doesn't solve the problem, because the consumer expects `product_id`, `product_name`, and `product_price` elements. This can be easily addressed just by aliasing the column names in SQL so that you get the following XSQL page:

```
<xsql:query connection="momnpup"
    xmlns:xsql="urn:oracle-xsql">
  SELECT id AS product_id,
         name AS product_name,
         price AS product_price
    FROM product
</xsql:query>
```

This gets you closer—you end up with the following output:

```
<ROWSET>
- <ROW num="1">
    <PRODUCT_ID>3</PRODUCT_ID>
    <PRODUCT_NAME>Step Ladder</PRODUCT_NAME>
    <PRODUCT_PRICE>30.00</PRODUCT_PRICE>
  </ROW>
- <ROW num="2">
    <PRODUCT_ID>4</PRODUCT_ID>
    <PRODUCT_NAME>Coffee Mug </PRODUCT_NAME>
    <PRODUCT_PRICE>20.00</PRODUCT_PRICE>
  </ROW>
```

Now you can use the `rowset-element` and `row-element` attributes in your XSQL to rename the `rowset` and `row` elements:

```
<xsql:query connection="momnpup"
    xmlns:xsql="urn:oracle-xsql"
```

```
     rowset-element="PRODUCTS"
     row-element="PRODUCT">
    SELECT id AS product_id,
           name AS product_name,
           price AS product_price
     FROM product
</xsql:query>
```

This gives the consumer the following output, which is almost perfect:

```
<PRODUCTS>
- <PRODUCT num="1">
  <PRODUCT_ID>3</PRODUCT_ID>
  <PRODUCT_NAME>Step Ladder</PRODUCT_NAME>
  <PRODUCT_PRICE>30.00</PRODUCT_PRICE>
  </PRODUCT>
- <PRODUCT num="2">
  <PRODUCT_ID>4</PRODUCT_ID>
  <PRODUCT_NAME>Coffee Mug</PRODUCT_NAME>
  <PRODUCT_PRICE>20.00</PRODUCT_PRICE>
  </PRODUCT>
```

There is only one problem with our output. Each product has an attribute num, but the schema requires that it be count. This can be fixed by setting the id-attribute in the xsql:query as follows:

```
<xsql:query connection="momnpup"
     xmlns:xsql="urn:oracle-xsql"
     rowset-element="PRODUCTS"
     row-element="PRODUCT"
     id-attribute="count">
    SELECT id AS product_id,
           name AS product_name,
           price AS product_price
     FROM product
</xsql:query>
```

For this simple example, the output is valid according to the schema, and you didn't need XSLT at all. The next example requires XSLT. You need to output data that looks like this:

```
<CATEGORY_LIST>
 <CATEGORY id="7">
  <NAME>Bathroom</NAME>
  <DESCRIPTION>Keep clean and healthy with these products</DESCRIPTION>

  <PRODUCT id="10">
   <NAME>Band-aids</NAME>
   <PRICE>5.31</PRICE>
  </PRODUCT>
```

```
  <PRODUCT id="3">
   <NAME>Tweezers</NAME>
   <PRICE>3.99</PRICE>
  </PRODUCT>

 </CATEGORY>

 <CATEGORY id="8">

  <NAME>Outdoor Clothing -- Men</NAME>
  <DESCRIPTION>Functional wear for the outdoorsmen</DESCRIPTION>

  <PRODUCT id="11">
   <NAME>Jeans</NAME>
   <PRICE>25.99</PRICE>
  </PRODUCT>

 </CATEGORY>
```

This query is immediately out of scope of the XSQL tricks, because the `id` is the product `id`, not the `row` number. Also, it has a tree format that isn't reproducible with XSQL. You can get all of the data with a single query by using cursors, but XSQL will put a `"_ROW"` suffix at the end of the cursor field. Here's the XSQL page that will get the data:

```
<?xml version="1.0" encoding="UTF-8"?>
<xsql:query connection="momnpup"
    xmlns:xsql="urn:oracle-xsql"
    rowset-element="PRODUCT_CATEGORIES"
    row-element="CATEGORY">
   SELECT pc.id, pc.name,pc.description,
  CURSOR(SELECT p.id,p.name,p.price
           FROM product p,prod_cat_joiner pcj
           WHERE p.id=pcj.product_id
                  AND
                 pc.id=pcj.product_cat_id) AS products
  FROM product_category pc
  ORDER BY pc.name
</xsql:query>
```

The output of this XSQL is as follows:

```
<PRODUCT_CATEGORIES>
 <CATEGORY num="1">
  <ID>7</ID>
  <NAME>Bathroom</NAME>
  <DESCRIPTION>Keep clean and healthy with these products</DESCRIPTION>
  <PRODUCTS>
  <PRODUCTS_ROW num="1">
    <ID>10</ID>
    <NAME>Band-aids</NAME>
```

```
      <PRICE>5.31</PRICE>
      </PRODUCTS_ROW>
    </PRODUCTS>
  </CATEGORY>
</PRODUCT_CATEGORIES>
```

The XSLT faces a couple of challenges. You have to rename several of the element names, and you have to add the id attribute for the CATEGORY and PRODUCT elements. It would be possible to create a highly verbose stylesheet that has a template for every single element. For this example, the stylesheet is much more concise. It assumes that all the elements are in the correct order, and it makes use of the xsl:element, xsl:attribute, and xsl:copy-of to translate the structure. The header information and the top-level template is as follows:

```
<?xml version = '1.0'?>
<xsl:stylesheet xmlns:xsl="http://www.w3.org/1999/XSL/Transform"
version="1.0">
<xsl:output method="xml"/>

<xsl:template match="/PRODUCT_CATEGORIES">
 <CATEGORY_LIST>
   <xsl:apply-templates select="CATEGORY"/>
 </CATEGORY_LIST>
</xsl:template>
```

The top-level template makes CATEGORY_LIST the root and then defers to the CATEGORY template to do the rest of the work. Of course, you could change the rowset-element to CATEGORY_LIST in the XSQL page. However, the preceding example illustrates an important point—if the element name is essentially static, you can always just name it in the template like this. If you don't mind verbosity, you can just structure the entire document with static text like this. But for this example, you can use a cleaner approach, as follows:

```
<xsl:template match="CATEGORY">
 <xsl:element name="CATEGORY">
  <xsl:attribute name="id"><xsl:value-of select="ID"/></xsl:attribute>
  <xsl:copy-of select="*[name()!='ID' and name()!='PRODUCTS']"/>
  <xsl:apply-templates select="PRODUCTS/PRODUCTS_ROW"/>
 </xsl:element>
</xsl:template>
```

The preceding template overcomes two challenges. First, it sets the id element as an attribute of the category element. Incidentally, you can use the id-attribute and id-attribute-column attributes of xsql:query to accomplish the same thing. You would set id-attribute to "id" and set id-attribute-column to "ID". Regardless, sooner or later you will probably have to use the preceding template. If you need to set more than one attribute, you'll have to use this template.

Second, it copies all the values of the children into the output, except for PRODUCTS and ID. You can use the xsl:copy-of element if the element name in the XSQL datagram is the same as the one desired and if you want to keep all the attributes (if there are any) and child nodes. In our case, the name in the datagram is `right`. This name is more than coincidental. You can control the names of elements in the result set by aliasing them to what you want. You can also control whether the element has child nodes. When you work at this level of a datagram, you will not have child nodes unless you reference a cursor, collection, or object. The `PRODUCTS` element does represent a cursor, so it is handled in the following template:

```
 <xsl:template match="PRODUCTS/PRODUCTS_ROW">
  <xsl:element name="PRODUCT">
   <xsl:attribute name="id"><xsl:value-of select="ID"/></xsl:attribute>
   <xsl:copy-of select="*[name()!='ID']"/>
  </xsl:element>
 </xsl:template>
</xsl:stylesheet>
```

This template handles the problem with the `PRODUCTS` and `PRODUCTS_ROW` elements. You don't need them, though you do want their children. This template creates a new element for each of the children and effectively skips two levels in the XSQL datagram. As before, an attribute is set by using a child value; the other elements are then copied. The `id` element isn't needed, so it is ignored in the `xsl:copy-of` element. This template is the last in the stylesheet, so the `closing` tag is included in the code snippet.

The two examples show a few ways how you can easily convert the XML datagram to the correct output. You can use the XSQL tricks described here to get the output close to if not entirely correct, and then you can greatly simplify your XSLT stylesheets by making use of `xsl:element`, `xsl:attribute`, and `xsl:copy-of`.

XML Handling Actions

The previous discussion showed how to create the XML that is sent to a Web services consumer. Just as important as that is dealing with the XML that is sent to XSQL as part of a Web services consumer's request. XSQL has three actions that handle the posted XML: `insert-request`, `update-request`, and `delete-request`. These actions are covered in detail in Chapters 5 and 7.

For each of these actions, you can specify a single stylesheet used to interpret the posted XML. The XML must be transformed into the canonical `row` format as discussed before. All of the XML handling actions use the same posted XML, but each can transform it with different stylesheets. This means that a single posted XML document can be used by multiple XML handling actions. Each action can use only the data that it needs out of the posted document.

The real work is transforming the data with XSLT as described in this chapter. The same XSLT techniques can apply but aren't necessarily as available. When you push the data into the database, you can't count on aliasing. The element names must be the same as they are in the table. Thus, it is more likely that you will need a verbose stylesheet that specifically changes each element's name and that the `xsl:copy-of` technique shown in this chapter won't be as useful.

Moving On

In this chapter you have learned about how Web services can work with XSQL. This and the previous chapter showed you that XSQL can be very useful beyond traditional Web pages. From the next chapter on, you'll start learning how to extend the XSQL framework with Java. The next chapter covers how to use XSQL from inside your applications. In Chapter 18, you'll see how to write your own custom action handlers and serializers.

CHAPTER

17

XSQL Beyond Web Browsing

So far, you've used XSQL as a framework. You encapsulate SQL and PL/SQL in an XSQL file, reference an XSLT stylesheet, and produce a result. In the next chapter, you'll see how to extend the framework by writing your own custom action handlers. This chapter looks at a completely different approach—how to use XSQL inside your programs.

Oracle provides a Java API for XSQL. You can instantiate an `XSQLPageRequest` object and then run it against the database. It will return the result as XML. At that point, you can transform it by using a stylesheet. This gives you some advantages. For example, you can keep the SQL outside of your programming logic. If you need to change the SQL, you can do so in an external file instead of having to recompile code. Now you have an XML document that can be used by other parts of your application. Instead of having to process a result set and create your own XML document, this is all done automatically. Also, you can transform the document programmatically by using a stylesheet.

This chapter looks at how to use XSQL programmatically, starting with a sample program. You will get an idea of what you can do with the APIs. Then the `XSQLPageRequest` class and `XSLTPageProcessor` class are studied in detail. The last two discussions look at the DOM and SAX APIs provided by Oracle, which give you two ways of processing XML documents.

A Sample Program

The sample program presented here runs from the command line. It loads an XSQL file, processes it against the database, outputs the XSQL datagram to the console, and transforms the datagram with a supplied stylesheet and outputs that as well. As with the example code for stylesheets given in the previous chapter, this sample program is very utilitarian. It shows you how to use some of the major functionality entry points. It should also serve as a good foundation for the other discussions in this chapter.

The usage of the program is as follows:

```
Usage: CommandLineExample XSQLPageURL [StylesheetURL] [Param=Val] ...
```

The program itself consists of two methods: the main method and a parameter setting method. The start of the class and the parameter setting method is as follows:

```
import oracle.xml.xsql.XSQLRequest;
import oracle.xml.parser.v2.XMLPrintDriver;
import oracle.xml.parser.v2.XMLDocument;
import oracle.xml.parser.v2.XMLDocumentFragment;
import oracle.xml.xsql.XSQLStylesheetProcessor;
import oracle.xml.parser.v2.XSLProcessor;
import oracle.xml.parser.v2.XSLStylesheet;
import oracle.xml.parser.v2.DOMParser;
import oracle.xml.parser.v2.XMLNode;
import oracle.xml.jaxp.JXDocumentBuilderFactory;


import org.w3c.dom.traversal.NodeIterator;
import org.w3c.dom.traversal.NodeFilter;
import org.w3c.dom.Document;

import java.util.Hashtable;
import java.io.PrintWriter;
import java.net.URL;
import java.net.MalformedURLException;

import javax.xml.parsers.DocumentBuilderFactory;
import javax.xml.parsers.DocumentBuilder;

import org.apache.xerces.jaxp.DocumentBuilderFactoryImpl;


   public class CommandLineExample {


    static URL stylesheetURL=null;
```

```
static Hashtable params=new Hashtable();
static String xsqlPageStr="";

private static boolean setParams(String[] args) {

 if (args.length==0) {
  System.out.println("Usage: CommandLineExample XSQLPageURL
[StylesheetURL] [Param=Val] ...");
  return false;
 }

 xsqlPageStr=args[0];

 int paramPos=1;

 if (args.length>1) {
  String secondParam=args[1];
  if (args[1].indexOf("=")==-1) {
    try {
     stylesheetURL=new URL(secondParam);
    } catch (MalformedURLException e) {
     System.out.println("Stylesheet argument is malformed");
    }
    paramPos++;
   }

 while (paramPos<args.length) {
  String paramStr=args[paramPos];
  int eqPos=paramStr.indexOf("=");
  String key=paramStr.substring(0,eqPos);
  String val=paramStr.substring(eqPos+1,paramStr.length());
  params.put(key,val);
 }
 return true;
}
```

This method gathers the parameters of the command line and readies them for processing by the main method. The real action is in the main method itself. Here, the XSQL page is read in and instantiated as an `XMLDocument`. The document is then used to create an `XSQLPageRequest` object, which is then processed. An XML document is returned and printed. Then a stylesheet, if one has been provided, is applied, and the result of the transformation is printed to the output.

```
public static void main( String[] args) throws Exception {
       // Set the parameters
       if (!setParams(args)) {
        return;
```

```
}

DOMParser parser=new DOMParser();
parser.parse(new URL(xsqlPageStr));
XMLDocument xDoc=parser.getDocument();
```

This code parses the document using the JAXP method. You get a document builder factory and then parse the results of the URL. As with the command line utility, you have to be careful when you use an HTTP URL. If the XSQL page at that URL references a stylesheet and the XSQL servlet is configured, you will get the transformed result. This will probably be HTML, which won't parse as an XML document at all. Even if it happens to be XML, it won't be what you want. If you use a `file://` URL, you will avoid this problem entirely.

The next few lines of code instantiate an `XSQLRequest` object, execute it, and prints the results to the console. The XML document that you instantiated in the previous line is passed to the `XSQLRequest` object along with the original URL. The URL is passed so that any URLs contained in the document can be properly resolved. You can also instantiate the `XSQLRequest` object based solely on the URL. The example does it this way so that you can see how to create an XML document from a file. If you want, you could modify the XSQL source itself before continuing with the `XSQLRequest` instantiation.

```
XSQLRequest req=new XSQLRequest(xDoc,new URL(xsqlPageStr));
XMLDocument xsqlDoc=(XMLDocument)req.processToXML(params);
System.out.println("++++++ XML Output +++++++++");
XMLPrintDriver pDriver=new XMLPrintDriver(System.out);
pDriver.printDocument(xsqlDoc);
```

At this point in the program, the resulting XML datagram has been printed to the screen. There is a lot more you can do with it if you like. You can take the `xsqlDoc` object and work with it through the Oracle XML DOM APIs. You can add, remove, and modify nodes, and you can even merge nodes with other documents. You'll see some of this functionality in the next chapter.

The last step for the code is to apply a stylesheet if one has been specified. This functionality is very simple and is more or less completely demonstrated in the following example. This code just executes the transformation, while the real code lies in the stylesheet itself. Here, the `XSLProcessor` is instantiated. Then a stylesheet object is created and is passed to the `processXSL` method along with the XSQL datagram and the output stream. In this case, the output stream is the console. Of course, you could also pipe the results over the network or in to a string object.

```
if (stylesheetURL!=null) {
 System.out.println("+++ XSLT Transformation +++");
 XSLProcessor xslProc=new XSLProcessor();
```

```
        xslProc.setBaseURL(stylesheetURL);
        XSLStylesheet
stylesheet=xslProc.newXSLStylesheet(stylesheetURL);
        xslProc.processXSL(stylesheet,xsqlDoc,System.out);

      }
    }
  }
```

This example shows you how the pieces can fit together in a simple application. The next section delves deeper into the XSQL classes used programmatically. You will use these same classes when, in Chapters 18 and 19, you develop custom action handlers and serializers.

Guide to the XSQL Classes

In the previous code, you used the `XSQLRequest` class to create the request and execute the page. This section acts as a guide for the various XSQL pages. You'll be making more use of these classes in the next chapter as you write action handlers. This section acts as a guide to the `XSQLRequest` class and the other classes in the oracle.xml.xsql package. You'll find the complete javadoc for all of the classes in the XSQL distribution.

When using XSQL programmatically, you'll have to use the `XSQLResult` class. In the previous example, you constructed it with an `XMLDocument`. `XMLDocument` objects are in-memory XML documents. You'll learn more about them later in this section. For now, it's important to note that you can use `XMLDocument` to create XML documents in your applications. This means that you can programmatically create XSQL pages—you don't have to define the XSQL in a file. You'll see an example of this later in this chapter.

You don't have to create an `XMLDocument` object to use the `XSQLResult` object. You can also construct an object from a URL. Although you won't have any programmatic control of the XSQL, you won't have to hassle with parsing the file first. Here's how you would use the `XSQLResult` class by just passing it a URL:

```
XSQLRequest req=new XSQLRequest(new URL(xsqlPageStr));
XMLDocument xsqlDoc=(XMLDocument)req.processToXML();
```

In the preceding example, you processed the XSQL request and got an `XMLDocument` object in return. This is convenient if you wish to do further processing on the result. You can use the DOM APIs that you'll learn about later. But again, you have flexibility in how to deal with the results. If you don't need to process the XML, you can have the `XSQLRequest` class write out the results directly to a stream. The following statement writes the results directly to the console when you execute from the command line:

```
req.process(System.out,System.err);
```

Almost every XSQL page that you've developed so far in the book has parameters. You need a way to pass parameters to the XSQL page that you wish to process. There are two ways to do this. First, both the `processToXml()` and `process()` methods allow you to pass a dictionary object. The keys and values inside the dictionary object are used as the parameter and parameter values inside the XSQL page. You used this method, with the dictionary subclass `Hashtable`, in the earlier example. In its simplest form, it looks like this:

```
Hashtable table=new Hashtable();
table.put("param1","value1");
table.put("param2","value2");
```

Then, you pass the parameters to either the `process()` or the `processToXML()` method:

```
req.process(table,System.out,System.err);
XMLDocument xDoc=req.processToXML(table);
```

The second way to pass parameters is as part of an `XSQLPageRequest` object. Each of the constructors described here can optionally take an `XSQLPageRequest` object as a parameter. The `XSQLPageRequest` has a variety of methods that are especially helpful when you write action handlers. In the next section, you'll get a sampling of how to use the `XSQLPageRequest` when you see how to use XSQL from servlets. If you wish to use the `XSQLPageRequest` in a nonservlet application, you'll need to implement the `XSQLPageRequest` interface. The easiest way to do that is by subclassing `XSQLPageRequestImpl`.

Using XSQL from Within Servlets

When you use XSQL in the simple manner, the XSQL servlet processes the URL and writes the output. But what if you want to use the capabilities of XSQL inside your own servlet? Obviously, you could do that with the method described earlier. But then you have to gather all of the parameters from the servlet and create a `Hashtable` yourself, as well as handle the XSLT transformation. There is an easier way. You create an `XSQLServletRequest` object, which implements the `XSQLPageRequest` interface, and pass that to the `XSQLRequest` constructor. Here is an example:

```
public class XSQLProgServlet extends HttpServlet {
  public void service(HttpServletRequest request,
                      HttpServletResponse response)
        throws IOException, ServletException
    {
```

```
        PrintWriter out = response.getWriter();
        ServletContext context=getServletConfig().getServletContext();
        String xsqlPageStr="http://localhost/xsql/momnpup/emp-
servlet.xsql.txt";
        XSQLServletPageRequest pageReq=new XSQLServletPageRequest(request,
response,
context);
        response.setContentType("text/html");
        XSQLRequest req=new XSQLRequest(xsqlPageStr,pageReq);
        XMLDocument xsqlDoc=(XMLDocument)req.processToXML();
        //Do stuff with the results
        XMLPrintDriver pDriver=new XMLPrintDriver(out);
        pDriver.printDocument(xsqlDoc);
       }
    }
```

As with the command line example, you can perform a transformation on the results. Just use the `XSLStylesheet` and `XSLProcessor` classes. You can also manipulate the data in any other manner that you like.

XML Parsing: DOM versus SAX

There are two primary models of XML parsing available today: DOM and SAX. The DOM model is based on a W3C standard and is object-based, while SAX is event-based. You used DOM in the previous examples. An XML document was created as a tree of objects. You can traverse and manipulate that tree of objects inside your code. When you finish manipulating the objects, you can save them, if you'd like, or perhaps write the result out to the network.

SAX works differently. Although DOM models consume a lot of memory, the SAX model is very lightweight. You register handlers that respond to events. The events are raised while the document is being processed. For instance, if you register a handler for elements with the name `foo`, the SAX parser will call your handler each time an element named `foo` is encountered. It is then up to you to decide what should be done.

XSQL doesn't provide a direct interface to SAX. However, you can use the SAX APIs in conjunction with streams. Just use `XSQLResult.process()` to write to a stream; then have your SAX parser consume that stream.

Oracle DOM API

Oracle provides an implementation of DOM. It is completely compatible with W3C DOM. It offers some advantages beyond DOM, including XPath integration and a simple way to import nodes from one document to another. If you have other code that uses DOM, any coding you do in Oracle DOM should be compatible. For instance, if a method expects a DOM object such as Node, you can always pass it an instance of Oracle's implementation, XMLNode. Thus, you can take advantage of the Oracle-provided extensions to DOM while your system still remains fully compatible with DOM. This section looks first at the DOM model and then how Oracle extends it.

DOM is a set of Java interfaces that extend one another. Since Java is a single inheritance language, interfaces are often used to specify a standard's implementation. Developers have a lot of freedom in how they design their code for implementing the DOM standard. Figure 17.1 describes the layout of the core classes of DOM.

The Oracle DOM API is a set of classes. There is a class that implements each of the interfaces in DOM. For instance, XMLDocument implements the document interface. Since the document interface extends the node interface, XMLDocument also implements the node interface. All the Oracle classes are prefixed with XML and live in the oracle.xml.parser.v2 package.

When using the Oracle DOM API, you can cast between the DOM type and its Oracle equivalent. The reverse is also true. In addition, you can also cast to any of the superclasses of the DOM equivalent, as illustrated by the following code:

```
Document w3cDoc=req.processToXML();
XMLDocument oraDoc=(XMLDocument)w3cDoc;
Document w3cDoc2=oraDoc;

Element w3cElem=w3cDoc.getDocumentElement();
XMLElement oraElem=(XMLElement)w3cElem;
XMLNode n=(XMLNode)w3cDoc.getDocumentElement();
```

One of the most useful aspects of the Oracle DOM is the integration with XPath. The XMLNode class has two sets of methods that will take XPath expressions as arguments—selectNodes() and valueOf(). The selectNodes methods return lists of nodes, while valueOf retrieves text values. This greatly simplifies the process of navigating a DOM tree.

There are a variety of other methods in the Oracle DOM API that are worth exploring. For instance, you can also apply a stylesheet to just a particular node by using the transformNode() method. This has a variety of uses. Also, you can import a node from one document in to another with just one method call—importNode() in XMLDocument.

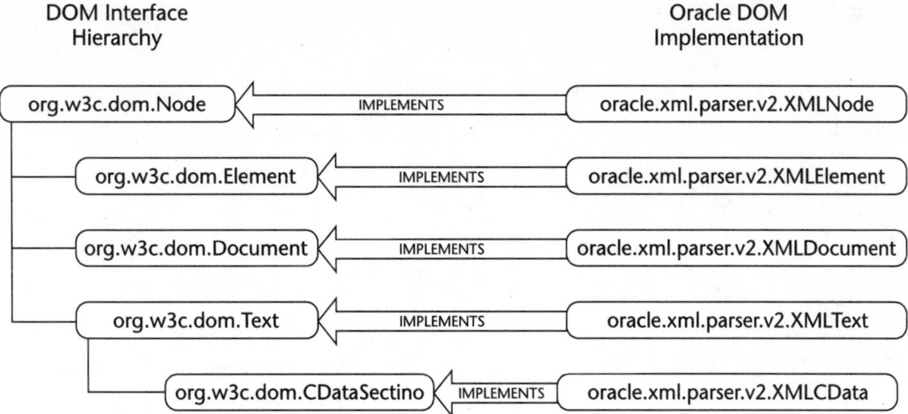

Figure 17.1 DOM interfaces.

Moving On

You learned in this chapter how to embed XSQL into your own applications. Even if you never actually embed XSQL in this manner, you probably have gained a lot of insight in how XSQL works. In general, you can find XSQL very useful in conjunction with your application code. You can configure the SQL and the presentation very easily, because the XSQL pages and the XSLT stylesheets are outside of your code. In the following chapters, you'll see how to extend XSQL with action handlers and serializers. You can use these in conjunction with XSQL that is invoked programmatically.

CHAPTER

18

Custom Action Handlers

The time has finally come! You've been using the built-in action handlers throughout the book; now it is time to make your own. As you've learned, custom action handlers are a valuable piece of the XSQL puzzle. You use them to extend the base functionality of XSQL in almost any direction that you wish.

The chapter starts with a simple action handler. You start with action handlers and get your environment set up. Next, the APIs that you use for developing action handlers are examined. You'll learn what functionality is available and how to use it. Then you'll see how your action handlers can interact with the database. Examples are given of how to use built-in actions such as `xsql:query`. The chapter ends by looking at parameters and input. You'll see how to receive and set parameters, handle input from the XSQL page, and pass objects to other action handlers.

Getting Started

Action handlers are simple to write once you understand the subtleties of their position in the XSQL architecture. In this section, you get your feet wet. The first step is to get a simple action handler working. Then you'll see how to add XML to the datagram. These two discussions should give you a good, basic understanding of how action handlers work. The next discussion compares action handler development to servlet development. They are both similar in a lot of ways yet have some important differences. Hopefully this discussion will solidify your understanding of the basic art and science of action handler development. The last section discusses how to debug action handlers.

Hello, Action Handler!

On any journey, there is a first step. The first step here is to create a working action handler. The goal of the action handler is simple: It is to add an empty element named `hello` to the datagram. As you read this discussion, you'll see how to write the code, deploy the class, and invoke the action handler.

The best place to start is on familiar ground. The following is the XSQL page that will invoke the action handler. When the XSQL page processor sees the `xsql:action` action, it loads the class specified by the handler attribute.

```
<?xml version="1.0" encoding="UTF-8"?>
<page xmlns:xsql="urn:oracle-xsql">
 <xsql:action handler="HelloActionHandler"/>
</page>
```

The name must be the fully qualified class name. For these simple examples, the classes aren't in a package. If your classes are in packages, you will need to specify the fully qualified name as follows:

```
<?xml version="1.0" encoding="UTF-8"?>
<page xmlns:xsql="urn:oracle-xsql">
 <xsql:action handler="org.ibiblio.mdthomas.HelloActionHandler"/>
</page>
```

In this particular example, there are no parameters, and the `xsql:action` element has no children. This particular action handler doesn't need them. If there were any present, they would be ignored. But the `xsql:action` element can have parameters and values. You'll see later in this chapter how to manipulate them from inside the action handler.

Before moving on to the action handler code itself, it's worth noting that the `xsql:action` element doesn't have to be a child element. It can be a top-level element just as any of the other actions can, as shown in the following code. You may have also noticed that there is no database connection specified. For the simple examples given in this chapter, you won't need a database connection. The "Database Interaction" section talks about connecting to the database from an action handler.

```
<?xml version="1.0" encoding="UTF-8"?>
 <xsql:action handler="org.ibiblio.mdthomas.HelloActionHandler"
            xmlns:xsql="urn:oracle-xsql"/>
```

Now it's time to write some Java code. The following is the `HelloActionHandler` class. A Java class is an action handler if it implements the `XSQLActionHandler` interface.

```
import org.w3c.dom.Node;
import oracle.xml.xsql.XSQLActionHandlerImpl;

public class HelloActionHandler extends XSQLActionHandlerImpl {

 public void handleAction(Node result) {
  addResultElement(result,"hello","hello!!");
 }
}
```

This code subclasses the `XSQLActionHandlerImpl` class, which implements the interface. This is the typical way to write action handlers, because the `XSQLAction-HandlerImpl` class gives you a lot of great methods to use. You use one of them in this example—the `addResultElement`. It takes care of all the details of creating an element and appending it to the result node.

You'll learn all the specifics about the `XSQLActionHandler` interface and `XSQLActionHandlerImpl` class in a few pages. The next step is to compile the class and deploy it. You compile the class just as you would any Java class. In this case, you need to make sure that all the Oracle jars are on your class path. These should be the same jars that your servlet engine uses; otherwise, you risk compiling code that won't run. The easiest way to set this up is to add to the classpath all the jars that are specified in the installation instructions.

With the classpath configured, you should be able to compile the action handler. Now you need to deploy the class. The class needs to live on the classpath of your servlet engine. The classpath can vary from servlet engine to servlet engine. If you want to package the classes in a jar or have the action handler classes in their own directory, you can alter the classpath for the servlet engine to point to the new jars and directories. If you used the default Apache/JServ install that comes with the Oracle database, the easiest thing to do is to put the class files in the `oracle/classes` directory. It should already be on the classpath, so you don't have to reconfigure anything. If you do wish to add to the classpath, you can do that on the default install by modifying the jserv.properties file. You can find it by going to the home directory for Oracle and then proceeding to `apache/jserv/conf`.

With the class compiled, you should be ready to go. Your final step is to access the code. First, you'll need to restart the servlet engine. With the default install, the easiest way to do this is to restart the Apache Web server. Then, you just go to the URL of the `hello.xsql` page. You should see the result seen in Figure 18.1.

As you modify the code, you will probably need to restart your servlet engine each time. For the default install, you will need to restart. Now that you have the simplest action handler possible working, you can move on to more advanced functionality.

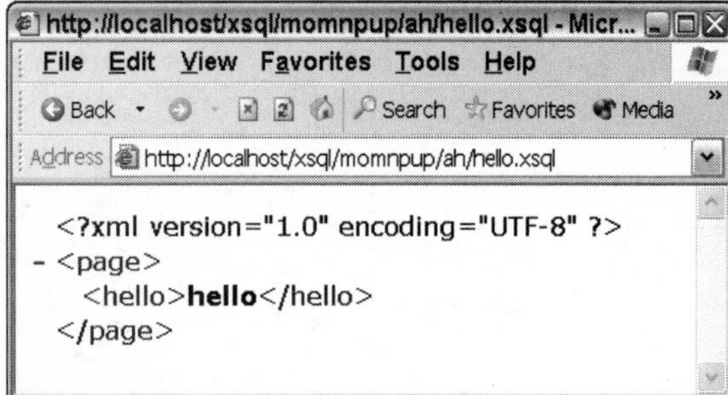

Figure 18.1 Your first action handler.

Adding XML to the Datagram

In the previous example, you added a single XML element to the datagram in place of the action handler. Adding data to the datagram is usually one goal of any custom action handler. This section looks at the specifics of adding data to the datagram. Some knowledge of the Oracle DOM classes, covered in detail in Chapter 17, is needed.

The simplest way to add an element to the datagram is by using the `addResultElement` method of the `XSQLActionHandlerImpl` class. This is what you used in the previous example. It creates an element that has the name of the first second argument and the value of the third argument, and it attaches the element as a child to the node argument. It's a great convenience method, but it isn't powerful enough to create complex element trees. There is no way to create attributes or children.

To create elements, you use the DOM APIs. The following example shows you how to create the same output as before, except that this time you have an attribute in the element:

```
import oracle.xml.xsql.XSQLActionHandlerImpl;
import oracle.xml.parser.v2.XMLDocument;
import oracle.xml.parser.v2.XMLElement;
import oracle.xml.parser.v2.XMLText;
import org.w3c.dom.Node;

public class ComplexHelloActionHandler extends XSQLActionHandlerImpl {

 public void handleAction(Node result) {

  XMLDocument doc=(XMLDocument)result.getOwnerDocument();
  XMLElement elem=(XMLElement)doc.createElement("hello");

  elem.setAttribute("attr1","val1");

  XMLText tNode=(XMLText)doc.createTextNode("hello!");
```

```
    elem.appendChild(tNode);
    result.appendChild(elem);

  }
}
```

In this example, the Oracle DOM classes are used. This is consistent with the discussion in the last chapter. You got some more functionality by using the Oracle classes, and can always interoperate with the base DOM interfaces.

The code itself is fairly straightforward. The node result, which is passed to the `handleAction` method, is the parent of the `xsql:action` element that invokes this action handler. If you want to provide XML back to the datagram, you will need to append it to the result node. To create elements and other node types, you will need to use the appropriate create method of the owner document. You can get a handle to the owner document through the `getOwnerDocument()` method of the node class.

The next example expands on the following one. This time, you create the same element as the preceding one and then add a couple of child elements. Since the first element has an attribute, you will need to create it from scratch. The second one doesn't have an attribute, so you can use the `addResultElement()` convenience method.

```
public void handleAction(Node result) {

   XMLDocument doc=(XMLDocument)result.getOwnerDocument();
   XMLElement elem=(XMLElement)doc.createElement("hello");
   result.appendChild(elem);

   elem.setAttribute("attr1","val1");
   XMLText tNode=(XMLText)doc.createTextNode("hello!");
   elem.appendChild(tNode);


   XMLElement child1=(XMLElement)doc.createElement("child");
   elem.appendChild(child1);

   child1.setAttribute("attr2","val2");
   tNode=(XMLText)doc.createTextNode("A child");
   child1.appendChild(tNode);

   addResultElement(elem,"child","another child");

  }
```

You can continue in this way to create as many elements as you want. You'll probably never write an action handler that doesn't output at least one element to the datagram. A lot of the examples in the rest of the chapter show you different ways to output elements. You won't always have to do it as manually as it was done in the previous example. As you'll see, you can use the built-in action handlers to ease this process.

Before moving on, it's important to note some practices that should be avoided. First, you'll notice that you can access the entire datagram. This means that you could append elements anywhere you like. The following code, for instance, appends an element off the document root:

```
public void handleAction(Node result) {

 XMLDocument doc=(XMLDocument)result.getOwnerDocument();
 XMLElement docElem=(XMLElement)doc.getDocumentElement();
 addResultElement(docElem,"bad","bad text");
 }
```

This is a bad idea. Instead, you should append only to the result node that is passed to the `handleAction` method. Once you start traversing the document in this manner, you open the potential for all kinds of conflicts. You may interfere with other action handlers and can make XSLT development very hard. Going beyond the result node to read data is likewise risky. You are making assumptions about the rest of the datagram that may or may not be true. It's best to operate within the confines of the result node that is passed to you. In fact, attempts to access siblings and the parent directly through the node methods will result in null pointer exceptions.

Another no-no is appending more than one element to the result node. In the following example, you add two elements to the result node:

```
public void handleAction(Node result) {

   addResultElement(result,"bad1","text");
   addResultElement(result,"bad2","text");
}
```

This code will work. It will even produce valid XML, as long the `xsql:action` action that invokes it has a parent. But what if the `xsql:action` is the root element of your document, as with this XSQL page?

```
<?xml version="1.0" encoding="UTF-8"?>
 <xsql:action handler="BadActionHandler" xmlns:xsql="urn:oracle-xsql"/>
</xsql:action>
```

This will result in an invalid XML document. An XML document can have only one root element, but the action element creates two root elements. Even if you decide that you are willing to live with an action handler that can never be a root element, you will still make writing XSLT stylesheets difficult. It is simpler to have a single element at the top of all XML elements that your action handler adds to the datagram. Your stylesheet will have an easier time finding the elements you add if they are kept under a single root element.

Comparing Action Handler and Servlet Development

Hopefully, you have a general feel for what action handlers can do and how they can do it. To flesh out this understanding a bit, it may be helpful to compare action handler development to servlet development. The two are similar yet different. Since servlet development is a model that you probably understand pretty well, you can use your servlet experience as a touchstone.

The first thing to note is that action handlers aren't strictly dependent on servlets. Though all the action handler examples in this section will be invoked through XSQL servlet-loaded pages, you can also load pages programmatically or with the XSQL command line utility. Servlets, on the other hand, are almost always invoked in response to an HTTP request.

Most of your action handlers will be invoked as part of an HTTP request. When they are, you can access all the servlet information. You'll learn in this chapter how to access the `ServletResponse`, `ServletRequest`, and `ServletContext` classes. So an action handler used from the Web has the same level of access as a servlet. In addition, it also has access to information from the invoking XSQL page.

Where action handlers differ decidedly from servlets is on the output side. A servlet can output whatever it wants, whereas an action handler can output only XML. While a servlet has full control of writing the output, the only thing an action handler can do is append XML to the node passed to `handleAction`. An action handler doesn't have control over when the data is written or what happens with the data.

If you're an experienced servlet writer, you'll find that you're able to leverage a lot of your experience. You should also find that your action handlers are more modular than the servlet code. You can easily swap action handlers in and out of different XSQL pages. Also, you don't have to deal with a lot of the messier aspects of outputting for the Web. You just push XML out and let the stylesheet take it from there.

Action Handler APIs

Oracle provides a rich set of functionality for action handlers. You've already gotten an introduction to some aspects of functionality in the previous section. This section looks at functionality in depth. Discussed first is the `XSQLActionHandler` interface, which defines a class as an action handler. In the next discussion, you'll see all the benefits of the `XSQLActionHandlerImpl` base class. The `XSQLPageRequest` class, which was covered in the last chapter, also plays an important role. Though the earlier discussion of this class won't be repeated, you will see how to use the class to access servlet functionality. The last discussion covers some other APIs that can play important roles in your action handler development.

`XSQLActionHandler` Interface

The `XSQLActionHandler` interface defines what an action handler is. You'll get an error if you specify a class in `xsql:action` that doesn't implement this interface. As mentioned before, the `XSQLActionHandlerImpl` base class implements this interface, so you don't have to worry about specifically implementing the interface. Nevertheless, it's important for you to know exactly what is defined in this interface. The two methods are described in Table 18.1.

Table 18.1 `XSQLActionHandler` Interface Methods

METHOD	DESCRIPTION
`public void init (XSQLPageRequest env, Element e)`	Called to initialize the action handler. The method is always called previously to `handleAction` and is called each time the action handler is invoked. The `env` argument is a handle to the current `XSQLPageRequest` and `e` is the element that is invoking the action handler.
`public void handleAction (Node result)`	Handles the action. The action handler should append a result element to a result that will be outputted as part of the datagram.

In general, you should subclass `XSQLActionHandlerImpl` rather than implement the `XSQLActionHandler` interface directly. As you'll see in the next section, you get access to a lot of great functionality by subclassing `XSQLActionHandlerImpl`. However, Java is a single-inheritance language. You might have cases where you'd rather subclass another class but it is impossible to subclass both. The following example implements the `XSQLActionHandler` interface rather than subclassing `XSQLActionHandlerImpl`.

```
import oracle.xml.xsql.XSQLActionHandlerImpl;
import oracle.xml.xsql.XSQLActionHandler;
import oracle.xml.xsql.XSQLPageRequest;
import oracle.xml.parser.v2.XMLDocument;
import oracle.xml.parser.v2.XMLElement;
import oracle.xml.parser.v2.XMLText;
import oracle.xml.parser.v2.XSLException;

import org.w3c.dom.Node;
import org.w3c.dom.Element;

public class InterfaceActionHandler implements XSQLActionHandler {

 XSQLPageRequest pageRequest;
 XMLElement actionElem;

 public void init(XSQLPageRequest env, Element e) {
  this.pageRequest=env;
  actionElem=(XMLElement)e;
 }
```

The `init` method in this case just saves the values to instance variables. They'll be referenced later in the `handleAction` method. You could also choose at this time to call other methods and do some of the work of the action handler.

```
public void handleAction(Node result) {

  XMLDocument doc=(XMLDocument)result.getOwnerDocument();
  XMLElement resultRoot=(XMLElement)doc.createElement("result-root");
  result.appendChild(resultRoot);
```

The preceding block of code creates the `resultRoot` element to which the rest of the elements will attach. You'll see these lines of code throughout the rest of the chapter. The code below pulls the text of the `xsql:action` element on the XSQL page and writes it to the datagram.

```
  try {
   String actionElemStr=actionElem.valueOf(".");
   actionElemStr=(actionElemStr.length()>0:actionElemStr:"");
   XMLElement actionElemVal=(XMLElement)doc.createElement("action-val");
   resultRoot.appendChild(actionElemVal);
   XMLText tNode=(XMLText)doc.createTextNode(actionElemStr);
   actionElemVal.appendChild(tNode);
   } catch (XSLException e) {
    // exception handling code
   }
```

This section makes use of the `XSQLPageRequest` object to get the `user agent` string, which is also added to the output.

```
  String userAgentStr=pageRequest.getUserAgent();
  XMLElement userAgent=(XMLElement)doc.createElement("user-agent");
  resultRoot.appendChild(userAgent);
  XMLText tNode=(XMLText)doc.createTextNode(userAgentStr);
  userAgent.appendChild(tNode);

 }
}
```

If you wish to implement the `XSQLActionHandler` interface directly, you need to grab the `XSQLPageRequest` and action element objects in the `init`. Then you can do almost anything that you'd like. But as you'll see in the next section, you'll have an easier time if you subclass `XSQLActionHandlerImpl` instead.

`XSQLActionHandlerImpl` Base Class

The `XSQLActionHandlerImpl` class implements the `XSQLActionHandler` interface. Any subclass of this class is a valid action handler. The `XSQLActionHandlerImpl` class also provides a lot of convenience methods so that you won't have to write new code to accomplish common tasks. This discussion looks more closely at the various methods and how to use them. It starts by looking at the two primary methods of the class—`init()` and `handleAction()`.

First, you don't have to have an `init()` method in your `XSQLActionHandlerImpl` subclass. Since it is defined in the `XSQLActionHandlerImpl` class, the implementation requirement for this method is already covered. If you do choose to have an `init()` method, you will need to call `super.init()`. If you don't, many of the other methods in the `XSQLActionHandlerImpl` class won't work correctly.

```
public void init(XSQLPageRequest env, Element e) {
   super.init(env,e);
   //your code
  }
```

In the previous example, the `init` method was used to capture the `XSQL-PageRequest` and action element objects. If you didn't capture those objects in the `init` method, you wouldn't be able to do anything with them. You don't face the same requirement when subclassing `XSQLActionHandlerImpl`. There are two convenience methods that make these objects available to you from the `handleAction` method:

```
public void handleAction(Node result) {

   XSQLPageRequest pageRequest=getPageRequest();
   XMLElement userAgent=(XMLElement)doc.createElement("user-agent");
   Element xsqlAction=getActionElement();

   //Other code

   }
```

These methods, `getPageRequest()` and `getActionElement()`, are just two of many methods that make life easier when you write action handlers. The upcoming text examines the various methods of the `XSQLActionHandlerImpl` class in terms of what they do for you. Table 18.2 covers methods such as `getPageRequest()` and `getActionElement()`, which make it easy for you to access the invoking environment.

Table 18.2 Environmentally Friendly Methods of `XSQLActionHandlerImpl`

METHOD	DESCRIPTION
`XSQLPageRequest getPageRequest()`	Returns the `XSQLPageRequest` object associated with the request. This object can provide a host of functionality.
`Element getActionElement()`	Returns the element that invoked the action handler. You can examine this element to get input.

Table 18.2 *(Continued)*

METHOD	DESCRIPTION
`String getActionElementContent()`	Returns the first child text of the action element, with parameters already substituted with the correct values.
`String getAttribute (String attrname, Element e)`	Get the attribute of a specified element.
`String getAttributeAllowingParam (String attrname, Element e)`	Get the attribute of the specified element with any parameters substituted with the correct values.
`String variableValue (String varName, Element e)`	Returns the value of a particular parameter. The `Element e` can be used to house default values.

Two of these methods, `getActionElementContent()` and `getAttribute-AllowingParam()`, interpolate the parameter values for you. This is valuable functionality to have. You'll work with these in greater detail later in the chapter, when parameters are covered in detail.

The methods described in Table 18.3 help you manipulate XML. The first, `addResultElement()`, is used in an earlier example. The `appendCopyOfSecondaryDocument()` and `appendSecondaryDocument()` methods make it very easy to work with any method that returns XML documents.

Table 18.4 describes two methods that make it easy to retrieve just a couple values from the result set of a SQL statement. These are useful if the query returns only one row and you are looking for only a couple pieces of information.

Table 18.3 XML Handling Methods

METHOD	DESCRIPTION
`void addResultElement (Node rootNode, java.lang. String elementName, java.lang.String content)`	Adds an element to `rootNode` with `elementName` as the name and content as the text value.
`void appendCopyOfSecondary Document(Node rootNode, Document d)`	Append a copy of another document to `rootNode`.
`appendSecondaryDocument (Node rootNode, Document d)`	Append another document to `rootNode` without copying.
`String valueOfXPathInPostedXML (java.lang.String xpath)`	Returns the results of an `Xpath` expression against a documented posted as part of the request.

Table 18.4 Database Value Retrieval Methods

METHOD	DESCRIPTION
`String firstColumnOfFirstRow (Node rootNode, java.lang. String statement)`	Returns only the first column of the first row as a string by using the database connection specified for the page.
`String[] firstNColumnsOfFirstRow (Node rootNode, java.lang. String statement, int n)`	Returns the first *n* columns of the first row as an array of strings.
`boolean requiredConnection Provided(Node rootNode)`	Returns true if a database connection has been provided.

Table 18.5 describes a set of methods that helps you write error messages. Error conditions may arise in your custom action handler. If they do, you want to be able to communicate them by using the standard error format. By using the standard format, you can reuse the same error handling stylesheets that you use for the XSQL built-in actions.

Table 18.5 Status and Error Handling Methods

METHOD	DESCRIPTION
`void reportError(Node rootNode, String message)`	Attaches a standard `xsl-error` element with the appropriate message.
`void reportFatalError (java.lang.String message)`	Using this stops all processing. A `SQLException` should be thrown after calling this method.
`void reportErrorIncluding Statement(Node rootNode, String statement, String message)`	Attaches a standard `xsl-error` element with the offending SQL statement and the appropriate message.
`void reportErrorIncluding Statement(Node rootNode, String statement, int ErrorCode, String message)`	Attaches a standard `xsl-error` element with the offending SQL statement, the error code and the appropriate message.
`void reportMissingAttribute (Node rootNode, String attrname)`	Reports that the specified attribute is missing using a standard `xsl-error` element.
`void reportStatus(Node rootNode, String statusAttr, String message)`	Reports the status as a standard `xsl-status`.

Of all of these methods, the `getPageRequest()` method is the most powerful. Through the `XSQLPageRequest`, you can access a wide range of data and functionality, which is covered in the next section.

XSQLPageRequest

The `XSQLPageRequest` object gives an action handler access to a large range of functionality. You access a `XSQLPageRequest` object in one of two ways. First, you can grab it in the `init()` method of the action handler. The other way is to call `getPageRequest()` of `XSQLActionHandlerImpl`. Of course, the second way works only if your action handler subclasses `XSQLActionHandlerImpl`.

Once you have an `XSQLPageRequest` object, you can use it for a variety of purposes. Table 18.6 outlines a few of the more important methods.

You'll be using these methods throughout the rest of the chapter. The `XSQLPageRequest` class is the gateway to a lot of interesting functionality.

Table 18.6 `XSQLPageRequest` Functionality

METHOD	DESCRIPTION
`String getJDBCConnection()`	Returns the JDBC connection for the request if one is defined for the page.
`String getPageEncoding()`	Returns the encoding for the source XSQL page.
`String getParameter (String name)`	Returns the value of the named parameter.
`Document getPostedDocument()`	Returns an XML document that may have been posted with the request.
`Object getRequestObject (String name)`	Gets an object associated with the request. Can be used to pass data between action handlers.
`setRequestObject(String name, Object val)`	Sets an object associated with the request. Can be used to pass data between action handlers.
`getRequestType()`	Returns `"Servlet"`, `"CommandLine"`, or `"Programmatic"`.
`String getStylesheetParameter (String name)`	Get the value of the named stylesheet parameter.
`setStylehseetParameter (String name, String val)`	Sets the value of a stylesheet parameter.

Accessing Servlet Functionality

Most of the action handlers that you write will probably be invoked from a servlet. Servlets have their own range of functionality that you can access. This section looks at how you verify that you are running under a servlet and how to access the servlet functionality.

WARNING **Don't write to the servlet response** `ServletOutputStream` **directly! Most servlets write to the** `ServletOutputStream` **to get data back to the client. Though you can access the** `ServletOutputStream` **for the XSQL servlet, you shouldn't write to it. This is the same stream that the XSQL servlet uses to output the datagram, so writing to it directly will have unpredictable results. Your output should be limited to the datagram XML and to session attributes and cookies.**

Before attempting to use servlet functionality, you first need to verify that you are being invoked from a servlet. Once you know that you are operating within a servlet, you can cast your `XSQLPageRequest` object to an `XSQLServletPageRequest` object. The following code shows how you can acquire all of the key servlet objects. Once you have those objects, you can do most anything you want—except writing output directly.

```
import oracle.xml.xsql.XSQLActionHandlerImpl;
import oracle.xml.xsql.XSQLPageRequest;
import oracle.xml.xsql.XSQLServletPageRequest;
import javax.servlet.http.HttpServletRequest;
import javax.servlet.http.HttpServletResponse;
import javax.servlet.ServletContext;
import javax.servlet.http.HttpSession;
import org.w3c.dom.Node;

public class ServletActionHandler extends XSQLActionHandlerImpl {

 public void handleAction(Node result) {

  XSQLPageRequest pageRequest=getPageRequest();

  if (pageRequest.getRequestType().equals("Servlet")) {

   XSQLServletPageRequest xspr=(XSQLServletPageRequest)pageRequest;
   HttpServletRequest req=xspr.getHttpServletRequest();
   HttpServletResponse resp=xspr.getHttpServletResponse();
   ServletContext ctx=xspr.getServletContext();
   HttpSession sess=req.getSession();

   //Now you can use any servlet functionality you want
   //But don't write to the output directly!
```

```
    //Here are some convenience methods for dealing with cookies

    String cookieVal=xspr.getCookie("some-cookie");
    xspr.setCookie("new-cookie","value",null,null, null,true);

   }
  }
 }
```

The last two lines of the code example show you two of the convenience methods that the `XSQLServletPageRequest` class provides. There are a few others that are described in Table 18.7. These are above and beyond the methods of the `XSQLPageRequest` class. These methods are covered in the last chapter.

The `XSQLServletPageRequest` class is your gateway to all of the servlet functionality. You may even find that you are able to reuse other code that works with the `ServletRequest` and `ServletResponse` objects. Of course, you can also set objects onto the session for use by other action handler invocations. As long as you are careful not to write output directly, you can create some powerful action handlers with a lot of the power of servlets.

Database Interaction

The discussions so far have provided a good background for how action handlers work. But you probably want your action handlers to access the database. This section covers how to reach the database effectively. Of course, you can always open a new JDBC connection. But it is far easier to reuse the built-in action handlers. It takes care of formatting the result as XML, and it is easy to merge the results into the datagram. If you have to use JDBC, you should use a connection provided by XSQL. Connection pooling is already taken care of. Each of these methodologies are discussed in this section.

Table 18.7 `XSQLServletPageRequest` Methods

METHOD	DESCRIPTION
`String getCookie(String name)`	Gets the named cookie
`void setCookie(java.lang. String name, String value, String maxage, String domain, String path, boolean immediate)`	Sets a cookie on the client
`String translateURL (java.lang.String path)`	Translates the URL using the invoking URL as a base
`void setContentType (java.lang.String mimetype)`	Sets the content type for the invoking servlet's output

Using Built-in Action Handlers

The built-in action handlers provide a great deal of functionality. You usually write an action handler because you can't do what you need to do with only the built-ins. But it's rare that you can't reuse one or more of the built-in action handlers. This section focuses on how to reuse the `xsql:query` and action within your custom action handlers. However, you can reuse all of the built-in action handlers in the same way.

The first step in reusing a built-in action handler is identifying the class name of the action that you need. All of the actions implement the `XSQLActionHandler` interface, so you don't have to relearn a new set of methods for each one. You need to know only the class name so that you can instantiate the object. The class name for each action is listed in Table 18.8.

Table 18.8 Action Handler Classes

ACTION	CLASS
<xsql:query>	oracle.xml.xsql.actions. XSQLQueryHandler
<xsql:dml>	oracle.xml.xsql.actions. XSQLDMLHandler
<xsql:set-stylesheet-param>	oracle.xml.xsql.actions. XSQLStylesheetParameterHandler
<xsql:insert-request>	oracle.xml.xsql.actions. XSQLInsertRequestHandler
<xsql:update-request>	oracle.xml.xsql.actions. XSQLUpdateRequestHandler
<xsql:delete-request>	oracle.xml.xsql.actions. XSQLDeleteRequestHandler
<xsql:include-request-params/>	oracle.xml.xsql.actions. XSQLIncludeRequestHandler
<xsql:include-xsql>	oracle.xml.xsql.actions. XSQLIncludeXSQLHandler
<xsql:include-owa>	oracle.xml.xsql.actions. XSQLIncludeOWAHandler
<xsql:action>	oracle.xml.xsql.actions. XSQLExtensionActionHandler
<xsql:ref-cursor-function>	oracle.xml.xsql.actions. XSQLRefCursorFunctionHandler
<xsql:include-param>	oracle.xml.xsql.actions. XSQLGetParameterHandler

Table 18.8 *(Continued)*

ACTION	CLASS
`<xsql:set-session-param>`	`oracle.xml.xsql.actions.XSQLSetSessionParamHandler`
`<xsql:set-page-param>`	`oracle.xml.xsql.actions.XSQLSetPageParamHandler`
`<xsql:set-cookie>`	`oracle.xml.xsql.actions.XSQLSetCookieHandler`
`<xsql:insert-param>`	`oracle.xml.xsql.actions.XSQLInsertParameterHandler`

To use a built-in action handler in your code, you do the following:

1. Import the appropriate class.
2. Instantiate the built-in action handler.
3. Call `init()` on the action handler object.
4. Call `handleAction()` on the action handler object, passing it a `DocumentFragment` object.
5. Do any processing you'd like to do on the result of the built-in action handler.
6. If you wish to include the result in the datagram, attach it to the result node that was passed to your `handleAction()` method.

The following class shows you how to use the `XSQLQueryHandler` action from inside the action handler:

```
import oracle.xml.xsql.XSQLActionHandlerImpl;
import oracle.xml.xsql.XSQLActionHandler;
import oracle.xml.xsql.XSQLPageRequest;
import oracle.xml.xsql.actions.XSQLQueryHandler;
import org.w3c.dom.Node;
import org.w3c.dom.DocumentFragment;
import org.w3c.dom.Document;
import org.w3c.dom.Element;
import java.sql.SQLException;

public class UseQuery extends XSQLActionHandlerImpl {

 XSQLActionHandler queryAction;

 public void init(XSQLPageRequest req, Element action) {
    super.init(req,action);

    queryAction = new XSQLQueryHandler();
    queryAction.init(req,action);

 }
```

The preceding `init` method instantiates the `XSQLQueryHandler` object and calls the `init()` method. The `queryAction` variable is actually of the `XSQLActionHandler` type. You don't need to call any of the methods besides those defined in the `XSQLActionHandler` interface, so there isn't much of a reason to have an `XSQLQueryHandler` variable.

You don't have to instantiate and initialize an action handler in the `init` method. If you would like, you can configure the action handler in the `handleAction` method. Just use the `getPageRequest()` and `getActionElement()` methods of the `XSQLActionHandleImpl` to grab the arguments that you need to pass to `init()`.

```
public void handleAction(Node result) {
    Document doc=result.getOwnerDocument();
    DocumentFragment resultFrag=doc.createDocumentFragment();
    XSQLPageRequest pageRequest=getPageRequest();

    try {
     queryAction.handleAction(resultFrag);
    } catch (SQLException e) {
      reportError(result,e.getMessage());
    }

    result.appendChild(resultFrag);
  }
}
```

In this method, you create a `DocumentFragment` object and pass it to the `handleAction` method of `queryAction`. The `queryAction` then appends the results of the query to it. You then append `resultFrag` to the result node and that outputs the XML to the datagram.

But where does the query come from? The query comes from the XSQL page, just as with a real `xsql:query` action. The XSQL below shows an example of this. The SQL query is inside the `xsql:action` element.

```
<?xml version="1.0" encoding="UTF-8"?>
<xsql:action handler="UseQuery"
             xmlns:xsql="urn:oracle-xsql"
             connection="momnpup">
 SELECT id,name FROM product where category_id={@category_id}
</xsql:action>
```

When you initialize the `queryAction` object with the `xsql:action` element, it treats it just as if it were an `xsql:query` object. You can even set parameters `xsql:query` parameters on the `xsql:action` element, as in the following example:

```
<?xml version="1.0" encoding="UTF-8"?>
<xsql:action handler="UseQuery"
             xmlns:xsql="urn:oracle-xsql"
             connection="momnpup"
             rowset-element="PRODUCTS"
```

```
              row-element="PRODUCT">
  SELECT id,name FROM product where category_id={@category_id}
 </xsql:action>
```

This results in the output shown in Figure 18.2. When one of the built-in action handlers is passed an element via the `init()` method, it doesn't care what the element name is. In the case of `XSQLQueryHandler`, it looks for all of the parameters that are allowed in the `xsql:query` element and treats the value as a SQL statement. It also automatically substitutes parameter values for any parameters it finds. The same is true for all the other built-in action handlers.

You gain great flexibility in your action handlers because they ignore the name. As you'll see in the "Parameters and Input" section later in this chapter, you can even pass non-`xsql` elements to a built-in action handler object and get the expected results. This next example demonstrates this flexibility in a largely theoretical way—you probably won't ever find any reason to do this in a real application. But it does prove beyond a shadow of a doubt that the built-in action handlers don't pay any attention to the name of the element that invokes the action handler. Here, the action handler passes the same element to two different built-in action handlers: `XSQLQueryHandler` and `XSQLSetPageParamHandler`.

```
import oracle.xml.xsql.XSQLActionHandlerImpl;
import oracle.xml.xsql.XSQLActionHandler;
import oracle.xml.xsql.XSQLPageRequest;

import oracle.xml.xsql.actions.XSQLQueryHandler;
import oracle.xml.xsql.actions.XSQLSetPageParamHandler;
import org.w3c.dom.Document;
import org.w3c.dom.DocumentFragment;
import org.w3c.dom.Node;
import org.w3c.dom.Element;
import java.sql.SQLException;

public class MultiActions extends XSQLActionHandlerImpl {

 XSQLActionHandler queryAction;

 XSQLSetPageParamHandler paramAction;

 public void init(XSQLPageRequest req, Element action) {

    super.init(req,action);

    queryAction = new XSQLQueryHandler();
    queryAction.init(req,action);

    paramAction = new XSQLSetPageParamHandler();
    paramAction.init(req,action);
 }
```

Both init() methods are passed the exact same arguments. The queryAction object considers the action element to be an xsql:query element, while the paramAction element considers the action element to be an xsql:set-page-param element.

```
public void handleAction(Node result) {

    Document doc=result.getOwnerDocument();
    DocumentFragment queryActionFrag=doc.createDocumentFragment();
    DocumentFragment paramActionFrag=doc.createDocumentFragment();

    try {

     queryAction.handleAction(queryActionFrag);
     paramAction.handleAction(paramActionFrag);

    } catch (SQLException e) {
      reportError(result,e.getMessage());
    }
    result.appendChild(queryActionFrag);
  }
}
```

The handleAction element is called on both. The XSQLSetPageParamHandler element doesn't actually write any XML data, so the paramActionFrag isn't appended to the datagram. The following XSQL page invokes the action handler:

```
<?xml version="1.0" encoding="UTF-8"?>
<page xmlns:xsql="urn:oracle-xsql"
      connection="momnpup">
 <xsql:action handler="MultiActions"
              rowset-element="PRODUCTS"
              row-element="PRODUCT"
              name="product_name">
   SELECT name
    FROM product
    WHERE id={@product_id}
 </xsql:action>
 <xsql:include-param name="product_name"/>
</page>
```

The xsql:include-param action is included to show that the parameter was actually set. The results of the query are shown in Figure 18.2.

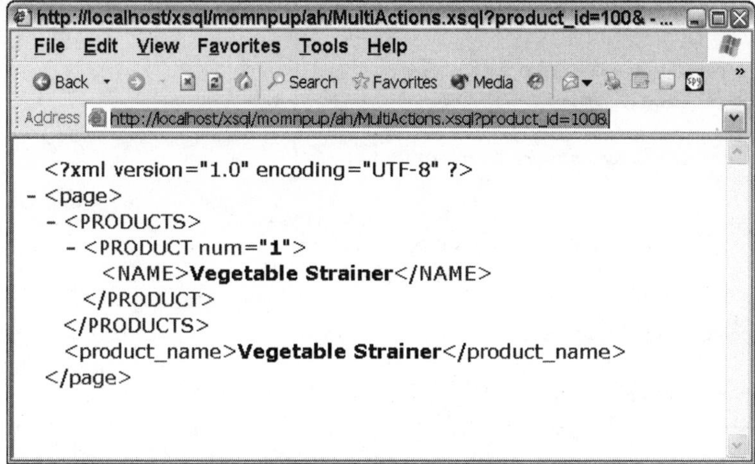

Figure 18.2 Results of multiple actions that use the same action element.

Before moving on from this discussion, it's worth noting that the action element doesn't have to be defined in the XSQL page. If you wish, you can construct an action element inside your code. The following example initializes the `XSQLQueryHandler` with an element that is created at runtime.

```
import oracle.xml.xsql.XSQLActionHandlerImpl;
import oracle.xml.xsql.XSQLActionHandler;
import oracle.xml.xsql.XSQLPageRequest;
import oracle.xml.xsql.actions.XSQLQueryHandler;
import oracle.xml.xsql.actions.XSQLSetPageParamHandler;
import org.w3c.dom.Document;
import org.w3c.dom.DocumentFragment;
import org.w3c.dom.Node;
import org.w3c.dom.Element;
import org.w3c.dom.Text;
import java.sql.SQLException;

public class NoXsqlQuery extends XSQLActionHandlerImpl {

 XSQLActionHandler queryAction;
```

```
  public void handleAction(Node result) {

   Document doc=result.getOwnerDocument();
   DocumentFragment queryActionFrag=doc.createDocumentFragment();

   XSQLPageRequest pageRequest=getPageRequest();

   Element queryElem=doc.createElement("my-special-query");
   Text queryStr=doc.createTextNode("SELECT name
                                     FROM product");

   queryElem.appendChild(queryStr);

   queryAction=new XSQLQueryHandler();
   queryAction.init(pageRequest,queryElem);

   try {

    queryAction.handleAction(queryActionFrag);

   } catch (SQLException e) {
     reportError(result,e.getMessage());
   }
   result.appendChild(queryActionFrag);
  }
}
```

In this case, you create the element named `my-special-query` and hard-code the SQL that you wish to pass. The result will be all of the names for all of the products. Since you don't use the action element at all, you can invoke the action handler with the following simple XSQL:

```
<?xml version="1.0" encoding="UTF-8"?>

 <xsql:action handler="NoXsqlQuery"
 xmlns:xsql="urn:oracle-xsql"
      connection="momnpup"/>
```

Hopefully, this discussion has given you a firm grasp of the various ways that you can reuse the built-in action handlers within your own action handlers. The process is simple and flexible. You've seen how to call multiple action handlers and even call action handlers that don't have their own element in the XSQL page. You'll see more use of built-in action handlers as the chapter progresses.

JDBC Connections

In the previous discussion, you used built-in action handlers to work with this the database. This approach is very easy if you wish to attach the result to the datagram. It hides the complexities of JDBC entirely. But there are many good reasons that you might need to use JDBC directly. If you wish to use the results in an intermediate step prior to returning data, then it may be easier to use a JDBC connection. This discussion examines the best way to do this.

The following class uses the page's JDBC connection to execute a simple SQL statement. The connection is named in the XSQL page and is already part of the JDBC connection pool. This is much easier than creating a JDBC connection from scratch and having to deal with connection pooling issues yourself. It is also easier to configure. The invoking XSQL page specifies the connection name and the details are kept in the `XSQLConfig.xml` file.

```
import oracle.xml.xsql.XSQLActionHandlerImpl;
import oracle.xml.xsql.XSQLActionHandler;
import oracle.xml.xsql.XSQLPageRequest;

import org.w3c.dom.Node;
import org.w3c.dom.Element;
import org.w3c.dom.Document;
import org.w3c.dom.Text;

import java.sql.PreparedStatement;
import java.sql.ResultSet;
import java.sql.Connection;
import java.sql.SQLException;

public class JdbcHandler extends XSQLActionHandlerImpl {

 Connection conn;

 public void init(XSQLPageRequest req, Element action) {

    super.init(req,action);
    conn=req.getJDBCConnection();

 }
```

You grab the connection from the `XSQLPageRequest` object. You don't have to do this in the `init` method, but it is a convenient place to do it. The connection will be null if there is no connection specified in the XSQL page. When you go to use the connection, you need to check to see it is null and generate an appropriate error message if it is.

```
 public void handleAction(Node result) {

  Document doc=result.getOwnerDocument();
  Element resultRoot=doc.createElement("result-root");

  if (conn!=null) {

   try {
```

```
        String sqlStr="SELECT name FROM product";
        Statement sql=conn.createStatement();
        ResultSet resultSet=sql.executeQuery(sqlStr);

        while  (resultSet.next()){
         String val=resultSet.getString("name");
         Element nameElem=doc.createElement("NAME");
         Text tNode=doc.createTextNode(val);
         nameElem.appendChild(tNode);
         resultRoot.appendChild(nameElem);
         resultSet.next();
        }

        result.appendChild(resultRoot);
       } catch (SQLException e) {
        reportError(result,e.getMessage());
       }

     } else {
      reportError(result,"No Database Connection");
     }
   }
 }
```

The handleAction method creates a simple statement, executes it, and grabs the result. Once you have the connection object, the full power of JDBC will be at your fingertips. You can do whatever you need to do. What may be new is building XML out of the result set data. This is a simple example in which an element is created for each name returned in the query. In the following text, you'll see how you can avoid this exercise entirely by using the XSU classes.

Using the XSU classes

The XSU classes allow you to imitate the behavior of the xsql:query and xsql:dml actions programmatically. They take you a step deeper than reusing the built-in actions. When you use the OracleXMLQuery and OracleXMLSave classes, you don't have to pass them an element object. Instead, you pass the SQL statement that you want, and the class returns a document. Then you just merge the document with the datagram.

This example uses the oracle.xml.sql.query.OracleXMLQuery class, which you use for select statements. The oracle.xml.sql.dml.OracleXMLSave class is used for DML statements. Only the handleAction method is shown. As in the previous example, the connection object, conn, is acquired in the init method.

```
 public void handleAction(Node result) {

   XMLDocument doc=(XMLDocument)result.getOwnerDocument();
   Element resultRoot=doc.createElement("result-root");

   if (conn!=null) {
```

```
    try {

      // Get an XML document based on a SQL query
      String sqlStr="SELECT name FROM product";
      OracleXMLQuery xQ=new OracleXMLQuery(conn, sqlStr);
      Document queryResultDoc=xQ.getXMLDOM();

      //Merge the resulting document in to the datagram
      Element queryRoot=queryResultDoc.getDocumentElement();
      Node n=doc.adoptNode(queryRoot);
      result.appendChild(n);

    } catch (Exception e) {
      reportError(result,e.getMessage());
    }

  } else {
    reportError(result,"No Database Connection");
  }
}
```

The result of this query is exactly the same as a plain `xsql:query` action with the same SQL query. Each row is contained in a `ROW` element, and all of the `ROW` elements are contained in a `ROWSET` element. If you wish, you can set the name for the `rowset` element and the `row` element just as you can with `xsql:query` action. All of the other options of the `xsql:query` action are available. The same is true for `OracleXMLSave`.

This example also contains a good example of when Oracle's XMLDocument class comes in handy. When you go to merge the documents, you can easily do so by using the `adoptNode` method of `XMLDocument`. Merging the document strictly through DOM is quite a bit harder.

Adding XMLType Objects

In the previous discussion, you merged two XML documents together. If you are storing XML documents in Oracle, this problem can arise often. You saw an example of this in the application that you built earlier in the book with the product document interface. In that case, you used the `xsql:include-owa` action along with a PL/SQL procedure to output the XML to the datagram. In an action handler, you don't have to do this. Instead, you create a document and merge it in to the document.

The following example shows you how to do this. You grab your JDBC connection as before. Then, you use the `extract()` function of the XMLType to get the data.

```
public void handleAction(Node result) {

  XMLDocument doc=(XMLDocument)result.getOwnerDocument();
  Element resultRoot=doc.createElement("product-set");

  if (conn!=null) {

    try {
```

```
      // execute the query
      String sqlStr="SELECT name,p.doc.extract('/product').getStringVal()
  AS product_xml FROM product p";
      Statement sql=conn.createStatement();
      ResultSet resultSet=sql.executeQuery(sqlStr);

      while  (resultSet.next()){

        String xmlStr=resultSet.getString("product_xml");
        InputSource xmlIn=new InputSource(new StringReader(xmlStr));

        // parse the xml string
        JXDocumentBuilderFactory dBF=new JXDocumentBuilderFactory();
        DocumentBuilder docBuilder=dBF.newDocumentBuilder();
        Document xDoc=docBuilder.parse(xmlIn);

        // merge the documents
        Element productRoot=xDoc.getDocumentElement();
        Node n=doc.adoptNode(productRoot);
        resultRoot.appendChild(n);
      }

      result.appendChild(resultRoot);
    } catch (Exception e) {
      reportError(result,e.getMessage());
    }

   } else {
    reportError(result,"No Database Connection");
   }
  }
```

The query is executed as in the straight JDBC example earlier. But the value can't be added to the datagram as a string. All of the special characters would be escaped and you wouldn't be able to use transformations against the XML. Instead, you parse the string into an XML document and then merge the two documents.

Parameters and Input

In the previous two sections, you learned how to attach XML to the datagram. This is only one part of action handler programming. You can also get and set the parameters of the XSQL page and a stylesheet, as well as access all of the attributes and text of the invoking `xsql:action` element. XSQL doesn't limit you to just the XSQL page. You'll learn how to access initialization parameters from the `XSQLConfig.xml` file. The last two parts of this section reveal how to interpolate parameters. You saw earlier that a built-in action element knows how to interpolate parameters found in the xsql:action element. Now, you'll see how to handle parameters in your own action handlers.

As you read this section, you'll see that XSQL gives you many ways to control your custom action handlers. You already know how to access all the information of a servlet; you're about to learn how to get input from the XSQL page and the XSQLConfig.xml, also. But that's only half the story. You can use both the XSQL parameters and the stylesheet parameters as a powerful output mechanism. By setting a parameter on a page, your action handler can communicate data with other action handlers.

Now, it's time to conquer parameters and input! This subject material might not seem as important as accessing the database and pushing data to the datagram. But here you understand how to control and modularize your action handlers and how your action handler can control other action handler's behavior. Just think: You could write the next xsql:query!

Accessing XSQL Data

In the previous section, you saw that a built-in action handler class can make use of the values of the action element. You pass the action element to the XSQLActionHandler object and it reads the data. But what if you aren't using a built-in action handler or if some of your code needs to access values of the elements directly? The XmlTypeHandler class developed earlier in the chapter is a good example for this. That class grabs sets of XML documents stored as XMLTypes and appends them to the datagram. But the SQL used to get the documents was hard-coded. Thus, the action handler was invoked like this from the XSQL page:

```
<xsql:action handler="XmlTypeHandler"/>
```

That's no good. If you want to use different SQL, you'll have to recode your action handler. One of the key benefits of XSQL is that you can keep the SQL statements outside of your compiled code. For something as generically applicable as the XMLTypeHandler, you want to be able to do something like the following:

```
<xsql:action handler="XmlTypeHandler" root-element-name="products">
 SELECT name,
        p.doc.extract('/product').getStringVal() AS product_xml
   FROM product p
</xsql:action>
```

The goal is that you can read the SQL statement in just as any other action handler can. The XSQL page author can also set the name of the root element that will be returned. Of course, you also want to be able to use XSQL parameters in the action element. You'll learn how to substitute parameter values in the next section. For this discussion, the focus is on accessing the values.

Your first step is to modify the `init()` method so that you grab the action element and the `XSQLPageRequest` object. Note that this time you cast the action element to an `XSQLElement` variable. You'll see why in a moment.

```
public class XmlTypeHandler extends XSQLActionHandlerImpl {

 Connection conn;
 XMLElement actionElem;
 XSQLPageRequest pageRequest;

 public void init(XSQLPageRequest req, Element action) {

    super.init(req,action);
    this.actionElem=(XMLElement)action;
    this.pageRequest=req;
    this.conn=req.getJDBCConnection();

 }
```

Now that you have the element captured, you'll want to grab the text value of the action element and the `root-element-name` attribute value. Here's how you do it:

```
public void handleAction(Node result) {

  try {

    String sqlStr=actionElem.valueOf(".");
    String resultRootName=getAttribute("root-element-name",actionElem);
    resultRootName=(resultRootName==null || resultRootName.length()==0?
                  "xml-doc-set":resultRootName);
```

From here, the code is like before. The difference is that now you are working with an SQL statement and `resultRootName` that are derived from the invoking XSQL page.

```
    XMLDocument doc=(XMLDocument)result.getOwnerDocument();
    Element resultRoot=doc.createElement(resultRootName);

    if (conn!=null) {

     Statement sql=conn.createStatement();
     ResultSet resultSet=sql.executeQuery(sqlStr);

     while  (resultSet.next()){

      String xmlStr=resultSet.getString("product_xml");
      InputSource xmlIn=new InputSource(new StringReader(xmlStr));

      // parse the xml string
```

```
        JXDocumentBuilderFactory dBF=new JXDocumentBuilderFactory();
        DocumentBuilder docBuilder=docBuilderFactory.newDocumentBuilder();
        Document xDoc=docBuilder.parse(xmlIn);

        // merge the documents
        Element productRoot=xDoc.getDocumentElement();
        Node n=doc.adoptNode(productRoot);
        resultRoot.appendChild(n);
       }
       result.appendChild(resultRoot);
      } else {
       reportError(result,"No Database Connection");
      }
     } catch (Exception e) {
     reportError(result,e.getMessage());
     }

   }
  }
```

In this example, you grabbed the text value of the action element. If your action element has child elements, you can certainly grab the values of those as well. For instance, if the name of a child element is "child", you can do the following to grab the value:

```
String s=actionElem.valueOf("child");
```

You'll learn more about creating nested action elements in the section after this next one. Now it's time to complete this example by making the preceding example parameter ready.

Substituting Parameter Values

One of the nicest features of XSQL is that you can pass parameters to action handlers. You can put them in the value of an attribute or in the text of an element itself. If you are writing an action handler, you want to have the same kind of power. For instance, it would be best if you could invoke the `XmlHandler` as follows:

```
<xsql:action handler="XmlTypeHandler"
 root-name="product-set">
  SELECT name,
         p.doc.extract('{@xPath-exp}').getStringVal() AS product_xml
    FROM product p
    WHERE p.id={@product_id}
 </xsql:action>
```

Oracle provides a couple of ways to substitute the parameters easily. For attributes, all you have to do is call the `getAttributeAllowingParam()` method. If there is no parameter set, you'll need to use a line like the second one to set the default value.

```
String resultRootName=getAttributeAllowingParam("root-name",actionElem);
resultRootName=(resultRootName==null || resultRootName.length()==0?
                "xml-doc-set":resultRootName);
```

You can get the same behavior by using `XSQLUtil.resolveParams()`. This is useful if you want to know what the original value of the attribute is without parsing.

```
String rootNameStr=getAttribute("root-name",actionElem);
String rootNameVal=XSQLUtil.resolveParams(rootNameStr,
                                          pageRequest);
rootNameVal=(rootNameVal==null || rootNameVal.length()==0?
                "xml-doc-set":rootNameVal);
```

This takes care of attributes. The next step is to handle the text of an element. Again, there are two ways to do this. If you are interested in resolving just the text value of the action element, you can do that with the `XSQLActionHandlerImpl` method `getActionElementContent()`. normalizes the text and returns a string with all parameters already substituted.

```
String s=getActionElementContent();
```

This method works only if you want the immediate child text of an element. What if the action handler has children and you want to access their text? Then you can use the `XSQLUtil.resolveParams()` method after grabbing the text.

```
XMLElement actionElem=(XMLElement)getActionElement();
String s=actionElem.valueOf("child");
String s=XSQLUtil.resolveParams(s, getPageRequest());
```

The following example shows you how to recursively descend an element, resolving all of the parameters. If you want children for your action handler elements, you'll need something like this. It takes a pure DOM approach.

```
public static void resolveElementParams(Element newElem,
                                        XSQLPageRequest pageRequest) {


    NamedNodeMap attribs=newElem.getAttributes();

    for (int i=0;i<attribs.getLength();i++) {

     Node attrib=attribs.item(i);
     String valStr=attrib.getNodeValue();
     valStr=XSQLUtil.resolveParams(valStr,pageRequest);
     attrib.setNodeValue(valStr);

     }
```

The preceding code resolves any attributes that the element may have. The next set of code works through all the children nodes. If they are text, the parameters will be resolved.

```
NodeList list=newElem.getChildNodes();
for (int i=0;i<list.getLength();i++) {

 Node n=list.item(i);

 // Text node
 if (n.getNodeType()==Node.TEXT_NODE) {
  log.println("found text node");
  String valStr=n.getNodeValue();
  log.println("valStr=="+valStr);
  valStr=XSQLUtil.resolveParams(valStr,pageRequest);
  log.println("valStr replaced =="+valStr);
  n.setNodeValue(valStr);
 }
```

The last two lines take care of the recursion. If the element has a child element, the method is called again on the child. The recursion stops and the method halts when no more children are encountered.

```
   if (n.getNodeType()==Node.ELEMENT_NODE) {
    resolveElementParams((Element)n,pageRequest);
   }
  }
}
```

This method gives you more flexibility when designing action handlers. For instance, you can invoke an action handler with this method. The hypothetical case is that your action handler chooses what action to take based on the test attribute. These could result in different SQL queries or maybe calls to other data sources. The problem solved is one of complexity. If you need to pass a lot of information to an action handler, why not use XML to help you keep it organized? This can be a more sane approach than having to parse text inside your action handlers.

```
<xsql:action handler="SomeActionHandler">
  <firstChoice test="{@test1}">{@valParam1}</oneChoice>
  <secondChoice test="{@test2}">{@valParam2}</secondChoice>
  <thirdChoice test="{@test3}">{@valParam3}</thirdChoice>
  <otherwise>{@valParam4}</otherwise>
</xsql:action>
```

In the Java code, you clone the action element first, then the `resolveElementParams`:

```
Element elem=getActionElement().cloneNode(true);
resolveElementParams(elem,pageRequest);
```

Having nested `xsql:action` elements like the one described previously does come at a price. The action handler will have to parse the nested action handlers on each call. If they are deeply nested, then you are adding that much more work for every action handler call.

Setting Page Parameters

You've already seen how to add to the datagram. In this section, you'll see another avenue of output for your action handlers—page parameters. When you set a page parameter from an action handler, it will be available to the other actions on the page. You can use it as input for queries, `dml`, or any other type of action.

This example code allows you to set any arbitrary header value as a parameter in your page.

```
import oracle.xml.xsql.XSQLActionHandlerImpl;
import oracle.xml.xsql.XSQLServletPageRequest;
import oracle.xml.xsql.XSQLPageRequest;

import org.w3c.dom.Node;
import org.w3c.dom.Element;

import javax.servlet.http.HttpServletRequest;

public class GetHttpHeader extends XSQLActionHandlerImpl {

 public void handleAction(Node result) {

  Element actionElement=getActionElement();

  if (getPageRequest().getRequestType().equals("Servlet")) {

   XSQLServletPageRequest servletPR;
   servletPR=(XSQLServletPageRequest)getPageRequest();
   HttpServletRequest req=servletPR.getHttpServletRequest();

   String header=getAttributeAllowingParam("header",actionElement);
   String paramName=getAttributeAllowingParam("param",actionElement);

   String headerValue=req.getHeader(header);
   headerValue=(headerValue==null?"":headerValue);
   if (paramName!=null && paramName.length()>0) {
    servletPR.setPageParam(paramName,headerValue);
   }

  }
 }
}
```

You can invoke this code with the following XSQL page, which uses the action handler.

```
<?xml version="1.0" encoding="UTF-8"?>
<page xmlns:xsql="urn:oracle-xsql"
      connection="momnpup">
 <xsql:action handler="GetHttpHeader"
      param="host-param"
      header="{@header}"
      />
 <xsql:include-param name="host-param"/>

</page>
```

The parameter `host-param` will hold the value of the host header that came with the HTTP request. Since the action handler uses the `getAttributeAllowingParam` method, you can dynamically set the header that you desire. Here is a simple example where you can specify that you want any header displayed just by setting the header name in the URL:

```
<?xml version="1.0" encoding="UTF-8"?>
<page xmlns:xsql="urn:oracle-xsql"
      connection="momnpup">
 <xsql:action handler="GetHttpHeader"
      param="host"
      header="{@header}"
      />
 <xsql:include-param name="host"/>

</page>
```

The header values aren't the most interesting values that come as part of the request. For instance, you can also access the name of a remote user if HTTP authentication is used. The following action handler makes all the various request variables available as page parameters:

```
import oracle.xml.xsql.XSQLActionHandlerImpl;
import oracle.xml.xsql.XSQLServletPageRequest;
import oracle.xml.xsql.XSQLPageRequest;

import org.w3c.dom.Node;
import org.w3c.dom.Element;

import javax.servlet.http.HttpServletRequest;

public class GetRequestVariable extends XSQLActionHandlerImpl {
```

```
public void handleAction(Node result) {

  Element actionElement=getActionElement();

  if (getPageRequest().getRequestType().equals("Servlet")) {

   XSQLServletPageRequest servletPR=


(XSQLServletPageRequest)getPageRequest();
   HttpServletRequest req=servletPR.getHttpServletRequest();

   String varName=getAttributeAllowingParam("var-name",actionElement);
   String paramName=getAttributeAllowingParam("param",actionElement);

   if (varName==null) {
    return;
   }

   varName=varName.toUpperCase();
   String varVal="";

   if (varName.equals("AUTHTYPE")) {
    varVal=req.getAuthType();
    }
   else if (varName.equals("CONTEXTPATH")) {
    varVal=req.getContextPath();
    }
   else if (varName.equals("METHOD")) {
    varVal=req.getMethod();
    }
   else if (varName.equals("PATHINFO")) {
    varVal=req.getPathInfo();
    }
   else if (varName.equals("PATHTRANSLATED")) {
    varVal=req.getPathTranslated();
    }
   else if (varName.equals("QUERYSTRING")) {
    varVal=req.getQueryString();
    }
   else if (varName.equals("REMOTEUSER")) {
    varVal=req.getRemoteUser();
    }
   else if (varName.equals("REQUESTURI")) {
    varVal=req.getRequestURI();
    }
   else if (varName.equals("REQUESTURL")) {
    varVal=req.getRequestURL().toString();
    }
   else if (varName.equals("SERVLETPATH")) {
```

```
      varVal=req.getServletPath();
      }
     varVal=(varVal==null?"":varVal);
     if (paramName!=null && paramName.length()>0) {
      servletPR.setPageParam(paramName,varVal);
     }
    }
  }
}
```

In these examples, the action handlers didn't travel to the database at all. Of course, you can set database data as a parameter value if you like. You may find `XSQLActionHandlerImpl`'s `firstColumnOfFirstRow()`, and `firstNColumnsOfFirstRow()` methods especially useful for this purpose.

You can also set stylesheet parameters from inside your action handlers. You use the `setStylesheetParameter()` method of the `XSQLPageRequest` class as follows:

```
XSQLPageRequest pageRequest=getPageRequest();
pageRequest.setStylesheetParameter("parameterName","parameterValue");
```

This has the same effect as the `xsql:set-stylesheet-param` action. If there is a stylesheet that has a top-level parameter of the specified name, it will be set to the specified value. Of course, if there isn't a parameter by the name you specify or if there isn't a specified stylesheet, this method call will have no effect.

Inter-action Handler Communication

XSQL action handlers can communicate data to one another by using the `getRequest-Object()` and `setRequestObject()` methods of the `XSQLPageRequest` class. Two action handlers never run at the same time, so you can't have true communication between them. But an action handler can use `setRequestObject()` to pass data to action handlers that will be invoked after it, and the action handler can use `getRequestObject()` to receive the data.

Here is a simple example of data passing. The following action handler grabs an integer object that represents a count. If there isn't such an object on the request, it creates it with a count set to zero. Each time this action handler is invoked, it increments the count and appends the value it set as an element in the datagram.

```
import oracle.xml.xsql.XSQLActionHandlerImpl;
import oracle.xml.xsql.XSQLPageRequest;

import org.w3c.dom.Node;
import org.w3c.dom.Element;

import javax.servlet.http.HttpServletRequest;

public class Counter extends XSQLActionHandlerImpl {
```

```
    public void handleAction(Node result) {

      int count;

      XSQLPageRequest pageRequest=getPageRequest();
      Integer countObj=(Integer)pageRequest.getRequestObject("count");

      if (countObj==null) {
        count=0;
      } else {
        count=countObj.intValue();
        count++;
      }

      pageRequest.setRequestObject("count",new Integer(count));
      addResultElement(result,"count",""+count);

    }
  }
```

When you invoke the action handler as follows,

```
<?xml version="1.0" encoding="UTF-8"?>

<page xmlns:xsql="urn:oracle-xsql"
      connection="momnpup">
  <xsql:action handler="Counter" />
  <xsql:action handler="Counter" />
  <xsql:action handler="Counter" />
  <xsql:action handler="Counter" />
  <xsql:action handler="Counter" />

</page>
```

you will get the results shown in Figure 18.3. Since you can pass any type of object, the application of this technique can get quite complex. However, passing data between action handlers also binds them. For instance, if you have action handler A and action handler B, and action handler B always expects data that action handler A sets, you might not be able to use B effectively without A. This may not be a problem for any given set of action handlers. However, such dependencies can reduce the potential for code reuse.

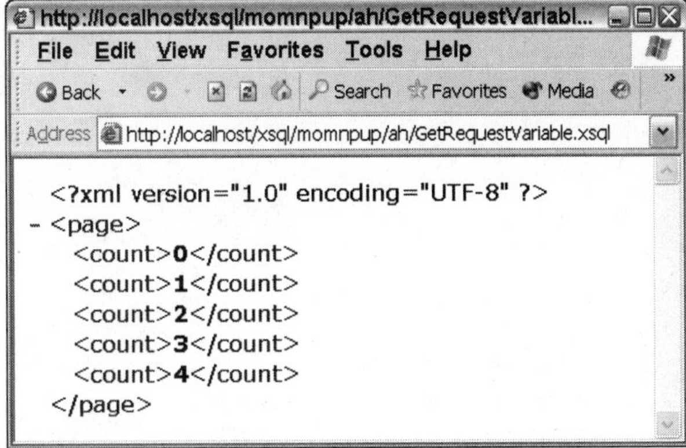

Figure 18.3 Data passing between action handlers.

Moving On

This chapter showed you how to create your own custom action handlers. This is the key point of extension for the XSQL framework. With a solid understanding of how to write your own action handlers, you have greatly increased your capabilities. If a built-in action can't handle your task, you can just write your own action. The next chapter discusses serializers and shows you how to use them to extend XSQL.

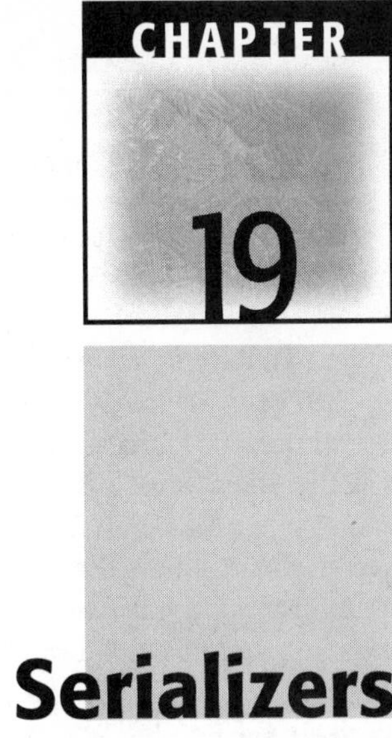

Serializers

Now that you've mastered action handlers, it's time for you to learn the last piece of the puzzle: serializers. A serializer controls precisely how a datagram is written to the output stream. The serializer can be called either after an XSLT transformation or prior to an XSLT transformation. This chapter shows you the ins and outs of serializers.

Before going further, it's important to put serializers into perspective. They are not as useful or as widely used as action handlers. They are capable of solving the same problems of stylesheets, but for most tasks stylesheets are better suited for the job. As you'll see, serializers are best utilized when you need to send binary data.

Now that serializers have been busted down to size, it's time to take a closer look at them. The first section serves as a general overview of serializers and also shows you how to write your own. The second section looks at a specific serializer: the FOP serializer. This serializer allows you create PDF documents. Used in combination with XSQL, you can use it to generate very nice reports of real-time data.

Serializer Overview

The best way to understand serializers is to create one. You'll do that in this section. The first step is learning the place of serializers in the overall XSQL architecture. With a solid understanding of how serializers fit in, you'll create a couple of your own. This section ends with a comparison of serializers and XSLT stylesheets. They occupy the same place in the overall framework, so it is important to know the best time to use each.

The Place of Serializers

Serialization is the act of taking data and serializing, or writing, it as output. XSQL typically serializes the results of an XSLT transformation as text data across the network. When you call the XSQL servlet, it does its job and its final act is to write a series of bytes to a network stream. If the requesting client is a Web browser, the browser reads in each of those bytes and then renders an HTML page. If the client is a Web services consumer, the process is essentially the same. However, the Web services consumer usually takes those bytes and interprets them into an XML document. The XSQL command line utility differs in that it doesn't write to a network stream. Instead, it either writes to a file or to the standard output.

In each of these cases, XSQL is serializing text data to an output stream. This is exactly what you want most of the time. It's what Web browsers expect, and any Web services consumer probably expects it as well. You get the data formatted correctly with an XSLT stylesheet and send it on. After the last byte goes out to the stream, XSQL closes the stream. Another happy customer served.

However, there are two big gaps in the architecture. The most important one is somewhat obvious: What if you want to send binary data, like images? By default, XSQL outputs text, not binary data. If you wish to send binary data, you'll need to use a serializer. Second, there are cases in which an XSLT stylesheet isn't going to do it for you by itself. This gives you the architecture illustrated in Figure 19.1. The serializer takes an XML document as input. If you want, you can perform a transformation before passing the XML document to the serializer.

If you want to output binary data, you will need to use a serializer. Text serializers, however, aren't as necessary. Most tasks that can be solved with a text serializer can be solved with an XSLT stylesheet. Though XSLT can be tricky to learn, it should be able to handle the vast majority of your needs. If it isn't working out for you, you may want to examine the XML that you are passing to it. If you're passing it poor XML in the first place, it will be simpler to fix the XML rather than to transfer the pain to a serializer. You can fix it either by reconsidering your SQL query or writing a custom action handler.

So when shouldn't you use XSLT? A good example is when you already have another subroutine of some sort that processes the XML into the desired format. Instead of reinventing the wheel and writing a stylesheet, you can just invoke the subroutine from the serializer. Another example is when you need to do something complex with the results of several actions. Maybe you want to do some mathematical processing on the end result, such as finding a standard deviation across a set of nodes. You certainly couldn't do that with a simple stylesheet, and even stylesheet extensions would be hard for such a problem. You could combine all the different actions into one action handler, but this can impact the modularity and freedom of the component action handlers. In such a case, it might be best to handle the processing in a serializer.

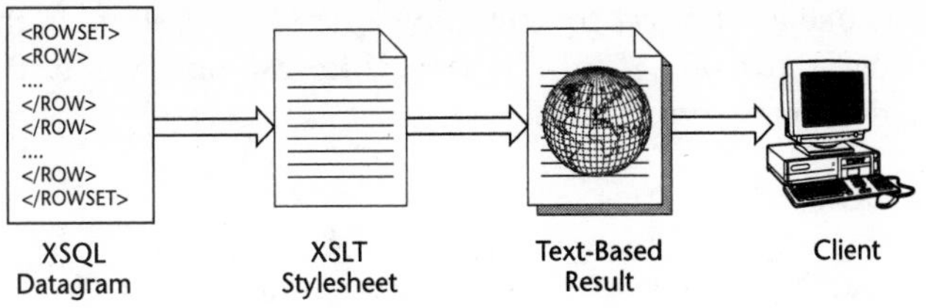

XSQL without a Serializer

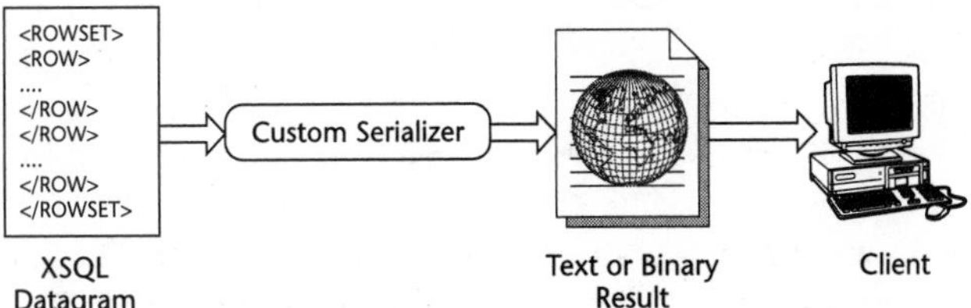

XSQL with a Serializer; No Stylesheet

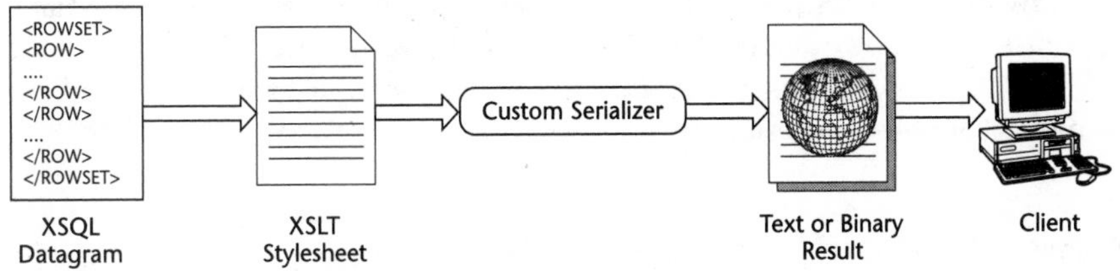

XSQL with a Serializer and a Stylesheet

Figure 19.1 XSQL with serializers.

Using Serializers

There are two ways you can invoke a serializer—after an XSLT transformation or in place of an XSLT transformation. Both methods are diagrammed in Figure 19.1. If you don't do an XSLT transformation first, your serializer will have to understand the raw XML datagram. If you are using the `xsql:query` action, for instance, the serializer will have to work with the canonical format. In most cases, you'll want to do some kind of transformation first. The FOP serializer works this way. Serializers that expect XML to be valid in accordance with a particular schema usually require an XSLT transformation.

In both cases, you invoke a serializer by including a handler attribute in the `xml-stylesheet` processing instruction. The following is an example where the XSLT processor is invoked prior to the serializer:

```
<?xml-stylesheet type="text/xsl"
                 href="someStylesheet.xsl"
                 serializer="java:some.pkg.SomeSerializer"?>
```

If you want the serializer to process the raw XSQL datagram, you can simply omit the `href` attribute:

```
<?xml-stylesheet type="text/xsl"
                 serializer="java:some.pkg.SomeSerializer"?>
```

In most cases, you will want to run a stylesheet before handing the XML over to a serializer. This is especially true for serializers that utilize other technologies, such as SVG or FOP. FOP, for instance, expects its data to be in agreement with a certain schema. If you are writing your own custom serializer, you may find it easier to just process the raw datagram. However, this does make your work less reusable. What if you want to use your code outside of XSQL? You might have to transform the data to match the canonical datagram schema. Instead, you'll probably want to create your own schema for your custom serializer.

Creating PDFs with Apache FOP

Many Web sites offer PDFs. They are better suited for printing and can be more polished than HTML Web pages. You have complete control over fonts, formatting, and images. But the PDF file format is binary, making it tough to code to directly. This is where the Apache FOP project comes in. You can use it to create PDF documents on the fly. By using XSQL and Apache FOP together, you can create dynamic PDF documents based on your database data. This section covers the architecture of Apache FOP and how to use the XSQL FOP serializer.

FOP Architecture

FOP uses the second part of the XSL family: XSL-FO. You're very familiar with XSLT, the first part. The aim of XSL-FO is quite different from XSLT. While XSLT is an XML application that gives you the ability to transform an XML document to some kind of output, XSL-FO is aimed at giving you great control over how the document looks. FOP is open source software that allows you to process and render XSL-FO documents.

You can think of XSL-FO as an attempt to overcome the presentation shortcomings of HTML and CSS. For instance, how many times have you struggled to get your elements positioned on the page just right? Once you get it right on one browser, you have to check other browsers. How many times have you printed a document and taken it with you to read, only to find that the printer had chopped off the last four words on the right-hand side? XSL-FO allows you to define exactly how items fit on a page and what the size and orientation of the page is. Assuming enough tool support, you could create a good-looking printed book by using XSL-FO. This isn't really true with HTML and CSS.

However, there isn't a lot of client software out there that understands XSL-FO directly. Maybe at some point, all the Web browsers will be able to accept and render XSL-FO documents just as they can handle HTML documents today. For now, you use XSL-FO to create one of the following established formats that meets the same goals as XSL-FO:

- PDF: Adobe Portable Document Format
- PCL: Printer Control Language from HP
- PostScript
- SVG: Scalable Vector Graphics
- AWT: Java Abstract Window Toolkit
- MIF: Marker Interchange Format for Adobe FrameMaker

You may be wondering, What does XSL-FO bring to the table? Why not just write one of these formats directly? First, you'd lose the benefits of a strong open standard. You'd also have to learn the intricacies of the underlying standard. Perhaps one the best benefits of XSL-FO is that you can easily use it in conjunction with XSLT stylesheets. You can transform an XSQL datagram in to an XSL-FO document. The XSQL FOP serializer hands it to FOP, which outputs the appropriate format. The architecture appears in Figure 19.2.

From the standpoint of the developer, you can consider that XSL-FO replaces HTML. Instead of writing an XSLT stylesheet that transforms the datagram in to HTML, you transform the datagram in to XSL-FO. Then, the serializer creates the output format. This is usually PDF. The XSQL FOP serializer that you'll look at in the next section writes to PDF. However, if you need to write to one of the other standards you can easily write your own serializer.

The details of XSL-FO aren't covered in this book. Appendix A points to some resources online that can help you learn and use XSL-FO.

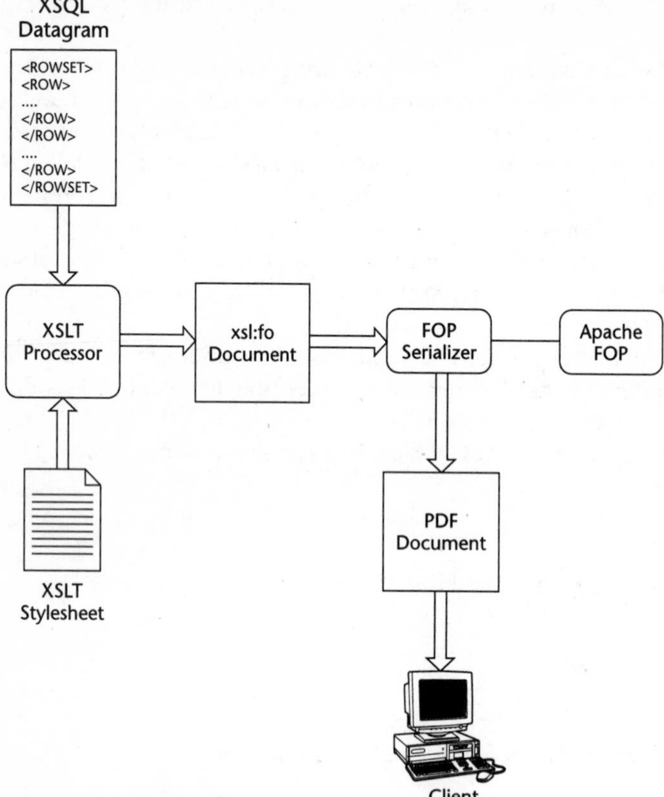

Figure 19.2 XSL-FO and FOP architecture.

Using the XSQL FOP Serializer

The XSQL FOP serializer comes with the XSQL distribution. You'll need to do a little work before you can use it, though. First, you'll need to download the release from Apache. Once that is installed, you need to set the classpath for your servlet engine so that it points to the correct jar files. From there, you should be able to verify your install by running the samples provided in the XSQL demos.

The home page for FOP is `http://xml.apache.org/fop`. Before downloading a distribution, you should first check your XSQL release notes. They will specify the appropriate version of FOP to use with the XSQL FOP serializer. At the time of this writing, XSQL supports FOP 0.19.0. Once it is downloaded, you simply expand the distribution file in to a convenient directory.

Now you need to set up the classpath. If you are using the Oracle Apache server, you should add the following to your `jserv.properties` file:

```
wrapper.classpath=c:\xsql\Fop-0.19.0-CVS\fop.jar
wrapper.classpath=c:\xsql\Fop-0.19.0-CVS\lib\avalon-framework-cvs-
20020315.jar
```

```
wrapper.classpath=c:\xsql\Fop-0.19.0-CVS\lib\batik.jar
wrapper.classpath=c:\xsql\Fop-0.19.0-CVS\lib\xalan-2.3.1.jar
wrapper.classpath=c:\xsql\Fop-0.19.0-CVS\lib\xercesImpl-2.0.1.jar
wrapper.classpath=c:\xsql\Fop-0.19.0-CVS\lib\xml-apis.jar
```

This takes care of FOP. You also need to make sure that the XSQL FOP serializer itself is installed. Here is the line that you need:

```
wrapper.classpath=C:\xsql\lib\xsqlserializers.jar
```

There should be a nickname for the XSQL FOP serializer in the `XSQLConfig.xml` file. You'll need to have the nickname in place for the samples to work correctly. You'll find it in the `serializerdefs` element. This is what it looks like:

```
<serializer>
  <name>FOP</name>
  <class>oracle.xml.xsql.serializers.XSQLFOPSerializer</class>
</serializer>
```

You should be ready to go. There should be an FOP directory underneath your demos. If you installed XSQL on a local Web server, you should be able to access the demo with `http://localhost/xsql/fop/emptable.xsql`. This produces the output shown in Figure 19.3.

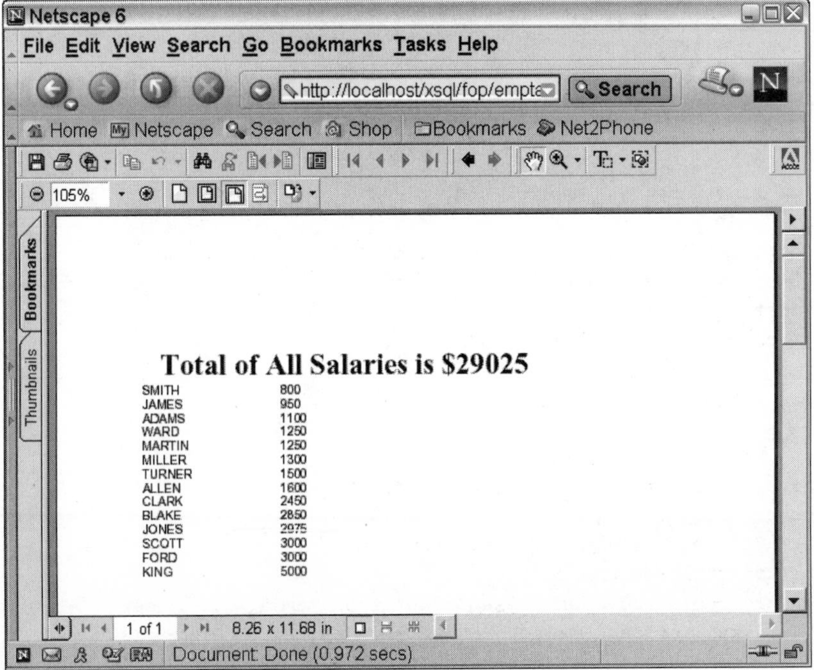

Figure 19.3 Demo PDF output.

Here's a closer look at what is going on. The XSQL looks quite like what you've seen before, except that a serializer is specified:

```
<?xml version="1.0"?>
<?xml-stylesheet type="text/xsl" href="emptablefo.xsl"
serializer="FOP"?>
<xsql:query connection="demo" xmlns:xsql="urn:oracle-xsql">
  SELECT ENAME, SAL FROM EMP
    ORDER BY SAL asc
</xsql:query>
```

The stylesheet looks quite a bit different, though:

```
<?xml version="1.0"?>
<fo:root xmlns:fo="http://www.w3.org/1999/XSL/Format" xsl:version="1.0"
         xmlns:xsl="http://www.w3.org/1999/XSL/Transform">


  <!-- defines the layout master -->
  <fo:layout-master-set>
    <fo:simple-page-master master-name="first"
                           page-height="29.7cm"
                           page-width="21cm"
                           margin-top="1cm"
                           margin-bottom="2cm"
                           margin-left="2.5cm"
                           margin-right="2.5cm">
      <fo:region-body margin-top="3cm"/>
    </fo:simple-page-master>
  </fo:layout-master-set>

  <!-- starts actual layout -->
  <fo:page-sequence master-name="first">

  <fo:flow flow-name="xsl-region-body">

      <fo:block font-size="24pt" font-family="Garamond" line-
height="24pt" space-after.optimum="3pt" font-weight="bold" start-
indent="15pt">
        Total of All Salaries is $<xsl:value-of
select="sum(/ROWSET/ROW/SAL)"/>
      </fo:block>

      <!-- Here starts the table -->
      <fo:block border-width="2pt">
        <fo:table>
          <fo:table-column column-width="4cm"/>
          <fo:table-column column-width="4cm"/>
          <fo:table-body font-size="10pt" font-family="sans-serif">
            <xsl:for-each select="ROWSET/ROW">
              <fo:table-row line-height="12pt">
                <fo:table-cell>
                  <fo:block><xsl:value-of select="ENAME"/></fo:block>
```

```
            </fo:table-cell>
            <fo:table-cell>
              <fo:block><xsl:value-of select="SAL"/></fo:block>
            </fo:table-cell>
          </fo:table-row>
        </xsl:for-each>
      </fo:table-body>
    </fo:table>
  </fo:block>
 </fo:flow>
</fo:page-sequence>
</fo:root>
```

The best way to get an idea as to what the serializer is doing is to look at the XML that the serializer processes. You can do this by simply commenting out the serializer attribute in the XSQL page. This yields a document like the following. The document here is an abbreviated version of the document used to produce the PDF in Figure 19.3; it includes only three of the rows.

```
<?xml version="1.0" ?>
 <fo:root xmlns:fo="http://www.w3.org/1999/XSL/Format">
  <fo:layout-master-set>
   <fo:simple-page-master master-name="first"
                          page-height="29.7cm"
                          page-width="21cm"
                          margin-top="1cm"
                          margin-bottom="2cm"
                          margin-left="2.5cm"
                          margin-right="2.5cm">
    <fo:region-body margin-top="3cm" />
   </fo:simple-page-master>
  </fo:layout-master-set>
  <fo:page-sequence master-name="first">
   <fo:flow flow-name="xsl-region-body">
    <fo:block font-size="24pt"
              font-family="Garamond"
              line-height="24pt"
              space-after.optimum="3pt"
              font-weight="bold"
              start-indent="15pt">
       Total of All Salaries is $14650
    </fo:block>
    <fo:block border-width="2pt">
    <fo:table>
     <fo:table-column column-width="4cm" />
     <fo:table-column column-width="4cm" />
     <fo:table-body font-size="10pt"
                    font-family="sans-serif">
      <fo:table-row line-height="12pt">
       <fo:table-cell>
        <fo:block>SMITH</fo:block>
       </fo:table-cell>
       <fo:table-cell>
```

```
          <fo:block>800</fo:block>
         </fo:table-cell>
        </fo:table-row>
        <fo:table-row line-height="12pt">
         <fo:table-cell>
          <fo:block>JAMES</fo:block>
         </fo:table-cell>
         <fo:table-cell>
          <fo:block>950</fo:block>
         </fo:table-cell>
        </fo:table-row>
        <fo:table-row line-height="12pt">
         <fo:table-cell>
          <fo:block>ALLEN</fo:block>
         </fo:table-cell>
        </fo:table-row>
       </fo:table-body>
      </fo:table>
     </fo:block>
    </fo:flow>
   </fo:page-sequence>
  </fo:root>
```

It looks quite a bit similar to HTML, but note that fonts and margins are defined precisely. This is the beauty of XSL-FO—that you are able to describe exactly what you want. A full treatment of XSL-FO is beyond the scope of this book. For more information, you should visit `http://xml.apache.org/fop/index.html`. This Web site not only describes the Apache FOP project but also provides links to resources for XSL-FO and describes the parts of the XSL-FO specification that aren't yet covered by Apache FOP.

Creating Custom Serializers

You can create your own custom serializers in a manner similar to that for action handlers. You implement an interface and then point to the Java class in the XSQL page. But instead of having multiple serializers in the same page you can only have one. This section walks you through the steps for writing serializers. You start by creating a simple text serializer. This should give you a good idea of how to program serializers. The second section shows you how to write binary serializers.

There isn't a lot of difference between writing text and writing binary serializers. In both cases, your class has to implement the `oracle.xml.xsql.XSQLDocumentSerializer` interface. These basic steps are expected for both text and binary serializers:

1. Set the content type.
2. Write the output.

You have to set the content type before writing any output. When outputting text, you can optionally specify a character encoding. You can write to either a stream or a writer, though you shouldn't try to write to both.

Now it's time for some examples, starting with a simple text serializer.

Text Serializers

As discussed previously, there isn't a lot that you can accomplish with a text serializer that you can't handle with an XSLT stylesheet. But from a learning perspective, the text serializer can be easier to understand. Here is a simple text serializer that outputs the skeleton of an XML document as HTML. Only the names of the elements are written.

```
import oracle.xml.xsql.XSQLPageRequest;
import oracle.xml.xsql.XSQLDocumentSerializer;
import org.w3c.dom.Document;
import org.w3c.dom.Element;
import org.w3c.dom.Node;
import org.w3c.dom.NodeList;

import java.io.PrintWriter;

public class SimpleTextSerializer implements XSQLDocumentSerializer {

public void serialize(Document doc, XSQLPageRequest env) {

      String mimeType="text/html";

      String encoding=env.getPageEncoding();
      if (encoding!=null && encoding.length()>0) {
       mimeType=mimeType+";charset="+encoding;
      }

      env.setContentType(mimeType);
      PrintWriter out=env.getWriter();
```

The content type is set in the preceding lines. If a page encoding is specified in the XSQL page, it will be attached to the `mime-type`. You get the PrintWriter from the XSQLPageRequest object. Optionally, you could call `getOutputStream()` and write to a stream instead. However, you should try to write only to one or the other. The remainder of the `serialize()` method sets up the beginning and ending HTML and calls the `displayElement()` method.

```
      Element docElem=doc.getDocumentElement();

      out.println("<html>");
      out.println("<head><title>"+docElem.getTagName()+"</title></head>");
      out.println("<body><H1>Document: "+docElem.getTagName()+"</H1>");
      out.println("<table>");
      displayElement(doc.getDocumentElement(),out,0);

      out.println("</table>");

  }
```

The `displayElement()` method is a recursive element that descends the document. The name for each element is printed, and then the method is called on each child of the `elem` element. The level argument represents the level in the tree at which the method is found. It is used to set the indentations properly.

```
private void displayElement(Element elem, PrintWriter out, int level) {

   out.println("<tr><td>");
   out.println(getSpaces(level)+"<b>"+elem.getTagName()+"</b>");
   out.println("</td><tr>");


   NodeList list=elem.getChildNodes();

   for (int i=0;i<list.getLength();i++) {

    Node n=list.item(i);

    if (n.getNodeType()==Node.ELEMENT_NODE) {
     displayElement((Element)n,out,level+1);
    }
   }
  }
```

The final method in the serializer is used to set the spacing. Three spaces are set for each level in depth.

```
  private String getSpaces(int num) {

   String s="";

   for (int i=0;i<num*3;i++) {
    s=s+" ";
   }
   return s;
  }

 }
```

Now you need to invoke your serializer. The following XSQL page will apply only the serializer to the XSQL datagram. Since no stylesheet is specified, no XSLT transformation will be performed prior to invoking the serializer.

```
<?xml version="1.0"?>
<?xml-stylesheet serializer="java:SimpleTextSerializer"?>
<page xmlns:xsql="urn:oracle-xsql" connection="demo">
  <xsql:query>
```

```
    select ename, job, sal from emp
    where deptno=20
    order by sal
  </xsql:query>
</page>
```

This produces the output shown in Figure 19.4. For this example, you can see that the elements for the raw datagram are listed.

You can also apply a serializer to the results of an XSLT transformation. The following XSQL page transforms the datagram with a stylesheet. The serializer is then called to process the results of that transformation.

```
<?xml version="1.0"?>
<?xml-stylesheet type="text/xsl" href="emp-serializer.xsl"
serializer="java:SimpleTextSerializer"?>
<page xmlns:xsql="urn:oracle-xsql" connection="demo">
  <xsql:query>
    SELECT ename, job, sal FROM emp
     WHERE deptno=20
     ORDER BY sal
  </xsql:query>
</page>
```

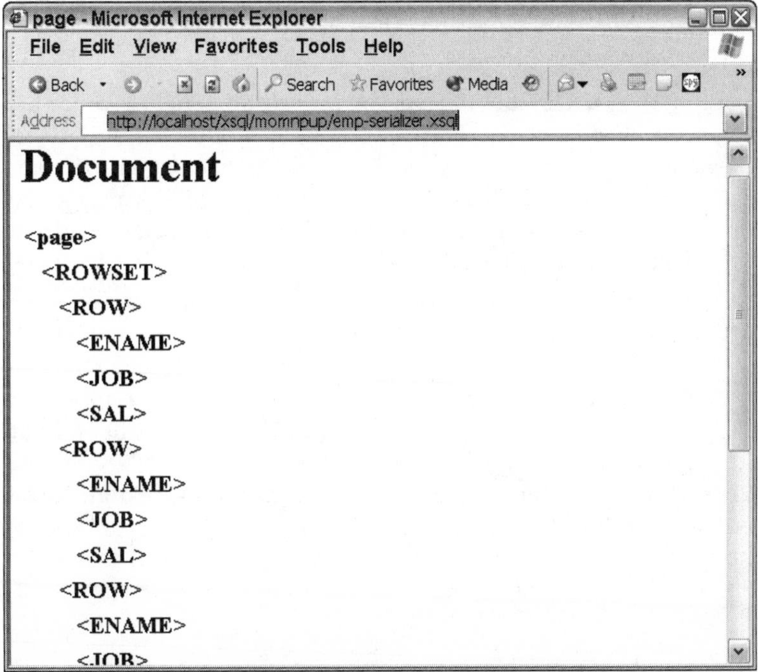

Figure 19.4 `SimpleTextSerializer` output.

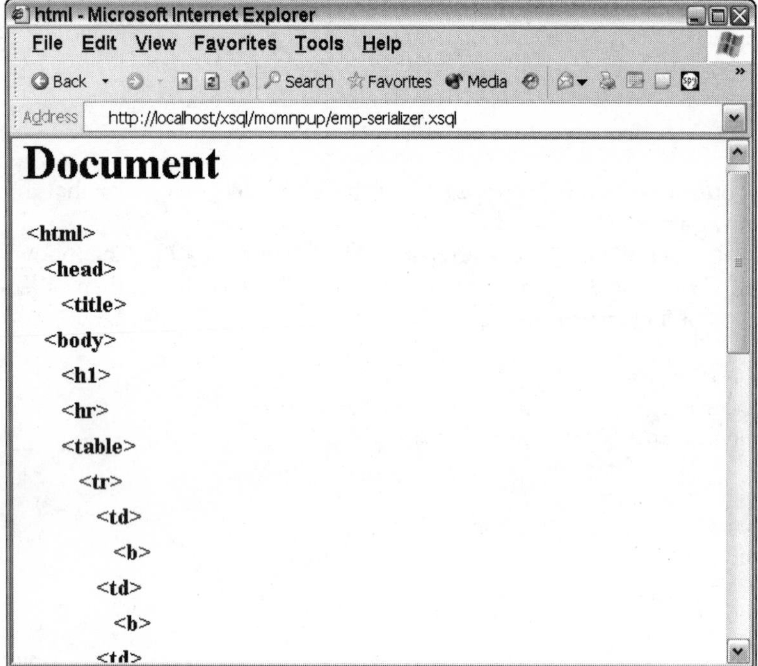

Figure 19.5 `SimpleTextSerializer` **and XSLT output.**

This produces the output shown in Figure 19.5. As you can see, the serializer processed the XHTML markup specified by the stylesheet.

These examples should give you a sense of how to use serializers, both with and without stylesheets. As with action handlers, the most important skill is learning how to navigate a document object. Once you learn how to navigate the DOM, you can do almost anything you want with a serializer.

Binary Serializers

Writing a binary serializer is almost exactly the same as writing a text serializer. You declare the content type and then write the output. Instead of using the writer for output, you use an `OutputStream`.

The following code is a simple binary serializer that reads an image file from the file system and writes it out. In this example, the XML input is ignored.

```
import oracle.xml.xsql.XSQLPageRequest;
import oracle.xml.xsql.XSQLDocumentSerializer;

import java.io.OutputStream;
import java.io.BufferedOutputStream;
import java.io.FileInputStream;
import java.io.BufferedInputStream;
```

```
import java.io.PrintWriter;

import org.w3c.dom.Document;

public class SimpleBinarySerializer implements XSQLDocumentSerializer {

 public void serialize(Document doc, XSQLPageRequest env) {

     String mimeType="image/gif";
     try {

      String fileName="c:\\data\\pics\\image.gif";
      FileInputStream fileIn=new FileInputStream(fileName);
      BufferedInputStream in=new BufferedInputStream(fileIn);

      OutputStream rawOut=env.getOutputStream();
      BufferedOutputStream out=new BufferedOutputStream(rawOut);

      env.setContentType(mimeType);

      for (int b=in.read();b!=-1;b=in.read()) {
       out.write(b);
      }

      out.flush();
      out.close();
      in.close();


    } catch (Exception e) {

    env.setContentType("text/plain");
    PrintWriter out=env.getWriter();
    out.println("An error has occurred");
    out.println(e.getMessage());

   }
 }
}
```

Obviously, this example doesn't do anything particularly useful. It does, however, show you the basic technique to use with a binary serializer. First, you set the content type to some binary mime-type. Then, you use `getOutputStream()` of `XSQL-PageRequest` to get the output. Although you arguably have a choice between using a writer or an `OutputStream` when you are writing a text serializer, you don't have a choice here. You should always use an `OutputStream` for a binary serializer.

In this case, you acquire your binary data from a file. In a real binary serializer, you would assemble the data in to some kind of buffer and then write the data out to the stream. In both cases, the basic technique is the same. You get the `OutputStream` object, write the bytes, flush, and close.

The following is an XSQL page that invokes this serializer. It follows the same rules as those of a text serializer. The only thing required is that you must specify the serializer in the `xml-stylesheet` processing instruction. Since the XML input is ignored in the simple example, it doesn't matter what XSQL is used or whether a stylesheet precedes transforms the datagram.

```
<?xml version="1.0"?>
<?xml-stylesheet serializer="java:SimpleBinarySerializer"?>
<dummy/>
```

Of course, a binary serializer can use the datagram or a transformation of the datagram. In this example, the file that this serializer writes is hard-coded. You could write the serializer so that the filename is derived from a database query of some sort. You dictate that the serializer expects the input XML to appear as follows:

```
<?xml version="1.0"?>
<binary-data>
 <content-type>image/gif</content-type>
 <file-name> c:\data\pics\image.gif</file-name>
</binary-data>
```

Instead of hardcoding the content type and the filename in the serializer, you can derive these from the XML input. This is how the new `serialize()` method will look:

```
public void serialize(Document doc, XSQLPageRequest env) {

     XMLElement docElem=(XMLElement)doc.getDocumentElement();

     try {

      String mimeType=docElem.valueOf("content-type");
      String fileName=docElem.valueOf("file-name");
      FileInputStream fileIn=new FileInputStream(fileName);
      BufferedInputStream in=new BufferedInputStream(fileIn);

      env.setContentType(mimeType);

      OutputStream rawOut=env.getOutputStream();
      BufferedOutputStream out=new BufferedOutputStream(rawOut);

      for (int b=in.read();b!=-1;b=in.read()) {
       out.write(b);
      }

      out.flush();
      out.close();
```

```
        in.close();

      } catch (Exception e) {

        env.setContentType("text/html");
        PrintWriter out=env.getWriter();
        out.println("<html><head><title>Error</title></head>");
        out.println("<body>");
        out.println("An error has occurred");
        out.println(e.getMessage());
        out.println("</body></html>");

     }
```

If you want to derive the content type and the filename from the database, you just query the database with an action, as follows:

```
<?xml version="1.0"?>
<?xml-stylesheet type="text/xsl"
                 href="binary-style.xsl"
                 serializer="java:SimpleBinarySerializer"?>
<xsql:query xmlns:xsql="urn:oracle-xsql" connection="demo">
    SELECT file-name, content-type
     FROM binary_table
     WHERE id={@some-param}
</xsql:query>
```

The last piece of the puzzle is the stylesheet that formats the query results so that the serializer can use them. The following stylesheet should do the trick:

```
<?xml version="1.0"?>

<xsl:stylesheet
 version="1.0"
 xmlns:xsl="http://www.w3.org/1999/XSL/Transform">

 <xsl:template match="/">
  <binary-data>
   <content-type>
    <xsl:value-of select="/ROWSET/ROW/content-type"/>
   </content-type>
   <file-name>
    <xsl:value-of select="/ROWSET/ROW/file-name"/>
   </file-name>
  </binary-data>
 </xsl:template>

</xsl:stylesheet>
```

In this example, you define a schema that your serializer accepts and then aim your XSQL and XSLT stylesheet to fit that schema. In this case, you used a built-in action to provide the data, but you could certainly write your own action handler to provide the data.

This example is still fairly simple, though. You aren't creating binary data based on the XML input. Instead, you are just choosing the source of binary data. In a lot of cases, you won't do much more than choose a source and stream it to the client with the correct content type. It's easy to create and mold text on the fly, but doing so with binary data is more difficult. If your serializer is truly going to create the binary data from scratch, you'll have to have a good understanding of the underlying binary standard of the data. In most cases, you'll probably be able to find some kind of encoder that knows how write the binary data, and then you just have to pass it to input. FOP generates the PDFs in this manner.

Examples of these cases are provided in the next sections. Because of the nature of binary data, your serializers tend to be either very simple or very complex.

If you are creating binary data from scratch, your serializer will be complex. You have to have detail.

Serializing BLOBs

In the previous example, you streamed an image that was stored on the file system. You can also stream binary data that exists in the database as a BLOB. In the text that follows, you'll see how to use a serializer to deliver BLOBs to your clients. In fact, if there is binary data in the database that you wish to push to the client, you will have to use a serializer both to write it and to fetch it from the database.

From our earlier discussions, it's obvious that you have to use a serializer to deliver binary data from XSQL. But in contrast to text data, you can't really provide binary data as input to a serializer. The serializer takes XML as input, and XML is a text format. You could encode the binary data in an action handler, but doing this is more trouble than its worth. It also avoids an important problem: Binary files tend to be large, and for large files, you would want to stream them rather than store them in memory.

If you wish to serialize a BLOB, your first challenge will be to determine what BLOB you want. You should be able to figure this out by examining the XML input that is provided. The following sample is a general-purpose serializer that takes an SQL statement as input.

```
import oracle.xml.xsql.XSQLPageRequest;
import oracle.xml.xsql.XSQLDocumentSerializer;
import oracle.xml.parser.v2.XMLElement;

import java.io.OutputStream;
import java.io.PrintWriter;
import java.io.InputStream;

import org.w3c.dom.Document;

import oracle.jdbc.driver.OracleResultSet;
import oracle.sql.BLOB;
```

```
import java.sql.ResultSet;
import java.sql.Statement;
import java.sql.DriverManager;
import java.sql.Connection;

public class SimpleBlobSerializer implements XSQLDocumentSerializer {

 public void serialize(Document doc, XSQLPageRequest env) {

     try {


      //Get the information from the input

      XMLElement docRoot=(XMLElement)doc.getDocumentElement();
      String mimeType=docRoot.valueOf("./mime-type");
      String cmd =docRoot.valueOf("./sql-statement");
      String connectStr=docRoot.valueOf("./connect-string");
      String username=docRoot.valueOf("./username");
      String password=docRoot.valueOf("./password");


      //Get the connection and execute the query

      Connection conn=DriverManager.getConnection(connectStr,
                                                  username,
                                                  password);

      Statement stmt = conn.createStatement ();
      ResultSet rset = stmt.executeQuery (cmd);

      //Get the blob data

      BLOB blob = ((OracleResultSet)rset).getBLOB(0);
      InputStream blobStream=blob.getBinaryStream();

      //Get the output stream and set the mime type

      OutputStream out=env.getOutputStream();
      env.setContentType(mimeType);

      //write the data

      for (int b=blobStream.read();b!=-1;b=blobStream.read()) {
       out.write(b);
      }

      blobStream.close();
      conn.close();

    } catch (Exception e) {
```

```
      env.setContentType("text/plain");
      PrintWriter out=env.getWriter();
      out.println("An error has occurred");
      out.println(e.getMessage());

    }
  }
}
```

This code uses JDBC to access the database and Oracle JDBC connections to handle the BLOB data. In this example, the connection is handled in the simplest manner. However, it does mean that you'll be opening and closing a connection on each request. Some kind of connection pooling mechanism would be better suited for this serializer.

To use the serializer, it needs an XML document that looks like this:

```
<?xml version="1.0"?>
<blob-serializer>

 <sql-statement>
  SELECT image FROM image_table
    WHERE id=5
 </sql-statement>

 <mime-type>image/jpeg</mime-type>
 <connect-string>jdbc:oracle:thin:@localhost:1521:ORCL</connect-string>
 <username>momnpup</username>
 <password>momnpup</username>

</blob-serializer>
```

This means that one of the products of your XSLT transformation is an SQL statement. To accomplish this, you can use the same techniques that you learned in Chapter 15. But first, you need an XSQL page. Here is a simple one that assumes that the `image_id` in the product table points to the `image_table`:

```
<?xml version="1.0"?>


<?xml-stylesheet type="text/xsl"
                 href="simple-blob-serializer.xsl"
                 serializer="java:SimpleBlobSerializer"?>

<xsql:query connection="momnpup"
            xmlns:xsql="urn:oracle-xsql"
            rowset-element="blob-serializer"
            row-element="row">

  SELECT image_id FROM product
   WHERE id={product_id}
</xsql:query>
```

This is just one possible example. The idea is that you get some data that can be used to locate the appropriate BLOB. The stylesheet then creates the XML that the serializer expects. Here is a stylesheet that creates a SQL query that grabs a JPEG image out of the image_table:

```
<?xml version = '1.0'?>
<xsl:stylesheet xmlns:xsl="http://www.w3.org/1999/XSL/Transform"
version="1.0">
<xsl:output method="xml"/>

<xsl:template match="/">
 <blob-serializer>

  <sql-statement>
   SELECT image FROM image_table
    WHERE id=<xsl:value-of select="/BLOB-SERIALIZER/ROW/IMAGE_ID"/>
  </sql-statement>

  <mime-type>image/jpeg</mime-type>
  <connect-string>jdbc:oracle:thin:@localhost:1521:ORCL</connect-string>
  <username>momnpup</username>
  <password>momnpup</password>

 </blob-serializer>

</xsl:template>
</xsl:stylesheet>
```

In this example, only one value is dynamic—the image_id. Of course, you could dynamically generate the other values. You could, for instance, store both GIF and JPEG images in the same table and then have a column that specifies the mime-type.

Creating JPEGs with Java AWT

The previous two examples were quite simple. You located a binary object, got an input stream for it, and wrote it to the output stream. Now a more complex case is presented. Instead of streaming an existing binary object, you'll create a completely new one. You'll use Java AWT to create a simple bar chart based on dynamic data. Then, you'll write this data out to the client. Since AWT gives you a way to write JPEGs, you won't have to figure out the JPEG standard itself.

NOTE **As you read this, you'll probably wonder if the task at hand could be more easily accomplished with the use of SVG. Absolutely. SVG gives you far more capability, with greater ease, than the serializer that you are creating here. You can even use the Batik package from Apache to directly render SVG images as JPEGs. This example is meant to demonstrate the basic process of integrating AWT with a XSQL serializer.**

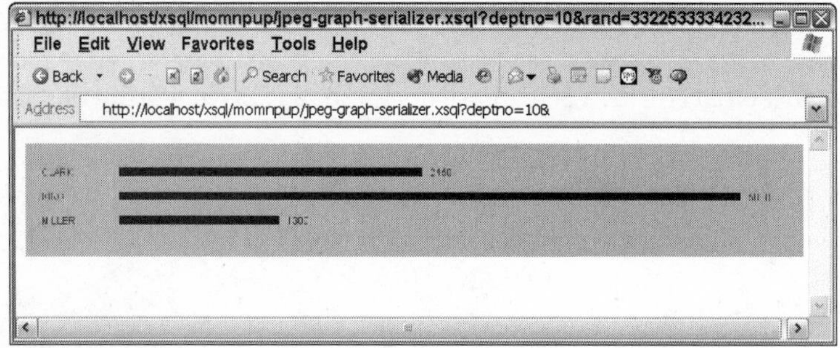

Figure 19.6 Output of the simple AWT serializer.

This serializer will create a bar chart of a series of data. Each bar will be labeled on the left, and the actual value will be written on the right after the bar. The serializer will also expect a scaling factor so that the bars can be rendered correctly for the image size. Figure 19.6 shows what the finished product can produce based on data in the database.

With these basic requirements, your first step is to define what the input will look like. Here is a sample XML file that meets the requirements:

```
<?xml version = '1.0'?>
<graph>
 <image height="140" width="1000" scale="0.16">
  <background red="200" green="200" blue="200"/>
 </image>
 <bar leftmargin="10"
      topmargin="10"
      bottommargin="10"
      height="10"
      value="2450">
  <title width="100">
   <text>CLARK</text>
    <textcolor red="255"
             green="0"
             blue="0"/>
  </title>
```

```
    <barcolor red="0"
              green="0"
              blue="255"/>
   </bar>
   <bar leftmargin="10"
        topmargin="10"
        bottommargin="10"
        height="10"
        value="5000">
    <title width="100">
     <text>KING</text>
     <textcolor red="255"
                green="0"
                blue="0"/>
    </title>
    <barcolor red="0"
              green="0"
              blue="255"/>
   </bar>
   <bar leftmargin="10"
        topmargin="10"
        bottommargin="10"
        height="10"
        value="1300">
    <title width="100">
     <text>MILLER</text>
     <textcolor red="255"
                green="0"
                blue="0"/>
    </title>
    <barcolor red="0"
              green="0"
              blue="255"/>
   </bar>
  </graph>
```

With an idea of what the input should look like, you can write the serializer. The basic design is much the same as the previous examples. You first interpret the inputted XML, and the last thing you do is write the data out to the client. What is added here is the actual creation of the binary object. You use the AWT libraries to create an image. You then write the text and draw the bars onto the image. The architecture of what you'll accomplish in the next few pages is diagrammed in Figure 19.7.

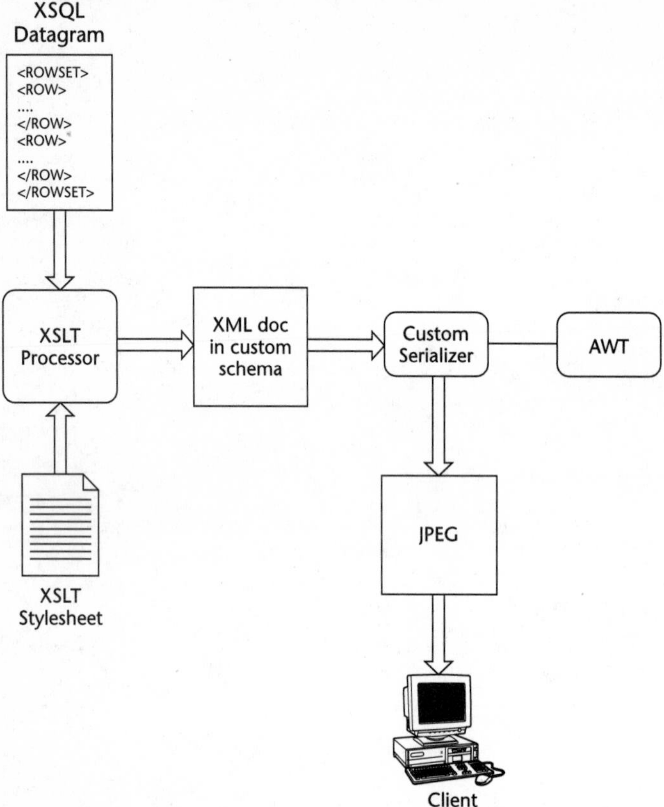

Figure 19.7 Architecture for the AWT custom serializer.

At this point, you know what your serializer should accept as input, so you can go ahead and start coding it. Here is the requisite class information and the `serialize` method:

```
import oracle.xml.xsql.XSQLPageRequest;
import oracle.xml.xsql.XSQLDocumentSerializer;
import oracle.xml.parser.v2.XMLElement;
import java.io.OutputStream;
import java.io.PrintWriter;
import com.sun.image.codec.jpeg.JPEGCodec;
import com.sun.image.codec.jpeg.JPEGImageEncoder;
import java.awt.image.BufferedImage;
import java.awt.Graphics2D;
import java.awt.geom.Rectangle2D;
import java.awt.geom.Line2D;
import java.awt.Color;
```

```
import org.w3c.dom.Document;
import org.w3c.dom.NodeList;
import org.w3c.dom.Node;

public class JpegGraphSerializer implements XSQLDocumentSerializer {

 float scale=1;


 /**
  * Takes an XML document that behaves the previously defined
  * schema and outputs a JPEG image created using AWT
  */

 public void serialize(Document doc, XSQLPageRequest env) {

     String mimeType="image/jpeg";
     try {

      XMLElement rootElem=(XMLElement)doc.getDocumentElement();

      // Get the top level information
      scale=getScale(rootElem);
      int width=getWidth(rootElem);
      int height=getHeight(rootElem);
      Node colorNode=rootElem.selectSingleNode("./image/background");
      Color bgcolor=getColor((XMLElement)colorNode);

      // Create an image and get the graphics used to draw with
      BufferedImage img=new BufferedImage(width,
                                          height,
                                          BufferedImage.TYPE_INT_RGB);
      Graphics2D g=img.createGraphics();

      // Set up the Image
      g.setPaint(bgcolor);
      Rectangle2D allRect = new Rectangle2D.Float(0,0,width,height);
      g.fill(allRect);

      // Draw the bars based on the input XML doc
      NodeList elems=rootElem.getElementsByTagName("bar");
      drawBars(g,elems);

      // Write the data
      env.setContentType(mimeType);
      OutputStream out=env.getOutputStream();
      JPEGImageEncoder encoder=JPEGCodec.createJPEGEncoder(out);
      encoder.encode(img);
      out.close();

     } catch (Exception e) {
```

```
        env.setContentType("text/html");
        PrintWriter out=env.getWriter();
        out.println("An error has occurred");
        out.println(e.getMessage());
        e.printStackTrace(out);
      }
    }
```

The preceding `serialize()` method sets up the initial image based on top-level parameters, calls the `drawBars()` method to do the actual drawing, and the uses the `JPEGCodec` class to write the JPEG data to the output stream. If any exception is thrown, an error message will be printed as an HTML file. The next method to examine is the `drawBars()` method:

```
private void drawBars(Graphics2D g, NodeList elems) throws Exception {

 int startX=20;
 int startY=20;

 for (int i=0;i<elems.getLength();i++) {

  XMLElement bar=(XMLElement)elems.item(i);
  startY=drawBar(g,bar,startX,startY);
 }
}
```

The main function of this method is to manage the position where the next bar should be drawn. The starting point is hard-coded in this example, but it could certainly be configurable. The real work of drawing is handled in the `drawBar()` method:

```
private int drawBar(Graphics2D g, XMLElement bar, int x, int y)
                 throws Exception{

 // Get the data from the XML element

 String topMarginStr=bar.valueOf("./@topmargin");
 int topMargin=Integer.parseInt(topMarginStr);
 String bottomMarginStr=bar.valueOf("./@bottommargin");
 int bottomMargin=Integer.parseInt(bottomMarginStr);
 String heightStr=bar.valueOf("./@height");
 int height=Integer.parseInt(heightStr);
 String valueStr=bar.valueOf("./@value");
 int value=Integer.parseInt(valueStr);
 String title=bar.valueOf("./title");
 String titleWidthStr=bar.valueOf("./title/@width");
 int titleWidth=Integer.parseInt(titleWidthStr);

 Node colorNode=bar.selectSingleNode("./barcolor");
 Color barColor=getColor((XMLElement)colorNode);
```

```
    colorNode=bar.selectSingleNode("./title/textcolor");
    Color textColor=getColor((XMLElement)colorNode);

    title=title.trim();

    // Do the drawing

    //Set the start position
    y=y+topMargin;

    // Write the title
    g.setPaint(textColor);
    g.drawString(title,x,y+height);

    // Draw the bar
    g.setPaint(barColor);
    Rectangle2D rect = new Rectangle2D.Float(x+titleWidth,
                                             y,
                                             value*scale,height);
    g.fill(rect);

    // Write the bar
    g.setPaint(textColor);
    g.drawString(""+value,x+titleWidth+value*scale+10,y+height);

    // Return the next starting position
    return y+height+bottomMargin;
  }
```

The code of this method is divided between two purposes: reading the data from the XML element for a particular bar and drawing the bar. A custom serializer will always need some strategy for reading its input from the XML document. What you do with that data varies widely. In this case, you are doing some simple drawing using AWT, but you are really unlimited in what you can do. The remainder of the class is displayed as follows. It consists of several helper functions.

```
  private int getWidth(XMLElement elem) throws Exception {

    String widthStr=elem.valueOf("./image/@width");
    return Integer.parseInt(widthStr);

  }

  private int getHeight(XMLElement elem) throws Exception {

    String heightStr=elem.valueOf("./image/@height");
    return Integer.parseInt(heightStr);

  }
```

```
private float getScale(XMLElement elem) throws Exception {

  String scaleStr=elem.valueOf("./image/@scale");
  if (scaleStr!=null) {
   return Float.parseFloat(scaleStr);
  } else {
   return 1;
  }

}

private Color getColor(XMLElement elem) throws Exception {

  String redStr=elem.valueOf("@red");
  String greenStr=elem.valueOf("@green");
  String blueStr=elem.valueOf("@blue");

  int red=Integer.parseInt(redStr);
  int green=Integer.parseInt(greenStr);
  int blue=Integer.parseInt(blueStr);

  return new Color(red,green,blue);

 }
}
```

Since this last snippet of code concludes the class, the last brace is the closing brace for the class. Your next steps are writing the XSQL and XSLT pages. It doesn't really matter what your XSLT pages look like, as long as they produce an XML document that obeys the schema for this serializer. The XSQL and XSLT pages presented here produce the chart displayed earlier in this chapter. Here's the XSQL page:

```
<?xml version="1.0"?>
<?xml-stylesheet type="text/xsl"
                 href="jpeg-graph-serializer.xsl"
                 serializer="java:JpegGraphSerializer"?>

<page connection="demo"
      xmlns:xsql="urn:oracle-xsql">

 <xsql:query>
  SELECT ename, sal FROM emp
   WHERE deptno={@deptno}
 </xsql:query>

 <xsql:set-stylesheet-param name="max-value">
  SELECT max(sal) FROM emp
   WHERE deptno={@deptno}
 </xsql:set-stylesheet-param>

</page>
```

This is pretty standard fare. The only thing that differs from what you've seen many times before is the serializer attribute in the stylesheet processing instruction. The stylesheet, displayed as follows, also requires the `max-value` parameter. This parameter isn't required of the serializer, but it is of the stylesheet.

```
<?xml version="1.0"?>

<xsl:stylesheet xmlns:xsl="http://www.w3.org/1999/XSL/Transform"
version="1.0">

 <xsl:param name="max-value"/>
 <xsl:param name="width">1000</xsl:param>
 <xsl:param name="title_width">100</xsl:param>
 <xsl:param name="scale-factor"><xsl:value-of select="800 div $max-
value"/></xsl:param>
 <xsl:param name="height"><xsl:value-of
select="count(/page/ROWSET/ROW)*30+50"/></xsl:param>


 <xsl:template match="/page">
  <graph>

   <image>
    <xsl:attribute name="height"><xsl:value-of
select="$height"/></xsl:attribute>
    <xsl:attribute name="width"><xsl:value-of
select="$width"/></xsl:attribute>
    <xsl:attribute name="scale"><xsl:value-of select="$scale-
factor"/></xsl:attribute>
    <background red="200" green="200" blue="200"/>
   </image>

   <xsl:apply-templates select="ROWSET/ROW"/>

  </graph>
 </xsl:template>

 <xsl:template match="ROW">
  <bar leftmargin="10" topmargin="10" bottommargin="10" height="10">
   <xsl:attribute name="value"><xsl:value-of
select="SAL"/></xsl:attribute>
    <title>
     <xsl:attribute name="width"><xsl:value-of
select="$title_width"/></xsl:attribute>
     <text><xsl:value-of select="ENAME"/></text>
     <textcolor red="255" green="0" blue="0"/>
    </title>
    <barcolor red="0" green="0" blue="255"/>
   </bar>
 </xsl:template>

</xsl:stylesheet>
```

The majority of this stylesheet works to create the bar elements needed by the serializer. The first few lines, though, are occupied in specifying the size correctly based on the number of rows of data and the correct scaling factor. By leaving this work to the stylesheet, you can have a simpler serializer that can handle a lot of different types of data.

Moving On

In this chapter you have learned how to use the final tool in the XSQL arsenal—serializers. They are especially apt for the creation of binary data. By using serializers, you can create any kind of data presentation that you wish. Often, this will mean leveraging existing tools such as FOP, but you are also free to write the binary formats directly from the ground up.

You now know all you need to know to easily create robust applications by using XSQL. You probably learned a number of new paradigms along the way, but hopefully you can now see how XSQL can make applications easily. Have fun!

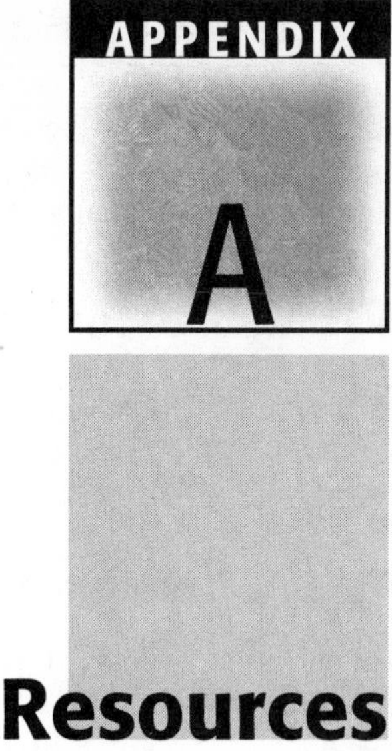

Resources

This appendix covers some resources that you should find useful as you develop XSQL applications.

Code Examples from This Book

All of the code examples from this book are available on the book's Web site. You can visit the Web site at `www.wiley.com/compbooks/thomas`. The code examples are indexed by the page numbers on which they appear.

Oracle Technet

The Oracle Technology Network's Web site resides at `http://technet.oracle.com`. You'll need to register. Once you've registered, you'll have access to a great variety of resources about Oracle, including white papers, product documentation, and discussion forums. The most relevant discussion forum for XSQL is the XML forum.

Oracle Database Resources

You'll find a lot of the best resources at http://technet.oracle.com, where you can find complete reference manuals for SQL, PL/SQL, Text, and XML functionality. Here are some especially useful links.

SQL Manual for Oracle 9i

This manual covers all the specifics of Oracle SQL. You'll find the manual at http://otn.oracle.com/docs/products/oracle9i/doc_library/release2/server.920/a96540/toc.htm.

PL/SQL Reference

This manual covers all you need to know about PL/SQL. You'll find the manual at http://otn.oracle.com/docs/products/oracle9i/doc_library/release2/appdev.920/a96624/toc.htm.

In this book, you used just a couple of supplied PL/SQL packages. Oracle offers a ton that you didn't use. They are described in a document at http://otn.oracle.com/docs/products/oracle9i/doc_library/release2/appdev.920/a96612/toc.htm.

Oracle XML DB

The Oracle XML DB offers information about the XML storage functionality of the Oracle database. There is a lot of information at this site about the Oracle XMLType that you learned about in Chapter 11, which discussed using Oracle Text with XML documents. You'll find the information at http://otn.oracle.com/docs/products/oracle9i/doc_library/release2/appdev.920/a96620/toc.htm.

Oracle XML Developer's Kit

You can find information about the Oracle XML Developer's Kit (XDK) at http://otn.oracle.com/tech/xml/xdkhome.html.

The XDK includes XSQL as well as the XML APIs that you used in the last three chapters of the book. If you are using XSQL in conjunction with Java—either by embedding XSQL in your code or writing custom action handlers or serializers—you can find the API documentation available in javadoc format at http://otn.oracle.com/docs/tech/xml/xdk_java/doc_library/Production9i/index.html.

The Oracle XDK and the Oracle XML DB are considered separate by Oracle. If you want information about storing XML in the database (e.g., XMLType), you should look at the foregoing XMLType link. The Oracle XDK covers XML that is derived from the database and focuses on how to create XML from data stored in the traditional relational format. It also includes the Oracle XML parser, XSLT processor, and other pieces that can be used with or without the database.

XSLT Resources

XSLT is extremely important in XSQL development. As a popular standard, there is a lot of information available on the Web. The definitive source of information is the XSLT Recommendation from W3C. You'll find the information at `http://www.w3.org/TR/xslt`.

However, this document covers a lot of information only needed by developers implementing an XSLT processor. A better starting point for the beginning XSLT developer is `http://www.xslt.com`.

Another great resource is available at `zvon.org`. This site provides an interactive guide to all of the XSLT elements and XPath. You'll find the guide at `http://www.zvon.org/xxl/XSLTreference/Output/index.html`.

Java Resources

The definitive resource for Java is `http://www.javasoft.com`. You can also find information that is specific to Oracle and Java at the XDK links listed earlier.

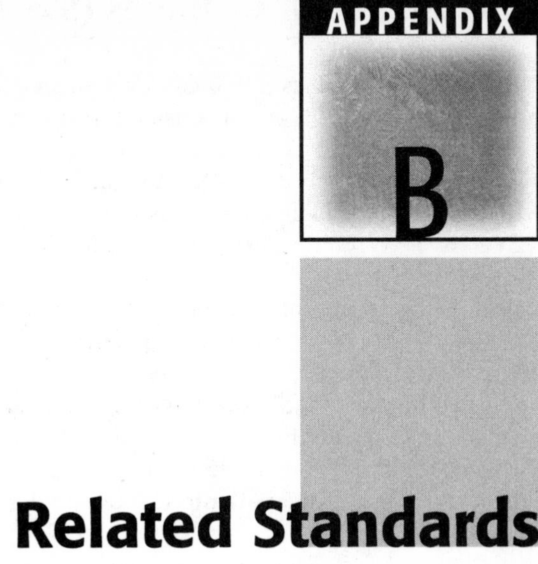

Related Standards

There were a few standards that were discussed briefly in the book. This appendix covers these in a little more depth, and provides links that you may find useful.

XSL-FO

You learned a little bit about XSL-FO in Chapter 19, "Serializers." You can use XSL-FO in conjunction with Apache FOP to create Portable Document Format (PDF) documents. There are also other formats that you can produce. XSL-FO is its own XML application that is quite similar to XHTML. The definitive source of information is from the World Wide Web Consortium (W3C) recommendation at `http://www.w3.org/TR/2001/REC-xsl-20011015/#`.

However, a beginner may not find the recommendation particularly useful. Also, Apache FOP doesn't fully implement the XSL-FO recommendation. For specific information about how Apache FOP implements the recommendation, you should visit the Apache FOP home page at `http://xml.apache.org/fop/`.

A good tutorial on creating XSL-FO documents is available from Dave Pawson at `http://www.dpawson.co.uk/xsl/sect3/bk/index.html`.

Scalable Vector Graphics (SVG)

Scalable Vector Graphics (SVG) creates an image based on an XML document. XSQL can easily produce SVG documents and thus gives you an easy way to create images based on dynamic data derived from your database. You simply write an XSLT stylesheet that converts the XSQL datagram to an SVG document. An example of how to do this is included in the XSQL distribution from Oracle.

SVG is a W3C recommendation and is available at `http://www.w3.org/TR/SVG/`.

Adobe has some of the best information about SVG on its Web site at `http://www.adobe.com/svg/main.html`.

There are two ways that you can use SVG. An SVG document can be sent directly to the client. The client requires an SVG plug-in to render the document. Adobe provides the most popular plug-in. It is also possible to render SVG on the server and create a JPEG file. You can do this using Batik, which is included in the Apache FOP distribution. You'll find additional information on Batik at `http://xml.apache.org/batik/`.

SQLJ and Java-Stored Procedures

This book showed you how to create stored procedures using PL/SQL. You can also create stored procedures using Java. This is known as SQLJ. You find the Oracle guide to SQLJ at `http://otn.oracle.com/tech/java/sqlj_jdbc/pdf/a96655.pdf`.

SQLJ is implemented with a precompiler. It translates statements in your Java source code to calls to the SQLJ APIs. These calls sit on top of JDBC. SQLJ allows you some of the convenience of PL/SQL's inline SQL statements. If Java is your primary development language, you may find it easier to work with SQLJ rather than learn PL/SQL from scratch.

Once a SQLJ class is compiled, it can run against the database as a Java stored procedure. However, you can have Java stored procedures whether you use SQLJ or not. You may be wondering which is better, PL/SQL or Java stored procedures? Java stored procedures take up a little more memory and can underperform PL/SQL when there are a lot of SQL statements. Java stored procedures have the disadvantage that statements have to be translated to SQL, whereas PL/SQL supports SQL natively. At the same time, Java is a much more predominant language than PL/SQL and has a richer native API set as well as lots of third-party and open source code. As with so many things, the choice between PL/SQL and Java is dependent on your projects, as well as on what you find most comfortable.

Index

B

D

J

Q

R